SOURCES
OF
ENGLISH
CONSTITUTIONAL
HISTORY

VOLUME I

SOURCES OF ENGLISH CONSTITUTIONAL HISTORY

*A Selection of Documents
from A.D. 600 to the Interregnum*

Revised Edition

EDITED AND TRANSLATED BY

CARL STEPHENSON AND
FREDERICK GEORGE MARCHAM

Cornell University

HARPER & ROW, *Publishers*
New York, Evanston, San Francisco, and London

SOURCES OF ENGLISH CONSTITUTIONAL HISTORY
REVISED EDITION, VOLUME I:
A SELECTION OF DOCUMENTS FROM A.D. 600 TO THE INTERREGNUM

Standard Book Number: 06-044202-6
Library of Congress Catalog Card Number: 72-84325

To the memory of
CHARLES HENRY HULL

CONTENTS

SECTION I
THE ANGLO-SAXON PERIOD

CONTENTS

SECTION II

THE NORMAN KINGS

SECTION III

HENRY II AND HIS SONS

SECTION IV

HENRY III AND EDWARD I

SECTION V
EDWARD II, EDWARD III, AND RICHARD II

SECTION VII

THE TUDORS

SECTION VIII
THE EARLY STUARTS

PREFACE

THIS book has been designed for use in any course that touches the growth of English institutions, a subject that almost inevitably demands a certain amount of source work. Before now the student has been provided with many collections of documents covering particular phases of English constitutional history. He has not, however, had one volume to illustrate all of it, combining extracts from the whole magnificent series that stretches back from the most recent acts of parliament to the dooms of the Kentish kings. Herewith is presented such a volume, which has been planned and carried out as a joint enterprise. Although Stephenson is mainly responsible for the portion before 1485, and Marcham for what follows, it is hoped that the close collaboration of the editors will be apparent from the result.

In organizing a book of this sort, and one that must be kept to a useful size for an elementary course, the most difficult task is that of selection. Possibly half the available space must be assigned to the great monuments that everybody considers essential. But from all the other accumulated records of thirteen centuries just what shall be taken? Constantly faced with the embarrassing duty of excluding one document in order to include another, we have in general sought to be guided by the experience of the class-room—to govern our choice by the needs of the ordinary student. And above all else we have prized direct information concerning the organs of government. Accordingly, we have preferred official to unofficial compositions, passing over most of the latter in order to keep more of the former. No doubt the absence of many a favourite passage from chronicler or essayist will be noted and regretted. Yet our primary concern is not the history of political opinion; and it is a sheer impossibility, in this brief source book, adequately to represent leading comment on English institutions from the Venerable Bede to Harold Laski. Eventually it may seem desirable to undertake some such project in a supplementary volume.

Except for the limitation just stated, our view of constitutional history has been comparatively broad. We have given attention to local as well as central government and, to show the enlarging interests of the state, we have from time to time included materials that can be classified under ecclesiastical, legal, economic, social, or colonial history. On the other hand, we have made no effort to give by way of examples any full or continuous account of the church, the common law, trade and industry, the classes of the people, or the separate parts of the empire. Nor have we so treated every well-known feature of the constitution narrowly defined. Any selection of documents such as this must emphasize the origin of institutions; from a series of records covering many centuries, the oldest are chosen because they explain the beginning of the governmental organ that produced them. To continue indefinitely with similar extracts would serve no useful purpose. In each succeeding period stress must be laid on the great new developments, while other matters receive illustration in whatever space happens to be left.

For the sake of convenience in study and teaching, we have divided our book into chronological sections, within each of which the documents have to a certain extent been topically arranged. But no analytic plan has been rigorously applied; the instructor will always prefer to select and recombine material to suit his particular needs. Nor has any systematic interpretation of the documents been attempted. The introduction that stands at the head of each section is intended merely as a brief guide to the principal sources of that period and to the pertinent historical literature. Footnotes have been added to explain or supplement the more difficult texts, to provide cross-references, and occasionally to indicate a special article or other commentary. Such references, as well as the citations placed after the separate documents, are abbreviated. For complete bibliographical descriptions the reader may consult the alphabetical list following p. 894. And immediately preceding it he will find a table of the feast days used for dating events in the earlier documents.

Words in parentheses should be read as part of the original text. Often they are quotations in the language of the original; less frequently, when so designated in a footnote, additions from a parallel source. Square brackets, on the contrary, always indicate words supplied for one reason or another by the editors. Omitted passages, without regard to length, are shown by three points (. . .). Sums in English money are printed in the usual way: with £, s., and d. for pounds, shillings, and pence. To these abbreviations has been added *m.* for marks. And to avoid the confusion that otherwise would be inevitable, spelling has been made to conform to British rather than purely American usage.

Throughout the latter portion of the book documents are given in their original language, except that, to facilitate study, the spelling, punctuation, capital letters, and paragraphs have been brought into greater harmony with modern practice. The earlier documents are nearly all translated from Anglo-Saxon, Latin, or Old French, and in every case the translation is a new one based directly on the printed record. Even the fifteenth-century writings in English have as a rule been treated in the same way, for otherwise they would be virtually unintelligible to the average student. Only the two royal speeches quoted in no. 66A and the excerpts under no. 72C have been preserved without essential change.

Translation is on the whole fairly literal, and in all passages of real importance an effort has been made to reproduce the meaning of the original with scrupulous care. But since this book is not intended for experts, liberties of a minor sort have often been taken to improve the sense of a text. When merely a verbal change is involved, singulars have sometimes been read as plurals, or vice versa. In many enumerations "and" or its substitutes have been inserted or omitted at will. "The latter," "the former," or occasionally a name in brackets has been put in place of an ambiguous pronoun. And the rhetorical preambles to various writs and charters have been given a decidedly free rendering. Logical uniformity in the translation of proper names is impossible. Christian names have regularly been changed to familiar forms. When the surname is essentially French, it has been given with "de"; when essentially English, with "of"—so Geoffrey de Mandeville and William of London. But inconsistencies are hard to avoid, and many names not easily identified have been left as they stand in the Latin. A little carelessness or inaccuracy in such matters may be pardoned because, in the present connection, it hardly affects the value of the documents.

For permission to incorporate in this volume numerous extracts from statutes, parliamentary proceedings, and other records published by the British government, we wish to express our gratitude to the Controller of H. M. Stationery Office. The precise derivation of such extracts is indicated by the references below them in the text, supplemented by the general bibliography. References given in the same way make plain our obligation to the Chetham Society, the Pipe Roll Society, the Royal Historical Society (successor to the Camden Society), the Selden Society, the Society of Antiquaries of Newcastle-upon-Tyne, the Staffordshire Record Society, the Incorporated Council of Law Reporting for England and Wales, the Corporation of the Borough of Nottingham, and the Worcestershire County Council—all of which have been good enough to place at our disposal their valuable publications. Through the courtesy of Messrs. J. E. Neale and G. O. Sayles and the editor of the English Historical Review, we have been able to make use of two documents that originally appeared in that journal. And the following publishers have kindly allowed us to include in our collection the various materials that are here briefly indicated: the Halifax Chronicle, no. 133B; John Murray, no. 133G,I; Longmans Green & Company, no. 87A; Cassell & Company (and Mr. Arthur Bryant), no. 113; the Cambridge University Press, nos. 51D, 59, 72C, 118B, 119; the Manchester University Press, nos. 52C, 57, 61I (in part); and the Oxford University Press, nos. 27F, 28C, 39A-B, 53A, 72D, 83I, 84, 89H, 133D,H.

Lastly, we wish to acknowledge our great indebtedness to those who have read and criticized all or parts of this book in manuscript: especially Dean Guy Stanton Ford, general editor of the series; Professors A. B. White, D. H. Willson, and Faith Thompson, also of the University of Minnesota; Dr. E. F. Bradford of Cornell University; Professors C. H. McIlwain and R. B. Merriman of Harvard University; Professor Paul Knaplund of the University of Wisconsin; and Professor R. L. Schuyler of Columbia University. Mr. H. H. King, Faculty Research Assistant in the Cornell University Library, has performed the invaluable service of verifying our documents from the printed originals. And we have received help in many ways from our departmental assistants, past and present: Messrs. Walter Balderston, Arthur B. Ferguson, Goldwin A. Smith, and Francis D. Wormuth. To these and the other friends whom we have consulted—so many that we shall not attempt to list them all by name—we extend our warmest thanks. Without their practical suggestions our book would have lost much, and without their constant goodwill and encouragement we ourselves should have lost infinitely more.

CARL STEPHENSON
F. G. MARCHAM

INTRODUCTION TO
THE SECOND EDITION

In preparing the second edition of the *Sources of English Constitutional History* for publication in two volumes I have had to make many decisions, and of these the most difficult was how to handle the original text. Should I change it? Should I substitute new documents for old? Should I alter the notes and bibliographical references from page to page to bring them up-to-date with modern scholarship? Or should I allow the original text to stand and make such observations and bibliographical changes as are necessary, outside the text so to speak, by way of introductory remarks and by changes in the general bibliography.

My decision in this matter, brought to its final stage after consultation with the publisher, is to leave standing virtually all the original text. The compelling reason for this decision is the wish to prepare a second edition that will become available to students in paperback form at a modest price.

To leave intact most of the original text is to retain the comments with which Professor Stephenson and I began each of the fourteen sections. These comments contained a few references to the student's tools of his trade: in one section a work of F. W. Maitland, in another, Conyers Read's *Bibliography*, or a specialized collection of documents. Many of the original suggestions for reading are still valid. I have added new titles here and there to make available to the student the work of a new generation of English constitutional historians. The new generation has accomplished much and much has occurred to change the setting in which a book such as ours can be used.

Of great help to the student are two extensive works: *English Historical Documents*, general editor David C. Douglas, 12 volumes, Oxford, London, 1953 and subsequent years (not all volumes are yet published); and *The Oxford History of England*, general editor G. N. Clark, 15 volumes, Oxford, 1933–1965. These two works make available either directly or indirectly much of the scholarship of the last thirty years.

The volumes of *The Oxford History of England* concern themselves little with constitutional history proper. Rather their value is that they provide, period by period, the general setting for the study of government. In some instances what the author has to say about constitutional topics is part of the pattern of his narrative and discussion, in others he separates it out into an individual chapter. The bibliographical notes to each volume contain separate sections on constitutional history.

The volumes of the *English Historical Documents* series have value of a different kind. Many of the documents in each volume illustrate the working of governmental institutions. Indeed, these volumes provide such a wealth of material that the student now has before him for each period a record rich in detail and varied in the range of sources presented. And while in each volume there are sections devoted to constitutional topics, many of the other sections, say in economics, religion, and social institutions, offer the chance to see government at work or to follow the evolution of ideas that bear upon government. In addition, each section dealing with a constitutional topic—for example, the crown, parliament—has its own introductory essay and a substantial bibliography.

Two other books are worthy of comment because they serve a special purpose in the study of recent English constitutional history. They are *British Government, 1914–1963*, editor G. H. L. Le May, London, 1964, and *Cases and Materials in Constitutional and Administrative Law*, G. Wilson, Cambridge, 1966. Together these two works deal fully with the period since the end of World War I and therefore offer material that much enlarges the range of the subject matter dealt with in the new Section XV.

In brief, thanks to these books, the student who uses *Sources of English Constitutional History* has readily available to him in his college library many hundreds of other documents of the same general nature. They open to him the opportunity to study firsthand not only major public institutions, but also lesser aspects of government; not only, for example, the courts and parliament, but modern applications of censorship law to movies and television. Yet the worth of the original selection of documents in *Sources of English Constitutional History* continues; these documents are foundation stones for the study of English constitutional history and they give examples of the basic governmental institutions at work.

Publication of new collections of documents has enlarged the field of study but brought no fundamental change in its proportions. However, those who have written during the past thirty years as interpretors of English constitutional history—exploring what they believe the documents to mean—have in some instances presented new judgments and significantly altered the pattern of interpretation. The whole range of study—from the Anglo-Saxons to the Tudors to the Victorians—has undergone reevaluation in a substantial literature. Evidence for this can be found in the bibliographies associated with the new works referred to above and in the bibliographies included in Bryce Lyon, *A Constitutional and Legal History of Medieval England,* New York: Harper & Row, 1960; and Frederick George Marcham, *A Constitutional History of Modern England, 1485 to the Present,* New York: Harper & Row, 1960.

The student will quickly see that reevaluation continues for all periods of English history; proof that the study of English governmental institutions continues to be vigorous. And this trend indicates more; that today, in the latter half of the twentieth century, debate is more active than ever regarding the effectiveness of the major institutions, of their structure, and of their relationship to one another both for the present and for the immediate future.

FREDERICK GEORGE MARCHAM

SOURCES
OF
ENGLISH
CONSTITUTIONAL
HISTORY

SECTION

I

THE ANGLO-SAXON PERIOD

OUR most valuable source for early English institutions is the matchless series of Anglo-Saxon dooms, which begin with the enactments of the first Christian king of Kent and end with those of Canute. Spanning close upon five centuries, they cannot be expected to reflect a uniform pattern either of state or of society. Furthermore, it must be remembered that in the main they are fragments of customary law rather than a code. Their tantalizing obscurity is due to the fact that the great body of familiar usages remained unwritten. So, although the present selection is at best a set of meagre excerpts, it is no more disconnected than the entire compilation. The student may be sure that he has before him all very significant references to the organs of government, especially those statements which are first of their kind. And he will find in addition a number of passages chosen to illustrate the working of the customary law and the status within it of the various social classes.

Compared with the dooms, the charters of the Anglo-Saxon period are of minor importance in the study of English constitutional history. From the great mass of such instruments that have come down to us, only seven are translated in the following pages. They may be regarded as typical examples, showing primarily how legal documents were drafted, how the formal decisions of courts were rendered, and how, through the alienation of public rights, the kings created immunities for their favoured subjects.

The definitive edition of the dooms is F. Liebermann's *Gesetze der Angelsachsen*, which is accompanied by a German translation and a wealth of learned comment. Text and English translation of nearly all the following excerpts are available, with useful notes, in F. L. Attenborough's *Laws of the Earliest English Kings* and A. J. Robertson's *Laws of the Kings of England from Edmund to Henry I*. There is, unfortunately, no well-edited general collection of Anglo-Saxon charters. Neither Kemble's *Codex Diplomaticus Aevi Saxonici* nor Birch's *Cartularium Saxonicum*

I

is at all adequate to meet the needs of modern scholars. The seven charters here given are all from Thorpe's *Diplomatarium Anglicum Aevi Saxonici*—a convenient volume of documents taken from Kemble's edition and provided with translations from the Anglo-Saxon, free use of which has here been made. For a much wider selection of such material, the student is referred to Miss Robertson's *Anglo-Saxon Charters*.

As may be seen by reading the first few of the *Supplementary Studies* by Petit-Dutaillis,[1] the work of Stubbs on the earlier centuries of English constitutional history has been largely superseded, but no single essay has been written to take its place. For the advanced student an indispensable guide to all phases of Anglo-Saxon institutions is to be found in Liebermann's exhaustive notes and *Sachglosser* (*Gesetze*, vols. I–II). And anyone who hopes to understand the dooms and other pre-Conquest sources should read F. W. Maitland's *Domesday Book and Beyond* and H. M. Chadwick's *Studies on Anglo-Saxon Institutions*. F. M. Stenton's *Anglo-Saxon England* and R. H. Hodgkin's *History of the Anglo Saxons* provide much information and interpretation regarding Anglo-Saxon government. *English Historical Documents, c.*500–1042, edited by D. Whitelock, presents in fuller form many of the laws and charters included in this section and adds to their number.

---

[1] In *Studies and Notes Supplementary to Stubbs' Constitutional History.* C. Petit-Dutaillis and G. Lefebvre. 1930.

1. DOOMS OF AETHELBERHT (601-04)

These are the dooms that King Aethelberht established in the days of Augustine.[1]

1. [One who steals] the property[2] of God and the church [shall

---

[1] The famous Roman missionary and archbishop of Canterbury, who secured the conversion of Aethelberht, king of Kent, and presumably inspired him to have the following dooms written down.

[2] *Feoh,* which originally meant cattle, but eventually came to be used for movable property in general.

pay] twelvefold compensation;[3] the property of a bishop, elevenfold; the property of a priest, ninefold; the property of a deacon, sixfold; the property of a [lesser] clergyman, threefold. [He who breaks] the peace (*friþ*) of the church [shall pay] double compensation; the peace of a public assembly (*maethl*), double compensation.

2. If the king summons his people[4] to him, and if any one there does them wrong, he shall pay double compensation [to the injured person] and 50s. to the king.

3. If the king is drinking in a man's house, and if any one commits any kind of misdeed there, he shall pay double compensation [to the householder].

4. If a freeman steals from the king, he shall pay ninefold compensation.

5. If a man slays another in a villa[5] of the king, he shall pay 50s. compensation [to the king]. . . .

8. The king's *mundbyrd*[6] is 50s.

9. If a freeman steals from a freeman, he shall pay threefold compensation [to the latter], and the king shall have the fine (*wite*) and all the goods [of the thief]. . . .

13. If a man slays another in a villa of a nobleman (*eorl*), he shall pay 12s. compensation [to the nobleman]. . . .

15. The *mundbyrd* of a *ceorl*[7] is 6s. . . .

17. If a man leads the way in breaking into some one's villa, he shall pay 6s. compensation; the one who next breaks in 3s.; and every one after that 1s. . . .

21. If a man slays another, he shall pay as compensation [to the kindred] the ordinary wergeld (*leodgeld*) of 100s. . . .

24. If any one binds a freeman, he shall pay [him] 20s. compensation. . . .

27. If a freeman commits hedge-breaking,[8] he shall pay 6s. compensation.

---

[3] Such compensation as is prescribed in these dooms was normally paid to the injured person or his kindred, in contrast to the fine, *wite*, paid to the king or his agent. The Kentish shilling, like the gold *solidus* of the Merovingians, was reckoned at twenty times the worth of a silver penny, *denarius* or *sceatt*.

[4] *Leode*, a quite general word, which could refer to any of the king's subjects.

[5] *Tun*, from which is derived our word town, was the ordinary term for an agricultural village during the later Anglo-Saxon period. Here, as in articles 13 and 17 below, it evidently refers to a house or an estate.

[6] Literally, right of protection; hence the payment for violating it.

[7] The ordinary freeman, often contrasted with the *eorl*, or nobleman.

[8] That is to say, forcibly enters a man's property surrounded by a hedge. Cf. Alfred, 40 (below, p. 11), and the later *hamsocn* (below, p. 22, n. 1).

28. If the man takes any property from inside, he shall pay three-fold compensation . . .[9]

(Anglo-Saxon) Liebermann, *Gesetze*, I, 3 f.

---

[9] Here follows in the doom an elaborate schedule of compensations for minor injuries: e.g., an ear, 12s.; an eye, 50s.; the chin-bone, 20s.; a front tooth, 6s.; a thumb, 20s.; a forefinger, 9s.; a fingernail, 1s.; a big toe, 10s.

2. DOOMS OF HLOTHAERE AND EADRIC (685-86)

1. If some one's servant[1] slays a man of noble birth, one whose wergeld is 300s., his master shall give up the slayer [to the kindred] and also pay [them] the value of three [ordinary] men.[2]

2. If the slayer escapes, he shall then add the value of a fourth man and shall clear himself with good oath-helpers, [proving] that he was unable to secure the slayer.

3. If some one's servant slays a freeman, one whose wergeld is 100s., his master shall give up the slayer and pay also the value of a second man. . . .

5. If a freeman steals a man, and he returns to accuse [the former], he shall make a personal accusation and the accused man shall then clear himself if he can: every [such] man shall have a number of free-men as oath-helpers, with [at least] one of them from the same vill to which he himself belongs. If he cannot thus clear himself, then he shall pay compensation to the best of his ability. . . .

7. If [presumably] one man steals property from another, and if the owner afterwards seizes it, the accused shall vouch to warranty at the king's hall,[3] presenting, if he can, the man who sold it to him. If he cannot do so, he shall give it up and the owner shall have [legal title].

8. If a man accuses another of a misdeed, and if he meets that [accused] man in an assembly (*medle*) or in a court (*þinge*), the [accused] man must regularly furnish the other with a surety[4] and submit to whatever justice the Kentish doomsmen[5] prescribe. . . .

---

[1] *Esne*, who was evidently unfree, although the ordinary word for slave in these dooms is *þeuw*. Cf. Wihtraed, 22 (below, p. 6).

[2] Because the slain man's wergeld was thrice that of an ordinary man. Cf. art. 3, below.

[3] *Sele*; cf. art. 16, below. Such a royal hall was apparently not a private residence, but rather an administrative centre in charge of a reeve, as is indicated at London. On the procedure known to the Anglo-Saxons as *team*, and later styled vouching to warranty, see Holdsworth, *History of English Law*, II, 100 f. See also the oaths under no. 14, below.

[4] The surety (*borh*) was a person who, if the accused man escaped, would be legally responsible for his obligations.

[5] A *dema*, whence is derived "deemster" and "dempster," was any one who rendered dooms, legal decisions of any kind. A royal official or judge might be called a *dema*, but in the courts of England and the continent at this time it was the suitors, rather than the presiding magistrate, who declared the law. See Pollock and Maitland, I, 139.

11. If a man in some one else's house calls another a perjurer, or accosts him insultingly with scandalous words, he shall pay 1s. to the householder, 6s. to the man whom he insulted, and 12s. to the king.

12. If, where men are drinking, one takes the tankard from another without any fault [on the part of the latter], by ancient custom he shall pay 1s. to the householder, 6s. to the man whose tankard he took, and 12s. to the king.

13. If, where men are drinking, one draws his weapon but inflicts no injury with it, he shall pay 1s. to the householder and 12s. to the king.

14. If the house is bloodied, he shall pay the *mundbyrd*[6] of the householder, and to the king [a fine of] 50s.

15. If any one entertains, as a guest in his own house, a trader or some other man from beyond the border, keeping him for three nights and supplying him with food, and if he then does wrong to some one, the man [of the house] shall bring him to justice or satisfy justice in his place.

16. If a Kentishman buys property in London-wick,[7] he must have as witnesses two or three reliable freemen or the king's wick-reeve. Then, should any one take it away from the man in Kent, he shall vouch to warranty at the king's hall (*sele*) in [London-]wick the man who sold it to him, if the man is known to him and can be produced for warranty. If he cannot do that, he shall swear on the altar, together with one of his witnesses or with the king's reeve, that he bought the property honestly and by public purchase in [London-]wick, and its value shall then be returned to him. If, however, he cannot justify himself by such lawful process, he must surrender it and the [rightful] owner shall have [legal title].

(Anglo-Saxon) *Ibid.*, I, 9 f.

---

[6] See above, p. 3, n. 6.
[7] *Wic* is a common equivalent of *tun*, to designate a settlement, big or little.

3. DOOMS OF WIHTRAED (695-96)

2. The *mundbyrd*[1] of the church shall be, like that of the king, 50s. . . .

16. The word of a bishop or of the king shall be incontestible [even] without an oath.

17. The head of a monastery shall clear himself by the same form as a priest.

18. A priest shall clear himself by his own [unsupported] affirmation: [dressed] in his sacred garments, he shall declare before the altar, *Veritatem dico in Christo; non mentior*.[2] In the same way shall a deacon clear himself.

19. A [lesser] clergyman shall clear himself with three [oath-

---

[1] See above, p. 3, n. 6.
[2] Before Christ I speak the truth; I do not lie.

helpers][3] of his own rank. But he alone shall have his hand on the altar; the others shall merely stand by to support the oath.

20. A stranger (*gest*) shall clear himself by his own [unsupported] oath at the altar.[4] In the same way shall a king's thegn clear himself.

21. An ordinary freeman (*ceorlisce man*) shall clear himself at the altar with three oath-helpers of his own rank. . . .

22. If any one accuses a bishop's or a king's servant (*esne*), the latter shall clear himself by the hand of the reeve,[5] so that the reeve shall either clear him or deliver him over [to the complainant] to be beaten. . . .

25. If any one slays a man in the act of theft, let him[6] lie without wergeld.

26. If any one catches a freeman in the act of theft, the king shall determine one of three [penalties]: that he be slain, that he be sold beyond the sea, or that he redeem his life through [payment of] his wergeld. The one who catches and holds him shall have half of what he is worth; or, if he should be slain, he [who captured him] shall be paid 70s.

27. If a slave (*þeuw*) steals and it is proposed to redeem him, 70s. [shall be paid] if the king is willing [to spare him]. . . .

28. If a man coming from afar, or a stranger, leaves the highway and then neither calls out nor blows a horn, he shall be considered a thief, to be slain or to be redeemed [by paying his wergeld].

(Anglo-Saxon) *Ibid.,* I, 12 f.

---

[3] Literally "as a foursome"—counting himself one of the four.

[4] The dooms normally regard a stranger as a suspicious person (cf. art. 28, below). In this instance, however, a man of honourable rank, a guest rather than a vagabond, seems to be thought of, for he is treated like a king's thegn. The latter title becomes increasingly common in the dooms, designating in particular a noble retainer.

[5] That is to say, the reeve of the estate to which the servant is attached may take an oath to clear him.

[6] The slain thief, for whose death the kindred had no right to compensation.

4. DOOMS OF INE (688-95)

I, Ine, by the grace of God king of the West Saxons, with the advice and instruction of Cenred, my father, of Hedde, my bishop, and of Eorcenwold, my bishop, together with all my aldermen,[1] the most distinguished *witan*[2] among my people, and also a great assembly of God's servants, have taken counsel concerning the welfare of our

---

[1] Royal officials of the highest rank, generally in charge of considerable districts, where they held courts, commanded troops, and performed other duties in the king's name.

[2] Literally "wise men"—the king's chief advisers, both lay and clerical. To what extent they constituted a formal council, with definite powers and privileges, has been a matter of controversy. See Chadwick, *Studies,* ch. ix, and F. Liebermann, *The National Assembly in the Anglo-Saxon Period;* cf. the formulae in the charters under no. 15. below.

souls and the state of our realm, in order that just laws and just royal dooms should be established and assured to all our people, and so that no alderman or subject of ours should henceforth pervert these our dooms. . . .

6. If any one fights in the king's house, he shall forfeit all his inheritance, and it shall be in the king's judgment whether or not he shall lose his life. If any one fights in a monastery, he shall pay 120s. compensation [to the monastery]. If any one fights in the house of an alderman, or of some other distinguished statesman (*witan*), he shall pay 60s. compensation [to the householder] and another 60s. as a fine [to the king]. If, however, he fights in the house of a rent-payer (*gafolgeldan*)[3] or peasant (*gebures*), he shall pay 30s.[4] as a fine and 6s. to the peasant. . . .

8. If any one demands justice before any shireman (*scirman*),[5] or any other judge, and cannot obtain it through default of a pledge [from the accused], he shall pay 30s. compensation [to the plaintiff] and within seven nights do him proper justice.

9. If any one wreaks vengeance [on his enemy] before demanding justice [in court], he shall give back anything he has seized together with as much again [to the injured party], and shall pay 30s. compensation [to the king]. . . .

12. If a thief is captured [in the act of thieving], let him suffer death or redeem his life through payment of his wergeld.

13. . . . By "thieves" (*þeofas*) we mean men up to the number seven; by "a band" (*hloð*) from seven to thirty-five; by "an army" (*here*) above thirty-five.

14. One accused of belonging to [such] a band shall clear himself through [an oath worth] 120 hides[6] or pay an equal amount[7] as compensation.

15. One accused of plundering with [such] an army shall redeem

---

[3] The ordinary meaning of *gafol* was rent, and it was often paid in kind (see no. 15A, below). The text seems to imply that the *gafolgelda* was a kind of *gebur*—the "boor" of our modern speech.

[4] This was apparently the original amount, although most manuscripts have 120. The West Saxon shilling was a weight of silver, at this time reckoned as 1/48 of a pound, but from the eleventh century on as 1/20 of a pound. At all times the pound was supposed to contain 240 silver pence (*denarii*).

[5] In the early dooms *scir* means any administrative district. The alderman was in charge of a large shire—whether or not it corresponded to one of the later counties is doubtful.

[6] Cf. art. 19, below, and Alfred, 39 (below, p. 11). According to this equation, the oaths of a *ceorl*, a six-hundred man, and a twelve-hundred man were computed respectively as 10, 30, and 60 hides. By this means any group of freemen could be quickly assessed at what may be called their swearing-worth. Note also that many dooms required the number of oath-helpers, or the total value of their oaths, to vary in proportion to the gravity of the offence; see especially Edward the Elder, I, 1 (below, p. 12). The determination of such matters was normally left to the doomsmen in the court.

[7] I.e., 120s.

his life through [payment of] his wergeld or shall clear himself by [an oath equivalent to] his wergeld. . . .

19. A king's *geneat*,[8] if his wergeld is 1200*s*., may swear for 60 hides if he is a regular communicant [at church].

20. If a man from afar, or a stranger, goes through the woods off the highway and neither calls out nor blows a horn, he may be considered a thief, to be slain or to be redeemed [by paying his wergeld].[9]

21. If then any one lays claim to the wergeld of the slain man, the slayer may prove [by an unsupported oath] that he slew the man as a thief; neither the geld-associates[10] nor the lord[11] [of the slain man] may avail themselves of an oath [to set aside such proof]. . . .

22. Should your *geneat* steal and then escape you, you may claim the *angyld*[12] from his surety, if you have one for him. If not, you must pay the *angyld*, but he shall not on that account be held guiltless.

23. . . . [The wergeld of] a Welsh rent-payer[13] [is] 120*s*.; of his son 100. A Welsh slave [is worth] 60, or sometimes 50. A Welshman's skin [is worth] 12.[14] . . .

25. If a trader does business among the people throughout the countryside, he must do so before witnesses. If stolen property is found in the possession of a trader, and if he has not bought it before good witnesses, he must pay a fine of 36*s*. or clear himself through [an oath equivalent to] the fine, swearing that he was neither the thief nor an accomplice. . . .

32. If a Welshman possesses a hide of land, his wergeld is 120*s*., if only half a hide, 80*s*.; if no land at all, 60*s*.

33. A Welsh horseman who rides in the king's service has a wergeld of 200*s*. . . .

36. If some one captures a thief or is given a captured thief [to

---

[8] The *geneat* might enjoy relatively high or low status, but was always a man of honourable rank. As described in the later sources, his chief duty was that of riding on errands; cf. no. 15C.

[9] A re-enactment of Wihtraed, 28 (above, p. 6).

[10] The meaning, obviously, is not "gild-brethren," as was assumed by older writers, but those persons who might have to pay compensation for a man's acts and so would have a claim on any wergeld that might be paid when he was slain. See Gross, *Gild Merchant*, I, 177.

[11] *Hlaford*, literally the "bread-keeper," while the lady is the "bread-kneader." The term was a vague one that could be used for any person of superior authority: God, the king, a husband, a great noble, one from whom land was held, one having rights of jurisdiction over another, or one to whom a man commended himself (cf. no. 14A). Just what sort of lord may be meant in a particular doom is often hard to determine.

[12] Literally "single payment"—the mere value of the stolen property. On the surety see above, p. 4, n. 4.

[13] *Gafolgelda;* see above, p. 7, n. 3.

[14] That is to say, he could buy off a beating with this sum. Cf. Alfred, 35 (below, p. 11), where flogging a Saxon *ceorl* involves the payment of 20*s*. compensation.

guard], and then lets the thief go or conceals the theft, he shall pay the thief's wergeld as compensation. If he is an alderman, he shall lose his shire, unless the king will pardon him.

37. If a *ceorl* has often been accused of theft, and is finally proved guilty, either through the cauldron[15] or through being caught in the act, he shall have his hand or his foot cut off.

38. If a *ceorl* and his wife have a child, and the *ceorl* dies, the mother shall keep her child and bring it up. She shall be given 6s. [a year] for its care—a cow in summer and an ox in winter.[16] The relatives shall keep the homestead until the child has grown up.

39. If any one leaves his lord without permission or steals away into another shire[17], and if he is then discovered, he must go back to where he was before and pay his lord 60s.

40. The landed property (*worðig*) of a *ceorl* shall be fenced both winter and summer. If it is not, and if his neighbour's cattle come through an opening that he has left, he shall have no claim to such cattle, he must drive them out and suffer the damage. . . .

42. If free peasants (*ceorlas*) have the task of fencing a common meadow or other land that is divided into strips (*gedalland*),[18] and if some have built their portions of the fence while others have not, and if their common acres or grasslands are eaten [by straying animals], then those responsible for the opening must go and pay compensation to the others, who have done their share of the fencing, for any damage that may have been suffered. . . .

45. [Compensation for] *burhbryce*[19] of the king, or of a bishop anywhere in his diocese, is 120s.; of an alderman 80s.; of a king's thegn 60s.; of a landed nobleman (*gesiðcundes monnes*)[20] 35s.: and according to these values [accusations of such offences] are to be cleared by oath. . . .

50. If a nobleman comes to an agreement with the king or with the king's alderman concerning the misdeeds of his dependents, or with his lord concerning slave or free, he shall have no share of such fines as they may pay through his own failure to restrain them from evil-doing at home.[21]

51. If a nobleman holding land neglects army service (*fierd*), he

---

[15] I.e., the ordeal of hot water; cf. no. 8B, below.

[16] It is not clear from the text whether the two animals were paid as the equivalent of the money or in addition to it. In Alfred, 16, a calf is valued at a shilling; a cow and an ox might well be worth 6s.

[17] See above, p. 7, n. 5; cf. Alfred, 37 (below, p. 11).

[18] The reference is to the division of arable into strips under the open-field system. It is noteworthy that in the present enactment the holder of the strip is styled a *ceorl*, the designation of the ordinary freeman.

[19] In these early dooms the *burh* is the fortified dwelling or estate of an important man; for the later *burh*, see below, p. 14, n. 7.

[20] This term is now substituted for the *eorl* of the Kentish dooms; see Chadwick, *Studies,* chs. iii, x.

[21] The doom seems to refer to some such arrangement as was later called *sac* and *soc*; see below, p. 30, n. 23.

shall pay 120s. and forfeit his land; one who holds no land shall pay 60s.; a *ceorl* shall pay 30s. as fine for neglect of service (*fierdwite*).

(Anglo-Saxon) *Ibid.*, I, 88 f.

5. DOOMS OF ALFRED (871-901)

I, then, King Alfred, have collected these [dooms] and ordered [them] to be written down—[that is to say,] many of those which our predecessors observed and which were also pleasing to me. And those which were not pleasing to me, by the advice of my *witan*, I have rejected, ordering them to be observed only as amended. I have not ventured to put in writing much of my own, being uncertain what might please those who shall come after us. So I have here collected the dooms that seemed to me the most just, whether they were from the time of Ine, my kinsman, from that of Offa, king of the Mercians,[1] or from that of Aethelberht, the first of the English to receive baptism; the rest I have discarded. I, then, Alfred, king of the West Saxons, have shown these [dooms] to all my *witan*, who have declared it is the will of all that they be observed. . . .

4. If any one plots against the king's life, either by himself or by harbouring outlaws or their men, he shall forfeit his life and all that he has.[2] If he wishes to clear himself, he must do so through [an oath equal to] the king's wergeld. So likewise we command with regard to all ranks of men, *eorl* or *ceorl*: he who plots against the life of his lord shall forfeit his life and all that he has, or else clear himself through [an oath equal to] his lord's wergeld. . . .

7. If any one fights or draws his weapon in the king's hall (*healle*) and is then caught, at the king's judgment he may be put to death or allowed his life in case the king is willing to forgive him. . . .

15. If any one fights or draws his weapon in the presence of an archbishop, he shall pay 150s. compensation; if this happens in the presence of some other bishop or in that of an alderman, he shall pay 100s. compensation. . . .

22. If any one at the popular court (*folces gemote*) brings an accusation [for theft] before the king's reeve and wishes to withdraw it, let him make his complaint against the right person if he can; if he cannot, he shall lose his *angyld*[3] and also pay a fine. . . .

34. It is further ordained with regard to traders that they shall bring before the king's reeve at the popular court all the men whom they are taking with them, declaring how many there are. And they should take with them such men as [when necessary] they can later bring to justice in the popular court. And in case they need more men

[1] The dooms of Offa have not come down to us.

[2] This crime may be called treason, but it should be noted that no idea of *lèse majesté* appears in the doom. As yet the king is treated like any other lord, and he has a wergeld like any other freeman.

[3] See above, p. 8, n. 12.

with them on their journey, as often as such need arises, a similar declaration must be made to the king's reeve in the popular court.

35. One who binds an innocent *ceorl* shall pay [him] 10s. compensation. One who flogs him shall pay [him] 20s. One who puts him under duress[4] shall pay [him] 30s. One who, as a shameful insult, cuts his hair shall pay [him] 10s. One who shears him like a priest, but without binding him, shall pay [him] 30s. One who cuts off his beard shall pay [him] 20s. One who binds him and then shears him like a priest shall pay [him] 60s. . . .

37. If any one wishes to go from one settlement[5] into another to seek a lord, he must first have as witness the alderman in whose shire he was at first a follower. If he does so without such witness, the lord who takes him as a man shall pay a fine of 120s., dividing his payment so that the king will get half in the shire where the man was at first a follower and half in that to which he comes. . . .

38. If any one fights at a court before the king's alderman, he shall pay whatever wergeld and fine (*wer ond wite*) may be due, but before that [he must pay] 120s. fine to the alderman. If he disturbs the court by [merely] drawing a weapon, [he shall pay] a fine of 120s. to the alderman. If anything of the sort occurs before a subordinate of the king's alderman, or before a priest of the king, 30s. fine shall be paid.

39. If any one fights in the house of a *ceorl,* he shall pay the *ceorl* 6s. compensation. If he draws his weapon but does not fight, the compensation shall be half as much. If either of these offences is committed in the house of a six-hundred man,[6] the compensation shall be three times that paid to a *ceorl*; if in the house of a twelve-hundred man, the compensation shall be twice that of the six-hundred man.

40. [Compensation for] *burhbryce*[7] of the king is 120s.; of an archbishop 90s.; of any other bishop or of an alderman 60s.; of a twelve-hundred man 30s.; of a six-hundred man 15s. [Compensation for] breaking through the hedge of a *ceorl* [is] 5s. If any of these offences occurs while the army is in the field or during the fast of Lent, the penalty shall be doubled. . . .

41. We now ordain that any one who has bookland[8] left him by his kinsmen is not to give it outside his kindred if there is written or oral evidence (*gewrit oððe gewitnes*) that to do so was forbidden by the man who originally acquired it or by those who gave it to him. And this should be proved in the presence of the kindred, and with the witness of the king or of the bishop, by any one [wishing to annul such an alienation].

---

[4] *On hengenne*—e.g., locks him up or fastens him in stocks.

[5] Cf. Ine, 39 (above, p. 9).

[6] One whose wergeld is 600s.

[7] Cf. Aethelberht, 27, and Ine, 45 (above, pp. 3, 9).

[8] Land held by book, that is to say, by charter; see the examples under no. 15, below.

42. We also command that any one knowing his enemy to be at home shall not fight him before demanding justice of him [in court]. If [the accuser] has strength to surround and besiege his enemy inside [the latter's house], let him be held there seven nights and not attacked so long as he will remain inside. Then, after seven nights, if the [besieged] enemy will surrender and give up his weapons, let him be kept unharmed for thirty nights while news of him is sent to his kinsmen and friends. . . . If, however, [the accuser] lacks the strength to besiege his enemy, he shall ride to the alderman and ask him for aid; if the latter refuses him aid, he shall ride to the king before beginning a fight. . . . We declare furthermore that one may fight for his lord without incurring blood-feud,[9] if the lord has been attacked. So also the lord may fight for his man. In the same way one may fight for his blood-relative, should the latter be unjustly attacked, except against his own lord—that we do not permit. . . .[10]

(Anglo-Saxon) *Ibid.*, I, 46 f.

---

[9] The lawful vengeance of the kindred.

[10] Here follows in the text a detailed schedule of compensations for physical injuries: e.g., an ear, 30s.; an eye, the tongue, a hand, or a foot, 66s. 3⅓d.; the nose, 60s.; a front tooth, 8s.; a molar, 4s.; an eye-tooth, 15s.; a thumb, 30s.; a thumbnail, 5s.; a first finger, 15s.; its nail, 3s.; a little finger 9s.; its nail, 1s.; a big toe, 20s.; a little toe, 5s.

6. DOOMS OF EDWARD THE ELDER (901·24)

I. King Edward's commands to all his reeves: that you deem such right dooms as you know to be most right and as stand in the doom-book.[1] Nor for any cause shall you fail to declare the customary law; and [you shall see to it] that a day is set for every cause, when that which you decide concerning it shall be carried out.

1. And I will that every man shall have his warrantor;[2] and that no one shall trade outside a port,[3] but shall have the witness of the portreeve or of other trustworthy men whose word can be relied on. And if any one trades outside a port, he shall be liable for the king's *oferhyrnesse*.[4] . . . A man who wishes to prove lawful title shall bring forward trustworthy witnesses to it, or he shall, if he can, provide an undetermined[5] oath such as shall satisfy the complainant. If, however, he cannot do this, he shall be assigned six men from the

---

[1] Presumably, as Liebermann suggests, Alfred's collection.

[2] *Getcaman;* see above, p. 4, n. 3.

[3] *Ceapige butan porte.* This is the first appearance in the dooms of the word port. Subsequently it is often used as the equivalent of *burh*, and the reeve of a borough was always styled portreeve; see below, p. 14, n. 7. A review of the literature in this connection will be found in C. Stephenson, *Borough and Town*, pp. 65 f.; cf. Tait, *The Medieval English Borough*, pp. 5 f.

[4] A special fine of 120s. for violation of a royal command.

[5] *Ungecorenne*—the term used when the defendant chose his own oath-helpers, as distinguished from the procedure required below.

same *geburhscipe*[6] in which he has his home. From these six he shall name [as oath-helper] one for each cow, or the equivalent in lesser beasts; and the number [of oath-helpers] shall be increased, as they are needed, in proportion to the property [in dispute]. . . .

3. Concerning perjurers we further declare that, if their guilt has been proved, whether oaths have failed for them or they have been oversworn [by better oaths], they shall no longer be oath-worthy, but must rely upon the ordeal [for clearing themselves of charges].

II. King Edward admonished his *witan,* when they were at Exeter, that all should consider how the peace of their country could be better kept than it had been; for it seemed to him that what he had previously ordained had not been enforced as it should have been.

1. . . . No man shall refuse justice to another. If he does so, let him pay compensation as has been earlier provided: the first time 30s., the second time the same amount, the third time 120s. to the king.

2. And if it is not exacted by the reeve lawfully, with the witness of such men as have been assigned to him for that purpose,[7] he shall pay 120s. as my *oferhyrnesse.* . . .

4. It is also my will that every one shall always have on his land men ready to guide those who wish to track their own [cattle], and that such guides shall in no way obstruct the search for the sake of bribes; nor shall they anywhere wilfully or wittingly protect or foster guilt. . . .

6. If, through conviction for theft, any one, deserted by his kindred and knowing no one who will pay compensation in his place, loses his freedom and places himself under the hand of another, then let him be liable for as much slave labour as may be due; and his kindred shall forfeit all claim to his wergeld [should he be slain]. . . .

8. It is my will that each reeve shall hold a court (*gemot*) every four weeks,[8] and that the reeves shall see that every man obtains folkright, and that every case shall have a day set when it is to be decided. And if any one [of my reeves] neglects this [duty], he shall be liable for the compensation already prescribed.

(Anglo-Saxon) *Ibid.,* I, 138 f.

---

[6] Presumably a district with a borough as its administrative centre; in any case, the region in which the accused dwelt.

[7] Probably by the court.

[8] This is the first definite mention of the monthly court which later dooms call the hundred; see below, p. 17, n. 5.

7. DOOMS OF AETHELSTAN (925-40)

II, 1. In the first place, no thief caught in the act is to be spared, [if he is] over twelve years old and [if the stolen property is worth] over 8d. . . .

2. And with regard to lordless men from whom no justice is to be obtained, we have ordained that their kindred be commanded to settle

them in homes [where they will be subject] to folkright, and to find them lords in the popular court (*folcgemote*). And if, by the day set. the kindred will not or cannot do so, he[1] shall thenceforth be an outlaw, to be treated as a thief by any one who meets him. . . .

3. Should a lord intervene on behalf of his guilty man and [thereby] deny justice [to some one], and should the [latter] man then appeal to the king, [the lord] shall pay [to the complainant] the value of the goods [in question], and to the king 120*s*. He, however, who appeals to the king before seeking justice [in the local court][2] as often as he should, shall pay the same fine as the other would have been liable for had he denied justice. . . .

4. And with regard to betrayal of the lord, we have declared that he who cannot deny it, or [having denied it] is convicted by the threefold ordeal,[3] shall forfeit his life. . . .

7. And with regard to the simple ordeal for men who have been often accused of theft, we have ordained that, if they are convicted, they shall be imprisoned and shall be released only on the conditions already stated.[4] . . .

10. And no one shall exchange any livestock without witness of the reeve,[5] the priest, the lord of the land (*londhlafordes*), the [lord's] steward, or some other reliable man. If any one does so, he shall pay a fine of 30*s*. [to the king], and the lord of the land shall seize whatever has been exchanged. . . .

12. And we have ordered that no one shall trade in goods worth more than 20*d*. outside a port;[6] but every one shall do his trading inside, with the witness of the portreeve or of some other trustworthy man, or else at the popular court (*folcgemote*) with the witness of the reeves.

13. And we have ordered that every borough (*burh*)[7] shall be repaired within a fortnight after Rogation. . . .

14. [We have also ordered] that one coinage shall have currency throughout all the king's realm and that no one shall mint [money] except within a port. . . . There shall be seven moneyers at Canterbury: four for the king, two for the archbishop, and one for the abbot. At Rochester [there shall be] three: two for the king and one for the bishop. At London [there shall be] eight, at Winchester six,

---

[1] A lordless man of this sort.

[2] Cf. Edgar, III, 2 (below, p. 19); Canute, II, 17 (below, p. 22).

[3] See no. 8B.

[4] When a surety has been found.

[5] The king's reeve is apparently meant; cf. art. 12, below. That the *hordere* of this passage was an ordinary rural steward, rather than some sort of treasurer, has been shown by R. L. Poole (*The Exchequer in the Twelfth Century*, pp. 22 f.).

[6] A modification of Edward, I, 1 (above, p. 12).

[7] This is the first appearance of the word in the dooms to refer to the official centres of defence and administration that are so frequently mentioned in the contemporary Anglo-Saxon Chronicle. It is clear from the following article that such a borough might also be called a port; see above, p. 12, n. 3.

at Lewes two, at Hastings one, another at Chichester, at Southampton two, at Wareham two, at Dorchester one, at Exeter two, at Shaftsbury two, and besides these one in [each of] the other boroughs (*burgum*). . . .

20. And if any one thrice neglects attendance at the court (*gemot*), he shall pay the king's *oferhyrnesse*.[8] And the holding of the court shall be announced seven days in advance. If, however, he will neither do what is right nor pay the *oferhyrnesse*, then all the chief (*yldestan*) men who belong to the borough shall ride against him and take all that he has and put him under surety. . . .

23. If any one is obliged to [go to] the ordeal, he shall come three days in advance to the priest in charge of the consecration; and before he does so, he shall feed himself on bread, water, salt, and herbs; and on each of the three days he shall attend mass; and on the day he undergoes the ordeal he shall make an offering and take communion; and then, before he goes to the ordeal, he shall swear an oath that, according to folkright, he is innocent of the charge made against him. And if it is [the ordeal of cold] water, he must sink an ell and a half on the rope [to clear himself].[9] If it is the [ordeal of] iron, three days must elapse before the hand is uncovered.[10] . . .

25. If, now, any of my reeves will not enforce this [ordinance], or shows less zeal [in the matter] than we have commanded, he must pay my *oferhyrnesse*, and I shall find another man who will [enforce it].

V, 1. . . . And in the district (*manunge*) of every reeve let there be named as many men as are known to be trustworthy, so that they may serve as witnesses in every suit. And their oaths shall count as those of trustworthy men, [to be numbered] acording to the value of the property without selection.[11]

(Anglo-Saxon) *Ibid.*, I, 150 f.

---

[8] See above, p. 12, n. 4.

[9] In this ordeal the accused was tied hand and foot and then lowered on the end of a rope into a pond or other still water. If he sank to the required depth, as marked on the rope, he was declared innocent, on the theory that a guilty person would not be received by the consecrated water. But a psychological factor may be detected in the possibility of a man's struggling to keep himself up.

[10] See below, p. 16, n. 5.

[11] See above, p. 7, n. 6; p. 12, n. 5.

8. ANONYMOUS DOOMS[1]

(A) Concerning Incendiaries and Murderers

With regard to incendiaries and murderers,[2] we have ordered that the difficulty of their oath shall be tripled;[3] likewise the iron for

---

[1] To judge from both the language and the subject matter, the two following dooms date from the time of Aethelstan.

[2] *Morpslyhtum*, those who slew by stealth or tried to conceal their offenses, cf. the later *murdrum* (below, p. 36, n. 2).

[3] That is to say, the required number of oath-helpers is to be tripled.

[trying such persons by] ordeal shall be brought up to three pounds in weight. The accused must go to the ordeal himself, and the accuser shall choose either ordeal by water or ordeal by iron, whichever he may prefer. If [the accused] fails in such oath and so is proved guilty, the chief men who belong to the borough[4] shall decide whether or not he shall be permitted to live.

(Anglo-Saxon) *Ibid.*, I, 388.

(B) Concerning Ordeals

And with regard to the ordeal, according to the commands of God and of the archbishop and of all the bishops, we order that, as soon as the fire has been brought to heat the [iron or water for the] ordeal, no one shall come into the church except the priest and the man to be tried. And [if the ordeal is by iron,] nine feet, according to the feet of the man to be tried, shall be measured from the [starting] post to the [final] mark.[5] If, on the other hand, it is to be [ordeal by] water, that shall be heated until it becomes boiling hot, whether the kettle is of iron or of brass, of lead or of clay. And if the process is "single," the hand shall be plunged in for the stone[6] up to the wrist; if it is "threefold,"[7] up to the elbow. And when the [water for the] ordeal is ready, two men from each party shall go in, and they shall agree that it is as hot as we have ordered.

Then an equal number of men from both parties shall go in and stand along the church on each side of the ordeal, and all of them shall be fasting and shall have held themselves from their wives during the previous night. And the priest shall sprinkle them all with holy water and give them to taste of the holy water; and he shall give them the Book to kiss and [shall make over them] the sign of Christ's cross. And no one shall build up the fire any more after the consecration has been begun, but the iron shall lie on the embers until the last collect. Then it shall be laid on the [starting] post. And nothing else shall be said inside the church except a prayer to God Almighty that He disclose the fullness of truth. And [after the man has undergone the ordeal,] his hand shall be [bound up and] sealed; and after the third day it shall be inspected to see whether, within the sealed wrapping, it is foul or clean (*ful swa claene*).[8] And if any one breaks these provisions, the ordeal shall be [counted] a failure for him, and he shall pay a fine of 120*s.* to the king.

(Anglo-Saxon) *Ibid.*, I, 386.

---

[4] Cf. Aethelstan, 20 (above, p. 15).

[5] It is stated below that the iron, when heated, was to be laid on the post. The accused picked up the iron in his bare hand and carried it for the specified distance.

[6] The one placed in the bottom of the kettle for this purpose.

[7] Cf. the previous doom.

[8] The cleanness of the hand was probably determined by its freedom from infection.

9. DOOMS OF EDMUND (942-46)

II, 1. Henceforth, if any man slays another, [we order] that he by himself shall incur the blood-feud,[1] unless he, with the help of his friends, buys it off by paying the full wergeld [of the slain man] within twelve months, no matter of what rank the latter may be. If, however, his kinsmen abandon him, refusing to pay anything in his behalf, then it is my will that the whole kindred, with the sole exception of the actual slayer, be free of the blood-feud so long as they give him neither food nor protection. If, on the other hand, one of his kinsmen later gives him such assistance, the former shall forfeit to the king all that he has, and he shall incur the blood-feud [along with the slayer] because the latter has already been disowned by the kindred. And if any one of the other kindred[2] takes vengeance on any men besides the true slayer, he shall incur the enmity of the king and all of the king's friends, and he shall forfeit all that he has.

III. This is the decree that King Edmund and his bishops, together with his *witan,* formulated at Colyton for the [maintenance of] peace and the swearing of an oath.[3]

1. In the first place [he commands] that all, in the name of God before whom this holy thing is holy, shall swear fealty to King Edmund, as a man should be faithful to his lord, without dissension or betrayal, both in public and in secret, loving what he loves and shunning what he shuns; and from the day on which this oath is sworn that no one shall conceal [the breach of] this [obligation] on the part of a brother or a relative any more than on the part of a stranger.

2. He also wills that, when a man is definitely known to be a thief, [both] twelve-hundred men and two-hundred men[4] shall join in taking him dead or alive, in whichever way they can. And whoever prosecutes a blood-feud against any one who has taken part in this search shall incur the enmity of the king and of all his friends. And if anybody refuses to present himself and give assistance, he shall pay a fine of 120*s.* to the king and of 30*s.* to the hundred [court],[5] unless he can prove that he had no knowledge of the affair by an oath of equal value.[6] . . .

---

[1] Cf. Alfred, 42 (above, p. 12).

[2] That of the slain man.

[3] Cf. no. 14A.

[4] Cf. Alfred, 39 (above, p. 11).

[5] This is the first mention of the hundred in the dooms. To what extent the name was new is a matter of controversy, but it was certainly connected with assessment of districts for military purposes in hundreds of hides, and much of this assessment system was the product of the Danish wars. So far as the institution was concerned, it is evident that many of the provisions henceforth applied to the hundred court were repetitions of those already applied to the *folcgemot.* See especially the analysis of the sources and literature in Liebermann, *Gesetze,* II, 516 f.; also Helen M. Cam, in the *English Historical Review,* XLVII. 370 f. On the payment to the hundred, cf. Edgar, I, 1-2 (below, p. 18). Since it is hardly credible that the hundred had a common chest, we must believe that the suitors to the court somehow shared the profits of justice.

[6] I.e., 120*s.*

7. And every man shall be responsible for his own men and for all who are under his protection and on his land. And all persons of bad repute, or those frequently accused of crime, shall be placed under surety. And reeve or thegn, *eorl* or *ceorl*, who refuses to carry out these orders, or neglects them, shall pay a fine of 120*s.* and suffer other penalties as stated above.

(Anglo-Saxon and Latin) Ibid., I, 186 f.

10. CORONATION OATH OF EDGAR

This writing has been copied, letter by letter, from the writing which Archbishop Dunstan gave our lord at Kingston on the day that he was consecrated as king, forbidding him to make any promise save this, which at the bishop's bidding he laid on Christ's altar:—

In the name of the Holy Trinity I promise three things to the Christian people my subjects: first, that God's Church and all Christian people of my realm shall enjoy true peace; second, that I forbid to all ranks of men robbery and all wrongful deeds; third, that I urge and command justice and mercy in all judgments, so that the gracious and compassionate God who lives and reigns may grant us all His everlasting mercy.

(Anglo-Saxon) Ibid., I, 214 f.

11. DOOMS OF EDGAR (946-63)

I. This is the ordinance as to how the hundred [court] shall be held.

1. In the first place, [we command] that they[1] shall assemble every four weeks and that all shall [there] give one another justice.

2. [We also command] that men shall ride forth in pursuit of thieves. If there is pressing need, notice shall be given to the hundredman, and he shall then inform the tithingmen;[2] and they shall all go forth, whither God may direct them, to find [the criminals]. Justice is to be done to the thief as already ordained by [King] Edmund. And the *ceapgyld*[3] shall be paid to the owner, and the rest [of the thief's property] shall be divided in two, half to the hundred and half to the lord—except the men [who belong to the thief]; they shall go to his lord.

3. And any one who disobeys this [command] and scorns the judgment of the hundred, should his guilt be later determined, shall pay to the hundred 30*d.*, and for the second offence 60*d.*, half to the hundred and half to his lord. If he does it a third time, he shall pay half a pound; on the fourth offence he shall forfeit all that he has

---

[1] The suitors to the court; cf. Edward, II, 8 (above, p. 13).

[2] The hundredman was the royal official in charge of a hundred; by analogy, the tithing may be understood as a subdivision of the hundred and the tithingman as its head. In this respect, however, the dooms are very obscure. See below, p. 23, n. 6.

[3] The value of the stolen property; cf. *angyld* (above, p. 8, n. 12).

and be outlawed, unless the king shall permit him [to stay in] the land.

4. And we have provided with regard to strange cattle that no one shall keep [any], unless he has the witness of the hundredman or the tithingman and such person is eminently trustworthy. And unless he has one of these [as witness], he shall not be permitted to vouch to warranty.[4]

5. We have also provided that, if a trail of lost cattle leads from one hundred into another, notice shall be given to the hundredman of the latter, and that he shall then join [in the search]. If he fails to do so, he shall pay the king 30s. . . .

7. In the hundred, as in [any] other court, we will that folkright shall be enforced in every suit and that a day shall be set for trying it. And he who fails to appear on this day, unless his absence is caused by a command from his lord, shall pay the king 30s. compensation and on a [newly] set day do what he should have done before.

III, 2. And no one shall appeal to the king on account of any suit unless he has failed to obtain justice at home.[5] If [however] the law is too severe, he may seek mitigation from the king. And no one shall forfeit more than his wergeld for any offence that can be paid for in money.

3. And a doomsman[6] who renders an evil doom against any one shall pay 120s. compensation to the king, unless he can prove by oath that he acted according to the best of his knowledge; and he shall lose forever his rank of thegn, unless he buys it back from the king by whatever payment the latter will allow. And the shire bishop (*scire biscop*) may exact the compensation on behalf of the king. . . .

5. And the hundred court shall be attended as has already been provided. And the borough court (*burhgemot*) shall be held three times a year and the shire court (*scirgemot*) twice.[7] And the shire bishop and the alderman shall be present and shall there administer both ecclesiastical and secular law (*Godes riht ge worldriht*). . . .

8. And one coinage shall have currency throughout all the king's realm and no one shall refuse it. And there shall be [as a standard]

---

[4] That is to say, only the designated persons could be called on to warrant his lawful possession; see above, p. 4, n. 3.

[5] In the hundred court; cf. Canute, II, 17 (below, p. 22).

[6] See above, p. 4, n. 5. The provision that the bishop could exact the compensation would indicate the alderman or the reeve as a possible offender. Cf. art. 5, below.

[7] This is the earliest specific mention of either the borough court or the shire court, both of which appear to have been courts of superior jurisdiction. Whether such a court was called *burhgemot* or *scirgemot*, and whether it met twice or three times a year, were perhaps matters of secondary importance. For evidence that at this time the shire was a comparatively large district, see Aethelred, II, 8 (below, p. 20). And on the controversial subject of the borough court, see C. Stephenson, *Borough and Town,* pp. 64-70; Tait, *The Medieval English Borough,* ch. ii.

one measure (and one weight), as used (at London and) at Winchester.[8] . . .

IV, 3. My will is then that every one, in borough or out of borough, shall be under surety. And witnesses shall be chosen for every borough and for every hundred: for every [great] borough thirty-six men shall be chosen as witnesses; for a small borough and for every hundred twelve—unless you wish [to have] more.[9] . . .

6. And under their witness every one shall buy and sell all the goods that he buys and sells either in a borough or in a wapentake.[10] And each of them, when he is first chosen as a witness, shall swear an oath that neither for fee nor for love, nor through fear, will he ever deny anything of which he is a witness or [will he ever] testify to anything but what he has seen or heard. And two or three of the men thus put on oath shall be present as witnesses at every transaction.

7. And he who rides out for the sake of any purchase shall announce to his neighbours what he is going for; and as soon as he comes home, he shall also announce under whose witness he made his purchase.

8. But if, while on some journey, he makes an unexpected purchase, without having made announcement [of it] when he set out, let him announce it when he comes home; and if it is livestock, he shall put it on the common pasture with the witness of his fellow villagers.[11] If he does not do so within five nights, the villagers (*tunes men*) shall notify the hundredman and shall [thereby] escape punishment, either for themselves or for their herdsmen. And he who brought the livestock there shall lose it, because he failed to notify his neighbours of it; and the lord of the land (*landrica*) shall take half and the hundred half.

(Anglo-Saxon) *Ibid.*, I, 192 f.

---

[8] The phrases in parentheses are additions to the original text. The insertion of London proves the growing importance of that city as a commercial centre in the eleventh century.

[9] Cf. Aethelstan, V, 1 (above, p. 15), which set up a select group of oath-helpers in the district later called the hundred. Note that such an oath-helper was often styled a witness and that a witness to a purchase served as an oath-helper when vouched to warranty; see the oaths under no. 14, below.

[10] A name by which the hundred was often known in Danish regions.

[11] *Tunescipe,* our "township." This is the sole appearance of the word in the dooms; see Maitland, *Domesday Book and Beyond,* p. 147.

12. DOOMS OF AETHELRED (980-1016)

II, 8. If any one seizes something that he lost, the man in whose possession it was seized shall give solemn engagement and provide surety that he will present his warrantor whenever formal claim [to the property] is made.[1] If he vouches a living person to

---

[1] See above, p. 4, n. 3.

warranty, and the one thus summoned is in another shire, he shall have as long a time [for his process] as may be necessary. . . . If he summons [a warrantor] from across one shire, he shall have a week's time; if he summons [one] from across two shires, he shall have two weeks' time; if he summons [one] from across three shires, he shall have three weeks' time—as many shires as he has to send across, so many weeks' time shall he have.

III. These are the laws (*laga*) that King Aethelred and his *witan* have drawn up at Wantage for the improvement of the peace. . . .

3. . . . And a court shall be held in every wapentake and there the twelve leading (*yldestan*) thegns,[2] together with the reeve, shall come forward and swear on holy things, to be placed in their hands, that they will neither accuse any innocent man nor spare any guilty one. . . .

6. And every accuser shall have the right to choose which [ordeal] he will [have the accused undergo], either water or iron. And every vouching to warranty (*team*) and every ordeal shall be held in a borough of the king. . . .

13. And if any man is accused of giving food to a man who has broken our [royal] lord's peace (*griô*), he shall clear himself with thrice twelve [oath-helpers], and the latter shall be named by the reeve [of the king]. . . . And that doom shall stand when the thegns [who declare it] are agreed; [or] if they disagree, that [doom] shall stand which is declared by eight of them, and those who are thereby outvoted shall each pay [a fine of] 6 half-marks.[3] . . .

IV, 5. They[4] have also declared that, to their eyes, no difference exists between counterfeiters and the merchants who take good money to the counterfeiters and pay them to make [from it] impure money of insufficient weight, and who then trade and bargain with it; [or between counterfeiters] and those who secretly make dies, engraving on them the name of some moneyer other than the guilty party, and who sell them to the counterfeiters. Wherefore it has been decided by all the *witan* that these three [kinds of] men shall be made liable for the same punishment. And if one of them is accused, whether he is English or comes from beyond sea, he shall clear himself through the full ordeal.[5] And they have decided that [convicted] counterfeiters shall [each] lose a hand, which shall be exhibited over the place where they made their coin. And moneyers who work in woods,

---

[2] On the possible connection between this doom and the Norman grand jury, see Pollock and Maitland, I, 139-43. Cf. the lawmen of Domesday and the *scabini* of the Frankish courts; Helen M. Cam, *Local Government in Francia and England,* pp. 31 f.

[3] The mark was a Danish unit of account, normally held to contain 8 ounces or ores of 20*d*. each, and so rated as two-thirds of a pound.

[4] The king's *witan.*

[5] See no. 8A.

or make coin in [other secret] places of the same sort, shall forfeit their lives, unless the king wishes to spare them. . . .

9. And it has been decided that there shall be fewer moneyers than heretofore: there shall be three moneyers in every principal port, and one in every other port.[6] . . .

VI, 31. Let us all, furthermore, give earnest attention to the improvement of the peace and the improvement of the coinage.

32. The improvement of the peace [shall be] such as is best for the husbandman (*bondan*) and worst for the thief. And the coinage shall be so improved that one coinage, free of all false [issue], shall have currency throughout the whole land. And weights and measures shall be made exactly right, to the exclusion in the future of all wrong ones. And the repair of boroughs (*burhbote*) and the repair of bridges (*bricbote*) shall be earnestly pushed in every region;[7] and likewise the maintenance of the army and the fleet, whenever there is need, and as may be ordered in our common necessity.

33. And it is well to have in readiness the ships for the fleet (*fyrdscipa*) soon after Easter in every year. . . .

35. And if any one, without leave, deserts the army when the king is there, he risks losing all his property.

(Anglo-Saxon and Latin) *Ibid.*, I, 224, f.

---

[6] Cf. Aethelstan, II, 14 (above, p. 14).

[7] On the borough as a fortification, see above, p. 14, n. 7. On the threefold obligation resting with all landholders, cf. Canute, II, 65 (below, p. 24), and the charters under no. 15, below. This was the famous *trimoda necessitas*, on which term see W. H. Stevenson, in the *English Historical Review*, XXIX, 689 f.

13. DOOMS OF CANUTE (1020-34)

II. Here now follows the secular ordinance which, by the counsel of my *witan*, I wish to be obeyed throughout all England. . . .

12. These are the rights which the king enjoys over all men in Wessex: namely, [compensations for] breach of his personal protection (*mundbryce*), housebreaking (*hamsocne*),[1] assault by ambush (*forsteal*), and neglect of army service (*fyrdwite*)—unless he wishes to honour some one in particular [by granting him even these rights]. . . .

14. And in Mercia he [likewise] enjoys the aforesaid rights over all men.

15. And in the Danelaw he enjoys the fines for fighting,[2] neglect of army service, breach of his personal peace (*gryðbryce*), and housebreaking—unless he wishes to honour some one in particular. . . .

17. And no one shall appeal to the king unless he fails to obtain

---

[1] More accurately, unlawful entry upon a person's premises, whether a house or land; cf. Aethelberht, 5-27 (above, p. 3), and Alfred, 40 (above, p. 11).

[2] *Fihtewite*, having to do especially with cases involving bloodshed.

justice in his hundred.[3] Every one, under pain of fine, must attend
his hundred court whenever attendance is demanded by law.

18. And the borough court shall be held three times [a year]
and the shire court twice unless there is need to hold it oftener. And
the shire bishop and the alderman shall be present and shall there
administer both ecclesiastical and secular law.[4]

19. And no one shall seize property [to enforce his rights] either
in the shire [court] or outside it, unless he has thrice sought justice
in the hundred. If he fails to obtain justice on the third attempt,
then, the fourth time, he shall go to the shire court, and the shire
shall set him a day for his fourth effort. And if this fails, then he
shall secure leave either here or there[5] to go after his property [in
any way he can].

20. It is our will that every freeman above the age of twelve shall
be brought within hundred and tithing,[6] if he wishes to be law-
worthy when accused by some one, or wergeld-worthy [when slain].
Otherwise he shall not enjoy any rights as a freeman, whether he is
a householder or a member of another's household. Every one shall
be brought within a hundred and under surety (borge), and his
surety shall keep him and see that he performs his legal obligations. . . .

22. And every trustworthy man, who is free of accusations and
has never failed in oath or ordeal, shall be law-worthy in the hundred,
[clearing himself] through a simple oath.[7] For an untrustworthy
man oath-helpers for the simple oath shall be chosen from three
hundreds, and for the threefold oath from [a territory] as wide as
belongs to the borough—or he must go to the ordeal. And a simple
oath of exculpation shall be introduced by a simple fore-oath [of
accusation]; a threefold oath by a threefold fore-oath.[8] . . .

24. And no one, either within a borough or in the open country,
shall buy anything worth more than 4d., whether living or not, without the trustworthy witness of four men. . . .

29. And if any one encounters a thief and wilfully lets him go
without making an outcry,[9] he shall pay the thief's wergeld as com-

---

[3] Cf. Aethelstan, II, 3 (above, p. 14), and Edgar, III, 2 (above, p. 19).

[4] A re-enactment of Edgar III, 5 (above, p. 19).

[5] Following Miss Robertson's suggestion that the hundred and shire courts are
referred to.

[6] Cf. Edgar, I, 2; IV, 3 (above, pp. 18, 20). One group of writers headed
by Liebermann, has held that the tithing of this passage refers to a group of
ten men combined for the sake of mutual suretyship; another that such a system
was a police measure introduced by the Normans and that the tithing here, as
in Edgar's dooms, was territorial. For a cogent presentation of the latter argument, see W. A. Morris, *The Frankpledge System*.

[7] And with oath-helpers chosen by himself, as appears from the following
provision.

[8] See the oaths under no. 14.

[9] That is to say, without raising hue and cry, as it was known in the later
law.

pensation, or shall clear himself by a full oath, [swearing] that he did not know him [whom he let go] to be guilty of anything. And if any one hears the outcry and neglects it, he shall pay the king's *oferhyrnesse* or clear himself by a full oath.

30. And if any man appears untrustworthy to the hundred, being discredited by accusations, and if now three men together bring charges against him, he shall have no recourse but to go to the three-fold ordeal. . . .

57. And if any one plots against the king or against his own lord, he shall forfeit his life and all that he has, unless he goes to the threefold ordeal and there clears himself.[10] . . .

65. If any one neglects the repair of boroughs, the repair of bridges, or army service,[11] he shall pay 120s. compensation to the king [in the region] under English law, and in the Danelaw whatever is customary [there]; or he shall clear himself with eleven oath-helpers out of fourteen named for him [by the court]. All the people shall, according to law, assist in the repair of churches. . . .

70. And if any one, whether through negligence or through sudden death, departs this life without having made a will,[12] his lord shall take no more of his chattels than his lawful heriot. Rather, by his direction, the goods are to be most justly apportioned to the widow, the children, and the near relatives—to each the share that is rightfully his.

71. And heriots shall be fixed in proportion to rank. The heriot of an earl [shall be] what belongs thereto: namely, eight horses, four saddled and four unsaddled; also four helmets, four shirts of mail, eight spears and as many shields, four swords, and 200 mancuses of gold.[13] For king's thegns, those who live close to him, the heriot shall be four horses, two saddled and two unsaddled; also two swords, four spears and as many shields, helmets, and shirts of mail; and 50 mancuses of gold. And for an ordinary thegn [the heriot shall be] his horse with its harness and his weapons, or, in Wessex, his *healsfang*;[14] in Mercia £2 and in East Anglia £2. And among the Danes the heriot of a king's thegn who enjoys soke[15] is £4. And if he lives in greater intimacy with the king, [it is] two horses, one saddled and the other unsaddled; also a sword, two spears, two shields, and 50 mancuses of gold. And for him who is not so well off [the heriot is] £2.

(Anglo-Saxon) *Ibid.*, I, 308 f.

---

[10] Cf. Alfred, 4 (above, p. 10).

[11] See above, p. 22, n. 7.

[12] Dying intestate was already considered exceptional. Many Anglo-Saxon wills have come down to us from earlier centuries.

[13] *Mancus* is derived from the Arabic and was originally used to designate an Arabic gold coin or an imitation of one. In the dooms, however, it is a weight of gold equal to 30d. in silver.

[14] A term normally used to mean a tenth of the wergeld.

[15] Jurisdictional rights over certain persons, or profits of justice in certain places; see below, p. 30, n. 23.

14. CUSTOMARY OATHS

(A) Oath of a Man to His Lord

By the Lord before whom this holy thing is holy, I will to N.[1] be faithful and true, loving all that he loves and shunning all that he shuns, according to the law of God and the custom of the world; and never by will or by force, in word or in deed, will I do anything that is hateful to him; on condition that he will hold me as I deserve and will furnish all that was agreed between us when I bowed myself before him and submitted to his will.

(B) Oath of an Accuser

By the Lord before whom this holy thing is holy, I thus bring my charge with full folkright, without deceit and without malice, and without any guile whatsoever, that stolen from me was this property, N., which I claim and which I seized in the possession of N.

(C) Oath of One Thus Accused

By the Lord . . . neither by counsel nor by deed had I knowledge of or part in this, that the property, N., was carried off. On the contrary, I possess the property for this reason, that I lawfully inherited it. . . . that he,[2] having the lawful right to sell it, sold it to me. . . . that it is the offspring of my own animals, my private property raised under my care.

(D) Oath of One Seizing Property

By the Lord . . . I seize N. neither through hate nor hostility, nor through unrighteous greed, and I know nothing truer than what my spokesman has said for me, and what I now myself state as truth, that he was the thief of my property.

(E) Oath in Reply to Such Seizure

By the Lord . . . I am guiltless, both in thought and in deed, of the accusation made against me by N.

(F) Oath of an Oath-Helper

By the Lord . . . the oath which N. has sworn is clean and without falsehood.

(Anglo-Saxon) *Ibid.*, I, 396 f.

---

[1] In these oaths *N.* represents either a person's name or the description of a particular article of property, usually an animal.

[2] Designating the person accused.

15. CHARTERS AND WRITS

(A) Offa, King of Mercia: Grant to Worcester Cathedral (741-96)

In the name of our Lord Jesus Christ who reigns throughout all time! I, Offa, for the health of my soul and the souls of my relatives

after my death and the soul of my son Egfrith, give to [the church of]
Worcester this land at Westbury with all that lawfully pertains to
it: namely, sixty hides, and in another place, at Hanbury, twenty
hides. [And this land is] lawfully to remain with the same endow-
ment of liberty in all things as when King Aethelbald earlier bestowed it on my grandfather, Eanulf. . . . In the name of Almighty
God we command that it shall be free from all power of kings and
princes, or of their subordinates, with the exception of these dues,
that is to say, the rent (gafol)[1] at Westbury: two tuns of clear ale,
a coomb of mild ale, a coomb of Welsh ale, seven oxen, six wethers,
forty cheeses, . . .[2] thirty ambers of rye corn, and four ambers of
meal at the king's manor (ad regalem vicum). This, with the advice
and consent of my prelates and counsellors, has accordingly been determined by firm covenant: no royal, princely, or secular official shall
in the future, by demands great or small, either through force or
through requisition, exact anything from them on account of [this]
our inheritance, with the sole exception of what is specified in this
present charter.

These are the witnesses. . . .[3]

(Latin and Anglo-Saxon) Thorpe, *Diplomatarium*, pp. 39 f.

(B) Aethelred, Alderman of Mercia: Grant to the Monas-
        tery of Berkeley (883)

    . . . Wherefore I, Aethelred, alderman, by the heartening grace
of God endowed and enriched with a portion of the Mercian realm,[4]
for love of God, for the remission of my guilt and sin, for the
prayers of the abbot and the congregation [of monks] at Berkeley,
and on behalf of all Mercia, free them forever of the *gafol* which
they still have to pay into the king's hand, [namely,] from that part
of the king's *feorm*[5] that has remained obligatory, whether in clear
ale, in beer, in honey, in cattle, in swine, or in sheep. And this I
have done for the sake of their godly prayers, and also because they
have granted to me in perpetuity a certain portion of their land,
that is to say, twelve hides at Stoke. Furthermore, they have given
me 30 mancuses of gold[6] so that I shall also free the monastery from

---

[1] See above, p. 7, n. 3.

[2] Certain words at this point are unintelligible.

[3] In the original the clerk wrote the names of the witnesses, together with
the variety of forms by which they attested the document. Each witness then
added a cross in the appropriate place. The present charter lists eighteen witnesses, including King Offa, his son, an archbishop, a bishop, four abbots, and
seven aldermen.

[4] Aethelred was descended from the royal line of Mercia and still held about
half of the old kingdom. His wife was the famous Lady of the Mercians,
Aethelflaed, daughter of King Alfred.

[5] The regular name for the payments of food owed the king from many of
his estates.

[6] See above, p. 24, n. 13.

all dues (*gafolum*) to which the lord of the people[7] is entitled, great or small, known or unknown, except simple compensation (*angilde*) to others,[8] and except repair of fortresses (*faestengewerce*), military service (*fyrdsocne*), and repair of bridges (*brycggeweorce*).[9] And this I do with the leave and witness of King Alfred, and with [the counsel of] all the Mercian *witan,* both clergy and laity.

Now, moreover, I give that same land at Stoke—namely, twelve hides—to Cynulf, son of Ceoluht, for 60 mancuses of pure gold, to be free of all obligations toward king or alderman or reeve: [that is to say,] of every burden, great or small, except military service, repair of fortresses, repair of bridges, and simple compensation to others, with naught out for *wite.* And we enjoin that no one, either relative or stranger, shall in any way rob [Cynulf][10] of it as long as he lives, for he has deserved it of the Mercian lords through righteous submission [to them].

And we now, in the name of Almighty God, command that this immunity for the monastery of Berkeley, as described above, and also the gift of land which we grant to Cynulf for three men's lives, shall continue unimpaired on this condition, that on the death of Cynulf and his two heirs, without any controversy, the twelve hides of land at Stoke are to be given in perpetual alms to the episcopal see of Worcester on behalf of Aethelred, alderman, and of all the Mercians. Also we beg and implore in the name of the Holy Trinity that, if there should be any man who with evil intent violates aught that is written in this charter, he may know that he does so to the displeasure of God and of all His saints, as well as of all men, both clerical and lay, who can think or will anything rightful; and that he shall make amends before the throne of the Eternal Judge if he has not already [in his lifetime] done so with just reparation to God and man.

Now this munificent grant was made in the year of the Incarnation of the Lord 883 . . . by the consent and attestation of the witnesses whose names are here noted. . . .[11]

This land, moreover, is bounded by the following bounds: first from Hazlewell in Hazledean, then to Woldeswell; from Woldeswell to Sweordes Stone in Ewcombe; from Ewcombe to Avon's stream; from Avon's stream again up, then to Ridgeley; from Ridgeley then to Penpau; from Penpau then to Severn's stream; from Hazle-

---

[7] Meaning, of course, the king.

[8] Cf. the similar phrase below, with the addition of "naught out to *wite*." As pointed out by Maitland (*Domesday Book and Beyond,* pp. 290 f.), the charter implies the grant of a judicial immunity: the church was to enjoy the profits of justice, including all fines normally paid to the king, but not including ordinary compensation paid by tenants for injuries to persons other than the grantee.

[9] See above, p. 22, n. 7.

[10] The text by error has Ceoluht.

[11] Besides the king and Aethelred, the list includes three bishops, an abbot, a priest, two aldermen, and eight other persons.

well again, then to Leadgedelf; from Leadgedelf to Millpool; from Millpool again to Avon's stream.

(Latin and Anglo-Saxon) *Ibid.*, pp. 129 f.

(C) Aethelred, Alderman of Mercia, and His Witan: Confirmation of a Title to Land (896)

Under the dominion of the Saviour Christ our Lord. After 896 winters had passed since His birth, then, in that year, . . . Aethelred, alderman, called together all the Mercian *witan* at Gloucester— bishops, aldermen, and all his magnates—and this he did with the leave and witness of King Alfred. And there they took counsel how, in the sight both of God and of the world, they could most justly rule their people; and [how they] could right [the wrongs of] man·· men, whether clerical or lay, whether in the matter of their lands or of other things that had been withheld from them.

Then Bishop Werferth complained to the *witan* that he had been deprived of nearly all the woodland belonging to Woodchester, which King Aethelbald had given to [the church of] Worcester in perpetual alms, [namely,] to Bishop Wilferth for mast and wood; and he said that, so far as he could tell, some of it had been taken at Bisley, some at Avening, some at Sherston, and some at Thornbury. Then all the *witan* declared that right should be done to this church as well as to any other. Whereupon Aethelwald at once announced that he would not hinder justice, saying that Bishops Aldberht and Alhmund had earlier been [concerned] about the same [matter], and promising that he would do his part in giving right to every church. So, with the utmost graciousness, he yielded to the bishop and bade his *geneat*,[12] named Ecglaf, ride with a priest of the Worcestermen (*ceastersetna*), named Wulfhun. And he then led him along all the bounds, while he read them to him from the old charters,[13] as King Aethelbald had earlier bounded that [woodland] in his grant. Then Aethelwald expressed the wish that the bishop and the [episcopal] household would kindly allow him to enjoy [the use of] it while he lived and [grant the same privilege] to Alhmund, his son; [so that] they might hold it by lease (*laen*) of [the bishop] and his household, and neither of them, during the time that God gave them [to live], would ever deprive [the bishop] of the mast to which he was entitled at Longridge. And Aethelwald then solemnly declared that only to the displeasure of God should any one but the lord of the church have that [woodland], saving [the rights of] Alhmund; and this only on condition that the latter should hold the same friendly relation with the bishop as he [himself] now held. If, however, it should happen that Alhmund did not hold that friendly relation, or if it should be proved that he was not worthy of the land, or,

---

[12] See above, p. 8, n. 8.

[13] Since Wulfhun was a priest, it must have been he who read the charters while Ecglaf showed him the boundaries.

thirdly, if his end should come, that then the lord of the church should take his land.

Thus the Mercian *witan* decided in the assembly, directing the [present] record concerning the land [to be drawn up] for him.[14] And this was done by the witness of Aethelred the alderman and Aethelflaed;[15] of Aethulf the alderman, Aethelferth the alderman, Alhelm the alderman, Eadnoth, Alfred, Werferth, Aethelwald the priest, and of his own kinsmen, Aethelstan and Aethelhun, as well as of his own son, Alhmund.

And thus the priest of the Worcestermen rode it,[16] and with him Aethelwald's *geneat*: first to Gemythley, and thence to Rodborough itself; thence to Smechcombe; thence to Sugley; thence to Hardley, [for which] there is another name, Dryganley; so to Nailsworth the smaller, and so to Aethelferth's land. Thus did Aethelwald's man show him the bounds as the old charters provided and indicated.

(Anglo-Saxon) *Ibid.*, pp. 139 f.

(D) Edgar: Grant to the Bishop of Winchester (963)[17]

Here, in this writing, is made known how King Edgar, with the counsel of his *witan*, confirmed the liberties at Taunton for the Holy Trinity, St. Peter and St. Paul, and the episcopal see of Winchester, as this freedom had earlier been established by King Edward: granting that men in that vill (*hame*) of God, whether two-hundred or twelve-hundred,[18] should enjoy the same rights as his own men enjoyed in his own royal vills; that all causes and rights should be given into the hand of God in the same measure as when they were brought into his own; [that] the [control of] trade in the vill (*tunes cyping*) and the income from [all other] rights in the port[19] should go to the holy see [of Winchester] as they earlier did in the days of my ancestors, and as they were collected for Bishop Aelfeage and for each of those who possessed the land. If any one will increase this liberty, may God increase his welfare during a long life here and in eternity. If, on the contrary, any one, through insolence and the instigation of the devil or his limbs, should seek to violate this liberty or to pervert it, unless he shall make amends before his death, may he with malediction be cut off from the communion of our Lord and of all His saints, and may he suffer eternal torment in hell along with Judas, who was Christ's betrayer.

---

[14] Presumably the bishop.

[15] See above, p. 26, n. 4.

[16] The boundary of the land in question.

[17] This document exists in two versions, Latin and Anglo-Saxon. The translation has been made from the latter.

[18] Cf. Alfred, 39 (above, p. 11).

[19] See above, p. 12, n. 3. In this case the reference is to the borough of Taunton which, together with all royal rights in market and court, remained in the hands of the bishop until after the Norman Conquest; see Round, in *Victoria History of Somerset*, I, 400 f.

. . . This was done at Cheddar on the holy Eastertide, in which year 968[20] years had passed since the birth of Christ, and in the tenth year of the reign [of Edgar], by the witness of the *witan* whose names are written below. . . .[21]

(Anglo-Saxon) *Ibid.*, pp. 235 f.

(E) Canute: Grant to St. Paul's, London (1036)

I, King Canute, give friendly greetings to my bishops, my earls,[22] and all my thegns in the shires where my priests of St. Paul's monastery hold land. And I make known to you my will that they shall enjoy their *sac* and *soc, toll* and *team*,[23] within tide and without tide, as fully and continuously as they best had them in any king's day, in all things, in borough and out of borough. And I will not permit any man in any way to do them wrong. And of this the witnesses are Aegelnoth, archbishop; Aelfric, archbishop; Aelwi, bishop; Aelwine, bishop; Duduc, bishop; Godwine, earl; Leofric, earl; Osgod Clapa, Thored, and many others.

May God curse him who shall pervert this [grant]!

(Anglo-Saxon) *Ibid.*, pp. 319 f.

(F) Confirmation of a Title to Land in the Shire Court of Hereford (1036)

Here, in this writing, it is made known that a shire court sat at Aegelnoth's Stone in the time of King Canute. There sat Aethelstan, bishop; Ranig, alderman; Edwin, [son] of the alderman; Leofwine, son of Wulfsige; and Thurcil the White (*Hwita*). And thither came Tofig the Proud (*Pruda*) on the king's errand. And there were Bryning the sheriff,[24] Aegelweard of Frome, Leofwine of Frome, Godric of Stoke, and all the thegns of Herefordshire. Then came faring to the court Edwin, son of Eanwen, and there claimed as against his own mother a portion of land, namely, Wellington and Cradley. Then the bishop asked who would speak for his mother. Then Thurcil the White answered, saying that he would if he knew

---

[20] The text mistakenly reads 978.

[21] The list includes, besides the king and the queen, the two archbishops, seven bishops, nine abbots, eight aldermen, and nine thegns.

[22] These officials henceforth appear in place of the aldermen; see Chadwick, *Studies,* ch. v.

[23] Such phrases as these now become characteristic of all formal grants of immunity; see Maitland, *Domesday Book and Beyond,* pp. 258 f. *Sac* and *soc* (more properly *sacu* and *socn*) together meant no more than the latter term alone, which ordinarily in modern English is given as *soke* or *soken;* see above, p. 24, n. 15. *Toll,* from the Latin *thelonium,* has come down to us with the spelling and the meaning alike unchanged. *Team* meant vouching to warranty, or the right to collect the fees for it on one's own land or elsewhere; see above, p. 4, n. 3.

[24] The shire-reeve, or sheriff, henceforth attains great importance in local government as the subordinate of the earl, who normally was in charge of several shires.

the defence [that she cared to make]. Since he did not know the defence, three thegns were chosen from the court [to ride to the place]
where she was, and that was Fawley. These [thegns] were Leofwine of Frome, Aegelsige the Red (*Reada*), and Winsige Sceagth-
man. And when they had come to her, they asked her about the land
which her son claimed. Then she said that she had no land which
in aught belonged to him, and she burst into a noble rage against her
son. Then she called thither her kinswoman Leoflaed, Thurcil's wife,
and before those [present] thus addressed her: "Here sits Leoflaed,
my kinswoman, to whom, after my day, I give both my lands and my
gold, both gear and garments, and all that I possess." After which
she said to the thegns: "Do nobly and well. Announce my message
to the court before all the good men, telling them to whom I have
given my land and all my belongings; and [that] to my own son
[I have] never [given] anything. And bid them be witness of this
[gift]." And they then did so, riding to the court and declaring to
all the good men what she had directed them [to say]. Then Thurcil
the White stood up in the court and prayed all the thegns to grant
his wife a clean title to all the lands which her kinswoman had given
her, and they did so. And Thurcil then rode to St. Aethelberht's
monastery, with the leave and witness of all the folk, and caused this
[grant] to be set forth in a Christ's book.[25]

(Anglo-Saxon) *Ibid.*, pp. 336 f.

(G) Edward the Confessor: Grant to Westminster Abbey
(1056)

I, King Edward, give friendly greeting to Bishop Wulfwig, Earl
Gyrth, and all my thegns of Oxfordshire. And I make known to
you that I have granted to Christ and to St. Peter of Westminster
the village where I was born, by name Islip, and half a hide at Marsh,
free of *scot* and *gafol*,[26] with all things thereto pertaining, in wood and
in field, in meadow and in water, with the church and the church-
soke,[27] as full and as complete and as free as it stood under my
own hand, and as Aelfgifa Emma, my mother, gave and bequeathed
it to me as a first gift on my birthday. And I grant them moreover
sac and *soc, toll* and *team, infangenepeof, blodwite,* and *weardwite,*
hamsocn, forsteall, gryðbryce and *mundbryce*,[28] and all the rights
which [there] belong to me. Now I greet well my beloved kinsman,
Wigod, at Wallingford, and I bid thee on my behalf ride around
these lands [and put them] into the possession of the saint; for I

---

[25] That is to say, formally recorded by a monastic scribe.

[26] The two words together cover all rents and taxes; see above, p. 7, n. 3.
Scot often appears in eleventh-century documents as the equivalent of *geld*;
see below, p. 38, n. 2.

[27] The territory subjected to the jurisdiction of the church.

[28] *Infangenepeof* was the right to punish thieves caught on the property;
blodwite the fine for wounding with bloodshed; *weardwite* the fine for neglect
of guard duty. For the other terms, see above, pp. 22, 30.

will on no account permit any man there to hold any authority, over anything or at any time, save only the abbot and the brothers for the sake of the monastery's worthy needs.

And whoever shall firmly hold this [grant in] alms, may God and God's Mother hold him in everlasting bliss. And whoever shall turn it aside, may he be turned aside from God to the bitter pains of hell's inmates, unless he the more painfully shall make amends on this earth.

May God and St. Peter keep you!

(Anglo-Saxon) *Ibid.,* pp. 368 f.

SECTION II

THE NORMAN KINGS

THE more important constitutional documents of the Norman period naturally fall into two divisions: those connected with the reign of William I (1066-87) and those connected with the reign of his talented son, Henry I (1100-35). Here included are such ordinances of the Conqueror as have survived, together with a selection of typical writs emanating from his chancery. The great inquest of 1086 is illustrated by the famous Cambridgeshire return, as well as by characteristic excerpts from the final condensation that became known as Domesday Book. Although Henry I's reign is especially noteworthy for the development of a more efficient central government, it has little to offer in the way of formal enactments. His Coronation Charter was, in all probability, never intended to be enforced, and is chiefly significant because it served as a precedent for Magna Carta. We have one brief ordinance, dealing with the shire and hundred courts, but it tells us almost nothing about their composition. For additional details we have to fall back on the wretched compilation misnamed *Leges Henrici Primi*. The few passages translated below (no. 26) are among those which apparently give authentic information on the legal usages of the early twelfth century. With regard to the organization of the exchequer, and the other financial measures now generally attributed to Henry I, our best source is the pipe roll of 1130;[1] so a considerable portion of it has been included in the following pages. And since Henry's reign marked the opening of a new era in British municipal history, three famous records of his activity in that respect have been placed under one heading, together with William I's vague grant to the Londoners.

Throughout the Norman period feudal tenures were established and regulated by oral agreement rather than by charter. We have,

---

[1] Originally published by the Record Commission in 1833 and reprinted by the Pipe Roll Society in 1929.

however, ample proof that enfeoffment for knight service and
serjeanty, as well as in free alms, was extended to all parts of his
conquered kingdom, and that the feudal aids and incidents—perhaps even scutage—were quite familiar features of the system
from the beginning. The illustrations here presented have been
chosen because they are among the earliest and most specific
available. Finally, within the present section, it has seemed well
to give a complete English version of the *Constitutio Domus
Regis* (no. 29), apparently an official survey of the king's household arrangements drawn up shortly after the death of Henry I.
It is a most remarkable document, graphically revealing how, in
a feudal age, matters of government and of domestic economy
were intimately combined.

An exhaustive catalogue of the acts of William I and William
II, with full bibliographical references, will be found in the *Regesta Regum Anglo-Normannorum* of H. W. C. Davis, additional volumes of which are promised in the near future. The
original texts of the Conqueror's ordinances, Henry I's Coronation Charter, his writ concerning the shire and hundred courts,
and the two charters to London are available, not only in the
books of Liebermann and Robertson already cited (above, p. 1),
but also in Stubbs, *Select Charters*. Along with the other Anglo-
Norman compilations, the *Leges Henrici Primi* are excellently
edited, though not translated, in Liebermann's *Gesetze*. The
greater part of Domesday Book is translated, and usually provided with valuable introductions, in the appropriate volumes of
the *Victoria History of the Counties of England*.

The constitutional history of this period can no longer be accepted as it appears in the classic pages of Stubbs. The revisions
forced by the penetrating criticisms of J. H. Round, F. W. Maitland, Paul Vinogradoff, R. L. Poole and others have been admirably summarized by Petit-Dutaillis. More recent interpretations of Anglo-Norman government appear in F. M. Stenton's
First Century of English Feudalism and A. L. Poole's *From
Domesday Book to Magna Carta. English Historical Documents*,
1044–1189, editors D. C. Douglas and George W. Greenaway, is
rich in original records, in comment, and in bibliographical information. Concerning legal history, the chapters in Pollock and
Maitland and in Holdsworth are to be considered the chief authority.

16. WILLIAM I: ORDINANCE CONCERNING TRIALS

William, king, gives friendly greeting to all before whom this writing may come throughout all England, bidding and urging all men throughout all England to observe it, to wit:—

If an Englishman challenges any Frenchman to combat for theft or for manslaughter or for any cause in which combat or judgment (*dom*) is customarily had between two men, he shall have full leave to accept [the challenge]. And if the Englishman rejects combat [as a mode of trial], the Frenchman whom the Englishman has accused shall clear himself by oath against him, with oath-helpers according to Norman law. Furthermore, if a Frenchman challenges an Englishman to combat, for [one of] the same causes, the Englishman shall have full leave to defend himself by combat, or by [the ordeal of] iron, if that suits him better. And if, being infirm, he will not or cannot engage in combat, he shall get him a lawful champion [to take his place]. And if the Frenchman is overcome, he shall give the king £3. And if the Englishman will not defend himself [either] by combat or with oath-helpers, he shall clear himself by [the ordeal of] iron. And in all cases involving outlawry the king ordains that the Englishman shall clear himself by [the ordeal of] iron. And if an Englishman accuses a Frenchman in a cause involving outlawry, and then wishes to prove the charge against him, the Frenchman shall defend himself by combat. And if the Englishman does not dare to challenge him to combat, the Frenchman shall defend himself by an unprescribed (*unforedan*) oath.[1]

(Anglo-Saxon) Liebermann, *Gesetze*, I, 484.

[1] One that did not have to be letter-perfect, at least not in Anglo-Saxon.

17. WILLIAM I: ORDINANCE ON CHURCH COURTS

W[illiam], by the grace of God king of the English, to R[alph] Bainard, G[eoffrey] de Mandeville, P[eter] de Valognes, and my other faithful men of Essex, Hertfordshire, and Middlesex, greeting.[1] Be it known to all of you, and to my other faithful men resident in England, that, by the common counsel of the archbishops, bishops, abbots, and all the princes of my realm, I have decided to amend the ecclesiastical law,[2] which up to my own time has not been rightly observed in England, nor in accordance with the holy canons. I ordain and, by my royal authority, command that henceforth, when ecclesiastical law is involved, no bishop or archdeacon shall hold pleas in the hundred [court], nor shall he bring to judgment before laymen any

[1] Similar writs were presumably sent to the other shires.

[2] *Leges episcopales*, literally "episcopal laws." For the presence of the bishop in the shire court during the previous period, see Edgar, III, 5 (above, p. 19), and Canute, II, 18 (above, p. 23). And on the "common counsel" in the earlier part of the sentence, see A. B. White, in the *American Historical Review*, XXV, 15 f.

cause that pertains to the cure of souls; but whoever has been accused in any cause, or of any offence, under ecclesiastical law shall come to the place named and selected for this purpose by the bishop, and shall there respond in such cause or concerning such offence, submitting to the justice of God and of His bishop, not according to the [judgment of the] hundred, but according to the canons and to ecclesiastical law. If indeed any one, puffed up with pride, neglects or refuses to come for justice before the bishop, let him be summoned once, twice, and thrice. But if, even then, he will not come to make amends, let him be excommunicated; and should there be need to enforce this [ban], let the power and justice of the king or of the sheriff be invoked. Moreover, he who, being summoned, refuses to come before the bishop for justice shall be fined for each [neglect of] summons as contempt of ecclesiastical law. I likewise prohibit and, by my royal authority, forbid that any sheriff or reeve or minister of the king, or any layman [whatsoever], shall interfere with the administration of law pertaining to the bishop. Nor shall any layman bring another man to trial [under such law] save by the judgment of the bishop. The trial, indeed, shall be carried out nowhere except at the bishop's see, or in such place as he shall appoint for that purpose.

(Latin) *Ibid.*, I, 485 f.

18. WILLIAM I: TEN (ATTRIBUTED) ARTICLES[1]

1. In the first place, he wishes above all else the one God to be venerated throughout his entire kingdom; the one Christian faith always to be kept inviolate; peace and security to be maintained between Englishmen and Normans.

2. We have also ordained that by covenant and oath every freeman shall promise within and without England to be faithful to King William, with him and before him to keep and defend his lands and his honour with all fealty against his foes.

3. It is also my will that all men whom I have brought with me, or who have come after me, shall be under my peace and protection. And if any one of them is slain, his lord[2] shall take the slayer within five days if he can; if, however, he cannot, he shall make a beginning of paying to me 46*m.*[3] of silver [and shall continue with his payment] as long as the property of that lord shall last. When, moreover, the property of that lord fails, the entire hundred in which the homicide

---

[1] This unofficial compilation apparently summarizes various authentic decrees of the Conqueror that have not come down to us. In some cases the provisions are confirmed by other sources. The parts omitted, for example, are approximate repetitions of no. 16.

[2] In the text as it stands the *eius* seems to refer to the slain man; but it is more likely that William put the responsibility on the slayer's lord, who would almost certainly be an Englishman. This document is our oldest source for the murder fine (*murdrum*), which is frequently heard of in later records; see particularly no. 26, art. 91.

[3] The Norman mark was two-thirds of a pound; see above, p. 21, n. 3.

was committed shall bear the common responsibility of paying what remains [of the debt].

4. And every Frenchman who was in England during the time of King Edward, my kinsman, [and was there] sharing the customs of Englishmen—what they call being in scot and lot—shall be paid for according to the law of the English.[4] This decree was enacted at Gloucester.

5. We also forbid that any livestock be bought or sold anywhere except within cities,[5] and this before three trustworthy witnesses; nor shall any used thing [be bought or sold] without a surety and a warrantor. And if any one does otherwise, let him pay double the value [of the goods] and afterwards a forfeiture [to us]. . . .

7. This likewise I wish and enjoin: that in [cases affecting] lands, as in all other matters, all shall keep and hold the law of King Edward, with the addition of those [amendments] which I have made for the benefit of the English people.

8. Every one who wishes to be considered a freeman shall be in pledge, so that his pledge shall hold and keep him for justice should he commit any offence.[6] And should any such [offender] escape, his pledges shall see to the payment of simple compensation toward the claim and shall clear themselves [by oath] of having been cognizant of any fraud in that escape. The hundred and county[7] [courts] shall be attended in accordance with the decrees of our predecessors. And let those who rightly owe attendance, but who refuse to attend, be summoned once. And if they refuse to attend on the second summons, let one ox be taken [as a fine] and let them be summoned a third time. And if they do not attend on the third summons, let a second ox be taken. If, however, they do not attend on the fourth summons, let the amount claimed [in the suit against them]—what is called *ceapgeld*[8]—be given [to the claimant], and to the king his forfeiture in addition.

9. I forbid, on pain of my full forfeiture, that any one shall sell a man outside his native land.

10. I also forbid that any one be slain or hanged for any offence,

---

[4] Such a Frenchman was to be regarded as a naturalized Englishman, for whom compensation had to be paid according to the customary law in force before the Conquest.

[5] The *civitas* of this passage is apparently a mere translation of *port* or *burh*, the official trading centre specified in the dooms since the days of Edward the Elder.

[6] Under the Norman system of frankpledge the lesser freemen throughout the countryside were organized into groups of ten, within which the members were mutually responsible for each other's misdeeds; see the references above, p. 23, n. 6, and no. 26, art. 8. Frankpledge appears prominently in the documents of the next two centuries.

[7] "County" is by derivation a French synonym for the English "shire."

[8] The simple compensation, or *angild*, referred to a few sentences earlier; see above, p 8, n. 12.

but let him be blinded or castrated. And this decree shall not be violated, on pain of my full forfeiture.

(Latin) *Ibid.*, I, 486 f.

19. RECORDS CONCERNING A SUIT (1079-86)

(A) WRIT OF WILLIAM I (1079-83)

William, king of the English, to Lanfranc, archbishop [of Canterbury], and Geoffrey, bishop of Coutances, greeting. See to it that *sac* and *soc*,[1] as between Bishop Wulfstan and Walter, abbot of Evesham, are determined as they were on the day that, in the time of King Edward, geld[2] was last taken for the building of a fleet. And for holding this plea, be you, Geoffrey, president (*praesul*) in my place; and be sure that Bishop Wulfstan fully has what is his right. Also see to it that the bishop justly has the houses in Worcester which he claims as against the abbot, and that all those who hold lands of him are always prepared for my service and his.

Witness, Roger d'Ivry.

(Latin) Bigelow, *Placita Anglo-Normannica,* p. 287.

(B) WRIT OF GEOFFREY, BISHOP OF COUTANCES (1086)

Geoffrey, bishop of Coutances, to Remi, bishop [of Lincoln], and Walter Giffard and Hendy de Ferrers and Adam [de Port] and the other barons of the king, greeting. Know that, as I now give testimony, when by the king's precept I held the plea between Bishop Wulfstan and the abbot of Evesham, the bishop proved the three hides at Bengeworth and the houses in the city [of Worcester] to belong to his fief, so that the abbot thence owes him service like his other vassals (*feudati*). And he proved that the *sac* and *soc* of Hampton belong to his hundred of Oswaldslaw; that the pleas [of Hampton] should be heard there; that geld, host,[3] and other lawful services should be rendered to him from those fifteen hides [at Hampton]; and that church-scot[4] and burial fees (*sepultura*) should be paid at his vill of Croppethorn. This was sworn and proved before me and Urse d'Abetot and Osbern Fitz-Escrop, and other barons of the kingdom, by the judgment and testimony of the whole county [court].

(Latin) *Ibid.*, p. 287.

(C) WRIT OF WILLIAM I (1086)

William, king of the English, to Urse, sheriff [of Worcestershire], and Osbern Fitz-Escrop and all men, French and English, of Worces-

---

[1] See above, p. 30, n. 23.

[2] *Geld,* like *scot,* was a general word that could be used to denote any tax or exaction; see above, p. 31, n. 26, and above, no. 27A. More specifically, as in Domesday Book, the term was used to refer to the Danegeld.

[3] *Expeditio*—the Anglo-Saxon *fyrd*, not the feudal service established after the Norman Conquest.

[4] Obscure payments in kind for the support of a local church; see Maitland, *Domesday Book and Beyond,* p. 321.

tershire, greeting. I will and command that Bishop Wulfstan shall have *sac* and *soc* and services and all customs belonging to his hundred and to his lands as fully as he best had them in the time of King Edward. And with regard to the lands which he has proved to be held of his fief by the abbot of Evesham—namely, the four[5] hides at Bengeworth and the houses in the city—I command that, if the abbot wishes to keep them, he must thence do service to the bishop like the other vassals of the latter. And with regard to the fifteen hides at Hampton, whence the bishop has proved soke and geld and host and other services of mine to belong to his hundred, and church-scot and burial fees to belong to his vill, I forbid any one to obstruct his tenure, but command that he shall enjoy all those [services] for my benefit and his, as was by my precept sworn and proved before Bishop Geoffrey and before you. By the witness of the said Bishop Geoffrey and of Roger d'Ivry.

(Latin) *Ibid.*, p. 19.

---

[5] Either this figure or the one given above is an error.

20. WILLIAM I: WRITS CONCERNING INQUESTS AT ELY

(A) CONFIRMATION OF LIBERTIES FOR THE ABBOT OF ELY (*c.* 1080)

William, king of the English, to all his faithful men and his sheriffs in those counties where the abbey of Ely possesses lands, greeting. I command that, in borough and out of borough, the abbey of Ely shall have all its customs: namely, *sac* and *soc, toll* and *team, infangeneþeof, hamsocn, gryðbryce, fihtwite, fyrdwite,*[1] and all other forfeitures within its own land and from its own men. These [liberties], I say, it shall have as it had them on the day that King Edward was alive and dead and as, according to my command, they were proved at Kentford by [the oaths of] various shires in the presence of my barons: namely, Geoffrey, bishop of Coutances; Abbot Baldwin, Ivo Taillebois, Peter de Valognes; Picot, sheriff [of Cambridge]; Tihel de Heluin, Hugh de Hosdeng, Jocelyn of Norwich, and many others.

Witness, Roger Bigod.

(Latin) Hamilton, *Inquisitio Comitatus Cantabrigiensis,* p. xviii.

(B) MANDATE FOR A RENEWED INQUEST (1082).

William, king of the English, to Lanfranc, archbishop [of Canterbury], and Roger, count of Mortain, and Geoffrey, bishop of Coutances, greeting. I command and instruct you that you again cause to be assembled all the shires that were present at the plea held concerning the lands of the church of Ely before my wife last came to Normandy. Let there also be present with them those of my barons who can suitably attend, those men who were at the afore-

---

[1] Cf. no. 156.

said plea, and those who hold lands of the same church. When these men have been brought together, let several be chosen of those Englishmen who know how the lands of the said church lay on the day that King Edward died, and let whatever they may say in that connection be testified to on oath. When that is done, let restitution be made to the church of those lands that were in its demesne on the day of Edward's death, except those which men shall claim as having been given them by me. These [lands] then signify to me by letters, [telling] what they are and who holds them. But those holding thegnlands[2] that beyond doubt should be held of the church shall make peace with the abbot as best they may; and if they refuse [to do so], the church shall keep their lands. Let the same be done with regard to those holding *sac* and *soc*. Lastly, order those men to repair the bridge of Ely who up to now, by my disposition and command, have been accustomed so to do.

(Latin) Ibid., p. xviii.

---

[2] Lands that before the Conquest had been held of the church by thegns. Men styled thegns occasionally appear in the Norman documents, but they were generally supplanted by French knights.

21. RETURN FROM THE DOMESDAY INQUEST (1086)

Here is written down the inquisition of the lands [of Cambridgeshire] as made by the king's barons:[1] namely, by the oath of the sheriff of the shire; of all the barons, their Frenchmen, and the whole hundred [court]; of the priest, the reeve, and six villeins of each vill.[2] Then [is set down] how the manor is called, who held it in the time of King Edward, who holds it now, how many hides there are, how many ploughs in demesne, how many ploughs of the men, how many men, how many villeins, how many cotters, how many serfs, how many freemen, how many sokemen, how much woods, how much meadow, how many pastures, how many mills, how many fishponds, how much has been added or taken away, how much it was worth altogether and how much now, and how much each freeman or sokeman had or has there. All this [information is given] three times over: namely, in the time of King Edward, when King William gave it out, and how it is now—and whether more can be had [from it] than is being had.

These men swore. . . .[3]

(Latin) Ibid., pp. 97 f.

---

[1] See Round, *Feudal England,* pp. 3 f., 118 f. On this fundamental criticism all subsequent study of Domesday has been based.

[2] Cf. no. 26, art. 7.

[3] Here follows a long list of names, arranged hundred by hundred. These groups were the juries that made the original returns. Domesday Book is a compilation made by condensing such material and rearranging it, so that the manors are enumerated as land of the king or land of a particular baron.

22. EXCERPTS FROM DOMESDAY BOOK

(A) HEREFORDSHIRE

In the city of Hereford, in the time of King Edward, there were 103 men dwelling together inside and outside the wall, and they had the customs hereinunder noted.[1] If any one of them wished to leave the city, he could, with the consent of the reeve, sell his house to another man who was willing to perform the service owed from it, and the reeve got the third penny from this sale. But if any one, because of his poverty, could not perform the service, he gave up his house without payment to the reeve, who saw to it that the house did not remain vacant and that the king did not lose the service. Every entire messuage (*integra masura*) inside the wall rendered 7½d., and [also] 4d. for the hire of horses; and [the holder] reaped for three days at Marden[2] and spent one day gathering hay wherever the sheriff wished. Whoever had a horse went thrice a year with the sheriff to the pleas and the hundred [court] at Wormelow.[3] When the king engaged in a hunting expedition, one man customarily went from each house to serve as a beater (*ad stabilationem*) in the wood. Other men, who did not have entire messuages, found guards for the [royal] hall when the king was in the city. On the death of a burgess who served with a horse, the king had his horse and arms.[4] From him who had no horse, when he died, the king had either 10s. or his land, together with the houses [on it]. If any one, overtaken by death, had not divided what he possessed, the king had all his chattels (*pecunia*). These customs were had alike by those living in the city and by those dwelling outside the wall, except that an entire messuage outside the wall rendered only 3½d. The other customs were common [to both groups].

Any man's wife who brewed inside or outside the city gave 10d. according to custom. There were six smiths in the city, each of whom gave 1d. for his forge. Each of them made 120 shoes (*ferra*) from the king's iron, and to each of them 3d. was customarily paid on that account, and these smiths were quit of all other custom. Seven moneyers were there; one of them was the bishop's moneyer. When the coinage was changed, each of them gave 18s. to obtain the dies, and from the day on which they returned each of them gave the king 20s. for one month;[5] and in the same way the bishop had 20s. from his moneyer. When the king came to the city, the moneyers

---

[1] On the interpretation of the following entries, see especially Round, in *Victoria History of Herefordshire*, I, 263 f.

[2] A nearby royal manor.

[3] This was south of Hereford, toward the wild region of Archenfield. On such a trip the sheriff needed an armed escort.

[4] The heriot of the ordinary thegn in Canute, II, 71 (above, p. 24). Cf. the moneyers of Hereford, the Welshmen of Archenfield, and the thegns of Nottinghamshire in the following passages.

[5] Presumably a pound a month, for relatively large sums were reported from mints elsewhere.

made for him as many pennies as he wished—that is to say, of the king's silver. And these seven had their *sac* and *soc*. When any moneyer of the king died, the king had 20*s*. as relief.[6] But if he died without having divided his cash (*censum*), the king had all of it. If the sheriff went into Wales with an army, these men [of Hereford] went with him. But if any one was summoned to go and did not do so, he paid 40*s*. fine to the king.

In this city Earl Harold[7] had 27 burgesses enjoying the same customs as the other burgesses. From this city the reeve rendered £12 to King Edward and £6 to Earl Harold, and he had in his farm all the aforesaid customs.[8] The king, however, had in his demesne three forfeitures: namely, breach of his peace, house-breaking, and assault by ambush. Whoever committed one of these [offenses] paid the king 100*s*. fine, whosesoever man he was.[9] Now the king has the city of Hereford in demesne,[10] and the English burgesses who dwell there have their previous customs. The French burgesses, however, are quit, through [payment of] 12*d*., of all forfeitures except the three aforesaid.[11] This city renders to the king £60 by tale in assayed money.[12] Between the city and the eighteen manors that render their farms in Hereford £335. 18*s*. are accounted for, besides the pleas of the hundred and county [courts].[13]

In Archenfield the king has three churches. The priests of these churches undertake the king's embassies into Wales, and each of them sings for the king two masses every week. When any one of them dies, the king customarily has 20*s*. from him. If any Welshman steals a man or a woman, a horse, an ox, or a cow, on being convicted, he first returns what has been stolen and [then] pays 20*s*. as a fine. For theft of a sheep, however, or of a bundle of sheaves, he pays 2*s*. fine. If any one kills a man of the king or commits house-breaking, he pays the king 20*s*. compensation for the man and 100*s*. as fine. If he kills any thegn's man, he gives 10*s*. to the lord of the slain man. But if a Welshman kills a Welshman, the relatives of the slain man come together and plunder the slayer and his kin and burn their houses until, toward

---

[6] The Anglo-Saxon heriot; see n. 4 on the previous page.

[7] The Normans refused to recognize Harold's title to the throne.

[8] The borough, including the revenues described above, was farmed by the portreeve for £18 a year, two-thirds to the king and one-third to the earl.

[9] The list of crown pleas varied from region to region; cf. the customs of Worcestershire and Nottinghamshire below, and Canute, II, 12 (above, p. 22).

[10] Earlier there had been three great border earls who enjoyed all regalian rights within their respective territories: Roger de Montgomery, earl of Shrewsbury; Hugh d'Avranches, earl of Chester; and William Fitz-Osbern, earl of Hereford. Before 1086, however, the third of these earldoms had been forfeited as the consequence of a rebellion.

[11] Cf. the entry for Rhuddlan, below.

[12] See below, p. 49, no. 25, n. 1.

[13] These manors had earlier belonged to Earl William, and so had been brought into a financial organization centering in Hereford.

noon on the following day, the body of the slain man is buried. Of this plunder the king has the third part, but they enjoy all the rest of it in peace. He, however, who burns a house in another fashion, on being accused of doing so, defends himself by [the oaths of] forty men. But if he cannot [clear himself], he has to pay 20s. fine to the king. If any one conceals a sester of honey out of a customary payment, and is convicted of it, he renders five sesters for one, should he hold enough land to warrant the payment. If the sheriff calls them to the shire court, six or seven of the better men among them go with him [as escort]. He who is summoned [to the court] and does not go gives the king 2s. or an ox; and whoever stays away from the hundred [court] pays the same amount. He who is commanded by the sheriff to go with him into Wales, and does not do so, pays a similar fine. But if the sheriff does not go, none of them has to go. When the army advances against the enemy, they customarily form the advance guard, and on return [they form] the rear guard. These were the customs of the Welshmen in Archenfield during the time of King Edward.

Here are set down those holding lands in Herefordshire and in Archenfield and in Wales. . . .[14]

The land of the king. . . . The king holds Leominster.[15] Queen Edith held it. . . . In this manor . . . there were 80 hides, and in demesne 30 ploughs.[16] In it were 8 reeves, 8 beadles, 8 ridingmen, 238 villeins, 75 bordars, and 82 serfs and bondwomen.[17] These together had 230 ploughs. The villeins ploughed 140 acres of the lord's land and sowed it with their own seed grain, and by custom they paid £11. 52d. The ridingmen paid 14s. 4d. and 3 sesters of honey; and there were eight mills [with an income] of 73s. and 30 sticks of eels.[18] The wood rendered 24s. besides pannage.[19] Now

[14] According to the regular plan, the king heads the list of landholders and is followed by his barons, first the ecclesiastics and after them the laymen. The lands held by each person in the list are then described in turn, manor by manor.

[15] On this "gigantic manor" see Maitland, *Domesday Book and Beyond*, p. 112.

[16] By *caruca* is meant, not merely the plough proper, but also the team of eight oxen. The hide in Domesday is a unit of assessment for geld and other royal services. It was divided into 4 virgates or yardlands, 8 bovates, and 120 acres.

[17] The beadle appears in Domesday as the subordinate of a manorial reeve. The *radcniht* or ridingman seems to have been much the same as a *geneat*; see above, p. 8, n. 8. The *villani* of Domesday, being distinguished from *servi*, were legally free; for it was only later that serfdom and villeinage came to be arbitrarily identified. According to Domesday, the normal villein holding was thirty acres of arable. The bordar or cotter, on the other hand, held only a hut and a garden plot. See especially Maitland, *Domesday Book and Beyond*, pp. 26 f.; Vinogradoff, *Villeinage in England*.

[18] About two dozen eels were counted as a stick. Most of them, obviously, were taken from mill-ponds.

[19] Swine were commonly allowed to run wild in woodland. Rent paid for the privilege was called pannage; see immediately below.

in this manor the king has in demesne 60 hides and 29 ploughs; and 6 priests, 6 ridingmen, 7 reeves, 7 beadles, 224 villeins, 81 bordars. and 25 serfs and bondwomen. Among them all they have 201 ploughs. They plough and sow with their own grain 125 acres, and by custom they pay £7. 14s. 8½d.; also 17s. [worth] of fish, 8s. of salt, and 65s. of honey. In it are eight mills [with an income] of 108s. and 100 sticks of eels less 10. A wood 6 leagues[20] long and 3 leagues wide renders 22s. Of these shillings 5 are paid for buying wood at Droitwich, and thence are obtained 30 mitts of salt.[21] Each villein possessing ten pigs gives one pig for pannage. From woodland brought under cultivation come 17s. 4d. An eyrie of hawks is there. . . . Altogether this revenue, except the eels, is computed at £23. 2s. This manor is at farm for £60 in addition to the maintenance of the nuns. The county[22] says that, if it were freed [of that obligation], this manor would be worth six score, that is to say, £120. . . .

(Latin) *Domesday Book,* I, 179-83[b].

(B) Cheshire

Earl Hugh[23] holds Rhuddlan of the king. There in the time of King Edward lay Englefield, and it was entirely waste. Earl Edwin held it [in the time of King Edward]. It was likewise waste when Earl Hugh received it. Now he has in demesne half the castle that is called Rhuddlan, and it is the administrative centre (*caput*) of this land. There he has eight burgesses and half of the church, half of the mint, half of the mining of iron wherever it may be found in this manor, half of the water of Clwyd in both mills and fisheries that may be conducted there—that is to say, in the part of the river that belongs to the earl's fief—half of the forests that do not belong to any vill of this manor, half of the toll, and half of the vill called Bryn. There is land for three ploughs and they are in demesne, together with seven serfs. . . . Robert of Rhuddlan holds of Earl Hugh half of the same castle and borough, in which Robert himself has ten burgesses. . . .

In this manor of Rhuddlan there was recently built a castle, likewise called Rhuddlan. A new borough is there, and in it [are] eighteen burgesses [divided] between the earl and Robert, as mentioned above. To these burgesses they granted the laws and customs that are [enjoyed] in Hereford and in Breteuil: namely, that during an entire year they shall give for any misdeed no more than 12d., except for homicide, theft, and premeditated house-breaking.[24] In the year of

---

[20] The Domesday league is a mile and a half, but these measurements are only rough approximations.

[21] Salt-wiches are a prominent feature of this region; see Tait, *The Domesday Survey of Cheshire,* pp. 39 f. The wood bought at Droitwich was for the furnaces used in connection with salt-pans. The mitt included two ambers of four bushels each.

[22] I.e., the jury that spoke for it.

[23] See above, p. 42, n. 10; and for illuminating comment on the whole entry, the introduction to Tait's work just cited.

[24] On the significance of these customs, see Mary Bateson, "The Laws of Breteuil," in the *English Historical Review,* vols. XV, XVI; C. Stephenson, *Borough and Town,* pp. 88 f., 120 f.

this description[25] the toll of this borough was placed at farm for 3s. The income of Earl Hugh from Rhuddlan and Englefield is valued at £6. 10s.; Robert's share at £17.

(Latin) *Ibid.*, I, 269.

(C) BERKSHIRE[26]

When geld was given in the time of King Edward, commonly throughout all Berkshire the hide gave 3½d. before Christmas and the same amount at Pentecost. If the king sent an army anywhere, only one soldier went from five hides, and 4s. were given him from each hide as food and pay for two months. This money, indeed, was not sent to the king, but was given to the soldiers. If any one was summoned for an expedition and did not go, he forfeited all his land to the king. But if any one, for the sake of remaining [at home], promised to send another in his place, and yet he remained who was to have been sent, his lord was quit through [payment of] 50s. On the death of a king's household thegn or *cniht*,[27] all his arms, as well as one horse with a saddle and one without, were sent to the king as relief. But if he possessed dogs or hawks, they were given to the king as a present, if the latter was willing to accept them. If any one slew a man enjoying the king's peace, he forfeited to the king both his body and all his substance. He who broke into a city[28] by night paid 100s. fine to the king, not to the sheriff.[29] He who was summoned as a beater for hunting, and did not go, paid the king 50s. fine.

(Latin) *Ibid.*, I, 56ᵇ.

(D) WORCESTERSHIRE

In this county, if any one knowingly breaks the peace which the king has given by his own hand, he is outlawed.[30] If any one knowingly breaks the king's peace given by the sheriff, he pays 100s. fine. He who commits assault by ambush pays 100s. fine. He who commits rape can offer no atonement save judgment upon his body. These forfeitures the king has in the said county except on the land of St. Peter of Westminster, to which King Edward gave whatever [rights] he had there[31]—so the county says. When the king advances against the enemy, any one who is summoned and who remains behind, if he

[25] The year of the Domesday inquest, 1086.

[26] Round (in *Domesday Studies*, pp. 77 f.) was the first to explain the significance of the Berkshire custom. For further comment on this and the following entries, see the appropriate volumes of the *Victoria County History*.

[27] See above, p. 41, n. 4. The *cniht* was a sort of lesser thegn; see Gross, *Gild Merchant*, I, 183 f.

[28] Cf. Ine, 45 (above, p. 9); and see above, p. 37, n. 5.

[29] The meaning of this provision and the similar ones below is probably that small fines were included in the sheriff's farm, while more extraordinary ones were not.

[30] Although the present tense is used, the customs described were those of the Anglo-Saxon period.

[31] Cf. no. 15G, above.

is so free a man that he has his *sac* and *soc* and can go with his land whither he pleases,[32] is in the king's mercy[33] for all his land. If, however, the freeman of some other lord remains away from the host, and if his lord takes another man in his place, he has to pay 40*s*. to his lord who received the summons. If, however, no one goes for him at all, he shall indeed give to his lord the 40*s*., but the lord has to pay the same amount to the king.

(Latin) *Ibid.*, I, 172.

(E) Nottinghamshire

. . . In Nottinghamshire and Derbyshire breach of the king's peace, given under [his own] hand or seal, is atoned for by [a fine of] 18 hundreds, each hundred [being] £8.[34] Of this fine the king has two parts, the earl the third; that is to say, 12 hundreds go to the king and 6 to the earl. If any one, on conviction of anything, is exiled according to law, no one except the king can restore peace to him. A thegn having more than six manors pays no relief for his land except to the king, [namely,] 3*m*. of silver—wherever he may live, in borough or out of borough. If a thegn having *sac* and *soc* forfeits his land, half of his land and his chattels is shared between the king and the earl; his lawful wife, together with his legitimate heirs if there are any, has the other half.

(Latin) *Ibid.*, I, 280.[b]

---

[32] That is to say, can commend himself, with his land, to a lord of his own choosing.

[33] See below, p. 48, n. 6.

[34] A method of reckoning peculiar to certain Danish regions; see Round, *Feudal England*, p. 73.

23. HENRY I: CORONATION CHARTER (1100)

Henry, king of the English, to Samson, bishop [of Worcester], and to Urse d'Abetot,[1] and to all his barons and faithful men of Worcestershire, both French and English, greeting.

1. Know that by the mercy of God, and by the common counsel of the barons of the whole kingdom of England, I have been crowned king of the same kingdom. And since the kingdom has been oppressed by unjust exactions, I, through fear of God and through the love that I have for you all, in the first place make the Holy Church of God free, so that I will neither sell nor put at farm nor, on the death of an archbishop, bishop, or abbot, take anything from the demesne of a church, or from its men, until a successor enters upon it.[2] And I henceforth remove all the bad customs through which the kingdom of England has been unjustly oppressed; which bad customs I here in part set down.

---

[1] Sheriff of Worcester. Other forms of address were of course used for the other counties.

[2] For examples of this feudal usage and of many others abolished or restricted in the Coronation Charter, see Henry's own pipe roll (no. 25).

2. If any one of my barons, earls, or other men who hold of me dies, his heir shall not redeem his land as he did in the time of my brother, but he shall relieve it by a just and legitimate relief. In the same way, furthermore, the men of my barons shall relieve their lands from their lords by just and legitimate reliefs.

3. And if any one of my barons or other men wishes to give in marriage his daughter, sister, niece, or [other] female relative, let him talk with me about the matter; but I will neither take anything from his property for this permission nor prohibit him from giving her [in marriage], unless he wishes to wed her to an enemy of mine. And if, on the death of a baron or other man of mine, a daughter remains as heiress, I will give her [in marriage], together with her land, by the counsel of my barons. And if, on the death of a husband, his wife survives and is without children, she shall have her dowry and marriage portion,[3] and I will not give her to a husband unless it is in accord with her own wish.

4. If, moreover, the wife survives with children, she shall yet have her dowry and marriage portion so long as she keeps her body legitimately, and I will not give her [in marriage] except in accord with her wish. And the guardian of the land and the children shall be either the widow or another one of the relatives who more rightly ought to be [in that position]. And I command that my barons shall conduct themselves in the same way toward the sons or daughters or wives of their men.

5. The common *monetagium*,[4] which has been collected throughout the cities and counties, and which did not exist in the time of King Edward, I utterly abolish for the future. If [however] any one, whether a moneyer or some one else, is taken with false money, let justice be done in the matter.

6. I pardon all pleas and debts that were owed to my brother, except my lawful farms and except those [payments] which were agreed on for the sake of others' inheritances or of those things that more rightly affected others.[5] But if any one has pledged anything for the sake of his own inheritance, that I pardon, as well as all reliefs that have been agreed on for the sake of rightful inheritances.

7. And if any one of my barons or men becomes infirm, as he himself may bestow his chattels or provide [by will] for their bestowal, so, I grant, shall they be bestowed. But if he, prevented by arms or

---

[3] The marriage portion (*maritagium*) was the land conferred on a woman by her father or other relative; the dowry that given her by her husband. To the former she had an absolute title if she survived her husband; in the latter she had only a life estate. Cf. no. 27E, G.

[4] The *monetagium*, which is obscurely referred to in Domesday, was an exaction introduced in England by William I. On the continent it was usually a tax on sales, paid for a term of years on condition that, during such time, no change in the coinage would be made.

[5] Presumably payments made to secure lands and perquisites that had reverted to the crown through escheat or forfeiture. But the clause might also refer to a sum paid by one man to advance the claim of another. For examples see Henry's pipe roll.

infirmity, has not bestowed his chattels or provided [by will] for their bestowal, his widow or his children or his relatives or his liegemen shall divide them for the good of his soul as may seem to them best.

8. If any one of my barons or men commits an offence, he shall not [be declared] in mercy [and required to] give a pledge from his chattels,[6] as he was in the time of my father and my brother; but he shall pay compensation according to the measure of the offence, as was done before the time of my father, in the time of my other predecessors. But if he is convicted of treason or disgraceful crime,[7] let him make amends as is just.

9. I also pardon all murders[8] [committed] before that day on which I was crowned king, and those that have been committed afterwards are to be paid for by just compensation according to the law of King Edward.

10. By the common counsel of my barons, I have kept in my hands the forests as they were held by my father.[9]

11. To knights who hold their lands by military service (*per loricas*) I grant, of my own gift, the lands of their demesne ploughs[10] quit of all gelds and of all work; so that, inasmuch as they are thus relieved of a heavy burden, they may the better provide themselves with arms and horses, to be fit and ready for my service and the defence of my kingdom.

12. I establish my firm peace throughout the whole kingdom and command that it be henceforth maintained.

13. I restore to you the law of King Edward, together with those amendments by which my father, with the counsel of his barons, amended it.[11]

14. If any one, since the death of my brother William, has taken anything from my property or from the property of any one else, let him at once restore it without penalty; but if any one keeps anything [of that sort], he on whom it may be found shall pay me heavy compensation.

Witnesses: Maurice, bishop of London; William, bishop elect of Winchester; Gerard, bishop of Hereford; Henry, earl [of Warwick]; Simon, earl [of Northampton]; Walter Giffard, Robert de Montfort, Roger Bigot, Odo the Steward, Robert Fitz-Hamon, Robert Malet. At Westminster, when I was crowned. Farewell!

(Latin) Liebermann, Gesetze, I, 521 f.

---

[6] This was a promise to abolish the system of amercement, or arbitrary fine, introduced by the Conqueror, and to revert to the older system of *bot* and *wite*, but it was not kept; see Pollock and Maitland, II, 513 f. Many examples of amercement will be found in the following documents.

[7] *Perfidiae vel sceleris*—offences for which there was no lawful compensation in money; cf. Alfred, 4 (above, p. 10), and the subsequent dooms.

[8] See above, p. 36, n. 2.

[9] See no. 35 and the references there given.

[10] Cf. no. 22A. If carried out, the reform would have been equivalent to a heavy reduction of hidage on all baronial manors.

[11] Cf. no. 18, art. 7.

24. HENRY I: ORDINANCE ON LOCAL COURTS

Henry, king of the English, to Samson, bishop [of Worcester], Urse d'Abetot, and all his barons of Worcestershire, French and English, greeting. Know that I grant and command that henceforth [the courts of] my counties and hundreds shall meet in the same places and at the same times as they did in the time of King Edward, and not otherwise. And I am unwilling that my sheriff, on account of any business that peculiarly concerns him, should have them meet in any other way. For I, when I please and on my own decision, will have them adequately summoned for the sake of my royal needs (*dominica necessaria*). And henceforth, if a plea arises concerning the division or occupation of lands, and if it is between my own barons (*dominicos barones meos*), let it be tried in my court.[1] And if it is between vassals of some baron who holds an honour of me, let the plea be tried in the court of their lord. And if it is between vassals of two lords, let it be tried in the county [court]. And this [trial] shall be by combat unless it is given up through their own fault (*nisi remanserit in eis*). Also I will and command that all men of the county shall attend the county [court] and the hundred [courts] as they did in the time of King Edward, and no peace or quittance of mine shall excuse them from following my pleas and judgments according to the usage of that time.[2]

Witnesses: R[ichard], bishop of London; Roger, Bishop [of Salisbury]; Ralph the Chamberlain; Robert, count of Meulan. At Reading.

(Latin) *Ibid.*, I, 524.

---

[1] His feudal court, made up of his vassals.

[2] Nevertheless, specific exemption from suit to shire and hundred courts was not infrequent in royal grants of immunity; e.g., no. 27A. For a general discussion of the principles involved, see Pollock and Maitland, I, 537 f.; and cf. no. 26.

25. PIPE ROLL OF 31 HENRY I (1130)

(A) WARWICKSHIRE ACCOUNT

Geoffrey de Clinton renders account of 44s. 8d. blanch[1] from the old farm. He has paid it into the treasury. And he is quit.

And the same man [renders account] of the new farm. In the treasury £100. 4s. 4d. by weight. And he owes £32. 9s. 4d. blanch.

And the same Geoffrey renders account of 310m. of silver for an office in the treasury at Winchester. In the treasury 100m. of silver. And he owes 210m. of silver.

And the same man owes 40m. of silver on behalf of the earl of Leicester for the debt of Ernald de Vétheuil.

---

[1] Payment by tale was made by counting out 240d. to the pound, as distinguished from payment by weight, when an actual pound of silver was demanded. If, furthermore, sample coins were melted down and an additional sum was thrown in as compensation for proved debasement, payment was said to be blanch. For a description of this procedure and of the whole exchequer system, see R. L. Poole, *The Exchequer in the Twelfth Century*.

And the same man owes 20*m*. of silver and 1*m*. of gold that the king will confirm in a charter for his church of Arden everything that the earl of Warwick gave him for the benefit of the said church.

And the same man owes £7. 13*s*. 8*d*. from the old farm of the land of William de Roumare.

And the same man owes 40*m*. of silver with which he should acquit Nicholas Fitz-Gundewin of Rouen.

Geoffrey Lovet owes £9. 13*s*. 4*d*. for the security that he unjustly took from a certain man; of which [money] the pledges are Geoffrey de Clinton and Robert de Neufbourg.

Osbert of Arden renders account of £10 for the pleas of William Hubold.[2] In the treasury 40*s*. And he owes £8.

And the same sheriff renders account of 100*s*. from old pleas and murders.[3] In pardon by the king's writ to the earl of Warwick 100*s*. And he is quit.

Hugh Fitz-Richard renders account of 200*m*. of silver and one valuable horse (*equo de pretio*) and two war-horses (*dextrariis*) for the land that Geoffrey de Lovet holds of him. In the treasury £30. And by the witness of Miles of Gloucester he has acquitted himself toward the king of the valuable war-horse (*dextrario pretioso*). And he owes 155*m*. of silver and two horses. And thereof [these men] are pledges: the earl of Warwick, 60*m*. of silver; Henry de Sai, 20*m*. of silver; Henry d'Armentières, 20*m*. of silver.

William Fitz-Ralph renders account of 113*s*. 4*d*. and one war-horse that he may have the land of his father. In the treasury 30*s*. And he owes £4. 3*s*. 4*d*. and one war-horse.

Robert Fitz-Ralph renders account of £4 for his portion of his father's land. In the treasury 20*s*. And he owes 60*s*.

The earl of Warwick renders account of £72. 16*s*. 8*d*. and two war-horses for pleas concerning stags;[4] and of 20*m*. of silver for the land which Geoffrey Lovet holds of him; and of 200*m*. of silver that the king will pardon him the surplus hidage of his manor of Brailles.[5] In the treasury £43. 6*s*. 8*d*. And he owes £176. 2*s*. 4*d*.

Guibert, steward of Roger de Mowbray, renders account of 1*m*. of silver from the pleas of Geoffrey de Clinton. He has paid it into the treasury. And he is quit.

Agnes de Clincamp renders account of 40*s*. that her sons may secure the inheritance of their father's land. She has paid it into the treasury. And she is quit.

And the same sheriff renders account of £8. 5*d*. from arrears of Danegeld. In the treasury 70*s*. 5*d*. And in pardons by the king's writ to the chancellor £4. 10*s*. And he is quit.

Walter Croc renders account of 33*s*. 4*d*. from the old rent of the

---

[2] Entries of this sort normally refer to trials held before the king's justices on mission—already an important source of revenue.

[3] See above, p. 36, n. 2.

[4] Violations of forest law. There are many such entries in the roll.

[5] A reduction of hidage would, of course, mean a reduction of Danegeld, which, as this roll testifies, was by now an annual exaction.

forest during four years. He has paid it into the treasury. And he is quit.

And the same Walter renders account of 10*m*. of silver from the new rent of the forest. In the treasury 106*s*. 8*d*. And he owes 26*s*. 8*d*.

And the same man owes 3*m*. of gold for having his office again; and £13. 11*s*. 5*d*. for the land of Richard Chienewe; and £7. 6*s*. 8*d*. for the plea of Roger, son of Eli the *scutellarius*;[6] and £18. 5*s*. from the pleas of William of Gloucester; and 10 horses and 106 oxen and 200 pigs which he took from the forest, and which did not belong to him but to the forester. And he is in the king's mercy unless the king will be his warrantor for the 30*s*. that he unlawfully took and did not return.

And the same sheriff renders account of £12. 3*s*. 10*d*. from arrears of Danegeld. In the treasury 19*s*. And in pardons by the king's writ: to Ralph the Butler 60*s*.; to the count of Meulan 24*s*.; to Geoffrey de Mandeville 60*s*. 9*d*.; to Curtis 10*s*.; to the earl of Warwick £4. 4*s*. Total £11. 4*s*. 10*d*. And he is quit.

And the same sheriff renders acount of 37*s*. 2*d*. from arrears of aid from the borough of Tamworth.[7] He has paid it into the treasury. And he is quit.

New Pleas and New Obligations[8]

Robert Tortran renders account of 60*m*. of silver for the chattels of William de Chenfara that he took. In the treasury 30*m*. of silver. And he owes 30*m*. of silver.

Hugh Hall (*de Hella*) renders account of 100*s*. for the claims of Leofric Lock. In the treasury 30*s*. And he owes 70*s*.

Rodbricht of Bradwell renders account of 100*s*. from. the same pleas. In the treasury 30*s*. And in pardon by the king's writ to the same Rodbricht 20*s*. And he owes 50*s*.

Ralph, son of Godwin Hall (*de Halla*) renders account of 10*m*. of silver from the same pleas. In the treasury 40*s*. And he owes 7*m*. of silver.

Fulk of Mauritania renders account of 30*m*. of silver for the plea concerning the chattels of Matilda of Stafford. In the treasury 5*m*. of silver. And he owes 25*m*. of silver.

Ivo, son of Hugh of Leicester, owes 20*m*. of silver for the grant of the land which belonged to William de Beaumont, and which the earl of Warwick gave him.

And the same sheriff renders account of Danegeld. In the treasury £78. 12*s*. 1*d*. And in pardons by the king's writ: to William Comyn 13*s*.; to the earl of Chester 24*s*. . . .[9] Total £50. 5*d*. And he is quit.

---

[6] Probably keeper of the dishes in the royal kitchen; see below, p. 67.

[7] On the annual *auxilia burgorum* that accompanied the Danegeld, see C. Stephenson, *Borough and Town*, pp. 160 f.

[8] *Conventiones* is the regular form, but it covered a variety of payments besides those based on agreement.

[9] Thirty-five other items enumerated.

And the same sheriff owes 30*s* from the aid of the borough of Tamworth.

Geoffrey de Clinton renders account of the farm of Wargrave. In the treasury £80. And he is quit.

And the same Geoffrey renders account of £20 from the old farm of Wallop. He has paid it into the treasury. And he is quit.

And the same Geoffrey renders account of the new farm of Wallop. In the treasury £20. And he owes £20.

And the same Geoffrey renders account of the revenues of the abbey of Evesham. In the treasury £40.

(Latin) Pipe Roll of 31 Henry I, pp. 104 f.

(B) Miscellaneous Entries

Oxfordshire. . . . Matthew de Vernon owes 100 *muids*[10] of wine for the settlement of his brother's duel. . . . The cordwainers of Oxford render account of 5 ounces of gold as a bonus (*gersoma*) for having their gild again. In the treasury 30*s*. in place of 2 ounces of gold. And they owe 3 ounces of gold. . . .

Nottinghamshire and Derbyshire. . . . Robert de Lusors renders account of £8. 6*s*. 8*d*. that he may marry the sister of Ilbert de Lacy. . . . Ralph Halselin renders account of 200*m*. of silver and 1*m*. of gold for the relief of his father's land. . . .

Wiltshire. . . . Humphrey de Bohun renders account of £22. 10*s*. for the relief of his father's land; and of 400*m*. of silver in order to be steward of the king.[11] . . . And the same sheriff owes 41*s*. 6*d*. from arrears of Danegeld. And the same sheriff owes £6. 18*d*. from arrears of the county's aid.[12] . . .

Yorkshire. . . . And the same sheriff owes £27. 10*s*. 7*d*. from arrears of the county's aid. . . . Walter de Chauncey renders account of £15 that he may marry a wife of his own choosing. . . . Thomas of York, son of Wulfgeat (*Ulvieti*), owes one hunting dog in order to be alderman of the gild merchant of York. . . .

Cambridgeshire. . . . Hervey, bishop of Ely, renders account of 7½*m*. of gold for the office of his nephew William. In the treasury £18 in place of 3*m*. of gold. And he owes 4½*m*. of gold. . . . And the same bishop owes £240 that the king will quitclaim him of the bishop's surplus of knights and that the abbey of Charteris may be quit of wardpenny.[13] . . .

Surrey. . . . And the same [John Belet] owes 60*s*. from old aid of his knights.[14] . . .

Essex. . . . And the same [Richard Fitz-Gilbert] owes 200*m*. of

---

[10] The *modius* seems to have been a large, rather than a small barrel; cf. the *modius* of grain, below, p. 67.

[11] See below, p. 66.

[12] *Auxilium comitatus*—a tax supplementary to the Danegeld, apparently raised through negotiation with the county court.

[13] Cf. no. 27D.

[14] Entries such as this, in the light of the one preceding, would appear to refer to scutage.

silver for the help that the king gave him in connection with his debt to the Jews. Juliana, wife of William of Hastings, owes £6 from old aid of knights from the fief of Waleran, her grandfather. . . .

Kent. . . . Turgis, [bishop of] Avranches, renders account of 300*m.* of silver and 1*m.* of gold and a war-horse for the land and the widow of Hugh d'Auberville and to have wardship over his son until the latter is twenty years old. . . .

Northamptonshire. . . . Osbert of Leicester owes 200*m.* of silver that the king will pardon him and Osbert, his clerk, for their malevolence. . . . Guy Maufé renders account of one war-horse that he may be justly treated in the court of his lord.[15] In the treasury 40*s.* in place of one war-horse. And he is quit. . . .

Norfolk. . . . Benjamin renders account of £4. 5*s.* that he may keep the pleas that belong to the king's crown.[16] In the treasury 56*s.* 8*d.* And he owes 28*s.* 4*d.*; and [guarantees] to make a profit of 500*m.* for the king. . . .

Suffolk. . . . William of Middlehall renders account of 4*m.* of silver from the pleas of Richard Basset. But he cannot be found in the county, nor has he anything. And so he is quit. . . .

Lincolnshire. . . . And the same sheriff renders account of 1*m.* of gold for the weavers' gild of Lincoln. In the treasury £6 in place of 1*m.* of gold. And he is quit. . . . Lucy, countess of Chester, renders account of £266. 13*s.* 4*d.* for the land of her father. In the treasury £166. 13*s.* 6*d.* And she owes £100; also 500*m.* of silver that she need not take a husband inside five years. And the same countess renders account of 45*m.* of silver for the same agreement, to be given to whom the king pleases. To the queen 20*m.* of silver. And she owes 25*m.* of silver. And the same lady owes 100*m.* of silver that she may hold justice in her court among her own men. . . . The burgesses of Lincoln render account of 200*m.* of silver and 4*m.* of gold that they may hold the city of the king in chief.[17] . . . Lambert Fitz-Peter renders account of one palfrey for the land of his father. In the treasury 30*s.* in place of one palfrey. And he is quit. . . .

Durham. . . . And the same Geoffrey renders account of the old farm of the bishropic for the previous year. . . . And the same Geoffrey renders account of the new farm of the bishropric.[18] . . .

London and Middlesex. The four sheriffs of London render account of the farm of London. In the treasury £16. 14*s.* 9*d.* blanch. And in fixed liveries £8. 2*s.* 1*d.* by tale. And in livery to the count of Mortain £12. 12*s.* 6*d.* by tale. And in clothes for the same count 65*s.* by tale. And in liveries to the serjeants who guard the count and to

---

[15] Cf. no. 33E.

[16] Keeping the crown pleas should be distinguished from trying them. The keeper, whose functions were later taken over by the coroner, had charge of a case until the time that it came to trial before a justice. •

[17] That is to say, farm the city direct from the king. The grant, presumably, was not in fee, as was that secured by the Londoners; see no. 28B.

[18] Taken into the king's hands during a vacancy despite his Coronation Charter.

watchmen and doorkeepers at the Tower £12. 3s. 4d. by tale. And in livery to the wife of Owen the Naperer[19] 46s. 8d. by tale. And in livery to Geoffrey the Engineer[20] £10. 12s. 11d. by tale. And in livery to Ralph the Arborer[21] £7. 12s. 1d. by tale. And to the goldsmiths of London for charcoal 60s. 10d. by tale. And in oil to burn before the queen's sepulchre 16s. 2½d. And in livery to the archbishop of Rouen and in clothes for the count of Normandy £23. 10s. by tale. And in herrings, unguent, oil, nuts, and transportation to Woodstock £8. 18s. 5d. by tale. And in the purchase of wine and in transportation £45. 6s. 2d. by tale. And in the purchase of pepper, cummin, ginger, towels, basinets, and linen cloth for the king's use £23. 19s. 9d. by tale. And in building two arches of London Bridge £25 by tale. And in work on the Tower of London £17. 6s. by tale. And in repairing the houses that belonged to Othweard (*Otuerus*), [in repairing] the chapel, and in other minor work 22s. 9d. by tale. And in quittances of toll[22] to the merchants of Thierry, count of Provence, 75s. 3d. by tale. And in the purchase of cloth to place on the queen's sepulchre 3s. by tale. And they owe £310. 9s. 2d. blanch. . . . Abraham and Deuslesalt,[23] Jews, render account of 1m. of gold that they may have their debts from Osbert of Leicester. . . . Rabbi Joseph (*Rubi Gotsce*), the Jew, and Jacob and Manasseh render account of 6m. of gold that the king will help them against Richard Fitz-Gilbert in the matter of his debts. . . . The men of London render account of 100m. of silver that they may have a sheriff of their own choosing.[24] . . . The Jews of London render account of £2000 for the infirm man whom they slew. . . . The abbot of Westminster renders account of 1000m. of silver to collect the goods of his church which were unlawfully dispersed, and to have the custody of them when collected. . . .

(Latin) *Ibid.*, pp. 4 f.

---

[19] See below, p. 67.

[20] *Ingeniator,* one in charge of a siege engine.

[21] *Arborarius,* the exact meaning of which remains doubtful.

[22] The tolls collected in the port of London were included in the farm of the city; hence any special pardon of such payments was charged off on the account as a credit to the sheriffs.

[23] *Dieu-le-saut,* the French equivalent of the Hebrew Isaiah.

[24] This liberty was subsequently confirmed by Henry's charter, no. 28B.

26. EXCERPTS FROM THE "LAWS OF HENRY I"[1]

7. Concerning the general pleas of the counties, how and when they should be held. . . . If any one of the king's barons or other men is lawfully present at the county [court],[2] he may acquit all the land that he there has in his demesne. The same is true if his steward is lawfully present. If both are of necessity absent, the reeve, the priest,

---

[1] Not a collection of royal enactments, but a private compilation which is often obscure or inaccurate: see above, p. 33, also Pollock and Maitland, I, 99.

[2] See below, art. 31.

and four of the better men of the vill shall attend on behalf of all who are not summoned to the court by name.[3] We have decreed the same to be observed in the hundred . . . with regard to the presence of the lord and his steward, or of the priest, the reeve, and the better men. . . .

8. Concerning the holding of the hundreds. If, however, there is need for a specially full session, all freemen shall assemble twice a year in their hundred . . . for the sake of determining, among other matters, whether the tithings are full. . . . The tenth man, indeed, is to be in charge of each group of nine,[4] and one of the better men, likewise, [is to be in charge of] the whole hundred, and he is called the alderman. . . .

15. Concerning Danegeld. If Danegeld, which earlier was given to the house-carls[5]—that is to say, 12d. annually from every hide—is not paid on time, compensation is made with a fine (wita). . . .

20. Concerning soke.[6] . . . For all soke is either exclusively or jointly held. In the custody [of subordinates], indeed, there is a threefold distinction [of soke]: under the reeves of manors in the appurtenant hall-motes,[7] under the men in charge of hundreds and boroughs, and under the sheriffs. Archbishops, bishops, earls, and other magnates in the lands under their own authority have *sac* and *soc*, *toll* and *team*, and *infangþeof*[8] over their own men and in their own [property], and occasionally over the men of another, especially when those men are seized or accused in [the act of] misdoing, and then they are to have adequate compensation; moreover, in other [lands], acquired by purchase or exchange or in any [such] way, they have *sac* and *soc* in ordinary cases and [such cases are tried] in the appurtenant hall-motes. Finally, jurisdiction in capital cases over all barons and magnates, clerical or lay, belongs to the king, no matter where they hold land and whether it is soke of the king or not.[9] . . .

25. Concerning the privileges of the nobles of England. If a plea arises between men of any baron having soke, in case of an ordinary action,[10] the plea is tried in the court of their lord. If it is between

---

[3] As Liebermann remarks (*Gesetze*, III, 316), this article may reflect the provisions of a lost ordinance of Henry I. See also Pollock and Maitland, I, 545 f., and cf. no. 21.

[4] The tithing was really a group of ten; see above, p. 37, n. 6, and below, pp. 78, 109, etc.

[5] Here called *þingemanni*, the members of the royal standing guard under Canute and Edward the Confessor.

[6] See above, p. 30, n. 23.

[7] On the nature and origin of these manorial courts, see Maitland, *Domesday Book and Beyond*, pp. 80 f.

[8] Cf. nos. 15G, 20A, 27F.

[9] The meaning is that in crown pleas the great men were personally subject to the king's justice, without regard to the privileges which they might enjoy within their own fiefs.

[10] One not reserved to the king or under ecclesiastical jurisdiction.

men of two lords having soke, the accused man shall respond in the court of his lord,[11] in case of an ordinary action. . . .

29. Those who should be the king's judges.[12] The king's judges are to be barons of the county, who there have freeholds; by them the cases of individuals should be decided on the prosecution of either party. But villeins, cotters, virgators,[13] or poor and mean persons of this sort are not to be included among the judges. . . .

31. Concerning capital pleas. . . . The county [court] should be attended by bishops, earls, and other magnates, who through just deliberation are to define God's laws and worldly concerns.[14] No one is permitted to dispute the record[15] of a court of the king; elsewhere it may be done by credible men of the court. And no one is to be convicted in capital pleas by testimony [alone].[16] . . . Every one ought to be judged by his peers[17] and [by men] of the same province [in which he lives]. . . .

32. That no one should judge his lord. . . . No one shall judge his lord or bring judgment against one of whom he is the liegeman, even if the case belongs to the prince.[18] If a lord brings suit against his man, he can, if necessary, make use of his counsellors as judges.[19]

33. Concerning the trial of a plea. If any one has a plea tried in his court or in any place of judicial business [under him], he shall summon the peers[20] and his neighbours, so that, when judgment is enforced, he may administer justice that is free and not liable to be contradicted by any one. . . .

51. Concerning the summoning of the hundred. . . . Moreover, as aforesaid, the hundred [court] ought to be assembled every month —that is to say, twelve times a year—and the county [court] twice, unless there is need for it more often. . . .

52. Concerning the king's own plea. If any one is impleaded by the king's justice in a crown plea, whosoever man he may be, he ought not to refuse the justice gage of right.[21] . . .

55. Concerning the privilege of a lord with regard to his man. It is lawful for every lord to summon his man for judgment in his court. Even if the man is residing at a more remote manor in the honour of which he holds, he shall go to court when his lord summons him. If the lord holds various fiefs, a man of one honour is not compelled

---

[11] But see Henry I's ordinance, no. 24.

[12] *Iudices regis,* meaning doomsmen or judgment-finders who declare the royal law.

[13] *Ferdingus (feorðing)* designated a man holding a fourth—presumably of a hide, i.e., a virgate. See above, p. 43, n. 16.

[14] A reflection of Edgar, III, 5 (above, p. 19); but see no. 17.

[15] Either written or oral testimony as to a previous action.

[16] Without ordeal, compurgation, or battle.

[17] His social equals; cf. Magna Carta, art. 39 (below, p. 121).

[18] That is to say, unless it is a crown plea.

[19] As well as his vassals who are to be specially summoned; cf. arts. 29, 55.

[20] The vassals who owed suit to the court.

[21] I.e., security for appearing in court and defending the suit.

by law to go to court in another, unless it is a case affecting some one else to which his lord summons him. If a man holds of various lords and honours, no matter how much he holds of the others, his primary obligation . . . is to the lord whose liegeman he is. Every man owes fealty to his lord for life and limbs and earthly honour and the keeping of counsel in all that is honest and worthy, saving fealty to God and to the prince of the land. Theft, treason, murder, and whatever is opposed to God and the catholic faith are, indeed, to be undertaken and carried out for no one. But fealty is to be kept toward all lords, and especially toward the lord of whom he is the liegeman, saving fealty to those mentioned above. . . .

80. Concerning homicide in the king's court, army, borough, or castle. If any one commits homicide in a house, court, borough, castle, army, or militia of the king, he shall be in the king's mercy[22] for his chattels or limbs. If assault is committed on any one in the king's highway, it is *forsteal*,[23] and compensation of 100*s*. shall be paid to the king. . . . And a royal highway is defined [as a road] which is always open, which no one can close or divert from its termination, and which leads to a royal city, borough, castle, or port. . . .

87. . . . If any one can prove by judgment of hot iron, or battle, or the production of lawful witnesses or oath-helpers, or [other] fit mode of proof, that he was assaulted and was forced to commit homicide in self-defence, such demonstration on his part shall be considered satisfactory and justice shall accordingly be done. . . .

88. . . . And no one shall forfeit his fief to the deprivation of his legitimate heirs except through felony[24] or the voluntary surrender [of the property]. . . .

91. Concerning the payment of murder [fine].[25] If any Frenchman or any Norman or, lastly, any man from beyond the sea is slain, and the affair turns out so calamitously that it is considered murder and the slayer is unknown and eventually flees, so that within seven days he is not handed over to the king's justice for the carrying out of whatever may be right, 46*m*. of silver shall be paid—40*m*. to the king and 6*m*. to the relatives of the slain man. If the relatives have no accusers or provers,[26] these [6*m*.] shall go to him who does prove [who committed] the murder. Where, however, [the slain man] is found, there must investigation be made according to the law, and the alderman of the hundred and [the lord] on whose land [the slain man] lies should give security that he will be paid for. . . . If the murder is discovered in a house or in a hall or in a close, when it comes to paying the aforesaid 46*m*., whatever is in that manor . . .

---

[22] See above, p. 48, n. 6.

[23] See Canute, II, 12 (above, p. 22).

[24] Default of feudal obligations. Because it involved forfeiture, felony was later made to embrace all sorts of crimes under English law; for examples see no. 54.

[25] See above, p. 36, n. 2.

[26] Through whom to determine the guilty party.

should first be sold. . . . And if thereby the 46m. are forthcoming, nothing is to be sought elsewhere; but if there is a deficiency, it is made up by the hundred in common. If, moreover, the manor in which the murder is discovered is of the king's demesne farm, and if the king so orders, composition for it shall be made by the entire hundred. If the murder is discovered in fields that are open and generally accessible, [the money] shall be supplied by the whole hundred in common, and not merely by him to whom the land belongs. If it happens on the boundary, [the obligation] shall fall on both [territories]. If it is on the king's highway, compensation is to be paid by him who owns the adjacent land. . . .

92. . . . [The death of] an Englishman is not regarded or paid for as murder, but only [that of] a Frenchmen; indeed, should there be no one to prove that the slain man is English, he is held to be French. . . . If the hundred wishes to prove concerning some one that he is not a Frenchman and that [accordingly] there is no murder, this [obligation] is to be entrusted to twelve of the better men from the same hundred, swearing [to that effect]. . . .

(Latin) Liebermann, Gesetze, I, 553 f.

27. WRITS CONCERNING FEUDAL TENURES[1]

(A) William I: Grant in Free Alms (1070-71)

William, king of England, to Baldwin, sheriff of Devonshire, and to all his barons and ministers of the province, greeting. Know that I have granted to my monks of Battle [Abbey] the church of St. Olave in Exeter, with all the lands of Sherford and Kenbury, and with all other lands and things belonging to that church. Wherefore I will and command that they shall hold it freely and peacefully, and that, as my royal alms (*elemosina dominica*), it shall be exempt from all custom of earthly service: [namely,] from all pleas and plaints and shires and hundreds,[2] and from all geld, scot, aid, gift,[3] Danegeld, and army [service], with *sac* and *soc*, toll and *infangenepeof*, and all work on castles and bridges.

Witnesses: Thomas, archbishop of York; William Fitz-Osbert. At Winchester.

(Latin) Oliver, Monasticon Dioecesis Exoniensis, p. 117.

(B) William I: Summons for Military Service (1072)

William, king of the English, to Aethelwig, abbot of Evesham, greeting. I command you to summon all those who are under your charge and administration[4] that they shall have ready before me at Clarendon on the octave of Pentecost all the knights that they owe

---

[1] See Pollock and Maitland, I, 240 f.

[2] See above, p. 49, n. 2.

[3] *Donum*, a frequent substitute in the pipe rolls for *auxilium* or *tallagium*; cf. no. 37B.

[4] As Round pointed out, the abbot commanded the military forces of a considerable region; his owed service was only five knights.

me. Come to me likewise yourself on that day, and bring ready with you those five knights that you owe me from your abbey.

Witness, Eudo the Steward. At Winchester.

(Latin) Round, *Feudal England*, p. 304.

(C) WILLIAM II: WRIT FOR THE COLLECTION OF RELIEF (1095-96)

William, king of the English, to all French and English who hold free lands of the bishopric of Worcester, greeting. Know that, since the bishop has died, the honour has reverted into my own hand.[5] It is now my will that from your lands you give me such relief as I have assessed through my barons: [namely,] Hugh de Lacy £20; Walter Punther £20; Gilbert Fitz-Turold £5; Robert, bishop [of Hereford], £10; the abbot of Evesham £30; Walter of Gloucester £20; Roger Fitz-Durand £10. . . .[6] And if any one refuses to do this, Urse and Bernard are to take both his lands and his chattels into my hand.

Witnesses: Ranulf the Chaplain, Odo the Steward, Urse d'Abetot.

(Latin) *Ibid.*, p. 309.

(D) HENRY I: GRANT CONCERNING SCUTAGE (1127)

Henry, king of the English, to his archbishops, bishops, abbots, earls, etc., greeting. Know that to the church of St. Aetheldreda of Ely, for the love of God, for the souls of my father and mother, for the redemption of my sins, and on the petition of Hervey, bishop of the same church, I have forgiven £40 of those £100 which the aforesaid church was accustomed to give for scutage whenever scutage was assessed throughout my land of England; so that henceforth forever the church shall on that account give no more than £60 when scutage is levied throughout the land. And so let the aforesaid church be quit in perpetuity of the aforesaid [40] pounds.[7]

Witnesses: Roger, bishop of Salisbury; Geoffrey, my chancellor; Robert, [keeper] of the seal; William de Tancarville; William d'Aubigny, steward; Ralph Basset, Geoffrey de Clinton, William de Pont-de-l'Arche. At Eling during my crossing.

(Latin) *Ibid.*, p. 268.

(E) HENRY I: GRANT OF AN HEIRESS WITH LANDS (1121)

Henry, king of the English, to his archbishops, bishops, abbots, earls, and sheriffs, to all his barons, French and English, and to all his faithful men of all England and Wales, greeting. Know that to

---

[5] The feudal custom of northern France quite justified the seizure by a lord of a vacant bishopric or abbacy, but not the collection of a relief from the prelate's vassals. Abuses such as this led to Henry I's exaggerated promises on his accession (see no. 23). It is apparent that reliefs from lay baronies were already customary in the time of William II.

[6] Here in the text follow twenty-two other names with amounts ranging down to 20s.

[7] Despite the pious language of this charter, Henry's concession was not gratuitous; see above, p. 52.

Miles of Gloucester I have given and firmly granted Sibyl, daughter of Bernard de Neufmarché, with all the land of her father Bernard and of her mother after their death, or earlier—that is to say, during their lifetime, if they wish—and with this marriage portion:[8] namely, Talgarth, the forest of Ystradyw, the castle of Hay,[9] and the whole land of Bryn as far as the boundaries of the land of Richard Fitz-Pons—that is to say, as far as Cantref Bychan and Cowarne, a certain vill in England—also the fee and service of Roger de Baskerville, the fee and service of William Revell, the fee and service of Robert de Turberville, and the fee and service of Picard. And I will and enjoin that all the tenants of the aforesaid [land given as] marriage portion shall perform liege homage to [the said Miles] as to their lord, saving my fealty. And all the tenants of all the aforesaid land of Bernard shall likewise perform liege homage to him as to their lord, saving my fealty and [saving the rights of] Bernard so long as he wishes to hold the land. And this I give and grant to [the said Miles] as the purchase of Bernard which he has given to me[10]—and this at the request of the said Bernard and of his wife and of his barons.[11] And I will and firmly enjoin that [the said Miles] shall hold it as well and as honourably, as quietly and as freely, as ever Bernard best and most honourably held it.

Witnesses: Roger, bishop of Salisbury; Robert, bishop of Lincoln; Ralph the Chancellor, Robert the King's Son, William de Tancarville, Nigel d'Aubigny, Payn Fitz-John, Geoffrey Fitz-Payn, Geoffrey de Clinton, Ralph Basset, William Brito d'Aubigny. In the same year that the king took in marriage the daughter of the duke of Louvain, between Easter and Pentecost.

(Latin) Round, *Ancient Charters*, p. 8.

(F) SUBINFEUDATION BY CHARTER (1121-22)

William Peverel of Dover to Hamund Peverel, his brother, and to William Peverel, his nephew, and to all his faithful men, French and English, as well as to all his friends, both present and future, greeting. Know that, for his service, I have given to Thurstan, my steward, and to all his heirs Gidding and Daywell, to be held of me and my heirs in fee and inheritance, with *sac* and *soc*, *toll* and *team*, and *infangenepeof*, in wood and in plain, in vill and in street, in fields and in meadows, in waters and in all other places, in return for the service of half a knight. Witnesses. . . .

(Latin) Stenton, *English Feudalism*, p. 273.

(G) EXCHANGE AND ENFEOFFMENT OF DOWER LAND (*c*. 1123)

We desire [hereby] to make known that Walter of Gloucester has given Little Hereford in fee to William de Mare, his nephew, for the service of two knights. But since Walter of Gloucester and Miles,

---

[8] See above, p. 47, n. 3.

[9] *Haia Talliata* (*Haie Taillé*) a trimmed hedge.

[10] So that the king might bestow it on Miles.

[11] Note that the term baron did not as yet refer solely to a vassal of the king.

his son, earlier gave that aforesaid [Little] Hereford in dower to
Sibyl, wife of the same Miles, they have given Bardsley in exchange
to the same Sibyl, by the favour and grant of the said Miles. Moreover, the said Sibyl, by the counsel of her good men, of her own will
and without any compulsion, has gratuitously ceded Little Hereford
to William de Mare on account of the above-named exchange, having received, by way of token and testimony, a certain gold ring
from the same William.

Now of this grant and donation the witnesses are. . . .

(Latin) Round, Ancient Charters, p. 19.

(H) Stephen: Confirmation of a Serjeanty

Stephen, king of the English, to the archbishop of York, to his
barons, sheriffs, and ministers, and to all his faithful men of Yorkshire, French and English, greeting. Know that I have granted and
confirmed to John, my larderer of York, and to David, his son, all his
land which he holds of me in chief together with his office of larderer
and his livery,[12] and all his lands, from whomsoever he holds them,
as he was seised of them on the day that King Henry was alive and
dead. Wherefore I will and command that he shall hold them well and
in peace, freely and quietly, in wood and in plain, in meadows and
pastures, in waters, mills, and marshes, in roads and in sown fields,
and in all other places, with *sac* and *soc*, *toll* and *team* and *infangenepeof*, and with all the customs and liberties with which he
ever held best and most freely in the time of King Henry.

Witnesses: Robert de Vere, Robert Fitz-Richard. At Nottingham.

(Latin) Calendar of Patent Rolls, 1385-89, p. 19.

---

[12] See below, p. 67; also Round, *The King's Serjeants and Officers of State*,
pp. 233 f. Besides his central larder, the king maintained various local larders,
the chief function of which was the preservation of meat from his forests.

28. GRANTS TO BOROUGHS

(A) William I: Charter to London

King William gives friendly greeting to William, bishop [of Lon-
don], to Geoffrey,[1] portreeve [of London], and to all the burgesses
(*burhwaru*) of London, both French and English. And I make known
to you that I wish you both [French and English] to enjoy all the
rights that you enjoyed in the days of King Edward. I will that every
child shall be the heir of his father after his father's lifetime. And I
will not permit any man to do you any wrong. God keep you!

(Anglo-Saxon) Libermann, Gesetze, I, 486.

(B) Henry I: Charter to London[2]

Henry, by the grace of God king of England, to the archbishop of

---

[1] That the Gosfregð of this charter was Geoffrey de Mandeville, constable of
the Tower and sheriff of London, was indicated by Round, *Geoffrey de Mandeville*, p. 439.
[2] For the dating of this charter after 1130, see J. P. S. Tatlock, in *Speculum*,
XI, 461 f.

Canterbury, and to the bishops, abbots, earls, barons, justices, sheriffs, and all his faithful men of all England, both French and English, greeting. Know that to my citizens of London I have granted the shrievalty of London and of Middlesex, to be held at farm for £300 on account at the exchequer, by them and their heirs of me and my heirs;[3] so that the said citizens may install a sheriff, whomsoever they please from among themselves, and a justice,[4] whomsoever they please from among themselves, to keep the pleas of my crown and to try them, and no other man is to be justice over the said men of London. And the citizens shall not be impleaded in any plea outside the walls of the city, and they are to be quit of scot and of Danegeld and of murder-fine,[5] and none of them shall wage battle.[6] And if one of the citizens is impleaded in connection with pleas of the crown, as a man of London, he shall prove his case by an oath to be determined in the city. And within the walls of the city no one is to be billeted; neither for one of my household nor for one of any other is lodging to be exacted by force. And all men of London, together with all their goods, are to be quit and free, throughout all England and throughout all the ports of the sea, from toll, passage, lastage, and all other [such] customs.[7] And churches, barons, and citizens shall well and peaceably have and hold all their sokes[8] together with all customs [of the latter]; so that the tenants who are settled in sokes shall owe customs to none except to him whose soke it is, or to his minister whom he may there appoint. And a man of London shall not be adjudged in mercy as regards his chattels except to the amount of his wergeld, namely, 100s.—that is to say, in a plea that concerns chattels (*pecuniam*).[9] And there shall no longer be [judgments of] *miskenning* in the husting, the folkmote, or in other courts within the city.[10] And the husting shall meet once a week, namely, on Mon-

---

[3] The text of the preceding sentence is that given by H. G. Richardson in the *English Historical Review,* XLII, 80 f. This is the earliest known grant of a borough in fee-farm to the burgesses; cf. Lincoln, above, p. 53, n. 17.

[4] See above, p. 53, n. 16.

[5] Exemption from scot and Danegeld would free the burgesses from all arbitrary taxation; see above, p. 38, n. 2. And on the *murdrum,* see above, p. 36, n. 2.

[6] That is to say, be held for trial by combat.

[7] *Passagium* and *lestagium* were particular forms of toll: the former term applied especially to taxes on the carriage of goods overland; the latter to those on the cargoes of ships.

[8] A soke in the mediaeval borough was a sort of manorial island—a territory under seignorial jurisdiction rather than the law of the privileged community.

[9] Cf. Edgar, III, 2 (above, p. 19).

[10] *Miskenning* or *stultiloquium* was the use, either by plaintiff or by defendant, of a wrong formula in a judicial process. The heavy penalty which it carried in Anglo-Saxon law would be especially irksome to the large French-speaking population of London; cf. William's concession to his French barons, above, p. 35, n. 1. The husting was the weekly court for the dispatch of ordinary business; the folkmote, we are told by later documents, met three times a year for extraordinary business, such as watch and ward, fire-prevention, and the election of municipal officials.

day. And I will see to it that my citizens have their lands and pledges and debts inside the city and outside it. And with regard to lands concerning which claims are made to me, I will on their behalf maintain justice according to the law of the city. And if any one takes toll or custom from a London citizen, the London citizens shall, within the city, take from the borough or the vill where the toll or custom was collected as much as the man of London gave for toll and thereby suffered in damage. And all debtors who owe debts to the citizens shall pay the same, or they shall prove in London that they do not owe [the debts]. But if they refuse to pay and do not come to prove their case [in London], then the citizens to whom the debts are owing shall take their pledges within the city, from either the borough or the vill or the county in which the man lives who owes the debt.[11] And the citizens shall have their hunting dogs for hunting, as [they were] best and most fully had by their ancestors—namely, in the Chilterns, in Middlesex, and in Surrey.

Witnesses: the bishop of Winchester, Robert Fitz-Richard, Hugh Bigot, Alfred of Totnes, William d'Aubigny, Hubert the king's chamberlain, William de Montfichet, Hagulf de Tany, John Belet, Robert Fitz-Seward. Given at Westminster.

(Latin) *Ibid.*, I, 524 f.

(C) Henry I: Charter to Beverley[12]

Henry, king of England, to his archbishops, bishops, justiciars, sheriffs, and all his faithful men, greeting. Know that I have granted and given and by this my charter have confirmed to the men of Beverley their free burgage[13] according to the free laws and customs of the burgesses of York; also their gild merchant,[14] together with their pleas and toll and all their other free customs and liberties in all things, as Archbishop Thurstan has granted and confirmed to them by his charter, inside the vill of Beverley and outside it, as well in wood as in field or in marsh and in other things. And it is my will that they, like the men of York, shall be quit of toll throughout the whole shire of York.

Witnesses: G[eoffrey] the Chancellor; R[obert], count of Meulan. At Woodstock.

(Latin) Gross, *Gild Merchant*, II, 21.

---

[11] For full discussion of this custom, see M. Bateson, *Borough Customs*, II, lii f.

[12] This is the royal confirmation of a grant to Beverley by Thurstan, archbishop of York (Stubbs, *Select Charters*, p. 131). The latter charter, in addition to the liberties mentioned here, farms the borough tolls to the burgesses for 18*m.* a year.

[13] That is to say, the customs and laws pertaining to a free borough, including beyond doubt burgage tenure.

[14] The archbishop's charter has *hans-hus*—the gildhall, in which the burgesses are authorized to enact statutes for the good of the town; see Gross, *Gild Merchant*, I, 192 f.

(D) THE LIBERTIES OF NEWCASTLE

These are the laws and customs which the burgesses of Newcastle-upon-Tyne enjoyed in the time of Henry [I], king of England, and should [now] enjoy.[15]

Burgesses can levy distraint upon foreigners (*foris habitantes*) inside their market and outside it, inside their homes and outside them, and inside their borough and outside it without the licence of the reeve, except when courts are held in the borough and except [when foreigners are summoned thither] for military service or castle-guard. A burgess may not levy distraint upon a [fellow] burgess without the licence of the reeve. If a burgess has lent anything of his to a foreigner, such a debtor must pay [his debt] in the borough if he admits it; if he denies it, he must give justice in the borough. Pleas that arise in the borough must be held and settled there, except those which are crown pleas. If any burgess is accused in any case, he shall not plead outside the borough except through default of [justice in the borough] court. And he need answer only when day and time are set, unless he has already been guilty of *miskenning*[16]—[that is to say,] except in matters pertaining to the crown.

If a ship that wishes to depart [at once] puts in at Tynemouth, the burgesses may buy [from it] whatever they please. If a plea arises between a burgess and a merchant [coming by sea], it must be settled before the third ebb-tide. Whatever merchandise a ship brings [to the borough] by sea should be carried ashore, except salt; and herring should [also] be sold on board the ship. If any one lawfully and without [adverse] claim holds land in burgage for a year and a day, he need not make reply to a claimant unless the claimant has been outside the kingdom of England, or unless he is a child not old enough to speak [in a judicial process]. If a burgess has a son, he shall share his father's liberty if he lives with his father.[17] If a peasant comes to dwell in the borough, and remains there as a burgess for a year and a day, he may permanently remain in the borough,[18] unless he or his lord has made a preliminary statement that he is to remain for a [fixed] term. If any one accuses a burgess of anything, he may not wage battle against the burgess, but the burgess shall defend him-

---

[15] In addition to the principal (or A) text of this document, published by Charles Johnson in *Archaeologia Aeliana*, Fourth Series, I, 170, there are three other versions (*ibid.*, 172 f.). The original record seems to have been made as the result of an inquest under Henry II. In place of the heading here given, the B text reads: "These are the laws and customs which King Henry [I] granted to his burgesses of Newcastle."

[16] See above, p. 62, n. 10.

[17] The A text is corrupt at this point, but the other versions make the meaning clear. B reads: "If a burgess has a son in his own home [eating] at his own table, the son shall have the same liberty as his father."

[18] . . . *in burgo ex toto remaneat*. The other versions agree in stating that he shall thenceforth remain there as a burgess. This is obviously a statement of the famous "law of a year and a day," by which the serf could attain freedom by completing a legal residence in a privileged town.

self by compurgation (*per legem*)—unless it is [an accusation of] treason, in which case he should defend himself by battle.[19] Nor can a burgess wage battle against a foreigner unless he has first abandoned his burgage.[20]

No merchant who is not a burgess can buy either wool or hides or other merchandise [in the country] outside the borough,[21] nor [can he buy them] inside the borough except from a burgess. If a burgess commits an offence, he shall give 6 ores[22] to the reeve. In the borough there is neither merchet nor heriot nor *blodwit* nor *stengesdint*.[23] Every burgess may have his own bake-oven and hand-mill if he wishes, saving the rights of the king's oven. If a woman commits a misdeed concerning bread or beer,[24] no one should intervene [in the matter] except the reeve. If she commits the offense twice, let her be punished by her [rightful] forfeiture; if she commits the offence a third time, let justice be done on her [by the common counsel of the burgesses].[25] No one who is not a burgess may buy cloths for dyeing or make them up or cut them.[26] A burgess may give or sell his land and freely and quietly go whither he pleases, unless a [legal] claim stands against him.

(Latin) *Archaeologia Aeliana,* Fourth Series, I, 170.

[19] See above, p. 62, n. 6.
[20] That is to say, given up his burgess status and burgage tenure.
[21] Burgesses normally had a monopoly of trade in certain articles within a specified region; in the case of Nottingham, for example, it was Nottinghamshire.
[22] 10s.; see above, p. 21, n. 3.
[23] The general meaning of this whole article is that the ordinary manorial custom has no force in the borough. At this time merchet and heriot were respectively the French *formariage* and *mainmorte*, which were eventually taken by the courts as marks of servile status. *Blodwit* was the old Anglo-Saxon fine for assault with bloodshed, which seems to have become essentially a seignorial perquisite. *Stengesdint* means beating with a stick; its exact implication here is not known.
[24] That is to say, violates the local regulations for baking or brewing.
[25] The phrase in brackets is added from the other versions.
[26] In order to sell by the piece, rather than in quantity.

29. THE CONSTITUTION OF THE KING'S HOUSEHOLD[1]

This is the constitution of the king's household regarding maintenance (*de procurationibus*).[2]

[1] Two copies of this document have been preserved: one in the *Liber Niger Scaccarii* (*Black Book of the Exchequer*), edited by Thomas Hearne; the other in the *Red Book of the Exchequer* (III, 807-13), edited by Hubert Hall. Both texts are badly jumbled and in places are almost unintelligible. With the exception of a few phrases, the following translation is based on the former, which is generally superior. For illuminating criticism of the document as a whole, see R. L. Poole, *The Exchequer in the Twelfth Century,* pp. 94 f., and J. H. Round, *The King's Serjeants and Officers of State.*
[2] The *domus regis*, it should be noted, was not merely the king's palace, for his court was still migratory. To eat in the *domus* was to take one's meals with the household. The understanding of many passages will be aided by comparison with the household ordinances of Edward I and Edward II (nos. 52C, 57).

The chancellor [is to have] 5s. a day, one demeine simnel,[3] two common [simnels], one sester of clear wine, one sester of ordinary wine,[4] one big candle (*grossum cereum*), and forty candle-ends. The master of the writing office (*scriptorium*) at first [received] 10d. a day, one common simnel, half a sester of ordinary wine, one big candle, and twelve candle-ends; but King Henry increased [the allowance] for Robert [keeper] of the seal to the extent that, on the day of the king's death, he was having 2s., one sester of ordinary wine, one common simnel, one little candle (*cereolum*), and twenty-four candle-ends. The chaplain[5] and the custodian of the chapel and of the relics [are to have] the allowance of two men, and four serjeants of the chapel [are to have] double food each. Two pack-horses of the chapel [are assigned] 1d. a day each and 1d. a month for shoeing. For the service of the chapel [are provided] two candles on Wednesday, two on the Sabbath, one candle every night [to be placed] before the relics, thirty candle-ends, and a gallon of clear wine for mass; also a sester of ordinary wine for washing the altar on the Day of Absolution,[6] and for communion on Easter a sester of clear wine and one of ordinary wine.

Concerning the stewards: the steward, if he eats outside the household, [is to receive the same] as the chancellor; if [he eats] inside, 3s. 6d., two common simnels, one sester of ordinary wine, and a full allowance of candles (*plenarie candelam*).[7] The clerk of the issue (*expensae*) of bread and wine [is to have] 2s. a day, one common simnel, one sester of ordinary wine, one little candle, and twenty-four candle-ends. Concerning the dispensers of bread: the master dispenser of bread in constant attendance (*assiduus*), if he eats outside the king's household, [is to have] 2s. 10d. a day, one common simnel, one sester of ordinary wine, one little candle, and twenty-four

---

[3] The *simenellus dominicus* is contrasted throughout with the *simenellus sal'* (occasionally *salat'*). The clerks who made the existing copies thus seem to have meant a "salt simnel," although, as remarked by Hubert Hall, one might prefer to find a connection with *salarium*, a salary or stipend, or with the French *salle*, the hall where most of the household ate. In any case, the original record clearly intended to make the same distinction as that found in a charter of William I, which grants to the abbot of Battle and two of his monks that, when summoned to the royal court, they shall have the following livery: two *panes similagines de dominico*, two *panes similagines de communi*, one sester of wine *de dominico*, one sester of wine *de communi*, six dishes of fish "or of whatever else may be at the court," two candles, and ten candle-ends (*Calendar of Charter Rolls*, III, 196; Davis, *Regesta*, no. 60). The later paragraph telling about the four bakers apparently makes the difference between the demeine and the ordinary simnel chiefly a matter of size. The liveries of food, drink, and candles were in addition to the regular meals; cf. no. 57.

[4] *Vinum expensabile*, wine of issue.

[5] Plural in the *Black Book*, singular in the *Red Book*—one of many such discrepancies.

[6] Holy Thursday.

[7] In the text the preceding sentence is obviously out of place, being inserted after the description of the master dispenser.

candle-ends; if, however, [he eats] inside, 2s., half a sester of ordinary wine, and a full allowance of candles. Concerning the dispensers who serve in turn: if [they eat] outside the household, [each is to have] 19d. a day, one common simnel, one sester of ordinary wine, one big candle, and twenty candle-ends; if [they eat] inside, 10d., half a sester of ordinary wine, and a full allowance of candles. Concerning the naperers: the naperer[8] [is to have] the customary food, 1½d. a day for his man, 1d. for a pack-horse, and 1d. a month for shoeing. The usher[9] of the dispensary [is to have] the same amount except [the allowance for] the pack-horse. The counter of bread[10] [is to have] the customary food. Concerning the four bakers who serve together in their turn: the two who serve in the household are to eat in the household; the two who go abroad are to have 40d. for procuring a Rouen *muid*,[11] from which they should supply 40 demeine simnels, 140 common [simnels], and 270 bakery loaves (*panes de pistrino*). A demeine simnel [is] for four men, a common [simnel] for two [men], a loaf for one man. The waferer[12] [is to have] the customary food and 1½d. for his man. The keeper of the tables (*bordarius*) [is to have] the same amount and in addition a pack-horse together with its livery. The bearer of the alms-dish is to eat in the household.

Concerning the dispensers of the larder: the master dispenser of the larder in constant attendance [is to have the same] as the master dispenser of bread and wine and in the same way. Likewise the dispensers of the larder who serve in turn [are to have the same] as the dispensers of bread and wine who serve in turn. The larderers who serve in turn [are to have] the customary food and 1½d. a day for their man. The usher of the larder [is to be treated] in the same way. The butchers [are to have] only the customary food. Concerning the cooks: the cook of the royal kitchen is to eat in the household [and is to have] 1½d. for his man. The keeper of the vessels (*vasarius*) is to eat in the household and [is to have] 1½d. for his man; also a pack-horse together with its livery. The somler[13] of the same kitchen [is to be treated] in the same way. The serjeant of the kitchen [is to have] only the customary food. The cook for the king's private family and the dispenser [are to be treated] in the same way.[14] Ralph de La Marche, who while cook died before the death of the

---

[8] The officer in charge of cloths for the tables and related services.

[9] *Ostiarius*, which at this time still retained its original meaning of doorkeeper.

[10] Evidently, as Round pointed out, the *pannetier*, whose title was eventually corrupted into pantler.

[11] The *modius* was also a measure of wine; see above, p. 52, n. 10. In the present instance it is obvious that a considerable quantity of grain or flour is meant.

[12] *Nebularius*—the maker of the sweet wafers that were the more highly prized in an age when sugar was a great rarity.

[13] *Sumelarius*, French *sommelier*—originally a person in charge of packing utensils or produce; cf. *sumarius*, a pack-horse.

[14] The text of this sentence and of the one following is badly corrupted.

king, ate in the household and [had] 1½d. for his man. Concerning the great kitchen: Owen Polchart[15] [is to have] the customary food and 1½d. for his man. Two cooks [are to have] the customary food each and 1½d. for their man. The serjeants of the same kitchen [are to have] only the customary food. The usher of the spit-house [is to have] the customary food and 1½d. for his man. The turnspit [is to be treated] in the same way and besides [is to have] a pack-horse together with its livery. The carter of the great kitchen [is to have] double food, and the rightful livery for his horse. The carter of the larder [is to be treated] in the same way. The serjeant who receives the venison[16] is to eat inside and [is to have] 1½d. for his man.

Concerning the butlery: the master butler [is to be treated] like the steward; they have the one livery and [receive it] in the same way. The master dispenser of the butlery [is to be treated] like the master dispenser of bread and wine. The dispensers of the butlery who serve in turn [are to be treated] like the dispensers of issue who serve in turn; but they have a larger allowance of candles, for they receive a small candle and twenty-four candle-ends. The usher of the butlery [is to have] the customary food and 1½d. for his man. The keepers of the hose[17] are to eat in the household and [are to have] 3d. each for their men. The keeper of the butts[18] [is to have] the customary food, 3d. for his men, half a sester of ordinary wine, and twelve candle-ends. The workmen under the keeper of the butts [are to have] only the customary food, but the serjeant [is to have] in addition 1½d. for his man and two pack-horses with their liveries. Concerning the cupbearers: four only should serve together in their turn, of whom two are to eat in the household and each [is to have] 1½d. for his man. The other two are to have the customary food and likewise 1½d. [each] for their men. The keepers of the mazers[19] [are to have] only double food. Concerning the fruiterer: the fruiterer is to eat in the household and is to have 3d. for his men. The carter [is to have] the customary food, and livery for his horse.

The master chamberlain is the equal of the steward in livery. The treasurer [is to be treated] like the master chamberlain, if he is at the court and serving as treasurer.[20] William Mauduit is to eat regularly in the household and [is to have] 13d. a day, one big candle, twelve candle-ends, and three pack-horses with their liveries. The porter of the king's litter[21] is to eat in the household and [is to have] 1½d.

[15] See Round, *King's Serjeants*, p. 58.

[16] *Venacionem;* see below, p. 87, n. 2.

[17] Probably wine-skins. At any rate, the *hosarii* were somehow connected with the receipt and distribution of wine; see Round, *King's Serjeants*, pp. 177 f.

[18] *Butarius,* presumably the man in charge of the casks in the cellar.

[19] Maple-wood cups.

[20] Originally a subordinate of the chamberlain, now his equal. The rise of this officer is eloquent testimony to the growing importance of financial administration.

[21] The man responsible for carrying the king's bedding when he went on journeys.

for his man and a pack-horse with its livery. The chamberlain who serves in his turn [is to have] 2s. a day, one common simnel, one sester of ordinary wine, one little candle, and twenty-four candle-ends. The chamberlain of the candles [is to have] 8d. a day and half a sester of ordinary wine. The king's tailor is to eat in the household and [is to have] 1½d. for his man. The chamberlains, if they wish, are to eat in the household without other livery. The ewerer[22] [is to have] double food and, when the king makes a journey, 1d. for drying the king's clothes; and when the king bathes, 4d., except on the three annual festivals. Concerning the launderer there is doubt.

The constables are to have liveries like the stewards and in the same way. William Fitz-Odo [is to have] one demeine simnel, one sester of clear wine, one little candle, and twenty-four candle-ends. Henry de la Pomerai, if he eats outside the household, [is to have] 2s. a day, one common simnel, one sester of ordinary wine, one little candle and twenty-four candle-ends. If, however, [he eats] inside, [he is to have] 14d., half a sester of ordinary wine, and a full allowance of candles. Roger d'Oilly [is to be treated] in the same way. The master marshal, namely John, [is to be treated] in the same way; and in addition he ought to have counterfoils for the gifts and liveries that are made from the king's treasury and chamber, and, as witness to everything, he ought to have tallies against all the king's officials. The four marshals who serve the king's household [including] both clerks and knights and also ministers, when they[23] take lodgings or stay outside the court on the king's business, [are to have] 8d. a day, one gallon of ordinary wine, and twelve candle-ends. If [the marshals] remain inside, [they are to have] 3d. a day for their men and a full allowance of candles. But if any one of the marshals is sent on the king's business, [he is to have] only 8d. The serjeant of the marshals, if they are sent on the king's business, are to have 3d. a day each; if not, they are to eat in the king's household. The ushers [who are] knights themselves are to eat in the household and [are to have] 1½d. for each of their men, and eight candle-ends. Gilbert Bonhomme and Ralph are to eat in the household and [are to have] 1½d. for their men. The other ushers, [who are] not knights, are to eat in the household without other livery. The watchmen [are to have] double food, 1½d. for their men, and four candles; and in addition each [is to have] of a morning two loaves, one dish [of meat], and a gallon of beer. The keeper of the hearth is always to eat in the household and, from Michaelmas to Easter, [is to have] 4d. a day for a fire. The usher of the chamber [is to have] 4d. for the king's litter on each day when the king makes a journey.[24] The curtainer[25] is to eat in the household; and when he had the curtains carried, he used to have

---

[22] *Aquarius,* water-bearer.

[23] The members of the household.

[24] Perhaps this and the following sentence are misplaced, belonging rather under the description of the chamber.

[25] *Cortinarius,* the man who cared for the tents and hangings used in connection with a royal progress.

livery for one man [and] one pack-horse. Each of the four trumpeters [is to have] 3*d*. a day. Twenty serjeants [are to have] 1*d*. a day each.

The velterers[26] [are to have] 3*d*. a day each; also 2*d*. for their men, and for each greyhound ½*d*. a day. The king's pack (*mueta*) [is assigned] 8*d*. a day. The knights huntsmen [are to have] 8*d*. a day each. The cat-hunters [are to have] 5*d*. each. The leader of the liam-hound [is to have] 1*d*., and ½*d*. for the liam-hound. The berner [is to have] 3*d*. a day. The hunters with harriers [are to have] 3*d*. a day each; and four big harriers should have 1*d*., and six little har-riers 1*d*. Two men [are required] for the big harriers and each [is to have] 1*d*. a day. The keepers of the brachs [are to have] 3*d*. a day each. The wolf-hunters [are to have] 20*d*. a day for horses, men, and dogs, and they should have twenty-four coursing dogs and eight greyhounds; also £6 a year for buying horses, but they themselves say £8. Concerning the archers who carry the king's bow: each [is to have] 5*d*. a day, and the other archers [are to have] the same amount. Bernard, Ralph le Robeur, and their fellows [are to have] 3*d*. a day each.

(Latin) *Liber Niger Scaccarii,* pp. 341 f.

---

[26] The berner had charge of the ordinary coursing dogs; the velterers of the larger greyhounds. These two groups both hunted the quarry by sight. The liam-hound, on the other hand, followed a track by scent, like a bloodhound. The brachs were smaller dogs of the same sort. Harriers were apparently used for hunting hares. On this whole subject, see Round, *King's Serjeants,* pp. 268 f.

SECTION

III

HENRY II AND HIS SONS

THE signal importance of Henry II's reign (1154-89) in the
constitutional history of England is well known to all students of
the subject. Such a collection as this can hardly omit the major
enactments of a king who restored the lost efficiency of the Norman monarchy, regulated anew the troubled relations of church
and state, enormously extended the resources of the crown, and
laid the foundations of the English common law. In addition to
the more familiar sources, such as the Constitutions of Clarendon
and Henry's famous assizes, the present section includes some of
the baronial returns that Round made the subject of a character-
istically brilliant study.[1] These are supplemented by a series of
scutage accounts from the pipe roll of 1187, and further examples of the king's financial measures are provided by entries concerning tallage and items of judicial income. Typical of this reign
were also two remarkable essays in Latin: the *Dialogue on the
Exchequer*[2] and the *Treatise on the Laws and Customs of England*,[3] attributed respectively to Richard Fitz-Nigel and Ranulf de
Glanville. However interesting and authoritative, such lengthy unofficial works cannot be incorporated in a brief volume of documents; only some of the commoner writs quoted by Glanville are
given here. For additional illustration and comment on these two
works, the student is referred to the scholarly introductions by
the editors, to R. L. Poole, *The Exchequer in the Twelfth Century,* and to Pollock and Maitland, *History of English Law.*

Constitutionally, the reigns of Richard and John (1189-1216)
were a mere prolongation of their father's reign. It is largely
by virtue of more systematic chancery enrolment that we henceforth gain fuller information with regard to the working of the
central courts and the activities of local officials. Alongside of
the pipe rolls, which are continuous from the second year of Henry
II, there appear by 1216 such great compilations as the charter

---

[1] *Feudal England,* pp. 236 f.

[2] Edited by Crump, Hughes, and Johnson (Oxford, 1902); translated in Hen-
derson, *Historical Documents,* pp. 20 f.

[3] Edited by G. E. Woodbine (Yale University Press, 1932).

rolls, patent rolls, close rolls, *curia regis* rolls, and fine rolls. From this formidable mass of material a few extracts are presented to illustrate, not only the general character of the records, but also, when possible, significant phases of legal and constitutional development. In the former connection particular reference should be made to the very helpful criticism of T. F. Tout, *Chapters in the Administrative History of Mediaeval England*, vol. I. In the latter connection the principal guides are the books already cited for the previous section—expecially those of Pollock and Maitland, Petit-Dutaillis, Round, and Stenton.

Thanks to a careful reworking of the pertinent records by a number of scholars,[4] the history of London and the other boroughs is much better known to us than it was to Stubbs. One result of their research has been to enhance our appreciation of Henry I's activity. Despite the increased output of borough charters under the Angevins, which may be readily perceived by a glance at Ballard's collection,[5] actual innovations within the field of municipal privileges were few in the later twelfth century. Lesser towns normally enjoyed customs like those of Newcastle; larger towns commonly received the liberties of London. But under Henry II the latter ceased to include exemption from arbitrary taxation and the right to choose magistrates. It was not until the closing decade of the century that the capital regained some degree of autonomy under an elected mayor and board of aldermen. The more definite of our meagre sources for that advance are given below. Meanwhile Henry II had apparently allowed a few boroughs to have elected reeves, and such arrangements were formally confirmed by Richard in charters which served as precedents for that of John to Ipswich. The latter grant has been selected for translation (no. 39A) because the ensuing action of the Ipswich burgesses is graphically described in a surviving record (no. 39B)—truly an outstanding monument in the history of local self-government.

This section appropriately ends with Magna Carta, which so

[4] J. H. Round, *Geoffrey de Mandeville*, pp. 347 f., and *The Commune of London*, pp. 219 f.; Mary Bateson, in the *English Historical Review*, XVII, 480 f.; M. Weinbaum, *Verfassungsgeschichte Londons*, and *London unter Eduard I und II*, vol. II. See also Petit-Dutaillis and Lefebvre, pp. 91 f.; F. M. Stenton, *Norman London*; W. Page, *London*; C. Stephenson, *Borough and Town*, pp. 179 f.; J. Tait, *The Medieval English Borough*.
[5] *British Borough Charters, 1042-1216*

admirably summarizes the developments of the previous century and introduces those of the century to come. And since the Great Charter has too often been thought of as an inflexible and definitive enactment, it has seemed advisable to indicate, by a sort of gloss on the original text, the changes made in the reissues.

W. S. McKechnie's *Magna Carta* and J. C. Holt's *Magna Carta* present the traditional and a more modern interpretation of the Charter. *English Historical Documents,* 1042–1189, editors D. C. Douglas and G. W. Greenaway, illustrates constitutional developments of the reign of Henry II.

30. THE CONSTITUTIONS OF CLARENDON (1164)

In the year 1164 from the Incarnation of the Lord, in the fourth year of the papacy of Alexander [III], and in the twelfth year of Henry II, most illustrious king of the English, there was made, in the presence of the said king, this record and recognition[1] of a certain portion of the customs and liberties and rights of his ancestors— namely, of King Henry his grandfather and of others—which ought to be observed and held in the kingdom. And on account of the dissensions and disputes that had arisen between the clergy and the justices of the lord king and the barons of the realm concerning [such] customs and rights, this recognition was made in the presence of the archbishops, bishops, clergy, earls, barons, and magnates of the realm. Furthermore, Thomas, archbishop of Canterbury, and Roger, archbishop of York, and Gilbert, bishop of London, and Henry, bishop of Winchester, and Nigel, bishop of Ely, and William, bishop of Norwich, and Robert, bishop of Lincoln, and Hilary, bishop of Chichester, and Jocelyn, bishop of Salisbury, and Richard, bishop of Chester, and Bartholomew, bishop of Exeter, and Robert, bishop of Hereford, and David, bishop of St. David's and Roger, [bishop] elect of Worcester, have granted and steadfastly promised, *viva voce* and on their word of truth, that the said customs, recognized by the archbishops, bishops, earls, and barons, and by the nobler and more venerable men of the realm, should be held and observed for the lord king and his heirs in good faith and without evil intent, these being present[2] . . . and many other magnates and nobles of the realm, both clerical and lay.

Now a certain part of the recognized customs and rights of the kingdom are contained in the present writing, of which part these are the chapters :—

1. If controversy arises between laymen, between laymen and

[1] *Recognitio,* the same word as is often used for the verdict of a jury; see, for examples, no. 33.

[2] Here follow in the text thirty-eight names.

clergymen, or between clergymen, with regard to advowson and presentation to churches, it shall be treated or concluded in the court of the lord king.

2. Churches of the lord king's fee[3] may not be given in perpetuity without his assent and grant.

3. Clergymen charged and accused of anything shall, on being summoned by a justice of the king, come into his court, to be responsible there for whatever it may seem to the king's court they should there be responsible for; and [to be responsible] in the ecclesiastical court [for what] it may seem they should there be responsible for—so that the king's justice shall send into the court of Holy Church to see on what ground matters are there to be treated. And if the clergyman is convicted, or [if he] confesses, the Church should no longer protect him.[4]

4. Archbishops, bishops, and parsons of the kingdom are not permitted to go out of the kingdom without the licence of the lord king. And should they go out [of it], they shall, if the king so desires, give security that, neither in going nor in remaining nor in returning, will they seek [to bring] evil or damage to the king or to the kingdom.

5. Excommunicated men should not give security for all future time (*ad remanens*) or take an oath, but [should] merely [provide] security and pledge of standing by the judgment of the church in order to obtain absolution.

6. Laymen should not be accused except through known and lawful accusers and witnesses in the presence of the bishop, [yet] so that the archdeacon shall not lose his right or anything that he should thence have. And if the guilty persons are such that no one wishes or dares to accuse them, the sheriff, on being asked by the bishop, shall have twelve lawful men from the neighbourhood, or the vill, placed on oath before the bishop to set forth the truth in the matter according to their own knowledge.[5]

7. No one who holds of the king in chief, nor any of his demesne ministers, shall be excommunicated; nor shall the lands of any of them be placed under interdict, unless first the lord king, if he is in the land, or his justiciar, if he is outside the kingdom, agrees that justice shall be done on that person—and in such a way that whatever belongs to the king's court shall be settled there, and whatever

---

[3] That is to say, the right of appointing to a living, or advowson, held in fee of the king.

[4] It was over this article that the famous controversy between the king and Thomas Becket took place. For the best interpretation, see Pollock and Maitland, I, 447 f.

[5] The article deals with trials in ecclesiastical courts, of which the lowest was that of the archdeacon. In the final clause we have our first clear reference to the accusation jury, but it is significant that the institution is described as a feature of established custom under Henry I; see Pollock and Maitland, I, 151, and cf. no. 31.

belongs to the ecclesiastical court shall be sent thither to be dealt with there.

8. With regard to appeals, should they arise—they should proceed from the archdeacon to the bishop, and from the bishop to the archbishop. And if the archbishop fails to provide justice, recourse should finally be had to the lord king, in order that by his precept the controversy may be brought to an end in the court of the archbishop; so that it should not proceed farther[6] without the assent of the lord king.

9. If a claim is raised by a clergyman against a layman, or by a layman against a clergyman, with regard to any tenement which the clergyman wishes to treat as free alms, but which the layman [wishes to treat] as a lay fee, let it, by the consideration of the king's chief justice and in the presence of the said justice, be settled through the recognition of twelve lawful men whether the tenement belongs to free alms or to lay fee. And if it is recognized as belonging to free alms, the plea shall be [held] in the ecclesiastical court; but if [it is recognized as belonging] to lay fee, unless both call upon the same bishop or [other] baron, the plea shall be [held] in the king's court. But if, with regard to that fee, both call upon the same bishop or [other] baron, the plea shall be [held] in his court; [yet] so that, on account of the recognition which has been made, he who first was seised [of the land] shall not lose his seisin until proof [of the title] has been made in the plea.[7]

10. If any one in a city, castle, borough, or demesne manor of the lord king is summoned by an archdeacon or a bishop for some offence on account of which he ought to respond to the said persons, and if he refuses satisfaction on their summons, he may well be placed under an interdict; but he should not be excommunicated until the chief minister of the lord king in that vill has been called upon to bring him to justice, so that he may come for satisfaction. And if the king's minister defaults in the matter, he shall be in the mercy of the lord king, and the bishop may then coerce that accused man through ecclesiastical justice.

11. Archbishops, bishops, and all parsons of the realm who hold of the king in chief have their possessions of the king as baronies and are answerable for them to the king's justices and ministers; also they follow and observe all royal laws and customs, and like other barons they should take part with the barons in the judgments of the lord king's court, until the judgment involves death or maiming.[8]

---

[6] Be appealed to the papal court.

[7] The article is obscurely phrased, but its general purport is clear. The preliminary question, whether the land is held in free alms or not, is to be decided in the king's court by a recognition jury—the procedure known as the assize utrum (see no. 33c). Jurisdiction over further litigation is to be determined by the jury's verdict.

[8] Clergymen were forbidden by canon law to take life or shed blood.

12. When an archbishopric, bishopric, abbey, or priory within the king's gift becomes vacant, it should be in his hands; and he shall thence take all revenues and income just as from his own demesne. And when it comes to providing for the church, the lord king should summon the greater parsons of the church, and the election should be held in the king's own chapel by the assent of the lord king and by the counsel of those parsons of the kingdom whom he has called for that purpose. And there the man elected should, before being consecrated, perform homage and fealty to the lord king as to his liege lord, for life and limbs and earthly honour,[9] saving the rights of his order.

13. If any of the magnates of the realm forcibly prevent an archbishop, bishop, or archdeacon from administering justice, either by himself or through his men, the lord king should bring them to justice. And if perchance any forcibly prevent the lord king from [administering] his justice, the archbishops, bishops, and arch-deacons should bring them to justice, so that they may satisfy the lord king.

14. Chattels of those who have incurred royal forfeiture should not be withheld in any church or churchyard against the king's justice; for they are the king's own, whether they are found inside churches or outside them.

15. Pleas of debt, owed under pledge of faith[10] or without pledge of faith, belong to the king's justice.

16. Sons of peasants should not be ordained without the assent of the lord on whose land they are known to have been born.

Now the [present] record of the aforesaid royal rights and customs was made at Clarendon by the archbishops, bishops, earls, and barons, and by the more noble and venerable men of the realm, on the fourth day before the Purification of the Blessed Virgin Mary, in the presence of the lord Henry, together with his father, the lord king. There are, moreover, other rights and customs, both many and great, of the Holy Mother Church, of the lord king, and of the barons of the realm, which are not contained in this writing; they are to be saved to Holy Church, to the lord king and his heirs, and to the barons of the realm, and are inviolably to be observed forever.

(Latin) Stubbs, *Select Charters*, pp. 163 f.

---

[9] Cf. no. 26, art. 55.

[10] See Pollock and Maitland, II, 189 f.

31. THE ASSIZE OF CLARENDON (1166)

Here begins the Assize[1] of Clarendon made by King Henry, namely the second, with the assent of the archbishops, bishops, abbots, earls, and barons of all England.

---

[1] In this context the word means an ordinance or set of instructions delivered to the king's ministers. The text comes to us on the authority of a chronicler and in many places lacks the precision and clarity that we should expect in a document issued by the royal chancery. See below, p. 80, n. 1.

1. In the first place the aforesaid King Henry, by the counsel of all his barons, has ordained that, for the preservation of peace and the enforcement of justice, inquiry shall be made in every county and in every hundred through twelve of the more lawful men of the hundred and through four of the more lawful men of each vill, [put] on oath to tell the truth, whether in their hundred or in their vill there is any man accused or publicly known as a robber or murderer or thief, or any one who has been a receiver of robbers or murderers or thieves, since the lord king has been king. And let the justices[2] make this investigation in their presence and the sheriffs in their presence.

2. And whoever is found by the oath of the aforesaid men to have been accused or publicly known as a robber or murderer or thief, or as a receiver of them since the lord king has been king, shall be seized; and he shall go to the ordeal of water and swear that, to the value of 5s., so far as he knows, he has not been a robber or murderer or thief, or a receiver of them, since the lord king has been king.

3. And if the lord of the man who has been seized or his steward or his men seek [to free] him under pledge, within the third day after he has been seized, let him and his chattels be remanded under pledge until he has made his law.[3]

4. And when robbers or murderers or thieves, or receivers of them, are seized in consequence of the aforesaid oath, if the justices are not soon to come into that county where they were seized, the sheriff shall, through some intelligent man, notify the nearest justices that he has seized such men; and the justices shall send back word to the sheriff that those [accused] are to be brought before them, wherever they please. The sheriff shall then take those [accused] before the justices, and with him he shall take two lawful men from the hundred or the vill where they were seized, to bring the record of the county and the hundred as to why they were seized; and there before the justices they shall make their law.

5. And with regard to those seized in consequence of the aforesaid oath of this assize, no one shall have jurisdiction or judgment or [forfeiture of] chattels but the lord king in his court and in the presence of his justices; and the lord king shall have all their chattels. With respect, however, to those seized otherwise than through this oath, let whatever is customary and right be done.

6. And the sheriffs who have seized them shall take them before the justice without other summons than shall be had from him. And when robbers or murderers or thieves, or receivers of them, whether seized in consequence of the oath or otherwise, are delivered to the sheriffs, the latter shall take them immediately and without delay.

7. And in every county where there are no jails let them be

---

[2] The king's itinerant justices who from time to time held full meetings of the county courts.

[3] That is to say, submitted to ordeal.

made within a borough or some castle of the king—with the king's money and with his wood if that is near at hand, or with some other wood close by, and by view of the king's serjeants—so that the sheriffs may have the seized men guarded in those [jails] by the officials accustomed to do so and by their serjeants.

8. The lord king also wills that all should come to the county [court] for the making of this oath; so that no one, on account of any liberty that he has, or on account of any jurisdiction or soke that he may enjoy, shall abstain from attendance for the making of this oath.[4]

9. And let there be no one, in castle or out of castle, or even in the honour of Wallingford,[5] who forbids the sheriffs to enter upon his jurisdiction or his land for view of frankpledge;[6] and let all men be placed under sureties, and let them be sent before the sheriffs under frankpledge.

10. And within cities or boroughs no one shall have men, or shall receive [men] within his house or his land or his soke for whom he will not be sponsor, [guaranteeing] that he will bring them before the justice, should they be summoned, or that they are under frankpledge.

11. And let there be no persons, either in a city or a borough or a castle, or outside them, or even in the honour of Wallingford, who forbid the sheriffs to enter upon their land or their soke for the purpose of seizing those who have been accused or publicly known as robbers or murderers or thieves, or receivers of them, or outlaws, or those accused under forest [law];[7] on the contrary, [the king] commands them to give assistance in seizing those [suspects].

12. And if any one is seized who possesses [the proceeds] of robbery or theft, should he be a notorious person and have a bad reputation, and should he not have a warrantor, let him not have his law.[8] And if he is not notorious, let him, on account of his [suspicious] possessions, go to the [ordeal of] water.

13. And if any one, in the presence of lawful men or of a hundred [court], has confessed robbery or murder or theft, or the reception of those [who have committed such crimes], and should he then wish to deny it, let him not have his law.

14. The lord king also wills that those who make their law and are cleared by the law, if they are of very bad reputation, being publicly and shamefully denounced by the testimony of many lawful men, shall abjure the lands of the king, so that they shall cross the sea within eight days unless they are detained by the wind; then, with the first [favourable] wind that they have, they shall

---

[4] Cf. no. 24.

[5] An important fief that was declared forfeit by Henry II and thenceforth held by a member of the royal house.

[6] See above, p. 37, n. 6.

[7] See no. 35.

[8] In other words, he is to have no chance of clearing himself.

cross the sea and thenceforth not return to England, except at the mercy of the lord king; [so that] they shall there be outlaws and shall be seized as outlaws if they return.

15. And the lord king forbids that any waif (*vaivus*)—that is to say, one wandering or unknown—shall be given lodging anywhere except in a borough; and he should not be given lodging there for more than one night unless he or his horse becomes ill there, so that he can show evident excuse [for his delay].

16. And if [otherwise] he stays there for more than one night, let him be seized and held until his lord may come to give pledge for him, or until he himself may find good sureties; and let him who provided the lodging be likewise seized.

17. And if any sheriff has notified another sheriff that men have fled from his county into the other county as the consequence of robbery or murder or theft, or of receiving those [who have committed such crimes], or of outlawry, or of accusation under the king's forest [law], let the latter [sheriff] seize them. Also, if he knows of himself or through others, that such men have fled into his county, let him seize them and guard them until he has good sureties for them.

18. And all sheriffs shall have the names of all fugitives who have fled from their counties written down, and this they shall do before [the courts of] their counties. And the names of those men, [thus] written down, they shall bring before the justices when first they report to those [justices], so that the latter may make inquiry throughout all England and may seize the chattels [of the fugitives] for the use of the king.

19. And the lord king wills that, as soon as the sheriffs have received the summons of the itinerant justices to come before the latter together with [the courts of] their counties, they shall bring together [the courts of] their counties and make inquiry concerning all who recently, after this assize, have come into their counties; and they shall put those [newcomers] under pledge to appear before the justices, or they shall guard those [newcomers] until the justices come to them, and then they shall bring [the newcomers] before the justices.

20. The lord king also forbids monks or canons or any religious community to receive any one from the lower classes (*de minuto populo*) as a monk or a canon or a brother until it is known of what reputation he may be, unless he is sick unto death.

21. The lord king also forbids that any one in all England shall receive under him within his land or his soke or his house any from the sect of those renegades[9] branded and placed under excommunication at Oxford. And if any one does receive them, he shall be in the mercy of the lord king; and the house in which they resided shall be taken outside the vill and burned. And every

---

[9] Heretics, probably Albigensians; see Pollock and Maitland, II, 547.

sheriff shall take an oath to obey this [command]; and he shall have this sworn by all his officials, by the stewards of barons, and by all knights and freeholders of the county.

22. And the lord king wills that, during his pleasure, this assize shall be observed in the kingdom.

(Latin) *Ibid.*, pp. 170 f.

32. THE ASSIZE OF NORTHAMPTON (1176)[1]

1. If, by the oath of twelve knights of the hundred—or, should knights not be present, by the oath of twelve lawful freemen—and by the oath of four men of every vill in the hundred, any one has been accused in the presence of the lord king's justices of murder or theft or robbery, or of receiving men who have committed such [crimes], or of falsification[2] or arson, he shall go to the ordeal of water; and if he fails [in the ordeal], he shall lose one foot. And to increase the severity of the law, it was added at Northampton that with the foot he should lose his right hand, and that he should abjure the realm and depart from it within forty days. And if he should be cleared by the [ordeal of] water, let him find sureties and remain in the kingdom, unless he has been accused of murder or other disgraceful felony by the community (*commune*) of the county and the lawful knights of his own countryside (*patria*). If [now] he has been accused in the aforesaid manner of this [sort of crime], although he has been cleared by the [ordeal of] water, let him nevertheless go out of the kingdom within forty days and take with him his chattels, saving the rights of his lords; and let him abjure the realm [on pain of being] in the lord king's mercy. This assize, moreover, shall hold good for all the time since the assize was made at Clarendon down to the present, and henceforward during the lord king's pleasure, with regard to murder, treason, and arson, and with regard to all [offenses in] the preceding chapters, except minor thefts and robberies which were committed in time of war, as of horses, oxen, and lesser things.

2. Item, no one, either in a vill or in a borough, shall be permitted to give lodging within his house for more than one night to any stranger for whom he is unwilling to be legally responsible, unless such lodger has a reasonable excuse which the master of the house may prove to his neighbours. And when he leaves, let him leave by day and in the presence of the neighbours.

3. If any one has possessed [the proceeds] of murder or theft or robbery or falsification, or of any other felony that he has committed, and confesses it before the reeve of a hundred or a borough and be-

---

[1] The document, as reported by the chronicler, is headed, "These are the assizes made at Clarendon and afterwards recorded at Northampton." That is to say, the earlier ordinance is regarded as still in effect, with certain amendments. But what is here stated about the Assize of Clarendon does not entirely agree with the text that we have.

[2] *Falsoneria*, meaning either counterfeiting or forgery.

fore lawful men, he may not afterwards deny it before the justices. And if, without [such] possession, he admits anything of the same sort in their presence, this likewise he may not deny before the justices.

4. Item, if any freeholder dies, his heirs shall remain in such seisin as their father had of his fee on the day that he was alive and dead; and they shall have his chattels, with which to carry out the testament of the deceased. And afterwards they shall go to their lord and shall perform to him their obligation for relief and other things owed from their fee. And if the heir is under age, the lord of the fee shall receive his homage and have wardship over him so long as is right. The other lords, if there are several, shall [also] receive his homage and he shall perform to them whatever obligations he owes. And the wife of the deceased shall have her dowry and the portion of his chattels to which she is entitled. And if the lord of the fee denies to the heirs of the deceased the seisin of the said deceased['s property] which they demand, the justices of the lord king shall have recognition made in the matter by twelve lawful men, as to what seisin in this respect the deceased had on the day that he was alive and dead.[3] And according to the recognition thus made, those [justices] shall make restitution to his heirs. And if any one acts contrary to this [command], and is convicted of so doing, let him remain in the king's mercy.

5. Item, the justices of the lord king shall have recognition made of disseisins contrary to the assize from the time that the lord king first came to England after the peace made between him and the king his son.[4]

6. Item, from the first Sunday after Easter to the first Sunday after Pentecost, the justices shall receive oaths of fealty to the lord king from all who wish to dwell in the kingdom: namely, from earls, barons, knights, freeholders, and even peasants. And whoever refuses to swear fealty is to be seized as an enemy of the lord king. The justices are also to command that all those who have not yet performed their homage and allegiance to the lord king shall come at the time assigned them and perform homage and allegiance to the king as to their liege lord.

7. Item, the justices, by writ of the lord king or of those acting in his place, shall enforce all rights and claims pertaining to the lord king and his crown to the amount of half a knight's fee and less, unless the case is so important that it cannot be decided without the lord king or [unless it is] such as, through their own uncertainty, the justices may report to him or to those acting in his place. They should, however, to the best of their ability strive to assure the king's interest. Also they shall hold assize concerning wicked thieves and [other] malefactors of the land—which assize, by the counsel of the

[3] This is known in law as the assize *mort d'ancestor*; see no. 33A.

[4] Apparently a reference to the assize of *novel disseisin*, the ordinance establishing which has not come down to us; see no. 33B.

king his son and of his men, is [to be held] throughout the counties to which they shall go.

8. Item, the justices shall see to it that the castles[5] [supposed to have been] razed are totally razed, and that those to be razed are well pulled down. And if they fail to do this, the lord king wishes them brought to judgment in his court as men in contempt of his command.

9. Item, the justices shall make inquiry concerning the escheats, churches, lands, and women[6] who are in the gift of the lord king.

10. Item, the bailiffs[7] of the lord king shall be answerable at the exchequer both for their fixed rents and for all sums acquired within their bailiwicks, except those belonging to the [farm of the] county.

11. Item, the justices shall make inquiry concerning the custody of castles: as to who owe [payments in this connection], how much [is owed], and where [it should be paid]. And afterwards they shall give the information to the lord king.

12. Item, [it is ordered that] a thief, from the time that he is captured, shall be delivered to the sheriff to guard. And if the sheriff is absent, he shall be taken to the nearest castellan,[8] and the latter shall guard him until he is turned over to the sheriff.

13. Item, the justices shall have investigation made, according to the custom of the land, as to those who have left the kingdom; and unless they are willing to return within a stated time and to stand trial in the court of the lord king, they shall then be outlawed; and the names of the outlaws shall be brought to the exchequer at Easter and Michaelmas, and shall thence be sent to the lord king.

(Latin) *Ibid.*, pp. 179 f.

---

[5] The so-called adulterine castles—those built without royal authorization during the anarchy under Stephen.

[6] Heiresses whom the king could bestow in marriage. For examples, see no. 40.

[7] Henceforth the ordinary title of an official in charge of a district less than a county. Bailiffs might be subordinates of the sheriff, but certain boroughs, escheated honours, and the like were regularly farmed as separate units.

[8] The official in charge of a castle, often called a constable.

33. FORMS OF ORIGINAL WRITS IN GLANVILLE

(A) Assize of Mort d'Ancestor

The king to the sheriff, greeting. If G., son of O., will give you security for prosecuting his claim, then summon through good summoners twelve free and lawful men from the neighbourhood of————, to be before me or my justices on————, prepared to recognize by oath whether O., father of the aforesaid G., was seised in demesne, as of his fee,[1] of one virgate of land in that vill on the day that he died, if he died after my first coronation, and whether the said G.

---

[1] See no. 32, art. 4. This assize gave redress only when the land was held in fee, rather than, for example, in villeinage or by lease.

is his nearest heir. And in the meantime they shall view that land, and you shall have their names written down. And summon through good summoners R., who holds that land, to be there in order to hear that recognition. And you are to have there the summoners and this writ.

(Latin) Glanville, Tractatus de Legibus, xiii, 3.

(B) Assize of Novel Disseisin[2]

The king to the sheriff, greeting. Complaint has been made to me by N. that R. has unlawfully and without judgment disseised him of his free tenement in————since my last crossing to Normandy; and so I command you, if the aforesaid N. will give you security for prosecuting his claim, to have restored to that tenement the chattels taken from it and [to let] the said tenement with its chattels remain in peace until————. And in the meantime you shall have twelve free and lawful men of the neighbourhood view that land, and you shall have their names written down. And summon them through good summoners to be before me or my justices, prepared to make recognition concerning it. And place under gage and good pledges the aforesaid R., or his bailiff if he himself cannot be found, to be there in order to hear that recognition. And you are to have there the summoners and this writ.

(Latin) Ibid., xiii, 33.

(C) Assize Utrum[3]

The king to the sheriff, greeting. Summon through good summoners twelve free and lawful men from the neighbourhood of————, to be before me or my justices on————, prepared to recognize by oath whether the one hide of land, which N., parson of the church in that vill, claims against R. in that vill as free alms of his said church, is lay fee of the said R. or church fee. And in the meantime let them view that land and have their names written down. And summon through good summoners the aforesaid R., who holds that land, to be there in order to hear that recognition. And you are to have there the summoners and this writ.

(Latin) Ibid., xiii, 24.

(D) Assize of Darrein Presentment[4]

The king to the sheriff, greeting. Summon through good summoners twelve free and lawful men from the neighbourhood of————, to be before me or my justices on————, prepared to recognize by oath what patron presented the last parson, now dead, to the church of that vill, which is thus said to be vacant, and of which N. claims the advowson. And have their names written down. And summon through

---

[2] I.e., recent dispossession; see above, p. 81, n. 4.

[3] See no. 30, art. 9.

[4] I.e., last nomination to a benefice; see no. 30, art. 1.

good summoners R., who is deforcing that claim, to be there in order to hear that recognition. And you are to have there the summoners and this writ.

(Latin) Ibid., xiii, 19.

(E) WRIT OF RIGHT

The king to Earl W., greeting. I command you without delay to give full right to N. with regard to the ten carucates of land in Middleton, which he claims to hold of you by the free service of one knight's fee for all service.[5] And unless you act in this matter so that I hear no further complaint as to default of justice, the sheriff of Nottingham will do so.

(Latin) Ibid., xii, 3.

(F) PRAECIPE[6]

The king to the sheriff, greeting. Command N. lawfully and without delay to restore to R. one hide of land in————, of which the same R. complains that the aforesaid N. is deforcing him. And unless he does so, summon him through good summoners to be before me or my justices on———— at————, in order to show good cause for not having done so. And you are to have there the summoners and this writ.

(Latin) Ibid., i, 8.

(G) DE NATIVO

The king to the sheriff, greeting. Complaint has been made to me by R. that N. is drawing him into villeinage, despite the fact that, according to his statement, he is a freeman. And so I command you that, if the said R. will give you security for prosecuting his claim, you shall then bring that suit before me or my justices on————, and in the meantime see that he enjoys peace in this matter. And summon the aforesaid N. through good summoners to be there in order to show cause for drawing him into villeinage. And you are to have there the summoners and this writ.

(Latin) Ibid., v, 2.

(H) PONE

The king to the sheriff, greeting. Bring before me or my justices on———— that suit which is in your county [court] between M. and N. concerning one hide of land in————, which the same M. claims against the aforesaid N. as her legitimate marriage portion.[7] And summon through good summoners the aforesaid N., who holds that

---

[5] Glanville here gives various examples of specific tenures. On the significance of the action, see Pollock and Maitland, I, 385.

[6] In full, *Praecipe quod reddat;* see art. 34 of Magna Carta, below, p. 120.

[7] See above, p. 47, n. 3.

land, to be there with his suit. And you are to have there the summoners and this writ.

(Latin) Ibid., vi, 7.

(I) PROHIBE

The king to the sheriff, greeting. Prohibit R. from proceeding in the court Christian with the plea begun between him and N. concerning the lay fee of the aforesaid R. in——, in which connection he complains that the aforesaid N. is impleading him in the court Christian before——. And if the aforesaid R. will give you security for prosecuting his claim, then place the aforesaid N. under gage and good pledges to be before me or my justices on——, to show cause for impleading him in the court Christian concerning his lay fee in——, although that plea pertains to my crown and dignity.[8]

(Latin) Ibid., xii, 22.

---

[8] See no. 30, art. 9.

34. THE ASSIZE OF ARMS (1181)

1. Whoever possesses one knight's fee shall have a shirt of mail, a helmet, a shield, and a lance; and every knight shall have as many shirts of mail, helmets, shields, and lances as he possesses knight's fees in demesne.[1]

2. Moreover, every free layman who possesses chattels or rents to the value of 16m. shall have a shirt of mail, a helmet, a shield, and a lance; and every free layman possessing chattels or rents to the value of 10m. shall have a hauberk, an iron cap, and a lance.[2]

3. Item, all burgesses and the whole community of freemen shall have [each] a gambeson,[3] an iron cap, and a lance.

4. Besides, each of them shall swear to have these arms before the feast of St. Hilary, to be faithful to the lord king Henry—namely, the son of the Empress Matilda—and to bear these arms in his service according to his command and in fealty to the lord king and his kingdom. And henceforth no one having these arms shall sell them or pledge them or lend them or alienate them in any other way; nor shall a lord in any way alienate them from his men, either through forfeiture or through gift or through pledge or in any other way.

5. If any one having these arms dies, his arms shall remain to his heir. If, however, the heir is not of age to use arms in time of need, that person who has wardship over him shall also have custody of the arms and shall find a man who can use the arms in the service of the lord king until the heir is of age to bear arms, and then he shall have them.

6. Any burgess who has more arms than he ought to have by this

---

[1] That is to say, as many knights as remain charged against his demesne; cf. no. 36.

[2] Presumably less elaborate armour than that required of the other group.

[3] A padded surcoat.

assize shall sell them, or give them away, or in some way alienate them to such a man as will keep them for the service of the lord king of England. And none of them shall keep more arms than he ought to have by this assize.

7. Item, no Jew shall keep in his possession a shirt of mail or a hauberk, but he shall sell it or give it away or alienate it in some other way, so that it shall remain in the king's service.

8. Item, no one shall carry arms out of England except by the command of the lord king: no one is to sell arms to another to carry out of England; nor shall a merchant or any other man carry them out of England.

9. Item, the justices shall have [a report] sworn by lawful knights, or by other free and lawful men of the hundreds and neighbourhoods and boroughs—as many as they see fit to employ—as to what persons possess chattels to the amount that they should have a shirt of mail, a helmet, a lance, and a shield according to what has been provided; so that they shall separately name for those [justices] all men of their hundreds and neighbourhoods and boroughs who are worth 16m. in either chattels or rents, and likewise those who are worth 10m. And then the justices shall have written down [the names of] all those jurors and other men, [recording] how much in chattels or rents they [each] have and what arms, according to the value of the chattels or rents, they should [each] have. Then, in their presence and in a common assembly of those men, they shall have read this assize regarding the possession of arms, and they shall have those men swear to have arms according to the value of the aforesaid chattels or rents, and to keep them for the service of the lord king according to this aforesaid assize, under the command of and in fealty to the lord king Henry and his kingdom. If, moreover, it should happen that any one of them, who ought to have these arms, is not in the county during the period when the justices are in that county, the justices shall set a time for him [to appear] before them in another county. And if he does not come to them in any county through which they are to go, and is not in that land [at all], they shall set him a time at Westminster toward the octave of St. Michael; so that, as he loves his life and all that he has, he shall be there for swearing his oath. And they shall command him, before the aforesaid feast of St. Hilary, to have arms according to the obligation resting on him.

10. Item, the justices shall have proclamation made in the counties through which they are to go that, with respect to those who do not have such arms as have been specified above, the lord king will take vengeance, not merely on their lands or chattels, but on their limbs.

11. Item, no one who does not possess 16m. [as specified above] or 10m. in chattels is to swear concerning free and lawful men.

12. Item, the justices shall command through all the counties that no one, as he loves his life and all that he has, shall buy or sell any ship to be taken away from England, and that no one shall carry any timber or cause it to be carried out of England. And the lord king

commands that no one shall be received for the oath concerning arms unless he is a freeman.

(Latin) Stubbs, *Select Charters,* pp. 183 f.

35. THE ASSIZE OF THE FOREST (1184)[1]

This is the assize of the lord king Henry, son of Matilda, with regard to his forest and venison[2] in England, [proclaimed] at Woodstock by the counsel and assent of the archbishops, bishops, and barons—earls and nobles—of England.

1. In the first place, he has forbidden that any one shall commit any sort of offence touching his venison and his forests, and he wills that no one shall take confidence from the fact that hitherto those who have committed offences touching his venison and his forests have been declared in mercy [only] as concerned their chattels. For henceforth, if any one commits any [such] offence against him and is convicted of it, he wills that full justice shall be had of that man as was had in the time of King Henry, his grandfather.

2. Item, he has commanded that no one shall have bows, arrows, dogs, or hounds in his forests, unless [such person] has the warrant of the king or of some other man who can [lawfully] be his warrantor.

3. Item, he forbids all persons to give or sell anything to the destruction or waste of their woods, which are within the forest of King Henry;[3] while fully conceding that, without waste, they may take from their woods whatever may be necessary for them, and this by view of the king's forester.

4. Item, he has commanded that all those who have woods within the bounds of the king's forest may put proper foresters in their woods; for which foresters those to whom the woods belong are to be sureties, or they are to provide such proper sureties as can pay compensation, should the foresters commit any offence touching what pertains to the lord king. And those who, outside the bounds of the [forest] visitation, have woods in which the venison enjoys the peace of the lord king are to have no forester unless they will swear [to respect] the king's assize, the peace of his venison, and whatever custodian is put in charge of his woods.[4]

5. Item, the lord king has commanded that his foresters shall exercise care over the forest of knights and others who have woods within the bounds of the king's forest, [to see] that the woods are not destroyed. For if on this account the woods are destroyed, let it be well known to those whose woods are destroyed that compensation

---

[1] On all phases of this assize see the chapters in Petit-Dutaillis and Lefebvre, pp. 149 f., and G. J. Turner's introduction to his *Select Pleas of the Forest* (Selden Society). No really good text of the document has come down to us.

[2] *Venatio,* meaning either game or hunting rights.

[3] The forest was a game preserve which might include all kinds of land, either inhabited or uninhabited. Within it might lie extensive woods that were the property of lay and clerical nobles. Such persons, under royal supervision, were entitled to any reasonable use of their own woods.

[4] Cf. articles 7, 13.

will be exacted from those men themselves or from their lands, and from none other.

6. Item, the lord king has commanded that all his foresters shall swear to the best of their ability to enforce the assize that he has established for his forests, and that they will not disturb knights or other good men in [the enjoyment of] what the king has granted them with regard to their woods.

7. Item, the king has commanded that, in each county where he has venison, twelve knights shall be appointed to guard his vert[5] and venison together with the forest; and four knights shall be appointed to have charge of agistment[6] in his woods, and to receive and keep his pannage. And the king forbids that any one shall provide agistment for his own woods within the bounds of the forest before agistment is provided for the king's woods. And [provision for] the lord king's agistment begins fifteen days before Michaelmas and lasts until fifteen days after Michaelmas.

8. And the lord king has commanded that, when a forester has the lord king's own woods in his charge, if those woods are destroyed and he can by no means show good cause for the destruction of the woods, vengeance shall be taken on the forester's own body and not otherwise.

9. Item, the king forbids all clergymen to commit any offences touching his venison or his forests. He strictly orders his foresters that, if they find such men committing offences, they shall not hesitate to lay hands on those men in order to hold them and put them under attachment;[7] he himself will give full warranty.

10. Item, the king has ordered that his assarts,[8] both new and old, are to be inspected; likewise his purprestures[9] and wastes of forests, and that each [class of offences] is to be recorded by itself.

11. Item, the king has commanded that, on summons of his master forester, archbishops, bishops, earls, barons, knights, freeholders, and all men, as they wish to be protected and not to be declared in the king's mercy, shall come to try the pleas of the lord king touching his forests, and to attend to his other business in the county [court].

12. At Woodstock the king has also commanded that, if any man commits a first offence touching the forest, good pledges shall be accepted from him, and so likewise if he commits a second offense. But if he does wrong a third time, for the third offence no further pledges shall be accepted from him, nor anything other than the body of the misdoer.

13. Item, the king has commanded that every man who is [at least]

---

[5] Green wood, or growing timber.

[6] The putting of animals, especially swine, into the woods to feed. For pannage, see above, p. 43, n. 19.

[7] Restraint either of the person or of his property, to assure his appearance in court.

[8] Clearings made for cultivation or some other purpose.

[9] Unauthorized uses of the royal land.

twelve years of age, and who dwells within the peace of the venison,[10] shall swear that peace; and clergy holding lay fees [shall do the same].

14. Item, he has commanded that the lawing of mastiffs[11] shall be carried out wherever his wild beasts enjoy his peace and have been accustomed to enjoy it.

15. Item, he has commanded that no tanner or bleacher of hides shall dwell in his forests outside a borough.

16. Item, the king has commanded that henceforth no one, either within or without a forest, shall engage in any kind of chase at night for the taking of wild beasts wherever his wild beasts live or enjoy his peace or have been accustomed to enjoy it, on pain of imprisonment for one year and of redeeming themselves by fine at at his pleasure; and that no one, under the same penalty, shall raise against his wild beasts any obstruction, either living or dead, between his forest and the woods or other regions disafforested by him or his ancestors.

(Latin) *Ibid.*, pp. 186 f.

---

[10] The region adjoining the forest, technically known as the purlieu, where hunting was restricted; see Petit-Dutaillis and Lefebvre, pp. 233 f.

[11] Mutilation of the dogs' feet so that they could not chase game; cf. no. 45, art. 6.

36. BARONIAL RETURNS (1166)[1]

(A) FROM THE ARCHBISHOP OF YORK

To his most beloved lord, Henry, by the grace of God king of England, duke of Normandy and of Aquitaine, and count of Anjou, his Roger, by the same grace archbishop of York and legate of the Apostolic See, greeting. Your majesty has commanded that all your faithful men, both clerical and lay, who hold of you in chief within Yorkshire, shall signify to you by their sealed letters patent[2] how many knights each of them has who were enfeoffed by old enfeoffment in the time of King Henry, your grandfather, namely, on the day and in the year that he was alive and dead; and how many he has who were enfeoffed by new enfeoffment after the death of your said grandfather of blessed memory; and how many knights are charged against the demesne of each. And the names of all those men, both of the new enfeoffment and of the old, are to be inscribed in that writ, because you wish that, if there are any who have not yet sworn fealty to you and whose names are not yet inscribed in your roll,

---

[1] On all problems of interpretation raised by these returns, see Round, *Feudal England*, pp. 236 f.; also his *Studies on the Red Book of the Exchequer* for criticism of the edition published in the Rolls Series.

[2] Letters patent had the seal attached to a strip of parchment run through the bottom of the document, so that it might be freely opened. For letters close the strip was run through the folded document, so that it should be read only by the person to whom it was addressed. Cf. no. 41 for examples of the difference in style. What here follows in the archbishop's letter obviously reflects the terms of the king's original mandate.

they should swear fealty to you before the first Sunday of Lent.
As one of which [faithful men], being subject in all things to your
command, I have with all diligence, and in so far as the brevity of
the time would permit, made investigation within my tenement and by
the present writing signify to you, my lord, [the results].

Wherefore, my lord, be it known to you in the first place that no
knight is charged against the demesne of the archbishopric of York,
since we have enough knights enfeoffed through whom to perform all
the service that we owe you, as also our predecessors had; and we
have more than we owe, as you may see from the present writing.
For our predecessors, not through necessity of the service that we
owe, but because they wished to provide for their relatives and
serjeants, enfeoffed more [knights] than they owed the king. Now
these are the names of those enfeoffed from the time of King Henry
[I].³ . . . After the death of King Henry, however, [the following
men] were enfeoffed: Peter the Steward with half a knight's fee; Earl
Peter with the twentieth of a knight; Geoffrey of Burton with the
twelfth of a knight; Gervaise of Bretton with the third of a knight.
And since, my lord, of these there are some from whom I demand
more service than they are performing, while others are withholding
what is said to belong to the table (*mensam*) and demesne of the
archbishop rather than to those men themselves, I humbly ask that
this writing shall not be held against me or my successors if we are
unable to restore or to retain the rights of the church. Fare thee well,
my lord!

(Latin) *Liber Niger Scaccarii,* pp. 303 f.

(B) FROM THE ABBOT OF ST. ALBANS

To his most benign lord, Henry, by the grace of God illustrious
king of the English, Brother Robert, humble minister of the church
of St. Albans, greeting and faithful service. With regard to the
knights, whose number and names you order reported to you in writing, we truthfully give you this information. We have six knights
enfeoffed from old enfeoffment of the time of King Henry [I], but
from new enfeoffment none. Nor have we any knight who performs
the full service of a knight except Hugh Wach, who holds of us one
knight's fee.⁴ . . . Our demesne, moreover, owes you no [knight].
May Almighty God preserve to you in peace and for long the integrity
of your realm!

(Latin) *Ibid.,* p. 244.

(C) FROM THE EARL OF ESSEX

To Henry, king of England, duke of Normandy and of Aquitaine,
and count of Anjou, Geoffrey, earl of Essex, greeting and faithful
service. Know that the names hereinunder written are those of the
knights who hold of me by old enfeoffment. . . . Total of the knights

---

³ The text here lists 39 tenants with over 41 knight's fees.
⁴ Various lesser holdings are enumerated.

by old enfeoffment, ninety-seven knights and the third of a knight. These are the names of the knights by new enfeoffment. . . . Total of those newly enfeoffed.[5] . . . And my men tell me that I owe the king sixty knights.

(Latin) *Ibid.*, pp. 228 f.

(D) FROM BADERON OF MONMOUTH

To his lord, Henry, king of the English, Baderon of Monmouth, greeting. Lord, I have heard your precept in the county [court] of Hereford: namely, that I should notify you, signifying to you by my letters patent under seal, how many knights I have who were enfeoffed by old enfeoffment. Accordingly, prepared to obey your precept, I have noted their names as follows. . . . These ten are of the old enfeoffment; of [knights] newly enfeoffed I have none. Besides, I am bound to furnish you five [knights] from my demesne.

(Latin) *Ibid.*, p. 152.

(E) FROM GILBERT OF PINKNEY

To his lord, the king, Gilbert of Pinkney gives this notification. It is ascertained that I have eleven and a half knights enfeoffed by old enfeoffment from the time of King Henry [I]: namely. . . . And afterwards, from my demesne, I gave to Henry, my son, one knight's fee; and to Gilbert, my son, half a knight's fee. In addition there remains against my demesne the service of two knights.

(Latin) *Ibid.*, p. 196.

(F) FROM PETER DE LA MARE

To Henry, by the grace of God king of the English, Peter de la Mare, greeting. Be it known to you that, by your grace, I hold Lavington in demesne for the service of two knights; but that I there have no knight enfeoffed, either by old or by new [enfeoffment]. Farewell!

(Latin) *Ibid.*, p. 113.

(G) FROM WILLIAM OF LONDON

To his dearest lord, Henry, by the grace of God king of the English, William of London, greeting. Know that I have no knight enfeoffed, either by old or by new enfeoffment; but that I am bound to defend my fief through the service of my body.

(Latin) *Ibid.*, p. 113.

37. PIPE ROLL OF 33 HENRY II (1187)

(A) ENTRIES CONCERNING SCUTAGE

From the scutage of the knights of Lincolnshire who did not depart with the king for the army of Galloway. The bishop of Lincoln renders account of £60 of scutage for his knights of the old enfeoffment, which he acknowledges he owes the king. . . . Oliver d'Ain-

---

[5] Twelve knights plus a number of fractions.

court owes £35 of scutage for his knights. Martin Martel renders account of 5s. for the fourth of a knight's fee. . . . William de Berville renders account of 3s. 4d. for the sixth of a knight's fee. . . .

Yorkshire. . . . Laurence, archdeacon of Bedford, and Master Roger Arundel render account of £20 of scutage for the knights of the archbishopric of York, which the archbishop acknowledges he owes the king.[1] They have paid it into the treasury. And they are quit. The same men render account of £27. 9s. 8d. for the knights which the archbishop does not acknowledge he owes the king, but which are accounted for because the archbishopric is in the king's hands. In the treasury £24. 9s. 8d. And they owe 60s. . . .

Gloucestershire. . . . Hugh Bardolf renders account of £327. 3s. of scutage for the knights of the honour of the earl of Gloucester, both of the old enfeoffment and of the new, for which account is rendered because the honour is in the king's hands. In the treasury £207. 8s. 10d. And in pardons by the king's writ.[2] . . . And in demesnes of the king, from which he has tallage, £6. And in pardons by the king's writ to the barons of the said honour enfeoffed in Wales £41. 15s. And he owes £62. 2s. 6d. . . .

Devonshire. . . . The bishop of Exeter renders account of £15. 10s. of scutage for his knights, which he acknowledges he owes the king. He has paid it into the treasury. And he is quit. The same man owes £18. 2s. 4d. for the knights which he does not acknowledge. Walter, abbot of Tavistock, renders account of £16 of scutage for the knights which he acknowledges. . . .

Cornwall. . . . Agnes, who was wife of Walter Hay, renders account of £12. 10s. of scutage for twenty knights: namely, 12s. 6d. for each knight. . . . Nicholas Fitz-Geoffrey renders account of £6. 5s. of scutage for ten knights with small fees. . . . William Fitz-Richard renders account of 62s. 6d. of scutage for five knights in the manner aforesaid. . . .

(Latin) Pipe Roll of 33 Henry II, pp. 75 f.

(B) Entries concerning Tallage

From the tallage of the king's demesnes and the lands which were then in his hands in Norfolk. The same sheriff renders account of 100s. from the contribution (*donum*) of Cawston.[3] . . . The same sheriff renders account of 4m. from the vill of Eresham. . . . The same sheriff renders account of £7. 10s. from the half-hundred of Eresham. . . . The same sheriff renders account of £25. 13s. 4d. from Yarmouth. . . . The same sheriff renders account of £93. 16s.

---

[1] The barons, especially the great ecclesiastics, refused to admit that they owed any service beyond that anciently charged against their fiefs, no matter how many knights they had subinfeudated. So, as may be seen from the entries below, the king often failed to collect all the assessed scutage, unless the honour was in his hands. See Round, *Feudal England*, pp. 242 f.

[2] Sums totalling £9. 16s. 8d. pardoned to five persons.

[3] About half of the assessed sum is normally paid into the treasury, with the remainder left for the following year.

8d. from the contribution of Norwich. . . . The same sheriff renders account of 1m. from two men of the king dwelling in Clacklose Hundred. . . .

Suffolk. . . . The same sheriff renders account of 2m. from Holbrook. . . . The same sheriff renders account of 2m. from Dunningworth. . . . The same sheriff renders account of 40s. from Little Framingham. . . . The same sheriff renders account of £20. 16s. 8d. from the contribution of Oreford. . . . The same sheriff renders account of £16 from Ipswich. . . . The same sheriff renders account of £30. 6s. 4d. from Lothingland. . . . The same sheriff renders account of £4. 13s. 4d. from the contribution of Eye. . . . The burgesses of Dunwich [owe] 100m. from the contribution promised by them in common. . . .

Lincolnshire. . . . From the tallage of the demesnes and lands which were then in the king's hands, [assessed] by Geoffrey de Lucy and Jocelyn, archdeacon of Chichester, and William le Vavasseur. The same sheriff renders account of £45. 15s. from the contribution of Grimsby together with the soke. . . . The same sheriff renders account of £31. 6s. 8d. from Caistor together with the soke. . . . The same sheriff renders account of 46s. 8d. from Stallingborough, demesne of the archbishopric [of York]. . . . The same sheriff renders account of 40s. from Benningworth, land of the archbishop. . . . The men of Sixhills and Henton owe 2m. of contribution. The same sheriff renders account of 103s. from Torksey. . . . The same sheriff renders account of 40s. from Surfleet, which belonged to Helpe the Crossbowman. . . . The citizens of Lincoln owe £176. 4s. from the contribution assessed by the justices on individual men. . . .

Yorkshire. . . . The same sheriff renders account of £226. 6s. 4d. from the contribution of the city of York, assessed by the justices on the men of the same city except the moneyers. . . .

(Latin) *Ibid.*, pp. 59 f.

(C) ENTRIES CONCERNING PROFITS OF JUSTICE

Northamptonshire. . . . From the pleas of Ranulf de Glanville, Jocelyn the Archdeacon, Thomas of Hurstbourne, and Michael Belet. The same sheriff renders account of 3s. 4d. from the amercement of Adam of Newton because he did not have the man for whom he was surety. . . . William of Stanford renders account of 8m., because, while he was serjeant of the hundred, he did not present to the sheriff a crown plea that had earlier been presented to him. . . . Ralph of the Churchyard renders account of 4s. 8d. for the flight of Richard. . . . Simon the Dean renders account of ½m. because he detained a [certain] man's slayers who were not in frankpledge. . . . The same sheriff renders account of 35s. from Sutton Hundred for a murder.[4] . . . Richard Blere renders account of 5s. 8d. for purpres-

---

[4] See above, p. 36, n. 2.

ture.[5] . . . Peter, son of Adam, renders account of 75*m.* for the same and because he took a certain woman and tortured her without the king's licence. . . . The burgesses of Northampton render account of 20*m.* for the concealment of a crown plea.[6] . . . Reginald, reeve of Weddon, owes ½*m.* because he first denied what he afterwards acknowledged. . . . Ralph of Aldewinc renders account of ½*m.* for a false claim. . . . William Caperum owes ½*m.* for false measure. Ralph, son of Bernard, renders account of ½*m.* because he withdrew [from his suit]. . . . Item, from offerings to the court. Hugh Ridel renders account of £93. 6*s.* 8*d.* to have such seisin of his land of Withering as he had when Peter de Saint-Médard died. . . . Gilbert de Wanleville owes 40*s.* for a recognition against William de Bere concerning sixteen virgates of land as to whether it is gage or fee. Geoffrey Brito renders account of 15*m.* for the wife whom he married without the king's licence when she was in the gift of the king. . . . Robert Reval renders account of 10*m.* that he may have in the king's court his suit against Adam Fitz-Warin concerning eight virgates of land in Cosgrove. . . .

Hampshire. . . . From the pleas of the forest [held] by Geoffrey Fitz-Peter. The same sheriff renders account of 25*s.* from the demesnes of the bishop and the prior of Winchester for transgression of the assize of the forest.[7] . . . Walter Waleran renders account of 2*s.* for an escape. . . . Robert d'Aumale renders account of 20*s.* for bows and arrows [kept] against the assize. . . . The same sheriff renders account of 56*s.* 10*d.* for wastes, assarts, purprestures, and pleas of the forest of Hampshire. . . . The prioress of Amesbury owes 3*s.* for vert.

London. . . . Bruno the Jew owes £340 of the amercement of 2000*m.* for which he fined with the king at Waltham.[8] Aaron the Jew of Lincoln owes 500*m.* of the same fine. But he is dead and the king has his chattels. . . . The Jews of England owe 5525½*m.* of amercement for Jurnet of Norwich, whose charters they have in order to acquit him. . . .

Norfolk. . . . Spreggi renders account of 100*m.* for not arresting Robert as the justices ordered. . . . William Fitz-William of Lynn renders account of 2*m.* for a recognition concerning the advowson of the church of Lynn.[9]

Lincolnshire. . . . Benedict Clarizia renders account of 20*m.* of amercement for the hauberk that his wife took in pledge contrary to the prohibition.[10] . . . Robert de Hardre owes 1*m.* of gold for recognition concerning two carucates of land in Hadley, as to whether it is free fee of the church or lay [fee].[11] . . .

[5] See above, p. 88, n. 9.
[6] That is to say, for failure to make presentation.
[7] For this and the following items, see no. 35.
[8] In connection with these entries, cf. no. 40A.
[9] See no. 33D.
[10] See no. 34, art. 7.
[11] See no. 33C.

Yorkshire. . . . The bishop of Durham owes 500*m*. because he held in the court Christian a plea concerning the advowson of a certain church.[12]. . . Robert of Sanford owes 40*s*. for recognition of his father's death with regard to the land of Ecclesfield, as against Reginald de Lucy. Ralph de Clare renders account of £80 to have the king's benevolence. . . .

Sussex. . . . Robert of Badbury renders account of £35. 9*s*. 10*d*. for disseisin against the assize. . . . The bishop of Chichester renders account of 10*m*. because he hunted without licence in woods of the king's escheat. . . . Warner de Sumery renders account of 20*s*. for right[13] concerning the service from one virgate of land in Bixley, as against Gilbert of Balliol. . . .

Essex and Hertfordshire. . . . The abbess of Barking owes 20*m*. for 180 oaks cut down in the forest against the assize. . . . Ralph of Dene owes 10*s*. for dogs [kept] against the assize. . . . Edwin Scaldhot renders account of 20*d*. because he unjustly vexed the jurors. . . .

Staffordshire. . . . Guy de Suinfen renders account of 1*m*. for having in the king's court his suit against Henry de Pirie, which was in the county [court]. . . .

Wiltshire. . . . The same sheriff owes 18*d*. from Kinwardstone Hundred for a murder and failure to prove Englishry.[14]. . . Walter de Saint-Germain renders account of 40*s*. for an investigation of the truth concerning the marriage of Margaret, wife of Ralph, his brother. . . .

Berkshire. . . . The same sheriff renders account of 2½*m*. from the vill of Letcombe because it received without frankpledge an unknown man who had slain five men. . . . Midwinter owes 20*s*. because it received a man who was not in frankpledge. . . .

(Latin) *Ibid.*, pp. 103 f., 197 f., etc.

---

[12] See no. 30, art. 1.
[13] See no. 33E.
[14] See no. 26, art. 92.

38. ORDINANCE OF THE SALADIN TITHE (1188)

1. Every one shall give in alms for this year's aid of the land of Jerusalem a tenth of his rents and movables, except the arms, horses, and clothes of knights, and except likewise the horses, books, clothes, vestments, and all sacred furnishings[1] of clergymen, and [except] the precious stones of both clergymen and laymen.

2. Moreover, this money is to be collected within each parish in the presence of the parish priest and the archpriest,[2] one Templar and one Hospitaller, a serjeant of the lord king and a clerk of the king, a serjeant of a baron and his clerk, and a clerk of the bishop— after excommunication has been proclaimed by the archbishops and bishops and by the archpriests, each in his own parish of every man

---

[1] *Capella*, whatever the priest needed for divine service.
[2] The chief priest of the diocese, otherwise known as the rural dean.

who will not lawfully give the aforesaid tenth in the presence and with the knowledge of those who, as already stated, should be present. And if any one, to the knowledge of these men, gives less than he should, let there be chosen from the parish four or six lawful men who, being sworn, shall determine the amount that he should have declared; then he must make up the deficiency in his contribution.

3. Clergy and knights who have taken the cross, however, shall give nothing toward the said tenth except from their own property and demesnes; whatever their men may owe shall be collected for their use by the aforesaid persons and given to them entire.

4. Moreover, on the day of the Nativity, [the day] of St. Stephen, and [the day] of St. John the bishops shall have announcement made through their letters in each parish of their bishoprics that every one is to assemble the aforesaid tenth at his own home before the Purification of the Blessed Virgin, and on the following day or thereafter pay [it] at the place to which he is summoned and in the presence of the aforesaid persons.

(Latin) Stubbs, *Select Charters,* p. 189.

39. BOROUGH CHARTERS AND RECORDS

(A) John: Charter to Ipswich (1200)

John, by the grace of God king, etc. Know that we have granted and by our present charter have confirmed to our burgesses of Ipswich our borough of Ipswich, with all its appurtenances and with all its liberties and free customs, to be held of us and our heirs by them and their heirs in hereditary right, paying to our exchequer every year at Michaelmas term, by the hand of the reeve of Ipswich, the just and accustomed farm and, at the same time, the increment of 100s. sterling by tale that they used to pay. We have also granted that all burgesses of Ipswich are to be quit of toll, stallage,[1] lastage, pontage, and all other customs throughout all our land and throughout the ports of the sea. We have granted to them that, with the exception of our officials, none of them shall be impleaded in any plea outside the borough of Ipswich, save only in pleas concerning foreign tenures; and that they shall have their gild merchant and their hanse;[2] that no one shall be lodged or shall take anything by force within the borough of Ipswich; that they shall justly have their lands and their pledges and all their debts, by whomsoever owed; that, with regard to their lands and tenures inside the borough, justice shall be assured them according to the custom of the borough of Ipswich and of our free boroughs; that, with regard to their debts established at Ipswich and their pledges made in the same place, the pleas shall be held at Ipswich; and that none of them shall be adjudged in mercy with respect to his chattels except according to the law of our free boroughs. We also forbid any one in all our land, on pain of £10

---

[1] Rent paid for stalls in a market or fair; not to be confused with tallage. Cf. no. 28B for a number of these privileges.

[2] See above, p. 63, n. 14.

forfeiture to us, to exact toll, stallage, or any other custom from the men of Ipswich. Wherefore we will and straitly command that the aforesaid burgesses shall have and hold the aforesaid liberties and free customs well and in peace, as they have been and are best and most freely enjoyed by the other burgesses of our free boroughs in England, saving in all things to our citizens of London their liberties and free customs.

Furthermore, we will and grant that our said burgesses, by the common counsel of their town, shall elect two of the more lawful and discreet men of their town and present them to our chief justice at our exchequer; which men shall well and faithfully keep the reeveship (*preposituram*) of our aforesaid borough of Ipswich. And so long as they well conduct themselves in that office, they shall not be removed except by the common counsel of the aforesaid burgesses. We also will that in the same borough, by the common counsel of the aforesaid burgesses, four of the more lawful and discreet men of the borough shall be elected to keep the pleas of the crown and other matters that pertain to us and to our crown in the same borough,[3] and to see that the reeves of that borough justly treat both rich and poor.

These are the witnesses. . . . May 25, in the second year of our reign.

(Latin) Gross, *Gild Merchant,* II, 115 f.

(B) RECORD OF PROCEEDINGS AT IPSWICH (1200)

On Thursday next after the feast of the Nativity of St. John the Baptist, in the second year of the reign of King John, all the townspeople (*tota villata*) of the borough of Ipswich assembled in the churchyard of St. Mary at the Tower to elect two bailiffs[4] and four coroners in the same borough according to the provision of the aforesaid charter of the lord king, which the same king had recently granted to the burgesses of the aforesaid borough. On which day the same burgesses, by common consent and in unanimity, elected two good and lawful men of their town—namely, John Fitz-Norman and William de Belines—who were sworn to keep the reeveship (*preposituram*) of the aforesaid borough, and well and faithfully to treat both rich and poor. On the same day, furthermore, they unanimously elected four coroners—namely, John Fitz-Norman, William de Belines, Philip de Porte, and Roger Lew—who were sworn to keep the pleas of the crown and to care for other matters that pertain to the crown in the same borough and to see that the aforesaid bailiffs justly and lawfully treat both rich and poor. On the same day, furthermore, it was ordered by the common counsel of the said town that henceforth there should be sworn in the aforesaid borough twelve chief portmen, as there are in other free boroughs of England, and

---

[3] See above, p. 53, n. 16; cf. no. 40A, art. 20.

[4] See above, p. 82, n. 7. It was obviously a matter of indifference to both king and burgesses whether their magistrates were styled *praepositi* or *ballivi*. For criticism of this whole document, see C. Stephenson, *Borough and Town,* pp. 174 f., and J. Tait, *The Medieval English Borough,* pp. 270 f.

that, for themselves and the whole town, they should have full power of governing and maintaining the aforesaid borough and all the liberties of the aforesaid borough, of rendering the judgments of the town, and also of keeping, ordering, and doing in the same borough whatever ought to be done for the welfare and honour of the said town. And besides it was announced by the aforesaid bailiffs and coroners that all the townspeople should come to the aforesaid churchyard on Sunday next after the coming feast of the Apostles Peter and Paul, to elect the aforesaid twelve chief portmen according to the provision of the same ordinance.

On Sunday next after the feast of the Apostles Peter and Paul, in the aforesaid year, the whole town of Ipswich assembled in the presence of the bailiffs and coroners of the same town, to elect twelve chief portmen in the same town, as previously ordered. And the aforesaid bailiffs and coroners, by the assent of the townspeople, chose four good and lawful men from each parish of the said town, who were sworn to elect twelve chief portmen from the better, more discreet, and more influential men of the aforesaid town, to make ordinances for the welfare of the town, as aforesaid. And the aforesaid sworn men of the parishes met and elected, for themselves and for all the townspeople, these twelve whose names are written below: namely, John Fitz-Norman, William de Belines, Philip de Porte, Roger Lew, Peter Everard, William Gotschalk, Ames Bolle, John of St. George, John le Mayster, Sayer Fitz-Thurstan, Robert Parys, and Andrew Pepper. Which men were sworn in the presence of all the aforesaid townspeople well and faithfully to keep and govern the borough of Ipswich and, to the best of their ability, to maintain all the liberties that had recently been granted to the burgesses of the same borough by the charter of the lord king aforesaid; also to maintain all other liberties and free customs of the aforesaid town and justly to render the judgments of the courts in the same town without respect to the person of any one; and, besides, to order and to do all else that ought to be done for the welfare and honour of the aforesaid town, justly and lawfully treating both rich and poor.

On the same day, as soon as the aforesaid twelve chief portmen had been sworn according to the aforesaid form, they had all the townspeople raise their hands towards the Book and in unison solemnly swear, from that hour onward, to be obedient, attentive, agreeable, and helpful with body and with goods to their bailiffs and coroners, and to all and singular of the twelve chief portmen aforesaid, for preserving and maintaining the aforesaid town of Ipswich and the aforesaid new charter, together with the honour and all the liberties and free customs of the aforesaid town, to the best of their ability as they justly and reasonably should, in all places and against all persons, saving, nevertheless, the king and his royal authority. On the same day it was agreed that the aforesaid new charter of the lord king should be given for safe keeping to two good and lawful men of the same town—namely, John Fitz-Norman and Philip de Porte—who were sworn faithfully to keep the said charter and to deliver it to the aforesaid townspeople whenever that should be necessary and when, on the request of the townspeople, they should be notified to do so. And since there was more to be ordered and done for the welfare and honour of the town than could properly be attended to on this one day, it was agreed that the bailiffs, the coroners, and all the chief portmen aforesaid should come and assemble here on Tuesday next after the feast of the Translation of St. Thomas the Martyr, to order and do whatever ought to be ordered and done for the welfare and honour of the said town.

On Thursday next after the feast of the Translation of St. Thomas the Martyr, in the aforesaid year, the bailiffs, coroners, and other chief portmen assembled to deliberate and ordain concerning the welfare of the town of Ipswich. In the first place, they ordered that all revenues of the aforesaid borough should thenceforth be collected by the hands of the bailiffs and of four good and lawful men of the same borough; and that every year, for the said townspeople, they should pay the right and accustomed farm at the exchequer of the lord king. Furthermore, they ordered that in the said borough two beadles should be sworn to carry out arrests, distraints, and all commands of the bailiffs, coroners, and chief portmen that ought to be carried out in the same borough; that one of the same beadles should be keeper of all prisoners to be placed under arrest by the bailiffs of the borough; and that such keeper should find security for the safe keeping of all his prisoners, etc. Furthermore, they ordered that, by the common counsel of the townspeople, there should be made in the said borough a common seal for use in important business affecting the community of the said borough, also. for signing affidavits on behalf of all and singular of the burgesses of the same borough, and for doing all else that ought to be done for the common honour and benefit of the aforesaid town; and that such common seal should be kept by three or four good and lawful men of the aforesaid borough, sworn to do so before the community of the same borough. Furthermore, they ordered that in the said borough, by the common counsel of its townspeople, one good and lawful and fit man should be elected to be alderman of the gild merchant in the same borough; that four good and lawful men of the same borough should be associated with him; and that the alderman and those four should swear well and faithfully to maintain the aforesaid gild and all pertaining to the gild. Furthermore, they ordered that the aforesaid new charter should be sent to the full county [court] of Suffolk and as far as Norwich to the full county [court] of Norfolk; and that the same charter should be publicly read in those counties, so that the liberties contained in the said charter should be generally known and published everywhere in each county. Furthermore, they ordered that no burgess of the aforesaid town should be quit of custom for his merchandise in the same town—that is to say, if he were a merchant—except one in scot and lot with respect to the common aids and obligations of the town.

On Sunday next after the feast of the Nativity of the Virgin Mary, in the aforesaid year, the community of the town of Ipswich assembled before the bailiffs, coroners, and other chief portmen of the same town to hear all the aforesaid ordinances, which were read before the people of the town in the churchyard of St. Mary at the Tower. And to the aforesaid ordinances, when they had there been read, the whole community aforesaid unanimously consented. And afterwards they elected their bailiffs to remain [in office] for the next year to come: namely, John Fitz-Norman and William de Belines. On the same day they elected four men to collect the customs of the town together with the aforesaid bailiffs: namely, Peter Pepper, Norman Halynoth, Clement le Palmer, and Leman de Pont. Likewise on the same day they elected two beadles—namely, John Prikehert and John Hawe—who were sworn well and faithfully to carry out arrests, distraints, and all commands of the bailiffs, coroners, and portmen, and [to do] all that pertained to their office. And the aforesaid John Prikehert was elected to keep the prisoners of the town; and he found sureties to be responsible for the escape of prisoners, should that—which God forbid!—occur: namely, Edmund Marsh (*de Marisco*), Peter Pepper, John Hawe, and Thomas de Horner. And since more could not be attended to on this day, it was agreed that the bailiffs and the whole community should be here on Thursday next after the coming feast of St. Faith, in order to elect an alderman and do the other things that could not at the moment be done. And it was announced by the bailiffs that in the meantime they would have a common seal made, as ordered above.

On Thursday next after the feast of St. Faith, in the aforesaid year, the bailiffs, coroners, and other chief portmen, as well as the whole community, assembled in the church of St. Mary at the Tower. And the bailiffs there showed the common seal of the town which had recently been made. And then three of the more lawful and influential men of the said borough were elected to keep that seal: namely, John Fitz-Norman, William de Belines, and Philip de Porte. Which men were sworn before the community well and faithfully to keep the aforesaid seal and not to sign any letter or other instrument with the same seal unless it was for the common honour and benefit of the town or of the burgesses of the town—and that with the assent of their peers. And besides it was agreed that the common charter of the town should remain in the keeping of the same men. On the same day an alderman was elected by the common counsel of the townspeople, namely, William Gotschalk. And four men were elected to be associated with him: namely, Peter Everard, John le Mayster, Roger Lew, and John of St. George. Which men were sworn, together with the alderman, well and faithfully to govern the gild merchant in the borough of Ipswich and all matters pertaining to the gild, and well and faithfully to treat all brothers of the gild. And afterwards it was announced by the alderman and his four associates, in the presence of the people of the town, that all who were of the liberty of the town should come before the alderman and his associates on a certain day— ·

when and where to be made known to them—in order to put themselves in the gild and pay their hanse[5] to the same gild. . . .

(Latin) Ibid., II, 116 f.

(C) Communal Oath of the Londoners[6]

Oath of the commune in the time of King Richard, while he was held captive in Germany. That they will bear faith to the lord king Richard for their life and limbs and earthly honour against all men and women who can live and die, and that they will keep and aid in keeping his peace. And that, in fealty to the king, they will support the commune and be obedient to the mayor of the city of London and to the *échevins*[7] of the said commune; and that they will follow and observe the decisions of the mayor, the *échevins*, and the good men who shall be [associated] with them, saving the honour of God and Holy Church, saving the fealty of the lord king Richard, and saving in all respects the liberties of the city of London. And that, neither for reward nor for family nor for any other consideration will they abstain from pursuing and maintaining right in all things to the best of their ability and knowledge; and that, in fealty to the lord king Richard, they will together endure good and evil, whether for life or for death. And if any one presumes to disturb the peace of the lord king and his realm, that they, by the counsel of the lady [queen mother][8] and of the lord [archbishop] of Rouen,[9] and of the mayor and of the other justices of the lord king, will support, to the best of their ability and knowledge, the faithful men of the lord king and those who desire to preserve the peace, saving always in all things the liberties of London.

(Latin) Weinbaum, London, II, 57.

(D) Levy of a Municipal Tax at London (1199)

A certain assessment (*assisa*) made to raise money for the lord king, when 3000*m.* were given him for the shrievalty.[10] It has been decided that each of the aldermen[11] and all men of their wards are

---

[5] The word is often used to mean a tax or a fee.

[6] First published and commented on by Round, *Commune of London,* pp. 235 f. For subsequent estimates of its significance, see the works cited above, p. 72, n. 4.

[7] A common name for groups of municipal magistrates in northern France. In this document the term probably applies to the aldermen who, along with the mayor, came to be elected by the citizens.

[8] Eleanor of Aquitaine.

[9] Walter, archbishop of Rouen, was royal justiciar from 1191 to 1193.

[10] An entry in the Fine Roll of 1 John shows that this payment was to secure a charter confirming the liberties of the city, and they, without doubt, included the right to elect magistrates and to farm London and Middlesex.

[11] When first heard of, in the early twelfth century, the aldermen were royal officials in charge of the city wards. By this time they had apparently come to be elected by the citizens assembled in wardmotes (cf. no. 72A)—the assemblies which had probably been used for a century or more to carry out such measures as are described in this and the following document.

to swear that, from rents which they have in the city and the Portsoken and which are in fee,[12] they will give 4s. on the pound, 2s. on
10s., 12d. on 5s., 6d. on 30d., and the proportionate amount on 12d.
And from rent of lodgers (*hospitum*) which is not in fee—whether a
reed, a rush, or anything else[13]—they will give 2s. on the pound, and
so on down to the proportionate amount on 12d. Besides, from all
their chattels and other things in their possession, either from what
lies in their houses or from other movable property, wherever it may
be—whether on this side of the sea or beyond it—they will give 2s.
on the pound and so on down to the proportionate amount on 12d.
And they are to swear that, on account of this assessment, they have
removed chattels neither from their houses nor from anywhere else,
and that they will not remove them until they have fully paid toward
this assessment whatever may be their obligation. And from all debts
known to be owed them, from whatever they know they have, they
shall give as much as from their other chattels. And from foreign
rents[14] which are held in the city and in the Portsoken and which
are in fee, they shall give 4s. on the pound, as provided above, and
from others which are not held in fee [they shall give] according to
what has been said above; and this should be charged against the
foreigners on their reception [in the city]. And they shall swear that
they will conceal no one who is of the city or who enjoys a claim (*se
advocet*) through the city and who does not make this oath and contribution as established and provided, so that they do not report the
fact to the aldermen and the wardens of the chest. Money-lenders,
men or women, shall not swear this oath.[15] [The names of] all are to
be written down—of those who come to the chest and of those who do
not come. And if any wish to swear that they do not have 12d. either
in rent or in chattels, let them prove this to the mayor and citizens,
and pay amends for [not doing] this. Each man shall swear for himself and for his wife and children, and he shall give the proper
amount for them; or, if he prefers, let them come before the mayor
and the citizens to swear and pay for themselves. And all the aldermen shall give strict orders to all in their wards that no one shall
leave the city, either by a street of the lord [king] or otherwise, until
he has acquitted himself and his [family] of this assessment. Moreover, if any of them does otherwise, let his name be recorded and
handed over to the mayor and the rest [of the officials], who shall

---

[12] Part of the text is destroyed at this point, and what remains is very bad;
but the general meaning can be guessed from what follows concerning foreign
debts. The Portsoken was the suburb lying east of the Roman wall to the north
of the Tower.

[13] *Arundine vel iunco vel alio*—does this mean that rents were actually paid
in reeds and rushes, or is it merely a rhetorical flourish?

[14] That is to say, rents enjoyed by persons who were not citizens of London.

[15] Presumably because the assets of all such persons were carefully set down
in official records; cf. no. 40A, art. 24.

seize all that he has, lands and chattels, for the use of the city. And every woman who is engaged in trading, in so far as she is manifestly acting for herself, shall carry out this [same set of instructions].

(Latin) *Ibid.*, II, 51 f.

(E) ORDINANCE FOR THE DEFENCE OF LONDON

A certain provision made for defending the city in the time of King John, at his request and with his approval. Each alderman shall hold his wardmote[16] for all his men who are aged fifteen years and more. And when they have assembled, each shall swear that, for every pound in movable property and in debts that he estimates he has [owed to him], he will give 2*d*., and for 10*s*. in movable property 1*d*. Item, for 20*s*. in rent each give 3*d*., and for 10*s*. [in rent] 1½*d*. Item, the alderman shall assemble all foreign merchants who are in his ward; and when he has explained to them the city's need, and how they and their chattels are safeguarded by the city, he shall urge them each by free will to contribute as much for the defence of the city as he has received from the city in favour. If, however, [he will] not [contribute], he shall be compelled to give 2*d*. for every pound in chattels which at the moment he has in the city. Item, from all rent of foreigners 12*d*. shall be taken for every pound, except from ecclesiastical rents. Item, to collect and receive this money, four good and discreet men shall be elected from each ward, who [in return] for a receipt shall pay that money at the gild-hall to Simon Blund and R. of Antioch.

Item, those persons who knowingly and deliberately break their oaths shall be excommunicated throughout all churches in the city. Item, each man, when his oath has been made, shall pay the money immediately or by the following Sunday at the latest; otherwise [his obligation] will be doubled on the next day.

Item, each alderman shall inspect the arms of all persons in his ward, so that they will have those [arms] ready for the defence of their bodies and their chattels and their city. And if any one is in default with respect to his arms, let his name be immediately enrolled, and let it be explained to the lord mayor and the other barons[17] of the city in what way, against the peace and security of the city, he has defaulted. Item, the alderman in his full wardmote shall command and provide that all have horses who ought to have them. Furthermore, a pennon shall be made in each ward, and the alderman shall have his banner. And when they have had the summons of the alderman, the men of each ward shall follow the banner of their alderman to the place assigned them for the defence of the city.

(Latin) *Ibid.*, II, 82 f.

---

[16] See above, p. 101, n. 11.

[17] An honorary title borne by the citizens of London and of the Cinque Ports. The usage perhaps arose because the burgesses of these towns were the first to hold liberties direct of the crown.

(F) John: Charter to London (1215)

John, by the grace of God king of England, etc. Know that we have granted and by our present charter have confirmed to our barons of our city of London that each year they may elect for themselves from among their own number a mayor who is faithful to us [and is] discreet and fit for the government of the city; so that, when he has been elected, he shall be presented to us, or to our justiciar if we are not present, and shall swear fealty to us. And they shall be permitted to remove him at the end of the year and to substitute another if they will, or they may retain the same man; yet so that he shall be presented to us or to our justiciar if we are absent. We have also granted and by our charter have confirmed to our said barons that well and in peace, freely, quietly, and fully, they shall have all the liberties which they have hitherto enjoyed, as well in the city of London as outside it, both on land and on water, and in all other places, saving to us our chamberlainship.[18] Wherefore we will and straitly command that our aforesaid barons of our city of London shall each year select for themselves from among their own number a mayor in the aforesaid fashion, and that they shall have all the aforesaid liberties well and in peace, fully and completely, with everything pertaining to liberties of this kind, as aforesaid. Witnesses. . . .

(Latin) Stubbs, *Select Charters*, p. 311.

40. JUDICIAL RECORDS OF 1194

(A) Articles for the General Eyre

In the first place, four knights are to be elected from the entire county, who on oath shall elect two lawful knights from each hundred or wapentake, and these two shall on oath elect ten [additional] knights—or free and lawful men, if knights are not available—from each hundred or wapentake; so that these twelve shall together make response concerning all the [following] articles for the entire hundred or wapentake.

1. Concerning the pleas of the crown, both old and new, and all those which have not yet been determined before the justices of the lord king.

2. Item, concerning all recognitions and all pleas which have been summoned before the justices by writ of the king or of his chief justice, or those which have been sent before them from the principal court of the king.

3. Item, concerning escheats, which now exist, and which occurred after the king set out for the land of Jerusalem, and which were then in the king's hands, and whether or not they are in his hands now; and concerning all escheats of the lord king, if they have been taken out of his hands, how and by whom [it was done] and into whose hands they have come, and who has thence had the revenue and how, what it was, what it has been worth, and what it is worth now;

---

[18] The king reserved the right to appoint to the profitable office of city chamberlain or treasurer.

and if there has been any escheat which belongs to the lord king and which is not in his hands.

4. Item, concerning churches which are in the gift of the lord king.

5. Item, concerning the wardships over children to which the king is entitled.

6. Item, concerning the marriages of girls or widows to which the lord king is entitled.

7. Item, concerning malefactors and their receivers and confederates.

8. Item, concerning falsifiers.[1]

9. Item, concerning the slayers of Jews, who they are; and concerning the pledges of the slain Jews, and their chattels, lands, debts, and charters . . . ; and all the pledges and debts of the slain Jews shall be taken into the king's hands; and those who were present at the slaying of the Jews, and who have not yet fined with the lord king or his justices, shall be arrested and shall be freed only by the lord king or his justices.

10. Item, concerning all aids paid for the ransom of the lord king, who made promises and to what amount, how much he has paid and how much is in arrears.

11. Item, concerning the adherents of Earl John,[2] which ones have fined with the lord king and which have not.

12. Item, concerning the chattels of Earl John or of his adherents, which have not been confiscated for the use of the lord king, how much the sheriffs or their bailiffs have received, and who has bestowed anything contrary to the ancient customs of the kingdom.

13. Item, concerning all the lands of Earl John, his demesnes, wardships, escheats, and grants, and why the grants were made; and such grants of Earl John and all of them shall be taken into the lord king's hands, except those which have been confirmed by the king.

14. Item, concerning debts and fines which were owed to Earl John, and why; and all of them shall be exacted for the use of the lord king.

15. Item, concerning money-lenders who have died, and their chattels.

16. Item, concerning wines sold contrary to the assize and concerning false measures both of wine and of other things.

17. Item, concerning crusaders who died before setting out for Jerusalem, who has had their chattels and what and how many these are.

18. Item, concerning grand assizes,[3] which involve 100s. worth of land, and which less.

---

[1] See above, p. 80, n. 2; and cf. art. 24, below.

[2] The king's brother, who had conspired against him and who had just been driven out of England.

[3] Trials in which a disputed title to land was settled by a jury of knights; see Pollock and Maitland, I, 147.

19. Item, concerning defaults.

20. Furthermore, in each county three knights and a clerk shall be elected as keepers of the crown pleas.[4]

21. And no sheriff shall be justice within his shrievalty or within any county that he has held since the first coronation of the lord king.

22. Furthermore, all the cities, boroughs, and demesnes of the lord king shall be tallaged.[5]

23. Moreover, the justices named[6] . . . shall cause to be summoned the knights of the county named in the roll to come on the day and to the place of which they shall make announcement, and in their presence they shall have those men swear to do all that is lawfully possible to restore the wardships and escheats of the lord king and to evaluate them for the advantage of the lord king, failing to do so for neither hate nor favour nor grace of any one.[7] . . .

24. All debts and pledges of Jews shall be enrolled, [also their] lands, houses, rents, and possessions. Moreover, a Jew who conceals any of these is to incur forfeiture to the lord king of his body and of what he has concealed, as well as of all his possessions and all his chattels. Nor shall it be permitted for the Jew ever to recover what he has concealed. Furthermore, six or seven places shall be provided, where [Jews] are to make their loans. And two lawful Christians, two lawful Jews, and two lawful scribes shall be provided, before whom and the clerk of William of St. Mary's Church and of William de Chimelli the loans are to be made. And the charters for the loans shall be made in the form of a chirograph:[8] one part, sealed with the seal of the borrower, to remain witn the Jew; the other to remain in a common chest, on which are three locks. Of the keys to these locks the two Christians shall have one, the two Jews a second, and the clerk of William of St. Mary's Church and of William de Chimelli the third. And besides [there shall be on the chest] three seals; those having the keys shall affix their seals.[9] . . . And henceforth no loan, no payment to Jews, and no change in the charters shall be made except in the presence of the aforesaid men or the majority of them, if all cannot be present. And the two Christians aforesaid shall have one receipt roll for payments henceforth to be made to Jews, and the two Jews shall have one, and the keeper of the roll [shall have] one. Furthermore, every Jew shall swear on his scroll[10] that he will

---

[4] That is to say, coroners. See above, p. 53, n. 16; also nos. 39B, 53D.

[5] See no. 37B.

[6] That is to say, those on eyre in that region.

[7] These knights are to choose twelve lawful men in each region of the county and the twelve are to choose enough of the freer men in each wardship or escheat to meet the needs of the king. From information thus obtained the manors are to be evaluated, restocked whenever necessary, and let to farmers.

[8] Two copies inscribed on one piece of parchment were separated by cutting through letters, such as CHIROGRAPH, written in between the two.

[9] Details follow in the text for enrolling such records and concerning the fees to be paid to the scribes.

[10] Of the Hebrew law.

enroll all his debts, pledges, and rents, and all his goods and possessions, and that he will conceal nothing, as aforesaid; and [that], if he should gain knowledge that any one has concealed anything, he will secretly reveal it to the justices on mission, that he will detect and denounce forgers of charters and clippers of coin whenever he learns of them, and [that he will act] in the same way with regard to the forged charters. . . .

(Latin) *Ibid.*, pp. 250 f.

(B) Excerpts from a Court Roll of 6 Richard I[11]

Wiltshire Pleas and Assizes. . . . The assize comes to make recognition whether Richard le Cras unlawfully and without judgment disseised Walter son of Philip of his free tenement in Melksham after the first coronation of the lord king. The jurors say that they do not know whether or not it is a free tenement. Let him ask other jurors if he wishes. . . .

The assize comes to make recognition whether the prior of Farley unlawfully and without judgment disseised William Burnel of his free tenement in Penly after the first coronation of the lord king. The jurors say that the prior of Farley did disseise him of it. Judgment: William to have seisin of it and the prior [to be] in mercy. . . .

The assize comes to make recognition whether Payn Burnel, uncle of Ralph de Berners, was seised in demesne as of his fee on the day that he died of one virgate of land with its appurtenances in Hillcot, and whether he died after the first coronation of Henry, the king's father, and whether Ralph is his nearest heir—which land is held by Henry de Berners. The jurors say that Payn was not seised of it on the day that he died. Judgment: Henry to hold in peace and Ralph [to be] in mercy for a false claim. . . .

The assize comes to make recognition whether Richard, uncle of William, was seised in demesne as of his fee on the day that he died of one virgate of land in Charlton, and whether he died after the first coronation of Henry, the king's father, and whether William is his nearest heir—which land is held by Isabel of Marlborough and Thomas, her son. And Isabel and Thomas have said that they claim nothing in that land of right,[12] but that they hold it as villeinage of the canons of Charlton, and [that it is] free alms of Reginald de Pavillon who gave that land to the aforesaid canons. And William asks the assize that recognition be made whether that land was free tenement or villeinage when that land was to be inspected and was inspected. The jurors say that, when by the king's writ that land was

---

[11] The first part is a record of civil pleas held before the itinerant justices; the second is a record of the returns made to the articles in the preceding document. See Maitland's introduction to the volume cited below. For the forms of action here illustrated, cf. no. 33.

[12] Since they hold in villeinage, which is not protected by the king's court; see above, p. 82, n. 1.

inspected, Isabel held that land as a free tenement. Judgment: William to have that land and Isabel [to be] in mercy. . . .

Hundred of Calne, inside and outside [the borough]. The jurors say that a certain man was found dead in the fields of Cherhill and it is not known who he was. Murder.[13]

Eli of Stodlegh and the forester of G[eoffry] Fitz-Peter, in the home of Herbert the Chamberlain (*de Camera*), took a certain Matthew who, they said, was an outlaw, and who was handed over to G[eoffrey] Fitz-Peter by writ of the archbishop of Rouen.[14] And the said Herbert was therefore put under gage and pledge. And the jurors say that they made no imputation against the said Herbert besides that reception of Matthew. And Herbert appears and acknowledges that he gave lodging [to Matthew] that one time when he was captured, not knowing that he was a malefactor. Herbert is to be quit.

Tova, wife of Ralph Jagard, has accused Ralph, nephew of Hugh de Brewer, and others of having stolen a certain pig, and she has withdrawn [from her suit]. In mercy.[15] . . .

Berwick is an escheat of the lord king and is worth £15. John Marshal had possession of it and thence took 75s. Then Henry de Longchamps had it and thence took £26. 5s., and after him the sheriff of Wiltshire thence took £7. 10s. . . . Again William de Braose held it and thence took £15, and he still has it. . . .

Richard, son of Elmer, and Alfred the Ploughman fled on account of the robbery of sheep from the castle of Marlborough, and they were in the tithing of Walter. . . . In mercy.[16]

The same [jurors] say that Philip and Arnold of Calne were at the taking of the sheep of Marlborough, together with others who fled, and that Arnold was not in any tithing. And Philip comes and acknowledges that he was there and that Arnold was with him. Philip is to be put under pledge, in case any one wishes to bring suit against him. . . .

Sum of the first aid[17] from the vill of Calne 4m., which the sheriff has received. Sum of the second tallage £4. 16s. 8d., which the sheriff has received.

Sum of the first aid from the hundred outside [the borough] £25. 18s. 11d., which the clerks of the sheriff have received. Sum of the second aid £4. 6s. 8d., [which] Thomas the clerk has received. Sum of the hidage £9. 18d. Adam, clerk of the sheriff, has received all except 23s., which Guy de Dives has received, and [except] 20s. from the hidage of Alan Basset. . . .

---

[13] See above, p. 36, n. 2.

[14] See above, p. 101, n. 9.

[15] Marginal notation.

[16] Marginal notation. Walter and his tithing are to be amerced because of the escape; see above, p. 37, n. 6.

[17] The following entries deal with the various taxes levied for Richard's ransom. *Auxilium* and *tallagium* sometimes appear as synonymous terms.

Manor of Malmesbury. Emma of Summerford was slain in the house of her mother, and Thomas and Richard of Malmesbury were on that account accused. And the whole jury, being interrogated concerning it, said that they did not suspect the aforesaid Thomas and Richard of Malmesbury of the death of the same Emma. And the knights of the whole county said that they did suspect the aforesaid Thomas and Richard, because the same men then proceeded to Gloucester, and they are convinced that the same men proceeded to Gloucester for the sake of there selling the chattels of that woman. Thomas and Richard are to clear themselves by the water.[18]

Sum of the first aid 67s. 6d.; sum of the second aid £5. 10s. 9d.—which [sums] Ralph Fitz-Stephen has received. Sum of the hidage 2s., which Laurence the serjeant of the hundred has received.

Hundred of Sedgelaw. The jurors say that a certain man was slain at Ashley, and his wife on that account accused John and Hugh, serjeants of the abbot of Malmesbury in the vill of Crudwell, and they fled. John was in the tithing of Walter Scarlet of Norton, and Hugh was a clerk. They are to be outlawed.

Fulling, land of Walter Maltravers, is escheat, and it is worth 50s. and is in the hands of Walter of St. Mary's Church.

Countess Margaret is in the gift of the lord king and has the wardship of her son by [grant of] the lord king. . . .

Hundred of Bradford. . . . In the vill of Bradford a certain woman was slain . . . , and Agatha was taken on the appeal of the mother and father of the slain woman and incarcerated at Salisbury. And when Earl J[ohn] broke the jail, then she escaped with the other prisoners and was never seen afterwards. . . . Englishry was presented at the [proper] term.

A certain infant of twelve years was drowned at Broughton, and Englishry was not presented. . . . Accident. . . .

Hundred of Devizes. The churches of Devizes were given to William de Furneaux by Earl John, and they are worth 3½m.

Sum of the first aid for the ransom of the lord king 3m., which Roger Fitz-Everard and Walter Giffard received. Sum of the second [aid] 100s. 7d., which Guy de Dives paid at the exchequer, and for which he has [a receipt].

Concerning the other articles [the jurors report] nothing.

(Latin) Maitland, Rolls of the King's Court, pp. 70-109.

---

[18] See no. 31, art. 2.

41. LETTERS CLOSE AND PATENT (1205-13)[1]

(A) Summons to a Great Council (1205).

The king, etc., to the bishop of Salisbury, etc. We command and pray you that as you cherish us and our honour, avoiding all excuse

---

[1] See above, p. 89, n. 2.

and delay, you come to us at London on Sunday next before the Ascension of the Lord, with us to consider our great and arduous concerns and the common good of our kingdom. And since, with regard to those demands from the king of France which have been brought to us by his messengers and ours[2]—and from which, by the grace of God, we hope to have a favourable outcome—it is needful to have your counsel and that of the other magnates of our land whom we have caused to be convoked on that day and at that place, you shall also cause to be summoned, on our part and on yours, the abbots and conventual priors of your whole diocese; so that, as they cherish us and the common good of the kingdom, they shall be present with us in the aforesaid council.

(Latin) Stubbs, Select Charters, p. 277.

(B) Summons of Service from the Cinque Ports (1206)

The king, etc., to all his beloved and faithful barons of Hastings, Dover, Sandwich, Hythe, and Romney, greeting.[3] We command you that as you cherish us and our honour and the peace of our kingdom and yourselves and all that you have, avoiding all excuse and delay, you be with us at Portsmouth on the eve of Pentecost, or as soon as you can, with as much service as you owe us, to go into our service as William of Wrotham, archdeacon of Taunton, will on our part instruct you. . . . May 12. . . .

(Latin) Rotuli Litterarum Patentium, I, 64.

(C) Levy of a Tax on Chattels and Rents (1207)[4]

The king to all, etc. Know that by the common counsel and assent of our council at Oxford, it was provided for the defence of our kingdom and granted for the recovery of our rights that every layman throughout all England, of whosesoever fee he may be, who has rent and chattels in England, shall give us as aid 12d. from every mark's worth of annual rent, and 12d. from [every mark's worth of] every sort of movable property that he had on the octave of the Purification of the Blessed Mary—namely, at the end of the council—and so in proportion whether more or less. And all stewards and bailiffs of the earls and barons shall swear in the presence of our justices to the value of the rents and movable property of their lords and likewise of their own. And every man besides the earls and barons shall swear to his own rents and chattels according to whatever [plan] our justices dispatched for this purpose shall find best suited to our advantage. . . . February 17.

(Latin) Stubbs, Select Charters, pp. 278 f.

---

[2] Having to do, of course, with the war between John and Philip Augustus.

[3] For references to sources and literature concerning these towns, see the recent book of K. M. E. Murray, <i>Constitutional History of the Cinque Ports;</i> also cf. no. 50c.

[4] On the significance of this tax, see S. K. Mitchell, <i>Taxation under John and Henry III</i>, ch. iii.

(D) Military and Naval Preparations (1212)[5]

The king to the bailiffs of ports, etc. We instruct you that henceforth you permit no ship, from whatsoever land it may be, to cross the sea from your bailiwick unless to that effect you have our special precept, in which is set down the number of men and horses that are to cross; and to suit the number of those whom we order to cross, you shall have a ship delivered to them. . . . March 23.

The king to G[eoffrey] Fitz-Peter, greeting. We command you that, on sight of these letters, you immediately send to Portsmouth with the utmost haste all the ships of your bailiwick, and others coming thither from anywhere, which can carry six horses or more, to go into our service as we have elsewhere directed, notwithstanding our last mandate given you, that you should not permit any ship, from whatsoever land it might be, to cross the sea without our special letters. . . . March 25.
Similar letters to all bailiffs of ports.

The king to the reeves and good men of Canterbury, etc. We command you that, as you cherish us, you have well prepared with horses and arms, forty of the solider and better men of our town of Canterbury, that they may well be fit and ready to cross the sea with us in our service when we send you orders, and so that we shall be grateful to you and to them. . . . June 15.[6]

The king to the sheriff of Lincoln, etc. We command you to see that we have from our city of Lincoln, from our demesnes and escheats, from those men who do not join the army with us, and from the abbeys and priories of your bailiwick two hundred good, strong, and vigorous men with axes, and that many among them are such as well know how to put themselves to carpentering, and for whom we shall be grateful to you; so that they shall be fit and ready for entering our service. And see that, by those on whose behalf they are sent, they are provided with victuals for forty days from the day on which they arrive at Chester. And you are to send with them one of your clerks and four serjeants to inspect and record those who have come and how they have come. And you are to inform us of their names and [tell us] on whose behalf they have been sent. . . . July 10.[7]

The king to the sheriff of Northumberland, etc. We command you

---

[5] In the course of this year John planned first a campaign in France and then one in Wales, but eventually all the orders were rescinded.

[6] Similar letters were sent to seventeen other boroughs for 10 men each, to thirteen for 20 men each, to three for 30 men each, to four for 40 men each, and to London for 100.

[7] Similar letters were sent to officials in charge of thirty-three other counties, vacant bishoprics, escheated honours, etc., for quotas of from 100 to 700 men equipped with axes or with spades and hoes.

to be with us at Chester on the Sunday next after the coming feast
of the Assumption of the Blessed Mary. And have orders given
throughout your whole bailiwick that, from the day on which you come
to Chester, there shall be no trading in victuals except for our army.
And see to it that, from that day, all dealers in victuals from your
bailiwick, as they prize their chattels, follow our army with all sorts
of victuals. . . . July 20.

Similar letters to all the sheriffs of England.

The king to the sheriff of Lincoln, etc. We command you to have
summoned through good summoners all those who hold of us by
serjeanty in your bailiwick, and whose names we have sent to you
in another writing, that they are to be with us at Chester on Sunday
next after the Assumption of the Blessed Mary, well equipped with
horses and arms and provided with victuals for going with us into
our service. And have this summons made by such witness that no
one shall be able to deny that he was summoned. And have there
this writ and the other writ. . . . July 21.

Similar letters to all the sheriffs of England.

The king to G[eoffrey] de Lucy, etc. We command you that, on
sight of these letters, you immediately send our eighteen galleys
toward Chester on a circuit of the coast of Llewelyn's land, to scatter
and destroy the ships, galleys, and boats of our Welsh enemies, and
to inflict evil upon them in all ways possible. But you are constantly
to beware lest you incur injury from the land or the forces of
W[illiam] Earl Marshal.[8] And you are to send to Bristol two galleys
with our supplies; and those who bring them are to notify us as
soon as they arrive at Bristol. And if you have need of money, you are
to let us know. . . . [August 17.]

(Latin) Rotuli Litterarum Clausarum, I, 121-33.

(E) Summons to a Great Council (1213)[9]

The king to the sheriff of Oxford, greeting. We command you
that you have all the knights of your bailiwick who were summoned
to be with us at Oxford a fortnight after All Saints' Day come
[thither] with their arms; and likewise the barons in person, but
without arms. And have four discreet knights of your county come
thither to us at the same time, to speak with us concerning the affairs
of our kingdom. . . . November 7.

Similar letters to all the sheriffs.

(Latin) Stubbs, Select Charters, p. 282.

---

[8] The earl of Pembroke, who was then in conflict with the king.

[9] As pointed out by Miss Levett (English Historical Review, XXXI, 85 f.),
Stubbs wrongly put homines for milites in the last sentence of this writ. For
the best interpretation of the document, see A. B. White, in the American Historical Review, XXII, 325 f.

42. HOUSEHOLD EXPENSE ROLL (1210)[1]

Sunday, at Clarendon. In harness bought for the lord king's use both in the great stable and in the stable of the chamber by Walter de Saint-Ouen and Nicholas of Wells, of which the particulars are endorsed on the roll, 41s. 9½d. To William of London, messenger of the lord bishop of Norwich, going to his lord, 5s., by William Brewer. Item, in alms to a hundred poor people, whom the king fed because he ate twice on Friday next after the feast of the Holy Trinity at Knappe, 9s. 4½d. Item, in alms to a hundred poor people because he ate twice on Friday next before the feast of St. John the Baptist, 9s. 4½d. Item, in alms to a hundred poor people because he ate twice on Friday next after the feast of St. John the Baptist, 9s. 4½d., paid to Brother Thomas. Item, at the same place, in a gift to William Le Pugneur, knight, 3m., by the king. . . .

On Tuesday next after the feast of All Saints, at Nottingham. To William the ewerer,[2] who has ½d. a day for 140 days—that is to say, from June 18 to November 4, both being counted—5s. 10d. To the same William for a bath of the lord king taken at Marlborough, 5d.; for a second bath at Nottingham, 5½d., for a third bath at Northampton, 5½d.; for a fourth bath at Gloucester, 5½d. Item, at the same place, in expenses of Adam and Gervaise, carters of the chamber, and of the man of Thomas the Marshal, and of two sumptermen with five cart-horses, two pack-horses, and a rouncey of Thomas the Marshal, staying with the wardrobe at Northampton and Rockingham for six days by the king's precept, while the lord king made a trip through the forests and river preserves, 18s. Item, in shoeing the said horses and in litter [for them] at Maldon, 4d., paid to Thomas the Marshal. . . .

On Thursday next after the feast of the Conception of the Blessed Mary, at Bristol, we paid to Engelard, sheriff of Gloucester, £400 to be put in the king's treasury. . . .

On the next Sunday, in the same place. In a gift to Walter de Marc, 5s., by the king. In a fur of vair[3] for trimming the tunic of the lord king, 20s. In gris for certain sleeves of the lord king, 9d. To a certain messenger going to the bishop of Winchester with letters concerning rumours about the Roman emperor, 3d. To Roger of the Tower going to Hugh de Neville with letters concerning the same, 3d. In two dozen [sheets of] parchment for making rolls concerning the bishoprics, 18d. . . .

On Sunday next before the [feast of the] Chair of St. Peter, at St. Bridget. In small expenses of Henry, son of the duke of Saxony, 20s., paid to Hugh of Barnwell by the king. In parchment at the same

---

[1] This is the oldest of the *mise* rolls, which anticipate the daily account-books of the later wardrobe; see Tout, *Chapters in Mediaeval Administrative History*, I, 44 f.

[2] See above, p. 69, n. 22.

[3] Vair and gris were two very popular kinds of fur: the former was grey and white, the latter grey.

place, 9d. On the same day, in repairs of the lord king's leggings furred with gris, 8d. . . . In a sack of cordovan to hold the lord king's robe, 7s. In four pairs of boots furred with lamb for the use of the lord king, 7s. 8d. In one pair of cowhide hose for the use of the lord king, 3s. In furbishing two swords of the lord king, 22d. In four pairs of iron spurs for the use of the same, 16d. . . . In a strap for the sword of the lord king, 8d. . . .

On Monday, [the feast of] the Chair of St. Peter, at Tweed-mouth. To Philip of Stradley, for buying a horse, 2m., by the king. In a fur of gris bought at Winchester for the lord king's overtunic [in which] to get up during the night, 20s., by the hand of William the Tailor. . . .

(Latin) Rotuli de Liberate ac de Misis, pp. 117-51.

43. JOHN: CHARTER TO THE CHURCH (1214)

John, by the grace of God king of England, lord of Ireland, duke of Normandy and of Aquitaine, and count of Anjou, to arch-bishops, bishops, earls, barons, knights, bailiffs, and all who may hear or see these letters, greeting. Since, by the grace of God, a full agreement with regard to damages and usurpations during the time of the interdict has been established, of the pure and free will of each party, between us and our venerable fathers—[namely,] Stephen, archbishop of Canterbury, primate of all England, and cardinal of the Holy Roman Church; and the bishops, William of London, Eustace of Ely, Giles of Hereford, Jocelyn of Bath and Glastonbury, and Hugh of Lincoln—we wish, not merely to give them satisfaction to the best, God willing, of our ability, but also to make sound and use-ful provision for the whole English Church in perpetuity. Accord-ingly, no matter what sort of custom has hitherto been observed in the English Church, either in our own time or in that of our pred-ecessors, and no matter what right we have hitherto asserted for ourself in the election of any prelates, we [now], on the petition of those [prelates], for the health of our soul and [the souls] of our predecessors and successors, kings of England, of our own pure and free will and by the common assent of our barons, have granted and established and by this our charter have confirmed that in all and singular of the churches, monasteries, cathedrals, and convents of our whole realm of England the elections of whatsoever prelates, both greater and lesser, shall henceforth and forever be free, saving to us and our heirs the custody of vacant churches and monasteries that belong to us. We also promise that we will not hinder, nor will we permit or authorize our men to hinder, the electors in any or all of the aforesaid churches and monasteries, when prelacies become vacant, from freely appointing a pastor over themselves whenever they please, providing, however, that permission to elect has first been sought from us and our heirs—which [permission] we will not deny or delay. And if perchance—which God forbid!—we should deny or delay [permission], the electors shall nevertheless proceed to make a canonical election. Moreover, after the election has been held, our confirmation is to be requested; which likewise we will not deny, unless we can bring forward and lawfully prove some reasonable cause for which we ought not to give confirmation. Wherefore we will and straitly enjoin that, when churches or monasteries are vacant, no one shall act or presume to act in any way contrary to this our grant and constitution. If, however, any one at any time or in any way shall act contrary to it, may he incur the malediction of Almighty God and our own!

These are the witnesses. . . . November 21, in the sixteenth year of our reign.

(Latin) Stubbs, *Select Charters*, pp. 283 f.

44. MAGNA CARTA (1215)[1]

John, by the grace of God king of England, lord of Ireland, duke of Normandy and of Aquitaine, and count of Anjou, to his archbishops, bishops, abbots, earls, barons, justiciars, foresters, sheriffs, reeves, ministers, and all his bailiffs and faithful men, greeting. Know that, through the inspiration of God, for the health of our soul and [*the souls*] *of all our ancestors and heirs, for the honour of God and the exaltation of Holy Church, and for the betterment of our realm, by the counsel of our venerable fathers*[2] *. . . , of our nobles*[3] *. . . , and of our other faithful men—*

1. We have in the first place granted to God and by this our present charter have confirmed, for us and our heirs forever, that the English Church shall be free and shall have its rights entire and its liberties inviolate. *And how we wish* [*that freedom*] *to be observed appears from this, that of our own pure and free will, before the conflict that arose between us and our barons, we granted and by our charter confirmed the liberty of election that is considered of prime importance and necessity for the English Church,*[4] *and we obtained confirmation of it from the lord pope Innocent III—which* [*charter*] *we will observe ourself and we wish to be observed in good faith by our heirs forever.* We have also granted to all freemen of our

[1] John's charter was reissued under Henry III in 1216 and again in 1217, at both times with considerable revision. The second reissue was confirmed with minor changes by Henry III in 1225, after he had been declared of age, and this remained the official Magna Carta of subsequent reigns. Parts of the original charter omitted after 1215 are here printed in italics. It has not been thought necessary to show how the introductory and final clauses were modified in each reissue, but noteworthy alterations of the numbered articles are given in the footnotes. The latter also include explanations of the more obscure words and phrases. For more detailed comment, see McKechnie, *Magna Carta;* and for all points connected with the reissues, see Faith Thompson, *The First Century of Magna Carta.*

[2] Here in the text follow the names of eleven ecclesiastics.

[3] Here in the text follow the names of sixteen lay nobles.

[4] Above, no. 43.

kingdom, for us and our heirs forever, all the liberties hereinunder written, to be had and held by them and their heirs of us and our heirs.

2. If any one of our earls or barons or other men holding of us in chief dies, and if when he dies his heir is of full age and owes relief, [that heir] shall have his inheritance for the ancient relief: namely, the heir or heirs of an earl £100 for the whole barony of an earl; the heir or heirs of a baron £100 for a whole barony; the heir or heirs of a knight 100s. at most for a whole knight's fee.[5] And let whoever owes less give less, according to the ancient custom of fiefs.

3. If, however, the heir of any such person is under age[6] and is in wardship, he shall, when he comes of age, have his inheritance without relief and without fine.[7]

4. The guardian of the land of such an heir who is under age shall not take from the land of the heir more than reasonable issues and reasonable customs and reasonable services, and this without destruction and waste of men or things. And if we entrust the wardship of any such land to a sheriff or to any one else who is to answer to us for its issues, and if he causes destruction or waste of [what is under] wardship, we will exact compensation from him; and the land shall be entrusted to two discreet and lawful men of that fief, who shall answer for the issues to us or the man to whom we may assign them. And if we give or sell the wardship of any such land to any one, and if he causes destruction or waste of it, he shall forfeit that wardship and it shall be given to two discreet and lawful men of that fief, who likewise shall answer to us as aforesaid.

5. Moreover, the guardian, so long as he has wardship of the land, shall from the issues of that same land keep up the houses, parks, preserves, fish-ponds, mills, and other things belonging to that land. And to the heir, when he comes of full age, [the guardian] shall give all his land, stocked with ploughs[8] *and produce,*[9] *according to what crops may be seasonable and to what the issues of the land can reasonably permit.*

6. Heirs shall be married without disparagement; *yet so that,*

---

[5] On the interpretation of this article, see J. H. Round, in *Magna Carta Commemoration Essays,* pp. 46 f.

[6] In the reissues this article ends as follows: "his lord shall not have wardship over him or over his land before receiving his homage. And when such heir, being under wardship, comes of age—that is to say, [attains] his twenty-first year—he shall have his inheritance without relief and without fine; so that, although he may become a knight while he is yet under age, his land shall nevertheless remain under the wardship of his lords until the term aforesaid."

[7] A term often used for an offering or a composition.

[8] In the reissues this article ends as follows: "and with all other things as, at least, he received it. All these [provisions] are to be observed with regard to custody over archbishoprics, bishoprics, abbeys, priories, churches, and vacant prelacies that belong to us, except that rights of this sort ought not to be sold."

[9] *Wainnagium,* by which the context forces us to understand chiefly harvested crops necessary for seed and the upkeep of the estate.

before the marriage is contracted, it shall be announced to the blood-relatives of the said heir.

7. A widow shall have her marriage portion and inheritance immediately after the death of her husband and without difficulty; nor shall she give anything for her dowry or for her marriage portion or for her inheritance—which inheritance she and her husband were holding on the day of that husband's death. And after his death she shall remain in the house[10] of her husband for forty days, within which her dowry shall be assigned to her.[11]

8. No widow shall be forced to marry so long as she wishes to live without a husband; yet so that she shall give security against marrying without our consent if she holds of us, or without the consent of her lord if she holds of another.

9. Neither we nor our bailiffs will seize any land or revenue for any debt, so long as the chattels of the debtor are sufficient to repay the debt;[12] nor shall the sureties of that debtor be distrained so long as the chief debtor is himself able to pay the debt. And if the chief debtor, having nothing with which to pay,[13] defaults in payment of the debt, the sureties shall be responsible for the debt; and, if they wish, they shall have the lands and revenues of the debtor until satisfaction is made to them for the debt which they previously paid on his behalf, unless the chief debtor proves that he is quit of such responsibility toward the said sureties.

10. *If any one has taken anything, whether much or little, by way of loan from Jews, and if he dies before that debt is paid, the debt shall not carry usury so long as the heir is under age, from whomsoever he may hold. And if that debt falls into our hands, we will take only the principal contained in the note.*

11. *And if any one dies owing a debt to Jews, his wife shall have her dowry and shall pay nothing on that debt. And if the said deceased is survived by children who are under age, necessities shall be provided for them in proportion to the tenement that belonged to the deceased; and the debt shall be paid from the remainder, saving the service of the lords. In the same way let action be taken with regard to debts owed to others besides Jews.*

12. *Scutage or aid shall be levied in our kingdom only by the common counsel of our kingdom, except for ransoming our body, for*

---

[10] Changed in the second reissue to "principal dwelling."

[11] See above, p. 47, n. 3. The second reissue adds: "unless it has been assigned to her earlier, or unless that house is a castle. And if she leaves the castle, she shall at once be provided with a suitable house, in which she may honourably dwell until her dowry is assigned to her as aforesaid. And in the meantime she shall have her reasonable estovers of common. Moreover, she shall be assigned as dowry one-third of all the land held by her husband during his lifetime, unless she was endowed with less at the church door." Estovers of common were a share of the produce.

[12] The reissues here insert the clause: "and the debtor is himself ready to satisfy [the debt] from them."

[13] The reissues here insert the clause: "or being unwilling to pay when he can."

knighting our eldest son, and for once marrying our eldest daughter; and for these [purposes] only a reasonable aid shall be taken. The same provision shall hold with regard to the aids of the city of London.[14]

13. And the city of London shall have all its ancient liberties and free customs, *both by land and by water.* Besides we will and grant that all the other cities, boroughs, towns,[15] and ports shall have all their liberties and free customs.

14. *And in order to have the common counsel of the kingdom for assessing aid other than in the three cases aforesaid, or for assessing scutage, we will cause the archbishops, bishops, abbots, earls, and greater barons to be summoned by our letters individually; and besides we will cause to be summoned in general, through our sheriffs and bailiffs, all those who hold of us in chief—for a certain day, namely, at the end of forty days at least, and to a certain place. And in all such letters of summons we will state the cause of the summons; and when the summons has thus been made, the business assigned for the day shall proceed according to the counsel of those who are present, although all those summoned may not come.*

15. *In the future we will not grant to any one that he may take aid from his freemen, except for ransoming his body, for knighting his eldest son, and for once marrying his eldest daughter; and for these [purposes] only a reasonable aid shall be taken.*

16. No one shall be distrained to render greater service from a knight's fee, or from any other free tenement, than is thence owed.

17. Common pleas shall not follow our court, but shall be held in some definite place.

18. Assizes of novel disseisin, of mort d'ancestor, *and of darrein presentment*[16] shall be held only in their counties [of origin] and in this way: we, or our chief justice if we are out of the kingdom, will send two justices through each county[17] *four times a year; and they, together with four knights of each county elected by the county*

---

[14] Literally, "in the same way let it be done. . . ." The Londoners had wanted a guarantee of exemption from forced taxes, but secured only this vague and ambiguous article; see C. Stephenson, *Borough and Town,* p. 183.

[15] The reissues here make specific mention of the barons of the Cinque Ports; see above, p. 103, n. 17.

[16] See no. 33.

[17] The second reissue substitutes the following provisions: "once a year; and they, together with the knights of the counties, shall hold the aforesaid assizes in the counties. And those matters which cannot be concluded during that visit in the county by the aforesaid justices, sent to hold the said assizes, shall be concluded by the same men elsewhere on their eyre. And those matters which, owing to the difficulty of some particulars, cannot be determined by the same men shall be referred to our justices of the bench and there concluded. Assizes of darrein presentment shall always be held before the justices of the bench and there concluded." The court of the bench (*de banco*) was that which became known as the court of common pleas; see Pollock and Maitland, I. 198 f.

[*court*], *shall hold the aforesaid assizes in the county, on the day and at the place* [*set for the meeting*] *of the county* [*court*].

19. *And if within the day* [*set for the meeting*] *of the county* [*court*] *the aforesaid assizes cannot be held, as many knights and free tenants shall remain of those present at the county* [*court*] *on that day as may be needed for holding the trials, according as the business is greater or less.*

20. A freeman shall be amerced for a small offence only according to the degree of the offence; and for a grave offence he shall be amerced according to the gravity of the offence, saving his contenement.[18] And a merchant shall be amerced in the same way, saving his merchandise; and a villein[19] in the same way, saving his wainage[20] —should they fall into our mercy. And none of the aforesaid amercements shall be imposed except by the oaths of good men from the neighbourhood.[21]

21. Earls and barons shall be amerced only by their peers,[22] and only according to the degree of the misdeed.

22. No clergyman shall be amerced with respect to his lay tenement except in the manner of those aforesaid, not according to the value of his ecclesiastical benefice.[23]

23. Neither vill nor man shall be distrained to make bridges on river-banks, except such as by right and ancient custom ought to do so.

24. No sheriff, constable, coroner, or other bailiff of ours shall hold the pleas of our crown.[24]

25. *All counties, hundreds, wapentakes, and trithings[25] shall remain at the ancient farms without any increment, with the exception of our demesne manors.*

26. If any one holding a lay fee of us dies, and if our sheriff or bailiff shows our letters patent of summons concerning a debt that the deceased owed to us, our sheriff or bailiff shall be permitted, by view of lawful men, to attach and record such chattels of the deceased as are found on the lay fief to the value of that debt; so that, moreover, nothing shall thence be removed until a debt that is manifestly owed shall be paid to us. And the residue shall be left to the executors for carrying out the will of the deceased. And if nothing is owed us from it, all the chattels shall be yielded to [disposition by] the deceased, saving to his wife and children their reasonable portions.

27. *If any freeman dies intestate, his chattels, under ecclesiastical*

---

[18] Sufficient property to guarantee sustenance for himself and his family.

[19] The second reissue here inserts: "of some one else, not our own."

[20] See above, p. 116, n. 9.

[21] Under such conditions the amercement was said to be afeered.

[22] Social equals.

[23] The wording of this article is changed in the reissues, but without affecting its meaning.

[24] See above, p. 53, n. 16.

[25] Certain large counties were divided into trithings or ridings, and these were subdivided into hundreds or wapentakes.

inspection, shall be distributed by the hands of his near relatives and friends, saving to each [creditor] the debts that the deceased owed him.

28. No constable or other bailiff of ours shall take grain or other chattels of any one without immediate payment therefor in money, unless by the will of the seller he may secure postponement of that [payment].[26]

29. No constable shall distrain any knight to pay money for castle-guard when he is willing to perform that service himself, or through another good man if for reasonable cause he is unable to perform it himself. And if we lead or send him on a military expedition, he shall be quit of [castle-]guard for so long a time as he shall be with the army[27] *at our command.*

30. No sheriff or bailiff of ours, nor any other person, shall take the horses or carts of any freeman for carrying service,[28] *except by the will of that freeman.*

31. Neither we nor our bailiffs[29] will take some one else's wood for [repairing] castles or for doing any other work of ours, except by the will of him to whom the wood belongs.

32. We will hold the lands of those convicted of felony only for a year and a day, and the lands shall then be given to the lords of the fiefs [concerned].

33. All fish-weirs shall henceforth be entirely removed from the Thames and the Medway and throughout all England except along the sea-coasts.

34. Henceforth the writ called praecipe shall not be issued for any one concerning any tenement whereby a freeman may lose his court.[30]

35. There shall be one measure of wine throughout our entire kingdom, and one measure of ale; also one measure of grain, namely, the quarter of London; and one width of dyed cloth, russet [cloth], and hauberk [cloth],[31] namely, two yards between the borders. With weights, moreover, it shall be as with measures.

36. Nothing henceforth shall be taken or given for the writ of

---

[26] Changed in the second reissue to read: "No constable or his bailiff shall take grain or other chattels of any one who is not of the vill where the castle is situated without immediate payment therefor in money, unless by the will of the seller he may secure postponement of that [payment]. If, moreover, he is of that vill, payment must be made within forty days."

[27] The reissues here substitute: "to perform the service owed from his fief."

[28] The reissues end the clause as follows: "unless he makes the anciently established payment [for such service]: namely, for a two-horse cart 10*d.* a day and for a three-horse cart 14*d.* a day. No cart from the demesne of any ecclesiastical parson or knight, or of any lady, shall be taken by the aforesaid bailiffs."

[29] The second reissue here inserts: "nor other men."

[30] That is to say, through which procedure a baron or other freeholder may lose jurisdiction over his men; see no. 33F.

[31] Perhaps cloth to be worn under a hauberk.

inquisition concerning life and limbs,[32] but it shall be issued gratis and shall not be denied.

37. If any one holding of us by fee-farm or by socage or by burg-age[33] holds land of some one else by military service, on account of that fee-farm or socage or burgage we are not to have the wardship of the heir or of the land that is another's fee, unless the said [land held by] fee-farm owes military service. By virtue of some little ser-jeanty held of us by the service of rendering knives or arrows or something of the sort, we are not to have wardship of any one's heir or of land that he holds of another by military service.

38. No bailiff shall henceforth put any one to his law[34] by merely bringing suit [against him] without trustworthy witnesses presented for this purpose.

39. No freeman shall be captured or imprisoned or disseised[35] or outlawed or exiled or in any way destroyed, nor will we go against him or send against him, except by the lawful judgment of his peers or[36] by the law of the land.

40. To no one will we sell, to no one will we deny or delay right or justice.

41. All merchants[37] may safely and securely go away from Eng-land, come to England, stay in and go through England, by land or by water, for buying and selling under right and ancient customs and without any evil exactions,[38] except in time of war if they are from the land at war with us. And if such persons are found in our land at the beginning of a war, they shall be arrested without injury to their bodies or goods until we or our chief justice can ascertain how the merchants of our land who may then be found in the land at war with us are to be treated. And if our men are to be safe, the others shall be safe in our land.

42. *Every one shall henceforth be permitted, saving our fealty, to leave our kingdom and to return in safety and security, by land*

---

[32] Also called the writ *de odio et atia*; it was designed to relieve a man of trial by combat when he had been appealed "through spite and hatred." At this point the third reissue inserts: "by him who seeks the inquisition."

[33] These three tenures were alike in being free, though non-military.

[34] See above, p. 77, n. 3. The second reissue expands this phrase to "mani-fest law or oath." The new provision was probably intended to cover substitutes for the ordeal, which had been abolished by the Lateran Council of 1215.

[35] The second reissue adds: "of any free tenement or liberties or free customs."

[36] Presumably meaning "and"; cf. art. 56. The interpretation is also aided by John's writ of May, 1215 (*Rotuli Litterarum Patentium,* I, 141): "Know that we have granted to our barons who are opposing us that we will neither capture nor disseise them or their men, nor will we go against them with force or with arms, except by the law of our kingdom or by the judgment of their peers in our court. . . ." See McIlwain, in *Magna Carta Commemora-tion Essays,* pp. 122 f.; and, for another interpretation, M. Radin, *Anglo-Amer-ican Legal History,* pp. 165 f.

[37] The reissues here insert: "unless they have earlier been given public prohibi-tion."

[38] *Malis toltis* (maltotes); see no. 51c.

or by water, except in the common interest of the realm for a brief period during wartime, and excepting [always] men imprisoned or outlawed according to the law of the kingdom and people from a land at war with us and merchants, who are to be treated as aforesaid.

43. If any one holds of any escheat—such as the honour of Wallingford, Nottingham, Boulogne, Lancaster, or the other escheats that are in our hands and are baronies—and if he dies, his heir shall give only such relief and shall render us only such service as would be due to the baron if that barony were in the hands of the baron; and we shall hold it in the same way that the baron held it.[39]

44. *Men dwelling outside the forest shall no longer, in consequence of a general summons, come before our justices of the forest, unless they are [involved] in a plea [of the forest] or are sureties of some person or persons who have been arrested for [offences against] the forest.*[40]

45. *We will appoint as justiciars, constables, sheriffs, or bailiffs only such men as know the law of the kingdom and well desire to observe it.*

46. All barons who have founded abbeys, concerning which they have charters from kings of England or [enjoy] ancient tenures, shall have the custody of those [abbeys] during vacancies, as they ought to have.[41]

47. *All forests that have been afforested in our time shall at once be disafforested; and the same shall be done with regard to river-banks which in our time we have placed under ban.*[42]

48. *Concerning all bad customs of forest and warrens, of foresters and warreners, of sheriffs and their officers, and of river-banks and their wardens, inquisition shall at once be made in each county through twelve knights of that same county placed under oath, who ought to be elected by the good men of the same county. And within forty days after the inquisition has been made, they shall be utterly abolished by the same [knights], so that they shall never be restored;*

---

[39] The second reissue adds: "Nor shall we, by virtue of such barony or escheat, have any escheat or [enjoy] wardship over any of our men unless he who held the barony or escheat [also] held of us in chief elsewhere." And after this a new article is inserted, as follows: "Henceforth no freeman shall give or sell to any one so much of his land that from what remains of it whatever service pertains to the fief cannot adequately be performed for the lord to whom it is owed."

[40] This became art. 2 of the Forest Charter, no. 45.

[41] Changed in the second reissue to read: "All patrons of abbeys who have charters from kings of England concerning their advowson, or [who enjoy] ancient tenure or possession [of that privilege], shall have custody of those [abbeys] when they are vacant, as they ought to have and as has been declared above."

[42] That is to say, reserved for the king's hawking. Part of this article was incorporated in the Forest Charter (no. 45); the rest was made into a new article in the second reissue.

in such fashion [however] that we may have prior notice, or our justiciar [may] if we are not in England.

49. *We will immediately restore all hostages and charters which were delivered to us by Englishmen as security for the peace or for faithful service.*

50. *We will utterly remove from their offices the relatives of Gerard d'Athée, Engelard de Cigogné, Peter and Guy and Andrew de Chanceaux, Guy de Cigogné, Geoffrey de Martigny and his brothers, Philip Marc and his brothers and his nephew Geoffrey, together with all their adherents, so that henceforth they shall have no office in England.*

51. *And immediately after the restoration of peace we will remove from the kingdom all alien knights, crossbowmen, serjeants, and mercenaries, who have come with horses and arms to the injury of the kingdom.*

52. *If any one, without the lawful judgment of his peers, has been disseised or deprived by us of his lands, castles, liberties, or rights, we will at once restore them to him. And if a dispute arises in this connection, then let the matter be decided by the judgment of the twenty-five barons, concerning whom provision is made below in [the article on] security for the peace. With regard, however, to all those [possessions] of which any one, without lawful judgment of his peers, was disseised or deprived by King Henry, our father, or by King Richard, our brother—which possessions we have in our hands or which are held by others whose possession we are bound to warrant—we are to have respite for the ordinary term of crusaders,[43] except those [possessions] concerning which suit was brought or inquest was made by our precept before we took the cross. Moreover, when we return from our journey, or if perchance we abandon our journey, we will at once administer full justice in such matters.*

53. *Moreover, we are to have similar respite and in the same way with regard to the disafforestation or retention of the forests which Henry, our father, or Richard, our brother, afforested; with regard to wardships over lands of another's fee, which sort of wardships we have hitherto enjoyed on account of a fee that any one holds of us by military service,[44] and with regard to abbeys which were founded in a fee other than our own, and over which the lord of the fee has asserted that he has the right. And when we return, or if we abandon our journey, we will at once give full justice to those making complaints in such matters.*

54. No one shall be seized or imprisoned on the appeal of a woman for the death of any one but her husband.[45]

---

[43] The three years' grace enjoyed by crusaders in meeting their obligations.

[44] Cf. art. 37.

[45] The second reissue adds three new articles:

"Henceforth no county [court] shall be held oftener than once a month; and wherever a longer time [between sessions] has been customary, let it be longer. Nor shall any sheriff or his bailiff make his tourn* through a hundred

55. *All fines which have been made with us unjustly and contrary to the law of the land, and all amercements made unjustly and contrary to the law of the land, are to be entirely pardoned; or decision is thereon to be made by the judgment of the twenty-five barons concerning whom provision is made below in [the article on] security for the peace, or by the judgment of the majority of them, together with the aforesaid Stephen, archbishop of Canterbury, if he can be present, and other men whom he may wish to associate with himself for this purpose—and if he cannot be present, the business shall nevertheless proceed without him; yet so that, if any one or more of the twenty-five barons aforesaid are [involved] in a dispute of this kind, they shall be removed so far as this judgment is concerned, and others, elected and sworn for this purpose, shall be substituted in their places by the rest of the twenty-five.*

56. *If, without the lawful judgment of their peers, we have disseised or deprived Welshmen of their lands, liberties, or other things in England or in Wales, [the same] shall be immediately restored to them. And if a dispute arises in this connection, then decision is thereon to be made in the [Welsh] march by the judgment of their peers—according to the law of England for their tenements in England, according to the law of Wales for their tenements in Wales, and according to the law of the march for their tenements in the march. Welshmen shall act in the same way toward us and our men.*

57. *Moreover, with regard to those [possessions] of which any Welshman, without the lawful judgment of his peers, was disseised or deprived by King Henry, our father, or King Richard, our brother.*[46] . . .

58. *We will at once restore the son of Llewelyn and all the [other]*

more often than twice a year; and [then he shall hold the court] only at the due and accustomed place [and time], namely, once after Easter and again after Michaelmas. And view of frankpledge shall without excuse be made then, at that Michaelmas term; and in such a way that every one shall enjoy the liberties which he was accustomed to have in the time of King Henry, our grandfather, or which he has subsequently acquired. The view of frankpledge, moreover, shall be made in this way: namely, so that our peace is maintained, the tithings are [kept] whole as has been accustomed, and the sheriff does not seek excuses [for additional revenue], but is content with what the sheriff was accustomed to have for making his view in the time of King Henry, our grandfather.

"Henceforth no one shall be permitted to give his land to any religious house in such a way as to receive it back, to be held of that house; nor shall any religious house be permitted to accept the land of any one on condition that it be given back, to be held by the man from whom it has been received. If, moreover, any one henceforth grants his land to any religious house in this way and is convicted of so doing, his grant shall be utterly quashed and that land shall be forfeit to the lord of the fief.

"Scutage shall henceforth be taken as it was customarily taken in the time of King Henry, our grandfather."

* See Pollock and Maitland, I, 530 f.

[46] The rest of this article repeats the ending of art. 52.

hostages of Wales, together with the charters that were given us as security for the peace.

59. *We will act toward Alexander, king of the Scots, in the matter of restoring his sisters and the [other] hostages, together with his liberties and rights in the same way as we act toward our other barons of England,*[47] *unless by the charters which we have from his father William, one time king of the Scots, the action ought to be otherwise—and this shall be [determined] by the judgment of his peers in our court.*

60. Now all these aforesaid customs and liberties, which we have granted, in so far as concerns us, to be observed in our kingdom toward our men, all men of our kingdom, both clergy and laity, shall, in so far as concerns them, observe toward their men.

61. *Since moreover for [the love of] God, for the improvement of our kingdom, and for the better allayment of the conflict that has arisen between us and our barons, we have granted all these [liberties] aforesaid, wishing them to enjoy those [liberties] by full and firm establishment forever, we have made and granted them the following security: namely, that the barons shall elect twenty-five barons of the kingdom, whomsoever they please, who to the best of their ability should observe, hold, and cause to be observed the peace and liberties that we have granted to them and have confirmed by this our present charter; so that, specifically, if we or our justiciar or our bailiffs or any of our ministers are in any respect delinquent toward any one or trangress any article of the peace or the security, and if the delinquency is shown to four barons of the aforesaid twenty-five barons, those four barons shall come to us, or to our justiciar if we are out of the kingdom, to explain to us the wrong, asking that without delay we cause this wrong to be redressed. And if within a period of forty days, counted from the time that notification is made to us, or to our justiciar if we are out of the kingdom, we do not redress the wrong, or, if we are out of the kingdom, our justiciar does not redress it, the four barons aforesaid shall refer that case to the rest of the twenty-five barons, and those twenty-five barons, together with the community of the entire country, shall distress and injure us in all ways possible—namely, by capturing our castles, lands, and possessions and in all ways that they can—until they secure redress according to their own decision, saving our person and [the person] of our queen and [the persons] of our children. And when redress has been made, they shall be obedient to us as they were before. And any one in the land who wishes shall swear that, for carrying out the aforesaid matters, he will obey the commands of the twenty-five barons aforesaid and that he, with his men, will injure us to the best of his ability; and we publicly and freely give licence of [thus] swearing to every one who wishes to do so, and to no one will we ever prohibit [such] swearing. Moreover, all those of the land who of*

---

[47] The Scottish king held the earldom of Huntingdon and other English fiefs of King John.

themselves and by their own free will are unwilling to take the oath for the twenty-five barons, with them to distress and injure us, we will by our mandate cause to swear [such an oath] as aforesaid. And if any one of the twenty-five barons dies or departs from the land, or in any other way is prevented from carrying out these aforesaid matters, the rest of the twenty-five barons aforesaid shall by their own decision choose another in his place, who is to be sworn in the same way as the others. Moreover, in all the matters entrusted to those twenty-five barons for execution, if perchance the same twenty-five are present and disagree among themselves in some respect, or if certain of those summoned are unwilling or unable to be present, that which the majority of those present may provide or command shall be held as settled and established, just as if all twenty-five had agreed to it. And the aforesaid twenty-five shall swear that they will faithfully observe all that has been set forth above. And neither of ourself nor through others will we procure from any one anything whereby any of these concessions and liberties may be revoked or diminished; and should anything of the sort be procured, it shall be null and void, and we will never make use of it either of ourself or through others.

62. And to all we freely pardon and condone all the ill-will, indignation, and rancour that from the beginning of the conflict have arisen between us and our men, both clergy and laity. Furthermore, to all, whether clergy or laity, we fully pardon and condone, in so far as pertains to us, all trespasses committed on account of the said conflict since Easter in the sixteenth year of our reign until the re-establishment of peace. And besides we have caused to be drawn up for them letters patent of the lord Stephen, archbishop of Canterbury, of the lord Henry, archbishop of Dublin, of the bishops aforesaid, and of Master Pandulf,[48] in witness of that security and the concessions aforesaid.

63. Wherefore we wish and straitly enjoin that the English Church shall be free and that the men in our kingdom shall have and hold all the aforesaid liberties, rights, and grants well and in peace, freely and quietly, fully and completely, for themselves and their heirs from us and our heirs, in all things and in all places forever, as aforesaid. Moreover, it has been sworn both on our part and on the part of the barons that all the aforesaid [provisions] shall be observed in good faith and without malicious intent.

By the witness of the aforesaid men and of many others. Given by our hand in the meadow that is called Runnymede between Windsor and Staines, June 15, in the seventeenth year of our reign.

(Latin) Ibid., pp. 292 f., 336 f., 341 f., 350 f.

---

[48] The papal legate.

SECTION
✾ IV ✾

HENRY III AND EDWARD I

THAT the period from 1216 to 1307 is one of the most important in the whole constitutional history of England has long been recognized. At the accession of Henry III the royal government was essentially that of his grandfather—an amazingly efficient system for the age, but one still contained within the prescriptive custom of feudalism. At the death of Edward I feudal principles, though by no means forgotten, had ceased to dominate political practice. The framework of what we know as the English constitution had been solidly built. How this development has tended to simplify the task of selecting illustrative material may at once be appreciated by turning to the documents in the following section. Our wealth of sources for the thirteenth century cannot so easily be classified.

One thread that can be followed throughout the confusion is Magna Carta, the reissues of which have already been summarized (no. 44). Intimately associated with them from the outset of Henry III's reign was his Forest Charter, here given in full. Another related document, the Provisions of Oxford, since it was never put into effect, has been considerably abbreviated. The Provisions of Westminster, being largely concerned with details of private law, have been cut down to a few articles. And it has not seemed necessary to retain more than the principal clauses in the famous settlements of 1264 and 1266 (no. 47D, E). Likewise the product of a baronial crisis was Edward I's Confirmation of the Charters, which, however, embodied much more than a reissue of Magna Carta and the Forest Charter. In it there clearly appeared an issue that was long to be of paramount interest—parliamentary control of taxation.

By 1297 the parliament of the ensuing centuries, or at least its constituent elements, had definitely emerged, and precedents had been set with regard to its deliberative, judicial, and fiscal powers. To explain when and how all these complicated developments took place is a difficult problem, to which no complete solution is possible in a brief source book. All that has been at-

tempted here is to illustrate its more significant phases through
a number of extracts from the rolls of Henry III and Edward I:
principally writs of summons for meetings with the king or his
ministers, ordinances for the collection of taxes, and demands
for the performance of other service. From such documents it
is hoped that the student may obtain a fairly accurate knowledge
of how the king made up his greater councils, together with a
few revealing glimpses of military, naval, and financial administration. Edward's major statutes are given at least in part, and a
good many pages have been devoted to a variety of judicial
records.

The materials available under this last heading are so extensive as to defy representative selection within brief scope. No
effort has been made to set forth in adequate fashion the growth
of the common law. Under no. 54 will be found merely some
typical entries in the rolls, illustrating such matters as manorial
justice and administration, the beginnings of jury trial in criminal cases, the local activities of the coroner, the gradual differen-
tiation of the central courts, and the adjudication of petitions in
parliament. For additional information on these subjects the student is referred, not only to the standard works on English law,
but also to the introductions of the volumes published by the
Selden Society—a series which includes various kinds of records
that have been entirely passed over in the present collection.

Of the enormous mass of other official writings produced in
the thirteenth century, lack of space prevents the inclusion of
more than a few extraordinary pieces. Thus the selections already
given from pipe rolls, household accounts, and similar records
must serve to exemplify the continuations of such enrolments
in the later age. And in the field of borough institutions an im-
pressive accumulation of charters and customals has also been
left to one side. How old privileges were extended to new communities and how more elaborate machinery came to be set up
for the government of the greater towns can be readily learned
from the second volume of Ballard's *British Borough Charters,*
which is provided with an admirable introduction by James Tait.
On the other hand, a place has been made for two early forms
of the oath taken by royal councillors and for Edward I's Household Ordinance—next to the *Constitutio Domus Regis* (no. 29)
the oldest regulation of the sort that has survived.

For the constitutional development of thirteenth-century England the work of Stubbs remains generally valuable, although some of his dominant ideas have now been abandoned by most historians. Among the books that have brought a new approach to the study of parliamentary origins may be mentioned the following :[1] G. B. Adams, *The Origin of the English Constitution;* C. H. McIlwain, *The High Court of Parliament;* D. Pasquet, *Essay on the Origins of the English House of Commons;* A. F. Pollard, *The Evolution of Parliament;* A. B. White, *Self-Government at the King's Command;* Petit-Dutaillis and Lefebvre *Studies and Notes Supplementary to Stubbs' Constitutional History.* This last work is particularly valuable for its concise review of the literature on parliamentary origins, as well as for its chapters on the forest and forest law. T. F. Tout's volumes on *The Administrative History of Medieval England* provide much information concerning the more routine phases of the royal government. Sir Maurice Powicke in his *The Thirteenth Century* and his *King Henry III and the Lord Edward* discusses constitutional issues with much authority, as do B. Wilkinson in *Studies in the Constitutional History of England in the Thirteenth and Fourteenth Centuries,* and G. O. Sayles in *The Medieval Foundations of England.*

---

[1] See also the numerous essays by H. G. Richardson and G. Sayles: *Transactions of the Royal Historical Society,* Fourth Series, XI, 137 f.; *Bulletin of the Institute of Historical Research,* V, 129 f., and VI, 71 f.; likewise those cited below, pp. 152, n. 4, 186, n. 18.

[2] *Parliamentary Taxes on Personal Property 1290-1334,* recently published by the Mediaeval Academy of America.

45. HENRY III: CHARTER OF THE FOREST (1217)[1]

Henry, by the grace of God king of England, lord of Ireland, duke of Normandy and of Aquitaine, and count of Anjou, to his archbishops, bishops, abbots, priors, earls, barons, justiciars, foresters, sheriffs, reeves, ministers, and all his faithful men, greeting. Know that[2] . . . we have granted and by this present charter have confirmed, for us and our heirs forever, these liberties hereinunder written, to be held in our kingdom of England forever:—

---

[1] Issued as a supplement to Magna Carta during the minority of Henry III and confirmed by him, with only slight revision, in 1225. For the meaning of many technical words, as well as the general significance of the articles, see no. 35 and the notes to that document.

[2] The introductory clauses are largely copied from Magna Carta.

1. In the first place, all the forests which Henry, our grandfather, afforested shall be visited by good and lawful men; and if he afforested any woodland other than that of his own demesne to the damage of him to whom the woodland belonged, let it be disafforested. And if he afforested his own proper woodland, let it remain forest, saving common of herbage and other things in the same forest to those who were accustomed to have them before.

2. Men dwelling outside the forest shall no longer, in consequence of a general summons, come before our justices of the forest, unless they are [involved] in a plea [of the forest] or are sureties of some person or persons who have been arrested for [offences against] the forest.[3]

3. All forests, however, which were afforested by King Richard, our uncle, or by King John, our father, down to the time of our first coronation, shall at once be disafforested, excepting our own demesne woodland.

4. Archbishops, bishops, abbots, priors, earls, barons, knights, and [other] freeholders, who have woodlands of theirs in the forests, shall have their woodlands as they had them at the time of the first coronation of the aforesaid King Henry, our grandfather; so that they shall forever be quit of all purprestures, wastes, and assarts made in those woodlands from that time down to the beginning of the second year of our coronation. And whoever henceforth makes any waste, purpresture, or assart in those [woods] without our licence shall be responsible for such wastes and assarts.

5. Our regardors[4] shall go through the forests for making their regard as was customarily done in the time of the first coronation of the said Henry, our grandfather, and not otherwise.

6. The investigation or view of the lawing of dogs living within the forest shall henceforth be carried out whenever the regard should be made, namely, every three years; and then it should be made by the view and testimony of lawful men and not otherwise. And he whose dog is then found not to be lawed shall give as amercement 3s., and henceforth no ox shall be taken for [default of such] lawing. Moreover, the lawing shall be carried out by common assize as follows: three toes shall be cut off a forefoot without [injuring] the ball [of the foot]; nor shall dogs henceforth be lawed except in the places where they were customarily lawed at the time of the first coronation of King Henry, our grandfather.

7. No forester or beadle shall henceforth levy scotale,[5] or collect sheaves or oats or any grain or lambs or pigs; nor shall he take up any kind of collection. And by the view and oath of twelve regardors,

---

[3] Originally art. 44 of Magna Carta.

[4] Inspectors, whose duties are described below.

[5] The exaction of ale, or the equivalent in money, on the pretext of some festivity—a common abuse on the part of public officials.

when they make their regard, as many foresters shall be appointed to keep the forests as reasonably appear sufficient for keeping them.

8. No swainmote[6] shall henceforth be held in our kingdom oftener than three times a year: namely, at the beginning of the fortnight before the feast of St. Michael, when the agistors meet for the agistment of our demesne woodlands; and about the feast of St. Martin, when our agistors ought to receive our pannage—at which two swainmotes are to assemble the foresters, verderers,[7] and agistors, but no one else by compulsion. And the third swainmote shall be held at the beginning of the fortnight before the feast of St. John the Baptist, for the fawning of our beasts; and for holding that swainmote the foresters and verderers shall assemble, but no others by compulsion. And the verderers and foresters shall also meet every forty days throughout the year to inspect attachments for [offences in] the forest concerning both vert and venison, through presentment by the same foresters and in the presence of those attached. The aforesaid swainmotes, however, are to be held only in the counties where they have been customarily held.

9. Every freeman shall at his own pleasure provide agistment for his woodland in the forest and have his pannage. We also grant that every freeman may freely and without interference drive his swine through our demesne woodland in order to agist them in his own woods or wherever else he pleases. And if the swine of any freeman spend one night in our forest, that shall not be made the excuse for taking anything of his away from him.

10. Henceforth no one shall lose life or limbs on account of our hunting rights; but if any one is arrested and convicted of taking our venison, let him redeem himself by a heavy payment, if he has anything with which to redeem himself. And if he has nothing with which to redeem himself, let him lie in our prison for a year and a day. And if, after the year and the day, he can find sureties, let him be freed from prison; but if he cannot, let him abjure the realm of England.

11. Any archbishop, bishop, earl, or baron who crosses our forest may take one or two beasts by view of the forester, if he is present; if not, let a horn be blown so that this [hunting] may not appear to be carried on furtively.

12. Henceforth every freeman, in his wood or on his land that he has in the forest, may with impunity make a mill, fish-preserve, pond, marl-pit, ditch, or arable in cultivated land outside coverts, provided that no injury is thereby given to any neighbour.

13. Every freeman may in his own woods have eyries of hawks, sparrow-hawks, falcons, eagles, and herons; and he may also have honey that is found in his woods.

14. Hereafter no forester who does not hold in fee, rendering to us

---

[6] Or swanimote—a court of the king's swineherds and other forest employees, with the functions here described.

[7] Men of the knightly class chosen in the county courts; cf. no. 35, art. 7.

a farm for his bailiwick, shall levy any road-tax (*chiminagium*) in his bailiwick. A forester, however, who holds in fee, rendering to us a farm for his bailiwick, may levy road-tax: namely, 2*d.* on a cart for a half-year, and 2*d.* for the other half-year; ½*d.* on a horse that carries loads for a half-year, and ½*d.* for the other half-year—and this only on those who, from outside his bailiwick, come by his licence into his bailiwick as merchants, to buy wood, timber, bark, or charcoal, and to carry it elsewhere to sell where they please. And road-tax shall not be levied on any other cart or pack-horse. And road-tax shall be taken only in the places where it has been anciently accustomed and owed. Moreover, those men who carry on their backs wood, bark, or charcoal for sale, although they may therefrom make their living, shall henceforth pay no road-tax. Moreover, no road-tax shall be paid to our foresters from the woods of other men, but only from our demesne woods.

15. All men outlawed merely for [offences against] the forest, from the time of King Henry, our grandfather, to our first coronation, may without interference return to our peace and provide good sureties that hereafter they will commit no offence with regard to our forest.

16. No castellan or other man [of the locality] shall hold pleas of the forest, concerning either vert or venison; but every forester holding in fee shall make attachments for pleas of the forest, concerning both vert and venison, and shall present them to the verderers of the provinces; and when they have been enrolled and closed under the seals of the verderers, they shall be presented to our chief forester when he comes into those parts to hold the pleas of the forest; and they shall be brought to conclusion before him.

17. Now these liberties with regard to the forest we have granted to all, saving to the archbishops, bishops, abbots, priors, earls, barons, knights, and other persons both ecclesiastical and lay, [also] to the Templars and the Hospitallers, the liberties and free customs in forests and outside them, in warrens and in other things, that they earlier had. Moreover, all these aforesaid liberties and customs, which we have granted to be observed, in so far as concerns us, toward our men, all persons of our kingdom, both clergy and laity, shall, in so far as concerns them, observe toward their men.

Since indeed we as yet have no seal, we have had the present charter sealed with the seal of our venerable father the lord Gualo, cardinal priest of the title[8] of St. Martin's and legate of the Apostolic See, and that of William Marshal, earl of Pembroke, rector of us and of our kingdom. By the witness of the aforesaid men and many others. Given by the hand of the aforesaid lord legate and of William Marshal at St. Paul's, London, November 6, in the second year of our reign.

(Latin) Stubbs, *Select Charters,* pp. 344 f.

---

[8] I.e., a parish in the city of Rome.

46. LETTERS CLOSE AND PATENT (1218-54)

(A) Collection of Scutage (1218)

The king to the sheriff of Worcester, greeting. We command you that, on sight of these letters, you immediately distrain all those men of your bailiwick who hold of us in chief, and who have not brought you our letters regarding the collection of their scutage by their own hand,[1] without delay to pay you the scutage owed us, namely, *2m.* from each knight's fee (*scuto*). And as you cherish your life and all that you have, see to it that you have all that scutage at our exchequer on Sunday next after the coming Mid-Lent. You are likewise to distrain all those of your bailiwick who have received our letters regarding the collection of their scutage by their own hand, for which they should have accounted at our exchequer at terms now passed, that on the same day, avoiding all excuse and delay, they account to us at our exchequer, under your inspection, for the scutage which they owe us. And you are there to have with you our letters which they bring you regarding the collection of their scutage by their own hand.

(Latin) *Rotuli Litterarum Clausarum,* I, 377.

(B) Summons Before the Itinerant Justices (1219)[2]

The king to the sheriff of York and Northumberland, greeting. Summon through good summoners all archbishops, bishops, abbots, earls, barons, knights, and freeholders of all your bailiwick, also four lawful men and the reeve from every vill and twelve lawful burgesses from every borough throughout your entire bailiwick, together with all other men of your bailiwick who by custom and right should come before our itinerant justices, to be at York before our justices a fortnight after St. Martin's day in order to hear and obey our precept. You are also to have brought before them at that time all pleas of the crown which have not been tried, and which have arisen since the assizes were last held in those parts before itinerant justices in the time of the lord king John, our father; likewise all attachments pertaining to those pleas, and all assizes and all pleas which have been assigned to the first assizes before the justices, together

---

[1] The tax was often passed on to the sub-tenants. See, for example, the royal authorizations of 1223 (*Rotuli Litterarum Clausarum,* I, 570 f.): "The king to the sheriff of Northampton, greeting. Know that we have granted to our beloved and faithful uncle, William, earl of Salisbury, that he may have from his knights who hold of him in your bailiwick his scutage for our army of Wales, in which he now is by our order: namely, *2m.* from a knight's fee. And therefore we command you that you cause him to have the said scutage as aforesaid. . . ." "The king to the sheriff of Middlesex, greeting. Know that we have granted to William, earl of Salisbury, that he may have from his freemen in your bailiwick a reasonable aid for maintaining himself in our service with our army of Wales, in which he now is by our order: namely, *2m.* from a knight's fee. And therefore we command you. . . ."

[2] This is a regular form, found year after year in the rolls.

with the writs for those assizes and pleas—so that, through your default or that of your summons, none of those assizes and pleas shall fail to be held. You are also to have it proclaimed and made known throughout your entire bailiwick that all assizes and all pleas for which a day has been set, but which have not been concluded before our justices at Westminster, shall be brought thither to York before the aforesaid justices in the same state as when, by our precept, they were held over at Westminster. Also summon through good summoners all those who have been sheriffs since the last eyre of the justices into those parts, to be present in the same place before the aforesaid justices, together with the writs concerning assizes and pleas which they received during their own time [of office], and to answer concerning their own time [of office] as should be done in the presence of the itinerant justices. And you are there to have the summoners and this writ. By the witness of W[illiam] Marshal, earl of Pembroke, rector of us and of our kingdom, at Westminster, November 4. In the presence of S[tephen], archbishop of Canterbury; P[eter], bishop of Winchester; and R[obert], bishop of Durham.

Similar letters to all the sheriffs of England except [those of] Gloucester, Worcester, Hereford, Stafford and Shropshire, and Leicester and Warwick; but with variation of place, as recorded on the dorse of the letters patent.[3]

(Latin) *Ibid.*, I, 403.

(C) Collection of Carucage[4] (1220)

The king to the sheriff of Northampton, greeting. Know that, on account of our great need and the urgent pressure of our debts, and for the sake of preserving our land of Poitou, all the magnates and faithful men of our entire kingdom have of their free will granted in common that a contribution (*donum*) shall be made to us: namely, 2s. from every plough-team, in so far as it was joined by the day after the last preceding feast of St. John the Baptist in the fourth year of our reign, to be collected by your hand and [the hands] of two lawful knights of your county, who shall be elected to do so by the will and counsel of all men of the county in full county [court]. And therefore we command you, firmly and straitly enjoining, that, having convoked your full county [court], you cause to be elected by the will and counsel of those men of the county two of the more lawful knights of the whole county who best have the knowledge, willingness, and ability to carry out this business to our advantage. And you, taking those [knights] with you, shall immediately cause that contribution to be assessed on and collected from every plough-team as aforesaid, excepting the demesnes of the archbishops and bishops and their peasants, and excepting the demesnes of the

---

[3] That is to say, on the reverse side of the patent roll.
[4] A tax levied on the plough-team (*caruca*) or on the plough-land (*carucata*). In the present writ the former is specified; but see Mitchell, *Studies in Taxation under John and Henry III*, p. 133.

Cistercian order and of the Premonstratensians. And see to it that you are able distinctly and clearly to account to us at London on the day after Michaelmas next how many plough-teams there are in your bailiwick from which we ought to have that contribution. And have the money due therefrom safely collected by the hands of the two knights aforesaid and by your own; and have it sent to London on the aforesaid day under your seal and the seals of the two knights aforesaid, and safely deposited in the house of the New Temple until provision is made as to what ought to be done with it. And as you cherish your life and all that you have, concern yourself with this matter so that, on account of no assessment or collection poorly carried out by you and the aforesaid knights, we shall later need to have severe inquisition made by faithful men sent from our court, to your grave confusion and that of those men associated with you in carrying out the aforesaid assessment and collection. Witness. . . .

Similar letters to all the sheriffs of England.

(Latin) *Ibid.*, I, 437.

(D) COLLECTION OF A FIFTEENTH (1225)

The king to . . . ,[5] greeting. We have assigned you as our justiciars to assess and collect for our use the fifteenth of all movables in the counties of Nottingham and Derby according to this form. Our sheriff of Nottingham and Derby will cause to be assembled before you at Nottingham all the knights of his counties on the Sunday next before Mid-Lent; on which day you shall cause to be elected four lawful knights from each hundred or wapentake—or more or less according to the size of the hundreds and wapentakes—who are to go through every hundred or wapentake to assess and collect the aforesaid fifteenth of all chattels. Nevertheless, from this fifteenth, for the benefit of archbishops, bishops, abbots, priors, and other men of religion, also of earls, barons, knights, and freeholders who are not merchants, are to be exempted their books of all kinds, the ornaments of churches and chapels, riding-horses, draught-horses, pack-horses, arms of all kinds, jewels, vases, utensils, hay, and [the contents of] larders and cellars; also grain bought for supplying castles. Likewise from this fifteenth, for the benefit of merchants who pay a fifteenth from all their merchandise and movables, are to be exempted the arms to which they are sworn,[6] their riding-horses, the utensils in their houses, and [the contents of] their larders and cellars [kept] for their sustenance. Likewise from this fifteenth, for the benefit of villeins, are to be exempted the arms to which they are sworn, their utensils, their meat and fish and drink that are not for sale, and their hay and fodder that are not for sale. Moreover, those knights shall not go into the hundreds or wapentakes of which they are residents, but into other adjacent hundreds or wapentakes. Furthermore, every person, with the exception of earls, barons, and

---

[5] Six collectors are named—one of many groups thus commissioned.

[6] See nos. 34, 46H.

knights, shall swear to the number, quantity, and value of his own movables and also of the movables belonging to two of his nearest neighbours. And if, perchance, dissension thereby arises between him who owns the movables and his neighbours who have sworn concerning the same movables, the said knights shall seek a verdict through the oaths of twelve good and lawful men of the neighbour-hood—or as many as they shall deem sufficient for a verdict in this matter—and according to that verdict they shall levy the fifteenth. But the serjeants and reeves of the lands of earls, barons, and knights—or just the reeves, if no serjeants are there—shall in the same way swear the same oath concerning the movables of their lords in each vill.[7] . . . Moreover, you are to follow the same procedure with regard to the fiefs of archbishops, bishops, abbots, priors, and other men of religion, except for their demesnes and their own vil-leins; so far as these are concerned, the archbishops and bishops shall have the fifteenth assessed and collected in the aforesaid form, and shall account for it to us at the same terms [as prescribed for the regular collectors]. And so we command and straitly enjoin you that, in the fealty by which you are bound to us, you give care and efficacious action to carrying out this matter as set forth above. By witness of the king, at Westminster, February 15.

(Latin) Patent Rolls, 1216-1225, pp. 560 f.

(E) Election of County Representatives (1227)[8]

The king to the sheriff of Northumberland, greeting. We com-mand you that in your full county [court] you tell the knights and good men of your bailiwick to elect from their own number four of the more lawful and discreet knights, who are to be before us at Westminster three weeks after the feast of St. Michael, there to set forth on behalf of the whole county their quarrel with you, should they have one, regarding the articles contained in the charter of liberty that has been granted to them.[9] And you are to be there yourself to show cause for the demand which in this connection you made upon them. And you are to have there the names of the knights and this writ. [By witness of the king at Northampton, August 13, in the eleventh year of the reign.]

(Latin) Rotuli Litterarum Clausarum, II, 213.

---

[7] The writ here gives details concerning the safeguarding of the money and the oaths to be sworn by the knights and justices.

[8] Copies of this writ were sent to the sheriffs of sixteen counties besides Northumberland; the instructions to the sheriffs of nineteen other counties contain additional clauses with regard to the perambulation of the forest. Mandates of the previous year had called for representatives from only eight counties, to meet at Lincoln; but the assembly had been postponed because the king had been unable to be at that city in time. On the significance of these writs of summons, see A. B. White, in the American Historical Review, XIX, 735 f.

[9] The reissue of Magna Carta, which the barons had demanded in return for the grant of a fifteenth.

(F) Collection of Tallage and Levy of Ships (1227)

The king to his beloved and faithful, the good men of his towns of Nottingham and Derby, and his other good men of his boroughs and demesnes in the same counties, greeting. Whereas opportunity has been given us of recovering, by the grace of God, our heritage in the lands across the sea, on which account it behooves us, God willing, soon to embark; we have assessed an efficacious aid in our city of London, so that, by the will of all our barons[10] of the said city, we have tallaged all men, whether greater or less, through their own agency (*per se*). And therefore we have provided that similar aid is to be assessed through all our cities, boroughs, and demesnes; so that in every one of our demesnes all men, according to their ability, shall be tallaged through their own agency. Thus we send to you our beloved and faithful William Basset, Eustace of Ludham, and the sheriff of Nottingham and Derby, to assess the tallage in the towns of Nottingham and Derby, and in our other boroughs and demesnes of the aforesaid counties, according to the mode and form described above; and we command and urge you to render us such prompt and efficacious aid in this urgent necessity that through your aid we may the more speedily recover our rights and may recognize ourself forever grateful to you—so that, indeed, as you cherish us and our honour, you let us have half of the aforesaid tallage at our exchequer on the approaching close of Easter in the eleventh year of our reign, and the other half on the feast of St. John the Baptist in the same year. By the witness of the king, at Westminster, January 30.[11]

The king to the bailiffs and good men of Dunwich, greeting. Know that, by the counsel of our faithful men, we are making preparations, God willing, to cross the sea in our own person. Wherefore we command and firmly enjoin you that, in the fealty by which you are bound to us, you have all good ships of your port, besides those which you owe us through your promise,[12] come to Portsmouth well equipped and supplied with arms and victuals; so that at the latest they shall be there on the approaching feast of St. James the Apostle, in the eleventh year of our reign, ready to cross the sea with our body. By witness of the king, at Westminster.[13]

(Latin) *Ibid.*, II, 208, 211.

---

[10] See above, p. 103, n. 17.

[11] Similar letters were sent to most of the other counties; also commissions to the various groups of justices, together with notifications to the sheriffs.

[12] From this writ and other records it appears that various boroughs had, as the result of separate negotiation, granted the king quotas of ships for his war, and in return had been given special concessions with regard to their tallage.

[13] The entry in the roll is rather confusing, but it seems to mean that similar letters were sent to Yarmouth, Ipswich, Oreford, Colchester, Pevensey, Seaford, Lynn, Southampton, Portsmouth, and the Cinque Ports (Dover, Sandwich, Hythe, Winchelsea, Rye, Hastings, and Romney); with the writs to the latter

(G) Collection of a Fortieth (1232)

The king to the sheriff of Kent, greeting. Know that the archbishops, bishops, abbots, priors, and clerks having lands that do not belong to their churches, [as well as] the earls, barons, knights, freemen, and villeins[14] of our kingdom, have granted to us as aid the fortieth part of all their evident movables as possessed on the morrow of St. Matthew the Apostle in the sixteenth year of our reign: namely, of grain, ploughs, sheep, cows, swine, studs, and cart-horses assigned to productive work on manors, excepting the property that the aforesaid archbishops, bishops, and other ecclesiastical parsons receive from parish churches belonging to them, from prebendal churches, from prebends, and from lands pertaining to prebends and parochial churches. Moreover, it has been generally provided by our faithful men aforesaid that the said fortieth is to be assessed and collected in this manner: namely, that from each entire vill four of the better and more lawful men shall be elected along with the reeves of those particular vills, and that by their oaths the fortieth of all the aforesaid movables is to be determined and assessed upon each person in the presence of the knights assessors commissioned for that purpose. And afterwards, by the oaths of two lawful men from [each of] the same vills, inquiry and assessment shall be made touching the fortieth of movable property possessed by the said four men and the reeves. And let it be distinctly and plainly recorded to whose barony or liberty each vill in whole or in part belongs.[15] . . . Nothing, however, shall be taken by way of a fortieth from any one who does not have movable property of this sort to the value of at least 40d. Now for the assessment and collection of the aforesaid fortieth in your county according to the plan aforesaid, we have assigned[16] . . . , whom, immediately on sight of these letters, you shall summon before you to hear our precept, and to whom you shall at once hand our letters patent which are directed to them for this purpose and which we send you to be handed to them. Moreover, you shall cause to come before them, on the particular days and at the [particular] places which they may then deem most convenient, [the men of] the various vills of your county in order diligently to carry out this matter. : . . By my own witness, at Westminster, September 28.[17]

(Latin) *Close Rolls, 1231-1234,* pp. 155 f.

---

changed to read "besides those which are owed us by way of service." Cf. nos. 41B, 50C.

[14] Presumably a grant by the magnates was held to bind their tenants, free and unfree.

[15] The writ here gives details concerning the collection of the money and the transmission of the records.

[16] Four persons are named.

[17] The roll also includes the forms used for notifying the knights assessors and for commissioning the itinerant justices. Similar letters were sent to all the counties.

(H) Ordinance for the Preservation of the Peace (1242)[18]

The king to the sheriff of Worcester, greeting. Know that, for the strict maintenance of our peace, it has been provided by our council that watches shall be kept in the various cities and boroughs and in all the other vills of your county from the day of the Ascension of the Lord to the day of St. Michael: namely, in every city by six armed men at each gate; in every borough by twelve men and in every vill by six men similarly armed, or four or less according to the number of the inhabitants. And they shall keep continuous watch throughout the whole night from sunset to dawn: so that, if any foreigner passes by them, they shall hold him until morning; then, if he is trustworthy, he shall be released, but if he is suspicious, he shall be turned over to the sheriff, who is to receive and safeguard him without difficulty or delay. If, however, foreigners of this sort, on passing through, do not allow themselves to be arrested, then the aforesaid watchmen are to raise hue against them on all sides and, with the whole force of the vill and of the neighbouring vills, are to follow them with hue and cry from vill to vill until they are captured. And then they are to be turned over to the sheriff as aforesaid; yet so that no one, on account of such arrest or capture of foreigners, shall be [unjustly] molested by the sheriff or his bailiffs. And the various cities, boroughs, and vills are to be warned to carry out each of the aforesaid watches and pursuits so diligently that, by reason of their default, we shall not have to inflict severe punishment.

It has also been provided that each sheriff, together with two knights especially assigned for that purpose, shall make the circuit of his county from hundred to hundred, [visiting] also the cities and boroughs; and in each hundred or city or borough they shall cause to be assembled before them the citizens, burgesses, freeholders, villeins, and other men aged from fifteen to sixty years. And they shall have them all assessed and sworn to arms according to their [respective] possessions in land and chattels: namely, for land worth £15, a shirt of mail, an iron cap, a sword, a knife, and a horse; for land worth £10, a hauberk, an iron cap, a sword, and a knife; for land worth 100s., a purpoint, an iron cap, a sword, a lance, and a knife; for land worth 40s. or more, up to a value of 100s., a sword, a knife, a bow, and arrows. Whatever persons have less than 40s. value of land are to be sworn to falchions (*falces*), halberds, knives, and other small arms. For chattels worth 60m., [a man shall possess] a shirt of mail, an iron cap, a sword, a knife, and a horse; for chattels worth 40m., a hauberk, an iron cap, a sword, and a knife; for chattels worth 20m., a purpoint, an iron cap, a sword, and a knife; for chattels worth 10m., a sword, a knife, a bow, and arrows; for chattels worth 40s. or more, up to a value of 10m., falchions, knives, halberds, and other small arms. Furthermore, all who, outside the forest, can have bows and arrows are to have them; but those in the forest [are to have] bows

---

[18] Wrongly dated 1252 in Stubbs, *Select Charters*, p. 362. Cf. no. 34.

and bolts.[19] And in the various cities and boroughs all men sworn to arms shall be obedient to their mayors, or to their reeves and bailiffs where there are no mayors.[20] In each of the other vills, moreover, there shall be established one or two constables,[21] according to the number of the inhabitants and the decision of the aforesaid [officials]. Besides, in each hundred there shall be established a chief constable, at whose command all men sworn to arms in his hundred shall be assembled; and to him they shall be obedient in carrying out necessary measures for the conservation of our peace. The chief constables of the various hundreds, moreover, shall be obedient to the sheriff and the two knights aforesaid, in coming at their command and in carrying out necessary measures for the conservation of our peace. . . .[22] By the witness of W[alter], archbishop of York, at Westminster, May 20.

(Latin) *Close Rolls, 1237-1242*, pp. 482 f.

(I) Naval Levies (1242)[23]

The king to the barons of Hastings, greeting. Whereas, on account of his continuous injuries, we are under no obligation to observe a truce toward the king of France, and whereas war between us has already broken out: we have decided, by your aid and counsel and by that of our other barons of the Cinque Ports, to assail the said king and his men both by sea and by land and to fight him in every way we can. Therefore, especially relying on your manliness and faith for willing and powerful aid in this affair, we command and urge you, in the fealty by which you are bound to us and as you cherish us and our honour, that as quickly as possible you have your ships prepared and well manned; and that, together with our other barons of the Cinque Ports, to whom we have sent the same mandate, you equip yourselves for assailing the said king of France along the coasts of Brittany, Normandy, and Boulogne, both by sea and by land, with fire and with other weapons at your command; yet so that you, on account of this our mandate, shall not presume to cause damage or injury to churches, or to any one who enjoys our protection or safe conduct—saving also to us the fifth which, as you know, belongs to us from booty acquired by you in our wars. . . . In testimony whereof, etc., to continue during our pleasure. By witness of the king, at Xanten, June 8.

Similar letters to the other barons of the Cinque Ports: namely, Sandwich, Dover, Hythe, Romney, Winchelsea, and Rye. Also to the good men of Dunwich. . . .

---

[19] *Pilettos*—apparently some sort of blunt arrows; cf. no. 35, art. 2.

[20] Cf. no. 39E.

[21] This seems to be the inauguration of rural constables as peace officers. On the earlier use of the word, see above, pp. 69, 82, n. 8.

[22] Details follow concerning the enforcement of these measures. Similar letters, together with the proper commissions of knights, were sent to all the counties.

[23] Cf. no. 41B, D.

The mayor and sheriffs of London are ordered to send 120 foot-soldiers with crossbows to Dover—to B[ertram] de Crioyl, constable of Dover [Castle], who on the part of the king will instruct them as to what they are to do. Witnessed as above [August 2].

The bailiffs of Dunwich are ordered with the utmost haste to send to Dover five ships well filled with [sea]men and crossbowmen—as many as they can supply—to do what B[ertram] de Crioyl, constable of Dover [Castle] will instruct them on the part of the king. Witnessed as above.

A similar mandate to the bailiffs of Yarmouth for five ships. Similar mandates to the bailiffs of Ipswich, Oreford, and Blakeney for four ships [each]. Witnessed as above.

(Latin) *Ibid.*, pp. 456, 495 f.

(J) WRITS OF SUMMONS (1253-54)

The king to B[oniface], archbishop of Canterbury, greeting. Whereas we have to communicate to you certain grave and urgent matters touching our interest and that of our kingdom, which we are unwilling to settle without your counsel and that of our other magnates, we command you that, in the fealty by which you are bound to us and as you cherish us and our honour, you do not fail to be at Westminster a fortnight after St. Hilary next—in the presence of our queen, our brother Richard, earl of Cornwall, others of our council remaining in England, and yet others of our council in Gascony, whom we are about to send for [the meeting on] the same day—to hear our good will and pleasure and, together with our said council, to take up the matters aforesaid. Nor are you to delay your arrival so that you fail promptly to attend on the same day. By witness of Queen Eleanor and of Richard, earl of Cornwall, at Westminster, December 27.

The king to the sheriff of Bedford and Buckingham, greeting.[24] Whereas the earls, barons, and other magnates of our kingdom have steadfastly promised to be at London with horses and arms three weeks from Easter next, prepared and well equipped to advance without delay towards Portsmouth in order to cross the sea to us in Gascony [and to support us] against the king of Castile, who in strength is to make hostile invasion of our land of Gascony next summer; and whereas we have ordered you to distrain for that same [service] all men of your bailiwick who hold land worth £20 of us in chief, or of others who are under age and in our wardship: [therefore] we straitly command you that, besides all those men aforesaid, you summon before our council at Westminster a fortnight after next Easter four lawful and discreet knights from the aforesaid counties, whom the same counties are to elect for this [purpose], to represent all and several of the same counties—namely, two from one county

---

[24] On the significance of this writ, see Pasquet, *Origins of the House of Commons*, pp. 33 f.

and two from the other—to provide, along with knights of the other counties whom we have caused to be summoned for the same day, what sort of aid they will give us in so great an emergency. And to the knights and others of the aforesaid counties you yourself shall explain our needs and the urgency of our business, and you shall induce them to render us efficacious aid that will suffice for the present; so that the four knights aforesaid can make a precise response to our aforesaid council at the aforesaid term with regard to the aforesaid aid on behalf of all men of the aforesaid counties. . . . By witness of the queen and of Richard, earl of Cornwall, at Windsor, February 11.

Similar letters were directed to all the sheriffs of England.

(Latin) Close Rolls, 1253-1254, pp. 107, 114.

47. RECORDS OF THE BARONIAL CRISIS (1258-66)

(A) Henry III: Letters Agreeing to Reform (1258)

The king to all, etc. You are to know that, through an oath given on our behalf[1] by Robert Waleran, we have granted to the nobles and magnates of our kingdom that, by twelve faithful men of our council already elected and by twelve other faithful men of ours elected on the part of those nobles, who are to convene at Oxford one month after the feast of Pentecost next, the state of our kingdom shall be ordered, rectified, and reformed according to what they shall think best to enact for the honour of God and our faith and the good of our kingdom. And if, perchance, any of those elected on our part are absent, those who are present shall be permitted to substitute others in place of the absentees; and the same shall be done [with regard to those elected] on the part of the aforesaid nobles and faithful men of ours. And whatever is ordained in this matter by the twenty-four elected by both sides and sworn to the undertaking, or by the majority of them, we will inviolably observe, wishing and henceforth straitly enjoining that their ordinance be inviolably observed by all. And whatever security those men, or the majority of them, may provide for the observance of this matter we will fully grant and cause to be granted. We also attest that Edward, our first-born son, through an oath personally taken, has by his letters granted that he will faithfully and inviolably observe, and will cause ever to be observed, all that has been expressed and granted above, so far as in him lies. Furthermore, the said earls and barons have promised that, on the completion of the business noted above, they will strive in good faith to see that a common aid is rendered to us by the community of our kingdom. In testimony whereof, etc. . . . Given at Westminster, May 2.

(Latin) Stubbs, Select Charters, p. 372.

---

[1] *In animam nostram;* kings very commonly named proxies to swear for them.

(B) The Provisions of Oxford (1258)

It has been provided that from each county there shall be elected four discreet and lawful knights who, on every day that the county [court] is held, shall assemble to hear all complaints touching any wrongs and injuries inflicted on any persons by sheriffs, bailiffs, or any other men, and to make the attachments that pertain to the said complaints [for keeping] until the first arrival of the chief justiciar in those parts: so that they shall take from the plaintiff adequate pledges for his prosecution [of the case], and from the defendant for his coming and standing trial before the said justiciar on his first arrival; and that the four knights aforesaid shall have all the said complaints enrolled, together with their attachments, in proper order and sequence—namely, for each hundred separately and by itself— so that the said justiciar, on his first arrival, can hear and settle the aforesaid complaints singly from each hundred. And they shall inform the sheriff that they are summoning all his hundredmen and bailiffs before the said justiciar on his next arrival, for a day and a place which he will make known to them: so that every hundredman shall cause all plaintiffs and defendants of his bailiwick to come in succession, according to what the aforesaid justiciar shall bring to trial from the aforesaid hundred; also as many men and such men— both knights and other free and lawful men—as may be required for best proving the truth of the matter. [This, however, is to be done] in such a way that all are not troubled at one and the same time; rather let [only] as many come as can be [used in cases to be] tried and concluded in one day.

Likewise it is provided that no knight of the aforesaid counties, by virtue of an assurance that he is not to be placed on juries or assizes, shall be excused by a charter of the lord king or be exempt from [the obligations of] this provision thus made for the common good of the whole kingdom.

Elected on the part of the lord king: the lord bishop of London; the lord bishop elect of Winchester; the lord H[enry], son of the king of Germany; the lord J[ohn], earl de Warenne; the lord Guy de Lusignan; the lord W[illiam] de Valence; the lord J[ohn], earl of Warwick; the lord John Mansel; Brother J[ohn] of Darlington; the abbot of Westminster; the lord H[enry] of Hengham.

Elected on the part of the earls and barons: the lord bishop of Worcester; the lord Simon, earl of Leicester; the lord Richard, earl of Gloucester; the lord Humphrey, earl of Hereford; the lord Roger Marshal; the lord Roger de Mortimer; the lord J[ohn] Fitz-Geoffrey; the lord Hugh le Bigot; the lord Richard de Gray; the lord W[illiam] Bardulf; the lord P[eter] de Montfort; the lord Hugh le Despenser. And if it should happen that of necessity any one of these cannot be present, the rest of them shall elect whom they please in place of the absentee, namely, another person needful for carrying on that business.

Thus swore the community[2] of England at Oxford. . . .
This is the oath [administered] to the twenty-four. . . .
Thus swore the chief justice of England. . . .
Thus swore the chancellor of England. . . .
This is the oath taken by the wardens of the castles. . . .
These are the men sworn [to be] of the king's council.[3] . . .

The twelve on the king's side have chosen from the twelve on the side of the community the earl Roger Marshal and Hugh le Bigot. And the party of the community has chosen from the twelve who are on the side of the king the earl of Warwick and John Mansel. And these four have power to elect the council of the king; and when they have made the election, they shall designate those [elected] to the twenty-four. And that shall hold on which the majority of these [four] agree.

These are the twelve who have been elected by the barons, on behalf of the whole community of the land, to consider common needs along with the king's council at the three annual parliaments. . . .

These are the twenty-four appointed by the community to consider aid for the king. . . . And if any one of these cannot or will not be present, those who are present shall have power to elect another in his place.

Concerning the state of Holy Church:—It should be remembered that the state of Holy Church is to be amended by the twenty-four chosen to reform the state of the kingdom of England—at what time and place they think best, according to the powers that they hold by writ of the king of England.[4]

Concerning the chief justice:—[It has been decided] furthermore that a chief justice—or two [chief justices]—shall be appointed; also what power he shall have; and that he shall be [in office] for only one year, so that at the end of the year he shall render account of his term before the king and the royal council and before the man who is to follow him [in office].

Concerning the treasurer and the exchequer:—The same [has been decided] with regard to the treasurer; so that he shall render account at the end of the year. And according to the ordinance of the said twenty-four, other good men are to be appointed to the exchequer, whither all the issues of the land are to come, and not elsewhere. And let that be amended which seems in need of amendment.

Concerning the chancellor:—The same [has been decided] with regard to the chancellor; so that he shall render account of his term at the end of the year, and that merely by the king's will he shall

---

[2] *Le commun*—a phrase which is shown by the context to have meant parliament or the baronial party. The oaths, which are here omitted, add nothing to the information given in the following articles.

[3] Fifteen men, of whom eleven were of the twenty-four named above.

[4] No. 47A, preceding.

seal nothing out of course,[5] but shall do so by [the advice of] the
council that surrounds the king.

Concerning the power of the justice and of the bailiffs:—The chief
justice has power to redress the misdeeds of all other justices, of
bailiffs, of earls, of barons, and of all other people, according to the
rightful law of the land. And writs are to be pleaded according to
the law of the land in the proper places. And [it has been decided]
that the justices shall accept nothing unless it is a present of bread
and wine and like things: namely, such meat and drink as have been
customarily brought for the day to the tables of the chief men. And
this same regulation shall be understood [to hold] for all the king's
councillors and all his bailiffs. And [it has been ordered] that no
bailiff, by virtue of his office or of some plea, shall take any fee, either
by his own hand or in any manner through another person. And if he
is convicted [of so doing], let him be punished; likewise the man
who gives [the fee]. And the king, if it is suitable, shall give [fees]
to his justices and to his people who serve him, so that they shall
have no need of taking anything from others.

Concerning the sheriffs:—As sheriffs there shall be appointed
loyal persons, good men who are landholders; so that in each county
there shall be as sheriff a feudal tenant of the same county, who
shall well, loyally, and justly treat the people of the county. And
[it is ordered] that he shall take no fee; that he shall be sheriff for no
more than a year in all; that during the year he shall render his
accounts at the exchequer and be responsible for his term [of office];
that the king, from the royal income, shall make [allowance] to him
in proportion to his receipts, so that he may rightly keep the county;
and that he shall take no fees, neither he nor his bailiffs. And if they
are convicted [of such wrongdoing], let them be punished. It should
be remembered that, with regard to the Jewry and the wardens of the
Jewry, such reforms are to be established as shall carry out the oath
in this respect.

Concerning the escheators:—Good escheators are to be appointed.
And [it is ordered] that they shall take nothing from goods of deceased persons whose lands ought to be in the king's hands; but that,
if a debt is owing to him, the escheators shall have free administration
of the goods until they have carried out the king's wishes—and this
according to the provision in the charter of liberties.[6] Also [it is
ordered] that inquiry shall be made concerning the misdeeds committed there by escheators, and that redress shall be made for such
[wrongs]. Nor shall tallage or anything else be taken, except as it
should be according to the charter of liberties. The charter of liberties
is to be strictly observed.

Concerning the exchange of London:—It should be remembered to
establish reforms touching the exchange of London; also touching

---

[5] That is to say, nothing but routine documents.
[6] Art. 26 of Magna Carta, above, p. 119.

the city of London and all the other cities of the king, which have been brought to shame and ruin by tallages and other oppressions.

Concerning the household of the king and queen:—It should be remembered to reform the household of the king and queen.

Concerning the parliaments, as to how many shall be held annually and in what manner:—It should be remembered that the twenty-four have ordained that there are to be three parliaments a year: the first on the octave of St. Michael, the second on the morrow of Candlemas, and the third on the first day of June, that is to say, three weeks before [the feast of] St. John. To these three parliaments the chosen councillors of the king shall come, even if they are not summoned, in order to examine the state of the kingdom and to consider the common needs of the kingdom and likewise of the king; and by the king's command [they shall come] also at other times, whenever it is necessary. So too it should be remembered that the community is to elect twelve good men, who shall come to the three parliaments and at other times, when there is need and when the king and his council summon them to consider the affairs of the king and the kingdom. And [it has been decided] that the community shall hold as established whatever these twelve shall do—and this is to reduce the cost to the community. Fifteen are to be named by these four men—that is to say, by the earl Marshal, the earl of Warwick, Hugh le Bigot, and John Mansel—who have been elected by the twenty-four to name the aforesaid fifteen, who are to form the king's council. And they are to be confirmed by the aforesaid twenty-four, or by the majority of those men. And they shall have the power of advising the king in good faith concerning the government of the kingdom and concerning all matters that pertain to the king or the kingdom; and of amending and redressing everything that they shall consider in need of amendment or redress. And [they shall have authority] over the chief justice and over all other people. And if they cannot all be present, that shall be firm and established which the majority of them shall enact.

These are the names of the principal castles of the king, and of those who have charge of them. . . .

(Latin and French) *Ibid.*, pp. 378 f.

(C) THE PROVISIONS OF WESTMINSTER (1259)

In the year 1259 from the Incarnation of the Lord, the forty-third of the reign of King Henry, son of King John, at a meeting of the lord king and his magnates at Westminster on Michaelmas fortnight, the provisions hereinunder written, by the common counsel and consent of the said king and his magnates, were enacted and published by the same king and his magnates in this form:—

1. With regard to the performance of suit to the courts of the magnates and of other lords who have such courts, it is provided and established by general agreement that no one who is enfeoffed by charter shall henceforth be distrained to perform suit to his lord's

court, unless he is specifically obliged by the tenor of his charter to perform the suit; with the sole exception of those whose ancestors were accustomed to perform suit of this kind, or who themselves [were accustomed so to do], before the first crossing of the said lord king into Brittany—after the time of which crossing twenty-nine and a half years had elapsed down to the time that this constitution was made. And likewise no one enfeoffed without charter since the time of the Conquest, or by other ancient enfeoffment, shall be distrained to perform suit of this kind, unless he or his ancestors were accustomed to perform it before the first crossing of the lord king into Brittany. . . .

4. With regard to the sheriff's tourn,[7] it is provided that, unless their presence is specially demanded, archbishops, bishops, abbots, priors, earls, and barons, or other men of religion, or women, shall not of necessity come thither. . . . And the tourns shall be held according to the form of the king's Great Charter, and as they were customarily held in the time of the kings John and Richard.

5. It is also provided that neither on the eyres of the justices nor in the [courts of the] counties nor in the courts of barons shall fines henceforth be taken from anybody for miskenning,[8] or for avoidance of trouble on that score. . . .

8. Moreover, with regard to charters of exemption and liberty, [to the effect] that those securing them are not to be put on assizes, juries, or recognitions, it is provided that, if their oath is so essential that without it justice cannot be administered . . . , they shall be forced to swear, saving to them their aforesaid liberty and exemption in other respects. . . .

11. Henceforth no one except the lord king and his ministers shall be permitted, for any cause whatsoever, to levy distraints outside his fief, or on a royal or a common highway. . . .

16. Hereafter no one but the king shall hold in his court a plea concerning false judgment rendered in a court of his tenant; for pleas of this sort especially pertain to the crown and dignity of the king. . . .

18. Without the king's writ, no one may henceforth distrain his free tenants to respond concerning their free tenements or anything that pertains to their free tenements. Nor may he cause his free tenants against their will to take oaths; so that no one may do this without the king's precept. . . .

21. Hereafter itinerant justices shall not amerce vills on their eyres because particular twelve-year-old persons do not come before sheriffs and coroners for inquests concerning a man's death or other matters pertaining to the crown; so long as, nevertheless, enough men come from those vills for satisfactorily carrying out such inquests.

22. No judgment of murder[9] shall henceforth be rendered before

---

[7] See above, p. 123, n. 45.

[8] See above, p. 62, no. 10.

[9] Cf. nos. 40B, 54D.

the justices in a case that is adjudged merely one of accident; but [a judgment of] murder shall be proper in the case of a man feloniously slain, and not otherwise. . . .

(Latin) *Ibid.*, pp. 390 f.

(D) The Decision of Louis IX (1264)

. . . In the name of the Father and the Son and the Holy Spirit. By our [present] decision or ordinance we quash and annul all the aforesaid provisions, ordinances, statutes, and obligations,[10] however called, and whatever has followed from them or by occasion of them, especially since it appears that the supreme pontiff by his letters has proclaimed them quashed and annulled; ordaining that as well the said king as all the barons and others who have consented to the present arbitration, and who in any way have bound themselves to observe the aforesaid [provisions], shall be utterly quit and absolved of the same. We likewise add that, by virtue or force of the aforesaid provisions or obligations or ordinances, or of any authority already granted by the king on that account, no one shall make new statutes or hold or observe those already made; nor ought any one, through non-observance of the aforesaid [provisions], to be held the enemy, either principal or otherwise, of any one else, or for that reason incur any penalty. . . . We also decree and ordain that the aforesaid king at his own volition may freely appoint, dismiss, and remove the chief justice, chancellor, treasurer, counsellors, lesser justices, sheriffs, and any other officials and ministers of his kingdom and his household, as he was used and able to do before the time of the provisions aforesaid. Furthermore, we repeal and quash the statute made to the effect that the kingdom of England should henceforth be governed by natives and that all aliens should leave the kingdom, never to return, except those whose residence the faithful men of the kingdom commonly agreed to, ordaining by our decision that aliens may safely remain in the said kingdom, and that the king may safely call to his counsel such aliens and natives as shall seem to him useful and loyal, just as he was able to do before the time aforesaid. Likewise we declare and ordain that the said king shall have full power and unrestricted rule within his kingdom and its appurtenances, and shall in all things and in every way enjoy such status and such full power as he enjoyed before the time aforesaid. By the present ordinance, however, we do not wish or intend in any way to derogate from royal privileges, charters, liberties, establishments, and praiseworthy customs of the kingdom of England existing before the time of the same provisions. . . .

Now this our ordinance or decision we have promulgated at Amiens on the morrow of the blessed Vincent the Martyr, A.D. 1263, in the

---

[10] The Provisions of Oxford, concerning which the French king had been called upon to arbitrate the quarrel between Henry III and the opposing party of the baronage.

month of January. In testimony whereof we have caused our seal to be attached to the present letters.

(Latin) Ibid., pp. 396 f.

(E) The Dictum of Kenilworth (1266)[11]

. . . 1. We declare and provide that the most serene lord prince Henry, illustrious king of England, shall have, fully receive, and freely exercise his dominion, authority, and royal power without impediment or contradiction of any one, whereby, contrary to the approved rights and laws and the long established customs of the kingdom, the regal dignity might be offended; and that to the same lord king and to his lawful mandates and precepts full obedience and humble attention shall be given by all and singular the men of the same kingdom, both greater and lesser. And all and singular shall through writs seek justice in the court of the lord king and shall [there] be answerable for justice, as was accustomed to be done up to the time of the recent disorders.

2. Furthermore, we ask the same lord king and reverently urge his piety that, for doing and rendering justice, he will nominate such men as, seeking not their own [interests] but those of God and the right, shall justly settle the affairs of subjects according to the praiseworthy laws and customs of the kingdom, and shall thereby strengthen with justice and restore the throne of royal majesty.

3. We likewise ask and urge the same lord king fully to guard and observe the liberties of the Church and the charters of liberties and of the forest, to keep and hold which he is expressly bound by his own oath.

4. Also the lord king shall provide that grants which up to the present he has made of his free will, and not under compulsion, shall be observed; and that he will firmly establish other necessary [measures] determined by his men and at his own pleasure. And furthermore the English Church shall be fully restored to its liberties and customs, which it had and rightly held before the time of such disorders, and shall be permitted to enjoy them freely. . . .[12]

37. All henceforth shall maintain firm peace, and none shall commit homicide, arson, robbery, or other transgression against the peace. And if any one does so and is convicted, let him have judgment and law according to the custom of the kingdom.

38. Likewise all interested persons shall swear on the Holy Gospels that, on account of the disorders, no one will take private revenge, nor will he procure or consent or tolerate that private revenge should be taken. And if any one takes private revenge, let him be punished

---

[11] The final settlement of the Barons' War, dictated by a commission of four bishops, two earls, and six other barons appointed for that purpose.

[12] The omitted articles take up in detail the restoration of lawful rights, the cancellation of Simon de Montfort's acts, and the rehabilitation, on various conditions, of those who had been disinherited.

by the court of the lord king, and let those who have injured the Church make satisfaction to it.

39. Also, if any one is unwilling to observe this decision, or to undergo judgment by his peers in the court of the lord king, such persons as thus declare themselves, and are accordingly disinherited, shall have no right of recovering their lands. And if any one holding lands of disinherited men rebels against the decision, he is to have no just claim, by the gift of the lord king, either to the land or to what is paid for redeeming it. Moreover, if any person does not consent to this decision, he is to be a public enemy of the lord king and of his sons and of the community; the people and clergy, in so far as is permitted by canon law, shall prosecute him as an enemy to the peace of the Church and of the kingdom. . . .

Given and published in the castle of Kenilworth on the day before the Kalends of November in the year of grace 1266, the fifty-first year of the reign of the lord Henry, king of England.

(Latin) *Ibid.,* pp. 407 f.

48. HENRY III: LATER WRITS OF SUMMONS

(A) MEETING WITH KNIGHTS OF THE SHIRE AT WINDSOR (1261)

The king to the sheriff of Norfolk and Suffolk, greeting. Whereas, on the part of the bishop of Worcester, the earl of Leicester, the earl of Gloucester, and certain other nobles of our realm, three knights have been summoned from each of our counties to be at St. Albans on the approaching feast of St. Matthew the Apostle, in order with them to deliberate on the common affairs of our kingdom; and [whereas] we and our nobles aforesaid shall come together on the same day at Windsor to treat concerning peace between us and them: we command you on our part to give strict orders to those knights from your bailiwick, who have been summoned before those [nobles] on the aforesaid day, that, avoiding all excuse, they come to us at Windsor on the aforesaid day; and you are also strictly to prohibit them from going elsewhere on the said day, by all means causing them to come before us on the aforesaid day to have a conference with us on the aforesaid matters, so that, as a consequence of this business, they may see and understand that we propose no undertaking but what we know to be for the honour and common benefit of our realm. By witness of the king at Windsor, September 11.

(Latin) *Ibid.,* pp. 394 f.

(B) FIRST PARLIAMENT OF SIMON DE MONTFORT (1264)

The king to Adam of Newmarket, greeting. Whereas the disturbance recently experienced in our kingdom has now subsided and, by the grace of divine co-operation, peace has now been ordained and established between us and our barons; and [whereas], in order that this peace may be inviolably observed througout our entire kingdom, it has been provided by the counsel and assent of our barons that in each of our counties throughout England keepers of our peace shall be appointed for the defence and security of those parts, until other provision for the state of our kingdom may be made by us and our barons; and whereas, relying on your fidelity as well as your industry, we, by the counsel of our said barons, have assigned you as our keeper in the county of Lincoln during our pleasure: we command and firmly enjoin that, in the fealty by which you are bound to us, you there diligently see to the keeping of our peace and to those matters which pertain to it, as aforesaid. . . .[1] And whereas in our approaching parliament, it is necessary for us to deliberate with our prelates, magnates, and other faithful men concerning our affairs and those of our kingdom: we command you to send to us on behalf of the entire county aforesaid four of the more lawful and discreet knights of the same county elected for that purpose by the assent of that county; so that they shall be with us at London on the octave of the approaching feast of the Holy Trinity at the latest, in order to deliberate with us on the aforesaid affairs. . . . By witness of the king at St. Paul's in London, June 4.

(Latin) *Ibid.,* pp. 399 f.

(C) Second Parliament of Simon de Montfort (1265)

Henry, by the grace of God king of England, lord of Ireland, and duke of Aquitaine, to the venerable father in Christ, R[obert], by the same grace bishop of Durham. Whereas, after the grave peril of the disorders recently experienced in our kingdom, Edward, our dearest first-born son, was delivered as a hostage to assure and strengthen the peace of our kingdom; and whereas, now that the aforesaid disorders have—thank God!—been quieted, we must hold a deliberation with our prelates and magnates to make salutary provision for his release, and to establish and consolidate full assurance of peace and tranquillity for the honour of God and the advantage of our whole kingdom, and to consider certain other affairs of our kingdom which we are unwilling to settle without your counsel and that of our other prelates and magnates: [therefore] we command and urge you, in the faith and love by which you are bound to us, that, avoiding all excuse and putting aside all other concerns, you come to us at London on the octave of St. Hilary next, together with us and with our aforesaid prelates and magnates whom we have summoned to the same place, to consider the matters set forth above and to give your counsel [regarding them]. And by no means fail to do this, as you cherish us, our honour, and your own, as well as the common tranquillity of our kingdom. By witness of the king, at Worcester, December 14 [1264]. . . .[2]

Similar mandates to the sheriffs throughout England, that by the

---

[1] The writ here includes details regarding the prevention of crimes and disorders.

[2] Here follow in the roll the names of the prelates and lay barons summoned by the same form.

same form they should cause two of the more lawful, upright, and discreet knights from every county to come to the king at London on the octave aforesaid.

Letters in the same form also to the citizens of York, to the citizens of Lincoln, and to the other boroughs of England, that in the same way they should send two of the more discreet, lawful, and upright citizens or burgesses.

A mandate in the same form to the barons and good men of the Cinque Ports, as is contained in the writ enrolled below. . . . [3]

(Latin) Reports Touching the Dignity of a Peer, III, 33 f.

(D) Council of 1268[4]

' Those same men who were not at Windsor have been ordered to be at Westminster on Wednesday before the quinzime of Easter. . . .[5]

Writs are to be issued for certain persons of the Cinque Ports, whom the lord R[ichard] of Lyburne[6] ought to name, and for certain persons of the cities and boroughs: namely, that the bailiffs and six others of the more discreet, better, and wealthier men in the same —that is to say, the nearer of the cities and boroughs—are to be at London on the quinzime of Easter, to treat and consult with regard to the affairs of the lord king and of the kingdom, which also concern [those men] themselves; and that they should bring with them letters patent of credence addressed to all persons and [respectively] sealed with the communal seals of the same cities and boroughs. . . .

The king to his beloved and faithful his mayor and citizens of York, greeting. Whereas, with regard to arduous affairs concerning us and the estate and community of our kingdom, and especially in the council summoned by the legate[7] at London on the approaching quinzime of Easter, we wish to have a special deliberation and conference with you and the other faithful men of our said kingdom, whom we have caused to be summoned for this purpose, and without whom we are unable to settle those affairs: [therefore] we command and firmly enjoin that in the fealty, homage,[8] and love by which you are bound to us, immediately on sight of these letters and setting aside all other concerns, you cause the said mayor, together with the bailiffs and six of the better and more discreet and more substantial men [of the said city] to come with all haste to us at Westminster, [bringing with them] your letters patent

---

[3] This writ is in substance much the same as the one quoted; each of the Cinque Ports is to send four representatives.

[4] See the article by G. O. Sayles in the review cited below. The following extracts are from a carelessly written memorandum of March, 1268, to which are appended the form of the summons to the boroughs and the form of the letters patent to be returned with the deputies.

[5] Various persons are named as having received the writ.

[6] Constable of Dover Castle and warden of the Cinque Ports.

[7] Ottobono, papal legate.

[8] The wrong form seems inadvertently to have been used by the clerk, for the burgesses owed no homage.

signed with the seal of your community according to the form sent
to you enclosed in the present letters; so that they shall be there
on the approaching quinzime of Easter at the latest, there in the
matters aforesaid to do whatever we shall see fit to provide by the
common counsel of our kingdom. And by no means fail to do this.
Witness.

[Such letters to] York, Lincoln, Northampton, Stafford, Norwich,
Cambridge, Lynn, Oxford, Worcester, Gloucester, Shrewsbury,
Hereford, Bristol, Winchester, Southampton, Canterbury, Chichester,
Rochester, Bath, Coventry, Lichfield, Exeter, Ely, Bury St. Ed-
munds, Yarmouth, Ipswich, Dunwich. . . .

To all faithful in Christ before whom these present letters shall
come, the mayor, bailiffs, and entire community of the city of York,
greeting in the Lord. For the sake of the affairs concerning our
lord King H[enry], illustrious king of England, his kingdom, the
community of England, and us, [to be considered] in the council
called by the legate at London on the approaching quinzime of
Easter, we have seen fit to send thither ———, our mayor, and ———,
our bailiffs, and ——— our citizens or fellow burgesses, so that
full faith may be given to them in everything which, with regard to
the aforesaid matters, they shall see fit on our behalf to set forth
in the council or on the occasion of the council. And we shall hold
as established and accepted whatever on our behalf those men do
in the aforesaid matters. In testimony whereof, etc. Given, etc.

(Latin) *English Historical Review,* XL, 583 f.

49. PARLIAMENTARY AND OTHER WRITS (1275-95)

(A) PARLIAMENT OF 1275

Edward, by the grace of God king of England, lord of Ireland,
and duke of Aquitaine, to the sheriff of Middlesex, greeting. Whereas,
for certain particular reasons, we have prorogued our general parliament[1] . . . at London with our prelates and the other magnates
of our realm . . . until the morrow of the Sunday after Easter
next; we command you that you summon to the same place, on the
morrow of the Sunday after Easter aforesaid, four knights from
your county of the more discreet and lawful, and likewise from
each of the cities, boroughs, and trading towns[2] of your bailiwick
six or four citizens, burgesses, or other good men, to consider, along
with the magnates of our kingdom, the affairs of the said kingdom.
On our part also you are without delay to have those letters of ours
that are addressed to various persons in your bailiwick given or sent
to them. And by no means neglect to do this and to give us full information touching the execution of this mandate at the term afore-

---

[1] Note that in this and the following writs *parliamentum* is used as a synonym
of *colloquium,* meaning a conference or deliberation.

[2] *Ville mercatorie,* not market towns; see Ballard and Tait, *British Borough
Charters,* II, lii.

said. By my own witness at Woodstock, December 26, in the third year of our reign.

(Latin) Stubbs, Select Charters, pp. 441 f.

(B) The New Customs (1275)

William de Valence, earl of Pembroke, to all faithful in Christ before whom the present writing may come, greeting in the Lord. Whereas the archbishops, bishops, and other prelates of the kingdom of England, as well as the earls and barons, and we and the communities of the said kingdom, at the suggestion and request of the merchants, have for a variety of reasons unanimously granted, for ourselves and our heirs, to the magnificent prince, our dearest lord Edward, by the grace of God illustrious king of England, ½m. for each sack of wool and ½m. for every three hundred wool-fells, which make a sack, and 1m. for each last of hides exported from the kingdom of England and the land of Wales, to be henceforth collected in each port of England and Wales, both within liberties and without: [therefore] we, at the request and suggestion of the aforesaid merchants, grant, for us and our heirs, that the same lord king and his heirs shall have within each of our ports in Ireland, both within liberties and without, ½m. from every sack of wool and ½m. from every three hundred wool-fells, which make a sack, and 1m. from every last of hides exported from the land of Ireland, to be collected by the hands of wardens and bailiffs of the said king; saving to us the forfeitures of those who, without the licence and warrant of the said lord king [given] by his letters patent and signed with the seal provided for that purpose, shall presume to take wool, wool-fells, or hides of this sort through our fiefs, where we enjoy liberties, [for export] out of Ireland. From which [articles] the said lord king and his heirs shall collect and keep the half-mark from wool and wool-fells and the mark from lasts of hides in the manner aforesaid; yet so that in each of our ports, where the writs of the aforesaid king do not run, two of the more discreet and faithful men of those ports shall be elected, and they, having taken an oath with regard to the seizure of wool, wool-fells, and hides in the said ports until the merchants of wool, wool-fells, and hides aforesaid have their warrant under the seal of the lord king provided for that purpose, shall faithfully collect and receive the said custom for the use of the said lord king, and shall therefor be answerable to him. In testimony whereof we have set our seal to the present writing. Given in the general parliament of the lord king aforesaid, at Westminster, on Sunday, the feast of St. Dunstan the Bishop, in the third year of the reign of the same king.[3]

(Latin) Ibid., pp. 443 f.

---

[3] Similar letters were issued by eleven other barons named in the roll, following the language of a royal ordinance which has come down to us in French (Palgrave, <i>Parliamentary Writs,</i> I, 1 f.). On the taxes mentioned in this writ, see Gras, <i>The Early English Customs System,</i> ch. iii.

(C) SUBSIDY OF 1282

The king to the sheriff of Warwick and Leicester, to the citizens, burgesses, merchants, mayors, bailiffs, and commmunities of the cities, boroughs, and trading towns, and to all other men of the aforesaid counties, greeting. Whereas we have sent our beloved John of Kirkby for the sake of orally explaining to you on our part and in our name, and of expediting through you, certain arduous and especial concerns of ours, which we have entrusted to him: we command and firmly enjoin you, in the fealty and affection by which you are bound to us, that you place firm trust in the same John with respect to the said matters and carry them out in all ways. Moreover we have enjoined the same John without delay to inform us concerning your response and your willingness. In testimony whereof, etc. By witness of the king, at Chester, June 19.[4]

The king to his beloved and faithful the mayor and citizens of Hereford, greeting. For the courteous subsidy that you have promised us for the sake of our present expedition into Wales—concerning which we have been informed orally by our clerk, John of Kirkby, whom we sent to you on this account with our letters of credence— we are exceedingly grateful to you, and through the grace of God we will indemnify you in this respect at an opportune time. But since at the present moment we greatly need the money, we command and firmly enjoin you, in the fealty and homage[5] by which you are bound to us, and according to the instructions drawn up under the seal of our clerk aforesaid and delivered to our sheriff of Hereford and to you, to cause the money of the aforesaid subsidy to be levied in all haste and paid to the same sheriff; so that it may be brought to us as we have commanded him through other letters of ours, and so that we may have it by the morrow of All Saints at the latest. And by no means neglect this, as you cherish your bodies and all that you have in the kingdom. And strive especially to prevent such an occurrence as that we and our army should presently retreat from the region of Wales through default of that payment of money, on which we are placing full reliance. By witness of the king, at Denby, October 28.

(Latin) *Ibid.,* pp. 456 f.

(D) PARLIAMENTS OF 1283

The king to the sheriff of Norfolk and Suffolk, greeting. Whereas Llewelyn, son of Griffith, and his accomplices, the other Welshmen, to us enemies and rebels, have so often in our own time and in the times of our progenitors, kings of England, disturbed the peace of our kingdom . . . ,[6] we command and firmly enjoin you to summon

---

[4] Similar letters were sent to the sheriffs of all the counties but Cornwall; likewise to all abbots, priors, and men of religion in all the counties except Cornwall: Palgrave, *Parliamentary Writs,* I, 384.

[5] See above, p. 152, n. 8.

[6] A number of rhetorical clauses are omitted.

to Northampton on the octave of St. Hilary, before us or before such of our faithful men as we may care to depute for this matter, all those of your bailiwick fit and able to bear arms who have land worth £20 and who are not with us on our Welsh expedition; also four knights from each of the aforesaid counties, having full authority [to act] on behalf of the communities of the same counties; also from each city, borough, or trading town two men similarly empowered on behalf of their communities—in order to hear and do what on our part we shall cause to be explained to them. And you shall not presume, through love, favour, reward, fear, or any other consideration, to grant pardon or postponement to any one of your bailiwick who has arms worth £20 and is fit and able to bear arms. Nor by any means shall you, on the aforesaid account, summon before us, or before our faithful men aforesaid, any one who does not have land worth more than £20, although he may be fit or able to bear arms. And through the four knights aforesaid you are to inform us, or our faithful men aforesaid, on the day and [at the] place aforesaid, of the names of all those whom you thus summon. And you are to have there the names of those four knights and this writ. And as you cherish your life and all that you have, do not fail to attend to all these matters. By witness of the king, at Rhuddlan, November 24 [1282].

Similar mandates to the sheriffs of Nottingham, Derby, Shropshire, Stafford, Cambridge, Huntingdon, Essex, Hertford, Buckingham, Bedford, Somerset, Dorset, Surrey, Sussex, Warwick, Leicester, Oxford, Berkshire, Kent, Middlesex, Northampton, Rutland, Lincoln, Cornwall, Devon, Wiltshire, Hereford, Worcester, Gloucester, and Hampshire, that they should summon, etc., at Northampton. And to the sheriffs of York, Cumberland, Westmorland, Northumberland, and Lancashire that they should summon, etc., at York.

The king to the venerable father in Christ, John, by the same grace archbishop of Canterbury and primate of all England, greeting. Whereas Llewelyn . . . ,[7] we command and urge you to summon to Northampton . . . your suffragans and the abbots, priors, and various other heads of religious houses, as well as proctors from the deans and chapters of your collegiate churches and [those] of the suffragans in your dioceses. And you are to be present on the same day and at the same place to hear and do what in this connection we shall cause to be explained to you and to them for the sake of the public good; also to give us your advice and assistance. . . .

Similar letters of the same date addressed to the archbishop of York, to summon his suffragans, etc., before the king at York on the aforesaid octave, or before faithful men whom the king, etc.

The king to the mayor and sheriffs and the whole community of his city of London, greeting. We are exceedingly grateful to you for having liberally granted to us, as a subsidy for our expedition in

---

[7] Here and immediately below the writ uses the preceding form.

Wales, a thirtieth of all your movable goods; aside from those which were excluded from the fifteenth recently granted to us, and excepting [the goods of] those three hundred persons in the aforesaid city who gave us a subsidy[8] for the sake of the warlike expedition aforesaid, on condition that our magnates would decide to grant the same. And we wish you to know that the same magnates, with respect to themselves, have granted and ratified the subsidy of the said thirtieth, as on our part they were requested to do. And since, as you know, we greatly need the money for the sake of our expedition aforesaid, we have assigned . . .[9] to lay and assess the said thirtieth and to collect it through themselves and through you, the mayor and sheriffs aforesaid. And so we command you in the said matter to be obedient, responsive, serviceable, and helpful to the same men . . . , according to the instructions which on our part they will give you. In testimony whereof, etc. Witnessed as above, February 28.

The king to the knights and freemen and the whole community of the county of Hampshire, greeting. We are exceedingly grateful to you for having, through the four knights sent to Northampton on the part of the community of the aforesaid county, courteously agreed to give us a subsidy for the sake of our present expedition in Wales, to the same amount as our magnates should provide and agree upon as a subsidy of this sort. And whereas the same magnates . . . have agreed upon a subsidy to us of a thirtieth . . . , we have assigned . . .[10] to lay and assess the said thirtieth and to collect it by their own agency and with the sheriff of the aforesaid county. And so we command you. . . . By witness of the king at Rhuddlan, February 28.[11]

The king to the mayor, citizens, and sheriffs of London. . . .[12] And since we wish to have a deliberation with our faithful men as to what should be done with the aforesaid David . . . , we command you to cause two of the wiser and fitter citizens of the aforesaid city to be elected, and to send them to us so that they shall come before us at Shrewsbury on the morrow of Michaelmas next, to talk with us concerning this and other matters. And by no means fail to do this. By witness of the king, at Rhuddlan, June 28.[13]

(Latin) Palgrave, *Parliamentary Writs,* I, 10-16.

[6] Presumably the subsidy or loan taken to anticipate the parliamentary grant; cf. no. 49c, preceding.

[9] Three collectors are named.

[10] Two collectors are named.

[11] Letters resembling one or the other of these forms were sent to the other counties.

[12] The writ contains a long preamble reciting the crimes of the Welsh and announcing the capture of Prince David.

[13] Similar letters were sent to twenty other boroughs; to nineteen persons requiring their individual attendance; and to the sheriffs of all the counties ordering the election in each of two knights to represent their respective communities at the same *colloquium.*

(E) Subsidies of 1294

The king to the knights and freeholders and the whole community of the county of Cumberland, greeting. Whereas the earls, barons, knights, and all other men of our kingdom have now courteously and graciously given us as a subsidy for our war . . . a tenth of all their movable goods, with the exception of those exempted from the fifteenth recently granted to us in the same kingdom[14] . . . , we have assigned our beloved and faithful Thomas of Newton, Robert of Whiteridge, or one of them, together with a certain clerk, to lay and assess and to levy and collect the said tenth in the aforesaid county, and to bring it to our exchequer and there pay it at the following terms. . . . And so we command you. . . .[15] By witness of the king at Westminster, November 12, in the twenty-second year of our reign.

The king to his beloved and faithful Robert of Ratford, greeting. Whereas our citizens and good men of London have graciously conceded to us as a subsidy for our war the sixth of their movables,[16] thus setting an example to the other men in our demesne towns for granting a similar subsidy, we have commissioned you to seek a sixth of this sort from each of our demesne cities and other towns in the counties of Kent, Sussex, Surrey, and Hampshire according to the assessment of the tenth already granted in our kingdom. And so we command you that, taking with you the sheriffs of the [respective] regions, you personally go to each of our demesne cities and other towns and on our part diligently urge and effectively induce the men of the said cities and towns—by whatever means you consider desirable—to give us the aforesaid sixth according to the aforesaid assessment. And you are without delay to report to us, or to our treasurer and our barons of the exchequer, what you accomplish in this undertaking. In testimony whereof we have caused to be drawn up these our letters patent. By witness of the venerable father [William, bishop of Bath and Wells], November 21, in the twenty-third year of our reign.[17]

(Latin) Brady, *Treatise of Boroughs,* pp. 63 f.

---

[14] The parliament of this year, like that of 1290, included no representatives of the boroughs, which were dealt with by separate negotiation. In 1290 a fifteenth was obtained both within and without boroughs, but in 1294 the latter were prevailed on to give a sixth, in contradistinction to the tenth of the knights and magnates. On the significance of this precedent, and on the general character of the assemblies concerned, see Willard, *Parliamentary Taxes,* pp. 3 f.; Stubbs, *Constitutional History,* II, 255 f.

[15] The form used is virtually the same as that in the writs of 1283. Similar letters assigned other commissioners in the rest of the counties.

[16] The writ appointing commissioners to levy the sixth in London states that the subsidy has been liberally and freely (*liberaliter et libenter*) granted by the citizens.

[17] Similar letters assigned other groups of collectors in six other regions; see Pasquet, *Origins of the House of Commons,* App. I (added by G. Lapsley).

(F) PARLIAMENTS OF 1295

Edward, etc., to the venerable father in Christ, R[obert], by the same grace archbishop of Canterbury and primate of all England, greeting. Whereas, with regard to certain arduous affairs touching us and our kingdom, as well as you and the other prelates of the same kingdom, which we are unwilling to settle without your presence and theirs, we wish to hold our parliament and to have a conference and discussion with you concerning these matters, we command and firmly enjoin you, in the fealty and love by which you are bound to us, to come to us at Westminster on the first day of the month of August next, or in any case within the third day following at the latest, in order with us to consider the said affairs and to give us your counsel. And by no means fail to do this. By my own witness at Whitchurch, June 24. By writ of the privy seal.

Similar mandates to the archbishop of York, to the bishops, abbots, and priors, to the masters of the order of Sempringham and of the Knights of the Temple in England, and to the prior of the Hospital of St. John of Jerusalem in England, as noted below: namely. . . .[18]

The king to his beloved and faithful brother Edmund, earl of Lancaster, greeting. Whereas, with regard to certain arduous affairs touching us and our kingdom, as well as you and the other nobles and magnates of the same kingdom, which, etc. (as above) : we command and firmly enjoin you, in the fealty and homage by which you are bound to us, to come to us, etc. (as above to the end). Witnessed as above.

Similar mandates individually by letters close to the following earls and barons: namely. . . .[19]

The king to his beloved and faithful Gilbert of Thornton, greeting. Whereas, with regard to certain arduous affairs touching us and our kingdom, as well as you and others of our council, which, etc. (as above) : we command you in the fealty and love by which you are bound to us, etc. (as above in the mandate for the bishops to the end). Witnessed as above.

Similar mandates to the justices of both benches,[20] the itinerant justices, the justices assigned as deans,[21] the men sworn of the council, the barons of the exchequer, and the other clerks of the council whose names are noted below: namely. . . .[22]

The king to the sheriff of Northampton, greeting. Whereas we wish to have a conference and discussion with the earls, barons, and

---

[18] Besides the archbishop and the heads of the great orders, the list includes eighteen bishops, forty-two abbots, and eleven priors.

[19] Ten earls and fifty-three other barons are enumerated.

[20] Later known as the courts of king's bench and common pleas; but cf. no. 54E.

[21] That is to say, chief justices on the circuits; see nos. 52G, 54E.

[22] Besides Gilbert, thirty-eight persons are named.

other nobles of our realm concerning the provision of remedies for
the dangers that in these days threaten the same kingdom—on which
account we have ordered them to come to us at Westminster on the
Sunday next after the feast of St. Martin in the coming winter, there
to consider, ordain, and do whatever the avoidance of such dangers
may demand—we command and firmly enjoin you that without delay
you cause two knights, of the more discreet and more capable of
labour, to be elected from the aforesaid county, and two citizens from
each city of the aforesaid county, and two burgesses from each borough, and that you have them come to us on the day and at the place
aforesaid; so that the said knights shall then and there have full and
sufficient authority on behalf of themselves and the community of the
county aforesaid, and the said citizens and burgesses on behalf of
themselves and the respective communities of the cities and boroughs
aforesaid, to do whatever in the aforesaid matters may be ordained
by common counsel; and so that, through default of such authority,
the aforesaid business shall by no means remain unfinished. And you
are there to have the names of the knights, citizens, and burgesses,
together with this writ. By witness of the king, at Canterbury,
October 3.

Similar letters addressed to each of the sheriffs throughout England
under the same date.

The king to the venerable father in Christ, R[obert], by the same
grace archbishop of Canterbury and primate of all England. . . .[23]
Wherefore, since darts cause less injury when they are foreseen, and
since your fortunes, like those of the other citizens of the same kingdom, are greatly concerned in this affair, we command and firmly
enjoin you, in the fealty and love by which you are bound to us, that
on Sunday next after the feast of St. Martin in the coming winter
you personally be present at Westminster; first summoning (*premunientes*) the prior and chapter of your church and the archdeacons
and all the clergy of your diocese, the said prior and archdeacons
to be present along with you in person, the said chapter [to be repre-
sented] by one fit proctor, and the said clergy by two—which proctors
are to have full and sufficient authority from the said chapter and
clergy to concern themselves, together with us, with the rest of the
prelates and magnates, and with other inhabitants of our kingdom,
in considering, ordaining, and deciding how such dangers and premeditated evils are to be obviated. By witness of the king, at Wing-
ham, September 30.[24]

The king to his beloved and faithful kinsman, Edmund, earl of

---

[23] The rhetorical preamble includes the famous phrase that "what concerns
all should be approved by all," but it is doubtful whether such flourishes had
any constitutional significance.

[24] Similar letters were sent to the other bishops and, with the omission of the
premunientes clause, to the heads of religious houses and the masters of the
military orders.

Cornwall, greeting. Whereas we wish to have a conference and discussion with you and with the other magnates of our kingdom to provide ways to meet the dangers that in these days threaten our entire kingdom, we command and firmly enjoin you, in the faith and love by which you are bound to us, to be present in person at Westminster on Sunday next after the feast of St. Martin in the coming winter, in order to consider, ordain, and decide, together with us, the prelates, and the rest of the magnates, and with other inhabitants of our kingdom, how such dangers are to be obviated.

Similar letters to those noted below: namely. . . .[25]

(Latin) Palgrave, *Parliamentary Writs*, I, 28-31.

---

[25] The roll lists eight earls and forty-one other barons.

50. MILITARY AND NAVAL RECORDS (1278-97)

(A) DISTRAINT OF KNIGHTHOOD (1278)[1]

The king to the sheriff of Gloucester, greeting. We command and firmly enjoin you without delay to distrain all men of your bailiwick possessing land to the value of £20 a year, who hold of us in chief and who ought to be knights but are not, to receive from us the arms of knighthood before the feast of the Lord's Nativity next or on that same day. You are also to distrain without delay all men of your bailiwick from whomsoever they hold, possessing land to the value of £20 or a whole knight's fee worth £20 a year, who ought to be knights but are not, to receive such arms on the same feast or before. And in this connection [see to it] that you obtain from the same men good and sufficient security, and have the names of all those men inscribed in a certain roll by the view of two lawful knights of the aforesaid county, and sent to us without delay under your seal and the seals of the two knights aforesaid. And we wish you to know that we shall make diligent investigation with regard to your conduct in the execution of this mandate, and according to it shall have an appropriate remedy to apply. By my own witness, at Westminster, June 26, in the sixth year of our reign.

(Latin) *Ibid.*, I, 214.

(B) COMMISSIONS OF ARRAY

The king to all his bailiffs and faithful men of the counties of Nottingham and Derby to whom, etc., greeting. Whereas we have sent our beloved and faithful William Wyther into the aforesaid counties there to select, both within and without liberties, three hundred footsoldiers from those more capable and fit to bear arms, and to lead those men to us as we shall instruct him: [therefore] we command that, when the same William comes to the aforesaid counties to select

---

[1] Precedents for such action can be found in the rolls of Henry III, but under Edward I the practice was systematized and extended; cf. no. 50D.

the said men as stated above, you are to be serviceable, helpful, attentive, and obedient to him, according to what on our part the same
William shall tell you. And as you cherish our interest and honour,
and as we trust in your fealty, by no means fail to do this. . . . By
witness of the king, at Rhuddlan, December 6 [1282].[2]

The king to the sheriffs of Hampshire, Dorset, and Wiltshire, and
to all his faithful men of the same counties, both within and without
liberties, greeting. Know that we have assigned our beloved and
faithful . . . , together with those whom they shall associate with
themselves, to select in the aforesaid counties three thousand men,
both archers and crossbowmen, capable for attack and defence and
well supplied with arms suited to them; and to have them come to
Winchelsea, so that they shall be there on the third or fourth day after
the feast of All Saints next, thus equipped and ready to set forth
on our fleet. . . . And so we command you. . . . By witness of the
king, at Canterbury, October 3 [1295].

(Latin) *Ibid.*, I, 245, 270.

(C) MEMORANDUM OF SERVICE FROM THE CINQUE PORTS (1293)

It is to be remembered that, on the octave of St. Hilary in the
twenty-first year of King Edward, son of King Henry, when Stephen
of Penchester, then constable of Dover [Castle] and warden of the
Cinque Ports,[3] in connection with the account for his aforesaid bailiwick was present in the exchequer before Master William de la
Marche, the treasurer, and the barons of the same exchequer, and
after the said Stephen had been interrogated at length concerning the
aforesaid Cinque Ports—namely, as to which were the ports and
which their members, and as to what services the said ports owed the
king, and how and in what way [they were owed]—the same Stephen
informed the aforesaid treasurer and barons to this effect:—

Sussex. Hastings is a chief port, the members of which are these:
Winchelsea, Rye, the lathe[4] of Pevensey, and Bulverhythe in the
county of Sussex; Bekesbourne and Grange in the county of Kent.
Which port, with its aforesaid members, ought on the king's summons
to find twenty-one ships; and in each ship there ought to be twenty-
one men, strong, fit, well armed, and prepared for the king's service;
but so that, on the king's behalf, summons should thereof be made
forty days before. And when the aforesaid ships and the men in
them have come to the place whither they have been summoned, they
shall there remain in the king's service for fifteen days at their own
cost. And if the king needs their service beyond the fifteen days afore-

---

[2] Many similar commissions were issued in this and the following years for
foot-soldiers, ditch-diggers, and carpenters, all of whom were normally paid
by the king. Cf. no. 41D.

[3] Cf. no. 48D.

[4] An administrative district peculiar to this region.

said, or wishes them to remain there longer, those ships with the men in them shall remain in the king's service so long as he pleases and at his cost: that is to say, a master shall receive 6*d*. per day, a constable 6*d*. per day, and each of the others 3*d*. per day.

Kent. Romney is a chief port, and Old Romney and Lydd are members of the same. Which port, with its members, shall find five ships for the king in the manner aforesaid. The port of Hythe owes the king five ships in the manner aforesaid. Dover is a chief port, the members of which are these: Faversham, Folkestone, and Margate. This port, with its aforesaid members, owes twenty-one ships in the manner aforesaid. Sandwich is a chief port, the members of which are Fordwich, Stonor, and Sarre. Which port, with its members, owes the king five ships in the manner aforesaid.

Total service of the Cinque Ports, fifty-seven ships.

(Latin) *Red Book of the Exchequer*, II, 714 f.

(D) GENERAL LEVY FOR SERVICE IN FRANCE (1297)

The king to the sheriff of York, greeting. Whereas by way of careful precaution against the peril and damage that might be incurred by us and our whole kingdom from the plots of our enemies, we recently commanded you to inform all men of your bailiwick possessing land and rent to the value of £20 a year, both within and without liberties, and likewise men having more—those not holding of us in chief as well as those so holding—that they should at once provide themselves with horses and arms and should hold themselves fit and ready to join us and to go with our own person for the safeguarding and defence of themselves and of our whole kingdom aforesaid, as soon as we should issue summons for them; and whereas, on account of the safeguarding aforesaid, we have now decided to set our crossing to the lands beyond the sea: [therefore] we command and firmly enjoin you, in the fealty by which you are bound to us, that on our part you immediately summon all and several of your bailiwick, both within and without liberties, who possess land and rent to the value of £20 a year or more, as aforesaid, from whomsoever they hold, urging and firmly enjoining them, on the first Sunday after the octave of St. John the Baptist next, to come to us at London with horses and arms—that is to say, each of them as befits his condition—prepared to cross the sea with our person to the lands aforesaid, for the honour of God and of themselves, and for the safeguarding and common benefit of the said kingdom. And so you are to devote yourself to the execution of this our mandate with all speed, lest—which God forbid!—our crossing be delayed through your default and we be obliged to chastise you severely. By witness of the king at Loders, May 15.

Similar letters to each of the sheriffs of England.

(Latin) Palgrave, *Parliamentary Writs*, I, 281.

51. RECORDS CONCERNING PARLIAMENT (1297-1306)

(A) CONFIRMATION OF THE CHARTERS (1297)

Edward, by the grace of God king of England, lord of Ireland, and duke of Aquitaine, to all who may see or hear these present letters, greeting. Know that, for the honour of God and of Holy Church and for the benefit of our entire kingdom, we have granted for ourself and for our heirs that the Great Charter of Liberties and the Charter of the Forest, which were drawn up by the common assent of the whole kingdom in the time of King Henry, our father, are to be observed without impairment in all their particulars. And we will that those same charters shall be sent under our seal to our justices—those of the forest as well as the others—to all sheriffs of counties, and to all our other ministers, as well as to all cities throughout the land, together with our writs providing that the aforesaid charters are to be published and announcement is to be made to the people that we have granted these [charters] to be observed in all their particulars; and that our justices, sheriffs, mayors, and other ministers, whose duty it is to administer the law of the land under us and through our agency, shall cause the same charters in all particulars to be admitted in pleas and judgments before them—that is to say, the Great Charter of Liberties as common law and the Charter of the Forest according to the assize of the forest, for the relief of our people. And we will that, if any judgment is henceforth rendered contrary to the particulars of the charters aforesaid by our justices, or by our other ministers before whom pleas are held contrary to the particulars of the charters, it shall be null and void. And we will that these same charters shall be sent under our seal to the cathedral churches throughout the kingdom and shall there remain; and twice a year they shall be read to the people. And [we will] that the archbishops and bishops shall pronounce sentences of greater excommunication against all those who, by deed or aid or counsel, shall violate the aforesaid charters, infringing them in any particular or violating them in any way; and the aforesaid prelates shall pronounce and publish these sentences twice a year. And if the same prelates—the bishops or any of them—prove negligent in making the aforesaid denunciation, by the archbishops of Canterbury and York who at the time hold office, they shall be reproved in a suitable manner and compelled to make this same denunciation in the form aforesaid.

And whereas some people of our kingdom are fearful that the aids and taxes (*mises*), which by their liberality and good will they have heretofore paid to us for the sake of our wars and other needs, shall, despite the nature of the grants, be turned into a servile obligation for them and their heirs because these [payments] may at a future time be found in the rolls, and likewise the prises that in our name have been taken throughout the kingdom by our ministers: [therefore] we have granted, for us and our heirs, that, on account of anything that has been done or that can be found from a roll or in some other way, we will not make into a precedent for the future any such aids, taxes, or prises. And for us and our heirs we have also granted to the archbishops, bishops, abbots, priors, and other folk of Holy Church, and to the earls and barons and the whole community of the land, that on no account will we henceforth take from our kingdom such aids, taxes, and prises, except by the common assent of the whole kingdom and for the common benefit of the same kingdom, saving the ancient aids and prises due and accustomed.[1]

And whereas the greater part of the community all feel themselves gravely oppressed by the maltote on wool—that is to say, 40s. from each sack of wool—and have besought us to relieve them [of the charge], at their prayer we have fully relieved them, granting that henceforth we will take neither this nor any other [custom] without their common assent and good will, saving to us and our heirs the custom on wool, wool-fells, and hides previously granted by the community of the kingdom aforesaid.[2]

In testimony whereof we have caused to be written these our letters patent. Given at Ghent, November 5, in the twenty-fifth year of our reign.

(French) Stubbs, *Select Charters,* pp. 490 f.

(B) PARLIAMENTARY BILL OF 1301

Bill of the prelates and nobles delivered to the lord king on behalf of the whole community in the parliament of Lincoln in the year aforesaid :[3]—

. . . Thus the said community is of the opinion that, if it please our lord the king, the two charters, of liberties and of the forest, shall henceforth be entirely observed in all particulars. [Response:] It expressly pleases the king.

And statutes contrary to the said charters shall be annulled and voided. [Response:] It expressly pleases.

And the power of the justices assigned to keep the charters in the counties shall be defined by the counsel of the prelates, earls, and barons. [Response:] It tacitly pleases.

---

[1] Cf. the first article in what used to be called the Statute *De Tallagio non Concedendo,* but which seems rather to have been a petition drawn up by the parliamentary opposition during the crisis of 1297: "No tallage or aid shall henceforth be imposed or levied by us or by our heirs in our kingdom except by the will and common assent of the archbishops, bishops, and other prelates, and of the earls, barons, knights, burgesses, and other freemen in our kingdom." On this subject see especially Pasquet, *Origins of the House of Commons,* pp. 109, 237 f. See below, p. 166, n. 6; and cf. no. 56, art. 10.

[2] See no. 49B.

[3] January, 1301. The king had first presented a bill to parliament, asking the latter to assume all responsibility that the new delimitation of the royal forest would not violate his coronation oath, and to provide means whereby the proposed disafforestment could be amended. This parliament bluntly refused to do, sending to the king instead the following articles. On this whole subject see Petit-Dutaillis and Lefebvre, pp. 217 f.; Pasquet, *Origins of the House of Commons,* p. 115.

And the perambulation that has already been made and ridden[4] by view of good men according to the form of the said charter of the forest shall stand and at the same time shall be carried out through prompt disafforestment according to the bounds determined by the perambulators, so that the community may at once be seised of them. [Response:] It expressly pleases.

And offences and trespasses committed by the king's ministers against the tenor of the said charters and prises extortionately taken without consent or payment, against the form of the lord king's statute made at Westminster during Lent just past, shall henceforth cease. [Response:] It expressly pleases.

And any offence by a minister shall be paid for in proportion to the trespass, according to [the judgment of] auditors who are not suspected on account of their past deeds and who are assigned for such purpose by the prelates, earls, and barons of the land, and this matter shall be undertaken at once. [Response:] The lord king wishes to provide another remedy in this connection, rather than through such auditors.

And henceforth sheriffs shall be answerable for their revenues according to the customary practice in the time of his father—which revenues have been and are now to the great impoverishment of the people. And sheriffs shall not be placed under increased charges. [Response:] It pleases the lord king that in this respect a fit remedy shall be provided by common counsel as quickly as is well possible.

And wherever the perambulation has in part been made, but has not been ridden, it shall be done between now and Michaelmas next. [Response:] It expressly pleases.

On condition that the aforesaid matters are carried out and firmly established and accomplished, the people of the realm grant him a fifteenth in place of the twentieth recently granted—yet so that all the matters aforesaid are carried out between now and Michaelmas next; otherwise nothing is to be taken. [Response:] It expressly pleases. . . .

(French and Latin) Palgrave, *Parliamentary Writs,* I, 104 f.

(C) MALTOTE OF 1303[5]

The king to the sheriff of Lincoln, greeting. Whereas we have learned that divers merchants of our kingdom, in order that they may be quit of our prises[6] and may use and enjoy the various liberties granted by us to foreign and alien merchants, are willing to give us from their goods and merchandise certain new payments and customs, which the said foreign and alien merchants give us from their merchandise within our kingdom and dominions: we [therefore],

---

[4] There were two steps in the procedure: juries first determined the theoretic extent of the forest; then commissioners fixed the bounds by riding along them.

[5] See above, p. 121, n. 38.

[6] The exactions of wine and other merchandise to which the king was entitled by ancient custom.

wishing to have a discussion and conference regarding these matters with the merchants of the said kingdom, command you to summon to our exchequer at York two or three citizens from each city, and two or three burgesses from each borough within your bailiwick, so that they shall be there on the morrow of St. John the Baptist next, with full power on behalf of the communities of the cities and boroughs aforesaid, to accept and to do what shall then be ordered in the foregoing connection by the counsel and assent of us and of them and of the merchants of the said kingdom. And you are then and there to have this writ. By witness of the king, at Newcastle-upon-Tyne, May 7.

Similar letters addressed to each of the sheriffs throughout England.

. . . And the aforesaid Walter, John, and Henry[7] appear for the city of London and . . . for Lincoln. For Winchester . . . ; for Salisbury . . . ; for Exeter . . . ; for Northampton . . . ; for Oxford . . . ; for Leicester . . . ; for Bristol . . . ; for Huntingdon . . . ; for Hertford . . . ; for Shrewsbury . . . ; for Stafford . . . ; for Lichfield . . . ; for Coventry . . . ; for Warwick . . . ; for Worcester . . . ; for St. Albans . . . ; for Plympton . . . ; for Bodmin . . . ; for Weymouth . . . ; for Canterbury . . . ; for Dunhaved . . . ; for Liskeard . . . ; for Dorchester . . . ; for Yarmouth . . . ; for Norwich . . . ; for Dunwich . . . ; for Lynn . . . ; for Colchester . . . ; for Cambridge . . . ; for Melcombe . . . ; for Chichester . . . ; for Grimsby . . . ; for Rochester . . . ; for the city of York . . . ; for Scarborough . . . ; for Nottingham . . . ; for Kingston-upon Hull . . . ; for Newcastle-upon-Tyne . . . ; for Whitby . . . ; for Richmond. . . . All of whom, by virtue of the summons in the aforesaid writ, appeared on June 25 before the council of the lord king at York, and said that by their unanimous opinion and will, on behalf both of themselves and of the communities of the cities and boroughs aforesaid, they would by no means agree to an increased maltote or to the customs mentioned in the aforesaid writ as having been granted to the lord king by foreign and alien merchants, but only to the customs anciently due and used.

(Latin) *Ibid.*, I, 134-35.

(D) MEMORANDUM OF PARLIAMENT (1306)

Memorandum that, after the lord king had recently ordered that Edward, his first-born son, should be decorated with the belt of knighthood at the feast of Pentecost in the thirty-fourth year of his reign, mandates were issued for the archbishops, bishops, abbots, priors, earls, barons, and other magnates to come before the lord king and his council at Westminster on the morrow of Holy Trinity next following, in order to deliberate and ordain with regard to giving the

---

[7] Commissioned by the mayor and community of London in a preceding writ. Similar groups of deputies are named from each of the other boroughs.

king an aid for the knighting aforesaid and in order to consent to those matters which should further be ordained in that connection, or for them then and there to send procurators or attorneys with sufficient instructions to carry out the aforesaid matters in their place; also each of the sheriffs of England was commanded to cause two knights from his county to come to the said place at the said time, and from each city of his bailiwick two citizens and from each borough of the same bailiwick two burgesses or one, etc., in order to deliberate, ordain, and consent as aforesaid. [Accordingly] there came in person before the king and his council at Westminster on that day[8] . . . ; also through procurators and attorneys[9] . . . ; and there came likewise two knights from each county of the same kingdom, two citizens from each city, and two burgesses from each borough, elected by the communities of the same counties, cities, and boroughs in the place of the same communities, to deliberate, ordain, and consent as aforesaid. And when all the aforesaid persons had assembled before the aforesaid council of the king, and it had been explained to them by the same council on behalf of the king that by right of the royal crown aid should be given the lord king on the occasion aforesaid, and besides that the lord king had incurred multifarious expenses and many other obligations toward suppressing the rebellion and malice of Robert Bruce, traitor to the same lord king, and of his adherents in the parts of Scotland, who were then presuming to make war against the king in those parts; the same prelates, earls, barons, and other magnates, as well as the knights of the shires, having discussed the matter with deliberation, and considering that aid was owed as aforesaid and that the king had incurred many obligations on account of the aforesaid war, at length unanimously granted to the lord king on behalf of themselves and the whole community of the land a thirtieth of all their movable temporal goods which they should happen to possess on Michaelmas next following, to be taken as a competent aid to the lord king for the knighting of his aforesaid son and also as an aid toward the expenditures that should be made in connection with the aforesaid war. This grant, however, [was made] on condition that it should in no way be held to their own prejudice or to that of their successors or heirs in future times, and that it should never be taken as a precedent in a case of this kind; also that in assessing the aforesaid goods all should be excepted which had been excepted in assessing the fifteenth granted by the community of the kingdom to the lord king in the eighteenth year of his reign for exiling the Jews. Moreover, the citizens and burgesses of the cities and boroughs aforesaid and others of the king's demesnes, being assembled and holding a discussion on the said matters, in consideration of the obligations incurred by the lord king as aforesaid, unanimously granted the lord

---

[8] Twenty persons, including the warden of the Cinque Ports "together with certain barons of the same ports."

[9] Twenty-seven named persons "and many other prelates, magnates, and nobles of the realm."

king for the reasons aforesaid the twentieth of their movable goods, to be taken as aforesaid.

(Latin) Pasquet, Origins of the House of Commons, pp. 234 f.

52. EDWARD I: STATUTES AND ORDINANCES[1]

(A) STATUTE OF GLOUCESTER (1278)

In the year of grace 1278, the sixth of the reign of King Edward, son of King Henry, at Gloucester in the month of August, the same king, having summoned the more discreet men of his kingdom, both greater and lesser, has made provision for the betterment of his kingdom and the fuller administration of justice, as is demanded by the kingly office. . . .

The sheriffs shall have it commonly proclaimed throughout their bailiwicks—that is to say, in cities, boroughs, trading towns, and elsewhere—that all those who claim to have any franchises by charters of the king's predecessors, kings of England, or by other title, shall come before the king or before the itinerant justices on a certain day and at a certain place to show what sort of franchises they claim to have, and by what warrant[2] [they hold them]. . . . And if those who claim to have such franchises do not come on the day aforesaid, those franchises shall then be taken into the king's hand by the local sheriff in the name of distress; so that they shall not enjoy such franchises until they come to receive justice. . . .

(French) Statutes of the Realm, I, 45 f.

(B) STATUTE OF MORTMAIN (1279)

The king to his justices of the bench, greeting. Whereas it was formerly enacted[3] that men of religion should not enter upon the fiefs of any persons without the consent and licence of the principal lords from whom those fiefs were immediately held; and whereas since then men of religion have nevertheless entered upon the fiefs of others as well as their own—by appropriating them, buying them, and sometimes by receiving them through gifts of other men— whereby the services which are owed from fiefs of this sort, and which were originally established for the defence of the kingdom, are wrongfully withheld and the principal lords [are caused to] lose their escheats: [therefore] we, seeking in this connection to provide

---

[1] *Statutum* had not as yet acquired the technical meaning of a legislative enactment in full parliament, as distinguished from an ordinance in council. The word was still vague, being generally applied to especially formal statements of law; see Holdsworth, *History of English Law,* II, 172 f., 244 f.; and cf. the examples cited below, no. 62.

[2] *Quo warranto* here and in the writ employed for legal proceedings of this sort. See especially H. M. Cam, *The Hundred and the Hundred Rolls,* ch. xiv; in which work the student will also find a full account of the inquests that led up to the formulation of this statute—e.g., the Articles of 1274, pp. 248 f.

[3] In the reissue of Magna Carta (above, p. 123, n. 45), somewhat extended by the Provisions of Westminster.

a suitable remedy for the good of the kingdom, by the counsel of the prelates, earls, and other faithful men of our kingdom who are members of our council, have enacted, established, and ordained that no man of religion or any other whatsoever shall buy or sell lands or tenements, or under colour of donation, lease, or other title of any sort shall receive them from any one, or presume artfully and craftily to appropriate them in any way whatsoever, whereby land and tenements of this sort may somehow come into mortmain[4]—under pain of forfeiting the same [lands or tenements]. . . . And so we command you to have the aforesaid statute read in your presence and henceforth strictly held and observed.

By witness of the king, at Westminster, November 25, in the seventh year of our reign.

(Latin) Stubbs, *Select Charters,* pp. 451 f.

(C) Ordinance for the Household (1279)

. . . It is ordained and commanded that the stewards, or one [of them] if both cannot be [there] together, with the treasurer,[5] or the comptroller if the treasurer cannot be [there], one of the marshals of the hall, and the clerks and serjeants of the offices[6] shall be present each night for [drawing up] the account of the household. And there, by the witness of the ushers of the hall, the servings of food in the hall (*mes de la sale*) are to be checked; and according to the number of the servings, the issues from the pantry, butlery, and kitchen are to be checked. And if there is irregularity, let it be corrected and the serjeants be reproved. Each night on the margin of the household roll is to be written the [amount of] wine dispensed during the day; so that, by the testimony of this roll which bears the record of the household, we may two or three times a year audit the account of the tuns of wine [dispensed]. Next the wages of the serjeants, squires, and grooms are to be there examined, as has been accustomed. And if at the account any wrongdoing is presented which is not so bad as to require being brought to the king's attention, let it be punished there at the discretion of the stewards and the treasurer—by the withholding of wages or in some other way according to what they may think best—so that the lord [king] shall not be bothered with affairs that can be settled by those [officials].

The treasurer, having called to him one of the stewards, or both of them, shall once or twice in every year audit the account of the chamberlain of wines; so that he may clearly know how many pieces come from each port and from each ship, and the names of the persons from whom the wines have been taken, parcel by parcel, and

---

[4] Literally, "dead hand"—permanent possession by a church or other corporation.

[5] Of the wardrobe, on which see Tout, *Chapters in Mediaeval Administrative History,* II, 27 f. More detailed information concerning most of the officials mentioned here will be found in the Household Ordinance of 1318, no. 57.

[6] *Mesters* (i.e., *métiers*), such as the pantry, butlery, kitchen, etc.

how much is through purchase and how much through prise.[7] And this account is to be audited and checked by the treasurer and one of the stewards in such fashion that the treasurer can present a summary of it in his account at the feast of St. Edmund the King, when he renders his account.

In the same way the treasurer shall draw up the account of the great wardrobe.[8] . . . And it is to be noted that the treasurer shall henceforth have all articles for the great wardrobe bought at three fairs a year by a certain man, who shall be keeper of the great wardrobe and shall go to fairs to make the purchases; and he shall be put on oath to the king for this particular office. And the usher of the wardrobe shall be comptroller for him, going to fairs with him to view his purchases and at the account witnessing liveries [made by him]. . . . And the aforesaid keeper shall not purchase anything or deliver anything to anybody without the special command of the treasurer, and this in the presence of the comptroller. . . .

The usher of the wardrobe should each day have the wax and candle-wicks weighed—what is to be made [into candles] and what is to be kept. And each night [he should] weigh what is given out in livery and on the morrow reweigh what is left; so that through such weights he may know what has been dispensed each night, and the sum of it all at the end of the year. . . . And the chandler shall have nothing in his charge except what is to be dispensed at night, as delivered to him by the usher.

And whereas it is rightful that the household of Madame [the queen] should be regulated according to the ordinance of the king's household, it is ordered that the steward of Madame, or the man who is in charge of her household, shall each night be present at the account for the king's household, together with the pantler, the butler, the chief cook, and the marshal of her chamber. . . .

Furthermore, it is ordained that the marshals, or one of them, shall make the circuit of the household each month of the year, or more often if they see fit, to clear it of rascally men and women, and of horses belonging to them, so that they shall take no hay, or oats, or wages. And [the marshals] shall do the same for the household of Madame. And the marshals of the hall and the ushers shall also see to it that the hall is well cleared of strange people and of rascals who should not eat [there], and that the hall is served well and for the common good (*comunaument*) and that no knight has more than one squire eating in the hall.

The evening livery of wine and candles shall all be made by the king's men, as well for the household of Madame as elsewhere. And the treasurer and the stewards shall see to it that no liveries are made outside except in a proper place, neither of bread nor of wine nor of candles, and each night they shall examine the liveries for the house-

---

[7] See above, p. 166, n. 6.

[8] "So-called not because of its importance, but because it dealt with bulky commodities": Tout, *Place of Edward II in English History*, p. 71.

hold of Madame as well as for other places and for the king's household.

Furthermore, it is ordained that no one shall sleep in the wardrobe except the treasurer; Sire Thomas Gunneys [the comptroller];[9] Master William of Louth, the treasurer's clerk; Master Simon, the surgeon; Orlandino,[10] when he comes to court; William of Blyborough and Sire Stephen of St. George [clerks of the wardrobe]; John Rede, chief usher of the wardrobe, and a footman under him—no others.

And it is ordained that no clerk who holds a benefice of the king shall henceforth receive wages from the king. And it is ordained that no one shall eat in the wardrobe except the under-usher; and the chamberlain, the treasurer, and all the other chamberlains [shall eat] in the hall unless they are lodged apart from the court.

With regard to the king's carriage [service], it is provided that for the wardrobe there shall be three long carts; for the pantry a long cart and a short one, which is to carry the demeine flour and the mills of the saucery;[11] for the butlery a long cart and a short one; for the kitchen a long cart and two short ones.

Twenty men are chosen as serjeants-at-arms . . . , and each is to receive 3½m. a year for robes. . . . Besides, it is ordained that each squire shall receive 10s. a year for robes, and each serving man (*valet de mester*) 1m. And each groom who receives 2d. a day as wages is to have 10s. for robes; and each groom who receives 1½d. a day, and all the others who ought to have robes, are to have ½m. . . .[12]

(French) Tout, *Mediaeval Administrative History*, II, 158 f.

(D) STATUTE OF MERCHANTS (1283)

Whereas merchants heretofore, on lending their goods to various people, have incurred poverty owing to the fact that no suitable law was provided whereby they could speedily recover their debt on the day set for payment; and whereas, on this account, many merchants have ceased coming into this land with their merchandise, to the damage of the merchants and of the whole kingdom: [therefore] the king, by himself and his council, has ordained and established[13] that the merchant who wishes to make sure of his debt shall cause his

---

[9] As appears from other entries in the record.

[10] Of Lucca, the king's banker.

[11] Demeine flour was that of superior quality for the king's use; cf. above, p. 66, n. 3. On the saucery see below, p. 204.

[12] Preceding the ordinance as printed is a memorandum of the wages and liveries enjoyed by the other officials, listed by name. The steward, the marshal, the surgeon, the chaplain, and the chiefs of the wardrobe received 8m. a year for robes, together with various fees, unless they had received lands or benefices. Subordinates usually received 3m. for robes, and wages of 7d. a day.

[13] Despite the phrasing of the act, it was actually drawn up in the assembly of burgesses first summoned to Shrewsbury (above, p. 157) and then transferred to Acton Burnell.

debtor to come before the mayor of London or York or Bristol—
[that is to say,] before the mayor and a clerk whom the king shall
depute for that purpose—to acknowledge the debt and the day of
payment; and the acknowledgment shall be enrolled by the hand of
the aforesaid clerk so that it may be known. Moreover, the aforesaid
clerk shall with his own hand write out a record of the obligation,
to which shall be attached the seal of the debtor, together with the
king's seal provided for that purpose, which seal shall remain in the
custody of the mayor and the clerk aforesaid. And if the debtor does
not pay on the day set for him, let the creditor come to the mayor
and the clerk with the record of the obligation; and if it is found by
the roll and the record that the debt was acknowledged and that
the set day has passed, the mayor shall at once, by view of worthy
men, have movables of the debtor sold to the amount of the
debt. . . .[14] And to meet the cost of the aforesaid clerk, the king
shall take a penny from every pound [of the debt]. This ordinance
and establishment the king wishes henceforth to be observed throughout his entire kingdom of England by all persons who shall freely
choose to make such acknowledgments, excepting Jews, to whom this
establishment does not apply. . . .

Given at Acton Burnell, October 12, in the eleventh year of our
reign.

(French) *Statutes of the Realm,* I, 53 f.

(E) STATUTE OF WINCHESTER (1285)

Whereas every day robbery, homicide, and arson are committed
more frequently than used to be the case, and felonies escape presentment by the oaths of jurors who would see the felonies committed
on strangers pass unpunished rather than accuse the offenders, many
of whom are persons of the same country[15] . . . : [therefore] our
lord the king, in order to abate the power of felons, has established
a penalty in such cases; so that henceforth, through fear of the penalty rather than of the oath, no one will be spared and no felony
will be concealed. . . .

Accordingly, inquests shall be held when necessary in a vill by him
who is lord of the vill, and afterwards in hundreds, franchises, and
counties—sometimes in two, three, or four counties, in cases where
felonies are committed on the borders of counties—so that the offenders may be brought to justice. And if the country will not answer
for criminals in this way, the penalty shall be such that each country—
that is to say, the people living in the country—shall be responsible
for the robberies committed and the damages [thus incurred]. . . .

And for better assuring the peace, the king has commanded that

---

[14] The statute includes detailed provisions for the attachment of property in
towns other than those mentioned, for imprisonment of debtors with insufficient
chattels, and the like.

[15] *Pays* (Latin, *patria*)—the neighbourhood in which a person had his home.

in great towns which are walled the gates shall be closed from sunset to sunrise; and that no man shall be lodged in the suburbs, or in the outskirts of the town, except in the daytime—nor even in the daytime unless his host will be responsible for him. And the bailiffs of towns each week, or at least every fortnight, shall make investigation concerning men lodged in the suburbs or in the outskirts of the towns; and if they find anybody harbouring or otherwise lodging persons suspected of being in any respect violators of the peace, the bailiffs shall have justice done in the matter. And the king has commanded that henceforth all watches shall be kept according to the ancient custom. . . .[16]

Furthermore, it is commanded that highways from one trading town to another shall be enlarged wherever there are woods, hedges, or ditches; so that there shall be neither ditches, underbrush, nor bushes for two hundred feet on the one side and two hundred feet on the other, where men can hide near the road with evil intent; yet so that this statute shall not apply to oaks or to any great trees, so long as they are cleared underneath. . . .

Moreover, it is commanded that every man shall have in his house arms for keeping the peace according to the ancient assize. . . .

Given at Winchester, October 8, in the thirteenth year of the king's reign.

(French) Stubbs, Select Charters, pp. 464 f.

(F) Statute of Quia Emptores (1290)

Whereas the buyers of lands and tenements belonging to the fiefs of magnates and other men have in times past frequently entered upon their fiefs to the prejudice of the same [lords], because the freeholders of the said magnates and other men have sold their lands and tenements to such purchasers to be held in fee by themselves and their heirs of the feoffors and not of the principal lords of the fiefs, whereby those same principal lords have often lost the escheats, marriages, and wardships of lands and tenements belonging to their fiefs; and whereas this has seemed very hard and burdensome to those magnates and other lords, being in such cases manifest disinheritance: [therefore] the lord king in his parliament at Westminister [held] after Easter in the eighteenth year of his reign. . . , at the suggestion of the magnates of his realm,[17] has granted, provided, and established that henceforth every freeman shall be permitted to sell his land or tenement, or a part of it, at pleasure; yet so that the feoffee shall hold that land or tenement of the same principal lord [of whom the feoffor held] and by the same services and customs by which the feoffor earlier held. . . .

(Latin) Ibid., p. 473.

---

[16] What is omitted here and in the second paragraph below is largely a repetition of Henry III's ordinance (no. 46H).

[17] The parliament was attended only by prelates and lay barons.

(G) Ordinance concerning Judicial Circuits (1293)

Whereas the lord king, in his recent statutes at Westminster[18] commanded that in each county certain justices, and no others, should be commissioned for the holding of assizes, juries, and certifications[19] at particular times in those counties; and whereas the justices of the two benches,[20] as well as the itinerant justices assigned to carry out the aforesaid [commissions] for limited periods, have often, when they were not on eyre, been hindered, both by their offices and by precepts of the lord king directed to them, from coming to the [appointed] places on the days announced by them; and whereas, on account of their absence, justice has long been withheld from many persons and misdeeds have gone unpunished: [therefore] the lord king, desirous that, in so far as he can [provide it], speedy justice shall be rendered to every one in his kingdom for the wrongs done to that person, commands that henceforth eight circumspect and discreet justices shall be commissioned to hold assizes, juries, and certifications throughout the whole kingdom of England—namely, two in the counties of York, Northumberland, Westmorland, Cumberland, Lancaster, Nottingham, and Derby; two in the counties of Lincoln, Leicester, Warwick, Stafford, Shropshire, Northampton, Rutland, Gloucester, Hereford, and Worcester; two in the counties of Cornwall, Devon, Somerset, Dorset, Wiltshire, Hampshire, Oxford, Berkshire, Sussex, and Surrey; and two in the counties of Kent, Essex, Hertford, Norfolk, Suffolk, Cambridge, Huntingdon, Bedford, and Buckingham. And the assizes, juries, and recognitions of Middlesex shall be held before the justices of the bench. . . .

(Latin) *Statutes of the Realm*, I, 112.

(H) Articles of 1300[21]

. . . Moreover, no common pleas shall henceforth be held in the exchequer, contrary to the form of the Great Charter. On the other hand, the king wills that the chancery and the justices of his bench shall follow him; so that he may always have near him certain men expert in the law, who, whenever the need arises, will know how rightfully to dispatch all such business as may come before the court. Henceforth no writ touching the common law shall be issued under the small seal.[22]

(French) *Ibid.*, I, 138 f.

---

[18] The reference is to art. 30 of the lengthy enactment known as the Second Statute of Westminster (1285). The article in question provided that for each county two justices should be commissioned to hold assizes three times a year. See Stubbs, *Const. Hist.*, II, 284.

[19] Certification was a process by which a vague or insufficient verdict was brought before a court for examination.

[20] Cf. 54E.

[21] Issued as an explanatory supplement to the Confirmation of the Charters (no. 51A).

[22] Cf. no. 54G, the last excerpt.

53. ROYAL COUNCILLORS' OATHS OF OFFICE

(A) OATH OF 1257

They have sworn in the first place to provide faithful counsel to the lord king as often as they shall perceive it to be useful. Item, they will reveal the counsel of the lord king to no one to whom it ought not to be revealed, whereby they believe harm might ensue. Item, they will consent to the alienation of none of those things which belong to the ancient demesne of the crown. Item, they will bring it about that justice is administered to all, both rich and poor, both great and small, according to the rightful laws and customs of the kingdom. Item, they will freely permit, with regard to themselves, their friends, and their relatives, that justice shall be provided to every one seeking it. Nor through them shall the administration of justice be impeded for prayer or price, for favour or spite; but they will in good faith strive to have the great and the small judged alike, according to the law and custom of the kingdom. Nor will they, either by word or by deed, support or defend evil-doers in their wrongs. Item, from no one whom they know to have business in the court of the king, or of his bailiffs, will they accept, either of themselves or through others, any gift or service on an occasion of this sort, in any way or by any means whatsoever. Item, should any one in the council discover for certain, or hear from reliable sources, that another councillor has received any reward or gift other than something to eat or drink,[1] he will bring it to the public attention of the whole council. And if [such councillor] is convicted of this [offence], he shall be forever excluded from the council and he shall lose his lands and his rents, or the income from his possessions, for one year. And if he has no such income, he shall be punished according to the decision of the councillors.

(Latin) Baldwin, *The King's Council*, pp. 346 f.

(B) OATH OF 1307

He who is to be sworn of the king's council shall be charged with regard to the particulars hereinunder written; and if he is to be a justice, he shall be charged [especially] with regard to the last particular:—

That well and loyally, according to your knowledge and ability, you will counsel the king. That well and loyally you will keep his counsel; and that you will not accuse another [on account] of anything that he may say in the council. And that, to the best of your ability, you will give and devote your care, aid, and counsel to keep and maintain, to safeguard and restore, the rights of the king and of the crown, in so far as you can without committing wrong. And that, whenever you know things of the crown and rights of the king to be concealed, wrongfully alienated, or withheld, you will bring it to the king's knowledge. And that, to the best of your ability and in loyal fashion, you will support the crown. And that you will take

---

[1] Cf. no. 47B, p. 145.

no part in court or council where the king deprives himself of something belonging to the crown, unless it is an action that you should approve. And that for no one, through love or hate, for good will or ill will, you will abstain from having right and justice done to every man, of whatsoever estate or condition, according to your knowledge and ability. And that you will take nothing from any one for doing wrong or delaying justice. And that, in judging or enforcing right there where you may be assigned, you will spare no one on account of grandeur, poverty, or wealth, so that justice shall not be done. And that, if you have formed an alliance through lordship or otherwise, so that you cannot do these things without breaking such alliance, you will tell the king or have him informed of it. And that henceforth you will make no alliance by oath with any one without the king's permission. And that you will take no gift from any one on account of a plea or anything else that is to be determined before you, unless it is food and drink for the day.

(French) *Statutes of the Realm*, I, 248.

54. JUDICIAL RECORDS (1220-83)

(A) Excerpts from the Curia Regis Roll of 122ᵒ

Hugh Hop-over-Humber appeals Thomas of Dean for [the following offense:] that on St. Giles's day, between the first and third hours, in the second year of the king's reign, while he, together with his cousin William of Leigh, was in the park of Cuckfield belonging to the earl de Warenne, for the purpose of guarding that park, the said Thomas came with a band [of accomplices], a multitude of men armed with bows and arrows, and assaulted them, aiming an arrow at the said William and hitting him in the leg, so that within nine days he died of the wound. And that [Thomas] did this wickedly and feloniously and in [violation of] the lord king's peace, [Hugh], as one who was present and saw it, offers to prove by his body, as the court shall decide. He also says that pursuit was made according to the law of the land and that hue was raised; that twelve jurors indicted [Thomas] on account of that death[2] before the itinerant justices on their last visit to these parts; and that the said William, while he was still alive after being wounded, stated that the said Thomas had struck him as aforesaid, and so blamed [Thomas] for his death.

And Thomas appears and denies the entire charge as an ordained clerk. And thereupon Robert of Dean, his brother, appears and presents letters close from the bishop of Chichester, in which it is set forth that the said Thomas has sufficiently proved before him by witnesses, etc., that the said Thomas was in due season promoted to the order of acolyte by Selfrid, one time bishop of Chichester, and that [the bishop] accordingly claims him as a clerk, so that justice may be

---

[1] On the nature of these records see Maitland's introduction; cf. immediately below, no. 54E, F.

[2] See no. 31, art. I.

administered with respect to him for all who may complain in the ecclesiastical court. Thomas is committed to R[alph], bishop of Chichester, who shall hold him for justice because he is a clerk. And it should be known that the lord [archbishop] of Canterbury, who earlier took the said Thomas into custody, is quit thereof.

William Smallwood[3] appeals Hugh the Large of Walthamstow for having received him together with two horses which he had [taken] from the chamberlain of Baldwin de Guisnes, whom he had slain; so that the said Hugh kept those two horses in his chamber for eight days, and for thus keeping them he received 6s., and a certain woman at the inn [received] 6d. for carrying water to the horses in order that they might not be seen. And that the same [Hugh] knew they were stolen property and received them as stated he offers to prove by his body. And Hugh denies the entire charge against him, [submitting to judgment] as the court shall decide; and he puts himself on the country[4] that he is held to be a trustworthy man. He is committed to the vill of Walthamstow, to be produced on summons.

The same [William] also appeals Nicholas of Trumpington as a receiver. . . . He is committed to the vill of Cheshunt, etc. . . .

The same [William] also appeals Robert Woodcock and William his son as receivers. . . . Let the sheriff take pledges for them.

The same [William] also appeals William, son of Henry Ware, as a receiver, but he is so old that he can hardly move; [evidently] the charge against him is trumped up. And so the matter should be discussed. The jurors say that they know nothing [bad] of him; and so let him go quit because he is old.

The same [William] also appeals John and Adam, sons of the priest, for being his associates and for homicide: namely, that they along with him slew a man of Alfred Gernon, scalding him in the house of Robert Woodcock and taking from him property to the value of £4 sterling. Likewise they killed another man in the same house and a third between Writtle and Chelmsford. Likewise Adam together with him broke into the house of Michael Smallwood, his brother, and robbed it, so that the said Adam [thence] received a blue cloak with a hood of doe-skin worth half a mark. And this he offers to prove by his body, and he takes as his first opponent Adam. And they appear and deny the entire charge word by word, and they put themselves on the country. And the sheriff says that he held an inquest and that, according to the inquest, they are of ill fame. The lawful knights of the county give the same testimony. So the combat is to proceed, in the first place against Adam, whom [William] appeals

---

[3] William, a confessed felon, has turned approver. That is to say, he now has to appeal and vanquish a certain number of persons—often five—in order to secure a pardon. In the present case, however, he is himself vanquished in his first duel. See F. C. Hamil, in *Speculum*, XI, 238 f.

[4] The ordinary phrase for submitting to jury trial, on the beginnings of which in criminal cases see Pollock and Maitland, II, 648 f.

for the death of the aforesaid men and for the robbery of his brother's house and [the theft of] the aforesaid cloak worth 7s., and who denies the entire charge [offering defense] by his body. . . . William Smallwood is vanquished and hanged; Adam and John are dismissed under pledge. . . .

Alice, wife of William Black, confesses that she was present with her husband at the slaying of three men and one woman at Barnet. And so let her be burned. . . .

Thomas of Lyminge, who was captured together with robbers, at St. Albans, appears and says that he has no lord, that he is not in frankpledge, and that he has no pledge [of any kind]. Furthermore, it is testified by the steward of the abbot of St. Albans and by [other] good men that he confessed the robbery in the abbot's court. Furthermore, he stated in the [court of the] bench that he knew no man who was so big a thief as Robert of Bermondsey, the archbishop's steward, and afterwards he withdrew the charge. And since he has nothing in his favour and refuses to put himself on the country, it is decided that he is to be hanged.

(Latin) Maitland, *Select Pleas of the Crown,* pp. 120-34.

(B) Excerpts from Assize Rolls of 1221

Agnes, who was the wife of Robert Wood, appeals Thomas, son of Hubert, for the death of her husband Robert. And because the same [Agnes] has a [second] husband named Robert de Verdun who makes no appeal, she has no power of appealing; so the truth is to be sought by the country. And Thomas appears and denies responsibility for the death, but does not wish to put himself on the country. And the twelve jurors say that he is guilty of that death, and twenty-four knights chosen for this purpose, other than the aforesaid twelve, say the same; and so let him be hanged. The chattels of Thomas [amount to] 34s. 6d., for which the sheriff is answerable.

And the jurors testify that the said Thomas, after that deed, continued to go back and forth from his house to cultivate his land; and [yet] he was not arrested, nor was his land taken into the king's hands until the day before the arrival of the justices. So the sheriff [is to be brought] to judgment. And [Thomas] was a villein and for that reason his land was not taken.[5] And the township[6] of Spernal does not appear; therefore it is in mercy for default, and is to appear tomorrow.

The same Agnes appealed as accessories Henry, son of Hubert; Michael, reeve of Spernal; Simon, the priest's son; Patecoc, son of Simon of Spernal; and Robert of Shortenhall. And none of them appears; and [yet] she sued at a number of county courts after the death of her husband, and [the accused men] were neither attached nor outlawed. So the county [is to be brought] to judgment.

---

[5] An addition to the record, to explain the sheriff's conduct.

[6] *Villata* meaning the people of the vill or their legal representatives.

Afterwards the township of Spernal appears and confesses that all the aforesaid men were residents in their vill after the death of Robert and were not arrested. So [the township is] in mercy. And all those appealed as accessories have fled, and they were in the frankpledge of the township of Spernal. So [the township is] in mercy. The chattels of Henry [amount to] nothing. The chattels of Michael [amount to] 14s., for which the sheriff is answerable. . . .

Simon of Coughton, on account of drunkenness, fell dead from his horse in the vill of Alcester. And Simon, his son, who was with him, does not appear, nor was he attached; he is not suspected. The township of Alcester confesses that they did not present the death [of Simon] at the county [court] or to the coroners. So the township is in mercy. No one is suspected. Judgment—misadventure. The township of Coughton confesses that the body was carried into their vill and that it was buried without the view of the serjeant [of the hundred] or of the coroners, and that they made no presentment at the county [court]. So [the township is] in mercy. The value of the horse is 1m., for which the sheriff is answerable. . . .

Richard Goky, accused of the death of Henry Lightfoot who was slain at Ling, appears and denies the entire charge and puts himself on the country. And the townships of North Curry, Bridgewater, Creech, and Newton, also the twelve jurors, say on oath that they suspect of that death no one but the same Richard, and they affirm that he slew [Henry]. And so let him be hanged. Inquiry is to be made as to his chattels. And the township of Ling and the twelve jurors in the first place presented a certain Robert Young as having killed [Henry]. And afterwards they appear and confess that they did so on the instance of Roger Baryl, serjeant of the hundred. And so [he is to be put in] custody, and the twelve jurors and the township of Ling are in mercy for their false presentment. The amercement of the jurors is pardoned.

(Latin) *Ibid.*, 99-117.

(C) Excerpts from Exchequer Plea Rolls of 1236-37

An assize, summoned and attached to make recognition on oath whether Richard of Hinton holds three-fourths of a knight's fee with appurtenances in Eastbury of the king in chief or of Ralph le Moyne, appears before the barons of the exchequer on the morrow of St. Hilary: namely. . . .[7] They declare on oath that the said Richard of Hinton holds the said three-fourths of a knight's fee with appurtenances in Eastbury of Ralph le Moyne in chief; that the said Richard and his ancestors always rendered to the same Ralph and his ancestors the service owed from this [fief]; and that the said Ralph holds that tenement of the lord king. And so it is decided that the said Richard is to be quit of the scutage exacted from him for the said tenement, and that the same Richard shall henceforth render

---

[7] The names of the twelve jurors are omitted.

service for the said tenement to Ralph le Moyne and his heirs as has been accustomed. . . .

Robert Musard has offered himself against Henry of the exchequer with respect to a plea of 6m. for the scutage of Poitou, as is contained in the writ. Henry, having been summoned and attached a number of times, has appeared and has acknowledged that he received from the aforesaid Robert 6m. for the aforesaid scutage of Poitou; and he states that he acquitted the said Robert for 40s. out of the 6m. aforesaid in the county of Nottingham when he was sheriff of Berkshire. And the barons have had inspection made of the account rolls of that county for the fifteenth and sixteenth years, during which the said Henry was sheriff of Berkshire; and from the rolls they have found that nothing was paid by the said Henry on behalf of the aforesaid Robert in the county of Nottingham for the aforesaid scutage, as he has alleged. . . .[8] Finally, however, they have come to an agreement by permission of the barons: to the effect that the same Henry will acquit Robert of the said scutage and will give him 4m. for his trouble and expense. And because the same H[enry] had rendered account in full and had pledged his faith to having rendered an honest account, when [actually] he had not fully accounted for the said scutage, because of his concealment, he is delivered to the marshal as a prisoner. Afterwards he is liberated from prison by the bishop of Carlisle. And the same Henry is in mercy, but is pardoned by the barons. . . .

Hubert of Wick and Walter of Hales, executors of the will of Richard of Brome . . . have appeared and declared that they have in deposit at Langley about 25m. from the goods of the said Richard, and they have undertaken to pay that sum at the exchequer within three weeks after Easter toward satisfaction of the debt that the same Richard owed the lord king. Moreover, they have declared that William Bernehouse, who lives in the county of Suffolk, owed the said Richard 20m.; that Nicholas Crawe, who lives in Norfolk, owed the same Richard 20s.; [and that] Ralph of Selton [owed him] four oxen worth 40s. Besides, as they say, the men of Earl R[oger] Bigot in Ditchling carried off the crop from five acres of corn belonging to the said Richard, worth 1m. And the sheriff is ordered to distrain the said debtors for the said debts to the king's use. . . . Afterwards the said executors paid £17. 4s. of the said debt, and they have declared that they have nothing more of his goods. And so they are acquitted, and the lord king is to recover the remainder of the said debt from the heir of the said Richard of Brome.

(Latin) Jenkinson and Formoy, *Select Cases in the Exchequer*, pp. 7-13.

(D) EXCERPTS FROM CORONERS' ROLLS OF 1266-67

Richard of Eltisley of the parish of Eaton came to the county

---

[8] Henry says he paid the rest of the money into the exchequer and a mistake was made in the tallies, but his explanation is found to be worthless.

[court] of Bedford on Monday next after Epiphany in the fiftieth year of King Henry [III] and appealed William Moring of Staplehoe for [the following offense:] that before the hour of vespers on Sunday next after the Lord's Nativity he came into the house of the said Richard and assaulted the said Richard wickedly, feloniously, and against the peace of the lord king by premeditated assault, striking him on the right shoulder with a willow stick and so knocking him to the ground; afterwards, falling upon the said Richard, [William] seized with his right hand [Richard's] finger—the one called index, next the thumb—and bit it, so that [Richard] believes himself to be maimed. This he offers reasonably to demonstrate and prove as a maimed man can and should, according to the decision of the lord king's court. The said Richard finds pledges for prosecution: [namely,] Henry of Basing from Staplehoe and John Poignant from the same [vill].

Item, at the county [court] of Bedford, on Monday next after the Purification of the Blessed Mary, Richard appears and sues, and the said William, having been called for the first time, does not appear. Item, at the county [court] of Bedford, on Monday next after the feast of St. Matthew the Apostle in the fiftieth year, the aforesaid Richard appears and sues, and William Moring, having been called for the second time, does not appear. Item, at the county [court] of Bedford, on Monday next after the Annunciation of the Blessed Mary in the aforesaid year, Richard appears and sues, and William Moring, being present, denies the entire charge and finds pledges: [namely,] Reginald, son of Walter of Honeydon, and William Allen of Staplehoe. . . .

It happened about bedtime on Sunday next before the feast of St. Bartholomew in the fiftieth year that Henry Colburn of Barford went out of his house in Barford to drink a tankard of beer and did not return that night; but early the next morning Agnes Colburn, his mother, looked for him and found the said Henry dead. And he was wounded in the body about the heart and in the belly with seven knife-wounds, and in the head with four wounds apparently made with a pick-axe, and also in the throat and the chin and the head as far as the brain. The aforesaid Agnes at once raised the hue and pursuit was made. And she finds pledges: [namely,] Humphrey Quarrel and Thomas Quarrel of the same Barford.

Inquest was held before S[imon] Read, the coroner, by four neighbouring townships: Barford, Boxton, Wilden, and Renhold. And they say that Gilbert, son of Margaret, killed the said Henry as aforesaid. They also say that they have suspicion of Hugh Cointerel, Agnes Cointerel, Hugh, son of the same Agnes, and Alice Wrong, who have appeared in the full county [court] and are delivered to G. Read, the sheriff, [to be put] in jail. . . . Gilbert had no chattels. Englishry was presented by Richard, brother [of Henry], on the side of his father and mother; and by Maurice Plane, his uncle, on the side of his father.

It happened in the vill of Wilden on Wednesday next before the feast of Simon and Jude in the fiftieth year that unknown malefactors came to the house of Jordan Hull of Wilden and broke into the said house while the said Jordan was absent. And the said malefactors wounded Agnes, wife of the said Jordan, and killed Emma, his eight-year-old daughter. Afterwards they carried off all the goods from the house. . . . Inquest was held before S[imon] Read, the coroner, by four neighbouring townships . . . , who said what has been reported, and that the malefactors were unknown. . . .

It happened at Eaton on Thursday next after the feast of the Apostles Peter and Paul in the fiftieth year that Reginald Stead of Eaton, reaper of John Francis, went into the meadows of Eaton to guard the meadow of his lord and, being taken with falling sickness, collapsed and died forthwith by misadventure. Alice, his wife, was the first to discover him, and she finds pledges. . . . Inquest was held before S[imon] Read, the coroner, by four neighbouring townships . . . , who say that he died by misadventure of the aforesaid disease, and they know nothing beyond that.

(Latin) Gross, *Select Cases from Coroners' Rolls*, pp. 2-6.

(E) MEMORANDUM OF JUDICIAL APPOINTMENTS (1278)

Justices of the bench for pleas of the king:

Ralph of Hengham, Chief [Justice], who is to receive annually in fee for maintaining himself in the king's service, at two terms, ... 60*m.*
Nicholas of Stapleton, at two terms, ... 50*m.*
Walter of Wimburn, at two terms, ... 40*m.*

Total 150*m.*

Justices of the bench at Westminster:[9]

Thomas of Weyland, Chief [Justice] .... 60*m.*
Walter of Helion .... 50*m.*
John of Lovetoft .... 50*m.*
Roger of Leicester .... 40*m.*
William of Brompton .... till now nothing

Total 200*m.*

Itinerant justices toward the north, namely, in the counties of Cumberland, Westmorland, and Northumberland:
The Abbot of Westminster, Chief [Justice][10]
John de Vaux
William of Saham .... 50*m.*
Roger Loveday .... 40*m.*

---

[9] This is the common bench; the court preceding is that of *coram rege,* or king's bench. Cf. no. 52G.

[10] The man heading the circuit, being a beneficed clergyman, receives no salary.

John of Metingham .... 40m.
Master Thomas of Sodington .... 40m.

Itinerant justices toward the south, namely, in the counties of
Hertford and Kent:
The bishop of Worcester, Chief [Justice]
John of Reigate .... 60m.
Geoffrey of Leukenore .... 40m.
William of Norburgh .... 40m.
Walter of Hopton .... 40m.
Solomon of Rochester .... 40m.
The aforesaid justices were installed by the king himself and
others of his council [at Gloucester]. . . .

(Latin) Palgrave, *Parliamentary Writs*, I, 382.

(F) Excerpts from the Coram Rege Rolls of 1281

Command was given to the mayor and sheriffs of London that
they should send to the king here on this day the record and process
of the suit recently held before them in their husting of London
between Edmund Trentemars, plaintiff, and Master Thomas of
Bread Street concerning a messuage with appurtenances in the suburb of London; which same record and process they sent to the following effect. . . . And Edmund, being asked why he had caused the
aforesaid record to come here, says it is because the lord king granted
by his Statute of Gloucester[11] that, if any one within the city of
London vouches any foreigner to warranty, he shall, according to the
Statute of Gloucester, sue against his warranty before the justices of
the bench, etc. Whereupon the said Thomas Trentemars was adjourned until the next arrival of the itinerant justices at the Tower
of London. And thereof he seeks remedy, etc. . . .

The abbot of Fécamp was summoned to answer to the lord king
by what warrant he holds the manor of Steyning, which is ancient
demesne of the crown of England, as is said, and concerning which
William of Pembridge, who sues for the king,[12] says that the lord
king Henry, father of the present lord king, was seised of the aforesaid manor, etc. . . . And the abbot now appears by his attorney and
says that he holds the aforesaid manor by this warrant: that St.
Edward [the Confessor], one time king, gave the aforesaid manor
with its appurtenances to the abbot and monks of Fécamp, which same
deed was confirmed by William [I], one time king of England, and a
certain Henry, king of England. . . . When this charter had been
read and understood, the attorney of the same abbot was told that
in such connection he might go *sine die*, etc. . . .

The jury [in the suit] between Hugh le Despenser, plaintiff, and
Roger le Bigot, earl of Norfolk and marshal of England, having
been chosen by the consent of the parties, [comes to make recogni-

---

[11] No. 52A.
[12] That is to say, acting as king's attorney.

tion] whether Alina le Despenser, who was wife of the aforesaid Roger, bore of the same Roger offspring since deceased that was heard to cry or raise its voice within four walls in the manor of Woking, or not; and if so, what kind of voice it raised, and whether that offspring was male or female, and in what house such child was born and in what church it was baptized, and when and at what time and in whose presence, and how long the same child lived, etc. . . .[13]

Command was given to the sheriff that he should cause to come here on this day the appeal which Wenthiliana, daughter of William le Prestre made in his county [court] against William d'Evreux for the death of Adam le Gouth, her husband, and also the appeal which Susan, daughter of Organ, made in the aforesaid county [court] against the aforesaid William for the death of her brother, John son of Organ, together with all appendant matters touching those appeals. . . .[14]

The lord king, by Walter of Wimbourne who sues for him, brings suit against Robert Banaster for the advowson of the church of Wigan with appurtenances. . . .[15]

Command was sent to John de Vaux and his associates, justices of the last eyre in the county of York, that under their seals they should send to the king the record and process of the suit brought before them on the aforesaid eyre by writ of right of the lord king between Peter de Mauley, plaintiff, and the abbot of Whitby, tenant, concerning the manors of Newholm, Stakesby, and Dunsley with their appurtenances. . . . Which same justices sent the record to the following effect. . . .[16]

Agnes Colle appeals Henry le Ternur and Gilbert of Grafham for the death of her son John. And she appeals them for this: that, while her aforesaid son was in the peace of the lord king on Saturday next after the feast of the Nativity of the Blessed Virgin in the eighth year of the present king's reign, at a place called Broneswellbrook between the vill of Offord Cluny and [that of] Offord Darcy, the aforesaid Henry le Ternur and Gilbert came with a certain Henry Nichol of Bedwin, and they held the aforesaid John by his hands and neck while the same Henry struck the aforesaid John with a Cologne sword [wounding him] to the brain, whereof he died. And that they wickedly and by felony aforethought committed the aforesaid felony on the aforesaid day in the aforesaid year she offers, etc. . . .[17]

(Latin) Sayles, *Select Cases in King's Bench*, pp. 74-91.

[13] The case did not go to the jury, for Roger surrendered Alina's lands to Hugh, her nearest heir. If she had borne Roger a living heir, he would have had a life estate.

[14] The cases were sent to the hundred court of Archenfield because of that district's ancient liberty.

[15] A jury of twelve awarded the right to Robert.

[16] A jury of twelve gave a verdict for Peter; the abbot was declared in mercy.

[17] The accused denied the charge and put themselves on the country. A day was set for trial.

(G) Excerpts from the Parliament Roll of 1283[18]

Aymer de Peche, who is ill, beseeches the lord king graciously to command the escheator to return to him the seisin of the manor of Steeple, the custody of which belongs to him because Hugh son of Otto ended his days holding of the said Aymer by military service the aforesaid manor, with which he had been enfeoffed by the same Aymer, who held the aforesaid manor of the lord king in chief.

[Endorsed:] Let it be restored because [Hugh] held nothing of the king in chief.

The lord William Martin seeks a writ of the lord king to the treasurer and the barons of the exchequer [permitting him] to pay the debt that he owes the king by instalments of £10 a year.

Let him pay 50*m*. a year in two [instalments]. . . .

When our lord the king was at Bristol on the festival of Easter in the eighth year of his reign, the mayor and community [of the town] made to him devout supplication, asking that he regard their condition which, through default of confirmation of the liberties obtained by grant and confirmation from the lord king Henry, father of the present lord king, and from his other ancestors, had been greatly injured by the divers oppressions of justices, sheriffs, and bailiffs; and requesting that the lord king would confirm their charters of liberties aforesaid. And the lord king promised them that he would do so when he first confirmed any liberties. We beseech you, lord chancellor, that you apply your counsel to whatever may be done in this matter for the sake of the community aforesaid.

The king will respond in the next parliament. . . .

The prior of Hexham beseeches the lord king to grant him licence[19] to enter upon land to the value of £20 in North Milburn within the county of Northumberland, which is held of Robert de Stuteville and Eleanor his wife for the service of 6*d*. a year for all service, and concerning which the sheriff of Northumberland was commanded to make diligent investigation as to what damage the lord king would suffer if the said prior took possession of the said land in fee. And the sheriff, having carried out an investigation, made a return in which it was stated that the lord king would thereby suffer no damage, except only to the amount of 6*d*. per year. And when [the result of] this inquest had been seen by the chancellor, the prior was told that he should come to this parliament.

[Endorsed:] The king will not grant the favour asked in the petition.

Thomas de Torneye, who had been in Wales to perform the service that the lord Gilbert de Bulebeke owed to our lord the king in connection with his recent expedition into those parts, was taken, after

---

[18] On the nature of these enrolments see the editors' introduction to the volume cited below; also that of Maitland to his *Memoranda de Parliamento*.

[19] Cf. no. 52B.

returning from Wales, and held in the prison of Aylesbury in the county of Buckingham on suspicion of a robbery suffered by Master John de Saint-Omer, of which he is not guilty; and by letters under the king's privy seal in the possession of the sheriff, to the effect that he is not to be released, he is being held in that prison until the delivery of the same prison.[20] Wherefore he beseeches our lord the king that he may be brought under the common law and have a jury trial;[21] for in the prison he is at the point of death on account of the duress with which he is treated.

[Endorsed:] Let a writ be issued for the two men imprisoned at Aylesbury; it is not to be neglected on account of a mandate under the small seal. Let an inquest be made by the justices through a good [jury of the] country.

(French and Latin) Richardson and Sayles, *Rot. Parl. Anglie*, pp. 17-25.

(H) Excerpts from Manorial Court Rolls (1246-49)[22]

Pleas of the manors . . . of Bec, Hokeday term, A.D. 1246:—

Bledlow [Buckinghamshire]. . . . The court made presentment that Simon Combe has raised a certain fence on the lord's land. Therefore let it be pulled down. . . . A day at the next court is given to Alice of Standen for producing her charter and her heir. . . .

Tooting [Surrey]. . . . The court made presentment that the following persons had encroached on the lord's land. . . .[23] Therefore [they are] in mercy. Godwin [is] in mercy because he neglected to do what he was ordered on behalf of the lord. Fine 12d. Roger Reed [is] in mercy for non-payment of rent. Pledge: Jordan of Streatham. Fine 6d. . . .

Ruislip [Middlesex]. . . . The court makes presentment that Nicholas Breakspeare is not in tithing, and he holds land. Therefore let him be distrained. Breakers of the assize [of beer]. . . .[24] Roger son of Hamo gives 20s. to have seisin of the land that was his father's and to have an inquest by twelve [men] as to a certain croft held by Gilbert Bisuthe. Pledges: Gilbert Lamb, William son of John, and Robert King. . . . Richard Maleville [offers to prove] at his law[25] as against the lord that he did not take attached property away from the lord's serjeants to the lord's damage and dishonour [amounting to] 20s. Pledges: Gilbert Bisuthe and Richard Hubert. Hugh Tree [is] in mercy for cattle of his taken in the lord's garden. Pledges: Walter of Hull and William Slipper. Fine 6d. Twelve jurors say that Hugh Cross has title to the bank and hedge over which there was a dispute between him and William White. Therefore let him hold

---

[20] By the itinerant justices.

[21] Literally "have his country (*pays*)"; see above, p. 178, n. 4.

[22] On the nature of these courts and their records, see the famous introduction by the editor, F. W. Maitland.

[23] Seven persons are named, with fines from 6d. to 2s.

[24] Thirteen persons are named, with a normal fine of 6d.

[25] That is to say, by compurgation; see above, p. 77, n. 3.

in peace, and let the said William be distrained for many trespasses. Later he fined for 12d. . . .

Pleas of the manors of Bec, Martinmas term, A.D. 1247:—

Weedon Beck [Northamptonshire]. . . . Elias Deynte resigned his land in full court and seisin of it was given to William Deynte, his son, who swore fealty and found pledges, named above, for his 5s. of relief. Later he paid it. The whole township gives 6m. for the abbot's tallage. . . . William Green and Guy Lawman have gallon measures that are too small. John Mercer will give three hens yearly at the feast of St. Martin to have the lord's patronage,[26] and he is received into a tithing. . . .

Wretham [Norfolk]. . . . Gilbert son of Richard gives 5s. for permission to marry a wife. . . . The following women have been violated and accordingly owe *leyrwite.* . . .[27] From the township 3m. for the abbot's tallage. . . .

Tooting [Surrey]. . . . The whole township gives 2½m. for the abbot's tallage. William Jordan [is] in mercy for badly ploughing the lord's land. Pledge: Arthur. Fine 6d. John Shepherd [is] in mercy for encroaching upon land bordering on his. Pledge: Walter Reeve. Fine 6d. Lucy Reed [is] in mercy for cattle of hers taken in the lord's pasture after ward had been set. . . .[28] Elias of Streatham [is] in mercy for default of autumn [labour] service. Fine 6d. Bartholomew Chaloner, who was at law against Reginald son of Swain, has defaulted in his law. Therefore let him be in mercy and let him satisfy the aforesaid Reginald for the latter's damage and dishonour, namely with 6s. Pledges: William Shoemaker and William Spendlove. Fine 6 gallons [? of beer].

Deveril [Wiltshire]. . . . William Miller [offers to prove] at his law that he was not pledge for William Scut of Hull, whose sheep were taken in the lambs' pasture. Pledges for his law: William Swineherd and Thomas Guner. Arnold Smith is in mercy for not producing the said William Scut, for whom he was pledge. The parson of the church is in mercy for a cow of his taken in the lord's meadow. Pledges: Thomas Guner and William Cook. The township gives 2m. for the abbot's tallage. From William Cobbe, William Cook, and Walter Dogskin 2s. for [neglect of] ward [in the case] of seven pigs belonging to Robert Gentil and for the damage that they did in the lord's corn. From Martin Shepherd 6d. for the wound that he inflicted on Pekin. . . .

Weedon Beck [Northamptonshire]. . . . The court made presentment that William son of Noah is the fugitive bondman of the lord and is living at Dodford. Therefore he is to be sought. They also say that William Askil, John Parsons, and Godfrey Green furtively carried off four geese from the vill of Horepoll. John Witrich [is]

---

[26] Meaning to be received as a manorial tenant.
[27] The fine for unchastity. Five girls are named, with fines from 6d. to 12d.
[28] That is to say, after it had been closed to such use.

in mercy for a colt of his taken in the lord's corn. Pledges: Guy Love and Simon Winbold. . . .

Pleas of the manors of Bec, A.D. 1249:—

Ogbourne [Wiltshire]. . . . Presentment was made that Stephen Shepherd by night struck his sister with a certain knife and badly wounded her. So let him be committed to prison. Later he fined for 2s. Pledge: Walter of Wick. Presentment was made that Robert son of Carter by night invaded [the property of] Peter Burgess and feloniously threw stones at his door, so that the same Peter Burgess raised hue [and cry]. Therefore let the aforesaid Robert be committed to prison. Later he fined for 2s. . . . Adam Moses gives half a sester of wine to have an inquest as to whether Henry Ayulf imputed to him the crime of larceny and used vile and insulting words [concerning him]. Later they came to agreement, and Henry gives security for amercement. Fine 12d. . . . From Ralph Joce ½m. for his son because [the latter] unlawfully took corn from the lord's court. . . . From Ralph Scales 6d. for carrying off timber. From William Cooper 12d. because without licence he ploughed his land with the lord's plough. From Hugh New 12d. for trespass in the wood. From Richard Penant 12d. for the same. From Helen, widow of Little Ogbourne, 6d. for the same. From Nicholas Seward 6d. for a false claim against William Pafey. From William Pafey 12d. for engaging in a fight with the same Nicholas. . . .

(Latin) Maitland, *Select Pleas in Manorial Courts*, pp. 6-20.

SECTION V

EDWARD II, EDWARD III, AND RICHARD II

THE period between the death of Edward I and the accession of Henry IV is chiefly significant for the rapid development of parliamentary institutions. This development involved, not only the definitive organization of a bicameral parliament, but also the assertion by that body of positive constitutional functions, principally directed toward restraint of the crown. And no matter what may have been the legality of such claims under Edward III, the triumph of parliament was assured by the Revolution of 1399.

That most of the materials presented below have a direct bearing upon this issue will be apparent without detailed comment. Edward II's reign is represented by five documents, of which only two run to any great length. The Ordinances of 1311, generally neglected by the compilers of source books, are here reproduced almost entire, because they provide a comprehensive criticism of the royal government and so link the parliamentary contests under Edward III with the baronial uprisings of the previous age. The Household Ordinance of 1318 is even less known.[1] Yet it gives us our most graphic picture of the royal *entourage* at which so many attacks were levelled and, by comparison with the *Constitutio Domus Regis* of about 1135 (no. 29), throws into historical perspective the whole intervening evolution of the English administrative system.

Aside from nos. 60 and 65, the remaining documents in this section fall under two main heads: statutes and ordinances, and excerpts from the rolls of parliament. In so far as possible, records of local government have been grouped in the following section and in those preceding; but the Durham Halmote Rolls are too important to be omitted, and their date necessitates an isolated position here. Although the chief value of the two writs of summons is merely that of typical examples, it should be noted that the great council of 1353 inaugurated some famous

---

[1] The French text, published without emendation by Tout, is corrupt in spots and is difficult throughout. Francis Tate's translation, reprinted by F. J. Furnivall in *Life Records of Chaucer*, Pt. II (Chaucer Society, 1876), is hopelessly inaccurate.

legislation (no. 62G, H). Such ordinances and statutes as are here included have been selected, first, on account of their actual provisions, that is to say, their reform or restatement of pre-existing law and custom; secondly, in order to show the methods by which enactments, more or less formal, came to be made. In the latter respect, however, statutes and ordinances serve at most to supplement the parliament rolls, which are unquestionably our best source for the constitutional history of the fourteenth and fifteenth centuries.

How rich and varied is the information supplied by these documents no one can possibly realize until he has worked through formidable volumes of Old French. What is translated in the following pages is, of course, but a small fragment of the whole series; yet the selections are extensive enough to reveal the characteristic features of the record and to illustrate many developments of great significance for the English monarchy. Among them may be mentioned the organization, powers, and procedure of the parliament as a whole and of its two houses separately; private suits, impeachment of ministers, and other judicial business in parliament; the growth of parliamentary control over taxation and expenditure; the constant agitation on the part of both houses for thorough reform of the royal administration; and the relation to all these matters of the king and his council. For it should not be thought that, on account of their name, the parliament rolls deal only with parliament in the modern sense. Throughout the fourteenth century parliament was still what the word originally implied—a specially important meeting of the king and his counsellors, including peers and deputies of the commons alongside of the more permanent advisers. To attempt a logical separation of parliamentary affairs from those of crown and council is futile. And a glance at the substance of the petitions and enactments in parliament will show that they were concerned with virtually all phases of the government, local as well as central.

Mainly because Stubbs was able to draw most of the material for his last six chapters from the parliament rolls, this portion of his *Constitutional History* remains authoritative—an indispensable commentary for one who would understand the purport of the following documents. But inevitably, through the advance of research, some of his views have been modified or superseded;

and the most useful guide in this connection is the volume of *Studies and Notes* by Petit-Dutaillis and Lefebvre, which contains an especially valuable essay on the Revolt of 1381. Particular reference may also be made to T. F. Tout, *Chapters in Mediaeval Administrative History,* vols. II-VI, and *The Place of the Reign of Edward II in English History*; J. C. Davies, *The Baronial Opposition to Edward II;* J. F. Baldwin, *The King's Council in England during the Middle Ages;* C. H. McIlwain, *The High Court of Parliament;* A. F. Pollard, *The Evolution of Parliament;* H. L. Gray, *The Influence of the Commons on Early Legislation;* M. V. Clarke, *Medieval Representation and Consent;* and M. McKisack, *The Parliamentary Representation of the English Boroughs during the Middle Ages. English Constitutional Documents,* 1307–1485, editors Eleanor C. Lodge and Gladys A. Thornton, and *English Historical Documents,* IV, editor A. R. Myers, add to the records provided in this section. May McKisack's *The Fourteenth Century,* 1307–1399 has a survey of constitutional developments.

55. EDWARD II: CORONATION OATH (1308)[1]

"Sire, will you grant and keep and by your oath confirm to the people of England the laws and customs given to them by the previous just and god-fearing kings, your ancestors, and especially the laws, customs, and liberties granted to the clergy and people by the glorious king, the sainted Edward, your predecessor?" "I grant and promise them."

"Sire, will you in all your judgments, so far as in you lies, preserve to God and Holy Church, and to the people and clergy, entire peace and concord before God?" "I will preserve them."

"Sire, will you, so far as in you lies, cause justice to be rendered rightly, impartially, and wisely, in compassion and in truth?" "I will do so."

"Sire, do you grant to be held and observed the just laws and customs that the community of your realm shall determine, and will you, so far as in you lies, defend and strengthen them to the honour of God?" "I grant and promise them."

(French) Statutes of the Realm, I, 168.

---

[1] This is the form actually followed at the coronation of Edward II, but the record provides an alternative in Latin to be used "if the king is literate." It is also stated that the archbishop of Canterbury put the questions before the king was crowned; and, after he had given his oral responses, he personally swore on the altar that he would keep all his promises. See B. Wilkinson, in *Historical Essays in Honour of James Tait,* pp. 405 f.

[2] *(aura elu).*

56. ORDINANCES OF 1311

. . . Whereas, through bad and deceitful counsel, our lord the king and all his men have everywhere been dishonoured and his crown in many ways has been debased and ruined, while his lands of Gascony, Ireland, and Scotland are on the point of being lost unless God improves the situation, and his realm of England has been brought to the verge of rebellion through prises[1] and [other] oppressive and destructive measures—which facts are known and proved—our lord the king of his free will has granted to the prelates, earls, and barons, and to the other good men of his realm, that certain persons should be elected to ordain and determine the condition of his household and of his realm, as appears more fully in the commission issued by our lord the king in this connection. Therefore we, Robert, by the grace of God archbishop of Canterbury and primate of all England, and the bishops, earls, and barons elected by virtue of the said commission, do ordain for the honour of God and Holy Church and of the king and his realm in the manner following:—

1. . . In the first place it is ordained that Holy Church shall have all its liberties as heretofore and as it should have them.

2. Item, it is ordained that the king's peace shall be firmly kept throughout the entire kingdom; so that every one may safely go, come, and remain according to the law and custom of the realm.

3. Item, it is ordained that, in order to acquit the king's debts, to relieve his estate,[2] and the more honourably to maintain it, no gift of land, rent, liberty, escheat, wardship, marriage, or office shall be made to any of the said Ordainers during their [tenure of] power under the said ordinance, or to any other person, without the counsel and assent of the said Ordainers or the majority of them—or of six of them at least—but that all sources of profit shall be improved for the benefit of the king until his estate is properly relieved and some other ordinance may be made for the honour and profit of the king.

4. Item, it is ordained that the customs of the kingdom shall be received and kept by men of the kingdom itself, and not by aliens; and that the issues and profits of the same customs, together with all other issues and profits pertaining to the kingdom from any source whatsoever, shall in their entirety come to the king's exchequer and be paid by the treasurer and the chamberlains for maintaining the king's household and [to be spent] in other ways for his benefit; so that the king may live of his own without taking prises other than those anciently due and accustomed. And all others shall cease. . . .

6. Item, it is ordained that the Great Charter shall be observed in all its particulars; so that, if there is any point in the said charter that is doubtful or obscure, it shall be interpreted by the said Or-

---

[1] See arts. 4 and 10, below.

[2] The word constantly used throughout these records to denote the king's legal position, including all powers and perquisites of the royal office.

dainers and other men whom they may see fit to call upon for that purpose.[3] . . .

7. And besides, since the crown has been so abased and ruined by numerous grants, we ordain that all grants made to the damage of the king and the impoverishment of the crown since the commission was given to us . . . shall be annulled; and we do annul them entirely, so that they shall not be given back to the same persons without the common assent [of the baronage[4]] in parliament. . . .

9. Whereas the king, on account of the many perils that he and his kingdom may incur, ought not to undertake an act of war against any one, or to go out of the kingdom, without the common assent of his baronage, we ordain that henceforth the king shall neither go out of the kingdom nor undertake an act of war against any one without the common assent of his baronage, and that in parliament. . . .

10. And whereas it is feared that the people of the land will rebel on account of the prises and divers oppressions recently established, . . . we ordain that henceforth all prises shall be abolished except the ancient and lawful prises due to the king and to others who are lawfully entitled to them. And if any prises are taken contrary to the ordinance aforesaid by any one whomsoever, no matter of what condition he may be—that is to say, if any one, under colour of purveyance for the use of our lord the king or of some one else, takes grain, wares, merchandise, or other goods against the will of those to whom they belong, and does not immediately give in return money to the true value [of the goods], unless he thereof has respite by the free will of the seller according to the provision in the Great Charter regarding prises taken by constables of castles and their bailiffs,[5] saving the accustomed prises aforesaid—notwithstanding any commission that may be [issued], pursuit with hue and cry shall be raised against him and he shall be taken to the nearest jail of the king, and the common law shall be enforced against him as against a robber or thief, should he be convicted of such [wrongdoing].

11. Also, [whereas] new customs have been levied and the old [customs] have been increased upon wool, cloth, wines, avoirdupois, and other things—whereby [our] merchants come more rarely and bring fewer goods into the country, while alien merchants reside longer than they used to, and by such residence things become dearer than they used to be, to the damage of the king and his people—we ordain that all manner of customs and maltotes levied since the coronation of King Edward, son of King Henry, are to be entirely removed and utterly abolished forever, notwithstanding the charter which the said King Edward granted to alien merchants, because it

was issued contrary to the Great Charter and contrary to the liberty of the city of London and without the assent of the baronage. . . .[6]

13. And whereas the king, as aforesaid, has been badly advised and guided by evil councillors, we ordain that all the evil councillors shall be put out and utterly removed, so that neither they nor other such persons shall be near him or shall be retained in any office under the king; and that other persons who are fit shall be put in their places. And the same shall be done in the case of domestics, officials, and other men in the king's household who are not fit.

14. And whereas many evils have been incurred through [the employment of] such councillors and such ministers, we ordain that the king shall appoint the chancellor, the chief justices of both benches, the treasurer, the chancellor[7] and the chief baron of the exchequer, the steward of the household, the keeper of the wardrobe, the comptroller and a fit clerk to keep the privy seal,[8] a chief keeper of the forests on this side of Trent and one on the other side of Trent, also an escheator on this side of Trent and one on the other side, as well as the king's chief clerk of the common bench, by the counsel and assent of the baronage, and that in parliament. And if by some chance it happens that there is need to appoint any of the said ministers before parliament meets, then the king shall make such appointments by the good counsel [of those] whom he shall have near him up to the time of the parliament. And so let it be done henceforth with regard to such ministers whenever there is need.

15. Item, we ordain that the chief wardens of ports[9] and of castles on the sea shall be appointed and installed in the aforesaid manner, and that such wardens are to be of the land itself.[10]

16. And whereas the lands of Gascony, Ireland, and Scotland are in peril of being lost through default of good ministers, we ordain that worthy and fit ministers to keep ward in the said lands shall be named according to the form set forth in the article before the last [preceding].

17. Moreover, we ordain that sheriffs shall henceforth be appointed by the chancellor, the treasurer, and others of the council who are present; and if the chancellor is not present, let them be appointed by the treasurer, the barons of the exchequer, and the justices of the bench. And such men are to be named and installed as are fit and worthy, and as have lands and tenements through which they may be held responsible for their actions to the king or to the people. And

---

[6] Saving to the king the ancient customs from wool and hides; see no. 51A.

[7] When, in the thirteenth century, the chancellor ceased to attend the meetings of the exchequer, his clerk became known as the chancellor of the exchequer.

[8] For further details concerning these and other household officials, see no. 57.

[9] Referring especially to the warden of the Cinque Ports and constable of Dover Castle; see no. 50C.

[10] I.e., England.

only such persons shall be appointed, and they shall have their commissions under the great seal. . . .[11]

24. And whereas the people feel much aggrieved because of divers debts demanded of them for the king's use by summons from the exchequer, of which debts, being actually paid, the people have various acquittances . . . ; we ordain that henceforth in the account of every sheriff, or other minister of the king who is answerable at the exchequer, such tallies, writs, and franchises as are allowable in the account shall be allowed. . . . And if the treasurer and the barons of the exchequer do not act in the manner aforesaid, the plaintiffs shall enjoy [the right of] recovery through petition in parliament.[12]

25. Whereas ordinary merchants and many others of the people are allowed to bring pleas of debt and trespass in the exchequer, through the fact that they are received by the ministers of the said court more favourably than they should be[13]—whereby accounts and other concerns of the king are greatly delayed and, in addition, a large number of people are aggrieved—we ordain that henceforth no pleas shall be held in the said court of the exchequer except pleas touching the king and his ministers: [namely] those answerable at the exchequer by reason of their offices, the ministers of the court itself, and their subordinates and servants who most of the time are with them in those places where the exchequer may be. And if anybody is received by the said court with permission to plead in the manner aforesaid, those impleaded shall have their [right to] recovery in parliament.

26. Item, whereas the people feel much aggrieved because stewards and marshals hold many pleas that do not pertain to their offices, and also because they will not receive attorneys for defendants as well as for plaintiffs, we ordain that henceforth they shall receive attorneys for defendants as well as for plaintiffs, and that they shall hold no pleas of freehold, debt, covenant, or contract, nor any common plea touching men of the people—saving [to their jurisdiction] only trespasses of the household itself and other trespasses committed within the verge,[14] and contracts and covenants which any one of the king's household may make with another of the same household within the household itself and not elsewhere. . . .[15]

28. Whereas the people feel much aggrieved because men are em-

---

[11] The next two articles provide for investigations concerning the misdeeds of forest officials and the enforcement of the Forest Charter (no. 45). Arts. 20-23 impose penalties on Piers Gaveston and three other persons named.

[12] Cf. nos. 54G, 61A.

[13] Cf. no. 54C.

[14] The area distinguished by the king's presence and thereby set apart from the common law.

[15] Various details follow in the text, including remedies at common law provided for aggrieved parties.

boldened to kill and rob by the fact that the king, through evil counsel, so lightly grants them his peace against the provisions of the
law; we ordain that henceforth no felon or fugitive shall be protected
or defended in any sort of felony by the king's charter granting his
peace, except only in case the king can give grace according to his
oath, and that by process of law and the custom of the realm. And
if any charter is henceforth made and granted to any one in any
other manner, it shall be of no avail and shall be held as null. And
no recognized malefactor against the crown and the peace of the
land is to be aided or maintained[16] by any one.

29. Whereas in the king's court persons find their cases delayed
because a party alleges that in the king's absence answer should not
be made to demands, and [whereas] also many persons wrongfully
suffer injuries from the king's ministers, with regard to which injuries one can secure recovery only in common parliament; we ordain
that the king shall hold a parliament once a year, or twice if need
be, and that in a convenient place. And [we ordain] that in those
parliaments pleas which are delayed in the said manner, and pleas
wherein the justices are of different opinions, shall be recorded and
settled. And likewise those bills[17] which are brought to parliament
shall be settled as heretofore in accordance with law and right.

30. Whereas all the people suffer greatly in many ways whenever
a change of money is made in the kingdom, we ordain that, when there
is need and the king wishes to make a change [of the money], he
shall do so by the common counsel of his baronage, and that in parliament.

31. Item, we ordain that all statutes which were made ·in amendment of the law and for the benefit of the people by the ancestors
of our lord the king shall be kept and maintained as heretofore in
accordance with law and right; provided that they are not contrary
to the Great Charter or to the Forest Charter or to the ordinances
by us made. And if any statute is made contrary to what has been
said, it shall be held as null and as utterly void.

32. Whereas, to the great injury of the people, the law of the land
and common right have often been delayed by letters issued under the
king's privy seal, we ordain that henceforth neither the law of the
land nor common right shall be delayed or disturbed by letters under
the said seal. And if, through such letters issued under the privy seal
contrary to right or to the law of the land, anything is done in any
session of the court of our lord the king, it shall be of no avail and
shall be held as null.

33. Whereas many of the people other than those known to be merchants feel much aggrieved and injured by the Statute of Merchants
made at Acton Burnell,[18] we ordain that hereafter this statute shall

---

[16] Cf. no. 64C.

[17] "Bill" and "petition" were at this time synonymous terms.

[18] No. 52D.

hold only as between merchant and merchant and with regard to dealings made between them. . . .[19]

38. Item, we ordain that the Great Charter of Liberties and the Forest Charter issued by King Henry, son of King John, shall be observed in all their particulars, and that points in the said charters of liberties which are doubtful shall be explained in the next parliament after this by the advice of the baronage, the justices, and other persons learned in the law. And this is to be done because we are unable to attend to the matter during our term [of office].

39. Item, we ordain that the chancellor, the treasurer, the chief justices of both benches, the chancellor of the exchequer, the treasurer of the wardrobe, the steward of the king's household, and all justices, sheriffs, escheators, constables, investigators [named] for any cause whatsoever, and all other bailiffs and ministers of the king, whenever they receive their offices and bailiwicks, shall be sworn to keep and observe all the ordinances made by the prelates, earls, and barons for that purpose elected and assigned—[to maintain] every one of those [ordinances] without contravening them in any particular.

40. Item, we ordain that in each parliament one bishop, two earls, and two barons shall be assigned to hear and determine all plaints of those wishing to complain of the king's ministers, whichever they may be, who have contravened the ordinances aforesaid. And if the said bishop, earls, and barons cannot all attend, or are prevented from hearing and determining the said plaints, then two or three of them shall do so. And those who are found to have contravened the said ordinances, in the interest of the king and in the interest of the plaintiffs, shall be punished at the discretion of the persons thus assigned.

41. Item, we ordain that the aforesaid ordinances are to be maintained and observed in all their particulars, and that our lord the king shall cause them to be issued under his great seal and sent into every county of England, to be published, held, and strictly kept as well within franchises as without. . . .

These ordinances, having been shown to us[20] and published on Monday next before the feast of St. Michael just past, we agree to, accept, and confirm. And we will and grant, for us and our heirs, that all and several of the said ordinances, made according to the form of our letters aforesaid, shall be published throughout our entire realm, henceforth to be strictly maintained and observed. In testimony whereof we have caused these our letters patent to be drawn up.

Given at London, October 5, in the fifth year of our reign.

(French) *Ibid.*, I, 157 f.

---

[19] The seals for authenticating such transactions are to be entrusted to groups of substantial citizens elected in certain specified towns: Newcastle-upon-Tyne, Nottingham, Exeter, Bristol, Southampton, Lincoln, Northampton, London, and Canterbury. The next four articles deal with reforms of the criminal law.

[20] King Edward II.

57. EDWARD II: HOUSEHOLD ORDINANCE (1318)[1]

. . . The king should have a fit steward of the household, who, if he is a banneret,[2] is to have a knight, three squires, and a clerk for the pleas that pertain to the stewardship, [all of them] eating in the hall. And each night he shall receive for his chamber a sester of wine, twelve candles, two *tortis pur viu*,[3] and one torch, and more when he needs them. And [he is to have] bedding for the whole year and wood for the winter season—from the eve of All Saints to the eve of Easter—[to be obtained] from the usher of the hall. And [he is to have] a livery for his chamberlain: namely, a portion of bread, a gallon of ale, and a general serving (*messe de gros*) from the kitchen. And [he is to have] dinners and suppers when he wants them; and as fees 20*m.* a year, in equal instalments on the feasts of Christmas and Pentecost. And if he is a simple knight, he shall receive fees and robes like the other simple knights of the household, and shall have two squires and his clerk eating in the hall.

A treasurer of the wardrobe, who is to have a chaplain, a clerk, and two squires eating in the hall. . . .[4]

A chamberlain, who, if he is a banneret, is to have a knight and three squires eating in the hall. . . .

Item, a comptroller, who is to keep a counter-roll against the treasurer of the wardrobe for all receipts and issues pertaining to the same wardrobe; and he is to witness them in the exchequer in connection with the account of the said treasurer. And he shall attend the receipt of wines in gross and shall supervise all the offices of the household, such as the pantry, butlery, cellar, larder, spicery, dispensary of oats (*avenerie*) and other offices, [to see] that the wines and victuals that he finds in the said offices are good and suitable for dispensing in the said household. . . . And he is to go into those same offices every Monday to examine the remainders [of supplies] and to see that they, with the amounts dispensed in the past week, agree with the receipts of the aforesaid week. And he shall be in the kitchen for the cutting of meat and the division of fish. . . . And every day, if he sees reasonable cause, he shall be present at the account,[5] to-

---

[1] The preamble explains that this ordinance was drawn up at the king's request by the steward, the chamberlain, the treasurer, and the comptroller of the wardrobe, to define the duties of the various officials and to establish needed reforms in the administration of the household. On the general significance of the document, see Tout, *Place of Edward II in English History,* ch. v, and *Chapters in Mediaeval Administrative History,* II, pp. 242 f.

[2] The banneret, as opposed to the simple knight or bachelor, had the right to bear a square pennon on his lance.

[3] Large candles "for view (? display)"; see *Oxford English Dictionary* under *tortis.* Henceforth the expression will be translated merely as "great candles."

[4] All the greater officials received liveries similar to that of the steward, but with considerable variation in the particular items. Besides, each normally had his own chamberlain, who was entitled to food and drink.

[5] Drawn up in the wardrobe; see no. 52c.

gether with the steward and the treasurer. And this same comptroller
of the wardrobe is to have a clerk and a squire eating in the hall. . . .

Item, a cofferer, who shall be appointed for the treasurer and shall
have a clerk eating in the hall. . . .

Item, two clerks of the counting table, well able to write and perform all duties touching the wardrobe and its account under the [di-
rection of the] cofferer. . . .

Item, a fit clerk keeper of the privy seal, who is to have a squire
eating in the hall. . . .[6]

Item, a clerk purveyor of the great wardrobe,[7] who should sleep on
guard when he is at court. And he shall have a squire eating in the
hall. . . .

Item, a clerk of the spicery, chief usher of the wardrobe, who shall
receive from the clerk purveyor of the great wardrobe the wax,
napery, linen, cloth, canvas, spices, and the other things of all sorts
that pertain to his office, [and this] by indenture expressly mention-
ing price, yardage, weight, and cost.[8] And he shall cause to be weighed
the wax which the chandler is to have worked, and shall reweigh it
after it has been worked. And he shall oversee and cause to be recorded by his under-clerk the liveries of chandlery made each day in
the wardrobe, and on the next day he shall supervise the putting away
of the torches, the great candles, and the mortars.[9] Each day he
shall record the parcels of all sorts of things delivered and dispensed
from his office, as counted since the day before, and he shall answer
concerning them at the account of the household. And he shall oversee the carriages belonging to the wardrobe, as well for the coffers
and other things of his office as for the beds of the wardrobe clerks
which ought to be carried. And he shall make allowance in his roll for
the carriage and transportation reasonably used in connection with
the king's journeys. . . .[10]

Item, a serjeant under-usher of the wardrobe, who shall live in the
wardrobe, sleeping within its door to safeguard all the things inside it.
And he shall be answerable if peril is incurred by his default. And he
shall obtain from the offices the liveries for all men of the wardrobe,
and he shall carry out their orders. . . .

Item, a porter of the wardrobe, who shall carry the coffers and the
other furnishings of the wardrobe to the carts, and shall load and
unload them. And he shall be on the cart [while it is] on the road.
And at night, if the cart is outdoors wandering through the country,
he shall remain on watch. . . .

Item, a squire fruiterer, who shall receive and take from the clerk
of the spicery confections and other spiceries, and figs and grapes for

---

[6] Also four under-clerks with liveries.

[7] See above, p. 171, n. 8.

[8] This was a newly established reform, as is explained in the next paragraph
of the text.

[9] Bowls of oil with floating wicks.

[10] Also an under-clerk to assist him.

the king's mouth. And each day he shall record for the said clerk what has been expended on the previous day: as well the said spiceries and fruit, thus received from the said clerk, as apples, pears, cherries, and other fruits which the said fruiterer shall purvey. . . .

Item, a serjeant chandler, who shall receive the wax and candle-wicks by weight from the clerk of the spicery, and shall have them worked according to the assize contained in the statute. . . .[11]

Item, a confessor of the king and his companion. . . .[12]

Item, a chief chaplain, who is to have a squire eating in the hall . . . and five chaplains . . . and six clerks. . . .

Item, an almoner chaplain, who is to have a squire eating in the hall. . . .[13]

Item, a physician. . . .

Item, a surgeon. . . .

Item, a clerk of the market, coroner of the king's household, who shall enforce the assize of bread, wine, and ale; also the assize of all sorts of measures, weights, and yards within the verge of our lord the king's presence. And he shall have wrongdoers who have broken the assize, or who are found with false measures, punished by imposition or fine. . . .

Item, the king shall have a squire inspector and keeper of viands for his mouth, and an inspector of his table; also a squire to carve before the king and a squire to serve him with his cup. . . .

Item, the king shall have two squires ushers of the chamber, one of whom shall be serjeant purveyor of wood and bedding for the office of the chamber. . . . And the serjeant purveyor shall have a serving-man to help him in making purveyance. . . .

Item, eight footmen of the chamber, who shall serve in the chamber making beds, holding and carrying torches, and [doing] various other things according to the commands of the king's chamberlain. . . .

Item, the king is to have thirty serjeants-at-arms, properly armed and mounted . . . , who shall daily ride armed before the king's person while he is journeying through the country, unless they have other commands from the king or the steward. . . .

Item, a knight chief usher of the hall, who shall have charge of the door of the hall, [seeing] that it is well kept by the serjeants and valets of the usher, as is fit. And he shall take care that the hall is well and honourably served, and that no one eats there except those who right-fully should, saving always that strangers are received and honoured as they ought to be. And each day he should enter and inspect the offices of the household, [to see] that the things sent by the purveyors are sufficient according to the purchase, and that no one is permitted in the same offices except those who ought to be there. And he shall have a squire eating in the hall. . . .

---

[11] I.e., a separate ordinance dealing with these matters. Two serving-men under the chandler worked the wax.

[12] With four horses and three grooms.

[13] Also a clerk and a serving-man.

Item, two serjeants ushers of the hall, of whom one shall be purveyor of wood and of bedding for the service of the hall.[14] . . .

Item, two knights marshals of the hall, of whom one shall have charge of lodgings and the other shall be on duty in the hall. . . .

Item, two serjeants marshals of the hall, of whom one shall have charge of lodgings and the other shall be on duty in the hall. . . .

Item, a serjeant overseer of the sideboard for the hall, who is to advise concerning the places that he serves, according as persons of high estate and others may be seated in the hall. . . .[15]

Item, a chief clerk of the pantry and butlery, who ought to keep the records of his office. And he is to respond each day at the account of the household. . . . He shall be present at the receipt of bread, wine, and ale; and he shall inspect and examine [them, to see] that they are of the proper weight, measure, and value. . . .[16]

Item, a serjeant chief pantler, who shall receive the bread in gross by view of the clerk or the under-clerk, and shall each day be answerable to the chief clerk for the enrolment of what has been dispensed. . . .[17]

Item, a serjeant pantler for the king's mouth, who each day shall receive from the great pantry the bread for the king and for his chamber, and for no other place. . . .[18]

Item, a waferer, who shall serve the king, the hall, and the chamber with wafers, as pertains to him. . . .

Item, a serjeant baker, who shall bake all sorts of bread for dispensing in the king's household—as well round loaves for all the commonalty as demeine loaves for the king's mouth. . . .[19]

Item, a serjeant naperer, who shall perform his office in the king's chamber and in the hall. And he shall receive the napery from the clerk of the spicery and shall be responsible for it at the account whenever he is asked. . . .[20]

Item, a ewerer for the chamber, who shall perform his office in the said chamber. . . .[21]

Item, a launderer for the king's chamber, who shall wash all sorts of linen cut for the king's body . . .[22] and the covers used in the service of the chamber. . . .

---

[14] Under the serjeants were two serving-men; under the knight was a sewer, who had charge of setting the table.

[15] He was assisted by two squires sewers, who served the meals in the hall. Besides, twenty-four squires were on duty in the hall, to carry out the commands of the high officials.

[16] Also an under-clerk, who kept tallies for all bread, wine, and ale received.

[17] Also a serving-man and two porters.

[18] Assisted by a serving-man for the chamber, and one for the rest of the household.

[19] Cf. above, p. 66, n. 3. The baker was assisted by two serving-men, one for the oven and the other for the mill.

[20] Also a serving-man.

[21] Also a serving-man, who acted as ewerer for the hall.

[22] This portion of the text is very corrupt.

Item, a launderer of napery, who shall wash all sorts of cut linen pertaining to the said office of napery, and the covers from offices connected with the hall. . . .

Item, a chief butler, serjeant purveyor of wines. . . . And he shall do that which pertains to him according to the content of the statute concerning his office below.[23]

Item, a serjeant butler of the household, who shall receive and dispense all wine and ale that are dispensed in the household. . . .

Item, a serjeant butler for the king, who shall receive from the butler of the household all the wine and ale that are dispensed in the king's chamber. . . .[24]

Item, a chief clerk of the kitchen, who ought to make the enrolments pertaining to his office. And every day at the account in the wardrobe before the steward and the treasurer he shall be responsible for the parcels delivered [in the kitchen] and for all other matters pertaining to his office. And he shall be present at the cutting of meat and the division of fish. And he shall oversee the purchase and the cost of meat and fish and of all other things pertaining to his office, with the aid of the comptroller, the knight usher of the hall or the knight marshal, and the sewer of the king's table. . . .[25]

Item, two serjeants cooks for the king's mouth. . . .[26]

Item, two serjeants cooks for the hall. . . .

Item, a serjeant larderer, who shall receive the meat and fish that the buyers cause to be brought to the larder, or which comes as a present; also the venison which comes thither from the king's huntsmen or from any other source. And he shall deliver the aforesaid meat and fish to be dispensed for the household in parcels, and [this] under the inspection of the comptroller, the knight usher of the hall or the knight marshal of the hall, the clerk of the kitchen, the sewer of the king's table, and the chief cook. And he shall keep the food on the sideboard and each day he shall give to the said clerk a record of the parcels of the aforesaid meat and fish dispensed in the manner aforesaid. . . .[27]

Item, a serjeant poulterer, who shall attend to purchases and purveyance of all sorts of things pertaining to his office. . . .[28]

Item, a serjeant of the scullery, who shall buy and purvey wood, charcoal, and all sorts of vessels of brass, iron, and wood that belong

[23] A separate ordinance added at the end of the survey.

[24] Also enumerated in the service of the butlery: a serving-man of the cup-house two drawers of ale and wine, a purveyor of ale, two serving-men of the pitcher-house. and two porters.

[25] As assistants he had an under-clerk and two buyers, who were to give money or tallies for anything taken by purveyance.

[26] Under each pair of cooks were five serving-men.

[27] Under him were an usher of the larder and two porters.

[28] Three serving-men assisted him in obtaining poultry and preparing it for the kitchen.

to the kitchen; also the pots and various other things pertaining to his office. . . .[29]

Item, a [second] serjeant of the scullery, who shall receive the silver vessels from the wardrobe by number and weight . . . , and shall keep them and be responsible for them by number and weight in the same wardrobe at the end of the year. . . .

Item, a serjeant of the saucery, who shall buy and purvey flour for all manner of sauces and other things needed for the office of the saucery and the king's household. . . .[29]

Item, a serjeant porter, who shall guard the door where the king sleeps, so that none may enter except those who by right should do so. . . .[29]

Item, a chief clerk of the marshalsea. . . .[30]

(French) Tout, *Edward II in English History*, pp. 270 f.

---

[29] Also two serving-men.

[30] Here the text gives a detailed account of all the services connected with the king's stables. The chief clerk, assisted by a purveyor of oats, had charge of all records pertaining to the office, including tallies given for oats, hay, straw, harness, etc. The actual care of the king's horses—palfreys, chargers, pack-horses, draught-horses, etc.—devolved on two serjeants harbingers and three serjeants marshals, under whom were numerous serving-men, porters, and grooms. The record then describes the officers in charge of the king's hunting, fishing, and fowling, and lists his trumpeters, musicians, messengers, and archers. It ends with a group of particular ordinances to regulate the duties of the chief butler, the arrangement of lodgings for the court, the daily account in the wardrobe, the exclusion from the household of undesirable persons, and many other matters.

58. EDWARD II: STATUTE OF YORK (1322)

Whereas our lord King Edward, son of King Edward, on March 16, in the third year of his reign, granted to the prelates, earls, and barons of his realm . . . ;[1] and whereas the archbishop of Canterbury, primate of all England, and the bishops, earls, and barons chosen for the purpose, drew up certain ordinances that begin as follows . . . , which ordinances our said lord the king caused to be rehearsed and examined in his parliament at York three weeks after Easter in the fifteenth year of his reign . . . ; and whereas, through that examination in the said parliament, it was found that by the ordinances thus decreed the royal power of our said lord the king was wrongfully limited in many respects, to the injury of his royal lordship and contrary to the estate of the crown; and whereas, furthermore, through such ordinances and provisions made by subjects in times past against the royal authority of our lord the king's ancestors, the kingdom has incurred troubles and wars, whereby the land has been imperilled: [therefore] it is agreed and established at the said parliament by our lord the king, by the said prelates, earls,

---

[1] Reciting the preamble to the Ordinances of 1311. On the significance of the following provisions, see G. Lapsley, in the *English Historical Review*, XXVIII, 118 f., and G. L. Haskins, *The Statute of York*.

and barons, and by the whole community of the realm assembled in this parliament, that everything ordained by the said Ordainers and contained in the said ordinances shall henceforth and forever cease [to be valid], losing for the future all title, force, virtue, and effect; and that the statutes and establishments duly made by our lord the king and his ancestors prior to the said ordinances shall remain in force. And [it is decreed] that henceforth and forever at all times every kind of ordinance or provision made under any authority or commission whatsoever by subjects of our lord the king or of his heirs against the royal power of our lord the king or of his heirs, or contrary to the estate of the crown, shall be null and shall have no validity or force whatever; but that matters which are to be determined with regard to the estate of our lord the king and of his heirs, or with regard to the estate of the kingdom and of the people, shall be considered, granted, and established in parliament by our lord the king and with the consent of the prelates, earls, and barons, and of the community of the kingdom, as has been accustomed in times past.[2]

(French) *Statutes of the Realm*, I, 189.

59. EDWARD II'S ABDICATION (1327)

Whereas Sire Edward, recently king of England, of his free will and by the common counsel and assent of the prelates, earls, barons, and other nobles, and of the whole community of the realm, has abdicated the government of the realm; and whereas he has granted and wills that the government of the realm should devolve upon his eldest son and heir, Sire Edward, who should govern, reign, and be crowned king; and whereas all the great men have performed their homage [to the said heir]: we proclaim and publish the peace of our said lord, Sire Edward, the son [of King Edward]; and on his part we command and firmly enjoin each and every one, on pain of disherison and loss of life or members, not to break the peace of our said lord the king; for he is and shall be ready to enforce right for each and every one of the said kingdom in all matters and against all persons, both great and small. So, if any one has some demand to make of another, let him make it by means of [legal] action, without resorting to force or violence.

(French) Lodge and Thornton, *English Constitutional Documents*, p. 21.

60. EDWARD III: WRITS OF SUMMONS

(A) PARLIAMENT OF 1337

The king to the venerable father in Christ, J[ohn], by the same grace archbishop of Canterbury and primate of all England, greeting. Whereas, on account of divers arduous matters especially affect-

---

[2] The ordinance was sent to all the sheriffs with commands for it to be read in full county court.

ing us and the state of our kingdom, we propose to hold our parliament at York on Monday next after the feast of St. Hilary and to have a conference with you and the other prelates, magnates, and nobles of the said kingdom; we command and enjoin you that, in the fealty and love by which you are bound to us, avoiding all excuse, you be personally present on the said day at the said place, in order with us and with the other prelates, magnates, and nobles aforesaid to discuss the said matters and thereupon give your counsel. And as you cherish us and our honour, as well as the peace and tranquillity of our kingdom, by no means fail to do this; first summoning (*premunientes*) the prior and chapter of your church of Christ at Canterbury and the archdeacons and all the clergy of your diocese, the said prior and archdeacons to be present in person, the said chapter [to be represented] by one fit proctor and the said clergy by two—which proctors are to have full and sufficient authority from the said chapter and clergy—on the said day and at the said place to determine and agree upon those measures which then and there, by the favour of divine clemency, may happen to be ordained through common counsel. By witness of the king of Bothwell, November 29.[1]

By the king himself.

(Latin) *Report Touching the Dignity of a Peer*, IV, 464 f.

(B) Great Council of 1353[2]

The king to the venerable father in Christ, S[imon], by the same grace archbishop of Canterbury, greeting. Whereas, on account of great and urgent matters recently come upon us, which intimately concern us as well as the condition and rights of our kingdom of England, and for which it behooves us to find a speedy and provident solution, we desire to have a conference and deliberation with you, with the rest of the prelates, magnates, and nobles, and with our other faithful men of the said kingdom, at Westminster on the morrow of the Assumption of the Blessed Virgin next to come: we firmly enjoin and command that, in the fealty, love, and allegiance by which you are bound to us, putting aside all other affairs, you be personally present at the said place on the said day in order, with us, with the rest of the prelates, magnates, and nobles, and with the other men aforesaid, to discuss the said business and thereupon give your counsel. And as you cherish us, our honour, and the salvation, defence, and best interest of our said kingdom, and as you wish to

---

[1] Similar mandates were sent to the archbishop of York, eighteen bishops, and the custodian of one vacant see; without the *premunientes* clause, to twenty-seven abbots and four priors; and with different forms of address, to fifty-eight lay peers and fifteen justices and councillors. Furthermore, by the usual form (see the writs of 1295, no. 49F) the sheriff of each county was ordered to cause the election of two knights of the shire, two citizens from each city, and two burgesses from each borough. The warden of the Cinque Ports was commanded to have two barons elected from each of the ports.

[2] Cf. no. 62G, H.

avoid its subversion, by no means fail to do this, then and there notifying us of the day on which you received these present letters and by whom they were brought to you. By witness of the king at Westminster, July 20.[3]

By the king himself and his council.

(Latin) *Ibid.*, IV, 593 f.

---

[3] Similar mandates were sent to nineteen bishops, the abbot of Westminster, the prior of the Hospital of St. John, thirty-seven lay peers, and sixteen justices and councillors. The sheriff of each county was ordered to have only one knight of the shire elected, so as to avoid disturbing the men engaged in their autumn work. Two citizens were to be elected from London, but only one—on account of the same autumn work!—from York and from each of nine other towns. Two barons were to be elected from the Cinque Ports as a whole.

61. PARLIAMENT ROLLS OF EDWARD III

(A) PARLIAMENT OF 1330

These are the treasons, felonies, and wrongs done to our lord the king and to his people by Roger de Mortimer and others of his following.[1] . . .

Accordingly, for the reasons aforesaid, and for many other reasons which may not all be set forth at present, our said lord the king, by the advice and aid of his privy and intimate councillors, had the said Roger taken in such fashion as he has often described to you. So our said lord the king charges you, earls and barons, the peers of the realm, that, with regard to these matters vitally affecting him and you and all the people of his kingdom, you render for the said Roger such right and lawful judgment as should be incurred by a man of this sort, who, as he believes, is truly guilty of all the crimes set forth above; and [he charges you] that the said matters are notorious and known to be true to you and all the people of the kingdom.

The which earls, barons, and peers, having examined the articles, returned to the king's presence in the same parliament and all declared through one of the peers [as spokesman] that all the matters contained in the said articles were notorious, being known to them and to the people, and especially the article touching the death of Sire Edward, father of our lord the present king. Wherefore, as judges of parliament, the said earls, barons, and peers, by the assent of the king in the same parliament, awarded and adjudged that the said Roger, as a traitor and enemy to the king and to the kingdom, should be drawn[2] and hanged. And thereupon the earl marshal was commanded to carry out the execution of the said judgment; and the mayor, aldermen, and sheriffs of London, also the constable of the Tower and those who had [the prisoner] in custody, [were ordered] to be of assistance to the said earl marshal in carrying out the said execution.

---

[1] See M. V. Clarke, in *Oxford Essays Presented to H. E. Salter,* pp. 164 f.
[2] On a hurdle to the place of execution.

Which execution was carried out and performed on Thursday next after the first day of parliament, namely, November 29. . . .

In the same parliament summoned at Westminster Sir Eblé Lestrange and Alice[3] his wife presented a petition in these words:—

To our lord the king and his council Eblé Lestrange and Alice his wife set forth that all the lands which he held of the inheritance of the said Alice, after the death of Thomas, one time earl of Lancaster . . . , were taken into the hands of the king, father of our lord the present king, and kept in his hands. . . . Wherefore they pray our lord the king that, for the salvation of his father's soul and for that of his own [soul], he will call before him his good council and the good and loyal men who were then in the council of his said father, and will examine them with regard to the matters aforesaid . . . ; and then that of his especial grace he will act toward them as may be his pleasure and as his good conscience may decide for him.

After the petition had been read and heard before our lord the king and the prelates, earls, barons, and other lords[4] of the same parliament, whereas it was testified by some of the said lords, trustworthy men, that the said Alice had then been subjected to such arbitrary will and severity . . . : our lord the king, having regard for good faith and conscience, with the assent of the said prelates, earls, barons, and other lords of the same parliament, granted to the said Sir Eblé and Alice, in order to constitute an estate for them, the lands which were still in their hands, to the value of 500*m.*, and lands of the same inheritance which were then in the king's hands, to the value of 700*m.*, to be had and held in fee forever . . . by the aforesaid Sir Eblé and Alice, and by the heirs of the said Sir Eblé, of our lord the king and his heirs, and of the other chief lords of the fief, for the services due and accustomed. . . . And thereupon our lord the king commanded the bishop of Winchester, his chancellor, to put into execution that which had thus been granted and agreed on. . . .

Item, in the same parliament summoned at Westminster Sir John of Clavering presented a petition in these words. . . .

After which petition had been read and heard before the council in the said parliament, whereas the lords and the other discreet men of the same [parliament] could not then agree on making a final disposition of that [case]; it was responded that this same petition and all the other petitions presented to the same parliament, together with the inquests returned in the chancery by the escheator . . . and with all the other certifications and memoranda of the exchequer

---

[3] Widow of Thomas, earl of Lancaster. The two following extracts are given as examples of the numerous private petitions introduced in this and the succeeding parliaments. Cf. no. 54G, and, on the jurisdiction of the chancellor, no. 71.

[4] *Granz,* the usual term for members of the original parliament; *seigneurs* came into general use a little later.

touching the said matter, should be remanded to the chancery, and that the chancellor, having summoned thither the discreet men of the king's council, should administer justice in the matter. . . .

(French) *Rotuli Parliamentorum,* II, 52-53, 57, 59.

(B) Parliament of 1332

These are the memoranda of the actions taken in the parliament summoned at Westminster on Wednesday, the morrow of the Nativity of Our Lady, in the sixth year of the reign of Edward III after the Conquest:—

. . . On which Thursday they held a discussion and deliberation: that is to say, the said prelates by themselves; and the said earls, barons, and other lords by themselves; and also the knights of the shires by themselves.[5]. . . And they advised for the sake of improvement[6] that our lord the king should remain in England and should betake himself toward the parts of the north, and that he should have with him discreet and forceful men for the salvation of the said kingdom and of his people, in case the men of Scotland or others should wish to invade it for the purpose of evil-doing. And they also advised that the king should send discreet and forceful men to the parts of Ireland, as well as money, to assist his lieges there. And whereas our lord the king could not carry out these matters except by the aid of his people, the said prelates, earls, barons, and other lords, as well as the knights of the shires and all the commons[7]—in order to carry out the said projects, and in order that our lord the king could live of his own and pay his expenses without burdening his people through outrageous prises or otherwise—of their free will granted to our lord the king a fifteenth, to be levied from the community,[8] and a tenth, to be levied from the cities, boroughs, and demesnes of the king. And our lord the king, at the request of the said prelates, earls, barons, and knights of the shires, for the relief of his said people, granted that the commissions recently issued for those appointed to assess a tallage in the said cities, boroughs, and demesnes throughout England should for the present be entirely repealed; and that for this purpose writs should be sent out in due form; and that in the future he would not have such tallage assessed except as had been done in the time of his ancestors and as he rightfully should.[9]

(French) *Ibid.,* II, 66.

---

[5] For the union of the knights and burgesses to form the house of commons, see the procedure in the parliaments of 1339-41 (no. 61C-E) and the definite statements concerning the parliaments of 1343 and 1348 (no. 61F, G).

[6] In the lamentable conditions previously described.

[7] *Tote la commune*—one of many expressions used to denote the members of the lower house.

[8] That is to say, from everybody outside cities and boroughs; see above p. 158, n. 14. For tallage, cf. nos. 37B, 46F.

[9] Despite the vagueness of this promise, tallage was never again levied; cf. no. 62B.

(C) PARLIAMENT OF 1339[10]

Memoranda of the parliament held at Westminster on the quinzime of St. Michael, in the thirteenth year of our lord the king's reign:—

In the first place a general proclamation was made in the great hall of Westminster according to the following form. . . .[11]

And then the reasons for the summons of this parliament were set forth and explained to the lords and to the commons, so that in this connection their counsel and advice might be obtained in the best manner possible. And three reasons were expounded, of which the first was that every one, whether great or small, ought to take up with himself the best way in which peace could and should be more securely preserved within the kingdom. The second reason was how the march of Scotland and the lands to the north could best be guarded and defended against the Scottish enemies. The third reason was how the sea could be guarded against enemies, so that they should do no damage and should not enter the kingdom to destroy it. . . .

And after that exposition[12] had been made, everybody, both great and small, was of the opinion that in this necessity [the king] would have to be aided with a large sum; otherwise he would be shamed and dishonoured, and he and his people would be ruined forever. . . . And afterwards they sought [to decide] how he could best be aided, to the least cost and grievance of his people, to his own greatest profit, and to the most efficacious advancement of the business aforesaid, considering the grave lack of money from which the country was suffering. And among other methods certain members of the council proposed the one that is described below: namely, that within two years each man of the kingdom, of whatever status or condition he might be, should pay to our lord the king a tithe of his sheaves, wool, and lambs, in the same way as he gave [tithe] to Holy Church. And the members of the council who best knew the estate of our lord the king, and his affairs both on this side [of the sea] and on that, were of the opinion that by this [tax] the king could be greatly aided and his said affairs improved and advanced in every way—on which matters there was prolonged discussion. And after that discussion the lords gave their response in the schedule which follows. . . .

This is the grant made by the lords to our lord the king in the present parliament: namely, the tenth sheaf of every sort of grain from their demesne lands, except the lands of their bondmen, [as well as]

---

[10] For a clear sketch of the complicated parliamentary history of the next few years, see Stubbs, *Constitutional History*, II, 400 f.

[11] To prevent riots and disturbances, the king forbids the carrying of arms in or near the palace of Westminster, or in the city of London and its suburbs, by any one except designated officials and except earls and barons, each of whom is entitled to carry a sword unless he is in the presence of the king or in the royal council chamber.

[12] Of the king's needs, made by the archbishop of Canterbury and other councillors. The king asked a large aid for the war in France.

the tenth fleece and the tenth lamb from their demesne stock during the coming year, to be paid in two years. And the said lords desire that the maltote, which recently has been levied on wool, shall be utterly abated and that the ancient custom shall be held to; that they shall have, by specific charter and by enrolment of parliament, [the promise] that no such custom [as the maltote] shall further be levied, and that neither this grant, which they have just made to our lord the king, nor any other grant made by them in times past shall be turned to their prejudice as a customary burden. . . .[13]

And the commons gave their response in another schedule, as follows:—

Lords, the men of the commons who are here at this parliament have well understood the position of our lord the king and the pressing need that he has of being aided by his people; and they are much enheartened and greatly comforted by the fact that he has made such progress in the enterprises which he has undertaken for his own honour and the salvation of his people; and they pray God that He will give him grace for successful continuation and for victory over his enemies. . . . And with regard to his need of aid from his people, the men of the commons who are here well know that he must be greatly aided, and they are of good disposition to do so, as they have ever been in times past. But in so far as the aid has to be large, they do not dare give consent until they have advised and consulted with the communities (*communes*) of their country. Wherefore the said men of the commons pray monseigneur the duke,[14] and the other lords who are present, that he will be pleased to summon another parliament on some convenient day; and in the meantime each [man of the commons] will return to his country. And they promise loyally, in the fealty which they owe to our lord the king, that they will all do their best, each in his own country, to obtain good and proper aid for our lord the king; and they are confident, with God's help, of a successful outcome. And they furthermore pray that a writ shall be sent to each sheriff of England [ordering] that two of the worthiest knights of the shire should be elected and sent to the next parliament for the commons, and that none of them should be either a sheriff or other minister.

And the men of the commons also presented two bills: one containing their response in the matters which they were charged to consider—that is to say, the peace of the land and the guarding of the Scottish march and of the sea—and the other [containing] the graces which they asked of the king. Of which [bills] the tenor is as follows. . . .[15]

[The commons also pray that] the king through his council will pardon his commons the murders, escapes, and chattels of fugitives

---

[13] Cf. nos. 49B, 51A, C.
[14] The Black Prince, duke of Cornwall, who had been placed in charge of the government during the king's absence.
[15] The first bill is omitted.

and felons and all trespasses in the forest of times past. Item, that they be pardoned aids for knighting the son of our lord the king and for marrying his daughter. Item, with regard to those men who, with or without commission, come to take prises either for the great horses of our lord the king or for other purposes, that they be arrested if they do not give immediate payment; and that [otherwise] they be treated as violators of the peace. Item, that pardon be given of all old debts up to the coronation of our lord the present king—as well scutages and reliefs as other debts owed for any reason whatsoever. And the commons pray that the maltote on wool and lead be levied as it used to be of old, since, as we understand, it has been increased without the assent of either commons or lords; and if it is demanded otherwise [than as aforesaid], that each man of the commons may forbid it with impunity; and that explanation be given them concerning the form of the security which they wish to be established for the commons in the aforesaid matters. . . .[16]

(French) *Ibid.*, II, 103-05.

(D) FIRST PARLIAMENT OF 1340

Memoranda of the parliament summoned at Westminster on the octave of St. Hilary in the thirteenth year of the reign of our lord the king, Edward III after the conquest. . . .

By virtue of which letters[17] the said treasurer, Richard [of Willoughby], John [of Stonor], and John [of St. Paul] had some of the lords and commons, who had arrived by that time, assembled in the Painted Chamber and had the said letters read. And those who had come were further told that, since the [rest of the] prelates, earls, barons, and other lords, as well as the knights of the shires and the citizens and burgesses of cities and boroughs, had been prevented by bad weather from coming on the said day, it would be necessary to await their arrival. And so the said parliament was postponed from day to day until Monday next after the said octave. . . .

On which day the reasons for calling the said parliament were set forth to the commons: namely, to make good and agreeable response concerning the promise which they had made at the last parliament, for giving suitable aid to our lord the king. . . . Upon this exposition they replied that they wished to talk together and consider the matter; and that, with God's help, they would make such response as would be to the pleasure of their liege lord and of all his council. Concerning which matter the commons delayed giving their response until Saturday, February 19.

On which day they offered to aid our lord the king in this necessity with 30,000 sacks of wool, on certain conditions put in the indentures drawn up in that connection and sealed under the seals of the prelates and other lords. . . . And since the matters contained in these indentures so intimately touched the estate of our lord the king, it was

---

[16] See the proceedings of the next parliament and no. 62B.

[17] From the duke of Cornwall naming as deputies the following men.

the opinion of the said council that our lord the king and the privy[18] council close to him should be advised of them. Wherefore it was granted and agreed that the said indentures should be sent to our lord the king, together with the advice of his council on this side [of the sea]; so that he could express his will in that connection. And it should be remembered that on the same day the earls and barons in attendance at the said parliament granted, for themselves and for their peers of the land holding by barony, the tenth sheaf, the tenth fleece, and the tenth lamb from all their demesne lands.

And whereas it was the opinion of the prelates, earls, barons, and other lords that, for carrying out the enterprises of our lord the king both on this side [of the sea] and on that, a large sum of money would have to be raised without delay, particularly for preparing a fleet of ships on the sea and equipping men-at-arms and archers for the defence of the kingdom, and that, if this were not done with haste, very great perils might arise; they asked the men of the commons how the latter wished to meet these perils and provide for their own salvation.

To which question, after a long discussion had taken place, they replied that they would vouchsafe to our lord the king 2500 sacks, to provide for the prompt raising of that [money], with this proviso: that, if the conditions set forth above were pleasing to our lord the king, those 2500 sacks should be counted as partial satisfaction of the said 30,000 sacks; and if not, they would vouchsafe these [2500 sacks] to our lord the king by their gift, as is more fully contained in another indenture made in this connection. . . .

(French) *Ibid.,* II, 107-08.

(E) PARLIAMENT OF 1341

In the first place it was agreed that Sir Thomas of Drayton should be clerk of the parliament.

Item, it was agreed by our lord the king and those of his council who had then arrived that a proclamation should be made against the bearing of arms by any person, according to the fashion customarily observed in other parliaments. . . .

Item, announcement was made that any one who wished to present a petition to our lord the king and to his council should present it between now and the next Saturday, the day stated in the announcement. And the following men were assigned to receive petitions from England: namely. . . .[19] And for petitions from Gascony, Wales, Ireland, Scotland, and the [Channel] Islands. . . . And to hear the petitions from England [the following men] were assigned. . . .[20]

---

[18] *Secrez*—that is to say, the intimate councillors who accompanied the king in France.

[19] Three chancery clerks constituted each group of receivers.

[20] In each case the hearers of petitions were a committee of bishops, earls, and barons, with the chancellor and treasurer as associates if needed.

Item, to hear the petitions from Gascony, Wales, Ireland, Scotland, and the [Channel] Islands, [the following men] were assigned. . . .

Item, it is to be remembered that, on account of debates arising in connection with certain articles which the lords and commons of the land asked of our lord the king, the parliament was continued day after day from the said Thursday[21] until the next Thursday following. On which Thursday a bill was brought in parliament by the lords of the land, containing certain requests which our lord the king graciously agreed to, as is more fully set forth below.

And whereas, among other matters contained in the petition of the lords, it was provided that peers of the land, whether officials or others, should not be held to answer concerning trespasses with which they had been charged by the king, except in parliament; [and whereas] it was the king's opinion that such provision would be improper and opposed to his rightful estate: therefore the said lords prayed the king to agree that four bishops, four earls, and four barons, together with certain men skilled in the law, should be chosen to consider in what cases the said peers should be held to answer in parliament and nowhere else, and in what cases they should not be; and to report their advice to him. And to do this [the following men] were elected. . . . Which twelve men reported their advice in full parliament on the Monday next following, in a schedule which is transcribed in this form. . . .[22]

Also they presented, before this same Monday, certain petitions affecting all the lords and commons of the realm, a copy of which is as follows:—

. . . That it may please his most high lordship . . . to command that the said Great Charter, together with the other ordinances and statutes made through great deliberation, shall be observed, maintained, and enforced in all particulars; and that the aforesaid persons who have been attached and imprisoned, and the other persons who have been deprived[23] as stated above, shall be fully liberated and restored to their benefices, lands, tenements, possessions, goods, and chattels, so that each may be lawfully tried according to his condition, without recourse in the future to such actions against the law and the tenor of the Great Charter and all the other ordinances and statutes.

Item, that the chancellor, the treasurer, the barons and chancellor of the exchequer, the justices of both benches and all other justices whatsoever, the steward and chamberlain of the king's household, the keeper of the privy seal, and the treasurer of the wardrobe shall, whenever they are installed in office, swear to maintain and keep without infringement the law of the land and the provisions of the

---

[21] When the king's request for aid had been presented to parliament.

[22] The report, guaranteeing the trial of peers in parliament, was embodied in a statute duly sealed by the king; but this was one of the acts annulled by the king in the following year (no. 62c).

[23] Of lands and other possessions, arbitrarily and without due process of law.

Great Charter and of the other statutes made by the assent of the peers of the land. . . .

Item, the lords and commons of the land . . . pray that certain persons shall be deputed by commission to audit the accounts of all those who have received the wool for our lord the king or the other aids granted to him; and likewise of those who have received and spent his moneys both beyond the sea and here, as well since the beginning of the war as at present; and that the rolls, memoranda, obligations, and other records made beyond [the sea] shall be delivered to the chancery, to be enrolled and recorded, as should be done at such times. . . .

Item, whereas many evils have arisen through bad councillors and ministers, the lords and the commons pray that it may please the king to ordain by the advice of the prelates, earls, and barons, that he will appoint in parliament the chancellor, the chief justices of both benches, the treasurer, the chancellor and the chief baron of the exchequer, the steward of his household, the keeper of the wardrobe, the comptroller, a clerk fit to keep his private seal, and the king's chief clerks of the common bench. And this shall henceforth be done in the case of such ministers whenever there is need, and they shall swear before the peers in parliament to observe the laws, as stated above, and this according to the ordinances previously made in such connection. . . .

And they besought the king that he would graciously make those concessions. And our lord the king, having deliberated on the matter contained in the same petitions, had certain responses made to the same petitions. When these responses, together with the aforesaid petitions, were reported in full parliament before the king and the lords and commons of the realm on the next Wednesday following, it was the opinion of the said lords and commons that the said responses were not so full or sufficient as was proper. Wherefore they besought the king that he would please to add an amendment. And our lord the king, yielding to their prayer, agreed with them that four prelates, four earls, and four barons, together with other men skilled in the law, should be assigned to review the said petitions and responses, and to report their advice to the king. And [the following men] were appointed. . . .

And on the same Wednesday the said archbishops and other prelates brought certain petitions before the king in his said parliament, whereof a copy is as follows. . . .

Responses to the clergy. . . .[24]
Responses to the lords. . . .[25]
Responses to the commons:—As to the first article, it is the will of our lord the king that the Great Charter and other statutes shall be observed in all their particulars. And he wills and grants for him-

---

[24] Made by the king after the prelates had declared earlier answers unsatisfactory.

[25] Dealing with only one important article; much the same as that below.

self and his heirs that, if any person does anything in the future contrary to the Great Charter, the statutes, or the rightful laws, he shall answer in parliament, or wherever else he should answer under the common law, as stated above. . . . And as to the oaths of ministers, it pleases the king that his ministers shall be sworn according to the form of the petition. . . .

Item, as to the second article—that is to say, with regard to the auditing of accounts from those who have received the king's wool, other aids, etc.—it pleases the king that the matter shall be attended to by good men deputed for the purpose, provided that the treasurer and the chief baron [of the exchequer] are added to them. And it shall be done in this case as has been ordained on previous occasions; and the lords [of the commission] shall be elected in this parliament. Furthermore, all rolls, memoranda, and obligations made beyond the sea shall be delivered into the chancery. . . .

It pleases the king that, if one of the king's great officials named in the petition is removed from office by death or other cause, he will secure the agreement of the lords who may be found nearest in the country, together with [that of] the good council which he shall have about him, and will place another fit man in the said office. And [such appointee] shall be sworn at the next parliament in accordance with the petition. And at every parliament their offices shall be taken into the king's hands and they [shall be held] to answer to those who may see fit to complain against them. And if complaint of any misdeed is made concerning any minister, and if he is thereof convicted in parliament, he shall be removed and shall be punished by the judgment of the peers, and another fit man shall be appointed to that [office]. And in such matters the king without delay will have execution pronounced and carried out according to the judgment of the peers in parliament.

It is to be remembered that, upon the aforesaid responses as well to the petitions of the lords as to those of the commons and of the clergy, the statutes hereinunder written were made by the said lords and commons and shown to our lord the king, together with certain conditions that the lords and commons asked of the king for the grant made to him of 30,000 sacks of wool in lieu of the ninth sheaf, lamb, and fleece of the second year.[26] Which statutes and conditions were then read before the king. And the chancellor, the treasurer, certain judges of both benches, the steward of the king's household, the chamberlain, and various others were sworn on the cross of Canterbury to hold and keep those [enactments] in so far as pertained to them. But the said chancellor, treasurer, and certain judges protested that they assented neither to the making nor to the form of the said statutes, and that they could not keep them in case the said statutes were contrary to the laws and usages of the realm, which they were sworn to preserve. And afterwards the same statutes and

[26] Cf. no. 62B.

conditions were sealed with the king's great seal and delivered to the lords and the knights of the shires. . . .[27]

(French) Ibid., II, 126-31.

(F) PARLIAMENT OF 1343

. . . Item, it is to be remembered that on the next Wednesday—namely, the last day of April—our lord the king and the archbishop aforesaid came into the Painted Chamber, together with the bishops . . . , and the earls . . . , and the other lords and commons there assembled. And the reasons for the summoning of parliament were explained to them by the chancellor of our lord the king in the manner following. . . . Whereupon the said prelates and lords were charged to meet by themselves in the White Chamber until Thursday, May 1, in order to treat, consult, and agree among themselves as to whether or not our lord the king should send messages to the court of Rome, setting forth and explaining his rights there before the said holy father the pope, as aforesaid. And in the same way the knights of the shires and the commons were charged to meet in the Painted Chamber in order to treat, consult, and agree among themselves on the same matter, and to report their answer and assent in parliament on the said Thursday. . . .

Item, it is granted and agreed that the statute made at Westminster on the quinzime of Easter, in the fifteenth year of the reign of our lord the king, shall be entirely repealed and annulled and shall lose the name of statute, as being prejudicial and contrary to the laws and usages of the realm and to the rights and prerogatives of our lord the king. But because certain articles were included in the same statute which are reasonable and in accord with law and right, it is agreed by our lord the king and his council that such articles and the others granted in this present parliament shall, by the advice of the justices and other learned men, be made into a new statute and held forever. . . .[28]

(French) Ibid., II, 135-39.

(G) PARLIAMENT OF 1348

. . . Whereupon the knights of the shires and the others of the commons were told that they should withdraw together and take good counsel as to how, for withstanding the malice of the said enemy and for the salvation of our said lord the king and his kingdom of England, our lord the king could be aided to his greatest advantage and to the least burdening of his people; and that, as soon as they had come to a decision, they should notify our lord the king and the lords of his council. The which knights and others of the commons

---

[27] Cf. no. 62c.

[28] Cf. no. 62c. No articles from the annulled statute are included in the statute of this year.

took counsel on the matter day after day and at last gave their response to the following effect:[29]—

. . . Thus the said poor commons, to their own excessive hurt, grant to our lord the king three fifteenths, to be levied during three years, beginning at Michaelmas next; on condition that in each of these years one fifteenth, and nothing in addition, shall be levied in equal portions at two terms of the year, Michaelmas and Easter, and that this aid shall be assigned and kept solely for the war of our lord the king and shall in no way be assigned to [pay] old debts. . . .

And afterwards the said commons were told that all individual persons who wished to present petitions in this parliament should present them to the chancellor; and that the petitions touching the commons [in general] should be presented to the clerk of the parliament. The which commons presented their petitions to the said clerk in the manner following:—

. . . Item, the commons pray that the petitions presented in the last parliament by the said commons and fully answered and granted by our said lord the king and the prelates and lords of the land, shall be observed; and that, by no bill presented in this parliament in the name of the commons or of any one else, shall the responses already granted be changed: for the commons acknowledge no such bill as may be presented by any one to effect the contrary. Response: At an earlier time the king, by the advice of the prelates and lords of the land, made answer to the petitions of the commons regarding the law of the land, [to the effect] that neither the laws held and accustomed in times past nor the process of the same [law of the land] so accustomed in the past could be changed without making a new statute—to do which the king could not then and cannot now see his way. But as soon as he can see his way [to do so], he will bring the lords and the skilled men of his council before him and by their advice and counsel will ordain concerning such articles and others that involve amendment of the law; so that right and equity shall be enforced for all and each of his lieges and subjects. . . .

(French) *Ibid.*, II, 200 f.

(H) PARLIAMENT OF 1372

. . . The petitions that the commons presented in Parliament and the responses to them were read, and also an ordinance made in the same parliament to the following effect:—

Whereas men of the law, who pursue a variety of business in the king's courts for the sake of individuals with whom they are [as-

---

[29] The address of the commons begins with a long list of the outrageous taxes and impositions laid upon them in the past contrary to the king's promises. Then follow a large number of specific conditions, including guarantees against other forms of taxation, restoration of 20,000 sacks of wool previously borrowed by the king, immediate settlement by commissioners of petitions left over from the last parliament, respite from all judicial eyres for three years, and the formal entry of these conditions in the roll of parliament.

sociated], take numerous petitions and have them presented before parliament in the name of the commons, although the latter are not at all concerned with them . . . ; and whereas sheriffs, who are the common ministers of the people and ought to stay by their offices to do right to every one, are named . . . and returned to parliament as knights of the shire by the sheriffs themselves: [therefore] it is agreed and granted in this parliament that henceforth no man of the law, pursuing business in the king's courts, or sheriff during such time as he is sheriff, shall be returned or accepted as a knight of the shire; nor shall those men of the law and sheriffs, who are at present returned to parliament, have wages. But the king wishes that the worthiest knights and serjeants of the country shall be returned as knights in parliament, and that they shall be elected in the full county [court].

And afterwards permission was given to the knights of the shires to depart and to sue for their writs of expenses. And so they departed. But the citizens and burgesses who had come to parliament were for certain reasons commanded to remain. To which citizens and burgesses, assembled on the very next day in a chamber near the White Chamber, it was shown how in the previous year a subsidy had been granted for a certain term to assure safe convoy of ships and merchandise coming to this country and leaving it by sea—that is to say, 2s. from each tun of wine coming to this country and 6d. from every pound of any merchandise whatsoever, either imported or exported[30]—[and how] this term had already passed. [So they were asked] that, considering the perils and mischiefs which might be incurred by their ships and merchandise from enemies on the sea, they would grant for the said causes a similar subsidy to continue for one year. Which subsidy they granted to the king, to be taken and levied in the same way as it had been taken and levied during the previous year. And so they departed.

(French) *Ibid.,* II, 310.

(I) PARLIAMENT OF 1376

. . . On the said morrow the prelates, the duke [of Cornwall], the earls, barons, and other lords, as well as the commons, justices, serjeants-at-law, and others, assembled in the Painted Chamber, where, before the king himself and all the others, Sir John Knyvett, knight, the chancellor of England, announced the causes for the summoning of the present parliament. . . . And in conclusion the chancellor besought them on behalf of the king that they would take diligent counsel regarding these matters—that is to say, the prelates and lords by themselves and the commons by themselves—and that, for the sake of prompter action by parliament, they would make good response in this connection as soon as they well might. And thereupon certain

---

[30] This tax, known as tunnage and poundage, was formally granted for two years by parliament in 1373: Stubbs, *Constitutional History,* II, 444 f., 556 f.

prelates and lords were assigned to be triers, and certain clerks to be receivers of bills in parliament, whose names here follow. . . .

Item, after the said prelates, lords, and commons had assembled in parliament, the said commons were told on behalf of the king that they should retire by themselves to their ancient place [of meeting], in the chapter house of the abbot of Westminster, and should there discuss and take counsel among themselves with regard principally to those matters of which, as stated above, declaration had been made in parliament on behalf of the king. And the prelates and lords on their part were likewise to hold a discussion; and they were told that report should be made from one group to the other concerning the acts and intentions of each. And so the commons departed to their said place [of meeting].[31]

(French) Ibid., II, 321 f.

. . . And on the said second day all the knights and commons aforesaid assembled and went into the chapter house and seated themselves about [the room] one next another. And they began to talk about their business, the matters before the parliament, saying that it would be well at the outset for them to be sworn to each other to keep counsel regarding what was spoken and decided among them, and loyally and without concealment to deliberate and ordain for the benefit of the kingdom. And to do this all unanimously agreed, and they took a good oath to be loyal to each other. Then one of them said that, if any of us knew of anything to say for the benefit of the king and the kingdom, it would be well for him to set forth among us what he knew and then, one after the other, [each of the rest could say] what lay next his heart.

Thereupon a knight of the south country rose and went to the reading desk in the centre of the chapter house so that all might hear and, pounding on the said desk, began to speak in this fashion: *"Jube domine benedicere, etc.*[32] My lords, you have heard the grievous matters before the parliament—how our lord the king has asked of the clergy and the commons a tenth and a fifteenth and customs on wool and other merchandise for a year or two. And in my opinion it is much to grant, for the commons are so weakened and impoverished by the divers tallages and taxes which they have paid up to the present that they cannot sustain such a charge or at this time pay it. Besides, all we have given to the war for a long time we have lost because it has been badly wasted and falsely expended. And so it would be well to consider how our lord the king can live and govern his kingdom and maintain the war from his demesne property, and not

---

[31] The official roll is here interrupted for the sake of inserting a portion of an anonymous chronicle preserved at St. Mary's Abbey, York. This account is especially valuable as our earliest description of procedure at a separate meeting of the commons, including the election of a speaker. See the remarks of the editor V. H. Galbraith, p. xliv.

[32] He begins and ends his speech with a conventional Latin grace.

hold to ransom his liegemen of the land. Also, as I have heard, there are divers people who, without his knowledge, have in their hands goods and treasure of our lord the king amounting to a great sum of gold and silver; and they have falsely concealed the said goods, which through guile and extortion they gained in many ways to the great damage of our lord the king and the kingdom. For the present I will say no more. *Tu autem domine meserere nostris.*" And he went back to his seat among his companions.

Thereupon another knight arose and went to the reading desk and said: "My lords, our companion has spoken to good purpose, and now, as God will give me grace, I will tell you one thing for the benefit of the kingdom. You have heard how it was ordained by common counsel in parliament that the staple of wool and other merchandise should be wholly at Calais, to the great advantage of our lord the king; and then the said town was governed and ruled by merchants of England, and they took nothing by way of payments to maintain the war or for the government of the said town. And afterwards the said staple was suddenly removed to divers cities and towns of England, and the merchants were ousted from Calais, together with their wives and their households, without the knowledge or consent of parliament, but for the benefit of a few, illegally and against the statute thereupon made; so that the lord of Latimer and Richard Lyons of London and others could have advantages.[33] And by concealment they took great sums of the maltote, which rightfully the king should have, because each year, to keep the town, the king spends sums amounting to £8000 of gold and silver, without getting anything there, where no expense used to be necessary. Wherefore it would be well to provide a remedy by advising that the staple should be restored to Calais." And he would say no more, but went back to his seat.

And the third man rose and went to the reading desk and said: "My lords, our companions have spoken very well and to good purpose. But it is my opinion that it would not be profitable or honourable for us to deliberate on such great affairs and such grievous matters for the benefit of the kingdom without the counsel and aid of those greater and wiser than we are, or to begin such procedure without the assent of the lords. Wherefore it would be well at the outset to pray our lord the king and his wise council in the parliament that they may grant and assign to us certain bishops and certain earls, barons, and bannerets, such as we may name, to counsel and aid us and to hear and witness what we shall say." And to this all agreed. Then two or three more arose in the same manner, one after the other, and spoke on various subjects. . . .

About the same time a knight from the march of Wales, who was steward to the earl of March and was named Sir Peter de la Mare, began to speak where the others had spoken, and he said: "My lords, you have well heard what our companions have had to say and what

[33] Cf. no. 62H.

they have known and how they have expressed their views; and, in my opinion, they have spoken loyally and to good purpose." And he rehearsed, word for word, all the things that they had said, doing so very skilfully and in good form. And besides he advised them on many points and particulars, as will be more fully set forth below. And so they ended the second day.

Then on the third day all the knights and commons assembled in the said chapter house and day after day until the next Friday held discussion concerning various matters and [particularly] the extortions committed by divers persons, through treachery, as they were advised. During which discussion and counsel, because the said Sir Peter de la Mare had spoken so well and had so skilfully rehearsed the arguments and views of his companions, and had informed them of much that they did not know, they begged him on their part to assume the duty of expressing their will in the great parliament before the said lords, as to what they had decided to do and say according to their conscience. And the said Sir Peter, out of reverence to God and his good companions and for the benefit of the kingdom, assumed that duty. . . .[34]

(French) Anonimalle Chronicle, pp. 80 f.

And thereupon the following prelates and lords were assigned in parliament . . . to go to the said commons and be of aid to them, joining with them and discussing the said matters that had been declared to them, as aforesaid. . . .[35]

Item, the commons, considering the sufferings of the land . . . , pray that the council of our lord the king may be afforced with lords of the land, prelates, and others, to remain constantly at the number of ten or twelve according to the king's will; so that no important business shall there pass or be determined without the advice and consent of all. . . . And our lord the king, believing the said request to be honourable and of good advantage to him and all his kingdom, has granted it. . . .

And afterwards the said commons came into parliament and made open protestation. . . .[36] Then the said commons made complaint in parliament especially of the persons mentioned below, affirming that many deceits and other wrongs had been inflicted upon the king and his kingdom, as appears below. . . .[37]

---

[34] The chronicle continues with a long and interesting account of the ensuing debates in parliament.

[35] The roll next records a grant of subsidy and certain ordinances concerning the council, although these enactments were presumably made after the protestation of the commons and the presentation of their petitions.

[36] Through their speaker, although the fact is not stated in the roll. The address summarized the complaints earlier made during the meeting of the commons, especially the restoration of the staple to Calais and the wasting of the royal revenues through the dishonesty of the king's advisers.

[37] Here the roll describes at length the impeachment of Lyons, Latimer, and others.

Hereafter follow the petitions presented in writing to the parliament by the commons, together with the responses made to those petitions in the same parliament. . . .[38]

(French) *Rotuli Parliamentorum,* II, 322-57.

[38] There were 140 of them; see Stubbs, *Constitutional History,* II, 453 f.

62. EDWARD III: STATUTES AND ORDINANCES

(A) SECOND STATUTE OF 1 EDWARD III: RESTRICTION OF MILITARY LEVIES, IMPROVEMENT OF JUSTICE, ETC. (1327)

. . . Item, the king wills that henceforth no one shall be charged to arm himself otherwise than was accustomed in the time of his ancestors, kings of England; and that no one shall be distrained to go outside his county except in case of necessity owing to the sudden invasion of enemy aliens into the kingdom, and such procedure shall then be followed as has been accustomed in times past for the defence of the kingdom. . . .

Likewise, whereas commissions[1] have been issued to certain people of the counties for arraying men-at-arms, and for taking them to the king in Scotland, in Gascony, or elsewhere at the cost of the counties—[for] up to this time the king has not provided wages for the said arrayers and commanders, or for the men-at-arms whom they have taken—whereby the commonalty of the counties has been greatly burdened and impoverished: the king wills that this shall no longer be done. . . .

Item, whereas the king wishes that common law should be administered to all, the poor as well as the rich, he commands and enjoins that none of his councillors or of his household or of his other ministers, nor any lord of the land . . . , nor any other man of the kingdom, small or great, shall undertake the maintenance of quarrels or suits in the country, to the disturbance of the common law. . . .

Item, for better keeping and preserving the peace, the king wills that in each county good and loyal men—such as are not maintainers of evil and fraud in the country—shall be assigned as keepers of the peace.[2] . . .

(French) *Statutes of the Realm,* I, 255 f.

(B) SECOND STATUTE OF 14 EDWARD III: PARLIAMENTARY CONTROL OF DIRECT TAXES (1340)

. . . Whereas the prelates, earls, barons, and commons of our realm, in our present parliament summoned at Westminster . . . , of their free will and grace have granted us, in aid of advancing the great enterprises that we have before us both on this side of the sea

[1] Cf. no. 50B.
[2] Cf. nos. 46H, 52E.

and beyond it, the ninth sheaf, the ninth fleece, and the ninth lamb[3] . . . ; and [whereas] the citizens of cities and the burgesses of boroughs [have granted] the true ninth of all their goods; and [whereas] foreign merchants and other[4] men who live neither from trade nor from flocks of sheep, [have granted] the fifteenth of their goods, rightly [assessed] according to value: we, desirous of providing indemnity for the said prelates, earls, barons, and others of the said commonalty, and also for the citizens, burgesses, and merchants aforesaid, will and grant for us and our heirs to the same prelates, earls, barons, and commons, [and to the same] citizens, burgesses, and merchants, that this grant now chargeable shall not at another time be treated as a precedent or work to their prejudice in the future; and that henceforth they shall be neither charged nor burdened to make common aid or to sustain charge except by the common assent of the prelates, earls, and barons, and of the other lords and commons of our said realm of England, and this in parliament; and that all profits arising from the said aid, and from wardships, marriages, customs, and escheats, together with other profits arising from the kingdom of England, shall be devoted and spent to maintain the safeguarding of our said kingdom of England and [to advance] our wars in Scotland, France, and Gascony, and nowhere else during the [continuance of] the said wars. . . .[5]

And whereas the said prelates, earls, barons, and commons, for the sake of the great enterprises which we have undertaken, have granted at our request that we may levy 40s. on each sack of wool passing beyond sea from now until the feast of Pentecost next; and 40s. on every three hundred wool-fells; and 40s. on a last of leather: we . . . have granted that, after the said feast of Pentecost to come in one year, neither we nor our heirs shall demand, assess, levy, or cause to be levied more than half a mark of custom on a sack of wool throughout all England, half a mark on three hundred wool-fells, and one mark on a last of leather. . . .

(French) *Ibid.*, I, 289-91.

(C) ANNULMENT OF THE STATUTE OF 1341[6] (1342)

The king to the sheriff of Lincoln, greeting. Whereas, in our parliament summoned at Westminster on the quinzime of Easter last, certain articles expressly contrary to the laws and customs of our kingdom of England, and to our royal rights and prerogatives, were drawn up in the form of a statute on the pretence that they had been granted by us: we, considering how we were bound by oath to observe and defend such laws, customs, rights, and prerogatives, and desiring

---

[3] Substituted for the tenth sheaf, lamb, etc., in the second parliament of 1340; see above, pp. 210 f.

[4] That is to say, other than those of cities and boroughs.

[5] The act continues with a general pardon of old debts, according to the commons' petition of 1339 (above, p. 211).

[6] Cf. no. 61E, F.

providently to revoke what had been improvidently done [and to restore conditions] to their proper state, thereupon held a council and deliberation with the earls, barons, and other skilled men of our said realm. [To them it was explained that] we never consented to the drawing up of the said pretended statute, but secured beforehand protests for the revocation of the said statute, should it proceed *de facto*;[7] and then, to avoid the dangers which we feared such a denial would provoke, we dissembled, as behooved us, promising that the said pretended statute should be sealed for the time being, since otherwise the said parliament would have been dissolved in bad feeling with nothing accomplished, and so—which God forbid!—our grave enterprises would in all likelihood have been ruined. [Therefore] it appeared to the said earls, barons, and skilled men that, because the said statute did not proceed of our free will, it was null and ought not to have the name or force of a statute. And so, by their counsel and assent, we have decreed the said statute to be null, considering that it ought to be annulled in so far as it proceeded *de facto*; wishing, nevertheless, that the articles in the said pretended statute which have already been approved in other statutes of ours, or [in those] of our ancestors, kings of England, should in all respects be observed according to the form of the said statutes, as is proper. And we do this solely to conserve and reintegrate the rights of our crown, as we are bound [to do]; and not in any way to oppress or burden our subjects, whom we desire to rule in kindness. And therefore we command you to have all these matters publicly proclaimed in such places within your bailiwick as you shall think best. By witness of the king at Westminster, October 1, in the fifteenth year [of our reign].

By the king himself and his council.

(Latin) *Ibid.*, I, 297.

(D) STATUTE OF LABOURERS (1351)

Whereas, to curb the malice of servants who after the pestilence were idle and unwilling to serve without securing excessive wages, it was recently ordained by our lord the king, with the assent of the prelates, nobles, and other men of his council, that such servants, both men and women, should be bound to serve in return for the salaries and wages that were customary in those places where they were obligated to serve during the twentieth year of the reign of our said lord the king, that is to say, five or six years earlier; and whereas the same servants, on refusing to serve in any manner, were to be punished by imprisonment of their bodies, as is more clearly set forth in the same ordinance . . . ; and whereas our lord the king has now, by the petition of the commons in this present parliament, been given to understand that the said servants have no regard for the said ordinance, but, to suit their ease and their selfish desires,

---

[7] That is to say, not of right, since the king had never really assented to it.

refrain from serving the lords or other men unless they receive double or triple that which they were accustomed to have in the said twentieth year and earlier, to the great damage of the lords and the impoverishment of all men of the said commons, who now pray for remedy of these matters: therefore in the same parliament, by the assent of the prelates, earls, barons, and the other lords, and of the same commons there assembled, the following measures are ordained and established to curb the malice of the said servants. . . .[8]

(French) *Ibid.,* I, 311.

(E) STATUTE OF PROVISORS (1351)

. . . Our lord the king, perceiving the mischief and damage mentioned above, and having regard to the said statute made in the time of his said grandfather[9] . . . , and also giving attention to the grievous complaints made to him by his people in various parliaments held in times past . . . , with the assent of all the lords and commons of his said kingdom, for the honour of God and the benefit of the said Church of England and [the welfare] of all his kingdom, has ordained and established that the free elections of archbishops and bishops, and [the elections to] all other dignities and benefices that are elective in England, shall continue to be held in such fashion as when they were granted by the ancestors of our said lord the king or founded by the ancestors of other lords; that all prelates and men of Holy Church, who hold advowsons of any benefices by gift of our lord the king and of his ancestors, or of other lords and donors . . . , shall freely have their collations and presentations according to the terms of the enfeoffment by the donors. And in case reservation, collation, or provision is by the court of Rome made of any archbishopric, bishopric, dignity, or other benefice whatsoever, to the disturbance of the elections, collations, or presentations aforesaid, [it is ordained] that, at the very time of the vacancies when such reservations, collations, or provisions should take effect, our lord the king and his heirs are to have and enjoy, for the time being, the collations to archbishoprics, bishoprics, and other elective dignities that are under his advowry, just as his ancestors had them before free election was granted. . . .[10]

(French) *Ibid.,* I, 317 f.

---

[8] The ordinance (*Statutes of the Realm,* I, 307) had fixed wages as here stated, at the same time prohibiting increased prices for victuals above the standard of the same years, forbidding alms to sturdy beggars, etc. The statute merely added details concerning the wages of agricultural labourers and of artisans, together with measures intended to secure the enforcement of the ordinance. See B. H. Putnam, *The Enforcement of the Statutes of Labourers.*

[9] The reference is to the Statute of Carlisle (1307) and the parliamentary petition against encroachments by the see of Rome: Stubbs, *Constitutional History,* II, 163.

[10] Similar enactment is made with regard to papal provision in religious houses; other lay patrons besides the king are given the same kind of protection; and means of enforcement is prescribed.

(F) Statute of Treasons (1352)

. . . Item, whereas until now there have been various opinions as to which cases should be called treason and which not, the king, at the request of the lords and the commons, has made the following declarations:—

If a man compasses or imagines the death of our lord the king, of our lady his consort, or of their eldest son and heir; or if a man violates the king's consort, the king's eldest daughter being as yet unmarried, or the consort of the king's eldest son and heir; or if a man makes war against our said lord the king in his kingdom, or is an adherent of enemies to our lord the king in the kingdom, giving them aid or comfort in his kingdom or elsewhere . . . ; or if a man counterfeits the great or the privy seal of the king or his money; or if a man, for the sake of trading or making payments in deceit of our said lord the king or of his people, brings into this kingdom false coin, counterfeit of the money of England, . . . knowing it to be false; or if a man slays the chancellor, treasurer, or justice of our lord the king . . . while [such official is] in his place and attending to his office—these cases specified above, it must be understood, are to be adjudged treason against our lord the king and his royal majesty; and in such [cases of] treason forfeiture of property pertains to our lord the king, as well lands and tenements held of another as those held of [the king] himself. . . .[11]

(French) *Ibid.*, I, 319 f.

(G) Ordinance and Statute of Praemunire (1353)[12]

Our lord the king, with the assent and by the prayer of the lords and commons of his kingdom of England, in his great council[13] held at Westminster on Monday next after the feast of St. Matthew the Apostle, in the twenty-seventh year of his reign—that is to say in England; in France the fourteenth—for the improvement of his said kingdom and for the maintenance of its laws and usages, has ordained and established the measures hereinunder written:—

First, whereas our lord the king has been shown by the clamorous and grievous complaints of his lords and commons aforesaid how numerous persons have been and are being taken out of the kingdom to respond in cases of which the cognizance pertains to the court of our lord the king; and also how the judgments rendered in the same court are being impeached in the court of another, to

---

[11] The statute also defines "another kind of treason"—the commission of similar offenses against a lord other than the king. The distinction is that known in law as between high and petit treason.

[12] Technically, this ordinance became a statute when it was confirmed by the parliament of the ensuing year; cf. the next document. For the name, see no. 64F; for interpretation, see W. T. Waugh, in the *English Historical Review*, XXXVII, 173 f., and E. B. Graves, in *Anniversary Essays by Students of C. H. Haskins*, pp. 57 f.

[13] Cf. nos. 60B, 62H (last paragraph).

the prejudice and disherison of our lord the king and of his crown and of all the people of his said kingdom, and to the undoing and annulment of the common law of the same kingdom at all times customary: therefore, after good deliberation held with the lords and others of the said council, it is granted and agreed by our said lord the king and by the lords and commons aforesaid that all persons of the king's allegiance, of whatever condition they may be, who take any one out of the kingdom in a plea of which the cognizance pertains to the king's court or in matters regarding which judgments have been rendered in the king's court, or who bring suit in the court of another to undo or impede the judgments rendered in the king's court, shall be given a day . . . [on which] to appear before the king and his council, or in his chancery, or before the king's justices in their courts, either the one bench or the other, or before other justices of the king who may be deputed for the purpose, there to answer to the king in proper person regarding the contempt involved in such action. And if they do not come in proper person on the said day to stand trial, let them, their procurators, attorneys, executors, notaries, and supporters, from this day forth be put outside the king's protection, and let their lands, goods, and chattels be forfeit to the king, and let their bodies, wherever they may be found, be taken and imprisoned and redeemed at the king's pleasure. . . .

(French) *Ibid.,* I, 329.

(H) Ordinance and Statute of the Staple (1353)

On Monday next after the feast of St. Matthew the Apostle, in the twenty-seventh year of the reign of our lord, King Edward III . . . , a great council was summoned at Westminster. . . .[14] On which Friday the prelates, dukes, earls, barons, and commons, assembled in the White Chamber of our lord the king, were told . . . the cause for the summons of the said council. . . .[15] Considering which mischief, our lord the king, by the assent of certain prelates and lords of his said kingdom . . . had ordained that the staple of wool, wool-fells, leather, and lead should be held in certain places within his kingdom of England and his lands of Wales and Ireland. And by the assent and advice of the said prelates and lords he had ordained for the maintenance and good government of the same staple certain particulars, which he caused to be read aloud before the prelates, lords, and commons, in order to obtain their assent. And [it was said] also that, if they wished to make any additions or subtractions, they should show [their desire] in writing. And thereupon the commons asked for a copy of the said particulars, which was given them—that is to say, one [copy] for the knights of the shires and another for the citizens

---

[14] Cf. no. 60B. The meeting was postponed from Monday until Friday.

[15] Principally the king's decision to change the staple, as is recited in the ordinance. On the procedure followed in drafting this statute, see H. L. Gray, *The Influence of the Commons on Early Legislation,* pp. 250 f.

and burgesses. And they, after long deliberation among themselves, presented their opinion to the council in writing. And after this writing had been read and debated by the lords, the ordinances of the staple were drawn up in the form following:—

Edward, by the grace of God king of England and France and lord of Ireland, to all our sheriffs, mayors, bailiffs, ministers, and other faithful men to whom these present letters may come, greeting. Whereas good deliberation has been held with the prelates, dukes, earls, barons, knights of the shires—that is to say, one from each for the whole shire—and commons of cities and boroughs of our kingdom of England, summoned to our great council held at Westminster . . . , concerning the damages which have been notoriously incurred by us and by the lords, as well as by the people of our kingdom of England and our lands of Wales and Ireland, because the staple of wool, leather, and wool-fells for our said kingdom and lands has been kept outside the said kingdom and lands; and also concerning the great profits that would accrue to our said kingdom and lands if the staple should be held within them and nowhere else: so, for the honour of God and the relief of our kingdom and lands aforesaid, and for the sake of avoiding the perils that otherwise may arise in times to come, by the counsel and common assent of the said prelates, dukes, earls, barons, knights, and commons aforesaid, we have ordained and established the measures hereinunder written, to wit:—

First, that the staples of wool, leather, wool-fells and lead grown or produced within our kingdom and lands aforesaid shall be perpetually held in the following places: namely, for England at Newcastle-upon-Tyne, York, Lincoln, Norwich, Westminster, Canterbury, Chichester, Winchester, Exeter, and Bristol; for Wales at Carmarthen; and for Ireland at Dublin, Waterford, Cork, and Drogheda, and nowhere else. . . .[16]

. . . For which grant our lord the king thanked the lords and commons. And then the said commons prayed the king that their petitions, which they had drawn up concerning divers grievances as well as benefits of his commons, should be answered. Which petitions our lord the king caused to be read and answered by the prelates, lords, and other men of his council in the following manner:—

. . . Item, whereas certain articles touching the state of the king and the common benefit of his kingdom have been agreed and assented to by him, and by the prelates, lords, and commons of his land in this council just held; the said commons pray that the aforesaid articles shall be recited at the next parliament and entered in the roll of the same parliament, with the intent that the ordinances and

---

[16] The following articles provide that all the said products, before being exported, must be taken to one of the staple towns, where they are to be officially weighed, sealed, and taxed. The prescribed customs are those of 1275 (no. 49B), except that 20s. worth of lead is to pay 3d., and that aliens are taxed at a higher rate.

agreements made in councils shall not be of record as if they had been made by a common parliament. . . .

As to the tenth article, it is the king's pleasure that all the ordinances made concerning the staple shall be published and proclaimed in each county of England, and in each place where a staple is [situated], so that they may be firmly kept; and at the next parliament, for the sake of greater stability, they shall be rehearsed and entered in the roll of parliament. . . .

Also the said commons in this parliament[17] prayed that the ordinances of the staple, and all the other ordinances made at the last council . . . , which they had examined with great care and deliberation, and which seemed to them good and advantageous for our lord the king and all his people, should be confirmed in this parliament and held as a statute to endure forever. To which prayer the king and all the lords unanimously agreed; to the effect that, whenever anything was to be added [to that statute], it should be added [in parliament], or whenever anything was to be subtracted, it should be subtracted in parliament, no matter at what time the need should arise, and never in any other fashion.

(French) *Rotuli Parliamentorum*, II, 246, 253, 257.

(I) STATUTE OF 34 EDWARD III: ON JUSTICES OF THE PEACE (1361)

These are the measures which our lord the king, the prelates, the lords, and the commons have ordained in this present parliament, held at Westminster on Sunday next before the feast of the Conversion of St. Paul, to be observed and publicly proclaimed throughout the kingdom, to wit:—

First, that for the keeping of the peace, there shall be assigned in each county of England one lord, and with him three or four of the most worthy men of the county together with certain men skilled in the law,[18] and they shall have power to restrain evil-doers, rioters, and all other miscreants; to pursue, arrest, capture, and chastise them according to their trespass or offence; to have them imprisoned and duly punished according to the law and custom of the kingdom, and according to what [the justices] may think best to do at their discretion and good advisement. Also [they shall have power] to inform themselves and to make inquiry concerning all those who have been pillagers and robbers in the regions beyond [the sea], and who have now returned to become vagrants, refusing to work as they used to in times past; and to take and arrest all whom they can find on indictment or suspicion, and to put them in prison. . . . Also [they shall have power] to hear and determine, at the king's suit, all manner of felonies and trespasses committed in the

---

[17] Of the next year, 1354.

[18] Cf. no. 62A, above; and for a résumé of the subject, together with citation of the pertinent literature, see Lodge and Thornton, *Constitutional Documents*, pp. 325 f.

same county, according to the laws and customs aforesaid. . . . And the fine to be assessed before the justices, because of trespass committed by any person, shall be just and reasonable, according to the gravity of the offence and as the causes leading to it are taken into account. . . .

Item, it is agreed that the men assigned to keep the peace shall have power to make inquiry concerning measures and also weights, according to the statute thereupon made in the twenty-fifth year of our lord the king's reign. . . .

Item, it is agreed in this present parliament that the Statute of Labourers earlier made shall stand in all its particulars, with the exception of the pecuniary penalty, in which connection it is agreed that henceforth labourers shall not be punished by fine and redemption. . . .

Item, with regard to labourers and artisans who run away from their [owed] services into another vill or county, [it is provided] that the [aggrieved] party shall have his suit before the justices [of the peace]. . . .

(French) *Statutes of the Realm,* I, 364 f.

(J) Statute of 36 Edward III: Regarding Purveyance, Customs, etc. (1362)

For the honour and gratification of God, for the reform of the outrageous wrongs and oppressions suffered by the people, and for the relief of their condition, King Edward, in his parliament held at Westminster on the quinzime of St. Michael in the thirty-sixth year of his reign, at the request of his commons and by their petition presented to him in the said parliament, with the assent of the prelates, dukes, earls, barons, and other lords assembled in the said parliament, has granted for him and his heirs forever the articles hereinunder written:—

First, that the Great Charter, the Charter of the Forest, and the other statutes made in his own time and in the times of his ancestors shall be well and firmly observed in all particulars.

Item, on account of the grievous complaint that has been made concerning purveyors of victuals for the households of the king, the queen, their eldest son, and other lords and ladies of the kingdom, the king, of his own will and without compulsion of lords or commons, has granted and ordained for the relief of his people that henceforth no man of the said kingdom shall take any prise except solely for [the king] himself and for the queen his consort. Furthermore, with the assent aforesaid, it is ordained and established that, in case of such purveyances to be henceforth made for the households of the king and the queen, prompt payment in hand shall be rendered—that is to say, the price at which such victuals are commonly sold in the neighbouring markets. [It is also ordained] that the heinous name of purveyor shall be changed to buyer; and if the buyer cannot well agree with the seller of that for which there is need, then the prises which are made for the said two households shall be made by the view, testimony, and appraisal of the lords, or of their bailiffs and constables, and four good men of each vill, and this through indenture to be made between the buyers and the said lords, or bailiffs and constables, and four good men, stating the amount of what has been taken, its price, and the persons from whom it was taken. And [it is ordained] that the prises shall be made in a proper and easy manner, without duress, compulsion, threats, or other villainy; that the prises and purchases shall be made in the regions and places where there is greatest plenty, and this at a convenient time; and that no more shall be taken than is needful at that season for the said two households. . . .[19]

Item, [it is ordained] that, with the exception of the king and queen, no lord of England or other man of the said kingdom, of whatsoever estate or condition, shall of himself or through any of his servants in any way take prises of any sort of victuals; but they shall buy what they need from those who of their own free will wish to sell, and for these [victuals] they shall pay promptly in hand according to what they may agree upon with the seller. . . .

Item, to maintain the said articles and statutes, and to redress divers mischiefs and grievances that recur day after day, parliament shall be held every year, as was earlier ordained by statute.

Item, by the assent aforesaid, the king, considering the great subsidy which the commons have granted him earlier in this parliament, to be levied for three years on wool, leather, and wool-fells, wills and grants that, after the said term has passed, nothing shall be taken or asked of the said commons except only the ancient custom of half a mark;[20] that neither the grant just made nor any that has heretofore been made shall be turned into a precedent or burden for the said commons in time to come; that resident as well as foreign merchants may pass with their wool free of restraint; and that henceforth no subsidy or other charge shall be levied or granted on wool either by merchants or by any other persons without the assent of parliament. . . .

(French) *Ibid.*, I, 371 f.

[19] The statute gives long and elaborate provisions for the commissioning of buyers, the prevention of abuses, etc.

[20] Cf. no. 49B.

63. PARLIAMENT ROLLS OF RICHARD II

(A) PARLIAMENT OF 1377

. . . And afterwards the commons came before the king in parliament, and there Sir Peter de la Mare, knight, who acted as speaker for the commons,[1] made his protestation, that what he had to say was not said on his own personal account, but by the initiative, as-

[1] See above, p. 222.

sent, and express will of all the commons there assembled.[2] . . . And since our lord the king—whom God save!—is at present innocent and of tender age, the said commons, for the redress of the wrongs aforesaid, as well as of others, and for the salvation of the kingdom, which at present is in great peril and more so than ever before, besought our lord the king and the lords of parliament with regard to three matters in particular:—

First, that it might please them to ordain and appoint in this present parliament eight fit persons of different estates, to remain continually along with the king's officials in council [to consult] on the needs of the king and the kingdom. . . .

Item, that it might please them to ordain and appoint in this parliament those who were to surround the person of our same lord the king, who is of such tender age. . . . And that it should also be ordained that our same lord the king and his household should be governed with good moderation of expenses, to be met solely from the [ordinary] revenues of the kingdom and from the other rights of his crown and his dominions; and that, for the aid and relief of his commons aforesaid, all which is or may be granted for his wars shall be used and expended in the wars and not otherwise.

Item, that the common law, as well as the special laws, statutes, and ordinances of the land made in earlier times for the common benefit and salutary governance of the kingdom, should in their entirety be kept, ratified, and confirmed. . . . Request is also made to the lords of parliament that whatever is ordained in this parliament shall not be repealed without [consent of] parliament. . . .

And thereupon answer was given that on these matters the prelates and lords would consult together; and the commons were instructed to return to their place and by themselves to consider their other business from now until the next Thursday. On which day they were commanded to return to parliament to hear the responses made to their aforesaid requests.

As to the first request presented by the said commons to our lord the king and to the lords of parliament, . . . our lord the king . . . has granted it, provided always that the chancellor, the treasurer, the keeper of the privy seal, the justices of both benches, and all the other officials of the king may perform and carry through the duties pertaining to their offices without the presence of such councillors. And our lord the king, for certain reasons that influence him at present, by the advice of the lords of parliament, wishes to have nine persons as such councillors for this present year only, and has had them elected in parliament: namely. . . . And as to the second request of the commons, . . . the lords of parliament respond, saying that to them it seems too severe and burdensome a request that any person should be placed near their lord the king other than one well pleasing to him for various reasons, or to remove

---

[2] The commons complained especially of the evils then being suffered by the knights and the merchants.

any of his officials or servants except by the express will of the said king. . . .[3] And as to the third and last request, it seems reasonable to all the lords that for the present it should be conceded and granted.

Item, the lords and commons of the kingdom of England, clearly perceiving the great peril of the kingdom . . . , of their free will have granted to our same lord the king two fifteenths outside cities and boroughs and two tenths within the same cities and boroughs.[4] . . . And it is the humble prayer [of the commons] to their liege lord and to the other lords of the parliament that for these moneys, as well as for the moneys from the tithes recently granted by the clergy of England and also for the moneys arising from the subsidies of wool, certain fit persons should be assigned on the part of the king to be treasurers or wardens, to such effect that these moneys shall be entirely devoted to the expenses of the war, and by no means to anything else. And it is to be remembered that this request was granted to them by the king. . . . And thereupon our lord the king had William Walworth and John Philipot, merchants of London, assigned to be wardens of the said sums to be used as aforesaid, and to render faithful account of their receipts and expenditures in such fashion as should be reasonably ordained by our lord the king and his said great council. . . .[5]

(French) Rotuli Parliamentorum, III, 5-7.

(B) Parliament of 1378

. . . And thereupon the commons, after some little deliberation, made another request of our lord the king, that it might please him to have demonstration made to his said commons how and in what way the said great sums thus given and ordered for the said war had been expended.[6] . . . To which it was replied by the said Sir Richard[7] . . . that, although it was unheard of that, for any subsidy or other grant made to the king by the commons in parliament or out of parliament, account should afterwards be rendered to the commons or to anybody besides the king and his officials, nevertheless, to please the commons, our said lord the king willed and commanded of his own initiative, without doing so as of right or through coercion on account of the said request recently made to him, that the said William Walworth,[8] there present, together with certain other persons from the council of our lord the king to be assigned

---

[3] But, they think, those about the king should be warned not to impose on him for their own selfish ends, and the officers of the household should be talked to about moderation of expenses.

[4] To be levied according to the ancient custom; see no. 61B.

[5] Sixty-nine petitions of the commons follow.

[6] This was after the commons had refused further aid and the king had protested their refusal.

[7] Richard le Scrope, steward of the king's household.

[8] See the preceding document.

for this duty by the king, should clearly show you in writing the receipts and expenditures made of those [sums]—on the understanding that this [action] should not thereafter be held a precedent, on the ground that it was taken otherwise than solely by the initiative and command of our lord the king, as aforesaid. . . .

Item, they prayed that five or six of the prelates and lords should come to the commons to discuss with them jointly the said matters concerning which they were charged.[9] And to this request the lords replied, saying that they were neither obliged nor willing to do this; for such manner of procedure had never been used in any parliament except in the last three parliaments recently held. But they said and declared that it had well been accustomed for the lords to choose from among themselves a certain small number, six or ten, and for the commons [to choose] another small number from among themselves; and for these lords and commons thus elected to meet together in easy manner, without murmurs, cries, and noise. And so by motions made among them they would quickly arrive at some good decision, which would then be reported to their companions of one or the other group. And in such fashion the lords would henceforth proceed, and in none other. . . . And thereupon the commons readily assented that certain lords and commons, a small and reasonable number, should be elected, as had anciently been accustomed. . . .[10]

(French) *Ibid.*, III, 35-36.

(C) PARLIAMENT OF 1379

. . . These are the names of the prelates and lords assigned on the request of the commons to examine the estate of the king: namely, . . .[11] First, [they are] to examine the revenues arising from the subsidy on wool, those received since the feast of St. Michael last and those presumably to be received before the feast of St. Michael next; item, to examine as well all the revenues of the kingdom received since the said time . . . and those which presumably can be received and levied before the said feast of St. Michael . . . ; item, to examine what sort of fees or wages the great and petty officers of the king were accustomed to have in the early days of King Edward, grandfather of our present king. . . .[12] And it should be remembered that the said lords thus assigned have the command of the same king in parliament to enter . . . the offices and courts of the king as may be necessary for this investigation, together with the officials and keepers of the same; and there, together with the

---

[9] See above, p. 222.

[10] The commons examined the royal accounts and approved them, except for a protest that too much had been spent outside the kingdom. Finally they granted the usual subsidy on wool.

[11] Three bishops, three earls, and three barons.

[12] Also annuities being paid by the king's grant, the furniture of the household, and other matters.

said officials, to search the rolls, accounts, and any other records that are concerned in this matter . . . ; and to make a distinct report to our said lord the king and to his council as to what they have done and have found, together with their good advice in this connection. . . .

Item, the lords and commons of the kingdom of England assembled in this parliament have granted for themselves and for the whole community of England the subsidy on wool, wool-fells, and leather; also another subsidy, to be taken from the goods of certain persons throughout the kingdom according to a certain form and in a certain manner prescribed in a schedule made in that connection and already presented in parliament, of which the tenor is word for word as follows. . . .[13]

(French) *Ibid.*, III, 57.

(D) PARLIAMENT OF 1380

. . . In the first place the lords and commons have agreed that, to meet the aforesaid necessities, every lay person[14] of the kingdom who has passed the age of fifteen years, whether male or female, of whatsoever condition or estate, both inside and outside franchises, shall give three groats[15]—with the exception of actual beggars, who are to be charged nothing—always providing that the levy shall be made under the regulation and form that each lay person is to be equally charged according to his ability and in the manner following: that is to say, in raising the total sum to be accounted for in each vill, the well-to-do shall according to their ability aid the lesser folk; yet so that the wealthiest man shall not pay more than the sum of sixty groats for himself and his wife and that no person shall pay less than a groat for himself and his wife. And no one shall be charged for payment except in the place where he and his wife and his children have their residence, or in the place where he remains in service. . . . And commissions shall be given to fit persons, as well in the counties as in the cities and boroughs, to be collectors and comptrollers of the aforesaid sum; and they are to be sworn well and loyally to perform their office. And it is the intention of the said commons to make the present grant solely for the support of the earl of Buckingham and the other lords and men of his company in the parts of Brittany, for the defence of the kingdom, and for the safeguarding of the sea.

(French) *Ibid.*, III, 90.

---

[13] The added subsidy was a graduated poll-tax, according to which dukes were to pay 10*m.*; royal justices £5; earls and the mayor of London £4; barons, bannerets, serjeants-at-law, aldermen of London, and mayors of larger towns £2; bachelors, squires, apprentices-at-law, mayors of smaller towns, and great merchants £1; other merchants, franklins, artisans, and the mass of the people lesser sums down to 4*d.*

[14] The clergy made a separate grant of £100,000.

[15] A silver coin worth 4*d.*

(E) PARLIAMENT OF 1381

. . . And the king commanded Sir Richard le Scrope, knight, the newly created chancellor of England, to rehearse for them the same charge touching the points aforesaid.[16] And so he clearly did; and especially with regard to the repeal thus made of the grant of freedom and manumission to the serfs and villeins of the land, it was again on the king's behalf plainly asked of all those present in full parliament whether this repeal pleased them or no.

To which the prelates and temporal lords, as well as the knights, citizens, and burgesses, unanimously responded that this repeal had been well made; adding that such [grant of] manumission or freedom could not be made without the assent of those who had the greatest interest. And to this they had never assented of their free will; nor would they have ever done so except to live and die all in one day.[17] And they—that is to say, the prelates and lords, as well as the commons—humbly besought our lord the king that these manumissions and enfranchisements, thus made and granted through coercion, to their disherison and the destruction of the kingdom, should be quashed and annulled by the authority of this parliament, and that the said repeal should be affirmed as one well and justly made. And this was then unanimously granted and agreed to by all. . . .

And it is to be noted that afterwards, when the king had secured advice from the lords of the kingdom and from his council with regard to these requests made to him [by the commons], as it truly appeared to him to be for his benefit and for that of his said kingdom, he willed and granted that certain prelates, lords, and other men should be assigned to survey and examine in privy council the estate and governance of our said lord the king's person, as well as of his said household, and to advise themselves of sufficient remedies, should he proceed with the matter [of reform], and thereupon to make report to the king aforesaid. And the lords in parliament then declared it seemed to them that, if reform of the government was to be made throughout the kingdom, attention should first be given to its principal member—namely, the king himself—and then [pass] from person to person, as well those of Holy Church as others, and from place to place, from the highest degree to the lowest, sparing no person, degree, or place.

And to do this for the said household, the following lords were elected. . . .[18]

(French) *Ibid.*, III, 100 f.

(F) PARLIAMENT OF 1386

. . . In this parliament all the commons, assembled as one body

---

[16] This was done at the request of the speaker of the commons.

[17] *Pur vivre et mourir touz en un jour;* the meaning obviously is "under threat of immediate death."

[18] The duke of Lancaster and seventeen others.

and with a single purpose, came before the king, the prelates, and the lords in the parliament chamber and made bitter complaint concerning the last chancellor of England, Michael de la Pole, earl of Suffolk, who was there present; accusing him by word of mouth in the manner following. . . . And on all these articles the commons asked the judgment of parliament. To which the said earl replied in the manner following. . . . And thereupon, after the response of the said earl to the accusations of the said commons, and the replies made to these [arguments] by the one side and the other, the said earl, at the request of the said commons, on account of the gravity of the offences thus charged against him, was arrested by the king's order and committed to the custody of the constable of England, and then released on bail. . . . And for the misdeeds and offences aforesaid, of which the said earl through the insufficiency of his said responses has thus been convicted, it is adjudged that he is to be committed to the king's prison, to remain there during the king's pleasure; and he shall not be liberated from the said prison until he has paid fine and redemption at the king's pleasure. . . .

The lords and commons of the realm assembled in this present parliament, for the defence of the kingdom and of the sea, and for the protection of trading, granted to our lord the king in full parliament certain subsidies and aids on certain conditions, according to the form and in the words that follow. . . .[19] And in addition the said lords and commons have for the said reasons granted another half a tenth and half a fifteenth, to be levied from laymen at the quinzime of St. Michael next, on a certain condition: namely, that the aforesaid grants, except the said latter half a tenth and half a fifteenth, together with the other income of the king, may [be made to] suffice for the charges and defences of the kingdom during the coming year, through the care and good administration of . . .[20], who have been ordained and assigned by our lord the king under his commission sealed with the great seal . . . to be of the continual council of our lord the king; and that until then the same latter half a tenth and half a fifteenth shall under no circumstances be levied or collected by any one in any way. . . .[21]

Item, the commons very humbly pray that, for the honour of God, for the maintenance of your crown, for your own profit and that of all the prelates and lords, and for the relief of the poor commons of your realm, it may please you to ordain and appoint in this present parliament fit officials: namely, the chancellor, the treasurer, the keeper of the privy seal, the steward of your household, and also

---

[19] The grant was of half a tenth and half a fifteenth, and of tunnage and poundage until the end of the next year.

[20] The dukes of York and Gloucester, two archbishops, two bishops, one abbot, one earl, one baron, two knights, the chancellor, the treasurer, and the keeper of the privy seal.

[21] Other provisions follow, prohibiting substitutions on the commission, interference with the members, etc.

the other lords of your great and continual council. [And they petition] that the said lords and officials may have power to correct and amend all the defects that so greatly blemish your crown . . . ; likewise that a statute be made that no one, of whatsoever dignity, estate, nation, or condition, shall in private or in public be so bold as to effect or counsel the contravention of what the said lords and officials see fit to decide, and this under severe penalty. Which matters, through your benignity, you have partially put into execution; it is prayed that at present you may please to carry out the remainder. . . . Response: The king so wills, providing that the commission and statutes asked in this petition shall be in effect for no more than one entire year. And as to the steward of his household, he will install a fit man by the advice of his council. . . .

It should be remembered that the king in full parliament, before its close, made public protest by personal word of mouth that, on account of anything done in the said parliament, he was unwilling that prejudice should be incurred by himself or by his crown, and that his prerogative and the liberties of his said crown should be saved and guarded. . . .

(French) *Ibid.,* III, 216-24.

(G) PARLIAMENT OF 1388[22]

. . . At the last parliament, on account of the great damages and terrible dangers which had been incurred through the bad government [of those] surrounding the king during all his earlier reign— [namely,] Alexander, then archbishop of York; Robert de Vere, then duke of Ireland; Michael de la Pole, then earl of Suffolk; Robert Tressilian, one time justice; Nicholas Brember, knight; and their adherents and others—whereby the king and all his kingdom had been almost wholly ruined and destroyed, . . . ordinance was made by statute and a commission was given to various lords for the benefit, honour, and salvation of the king, his royal authority, and all his realm, the tenor of which commission and statute is as follows. . . . And thereupon the aforesaid Alexander, Robert, Michael, Robert, and Nicholas, and their aforesaid adherents and others . . . devised, plotted, and proposed various horrid treasons and wrongs against the king, the aforesaid lords thus assigned, and all the other lords and commons who had agreed to set up the aforesaid ordinance and commission, [thus conspiring] for the defeasance of the king, his royal authority, and all his realm.

Whereupon Thomas, duke of Gloucester, uncle of our lord the king, and son of King Edward—whom God assoil!—Richard, earl of Arundel, and Thomas, earl of Warwick, perceiving the evil purposes of the traitors aforesaid, assembled in force to safeguard their persons, to show and declare the said treasons and evil purposes, and to provide remedy according to the will of God. And they came

---

[22] The following recitation constitutes the preamble to the petition, which is here placed in the third paragraph.

into the presence of our aforesaid lord the king and appealed the said five traitors for high treason committed by the latter against the king and his kingdom. Upon which appeal, our said lord the king adjourned the aforesaid parties until this present parliament. . . .[23] Which five traitors were attainted in this present parliament of the treasons and wrongs aforesaid, at the suit and appeal of the said duke of Gloucester, the said earls of Derby, Arundel, and Warwick, and the earl marshal.

[Therefore] may it please our said highly respected lord the king to accept, approve, and confirm in this present parliament all that was done in the last parliament, as set forth above, and whatever has been done since the said last parliament through force of the statute, ordinance, or commission aforesaid, as well as what has been done by the aforesaid duke of Gloucester, earls of Derby, Arundel, and Warwick, and earl marshal. Response: Our lord the king, considering the matter of the said petition to be true and the request of his said commons in this affair to be for the honour of God and to his own advantage and that of his realm, by assent of the prelates, dukes, earls, barons, and all others in this present parliament, granted the request of the said commons in all particulars according to the form of the said petition. . . .[24]

(French) *Ibid.*, III, 248 f.

(H) PARLIAMENT OF 1397

. . . Item, with regard to the fourth article,[25] concerning the expense of the king's household and the residence of bishops and ladies in his company, the king was greatly aggrieved and offended at the fact that the commons, his lieges, should take unto themselves or presume [to make] any regulation or government of the king's person, or of his household, or of any person of the state whom he pleased to have in his company. And it seemed to the king that the commons herein committed a great offence against his regality and his royal majesty and the liberty both of himself and of his honourable progenitors, which he had held and by the aid of God would maintain and support. Wherefore the king commanded the said lords spiritual and temporal on the following Saturday morning fully to show and declare the king's will in this matter to the said commons. Furthermore, the king, hearing how the said commons had been moved and excited by a bill presented before them to express and demonstrate the said last article, commanded the duke of Guienne and Lancaster to charge Sir John Bussy, speaker of the commons, by

---

[23] The record here recites how the said traitors violated the king's protection by open revolt, and how the Lords Appellant were forced to take arms against them.

[24] Here follow a complete pardon for the Lords Appellant and the royal assent to various other petitions providing for punishment of the traitors, the purification of the government, etc.

[25] In the address by the speaker of the commons.

the fealty [owed to the king] to report to him the name of the man who had presented the said bill before the commons.

Item, on Saturday, the morrow of Candlemas, the lords spiritual and temporal were [assembled] together with the commons, to whom they explained the will and command of the king; and the said commons delivered the said bill to the lords, with the name of the man who had presented it to them, that is to say, Sir Thomas Haxey. Which bill was afterwards at the king's command delivered by the clerk of parliament to the clerk of the crown. Then, by the king's order, the commons came before the king in parliament; and there, with all the humility and obedience of which they were capable, they expressed deep grief, as appeared from their demeanour, that the king had formed such an opinion of them. And they humbly besought the king to hear and accept their apology: that it had never been their intention or will to express, present, or do anything which would offend or displease the king's royal majesty, or would contravene his royal estate and liberty, either in this matter concerning his own person and the government of his household, [in that] concerning the lords and ladies in his company, or in any other matter touching [the king] himself; for they well knew and understood that such matters pertained to them not at all, but solely to the king himself and to his [power of] ordinance. . . .[26]

(French) *Ibid.*, III, 339.

(I) PARLIAMENT OF 1398[27]

. . . Item, on the same Thursday the commons prayed the king that, since they had before them divers petitions, as well for individual persons as others, which had been neither read nor answered, and also since numerous other matters and proposals had been brought up in the king's presence, which for lack of time they could not at present well terminate, it might be the king's pleasure to commit full power to certain lords and such other persons as should please him, to examine, answer, and determine the said petitions and the matters and proposals aforesaid and all related questions. To which prayer the king agreed. And thereupon, by the authority and assent of parliament, he appointed and assigned. . . .[28]

Item, on the same day the commons of the realm, by the assent of the lords spiritual and temporal, granted to the king the subsidy on wool, wool-fells, and leather for his lifetime; also a fifteenth and

[26] The commons formally submitted to the royal grace, which was granted through the chancellor. The king personally promised not to request tenths and fifteenths just for himself and his household.

[27] First summoned at Westminster, September, 1397; adjourned to Shrewsbury, January, 1398. During the first session the statute and commission of 1388 were repealed and the Lords Appellant convicted of high treason. See J. G. Edwards, in the *English Historical Review*, XL, 321 f.

[28] Twelve peers, or six of them, and six knights, or three of them, with power as aforesaid.

tenth and half a fifteenth and half a tenth, in the manner and form following. . . .[29]

(French) *Ibid.*, III, 368.

[29] They were thanked and dismissed by the king on the same day.

64. RICHARD II: STATUTES AND ORDINANCES

(A) APPOINTMENT OF COUNCILLORS (1377)

The king to all who shall see these letters, greeting. By the assent of the prelates, dukes, earls, barons, and others assembled beside us in our council held at Westminster on the morrow of our coronation, we recently ordained that twelve persons—that is to say, two bishops, two earls, two barons, two bannerets, and four bachelors—should be elected by us and them as our councillors to aid our chancellor and treasurer in affairs touching the estate, honour, and advantage of us, and of our kingdom, lordships, and lands; and that the said councillors thus to be elected should have, after their election, our letters patent [commissioning them] to carry out and execute the said matters; and that the said chancellor and treasurer should duly enforce the measures ordained by them and by the said elected [councillors], or by the majority of them. Whereupon [the following men] were elected by us and by the prelates and lords aforesaid. . . . And in our presence they were sworn as our councillors, to carry out and execute the said matters according to the form stated above so long as it should be our pleasure. We, wishing the said ordinance to be put into effect, have constituted and assigned the aforesaid men, thus elected, as our councillors to carry out and execute the said matters according to the form of the ordinance aforesaid.[1] . . . And so we shall hold firm and good whatever the said elected [councillors], together with the aforesaid chancellor and treasurer, or the majority of them, shall do in our name as stated above and in each and all of the aforesaid matters, and we will that it be strictly observed. In testimony whereof we have caused to be drawn up these our letters patent, to continue at our pleasure. Given at our palace of Westminster, July 20.

By writ of the king himself under the signet.

(French) *Ibid.*, III, 386.

(B) STATUTE OF 7 RICHARD II: FOR THE IMPROVEMENT OF JUSTICE (1384)

. . . Item, it is agreed and established that no man of law shall henceforth be justice of assize or of common jail delivery in his own country (*patria*), and that the chief justice of the common bench, among others, shall be assigned to hold assizes of this sort and to deliver jails; but with regard to the chief justice of the king's bench,

[1] They were especially commissioned to borrow money for the king's immediate needs.

let such action be taken as has been customary for the greater part of the past hundred years.

Item, . . . after the said ordinance [of Edward III] had been recited in parliament, it was agreed and established that no justice of the king's bench or of the common bench, or any baron of the exchequer, so long as he held the office of justice or baron, should henceforth take, either by himself or through others, whether openly or in secret, any robe, fief, pension, gift, or reward from anybody except the king; nor [should he take] any present from anybody except one of food and drink which is not of great value. And [it is established] that henceforth [such justices and barons] shall not give counsel to any one, whether great or small, in causes or concerns to which the king is a party or which in any way touch the king; and that they are not to be of counsel to any one in any case, plea, or dispute pending before themselves or in any other great court or tribunal of the king, on penalty of forfeiting office and of paying fine and ransom to the king.[2]

Item, on complaint made by the same commons to the lord king in parliament, to the effect that great disherison of people had been caused in times past, and might yet be caused, through false entry of pleas, erasure of rolls, and alteration of verdicts, it was agreed and established that any one, whether judge or clerk, properly convicted before the king and his council . . . of an offence of this sort . . . should be punished by fine and redemption at the king's pleasure and should satisfy the party [defrauded]. . . .

Item, whereas various pleas which touch the common law, and which ought to be discussed and determined according to the common law, are now by way of innovation coming to be drawn before the constable and the marshal of England,[3] to the serious damage and disturbance of the people: it is agreed and established that all pleas and disputes which touch the common law of the land, and which ought to be discussed and determined according to the common law, shall henceforth by no means be drawn or held before the aforesaid constable and marshal; but that the court of the same constable and marshal shall have [jurisdiction over] that which pertains to the said court, and the common law that which pertains to it; and let such action and usage continue as was customary in the time of the lord king's ancestors.

(Latin) *Statutes of the Realm,* II, 36 f.

(C) Ordinance concerning Livery and Maintenance (1390)

Whereas . . . in many of our parliaments previously held . . . grievous complaint and great clamour has been made to us by the lords spiritual and temporal, as well as by the commons of our kingdom, concerning the great and outrageous oppression of maintenance, carried on to the damage of us and our people in various parts of

---

[2] Cf. no. 53.
[3] Cf. no. 56, art. 26.

the same kingdom by divers supporters . . . of suits and inquests
. . . , among whom many are the more encouraged and emboldened
in their aforesaid maintenance and wrongdoing because they are in
the retinues of lords and others of our said kingdom [and are pro-
vided] with fees, robes, and other liveries called company liveries:[4]
[therefore] by the advice of our great council, we have ordained
and straitly enjoined that neither prelate nor other man of Holy
Church, nor bachelor, nor squire, nor other man of less estate shall
bestow any sort of such livery as is called company livery; and that
no duke, earl, baron, or banneret shall bestow such company livery
on knight or squire, unless he is retained for the term of his life
during peace and war and through indenture [made] without fraud
or malice, or unless he is a domestic and family retainer living in
the household; nor [shall such a nobleman bestow such livery] on
any valet called "yeoman archer," or on any person of less estate,
unless he is similarly a family retainer living in the household. . . .
And [it is ordained] that no lord spiritual or temporal or other person, who has or shall have men in his retinue, shall suffer any who
are with him to be in any way supporters . . . of suits and inquests
in the localities; but, as aforesaid, he shall oust them from his service
and retinue as soon as it can be perceived [that they are wrongdoers of this sort] . . . ; and that none of our lieges, great or
small, of whatsoever condition he may be, whether he is the retainer
of some lord or is any other sort of person belonging to no retinue,
shall undertake any quarrel other than his own or shall maintain it,
by himself or through others, either openly or in secret; and that all
those who, contrary to this our ordinance, use or wear such livery
as is called company livery shall utterly abandon it within ten days
after the proclamation of this same ordinance. . . . Given under
our great seal at Westminster, May 12.
    By the king himself and the council.

(French) Ibid., II, 74 f.

(D) ORDINANCE CONCERNING THE KING'S COUNCIL (1390)

In the first place, the lords of the council shall take pains to appear
at the council by eight or nine o'clock at the latest.

Item, the affairs of the king and the kingdom are to be examined in
preference to all others when the greater men of the council and the
other officers are present.

Item, matters touching the common law are to be sent for determination before the justices.

Item, matters touching the office of chancellor are to be sent for
determination before him in the chancery.

Item, matters touching the office of treasurer are to be sent for
determination before him in the exchequer.

---

[4] This ordinance was one of many futile efforts to check the practice of keeping bands of uniformed retainers, organized like the notorious free companies
in the French wars.

Item, all other matters, which cannot be settled without the special grace and permission of the king, are to be laid before him in order thereon to have his opinion and pleasure.

Item, no gift or grant that may be turned to the diminution of the king's profit shall be passed without the advice of the council and the assent of the dukes of Guienne, York, and Gloucester and of the chancellor, or of two of them.

Item, all other matters presented to the council in order to have their advice, and other matters of great weight, are to be determined by those of the council who are present, together with the officers.

Item, all other bills of less weight from the people[5] are to be examined and determined before the keeper of the privy seal and others of the council who may be present at the time.

Item, ordinances previously made by the assent of the king and of his council with regard to offices in his gift are to be held and observed.

Item, no steward or justice is henceforth to be appointed for the term of his life.

Item, bachelors who are of the king's council shall have reasonable wages for the time spent in work connected with the same council.

Item, lords who are of the same council shall receive consideration for their labour and expense by the advice of the king and his council.

Item, after one matter has beeen introduced in the council, they shall not pass on to any other matter until an answer has been given in the matter first introduced.

On March 8, in the thirteenth year, etc., this ordinance was made at Westminster in the presence of the king, there being in attendance the duke of Guienne, the duke of York, the earl of Salisbury, the earl of Northumberland, the earl of Huntingdon, the chancellor, the treasurer, the [keeper of the] privy seal, the steward, Lovell, Stury, and Dalynrigg.

(French) Nicolas, Proceedings of the Privy Council, I, 18a f.

(E) Statute of 15 Richard II: Restriction of Uses[6] (1391)

. . . Item, whereas it is contained in the statute *De Religiosis*[7] that no man of religion or other man whatsoever shall buy or sell, or under colour of gift or lease or other title of any sort shall receive from any one or in any way, by artifice or stratagem, cause lands or tenements to be appropriated to himself from any one . . . , so that the said lands and tenements come into mortmain: . . . it is granted and agreed that all those who are possessed of lands, tenements, fiefs, advowsons, or other possessions by enfeoffment or in other fashion for the use of men of religion or of other spiritual persons . . . shall, between now and the feast of St. Michael next, have them amortized

---

[5] That is to say, private petitions; see, for example, no. 70.

[6] On the law of uses, see Holdsworth, *History of English Law,* IV, 407 f.

[7] The Statute of Mortmain, no. 52B.

by licence of the king and the lords [of the lands]; or, otherwise, [the holders] shall sell them and alienate them for another use between now and the said feast, on pain of their being forfeit to the king and the lords as tenements purchased by men of religion, according to the form of the statute *De Religiosis*. And from this time on, under the same penalty, no such purchase shall be made, so that such men of religion or other spiritual persons shall thereof enjoy the profits as aforesaid. And this same statute shall extend to and hold for all lands, tenements, fiefs, advowsons, and other possessions purchased or to be purchased for the use of gilds or fraternities.[8] . . .

(French) *Statutes of the Realm*, II, 79 f.

(F) SECOND STATUTE OF PRAEMUNIRE (1393)[9]

. . . Wherefore our said lord the king, by the assent aforesaid and at the prayer of his said commons, has ordained and established that, if any one purchases or pursues, or causes to be purchased or pursued, in the court of Rome or elsewhere, any such translations,[10] processes, sentences of excommunication, bulls, instruments, or anything else touching our lord the king that is inimical to him, his crown, his regality, or his aforesaid kingdom, as aforesaid; or if any one brings them into the kingdom, receives them, or thereof makes notification or any other execution, either within the said kingdom or outside it; such persons, their notaries, procurators, partisans, supporters, abettors, and counsellors are to be put outside the protection of our said lord the king, and their lands, tenements, goods, and chattels are to be forfeit to our lord the king. And [it is ordained] that, if they can be found, they are to be bodily attached and taken before the king and his council, there to respond in the cases aforesaid; or that process shall be brought against them by *praemunire facias*[11] in the manner provided by other statutes concerning provisors and other men who, in derogation of our lord the king's regality, bring suit in the court of another.

(French) *Ibid.*, II, 85 f.

---

[8] The prohibition also extended to municipalities.
[9] The extremely long preamble is omitted.
[10] Removals of ecclesiastics from one office to another.
[11] The special writ after which the statute came to be named; cf. no. 62G.

65. DURHAM HALMOTE ROLLS (1375)[1]

Pittington. . . . Inquest: it was proved by oath . . . that Thomas, son of John Widowson of West Rainton, is a freeman of free condition and of free status and not a bondman of the said lord prior.

Ferry. It was ordered[2] that no cotters of the vill should leave the vill while any of the tenants had work to be done. . . .

---

[1] On the significance of these records see Pollock and Maitland, I, 624 f.; and cf. no. 54H.
[2] *Ordinatum est*—the usual form used to introduce a local ordinance or by-law. Before too much communal self-government is read into these extracts, it

Wallsend. From Alan of Durham and John del Rawe 2s. for breach of the peace in gathering peasecods. And it was ordered that no tenants of the vill should gather peasecods except for their own use, and not for sale at Newcastle—and this in the place ordered by the reeve. . . .

Westoe. Increase of rent 6d.: John Gray took a cottage last in the holding of Thomas Wright, to have and to hold at the will of the lord, at annual rent of 2s. Catherine of Brenklaw took half a cottage, last in the holding of William Souter, to have and to hold at the will of the lord, at annual rent of 18d. . . .

Coupon. It was ordered that no tenants of the vill should enter the park without licence. . . .

Aycliffe. It was ordered that all cotters, and all other tenants of the lord who had no corn of their own to harvest, should reap with the lord at Ketton, on pain of 40d. . . . And it was ordered that William Power, the reeve, and the forester should have all such tenants, servants, and labourers of the vill stopped from going outside the vill for harvesting, except with the lord and his tenants, on pain of 20s. William Power, John Taylor, Gilbert Randolf, and Thomas Watson were made constables of the vill. . . .

Willington. From the tenants of Willington and Wallsend 2s. amercement because they did not have a common smith as they had been ordered in many halmotes. It was ordered that [the men] of this vill and township should have a common smith before the feast of St. Martin and that henceforth none of them should work on ploughshares, under penalty of 20s. . . .

Hebburn. John of Hedworth rendered homage and fealty in the church of Jarrow to the lord Robert, prior of the church of Durham . . . , for his land which he holds of the aforesaid [prior] in Hebburn. Item, John Wiley rendered homage and fealty to the same lord Robert in his court at Harton. . . .

Aycliffe. It was ordered for all tenants of the vill, namely for brewers, that they should not sell a gallon of beer for more than 1½d. . . .

West Merrington. It was ordered that no tenants of the vill should insult one another by word or deed.

Mid Merrington. . . . It was ordered that no tenants of the vill should cut down thorns in the fields of Mid Merrington. . . .

Moorsley. Presentment was brought that Alice, daughter of John Hudson, was married on free land; therefore let inquiry be made whether the same Alice should give merchet[3] or not. John son of Roger was claimed as the lord's bondman of the vill of Little Haswell. And he says he is a freeman; so he shall swear not to remove himself before the next court. . . .

Coupon. Little-Stephen took a cottage once in the holding of Geoffrey Ladman. Gilbert son of John was elected to the office of reeve, and John de Raw is his associate. And they were sworn.

---

should be noted that the village obligations, though declared "by common assent," often carried a penalty of 20s. for disobedience. See the entries below.

[3] A fine for permission to marry, at this time a mark of servile condition.

Aycliffe. It was ordered by common assent that they should have a common harvester[4] before the feast of St. Cuthbert in March, on pain of 20s.; also that they should have a common harvester before the feast of St. Helen, on pain of 20s.; also that no tenant of the said vill should do wrong to the said harvester or unlawfully take from him animals under pledge or remove animals from his fold without the licence of the said harvester, on pain of 20s.; also that every tenant should act toward the shepherds of the vill as was agreed in common. . . .

Ferry. It was ordered that no tenants of that vill or of the townships of East Merrington, Mid Merrington, West Merrington, and Chilton should implead one another in any court except the court of the prior, that is to say, in his lay and secular [court]. . . .

West Rainton. . . . From Thomas Rois 18d., because his dog ate a pea-hen. . . .

Hedworth. . . . It was ordered that no tenant of the vill should permit his wife to vilify or insult any persons of the neighbourhood. . . .

Hesleden. . . . It was ordered by common assent that everything gathered in the field, whether corn or herbs, should be brought openly through the centre of the vill and not secretly behind the gardens. . . . It was ordered that all women of the vill should hold their tongues and should not scold or curse any one.

Dalton. From Joan, wife of William Smith, 12d. for merchet. From Margaret, servant of the farmer, 12d. for *leyrwite*[5] [incurred] with two men. From Joan Woodcock 6d. for the same. From the wife of John Dawson 6d. for breach of the assize of beer. . . . Marjory, widow of John Dawson, deceased, took a kiln built by the same John in the lord's waste, to have and to hold for the term of her life, at annual rent of 12d., but the lord prior of his grace remitted to the aforesaid Marjory all but 8d., to be paid annually during the life of the said Marjory. And she gave as fine 12d., which was pardoned except 3d. Item, the aforesaid Marjory took a villein tenement (*terram husbandorum*): namely, a messuage and eighteen acres of land with appurtenances, which the said John Dawson, formerly husband of the said Marjory, once held, to have and to hold for the term of her life, and paying annually the ancient farm. And within a year she will build a house at her own expense. And she gives as fine 13s. 4d., which is pardoned except 40d. . . . John, son of John Dawson, took two villein tenements, each containing eighteen acres, which the said John Dawson earlier held, to have and to hold for the term of nine years, rendering annually the ancient farm. And he gives 40d. as fine for the said term of nine years. . . .

(Latin) *Halmota Prioratus Dunelmensis,* pp. 126-32.

---

[4] *Messor*—apparently a superintendent of the harvest who incidentally acted as keeper of the pound.

[5] See above, p. 188, n. 27.

SECTION VI

THE HOUSE OF LANCASTER AND YORK

IN THIS section, as in the one before it, pre-eminence has been accorded to statutes and excerpts from the rolls of parliament; so what has been said of those sources in the previous introduction is to a large degree applicable here also. With particular regard to the following selection, it need only be remarked that the bulk of the material is drawn from the early Lancastrian period, when so many important precedents were established for subsequent ages. Emphasis has thus been placed on the Revolution of 1399, its formal justification and its immediate results (no. 66A); parliamentary control of the council and the household (nos. 66C, D; 67A, B); parliamentary appropriation and audit (no. 66D, E); and the assertion by the commons of various rights and privileges—that redress should precede supply (no. 66B, E); that grants of money should originate in the lower house (no. 66E); that petitions agreed to in parliament should not be changed without parliamentary consent (no. 66F); that election returns should not be tampered with by officials (no. 66C); that members should enjoy freedom of petition (no. 66A), freedom of discussion (nos. 66B, 67C), and, to a certain extent, freedom from arrest (nos. 66C, 67C). No. 67E is included as an example of the parliamentary attainders that became all too common in the later fifteenth century. Finally, the acts of Richard III's parliament have been summarized in order to show the development of what we know as bill procedure (no. 68).

On some of these matters additional information is provided by the acts of the privy council, which henceforth attain increasing importance as a source for constitutional history. Under no. 70 will be found a variety of excerpts: a few chosen, as just remarked, because they supplement the parliament rolls; others because they are typical of the council's daily work, administrative or judicial. And a comparison of the entries under nos. 70 and 71 will quickly show how vague and fluctuating was as yet the distinction between justice in council and justice in chancery. The technicalities of equitable procedure, like those of the common law, must here be passed over; nevertheless, several cases are presented as instances of appeal to the chancellor's conscience when no remedy could be had in the ordinary courts, and of the discretionary authority retained by the king in council—the basis of an enhanced star chamber jurisdiction under the Tudors.

Concluding this section are a number of documents concerning the boroughs. A few excerpts from the *Liber Albus,* in default of a better source, reveal the growing complexity of the London government. Henry VI's charter to Nottingham is typical of the formal acts of incorporation then being secured by the greater towns. The Leicester ordinances are homely examples of municipal by-laws. The indentures for the parliament of 1437 illustrate the varieties of electoral processes that prevailed in England until the Reform Act of 1832. Although an indefinite amount of other such material could be assembled, it would include little that was fundamentally new. In the history of English municipal institutions the formative period is the twelfth, rather than the fifteenth century. The maturing of the local administrative system can well be left for more vivid portrayal in connection with the reorganization of the Tudors.

The list of authorities cited for the preceding section is applicable for the present one, with the addition of the following: S.B. Chrimes, *English Constitutional Ideas in the Fifteenth Century;* John Fortescue, *De Laudibus Legum Angliae,* editor, S. B. Chrimes; G. Lapsley, *Crown, Community and Parliament in the Later Middle Ages,* editors H. Cam and G. Barraclough; E. F. Jacob, *The Fifteenth Century,* 1399–1485; B. Wilkinson, *The Constitutional History of England in the Fifteenth Century,* 1399–1485.

66. PARLIAMENT ROLLS OF HENRY IV AND HENRY V

(A) PARLIAMENT OF 1399

At the parliament summoned and held at Westminster by King Henry IV on Monday, the day of St. Faith the Virgin . . . , in the presence of the same king seated on his royal throne in the great hall of Westminster, and of all the lords spiritual and temporal, and of the commons who had come thither by virtue of their summons to parliament, and of many other gentlemen and commoners there present in large numbers, Thomas of Arundel, archbishop of Canterbury, related how King Richard II after the Conquest had summoned his parliament to be held there on the previous Tuesday . . . ; which summons was without force and effect through the acceptance of the renunciation made by the same King Richard, and through the deposition of the same King Richard made on the aforesaid Tuesday, as more fully appears in the record and process drawn up in this connection and enrolled in this roll of parliament. . . .

Here follow the record and process of the renunciation by King Richard II after the Conquest, and of the acceptance of the same renunciation; likewise of the deposition of the same King Richard. . . .[1] On the next day, however . . . , in the great hall at Westminster, honourably prepared for the holding of parliament, in the presence of the said archbishops of Canterbury and York, of the duke of Lancaster, of other dukes and lords both spiritual and temporal whose names are inscribed below, and of the people of the said kingdom then and there assembled in a very great multitude for the sake of [witnessing] the deeds of parliament, while the aforesaid duke of Lancaster occupied the place due and accustomed to his estate and while the royal throne, solemnly prepared with cloth of gold, stood vacant in the absence of any presiding officer whatsoever, the aforesaid archbishop of York . . . had the said cession and renunciation read by another, first in Latin and then in English. And immediately it was asked of the estates and the people then and there present[2] . . . whether for their own interest and for the benefit of the kingdom, they wished to accept the same renunciation and cession. And the same estates and people, considering, for the reasons specified by the king himself in his aforesaid renunciation and cession, that to do so would be highly expedient, all singly and in common with the people unanimously and with one accord accepted such renunciation and cession. After this acceptance, however, it was then publicly set forth that, besides the renunciation and cession accepted as aforesaid, it would in many ways be expedient and advantageous for the said kingdom if, in order to obviate all scruple and evil suspicion, the many crimes and defaults frequently committed by the said king in connection with the bad government of his kingdom—on account of which, as he himself had asserted in the cession made by him, he merited deposition—should be written down in the form of articles, to be publicly read and declared to the people. And so a large part

---

[1] The long account of Richard's abdication and how it was brought to parliament is here omitted. On the significance of this whole proceeding, see M. V. Clarke and V. H. Galbraith, "The Deposition of Richard II," in *Bulletin of the John Rylands Library*, XIV, 125 f.; also G. Lapsley, in the *English Historical Review*, XLIX, 423 f., 577 f.

[2] The archbishop of Canterbury was first asked for his opinion; then, apparently, the others were interrogated one after the other.

of those articles was then publicly read, of all which articles the tenor is as follows. . . .[3]

Item, in the parliament recently held at Shrewsbury[4] the same king, proposing to oppress his people, subtly procured and caused it to be granted that, by the counsel of all the estates of his realm, the power of parliament to decide certain petitions, which had been presented in the same parliament but on which no progress had as yet been made, should devolve upon certain persons. By colour of which concession the persons thus deputed proceeded with other matters of common concern to that parliament—and this at the will of the king and in derogation of the estate of parliament, to the great damage of the entire kingdom, and [by way of setting] a pernicious example. And in order that [these persons] might seem to have a certain colour of authority for such deeds, the king had the rolls of parliament deleted and changed to suit himself and contrary to the terms of the aforesaid concession. . . .

Item, when the king of England was able, without oppressing his people, to live honourably from the issues of his kingdom and from the patrimony belonging to his crown, since the kingdom was not burdened with the expense of wars, the same king, while truces between the kingdom of England and his adversaries continued during almost his entire reign, not only gave the greater part of his said patrimony to unworthy persons, but also, on that account, threw such burdens of taxation on his subjects in nearly every year of his reign that he widely and outrageously oppressed his people, to the impoverishment of his kingdom. And the income thus obtained was not used for the benefit and advantage of the kingdom of England, but was prodigally dissipated for the sake of his own ostentation, pomp, and vainglory. And great sums of money were owed in his kingdom for the victuals of his household and other purchases of his, although, more than any of his progenitors, he enjoyed an abundance of treasure and riches. Item, the same king, refusing to keep and defend the just laws and customs of his kingdom, but [wishing] at his own arbitrary will to do whatever appealed to his desires, sometimes—and very often when the laws of the kingdom had been declared and explained to him by his justices and others of his council, and when, according to those laws, he was to administer justice to those seeking it—expressly said, with an austere and determined countenance, that his laws were in his own mouth or, occasionally, in his own breast; and that he alone could establish and change the laws of his realm. And he, seduced by that opinion, would not permit justice to be done to many of his lieges, but by threats and intimidation compelled many to abstain from the pursuit of common justice. . . .

Item, although, according to the statutes and custom of his realm,

---

[3] The record here inserts the coronation oath (no. 55) and then justifies the deposition by thirty-three articles, of which five are translated below.

[4] See no. 63 i.

his people in all the counties of the kingdom ought, on the summoning of every parliament, to be free to elect and depute knights on behalf of such counties to attend parliament, explain their grievances, and in that connection sue for remedies as may seem best to them; nevertheless, the aforesaid king, in order that he might be able the more freely to carry out his own headstrong will, very often sent mandates to his sheriffs that they should cause certain persons, nominated as knights of the shires by the king himself, to come to his parliaments. And these knights, since they favoured the same king, he was able to induce—as he very often did, sometimes by divers threats and intimidation and sometimes by rewards—to support matters prejudicial to the kingdom and extremely burdensome to the people, especially the grant to the same king of a subsidy on wool for the term of his life and another subsidy for a number of years, to the excessive oppression of his people. . . .

Item, although the lands, tenements, goods, and chattels of every freeman, according to the laws of the realm accustomed throughout all times past, ought not to be seized unless they have been [lawfully] forfeited, nevertheless the said king, proposing and determining to undo such laws, in the presence of very many lords and of other men from the commonalty of the realm, often said and affirmed that the life of every one of his lieges, together with the lands, tenements, goods, and chattels of such men, was subject to his own pleasure, apart from any [lawful] forfeiture—which is wholly contrary to the laws and customs of his kingdom aforesaid.

Item, although it is established and ordained that no freeman shall be seized, etc., or in any way destroyed, and that the king will neither go against him nor send against him, except by the lawful judgment of his peers, or by the law of the land;[5] nevertheless, by the will, mandate, and order of the said king, very many of his lieges, maliciously accused of having publicly or secretly said something that might lead to the slander, shame, or humiliation of the said king's person, were seized and imprisoned and taken to a military court before the constable and marshal of England. . . . Wherefore, since the aforesaid king wilfully contravened such statute of his realm, it is not to be doubted that he thereby committed perjury. . . .

And since it seemed to all these estates, thereupon interrogated singly and in common, that those statements of his crimes and defaults were notoriously sufficient for deposing the same king, considering also his own confession with regard to his incompetence and other matters contained in the said renunciation and cession which had been openly published, all the estates aforesaid unanimously agreed that the deposition of the said king was abundantly justified in order to secure the greater safety and tranquillity of the people and the good of the kingdom. . . .[6]

---

[5] Art. 39 of Magna Carta, above, p. 121.

[6] A commission was then appointed to draw up the formal deposition of Richard and, in the name of all, to withdraw the homage and fealty of his subjects.

And immediately, as it appeared from the foregoing [actions] and their result that the kingship of England, together with its appurtenances, was vacant, the aforesaid Henry, duke of Lancaster, rising from his place and standing so erect that he could be well seen by all the people, humbly signing himself on the brow and breast with the symbol of the Cross and first invoking Christ by name, laid claim to the said kingship of England, thus declared vacant, together with the crown and all its members and appurtenances; [and this he did] in his mother tongue by the form of words following:—

"In the name of Fadir, Son, and Holy Gost, I, Henry of Lancaster chalenge this rewme of Yngland and the corone with all the membres and the appurtenances, als I that am disendit be right lyne of the blode comyng fro the gude lorde Kyng Henry Therde, and thorghe that ryght that God of his grace hath sent me, with the helpe of my kyn and of my frendes, to recover it—the whiche rewme was in poynt to be undone for defaut of governance and undoyng of the gode lawes."

After which declaration and claim the lords both spiritual and temporal, and all the estates there present, were asked singly and in common what they thought of that declaration and claim; and the same estates, together with all the people, unanimously agreed without difficulty or delay that the aforesaid duke should reign over them. And immediately . . . the aforesaid archbishop, taking the said King Henry by the right hand, led him to the royal throne aforesaid. And after the said king, kneeling before the said throne, had made a short prayer, the same archbishop of Canterbury, with the assistance of the aforesaid archbishop of York, placed the said king and caused him to sit on the aforesaid royal throne, while the people in their excessive joy loudly applauded. And then the said archbishop of Canterbury, when silence had with difficulty been obtained, on account of the joy of all the bystanders, preached a brief sermon, speaking in these words. . . . And when this sermon had been ended, the said Lord King Henry, in order to put at rest the minds of his subjects, in the same place publicly spoke the following words:—

"Sires, I thank God and yowe, spiritual and temporal and all the astates of the lond, and do yowe to wyte[7] it is noght my will that no man thynk that be waye of conquest I wold disherit any man of his heritage, franches, or other ryghtes that hym aght to have, no put hym out of that that he has and has had by the gude laws and customs of the rewme—except thos persons that has ben agan the gude purpose and the commune profyt of the rewme."

. . . On Monday, which was the day of St. Edward the King and Confessor, the said King Henry was crowned at Westminster with all due honour and solemnity; and certain lords and others, in accordance with their tenures, severally performed their service to the same

---

[7] Would have you know.

King Henry after the fashion accustomed at the time of such coronation.

Item, on the following Tuesday, the commons of the realm presented to the king Sir John Cheyne as their speaker and procurator in parliament, to whom the king well agreed. . . .[8]

Item, on the same Wednesday, the said commons set forth to our lord the king that on Monday next after the feast of the Exaltation of the Holy Cross, in the twenty-first year of the reign of the recent King Richard, a parliament was summoned and held at Westminster and then adjourned to Shrewsbury,[9] at which town, by the authority of parliament, certain power was committed to various persons to proceed with divers articles and matters contained in the roll of parliament made in that connection, as appears from the said roll. In which parliament, also by the aforesaid authority, divers statutes, judgments, ordinances, and establishments were made, ordained, and rendered, erroneously and very grievously, to the great disherison and to the ultimate destruction and undoing of numerous honourable lords and other lieges of the kingdom and of their heirs for all time. Wherefore the same commons prayed our lord the king, and all the lords spiritual and temporal in this present parliament, that it might please them by their common assent to revoke, annul, quash, delete, and repeal everything whatsoever that had been done in that same parliament held in the said twenty-first year or [enacted] by its authority. . . . Whereupon our said lord the king, having deliberated and advised with all the lords spiritual and temporal, severally examined in full parliament with regard to the matters aforesaid, by the common assent of the same lords, adjudged the said parliament held in the said twenty-first year and the authority thereby given as described above, together with all its other consequences and effects, to be of no force or validity. . . .[10]

Item, on the same Wednesday the said commons prayed our said lord the king that the [acts of the] parliament held at Westminster in the eleventh year of the said King Richard,[11] which parliament was held for the great honour and common profit of the whole kingdom, should be of full force and validity. To which prayer the king, by the common assent of all the lords aforesaid, severally examined in parliament concerning the matter, has well agreed; and he wills that the [acts of the] said parliament, held in the said eleventh year, shall be observed and kept in all particulars. . . .

On Monday, the morrow of All Souls, which was the third day of November, the commons made their protestation in the same manner as at the opening of the parliament; and besides they set forth

---

[8] On Wednesday the speaker made his usual address and the commons voted various customs for three years as well as a tenth and fifteenth.

[9] See no. 63 I.

[10] Richard II's statute of treasons was also repealed, leaving the law as it had been established in 1352 (no. 62F).

[11] See no. 63G.

to the king that, whereas the judgments of parliament pertained solely
to the king and to the lords, and not to the commons except in case
it pleased the king of his special grace to show them the same judgments for their satisfaction, no record should be made in parliament
concerning the said commons to the effect that they are or shall be
parties to any judgments henceforth to be given in parliament. To
which, at the king's command, response was made by the archbishop of Canterbury, to the effect that the commons are petitioners
and demandants, and that the king and the lords have always had
and of right shall have the [rendering of] judgments in parliament,
after the manner described by the same commons; except that the
king especially wishes to have their advice and assent in the making
of statutes, or of grants and subsidies, or [other] such matters for
the common good of the realm. . . .

Item, since divers statutes and ordinances have been framed in
times past . . . touching provisions [made] at the court of Rome,[12]
the commons of the realm of England assembled in parliament,
through the great trust which they have in the person of our lord
the king, in his most excellent sense and discretion, and in the great
tenderness and affection which above all others he has for his crown
and its rights and the salvation of his royal estate, have of their
free will agreed in full parliament that our said lord the king,
with the consent and advice of such wise men and worthy persons as
in this connection it may please him to call upon for counsel, shall
have power to effect such permission, ordinance, and moderation with
regard to the said statute as may seem to him most reasonable and
advantageous for the satisfaction of God and the salvation of Holy
Church; and even to quash, repeal, delete, and wholly annul the
same statute according to his high discretion and according to what
shall seem to him for the honour of God and most expedient and
necessary for the honour and profit of his royal estate, of his said
realm, and of his people. . . .

Item, it is to be remembered that Thomas of Haxey, clerk, presented to our lord the king in parliament a petition in the following
words:[13]—

To our most respected lord the king and to his lords of parliament
your poor clerk, Thomas Haxey, sets forth that the said Thomas, in
the parliament held at Westminster on the day of St. Vincent in
the twentieth year of King Richard II, presented a bill to the commons of the said parliament for the honour and profit of the said
king and of all his realm, on account of which bill, at the desire of
the said king, the said Thomas was adjudged traitor and forfeited
everything that he had, in violation of right and of the usage that
had hitherto prevailed in parliament (and to the undoing of the
customs of the commons). Therefore may it please your very gracious

---

[12] See nos. 62E, 64E.
[13] Cf. no. 63H. Two versions of this petition are included in the roll. The
clauses given below in parentheses are added by the second version.

lordship to have the record and process of the said judgment, together with all appendant matters, brought before this present parliament, to have that judgment quashed and annulled as erroneous, and to have the same Thomas entirely restored to his rank, estate, goods, chattels, farms, annuities, pensions, lands, tenements, rents, offices, advowsons, and possessions of all sorts, together with their appurtenances . . . ; and that he may hold them for himself and his heirs as he held them on the day that the said bill was drawn up . . . (as well for the enforcement of right as for the salvation of the liberties of the said commons).

Response: When this petition, together with the record and process of that [judgment], had been read and heard, our same lord the king, by the advice and consent of all the lords spiritual and temporal, ordained and decided that the judgment rendered against the said Thomas in the parliament held at Westminster in the said twentieth year of Richard, recently king, should be utterly quashed, reversed, repealed, and annulled, and be held as of no force or effect; that the said Thomas should be restored to his name and fame, and that he and his heirs should be entitled to seek, demand, and have their inheritance as heirs of their ancestors in such fashion as the said Thomas was [seised] before the said judgment thus rendered against him, notwithstanding the same judgment, according to which the [right of inheritance by] blood was broken as between the said Thomas, together with his heirs, and any of their ancestors.[14]

(Latin, French, English) *Rotuli Parliamentorum,* III, 415-34.

(B) PARLIAMENT OF 1401

It is to be remembered that, in the parliament held at Westminster on Thursday, the octave of St. Hilary, which was the twentieth day of January, in the second year of King Henry IV since the Conquest, the knights of the shires, the citizens of the cities, and the burgesses of the boroughs, who had come by virtue of summons to parliament, were proclaimed by their names in the chancery of the king within the hall of Westminster and in the presence of the chancellor of England and of the steward of the king's household. And on their appearance the same parliament, for certain good reasons affecting the king, was adjourned until the next Friday. . . . On Friday, January 21, Sir William Thirning, chief justice of the common bench, at the king's command declared the cause for the summoning of parliament, in the form that follows:[15]—

. . . And, finally, the king wills and commands that no lord, knight of the shire, citizen, or burgess, who has come to parliament by virtue of summons, shall absent himself from the same parlia-

---

[14] The reference is to the so-called corruption of blood resulting from conviction of treason; cf. the attainder of John Cade, no. 67E.

[15] The chief cause was financial: the great expense of the government and the cost of restoring the kingdom, putting down rebellions, defending the frontiers, etc.

ment or depart from it out of the city until it is finished; and that
they shall come on time every day to their places assigned for the
parliament; and that forthwith the said commons shall among themselves effect the election of their common speaker and, according to
custom, bring him into the [king's] presence on next Saturday at
ten o'clock. . . .

On Saturday, January 22, the commons of the realm presented
to the king Sir Arnold Savage as their speaker and procurator in
parliament, to whom the king well agreed. . . .[16]

Item, on the same day[17] the said commons set forth to our lord
the king that, in connection with certain matters to be taken up among
themselves, one of their number, in order to please the king and to
advance himself, might perchance tell our lord the king of such matters before they had been determined and discussed, or agreed on
by the same commons, whereby our same lord the king might be
grievously moved against the said commons or some of them. Therefore they very humbly prayed our lord the king that he would not
receive any such person for the relating of any such matters. . . .
To which it was responded on behalf of the king that he wished the
same commons to have deliberation and advisement in treating all
their affairs among themselves, in order at their convenience to arrive at the best end and conclusion for the welfare and honour of
him and of all his kingdom; and that he would not listen to any
such person or give him credence until such matters had been presented to the king by the advice and consent of all the commons, according to the purpose of their said petition. . . .

Item, on the same Saturday the said commons prayed our lord the
king that the business done and to be done in this parliament should
be enacted and engrossed before the departure of the justices, and
while they had it in their memory. To which it was replied that the
clerk of parliament should, by the advice of the justices, do his
duty in enacting and engrossing the substance of [the proceedings of]
parliament, and then show it to the king and to the lords of parliament in order to know their opinion. . . .

Item, on the same Saturday the said commons set forth to our
said lord the king that in several parliaments during times past their
common petitions had not been answered before they had made
their grant to our lord the king of some aid or subsidy. And therefore they prayed our same lord the king that, for the great ease and
comfort of the said commons, our lord the king might be pleased to
grant to the same commons that they could have knowledge of the
responses to their said petitions before any such grant had thus
been made. To which it was replied that the king wished to confer on
this matter with the lords of the parliament and thereupon do what
seemed best to him by the advice of the said lords. And afterwards,

[16] The speaker then made his address and the commons voted tunnage and
poundage for two years, together with a tenth and fifteenth.
[17] Tuesday, January 25.

that is to say, on the last day of the parliament, the response was given that such procedure had been unknown and unaccustomed in the time of any of his progenitors or predecessors—[namely] that they should have any answer to their petitions, or knowledge of it, before they had set forth and completed all their other business in parliament, whether it was the making of any grant or something else. And, in conclusion, the king wished in no way to change the good customs and usages of ancient times. . . .[18]

(French) *Ibid.,* III, 454-58.

(C) PARLIAMENT OF 1404

. . . Item, upon certain prayers and requests earlier made by the commons at various times regarding the removal of divers persons, as well aliens as others . . . , it was in particular agreed by the said lords that four persons—namely, the king's confessor, the abbot of Dore, Master Richard Durham, and Crosby of the chamber—should be entirely ousted and removed from the king's household. Whereupon, on Saturday, February 9, the said confessor, Master Richard, and Crosby came before the king and the lords in parliament. And there the king, excusing the said four persons, said openly that, so far as he was concerned, he knew of no special reason or occasion why they should be removed from his household. Nevertheless, our same lord the king, well understanding that what the said lords or commons should do or ordain was for his good and that of the kingdom, and, finally, wishing to conform to their desires, he well agreed to the same ordinance and charged the said confessor, Master Richard, and Crosby to leave his said household. And a similar charge would have been given to the said abbot if he had been present. And our same lord the king further said that he would act in the same way with regard to any one else near his royal person, should that one incur the hatred or indignation of his people. . . .

Item, on the same Saturday the said commons prayed our said lord the king that, in the ordinance to be drawn up for the household of our same lord the king, nomination and appointment should be made of honest, virtuous, and reputable persons, concerning whom notice might be given to the said lords and commons in this parliament; and that such an ordinance should be made as might be pleasing to God and be of honour and advantage to the estate of the king and of his kingdom. . . .

Item, with regard to the commission of array[19] . . . of which a copy was delivered to the said commons, so that they might be advised concerning it and might correct it according to their desires, the same commons, having thereupon deliberated and consulted, caused to be cancelled certain clauses and words contained in it. And they prayed the king that henceforth no commission of array should

---

[18] How the commons largely gained their point by voting subsidies on the last day of parliament is illustrated below, p. 263.

[19] Cf. no. 50B.

be issued otherwise, or in other words than were contained in the same copy. . . . Which prayer our said lord the king, by the advice of the lords and after consultation on the matter with the judges of the realm, very graciously granted in parliament. Of which copy the tenor follows in these words. . . .

Item, it should be remembered that, on March 1, it was granted by the king and the lords spiritual and temporal in parliament that certain farms, revenues, issues, profits, and emoluments, specified in the enrolment of the letters patent below, should be devoted to and spent for the expenses of the king's household. . . .[20]

Item, on Saturday, March 1, in the presence of the king and the lords of parliament, the archbishop of Canterbury at the king's command explained to the said lords our same lord the king's intention regarding his government. . . . He told them that it was our said lord the king's desire that the laws should be kept and observed; that equal right and justice should be administered to poor and rich alike; that, on account of any letters under the secret seal[21] or the privy seal, or on account of any command or signed instruction whatsoever, the common law should not be disturbed, or the people in any way delayed in their pursuit [of justice]. And besides, our same lord the king, wishing that good administration should be maintained in his household, prayed the said lords that they would give their aid and care to placing it under good and satisfactory government, and one by a suitable number [of persons]; so that the people could be paid for their victuals and for the [other] expenses of his said household. . . . And it was furthermore our same lord the king's will that, with regard to the grant to be made in this present parliament by the lords and commons for the wars and for the defence of the kingdom, certain treasurers for the same grant should be appointed by the advice of the said lords and commons, so that the money thence arising should be expended for the wars and for nothing else. . . .

Item, for the sake of good and just government and of a remedy to be provided for the numerous complaints, grievances, and mischiefs shown to our lord the king in this parliament, our same lord the king, in reverence to God and in response to the very insistent and especial requests brought to him at various times in this parliament by the commons of his realm, for the ease and comfort of all his people has appointed certain lords and other persons, hereinunder written, to be of his great and continual council: namely, the archbishop of Canterbury; the bishop of Lincoln, chancellor of England; the bishop of Rochester, the bishop of Worcester, the bishop of Bath, the bishop of Bangor, the duke of York, the earl of Somerset, the earl of Westmorland; the lord of Roos, treasurer of England; the keeper of the privy seal, the lord of Berkeley, the lord of Willoughby, the lord of

---

[20] The total amount was £12,100, drawn from seven specified sources.

[21] Normally used for the king's personal correspondence. One form of the secret seal became known as the signet in the fifteenth century; see Tout, *Chapters in Mediaeval Administrative History*, V, 195 f.

Furnivall, the lord of Lovell, Sir Piers Courteney, Sir Hugh Waterton, Sir John Cheyne, Sir Arnold Savage, John Northbury, John Durward, John Curson.

Item, whereas the writ of summons to parliament returned by the sheriff of Rutland was not satisfactory or properly returned, as the said commons understood, the same commons prayed our lord the king and the lords in parliament that this matter might be properly examined in parliament, and that, in case default was therein discovered, such punishment should thereof be made as should serve for an example to others against trespass in such ways on some other occasion. Whereupon our said lord the king, in full parliament, commanded the lords of parliament to examine the said matter and at their discretion to deal with it as they thought best. And thereupon the said lords caused to come before them in parliament as well the said sheriff as William Ondeby, who had been returned by the said sheriff as one of the knights of the said shire, and also Thomas of Thorpe, who had been elected in full county [court] as one of the knights of the same shire for the said parliament and had not been returned by the said sheriff. And after the same parties had been duly examined and their cases well heard in the said parliament, it was decided by the same lords that, whereas the same sheriff had not satisfactorily made return of the said writ, he should amend the same return and should return the said Thomas as one of the knights, since the latter had been elected to the parliament in the county [court]; and besides that the said sheriff, on account of this default, should be discharged from his office and committed to Fleet Prison, and that he should be subjected to fine and redemption at the king's pleasure. . . .

May it please our most excellent and respected lord the king to grant to your poor commons of the parliament held at Westminster on the morrow of St. Hilary, in the fifth year of your reign, the following petitions for their relief:—

. . . Item, the commons pray that, whereas all the lords, knights, citizens, and burgesses attending parliament by the king's writ, together with their servants, are under royal protection while coming, remaining, and returning; and [whereas] the said lords, knights, citizens, burgesses, and their household servants have at the aforesaid times often suffered numerous mischiefs and molestations, such as murder, mayhem, and battery, from men lying in ambush or otherwise, for which due remedy has never been provided. . . .[22] : may it please [the king] to ordain sufficient remedy in this matter and in other similar cases, so that the punishment may serve as a terrible example to others who commit such misdeeds in times to come—that is to say, if any one kills or murders a man who has thus come to parliament under your protection, he shall be adjudged [guilty of]

[22] The petition then describes in detail the "horrible battery" recently suffered by Richard Cheddar while coming to parliament as knight of the shire for Somerset.

treason; if any one maims or disfigures such a man thus come under your protection, he shall lose a hand; and if any one assaults or beats such a man thus come, he shall be subjected to a year's imprisonment as well as fine and redemption to the king. And [the commons pray] that it may please you of your special grace henceforth to abstain from grants of pardon in such cases, unless the parties concerned have come to full agreement. . . .[23]

(French) *Ibid.*, III, 523-42.

(D) PARLIAMENT OF 1406

. . . Item, on Saturday, May 22, the commons came before the king and the lords in parliament, and there the said Sir John[24] related how, at the opening of parliament and afterwards, he had petitioned the king with regard to a satisfactory government; and he prayed our same lord the king to proceed with its establishment. And he also related how the archbishop of Canterbury had reported to them that the king wished to be counselled by the wisest lords of the realm, who were to have the supervision of everything that should be done for the good government of his kingdom. To do which the king agreed; and he declared by his own mouth that it was wholly his pleasure [so to do]. And thereupon a bill was drawn up by the king himself and of his own will was read, with the names of the lords who were to be of his council. Of which bill the tenor follows. . . .[25]

And thereupon the said lords prayed the king that, since this bill was the king's desire and [resulted] from his own initiation and not at all from their suit, the said bill might be entered as of record in the roll of parliament. And they also prayed that all matters contained within the said bill might be executed according to its provisions. Which [requests] the king granted. Furthermore, the king commanded that, as requested by the said lords, the said bill should well be enacted and enrolled in the same roll of parliament. . . .

Item, on the same day,[26] the said Sir John Tibetot, in the name of the said commons, prayed our said lord the king and all the lords in parliament that certain lords spiritual and temporal, whom they should be pleased to name, and also certain of the commons whose names he had written on a schedule in parliament . . . , might be assigned to be present at the enactment and engrossing of the roll of parlia-

---

[23] The king replies that the assailant is to be summoned before the king's bench; if he does not come, he is to pay double damages and be subject to ransom at the king's pleasure. Similar action is to be taken in future cases of the same sort.

[24] Tibetot, speaker of the commons.

[25] The list of councillors includes three prelates, six peers, three knights, the chancellor, the treasurer, the keeper of the privy seal, the steward, and the chamberlain. Instructions to all officials must be drawn up in council or endorsed by some of the members. Certain specified actions can be taken only by the advice of the council. Note this early example of what was to become known as bill procedure; cf. nos. 51B, 70B.

[26] December 22.

ment. And he further asked that this prayer and petition should be enacted as of record in the roll of parliament. Which prayers the king graciously conceded. . . .

In reverence to God and for the great love and affection that your poor commons of your realm of England have for you, our very sovereign and very gracious lord the king, and on account of the great trust that your said commons have in the lords recently elected and ordained for your council in order to provide better government than has been had, your said poor commons, by the assent of the lords spiritual and temporal, on December 22 of the eighth year of your reign, grant to you, most sovereign lord, for the salvation and defence of your kingdom of England against all enemies and rebels . . . , an entire fifteenth and tenth to be levied from laymen in the accustomed manner. . . .[27] [And this grant is made] on condition that the said fifteenth and tenth, the said subsidies, and all that remains unspent of the previous grant made at Coventry shall, by the advice of the lords and officials named and elected to the council by our lord the king in this present parliament, be disbursed and expended in the most advantageous places for the defence of the kingdom and the safeguarding of the sea, and in no other way. . . .[28]

(French) *Ibid.*, III, 568, 572-85.

(E) PARLIAMENT OF 1407

. . . Item, on Wednesday, November 9, the commons came before the king and the lords in parliament, and there Thomas Chaucer, speaker for the said commons, made protestation. . . .[29] To which the chancellor of England replied, saying that with regard to all these matters the same chancellor had already accounted to them in the refectory, the place assigned to the said commons for this proceeding—first orally and then in writing, by means of a schedule presented to the said commons voluntarily by the said lords of the council and at neither the instance nor the request of the said commons, [explaining] how and in what manner the said tenth and fifteenth, as well as the subsidy and the tunnage and poundage, had been spent. . . .

Item, on Friday, December 2, which was the last day of the parliament, the commons came before the king and the lords in parliament and there, by the king's command, a schedule of indemnity was read touching a certain altercation that had arisen between the lords and the commons; and at the command of our same lord the king the same schedule was entered as of record in the roll of parliament. Of which schedule the tenor is as follows:—

It is to be remembered that on Monday, November 21, while our

---

[27] Also tunnage and poundage and the ordinary customs on wool, etc., for one year.

[28] Although recorded toward the beginning of the roll, this grant was made at the end of the session; cf. no. 66B.

[29] In this address, the usual formality, he reminded the king of promised reform in the government, the reconstitution of the council, etc.

sovereign lord the king was in the council chamber within the abbey
of Gloucester, and while the lords spiritual and temporal assembled
for this present parliament were there before him, a conference was
held among them regarding the state of the kingdom and the defence
of the same. . . . And thereupon the aforesaid lords were asked by
way of interrogation what aid would be necessary and [how much]
might suffice in this case. To which demand and question the same
lords severally responded that, in consideration on the one hand of
the king's need and on the other of the poverty of his people, less
aid would not suffice than a tenth and a half [a tenth] from the
cities and boroughs and a fifteenth and a half [a fifteenth] from other
laymen, and besides this an extension of the subsidy from wool,
leather, and wool-fells, and of [tunnage and poundage at] 3s. the tun
and 12d. the pound, from the feast of St. Michael next to the feast
of St. Michael two years hence. Whereupon, by the command of our
said lord the king, word was sent to the commons of this present
parliament to cause a certain number of persons from their member-
ship to appear before our said lord the king and the said lords, in
order to hear and to report to their companions what they might
have by way of command from our said lord the king. And thereupon the said commons sent into the presence of our said lord the
king, and of the said lords, twelve of their members, to whom, at the
command of our same lord the king, the aforesaid question was set
forth, together with the response severally made to it by the lords
aforesaid. Which response, it was the pleasure of our said lord the
king, they should report to the rest of their companions in order
that action might be taken to conform as nearly as possible with
the opinion of the lords aforesaid. When this report had thus been
made to the said commons, they were thereby greatly disturbed, saying and affirming that it was to the great prejudice and derogation of
their liberties. And as soon as our said lord the king had heard this,
desirous that neither at the present time nor in that to come anything
should be done that in any way could be turned against the liberty
of the estate [of the commons], under which they had come to
parliament, or against the liberties of the lords aforesaid, willed,
granted, and declared, by the advice and consent of the same lords,
to the following effect: namely, that in the present parliament and
in all those to come the lords may well confer among themselves in
the king's absence regarding the state of the kingdom and the remedies thereby demanded, and that in the same way the commons on
their part may well confer among themselves with regard to the state
and remedies aforesaid; always provided that neither the lords on
their part nor the commons on their part shall make any report to our
said lord the king of any grant made by the commons and assented
to by the lords, or of the discussions in connection with the said grant,
until the same lords and commons are of one mind and accord in this
matter, and then [the report shall be made] in the manner and form
accustomed, that is to say, by the mouth of the speaker of the said

commons for the time being, so that the said lords and commons may hear the pleasure of our said lord the king. Furthermore, our said lord the king, by the assent of the lords aforesaid, wills that the conference held in this present parliament, as aforesaid, shall not be made a precedent for times to come or be turned to the prejudice or derogation of the liberty of the estate, under which the same commons are now in attendance—neither in this present parliament, nor in any other throughout the future. . . .[30]

(French) *Ibid.*, III, 609-11.

(F) PARLIAMENT OF 1414

Item, it is to be remembered that in this parliament the commons presented to our most sovereign lord the king a petition of which the tenor is word for word as follows:—

Our sovereign lord, your humble and true lieges who have come on behalf of the commons of your land pray your righteousness that— whereas it has ever been their liberty and freedom that no statute or law should be made unless they have thereto given their assent, and in consideration of the fact that the commons of your land, who now are and ever have been a member of your parliament, have the power of assenting as well as of petitioning—from this time forward, on complaint by the commons asking remedy for any mischief either by the mouth of the speaker of the commons or else by written petition, no law shall thereupon be made and engrossed as a statute and a law with either additions or subtractions which in any particular or particulars change the meaning and intent as requested by the mouth of the speaker or the aforesaid petitions drawn up in writing after the manner aforesaid, without the assent of the aforesaid commons. It is to be understood, our sovereign lord, that if the commons either orally or in writing make two or three requests of you, or as many as please them, they have no intention whatsoever but that it shall always be in the freedom of your high regality to grant whichever of them you please and to refuse the rest.

Response: The king grants of his especial grace that, in connection with the petitions of his commons, nothing contrary to their request shall henceforth be enacted, whereby they shall be bound without their assent; saving always to our liege lord his real prerogative to grant and deny what may please him of their petitions and requests aforesaid. . . .

(French and English) *Ibid.,* IV, 22.

67. PARLIAMENT ROLLS OF HENRY VI

(A) PARLIAMENT OF 1422

. . . It is to be remembered that, on the twenty-seventh day of this parliament, in consideration of the tender age of our most honoured lord, King Henry VI after the Conquest—on which account he could

---

[30] A parliamentary grant in the regular form follows.

not for the time being personally see to the protection and defence of his kingdom of England and of the English Church—the same lord king, fully trusting in the wisdom and industry of his dearest uncles, John, duke of Bedford, and Humphrey, duke of Gloucester, by the advice and consent of the lords both spiritual and temporal assembled in the present parliament, and also by the assent of the commons of the English realm assembled in the same, ordained and constituted his said uncle, the duke of Bedford, now absent in foreign parts, as protector and defender of his kingdom and the English Church aforesaid, and as chief councillor of the said lord king; and [he ordered] that the said duke, when he returned to England and came into the king's presence, and for so long a time as he there remained and it was pleasing to our same lord the king, should be and should be styled protector and defender of the same kingdom and chief councillor of the said king. And furthermore the same lord king, by the advice and consent aforesaid, in the absence of his aforesaid uncle, the duke of Bedford, ordained and constituted his aforesaid uncle, the duke of Gloucester, who was then present in his said kingdom of England, as protector and defender of his said kingdom of England and the English Church, and as chief councillor of the said lord king; and [he ordered] that the same duke of Gloucester should be and should be styled protector and defender of the same kingdom of England and the Church aforesaid during the king's pleasure, and besides that letters patent of the said lord king should be drawn up in the form here following. . . .

Now when this act had thus been drawn up and the commission had been secured, and after their contents had been read and recited in the presence of the said lord duke of Gloucester, as well as of the aforesaid lords spiritual and temporal, the same lord duke of Gloucester, having thereupon deliberated, agreed to assume, in so far as pertained to him, the obligation and exercise of such office for the honour of God, for the benefit of the king and the kingdom aforesaid, and at the request of the aforesaid lords; and he then and there did assume it according to the form of the act aforesaid—protesting, nevertheless, that such assumption of his, or consent in this matter, should in no way serve to the prejudice of his aforesaid brother, but that the same brother might freely deliberate and decide for himself whether or not to assume such responsibility. . . .[1]

Be it known that afterwards . . . , on the request of the said commons, and by the advice and consent of all the lords aforesaid, certain persons of rank, both spiritual and temporal, were named and elected as councillors to assist in the government, whose names, written in a small schedule and publicly read in this parliament, here follow: the duke of Gloucester, the archbishop of Canterbury, the bishop of London, the bishop of Winchester, the bishop of Norwich, the

---

[1] Here follows a memorandum limiting the discretionary authority of the protector to minor appointments in church and state; all important offices were to be filled only by the advice of the council.

bishop of Worcester, the duke of Exeter, the earl of March, the earl of Warwick, the earl marshal, the earl of Northumberland, the earl of Westmorland, Lord Fitz-Hugh, Sir Ralph Cromwell, Sir Walter Hungerford, Sir John Tiptoft, Sir Walter Beauchamp.

And be it known also that the same persons, thus named and elected as assistant councillors, after this nomination and election, agreed to accept such assistance in the government in the manner and form set forth in a schedule written in English on paper, containing not only all their names, but also five special articles presented in this same parliament by the same persons named as assistant councillors; of which schedule the tenor is as follows. . . .[2]

(Latin and French) *Ibid.*, IV, 174-76.

(B) PARLIAMENT OF 1427

. . . It is to be remembered that, on March 3 of the present year, the illustrious prince, my lord Humphrey, duke of Gloucester . . . immediately after the opening of the same parliament, among other matters, declared that he, in the absence of the illustrious prince, my lord John, duke of Bedford, his dearest brother, acted as protector and defender of the kingdom of England and chief councillor of the lord king, and that, through the relation of certain persons, he had heard there were diverse opinions concerning his authority and power. The aforesaid duke of Gloucester, therefore desirous of being more fully informed in this matter of his power and authority, particularly urged and requested all the lords spiritual and temporal assembled in the present parliament that they, through the good discretion and advisement of all, would discuss and consider such power and authority of his and with all possible speed give him sure information in that matter, stating that he would absent himself from the chamber of the parliament aforesaid until response should be made to him in this connection. When this declaration and request had been heard . . . , all and singular of the lords spiritual and temporal had a certain response drawn up in writing and put into an indenture, which afterwards . . . was delivered to the aforesaid duke of Gloucester by the venerable father, Henry, archbishop of Canterbury; of which response the tenor follows in these words:—

High and mighty prince, my lord of Gloucester, we, lords spiritual and temporal assembled by command of the king our sovereign lord in this his present parliament, well remember how[3] . . . , in the first

---

[2] These articles specify that the council is to have control of appointments to financial offices and the leasing of wardships, marriage rights, etc. A record is to be kept of the councillors present each day and nothing is to be done without the agreement of at least four of them; a majority is required for important matters. A new election was made in the parliament of the next year and eight additional articles were passed, further defining the necessary procedure of the council.

[3] The address first recites the parliamentary action of 1422; see the previous document.

parliament held at Westminster by our sovereign lord the king who now is, you desired to have the government of this land, affirming that it belonged to you of right, as well by virtue of your birth as by the last will of the late king, your brother—whom God assoil! . . . Whereupon the lords spiritual and temporal then assembled in parliament . . . held great and long deliberation and advisement, sought precedents in the government of the land for similar times and cases when kings of this land had been of tender age, also obtained information concerning the laws of the land from such persons as were notably learned therein, and finally found your said desire unjustified and groundless according to precedent and the law of the land, which the late king during his lifetime could not alter, change, or abrogate by his last will or otherwise without the consent of the three estates ;[4] nor could he commit or grant to any person the government or rule of this land for a longer term than that of his own life. . . . Nevertheless, to preserve peace and tranquillity, and in order to ease and appease you, it was ordained and established by the authority of the king with the assent of the three estates of this land that, in the absence of my lord your brother of Bedford, you should be chief of the king's council; and accordingly a title was devised for you different from that of the other councillors—not the title of tutor, lieutenant, governor, or regent, nor any title that would imply authority of government over the land, but the title of protector and defender, which implies a personal duty of attending to the actual defence of the land, as well against outward enemies, if the case requires, as against inward rebels, should there be any—which God forbid! And therewith you were granted certain power, which is specified and contained in an act of the said parliament, to continue as long as might be the king's pleasure. And if the intent of the said estates had been for you to have more power or authority, more would have been expressed therein. . . .[5] With all our hearts we marvel that, considering the open declaration of the authority and power belonging to my lord of Bedford, to you in his absence, and to the king's council, to which [declaration] both my lord of Bedford aforesaid and you purely and simply subscribed, you should in any way be stirred or moved not to content yourself therewith, or to lay claim to any other. . . . Accordingly, considering the facts and causes aforesaid and many others too long for enumeration, we, the lords aforesaid, pray, exhort, and require you to content yourself with the power set forth and declared above . . . and that you neither desire nor exercise any larger power; giving you, as our answer to your aforesaid demand, that which is above written, and which without variance or change we will keep and abide by. . . .

Item, on March 25, which was the last day of this present parliament, another petition was presented to our lord the king in the said

---

[4] The lords spiritual and temporal and the commons.

[5] The address then relates at length how the duke had agreed to all these earlier arrangements.

parliament by the commons of the same, the tenor of which petition here follows:—

May it please our sovereign lord the king, considering how, in order to obtain suitable remedies, numerous petitions have been introduced and presented to your most noble highness by the commons of this present parliament, and how they have not as yet been settled, to ordain by the advice of the lords spiritual and temporal, and by the consent of the aforesaid commons, that the said petitions may be delivered to the lords of your most wise council, who, calling unto themselves, if need be, the justices and other persons skilled in your law, shall have power through the authority of the said parliament between now and the coming feast of the Nativity of St. John the Baptist to hear and determine the said petitions; and that the latter, thus determined by the advice and consent aforesaid, may be enacted, enrolled, and placed as of record in the roll of your same parliament.

Response: *Le roi le voet.*[6]

Afterwards, that is to say, on June 15 next following, in the presence of divers lords of our lord the king's council[7] . . . assembled in the Star Chamber[8] at Westminster, a number of the said petitions . . . were read and heard; and by virtue of the authority given to the said lords, as aforesaid, they were answered and determined, as is more clearly set forth in the endorsement of the same petitions. . . .

(Latin, French, English) *Ibid.,* IV, 326-34.

(C) PARLIAMENT OF 1429

The commons pray that—whereas one William Larke, servant to William Melrede, attending your present court of parliament for the city of London, through the subtle imagination and conjecture of one Margery Janyns, and while he was then in the service of the said William Melrede, was arrested by the local officers in the court of piepowder[9] belonging to the abbot of Westminster and, at the suit of the said Margery, was thence removed to your [court of] common bench . . . , and by the justices of your said bench was committed to your Fleet Prison and there detained in prison until the present . . . —it may please your royal majesty, considering how the said William Larke was in the service of the said William Melrede at the time of the said arrest and truly supposed that, by the privilege of your court of parliament, he was quit of all arrest during [the session of] your said court except for treason, felony, or surety of the peace, to ordain by the authority of your same parliament that the said

---

[6] The king so wills—the form still used for the royal assent to an act of parliament.

[7] Seven bishops, five lay peers, the justices of both benches, the chief baron and two other barons of the exchequer.

[8] Cf. no. 70G.

[9] A corruption of *pied poudré*, dusty foot. The court was so called because it was held to settle the disputes of those attending a fair.

William Larke shall be liberated from your Fleet Prison, notwithstanding the said condemnation, judgment, and execution, or anything thereby pending against or upon him; saving always to the said Margery and her executors their right to execute the said judgment against the said William Larke after the end of the same parliament. And [the commons pray the king] also to grant, by the aforesaid authority, that none of your said lieges—that is to say, lords, knights of your shires, citizens, or burgesses in your parliaments to come, together with their servants or menials—shall in any way be arrested or detained in prison during the time of your parliaments, except for treason, felony, or surety of the peace, as aforesaid.

Response: The king, by the advice of the lords spiritual and temporal, and at the especial request of the commons assembled in this present parliament, and also with the assent of the counsel of the Margery Janyns named in this petition, wills and grants by the authority of the said parliament that William Larke, named in the said petition, shall for the time being be liberated from Fleet Prison. . . .[10] And as to the remainder of the petition, *le roi s'avisera*.[11]

(French) *Ibid.*, IV, 357-58.

(D) PARLIAMENT OF 1439

. . . Item, by command of the said lord king, a certain schedule or bill was presented and delivered to the commons in words to this effect. . . .[12] To which schedule or bill and the matter therein contained the said commons gave their assent in these words: To this bill the commons have assented. When this schedule or bill and the assent thereto had been read and fully made known before the same lord king in his aforesaid parliament and the lords spiritual and temporal there assembled, the same lord king, having thereon had mature and careful deliberation with the same lords, by the advice and consent of the same lords and commons, on the authority of the aforesaid parliament, granted all and singular of the matters specified and contained in the aforesaid bill or schedule and the assent thereto, and he willed and granted that they should be enacted as of record in the aforesaid parliament. . . .

(Latin and French) *Ibid.*, V, 8-9.

(E) PARLIAMENT OF 1451

. . . Your commons of this present parliament pray that—whereas the false traitor John Cade, who named himself John Mortimer and

---

[10] Details follow with regard to the execution of the judgment after the termination of parliament and the recommitment of Larke to prison.

[11] The king will deliberate—the form that became customary for a royal denial of a petition.

[12] Here follows a formal act in English to provide greater income for the household and so to relieve the people of continued exactions from royal purveyors. Compare this procedure with what had become customary by 1483 (no. 68).

was lately called captain of Kent, on July 8 in the twenty-eighth year of your reign at Southwark in the shire of Surrey, and on July 9 of the year aforesaid at Dartford and Rochester in the shire of Kent, also at Rochester aforesaid and elsewhere on July 10 and 11 next following, within this your noble realm of England falsely and traitorously imagined your death and the destruction and subversion of this your said realm, by gathering and raising a great number of your people and inciting them falsely and traitorously to rise against you in the places aforesaid and at the times aforesaid, contrary to your royalty, crown, and dignity, and then and there made and raised war falsely and traitorously against you and your highness; and whereas, although dead and mischieved, he has not yet been punished by the law of your said land—you consider the premises and warn such traitors against so doing in times to come and, for the salvation of yourself and your said realm, by the advice of your lords spiritual and temporal in this your present parliament assembled and by authority of the said parliament, ordain that he be attainted of these treasons, that by the authority aforesaid he forfeit to you all goods, lands, tenements, rents, and possessions which he had on the said July 8 or thereafter, that his blood be corrupted and disabled forever, and that he be called false traitor within your said realm forevermore.

Response: *Le roi le voet. . . .*

(English) *Ibid.*, V, 224.

(F) PARLIAMENT OF 1455

To the right wise and discreet commons in this present parliament assembled Thomas Young humbly makes this prayer:—[13]

Whereas, having of late been one of the knights for the shire and town of Bristol[14] in divers parliaments held before this time, in his speech at the same [parliaments] he conducted himself as well and faithfully, and with all such true and diligent labour, as in his simplicity he could or might, for the welfare of the king our sovereign lord and of this his noble realm; and whereas, notwithstanding the fact that, by the ancient liberty and freedom held, enjoyed, and prescribed by the commons of this land from time out of mind, all such persons as for the moment are assembled for the same commons in any parliament ought to have their freedom to speak and say in the house of their assembly whatever they think convenient or reasonable without in any way incurring any sort of challenge, charge, or punishment, nevertheless, through false and sinister reports made to the king's highness concerning him, your said petitioner, on account of matters presented by him in the house customarily used by the

---

[13] Recorded among the petitions of the commons and endorsed: "To be presented to the lords."

[14] Bristol and the environs had been created a separate county in 1373; since then its two representatives had been ranked as knights of the shire. Cf. no. 72B.

commons in the said parliament, was taken, arrested, and rigorously
and publicly led to the Tower of London, where, contrary to the said
liberty and freedom, he was grievously and in great duress imprisoned
for a long time, and was put in great fear of unbearable punishment
of his body and in dread of the loss of his life, without any indictment, presentment, appeal, due original, accusation, or lawful cause
held or sworn against him . . . , whereby he not only suffered great
hurt, pain, and discomfort of body, but was . . . put to excessive loss
and expense of goods amounting to the sum of 1000m. and much
more: [therefore] may it please you in your great wisdom to give
sympathetic consideration to the premises and thereupon to pray the
king our sovereign lord that his highness and most noble grace will be
pleased to grant and provide, by the advice of the lords spiritual and
temporal in this present parliament, that for the said losses, costs,
damages, and imprisonment your said petitioner shall have sufficient
and reasonable compensation, as is required by good faith, truth, and
conscience.

Response: The king wills that the lords of his council shall act and
provide for the said petitioner in this matter as at their discretion they
shall think convenient and reasonable.

(French and English) Ibid., V, 337.

68. PARLIAMENT ROLL OF RICHARD III (1483)

. . . It is to be remembered that a certain bill was presented before
the lord king in the aforesaid parliament to this effect.[1] . . . Which
bill was taken to the commons of the realm of England assembled in
the said parliament, and to it the same commons gave their assent in
these words: To this bill the commons have assented. When this bill
and the assent thereto had been read, heard, and fully made known
before the king in the aforesaid parliament, by assent of the lords
spiritual and temporal likewise assembled in the said parliament, and
of the commons aforesaid, and by the authority of the same parliament, it was pronounced, decreed, and declared that all and singular
of the contents of the aforesaid bill were true and undoubted; and
the same lord king, by the assent of the said three estates of the
realm, and by the authority aforesaid, granted all and singular of the
premises contained in the aforesaid bill, pronouncing, decreeing, and
declaring them all to be true and undoubted. . . .

Item, a certain petition with a certain schedule attached to it was
presented to the same lord king in the said parliament by Henry
Percy, now earl of Northumberland, in these words.[2] . . . When this
petition and this schedule had been read, heard, and fully made known
in the aforesaid parliament, by the advice and consent of the lords

---

[1] A recapitulation of the king's title and settlement of the crown on him
and his heirs. The same procedure was used for an act of resumption, an act
of attainder against all his enemies, and others.

[2] The extract is typical of numerous private petitions introduced in this
same parliament.

spiritual and temporal, and of the commons of the realm of England assembled in the same parliament, answer was made to them in these words: Let it be done as is desired. . . .

Item, a certain other petition was presented to the aforesaid lord king in the said parliament by the commons of the realm of England on behalf of the inhabitants of the town of Croyland in Lincolnshire, to the following purport.[3] . . . When this petition had been read, heard, and fully made known in the aforesaid parliament, by the assent of the lords spiritual and temporal, and of the aforesaid commons assembled in the said parliament, and by the authority of the same persons, answer was made to it in the following form: *Le roi le voet.* . . .

It is to be remembered that the commons of the realm of England assembled in the present parliament appeared before the lord king in the full parliament aforesaid on February 20 of the aforesaid year— that is to say, on the last day of the present parliament—and declared through William Catesby, their speaker, that they, by the assent of the lords spiritual and temporal assembled in the parliament aforesaid, granted to the aforesaid lord king certain subsidies, to be levied from both natives and aliens according to the form specified in a certain indenture drawn up in that connection, the contents of which were then and there exhibited to the same lord king. The tenor of which indenture follows in these words. . . .[4]

Response: Our lord the king, thanking his commons for their kindness in making the aforesaid grants, has accepted those grants and has conceded everything specified in the aforesaid indenture, with the provisions here following. . . .[5]

(Latin, French, English) *Ibid.,* VI, 238-63.

---

[3] This is the form used for the commons' petitions, of which some fifteen are entered in the statute roll of Richard III; e.g., no. 69H.

[4] A formal grant of tunnage and poundage and of customs on wool, woolfells, and hides for the king's lifetime, but with many restrictions set forth in great detail.

[5] Clauses saving the privileges in England of the German Hansa and of the merchants from Spain.

69. STATUTES (1399-1483)

(A) 1 HENRY IV: RESTRICTION OF APPEALS (1399)

14. Item, on account of the many great inconveniences and mischiefs that have occurred in consequence of the numerous appeals[1] heretofore made in the kingdom of England, it is ordained and established that henceforth all appeals for acts accomplished within the kingdom shall be tried and determined according to the good laws of the kingdom made and used in the time of the most noble progenitors of our said lord the king; and that all appeals for acts accomplished outside the kingdom shall be tried and terminated before the constable and marshal of England for the time being. And besides it is granted

---

[1] That is to say, for felony and treason; cf. no. 63G.

and agreed that henceforth no appeals shall in any way or at any
time be made or pursued in parliament. . . .

(French) Statutes of the Realm, II, 116.

(B) 3 HENRY IV: FOR THE BURNING OF HERETICS (1401)

15. . . . With regard to which innovations and excesses,[2] set forth
above, the prelates and clergy aforesaid, and also the commons of the
said realm assembled in the same parliament, prayed the said lord
king that his royal highness would in the said parliament deign to
make provision for a suitable remedy. The same lord king then . . . ,
by the assent of the magnates and other nobles of the said realm assembled in parliament, has granted, ordained, and established . . .
that no one within the said kingdom or the other dominions subject
to his royal majesty shall presume to preach in public or in secret
without having first sought and obtained the licence of the local diocesan,[3] always excepting curates in their own churches, persons who
have hitherto enjoyed the privilege, and others to whom it has been
granted by canon law; and that henceforth no one either openly or
secretly shall preach, hold, teach, or impart anything, or compose or
write any book, contrary to the catholic faith or the decisions of Holy
Church, or anywhere hold conventicles or in any way have or maintain schools for such a sect and its nefarious doctrines and opinions;
and also that in the future no one shall favour anybody who thus
preaches, holds such or similar conventicles, has or maintains such
schools, composes or writes such a book, or in any such fashion
teaches, instructs, or excites the people.[4] . . . And if any person
within the said kingdom and dominions is formally convicted before
the local diocesan or his commissioners of the said nefarious preachings, doctrines, opinions, [holding of] schools, and heretical and erroneous instruction, or any of them, and if he refuses properly to abjure
the same . . . , or, after abjuration has been made by the same person, he is declared by the local diocesan or his commissioners to have
relapsed, so that according to the sacred canons he ought to be re-
linquished to the secular court . . . , then the sheriff of the local
county and the mayor and sheriffs or sheriff, or the mayor and bailiffs
of the city, town, or borough of the same county nearest the said diocesan or his said commissioners . . . , shall, after the pronouncement
of such sentences, receive those persons and every one of them and
shall have them burned before the people in some prominent place,
so that such punishment shall inspire fear in the minds of others and
prevent such nefarious doctrines and heretical and erroneous opinions,

---

[2] Of the Lollards, "a certain new sect," accused in the long preamble of holding
damnable opinions concerning the sacraments and the authority of the Church
and of doing all the things which the statute proceeds to forbid.

[3] That is to say, the bishop.

[4] Such persons are to be subjected to canonical trial in the episcopal court
and, if convicted, to imprisonment in ecclesiastical prison as well as to royal
fine.

or their authors and protagonists in the said kingdom and dominions, from being supported or in any way tolerated against the catholic faith, the Christian religion, and the decisions of Holy Church—which God forbid! And in all and singular of the aforesaid matters regarding the said ordinance and statute, the sheriffs, mayors, and bailiffs of the counties, cities, towns, and boroughs aforesaid are to be attentive, helpful, and favourable to the said diocesans and their commissioners. . . .

(Latin) *Ibid.*, II, 126-28.

(C) 7 HENRY IV: ON SUCCESSION TO THE THRONE AND ELECTIONS TO PARLIAMENT (1406)

2. Item, it is ordained and established in the said parliament at the request and by the assent of the said lords and commons that the inheritance of the crown and of the kingdoms of England and France and of all the other dominions of our said lord the king beyond the sea, together with all their appurtenances, shall be settled upon and shall remain with the person of our same lord the king and the heirs of his body. And at the request and by the assent aforesaid it is especially ordained, established, pronounced, decreed, and declared that my lord Prince Henry, eldest son of our said Lord the king, is to be heir apparent of our same lord the king to succeed him in [the possession of] the aforesaid crown, kingdoms, and dominions, and, after the death of our said lord the king, to have them with all their appurtenances for himself and the heirs of his body. And if he dies without heir of his body, then the aforesaid crown, kingdoms, and dominions, together with their appurtenances, shall all remain to my lord Thomas, second son of our said lord the king, and to the heirs of his body. And if he dies without heir of his body, then the aforesaid crown, kingdoms, and dominions, together with their appurtenances, shall all remain to my lord John, third son of our same lord the king, and the heirs of his body. And if he dies without heir of his body, then the aforesaid crown, kingdoms, and dominions, together with their appurtenances, shall all remain to my lord Humphrey, fourth son of our said lord the king, and to the heirs of his body. . . .

15. Item, on the grievous complaint of the commons regarding improper election to parliament of knights of the shires, which, to the great scandal of the counties and to the retardation of the business of the community in the said courts, is sometimes made through the favouritism of the sheriffs or in other ways contrary to the writs directed to the said sheriffs, our sovereign lord the king, wishing to provide a remedy for these [abuses], by the assent of the lords spiritual and temporal and of all the commons in this present parliament, has ordained and established that henceforth elections of such knights shall be carried out according to the form that follows. That is to say, at the next county [court] to be held after the delivery of the writ for [elections to] parliament, proclamation shall be made in the full county [court] of the day and the place of the parliament;

and all who are there present, as well suitors duly summoned for this purpose as others, shall attend to the election of their knights for the parliament, then freely and impartially proceeding with that election, any command or request to the contrary notwithstanding. And after the election has been held, whether the persons elected are present or absent, their names are to be written in an indenture under the seals of all who elected them, and [this indenture is to be] attached to the said writ for parliament. Which indenture, thus sealed and attached, shall be kept [by the sheriff] for return of the said writ when it comes to [certifying] the knights of the shire.[5] . . .

(French) *Ibid.,* II, 151-56.

(D) 1 HENRY V: ON ELECTIONS TO PARLIAMENT (1413)

First, that the statutes made concerning the election of knights of the shires to attend parliament shall be held and kept in all particulars, with the addition that henceforth in each county no knights of the shire shall be elected unless, on the date of the writ of summons to parliament, they are resident within the county where they are thus to be elected; and that the knights, squires, and others who are to be electors of such knights of the shires shall also be residents within the same counties in the manner and form aforesaid. And it is furthermore ordained and established that men, citizens, and burgesses resident, domiciled, and enfranchised in the same cities and boroughs are to be elected as citizens and burgesses of cities and boroughs [to attend parliament], and by no means any others. . . .

(French) *Ibid.,* II, 170.

(E) 8 HENRY VI: ON ELECTIONS TO PARLIAMENT (1429)

7. Item, whereas in many counties the elections of knights of the shires, those chosen to attend the king's parliaments, have of late been carried out by too great and excessive a number of people dwelling within those same counties, of whom the larger part have been people of little substance or of no worth, each pretending to have the same voice in such elections as the most worthy knights or squires dwelling in the same counties, whereby homicides, riots, assaults, and feuds are very likely to arise among the gentlefolk and other people of the same counties unless a suitable remedy is provided in this connection: [therefore] our lord the king, considering the premises, has provided and ordained by the authority of this parliament that knights of the shires, elected to attend parliaments hereafter to be held in the kingdom of England, shall be chosen in each county by persons dwelling and resident therein, each of whom shall have a freehold to the value of at least 40s. a year beyond the charges [on the estate][6] . . . ;

---

[5] Cf. no. 72D.

[6] That is to say, clear annual income. The act then repeats the requirement of the preceding statutes, that knights of the shire must be resident in the county and that the sheriff must make returns by indenture.

and that every sheriff of England shall, by the aforesaid authority, have power to examine on the Holy Gospels each such elector, [to determine] how much he is able to spend annually.[7] . . .

(French) Ibid., II, 243 f.

(F) 23 HENRY VI: ON ELECTIONS TO PARLIAMENT (1445)

14. Item, . . .[8] the king, considering the premises, has ordained by the aforesaid authority that the said statutes shall be duly kept and observed in all particulars; and furthermore that each sheriff, after the delivery to him of every such writ [for elections to parliament], shall without fraud draw up and deliver a sufficient precept under his seal to each mayor and bailiff, or to the bailiffs or bailiff where there is no mayor, of the cities and boroughs within his county, reciting the same writ and commanding them by the same precept to have two citizens elected to attend parliament by the citizens of the same city, in case it is a city, or [two] burgesses in the same way, in case it is a borough[9] . . . ; and that the knights of the shires henceforth to be elected to parliament shall be notable knights of the same counties from which they are elected, or else such notable squires of those counties, gentlemen by birth, as are able to be knights;[10] and that no man who is of the rank of valet or lower is to be such knight [of the shire]. . . .

(French) Ibid., II, 340-42.

(G) 1 EDWARD IV: VALIDATION OF LANCASTRIAN ACTS (1461)

. . . First—for the avoidance of ambiguities, doubts, and differences of opinion that might arise, ensue, or be entertained concerning the judicial acts . . . made or secured in the time of Henry IV, of his son Henry V, and of his son Henry VI, recently in succession *de facto* and not rightful kings of England, or any of them—our said lord the king, by the advice and consent of the lords spiritual and temporal, and at the special request of the said commons in the said parliament assembled, and by the authority of the same, has declared, established, and enacted in the same parliament that all fines and final concords[11] levied or made concerning any lands, tenements, possessions, rents,

---

[7] Enforcement is provided through the justices of assize, with a penalty of £100 on the sheriff for a false return.

[8] A long preamble recites the statutes of 1413 and 1429, enumerating their defects and the misdeeds of the sheriffs.

[9] The mayors and bailiffs are to make return by indenture to the sheriff; the latter is to make similar return to the king. Heavy penalties are provided for infraction of the law; also new legal remedies for persons aggrieved in fraudulent elections.

[10] That is to say, persons having the requisite income; distraint of knighthood (see no. 50A) had by now pretty well lapsed.

[11] Sums of money paid in the king's courts in order to secure legal records of agreements.

inheritances, or other things, and all judicial acts, recoveries, and processes . . . made or secured in any court or courts of record . . . during the pretended reign of any of the said recent kings *de facto* and not of right[12] . . . shall have the same force, validity, and effect as if the said fines, final concords, acts, recoveries, processes, and other premises . . . were begun, sued, had, or determined in the time of any king lawfully reigning in this kingdom and obtaining the crown of the same by just title. And [it is ordained] also that all letters patent made by any of the pretended kings to any person or persons for the creation, appointment, or promotion of any of them to any estate, dignity, or pre-eminence shall have, for the said person or persons or for such of their heirs as are specified in the said letters patent, the same force, validity, and effect with regard to such creation, appointment, or promotion as if the same letters patent had been made or granted to any of them by any king lawfully reigning in this kingdom and obtaining the crown of the same by just title; and that persons thus created, appointed, or promoted shall have from the king new grants of annuities for the support of their estates as has been anciently accustomed; always excepting the persons, and each of them, whom our said lord the king considers and holds as rebels or enemies. . . .

(French) *Ibid.,* II, 380 f.

(H) 1 RICHARD III: ABOLITION OF BENEVOLENCES (1483)

. . . Item, our lord the king, remembering how the commons of this his realm, through new and unlawful inventions and inordinate avarice, against the law of the realm have been subjected to great servitude and unbearable charges and exactions, and especially so through a new imposition called benevolence, whereby in divers years the subjects and commons of this land have, against their will and freedom, paid great sums of money to their almost complete ruin— for many and divers honourable men of this realm were on that account compelled of necessity to break up their households and to live in great penury and wretchedness, with their debts unpaid and their children unpreferred, and such memorials as they had ordered for their souls' health were set at naught, to the great displeasure of God and the destruction of this realm—therefore wills and ordains by the advice and consent of his said lords and commons in the said parliament assembled, and by the authority of the same, that henceforth his subjects and the commonalty of this his realm shall in no way be burdened with any such charge or imposition called benevolence, or anything like it; and that such exactions called benevolences as before this time have been taken shall not be held as a precedent for placing such or similar charges upon any of his said subjects of this realm in the future, but that they are to be condemned and annulled forever.

(French) *Ibid.,* II, 478.

---

[12] Judicial acts in parliament are excepted from the force of this statute.

70. RECORDS OF THE PRIVY COUNCIL

(A) Petition and Judgment (1401)

To the most wise council of our lord the king his poor chaplain, Nicholas Hogonona of the land of Ireland, humbly prays [as follows] :—

Since, by reason of certain vows that he had made, he recently decided to go on a pilgrimage to the court of Rome, he so came into England; and when he had come to Oxford, he took as companion an Austin friar, to whom he gave 40*d.* and expenses to conduct him to London; and he also delivered to the said friar 40*d.* to keep [for him]. And when they had come to London, the said poor chaplain asked for the delivery of his said money, and would have sued for his writ of passage;[1] but in the meantime the said friar went to certain people of London and made a false allegation, stating that he was a "wild Irishman"[2] and an enemy to our said lord the king—and this with the intent of having his said money and his book called a *porthous*,[3] which is still retained [by the said friar], together with part of his money. On account of which statement he was taken and committed to prison, and is there detained in great duress, trouble, and discomfort, although he is a loyal man and a supporter of our said lord the king, as he can well prove if he may come to answer [for himself]. [Accordingly] may it please the said most wise council to grant and command that the said poor chaplain may come before you to give answer to all that any one shall wish to charge against him; and afterwards [may it please you] to ordain concerning his liberation as in your wise discretion may seem demanded by reason and good faith, for the sake of God and as a work of charity.

[Endorsed:] August 25 of the second year, etc. It was agreed by the council—attended by my lords the chancellor, the bishops of Durham, Hereford, and Bangor, the earl of Northumberland, the treasurer, and Master John Prophet—that a writ should be issued to the sheriffs of London for the release from prison of the petitioner in the record, if he is therein detained for the cause here stated and for no other.

(French) Leadam and Baldwin, *Select Cases before the Council,* pp. 85 f.

(B) Minutes of December 8, 1406[4]

On December 8 of the eighth year, etc., in the afternoon, assembled in council at Westminster my lord the honorable Prince [Henry] and my lords the archbishop of Canterbury, the bishop of Durham, chancellor, the duke of York, and the earl of Somerset; also the

---

[1] The license to cross the sea required of ordinary travellers.

[2] Such persons, as distinguished from law-abiding subjects of the king, had been excluded from England by act of parliament.

[3] A portable breviary.

[4] Cf. no. 66D.

treasurer, and the steward, chamberlain, and treasurer of the household—where they had certain ordinances drawn up.

And in the first place, with regard to the good government of our lord the king's household, it seemed to the council most expedient that good and loyal officers should be placed and ordained in the said household; and especially that there should be a good comptroller, and for that [office] were named Sir Thomas Bromflete and Sir Arnold Savage, one of whom, if it pleased the king, should be comptroller. And since the said council lacked advice for the nomination of other fit persons to be appointed to other offices in the said household according as there might be need for them, the said steward and treasurer were requested to advise them of such fit persons, whose names could be presented to our said lord the king and his said council.

Item, [it was decided] that provision should be made of a certain sum appropriate for the expenses of the said household against the approaching feast of Christmas.

Item, it seemed necessary that, after the said feast, the king should be pleased to withdraw to some convenient place where, by the advice and deliberation of himself and his council and his officials, such moderate government could be ordained for the said household as should henceforth continue to the pleasure of God and of the people.

(French) Nicolas, *Proceedings of the Privy Council,* I, 295 f.

(C) MINUTES OF AUGUST 18, 1409

Matters to be considered by the council: First, regarding the response to be given to the messages from Prussia.[5]

Item, regarding the conference to be held with the king of Castile and the sending of commissioners and deputies on the part of our lord the king to the said conference; also the estates of the great commissioners, etc.—that is to say, a bishop, a baron, a knight, and a clerk, if it please the king.

Item, regarding the land of Ireland.

Item, regarding my lord John, son of the king, and the state of the east march against Scotland.

Item, regarding the truces lately established between our lord the king and the Scots.

Item, regarding the regions of Guienne.

Item, regarding the steward of Guienne.

Item, regarding the dispute between the said steward and the man of La Motte.

Item, regarding Master John Bordin in connection with his office as lieutenant of the constable of Bordeaux and as chancellor of the regions of Guienne.

Item, regarding the Sire de Barde, whose petition has been granted by the advice of the council.

---

[5] Having to do with prises unjustly taken from Prussian merchants—as appears from subsequent minutes.

Item, regarding William Brewer, captain of Trawe Castle.

Item, regarding the finding of proper security by the Scot, Richard Maughlyn, who desires to be English; to whom the king has granted for this purpose 20*m.* a year, to be taken from the issues of the county of York, in case he will agree to it.

Item, regarding charters of pardon for murder.

(French) *Ibid.,* I, 319 f.

(D) MEMORANDUM OF MAY 6, 1421[6]

Sum of all the custom, subsidy, and revenue aforesaid, £55,743. 10*s.* 10*d.* ; out of which [the following expenditures must be made] for annual upkeep, to wit :—

For guarding the kingdom of England, annually 8000*m.*

Item, for Calais and the march of the same in wartime, £19,119. 5*s.* 10*d.*

Item, for guarding the east march and the west march of Scotland, together with Roxburgh Castle in wartime, £19,500.

Item, for guarding the land of Ireland, 2500*m.*

Item, for guarding Fronsac Castle, 1000*m.*

Item, for the fees of the treasurer, the keeper of the privy seal, the justices of both benches, the barons of the exchequer, and other officials of the king's court, £3002. 17*s.* 6*d.*

Item, to the collectors and comptrollers of the king's customs and subsidies in the various ports of England, for their annual rewards enjoyed by virtue of their offices and received at the exchequer, £547.

Item, to divers dukes, earls, knights, and squires, to the abbess of Shene, and to divers other persons for their annuities enjoyed yearly and received at the exchequer, £772. 12*s.* 7½*d.*

Item, to divers persons for their annuities yearly enjoyed from divers customs in the various ports of England, £4374. 4*s.* 3*d.*

Item, for the fees of the collectors and comptrollers of customs in the various ports of England yearly allocated to them at the exchequer on account of their offices, £274. 3*s.* 4*d.*

Sum of the total annual obligation, £52,235. 16*s.* 10½*d.* And so the sum of the aforesaid income exceeds the aforesaid obligation [by] £3700. 13*s.* 11¾*d.* From which amount provision must be made [for the following needs] to wit :—

For the chamber of the king and the queen.

Item, for the household of the king and the queen.

Item, for the wardrobe of the king and the queen.

Item, for the king's works.

Item, for the construction of a new tower at Portsmouth.

Item, for the office of clerk of the king's ships.

Item, for keeping the king's lions and the fee of the constable of the Tower of London.

---

[6] Submitted on this date to the king and his council. Only a fragment remains of the itemized statement of receipts.

Item, for artillery and divers other matters ordained for the king's wars.

Item, for the custody and support of the king's prisoners.

Item, for the king's embassies.

Item, for divers messengers, parchments, and other expenses and necessities.

Item, for the expenses of the duchess of Holland.

And no provision has as yet been made [for the following matters], to wit:—

For the old debts of the city of Harfleur.

Item, for the old debts of the city of Calais.

Item, for the old debts of the king's wardrobe.

Item, for the old debts of the king's household.

Item, for the old debts pertaining to the office of clerk of the king's ships.

Item, for the old debts pertaining to the office of clerk of the king's works.

Item, for arrears of annual fees.

Item, for executing the will of King Henry IV with regard to the debts of the same king.

Item, for the debts of the king while he was prince.

(French) *Ibid.,* II, 312 f.

(E) MINUTES, MARCH TO JUNE, 1422

On March 9 in the ninth year, it was advised and agreed by the council that the keeper of the king's great wardrobe[7] should provide for the clothing of all those crossing with the lady queen to the king in the parts of France. . . .

Memorandum that, on March 1 in the ninth year of our sovereign lord Henry V after the Conquest, Ralph, son of Nicholas of Langford, knight, set forth to the lords of the council of our said lord the king how Margaret of Langford . . . , mother of the said Ralph, had, as well by indenture as otherwise, given and delivered to the prior of Gisburn divers things, goods, and jewels to keep for the use and profit of the said Ralph; which prior was unwilling to deliver the said things, goods, and jewels to the said Ralph, according to his allegation; wherefore he prayed the said lords for remedy.[8] . . .

On March 30 in the tenth year,[9] it was agreed by the council that the persons designated below should have, in the name of reward for their crossing to France with the lady queen, the following sums: namely, Lady Margaret of Roos, 100*m.*; Elizabeth Fitz-Hugh, £20; Catherine Chideok, 40*m.* And on the same day £10 were also granted to Friar Walden, newly elected confessor, for his crossing to the king.

---

[7] See above, p. 171, n. 8.

[8] The prior was summoned to appear before the council and to bring with him the articles in question. He did so through an attorney. The articles were delivered to Ralph in return for his copy of the indenture.

[9] Henry V's regnal year ended on March 20, the day of his father's death.

On May 6 in the tenth year, the lord of Willoughby, [appearing] in person before the lords of the council at Westminster, promised that, by indenture between the king and himself, he would retain for a year's service thirty men-at-arms with the usual quota of archers, that is to say, three to the lance. . . .

On the same day Robert Scot, esquire, undertook to be lieutenant keeper of the Tower of London and of all the prisoners therein contained, for the faithful performance of which [duty] he was personally sworn on holy things at Westminster, and the aforesaid custody was straitly committed to him. . . .

On May 16, in the presence of the lords at Westminster, certain dies (*ferra*) for making the king's coinage in his town of Calais were delivered to a certain William Latchford, servant of Richard Buckland, the treasurer of Calais: namely, one die for the gold noble, another for the half-noble, and another for the gold farthing, as well as a die for coining the silver groat, another for the half-groat, another for the penny, another for the halfpenny, and another for the silver farthing—[placed] in divers sealed bags, which in the same place the same [William] promised to convey with all possible haste to the said town of Calais.

On May 17 it was agreed by the lords that the seigneur de Gaucourt should be transferred to Pontefract Castle . . . in the custody of Robert of Waterton, esquire.

Item, on the same day it was ordained that John Mortimer, knight, should be committed to the king's castle of Pevensey in the custody of John Pelham, knight. . . .

On May 25, in the presence of the lord [duke] of Gloucester and the other lords at Westminster, John, bishop of Hereford, took the oath of fealty that he owed to the king. . . .

On May 28 in the tenth year, in the case [pending] before the lords between John Middlemore, plaintiff, and Richard Clodeshalle, defendant, concerning the manor of Edgebaston with its appurtenances in the county of Warwick . . . , the aforesaid parties were dismissed by the lords to prosecute [their case] at common law if they saw fit.[10]

On the same day the case between the mayor and community of the city of York, plaintiffs, and the lord archbishop of York, defendant, was continued *in statu quo* until the quinzime of Michaelmas next. . . .

On June 29, in the aforesaid year, it seemed to all the lords, being individually examined and making individual responses with regard to the fine that should be paid to the king by Lady Clarence for the demesne of Holderness, once belonging to the lord duke of Clarence,

---

[10] This agreement was reached after the defendant, a tenant of the duke of Bedford, had promised not to allege the king's special protection or to make any other "frivolous or exorbitant" claim by which the case should be excluded from the ordinary courts.

her husband, that one year's income from the said demesne would be
sufficient as fine therefrom to be paid by the said Lady Clarence.

On June 30 William Wynart presented before the lords an indenture with an attached schedule, containing the names of the king's
prisoners taken in the market of Meaux in France and sent by the
king . . . to England for safekeeping there—who, according to what
is stated in the said indenture . . . , are to the number of 151. . . .

(Latin and French) *Ibid.*, II, 328-35.

(F) MINUTES OF NOVEMBER 12. 1437

November 12 in the sixteenth year, etc., in the presence of the king
at the hospital of St. John near Clerkenwell, [the following persons]
being in attendance: the lord duke of Gloucester, the lord cardinal
[Beaufort], the archbishop of York; the bishops of London, Lincoln,
Salisbury, Norwich, and Worcester; the earls of Huntingdon, Stafford, Northumberland, Salisbury, and Suffolk; the lords of Hungerford, Tiptoft, and Fanhope; the chancellor, the treasurer, the keeper
of the privy seal, and William Philip, knight.

[It is agreed that] they who were of the council before are to be
of the council now; [and that the following men are] also to be of
the council: the bishop of St. David's, the earl of Salisbury, the keeper
of the wardrobe, Sir John Stourton. And the king wills that the
present councillors of the king are to have such power as King Henry
IV gave to his councillors, according to a schedule passed in parliament during the time of the same king, which [schedule] was read
there [in the council]. . . .[11]

The keeper of the privy seal and others have sworn and given
their faith to the king, to counsel him well and truly in such matters
as shall come before them by way of the king's council, to keep secret
the king's counsel, and in short to counsel and do all that good councillors should counsel and do for the king their sovereign lord. . . .[12]

(French and English) *Ibid.*, V, 71 f.

(G) JUDGMENT IN THE STAR CHAMBER[13] (1482)

In the Star Chamber at Westminster, on May 2 in the twenty-
second year of the reign of our sovereign lord King Edward IV—
being present my lords the archbishop of York, chancellor of England; the bishops of Lincoln, [lord] privy seal, and of Worcester,
Norwich, Durham, and Llandaff; the earl Rivers; the lords Dudley,
Ferrers, and Beauchamp; Sirs Thomas Burgh, William Parr, Thomas
Vaughan, and Thomas Grey, knights—the judgment and decree
earlier rendered by the lords of our said sovereign lord's council for
the cause of Richard Whele, otherwise called Richard Pierson . . .

---

[11] Cf. no. 66D. This act, at least in theory, marked the resumption of personal
government by the king; see Baldwin, *The King's Council*, pp. 184 f.

[12] Cf. no. 53.

[13] Cf. no. 67B, last paragraph.

against John Fortescue, esquire, . . . was openly read in full and plenary council. . . . The said John Fortescue alleges and says that the said Richard is a Scot born and is under allegiance to the king of Scots, and as such [the said John] has taken him and holds him prisoner. The said Richard [denies this], evidently proving the contrary, that he is an Englishman born and no Scot. . . .[14] And after each of the said parties . . . had at divers times been diligently heard in all that they could or would allege and say in their behalf, it appeared to the lords of the said council that the said Richard Whele, otherwise called Pierson, is and was an Englishman born and no Scot. . . . And therefore it is considered, adjudged, and decreed by the same lords that the same Richard is so to be held, taken, and reputed among all the king's liege people and subjects; he is to be regarded and treated in all places as the king's liegeman and not otherwise; and he is to be wholly free to do whatever he thinks good for a king's subject to do, without trouble, let, or impeachment. And the said John Fortescue is to be commanded, and was so commanded, to perpetual silence in respect to any further . . . vexation of the said Richard in any way and at any time to come for the cause alleged above. . . .

(English) Leadam and Baldwin, *Select Cases before the Council*, pp. 117 f.

[14] The case had been argued at length in the Star Chamber on the previous November 21.

71. CASES IN CHANCERY

(A) Petition for General Relief (1399)

To the most reverend father in God and most gracious lord, the bishop of Exeter, chancellor of England, Simon Hilgay, parson of the church of Hilgay, humbly makes petition [as follows]:—

Whereas he has charge and cure of souls in the same parish and is menaced by one Robert of Wesnam and by . . . ,[1] associates and confederates of the same Robert, who daily menace him to the extent that, through fear of unmerited death, he does not dare to approach the said parsonage to hear the confessions of his parishioners in this most holy time of Lent . . . ; and whereas, furthermore, the said Robert of Wesnam, with so many miscreants for associates and confederates, has such horrid maintenance that the said petitioner will never be able at common law to secure recovery against him and the rest without your most gracious aid: [therefore] may it please your most gracious lordship to consider the aforesaid matter and therein, at your most wise discretion, to provide remedy for the said petitioner —for the sake of God and as a work of charity.

[Endorsed:] By virtue of this petition the herein named Simon Hilgay, parson of the church of Hilgay, obtains four writs directed to the herein named persons, [summoning them] to appear before the said king and his council in his chancery on Tuesday next after

[1] Six other persons named.

the coming feast of St. Gregory, to make answer regarding the content [of the said petition].

(Latin and French) Baildon, Select Cases in Chancery, pp. 44 f.

(B) Petition for Injunction

To the most reverend father in God and most gracious lord, the bishop of Exeter, chancellor of England, Esmond Francis, grocer and citizen of London, humbly makes petition [as follows] :—

Whereas, on account of a certain debt owed to him . . . , the said Esmond for the past two years has been executor over certain lands and tenements within the parish of Madesden in the county of Gloucester, once belonging to John Madesden, dyer of London, of which lands and tenements, according to the requirement of the common law, he had livery by the king's writ; and whereas it now happens that, through the maintenance and conspiracy of James Clifford and Hugh Bisley of the same county, no man or farmer of the said county . . . dares to occupy or administer the said lands and tenements for the use and profit of the said Esmond: [therefore] may it please your most noble and gracious lordship to grant a writ of our lord the king directed to the sheriff of the said county and to the justices of the peace in the same locality, instructing them, on behalf of our said lord the king, to charge and command the same James and Hugh, on peril of the consequences, to permit the said Esmond and his servants and farmers to occupy and administer the said lands and tenements thus delivered to him by the law, without any interference or disturbance by the said James and Hugh; so that the said Esmond may have his profit from the said lands ahd tenements as awarded to him under the law—for the sake of God and as a work of charity.

(French) Ibid., pp. 68 f.

(C) Petition with Regard to a Trust

To the chancellor of England John Horsemonger humbly makes petition as follows:—

Whereas one John Peckham enfeoffed, among others, Reginald Pympe and Walter Judde with certain lands and tenements in the county of Kent on certain conditions, among which was contained the wish of the said John Peckham that, when the said lands were sold, he who was next of blood to the said John Peckham, and to whom the inheritance of the lands and tenements would have descended, was to have £40 to relieve his estate; [and whereas] the said lands and tenements have now been sold by the said feoffees for 500m., which sum the said Reginald has in his own possession, and, although the said petitioner, as kinsman and heir of the said John Peckham . . . , has often requested the said Reginald to pay and deliver to him the said £40 according to the wish of the said John Peckham, [the said Reginald] is nevertheless unwilling to pay him a penny of it, to the great damage of the said petitioner: [therefore] may it please your most gracious lordship, for the honour of God and the cause of righteousness, to grant writs summoning the said Walter and Reginald to appear before you in the king's chancery, which is a court of conscience, there to make answer in this matter, as is demanded by reason and conscience; otherwise the said petitioner is and shall be without remedy—which God forbid!

(French) *Ibid.*, pp. 120 f.

(D) PETITION AND JUDGMENT REGARDING A MORTGAGE (1456)

To the right reverend and worshipful father in God, the archbishop of Canterbury, chancellor of England, Robert Bodenham humbly makes petition [as follows] :—

Whereas he lately borrowed £80 from John Hall of Salisbury, for which [sum] the said John, through subtle promises, caused the said Robert, on May 1 in the thirty-third year of the reign of our sovereign lord the present king,[2] trustingly to enfeoff the said John with the manor of Shipton-Bellinger in the shire of Suffolk, to have and to hold for the said John and his heirs and assigns, on condition that, if the said Robert or his heirs or executors would pay to the said John or his assigns £100 at the feast of St. John the Baptist in the year of our lord 1461, the said feoffment should then be void,[3] as plainly appears from an indentured deed made in that connection, so that the said John thereby intends to receive and have the issues of the said manor until the said day of payment, which will amount to the sum of 85*m.*, and also £100 by way of usury for the loan of the said £80, or else the said manor is to be lost and forfeited [by the said Robert] ; [and whereas,] moreover, the said John, imagining further deceit for the injury of the said Robert, by subtlety caused himself to be bound to the said Robert by an obligation for £300 under the law merchant of Salisbury dated on the second day of the said month of May, which [obligation] the said Robert delivered to one John Gardner to keep until satisfactory indentures in defeasance thereof were made by learned men between the said Robert and John, that the said condition should be performed ;[4] and [whereas], although the said indentures are not yet made and the said obligation remains with the said John Gardner, the said John Hall has sued for execution upon the said obligation for the said £300 and by virtue thereof has taken the said Robert and straitly imprisoned him at Salisbury, so that the said John intends to have from the said Robert £450 and more for the lending of £80, against right and conscience and to the utter ruin of the said Robert, who in this matter has no remedy at common law: [therefore] may it please

[2] 33 Henry VI, 1455.

[3] This transaction constituted the mortgage, on the law of which see Holdsworth, *History of English Law,* III, 108 f.

[4] That is to say, Robert signed in favour of John a bond for £300, which was to be cancelled when further agreements had been drawn up in connection with the mortgage. On the law merchant, see *ibid.,* II, 158 f.

your gracious lordship to summon the said John by a writ of *sub poena* to appear before you on a certain day to make answer to the premises; and [may it please] you thereupon to execute justice as required by good faith and conscience—for the love of God and as a work of charity.

This is the answer of John Hall to the bill of Robert Bodenham. . . .

This is the replication of Robert Bodenham to the answer of John Hall to the bill of the said Robert. . . .

This is the rejoinder of John Hall to the replication of Robert Bodenham.[5] . . .

[Endorsed:] Memorandum that, on February 18 in the thirty-fourth year of the reign of King Henry VI after the Conquest, after the matters in the herein-written petition . . . , as well as the matters in the answer, replication, and rejoinder . . . , had been fully read and made known in the said chancery, and after deliberation and advisement . . . had been held with the lord king's justices of both benches and with divers serjeants-at-law and other persons then and there appearing as counsel for the parties aforesaid, by the advice of the said justices, it was then and there decided that, in so far as the said Robert then and there in the same chancery paid to the said John Hall the said £80 . . . , the same John Hall should cause the same Robert to be liberated from prison . . . and should quash, annul, and cancel the said obligation [for £300]; and that the said John Hall should re-enfeoff the said Robert with the said manor and its appurtenances. , . .

(Latin and English) *Ibid.,* pp. 137 f.

---

[5] In the course of this debate, the regular procedure in such cases, John admitted at least the principal transaction and advanced little more than trifling arguments in defense. Robert offered to repay the £80 in court, together with reasonable costs, for the recovery of the manor and the quashing of the bond.

72. BOROUGH RECORDS

(A) Extracts from the London Liber Albus[1]

. . . It has been the custom that . . . the commoners, on being summoned for such an election [of a mayor], and after the occasion for the summons has been explained to them by the recorder on behalf of the mayor and aldermen, cross to the other end of the hall[2] . . . and there nominate two aldermen, each of whom has served as sheriff and has proved his fitness for the office of mayor. Having done so, they return and by their common spokesman present to the mayor and aldermen the names of the two men . . . , asking them

---

[1] I.e., White Book, composed by John Carpenter, city clerk, in 1419. This customal contains some fanciful explanation of earlier constitutional history, but in the main was based on authentic records and Carpenter's expert knowledge.

[2] The chamber in the gildhall that was used for sessions of the husting. Cf. nos. 28B, 39D-F.

to admit whichever of the two they please to the office of mayor for the ensuing year. The mayor and the aldermen, mounting to the upper part of the chamber, then choose one of the two by majority vote, with the common clerk noting the result under the supervision of the recorder; and then, once more descending, they announce through their recorder to the people in the gildhall who has been elected mayor for the next year. . . .

Now this has been the process used in holding a wardmote at London. The alderman, after receiving a warrant, orders his beadle to summon all men possessing houses, as well as all paid servants, within his ward to come before him on a certain day at a certain hour and in a certain place . . . within the same ward for the meeting of the wardmote. The names of which persons, after they have been summoned, the beadle shall have inscribed in a certain roll: that is to say, [the names of] the freemen dwelling in that ward of the city by themselves, and [the names of] the paid servants, not freemen,[3] by themselves. And when they have assembled at the assigned hour, with the alderman and the more substantial men of the ward seated in the proper places, the alderman's clerk shall order the beadle on behalf of the alderman to proclaim peace.[4] . . . And by the alderman and the good men of the ward, and also by the jurors at the said wardmote, should be elected the constables, scavagers, aleconners,[5] beadle, and other officers, who shall take suitable oaths of office at the general court. . . .

In electing an alderman it has been the custom for the mayor to go to the ward that has been vacated[6] and, if he pleases, have all free inhabitants of the aforesaid ward summoned through the beadle to the place where the wardmote of that ward is customarily held; and there, at once if it is possible and desirable, or else on a day to be set, the alderman should be elected by the major and better part of those men; yet so that fifteen days shall not be exceeded in making an election, for then the mayor, with the advice of the aldermen, his associates, ought and has been accustomed to install an honest, rich, and discreet man as alderman of that ward. . . .

This is the method of holding the common council. On the day before it is to meet, the mayor and the aldermen, through the servants of the chamber, should cause a certain number of the wiser and wealthier men to be summoned from each ward of the city to meet at the gildhall on the next day—sixteen, twelve, eight, or four, according as the ward is large or small. And no one, unless he has been

---

[3] That is to say, men who did not enjoy the freedom of the city. They had no right of voting at elections; see immediately below.

[4] A jury empanelled by the constables then carries out an inquest to present various offenses for subsequent trial before the city courts.

[5] The scavagers collected "showage," dues paid for displaying goods in the market. The aleconners were inspectors of brewing.

[6] The aldermen enjoyed life tenure of their offices.

summoned, is to come or is to presume to attend such council under pain of imprisonment. . . .

For the purpose of electing sheriffs, the mayor, recorder, aldermen, and commons are to be assembled on the day of St. Matthew the Apostle in such manner as is ordained for the election of the mayor. And first of all, the mayor shall of his own free will choose a worthy freeman of the city to be one of the sheriffs for the ensuing year, on whose behalf he is willing to be responsible for half the farm of the city, should he who is chosen by the mayor be in default. But if the mayor chooses the man by the counsel and consent of the aldermen, they must share his responsibility. And those elected to the common council . . . shall choose for the commons another sheriff, on whose behalf all the commons should be responsible for the other half of the farm owed to the king, if he should be in default. . . .

(Latin and French) *Munimenta Gildhallae Londoniensis*, I, 20-47.

(B) HENRY VI: CHARTER TO NOTTINGHAM (1448)[7]

. . . Furthermore, of our richer grace, on our own initiative, and from our certain knowledge, we have granted and by our present letters have confirmed for us and for our heirs and successors in perpetuity to the existing burgesses of the same town of Nottingham, which has now and has long had a certain corporate form,[8] and to the heirs and successors of the same burgesses, being burgesses of that town, that the said town, [consisting] of a mayor and burgesses, shall henceforth and forever be incorporate, and that the same mayor and burgesses and their successors, being mayors and burgesses of that town thus incorporated, are to be a community perpetually incorporate in fact and in name, known as the Mayor and Burgesses of the Town of Nottingham, and having perpetual succession; and that the mayor and burgesses of that town and their aforesaid successors shall, under that same name, be competent and able to prosecute and defend all manner of pleas, suits, complaints, and demands . . . in any courts whatsoever of us, or of our heirs or successors, or of any other persons whatsoever. . . .

Furthermore . . . we have granted . . . that the same town of Nottingham and the precincts thereof . . . , which now exist and are contained within the county of Nottingham, shall be forever separated . . . from that county . . . ; that the same town of Nottingham and its precincts . . . shall forever be known as the county of the town of Nottingham; that the said burgesses of the same town and their successors . . . shall forever have two sheriffs . . . , to be elected from among themselves in place of the two bailiffs . . . ; that here-

---

[7] These provisions follow a detailed confirmation of Henry V's charter and various subsequent grants. Henry VI's own charter covers some ten pages of print; only the merest skeleton is given here.

[8] The larger boroughs had long been *de facto* corporations; the charters of the fifteenth century only confirmed the status in the formal language of that age: see the forthcoming book on the subject by M. Weinbaum.

after each burgess . . . to be elected mayor of that town . . . shall be escheator for us and our heirs and successors[9] . . . ; and that the same existing burgesses of that town and their successors forever shall there have a court [for the settlement] at their pleasure of all and singular contracts, agreements, transgressions made against the peace as well as otherwise, and all other things, causes, and matters whatsoever in any way arising or happening within the same town or its precincts . . . , to be held from time to time in the gildhall of the same town before the mayor . . . and sheriffs of that town for the time being. . . .

Furthermore . . . we have granted . . . that the same burgesses and their heirs and successors may from time to time elect from among themselves seven aldermen, of whom a certain one is to be elected as mayor of that town . . . ; that the aldermen thus elected shall remain in such offices . . . during their lifetimes . . . ; and that the aldermen of the same town for the time being shall be justices for us and our heirs and successors to keep the peace within the same town and its liberty and precincts . . . , having full power and authority for investigating, hearing, and determining all felonies, murders, trespasses, and misprisions, as well as all sorts of other causes, complaints, contempts, and misdeeds, and everything else pertaining to other justices of the peace within our kingdom of England. . . .[10]

(Latin) Stevenson, *Records of the Borough of Nottingham,* II, 186 f.

(C) Municipal Ordinances at Leicester (1466-67)

Hit was ordeyned and agreed at a comen hall[11] holden at Leycestre the xxv day of Octobre, the 6ᵗᵉ yere of the regne of the kyng oure sovereyne lord Edward the IIIIᵗᵉ, in the time of mairaltie of Roger Wygston than beyng maire of the seyd towne of Leycestre, by a generall assent and agrement as wele of the same maire, his brethern,[12] and all the comens of the same toune then being at the forsaid comen hall, that from that tyme forth no man presume to entre into the gilde hall, otherwise cald the maires hall, at eny comen hall ther holden or to be holden but oonly thoes and siche as ben frraunchest, that is to say, men entred into the marchaundes gild; on payne of

---

[9] London and Middlesex had been combined under one government since before the Norman Conquest (see above, nos. 25B, 28B). Bristol had been made a county in 1373, York in 1398, Norwich in 1404, Lincoln in 1409, and Southampton in 1448. For a much more complete statement of what was involved in such a grant, the student is referred to Edward III's charter to Bristol, clearly translated by N. D. Harding in *Bristol Charters,* pp. 119 f. See also McKisack, *Parliamentary Representation of English Boroughs,* pp. 32, 48 f.

[10] The judicial revenue accruing through acts of the justices of the peace was to go to the town; other revenue collected by the escheator and sheriffs as county officers was reserved by the king.

[11] I.e., the general court.

[12] The twenty-four jurats who had long formed what amounted to a closed corporation for governing the town; see M. Bateson's introduction.

inprisonment as long as the maire lykes forthwith doon upon every suche persone doing the contrary at eny comen hall. . . .

The ordenance made by Richarde Gillot, maire of the town of Leycestre, and his brethern, and by the advise and assent of all the comons of the same town, at a comon halle holden at Leycestre the Thursday next afore the feste of Symonde day and Jude, in the yere of the reigne of our soverayn lorde Kyng Edwarde the Fourth after the Conquest off Ynglond the vii.

The maire commaundeth, on the kynges behalfe, that all maner of men kepe the pees of our soverayn lorde the kyng, and that no man disturbull hit withynne the fraunches of this town as be armour or wepon beryng, as halbergon, salett,[13] bylle, swyrd, longe staff, or dager, or any other maner of wepon, where thurgh the kynges pees should be disturbelyd or lettyd,[14] yn payne of forfeture of his wepon and his body to preson, sauf in supportacion of the maire, but yf hit be a knyght or a squyer a swyrde borne after hym; and that every man of the contrary that bryng any wepon to the town leve hit at his in and bere hit not withynne this town, neyther swyrde, bille, ne long staffe, but in the supportacion of the mayre aforesaid, in payne of forfeture of his wepon and his body to preson as long as the mayre lykes; and that no man walke after ix of the belle be streken in the nyght withoute lyght, or withoute cause resonable, in payne of inpresonment.

Also, alle bakers that bake shall bake symnell, wastell, coket lovys[15] iiii for a peny of good paste, good bulture,[16] and well baken . . . ; and of all other kyndes of breed sesonable and of good weyght and pryse after the form aforsaid. . . .

Also, that alle brewers that brewe shall brewe good ale and se that it be neyther rawe, roppy, ne red, but holsum for mannys body, selling a galon of the best for i*d., ob.,*[17] a galon of the secunde for i*d.,* and a galon of the thirde for *ob.*; and that they selle non by measure unlawfull nor unseled,[18] in payne of inprisonment. . . .

Also, that every bocher of the cuntray that bryng flesshe to the market bryng the skynnes and talowe of the same flesshe with hem, in payne of forfetyng theroff; and that no bocher bryng no flesshe to selle withinne this town that is corupte with eny maner of sekenes, in payne of forfeture of the same flesshe and there bodyes to preson as long as the mayre lykes. . . .

Also, that no man ley owte no muke at his dore—stokkys ne stoyns, tymbre ne clay, ne non other maner of thing to the anuysauns of the

---

[13] A halbergon, or halberd, was a combined lance and battle-axe; a sallet was an iron head-piece.

[14] Obstructed.

[15] Simnel, wastel, and cocket were three varieties of first-class bread, but exactly what each term designated is not known; cf. above, p. 66, n. 3.

[16] I.e., well-bolted flour.

[17] *Obulus,* the Latin word for a halfpenny.

[18] Without the official seals that designated true measures.

kynges peple, but yf hit be a bygger[19] in the stretes of the town—
neyther withinne the iiii yates ne withinne the iiii stretes of the
subberbis, but yf hit be remeved withinne iii dayes, in payne of
imprisonment as long as the maire likes, etc.

Also, that no man nor woman suffre no corrypcion to lye before
his dore, ne keste non owte of his dore by nyght ne by day—that is
to say hors, swyn, dogge, ne catte, nor non other corypcion—withinne
the iiii yates, ne withinne the iiii stretes of the subbarbys, but voyde
hit forthe into the fylde from the course of the peple, yn payne of
inprisonment while the mair lykes, etc.

Also, that no man ne woman, ne non other persone, swepe ne
throwe owte swepynges whan hit rayneys upon his neghbour for dis-
turbelyng of his neybur, in payne of inprisonment as long as the
mayre lykes of the persone or persones that is founden so gylty.

Also, that no man of the town nor of the cuntray play withinne the
fraunchys of this town for sylver at no unlaufull gamons . . . , that
is for to sey, at dyce, haserdyng, tenes, bowlys, pykking with arowes,
coytyng with horsshon, penypryk, foteball, ne cheker in the myre,[20]
in payne of inprisonment. And the owner of the hows, gardens, or
placez where the plays been used, as often as hit is so founden and
used, shall paye to the chamberlens iiii*d*., and every player vi*d*. to
the same chamberlens, to the use of the comons. . . .

Also, that no woman use to wasshe no clothes ne none other cor-
ripcion at the comon wellys of the town ne in the hye strete, in
payne of inprisonment.

Also, that alle maner scholdys that are dwellyng withinne this town,
man or woman, that are founde defectyf by sworne men before the
maire presented, that than hit shall be lefull to the same mayre for to
ponyssh them on a cukstool[21] afore there dore as long as hym lyketh
and thanne so to be caried forth to the iiii yates of the town. . . .

Also, all maner men, women, and children that bryngeth any hors
or mares to the market laden with corne or other vitaill, that they,
after the tyme they be unladen, to lede them owte of the markett
place to the innes, in payne of every best ii*d*., to by levied by the
chamberlens to the use of the comons. . . .

Also, that no man latt no swyne ne neet[22] goo abrode, neythere
before the herde[23] goo afylde ne after he come hom, but kepe them
inne týll the herde come, in payne of losyng of every best ii*d*., and
that to be levied by the chamberlens to the use of the comons. . . .

Also, that no dukkes be letyn abrode in any stret withinne the iiii
yates of the town, on payne of forfeture of every duk *ob*., that to be

---

[19] Builder.

[20] Picking with arrows was apparently throwing darts at a target; quoiting
with horseshoes is obvious; in penny-prick the players threw at a penny; checker
in the mire remains unidentified.

[21] A chair in which the culprit was bound before being ducked or otherwise
punished.

[22] Cattle.

[23] Herdsman.

levied by the chamberlens to the use of the town as ofte as eny dukkes been founden or takyn goyng abrood withinne the said stretes of the town.

Also, that no man in the town dwellyng, fraunchysed ne un-fraunchesed, drawe to no conventicles, ryotes, ne assembles withinne the town, ne rydyng withoute, agayen the kinges pees; ne take no lyveres, gownyng ne hodyng, of no man of non astate ne degre for maintenaunce of no man ne of no maner matire; but that they gyf assistence to the maire in sustentacion of the kynges pees, good rule, and honoure of this town. . . .

Also, whatsomever persone or persones that dysobeyeth the maire and his officers and wil nott come to hym when he is sent for, that than hit shall be lefull to the same maire, with all the powre that he can make, to fecche hym, and yf he close his dore, to breeke hit oppen & than to enprison hym whiles the maire lyketh. . . .

Bateson, *Records of the Borough of Leicester*, II, 285 f.

(D) Returns of Borough Elections (1437)[24]

This indenture, made between Richard Sherwood and William Burton, sheriffs of the city of York, on the one part, and . . . ,[25] citizens of the aforesaid city, on the other part, testifies that the aforesaid sheriffs, in the presence of the aforesaid county[26] at the last county [court] of the aforesaid city held there immediately after the receipt of a certain writ of the lord king, which is sewed to this indenture—namely, at the county [court] of the aforesaid city held there on Monday, Christmas eve, in the fifteenth year of the reign of King Henry VI after the Conquest of England—made proclamation of a certain parliament of the lord king to be held at·Westminster on January 21 next to come, and in the same court they caused to be elected two of the more discreet and substantial citizens of the aforesaid city—namely, William Bowes, jr., and Richard Louth—having full and sufficient authority, for themselves and the community of the city aforesaid, to attend the aforesaid parliament and to do and agree to whatever then and there may happen, God willing, to be ordained. In testimony whereof the aforesaid parties have individually placed their seals on portions of this indenture.

Given at York on the day and in the year aforesaid.

This indenture, made between Richard Winsley, bailiff of the liberty of the abbot of Reading at Leominster, on the one part, and John Walter, bailiff of the borough of Leominster, and . . . ,[27] burgesses of the aforesaid borough, on the other part, testifies that the aforesaid burgesses, with the assent of the whole community of the same borough, on Friday next before the feast of Epiphany in the fifteenth year of the reign of King Henry VI after the Conquest,

---

[24] Cf. no. 69c.
[25] Fifteen names.
[26] Of the city of York; see above, p. 291, n. 9.
[27] Eleven names.

in the gildhall of the same borough elected William Rabys and John Crewe, burgesses of the aforesaid borough, to attend the parliament of the lord king which is to be held at Westminster on January 21 next to come, having full and sufficient authority, for themselves and the community of the same borough, to consider, advise, and agree to whatever may happen, God willing, to be ordained by the common council of the king of England concerning matters there to be considered and moved. In testimony whereof the aforesaid burgesses have in turn placed their seals on this portion of the indenture.

Given on the day and in the year aforesaid.

This indenture, made in the full county [court] of Devon—held in the castle of the lord king in the city of Exeter on Tuesday, December 28, in the fifteenth year of the reign of King Henry VI—between Thomas Beaumont, knight, sheriff of the aforesaid county, on the one part, and William Wonard, John Copleston . . . ,[28] [on the other part,] by virtue of a certain writ of the lord king, directed to the said sheriff and [now] sewed to this indenture . . . ,[29] testifies that the aforesaid William Wonard, John Copleston, and others have elected John Speke and Roger Champernoun, knights, to attend the aforesaid parliament on the day and at the place aforesaid on behalf of the community of the aforesaid county; also Thomas Cook and Walter Pope, citizens of the city of Exeter; John Searle and Richard Strode, burgesses of the borough of Plympton; Thomas Aysheldon and John Walsh, burgesses of the borough of Tavistock; John Worthy and John Wick, burgesses of the borough of Totnes; John Bearl and Hugh Champernoun, burgesses of the borough of Barnstaple—[all elected] according to the provisions of the said writ.[30] In testimony whereof the aforesaid William Wonard, John Copleston, and all the others named below, who were present at that election, have attached their seals to the present letters. To the other portion of this same indenture, remaining with the aforesaid sheriff, the aforesaid sheriff has attached his seal.

Given on the day and in the place and year aforesaid.

(Latin) McKisack, *Representation of English Boroughs,* pp. 158 f.

---

[28] Seventeen others.

[29] The text here states the substance of the writ of summons.

[30] That is to say, by the men of their respective boroughs and so reported to the sheriff.

SECTION
VII

THE TUDORS

THE present section is a long one for good reason. England was ruled by the Tudor house for well over a hundred years, from 1485 to 1603, and during all but a few of these years the throne was occupied by masterful and energetic sovereigns. Furthermore, this was an age when the rapid diffusion of wealth and of Renaissance learning within the upper and middle classes led them to take a livelier interest in the study of government and the discharge of its responsibilities. As a consequence, a collection of only the more important constitutional sources must include a relatively large proportion of Tudor documents.

The primary object of the new dynasty was to restore a monarchy that had been weakened by the disorders of the previous age. Henry VII accomplished this first task by re-establishing the traditional authority of the crown. Building upon his success, Henry VIII and Elizabeth greatly extended the royal prerogatives. Yet, though the Tudors developed and controlled a strong royal government, they were by no means tyrannical in their methods. Above all else they desired the actualities of power. Accordingly, they sought to invigorate existing institutions rather than to create an entirely new system. They constantly appealed to ancient custom and the rule of law. They preserved the old governmental agencies, both central and local, with but slight formal change. Occasionally they resorted to frankly despotic measures, but generally they were content with putting to new uses constitutional practices that depended upon the co-operation of the people. Thus the Tudors strengthened the administration of the common law as well as of more arbitrary justice through special courts. They increased the efficiency, not only of their council, but also of their parliament. Even while accomplishing a revolutionary settlement for the Church of England, they anxiously cited precedent and legalized innovation by statute.

Nevertheless, whatever their content, the Tudor records are pervaded by a spirit of newness. For one thing, they were composed in a vigorous English which, despite some archaic expressions, is essentially our own. Thanks to a familiar language, we come more intimately to know the kings and queens of the sixteenth century, their ministers and justices, the members of their parliaments, even their humbler subjects in town and country. Perhaps it is mainly due to this fact that the documents henceforth seem to reveal more vivid personalities. But there is another factor to be taken into account—the improved education of the sixteenth century. Inspired by the constant encouragement as well as by the example of their sovereigns, Englishmen turned with enthusiasm to the writing of books and the making of speeches upon matters affecting the public life. Such a development stimulated political discussion and led to the keeping of better records.

After the plan followed in previous sections, the materials for the Tudor period have been grouped according to the nature of the documents, rather than according to an attempted analysis of contents. The chronological lists of statutes thus include a variety of formal enactments, and they are supplemented by a few characteristic ordinances for the guidance of courts and the regulation of printing (nos. 75, 84, 85). The excerpts placed under nos. 79 and 83 have been selected, in default of earlier examples, to illustrate the routine work of the privy council and to bring out the diversity of its activities. The star chamber records under no. 80 are of somewhat the same sort—a typical collection of matters brought before that court soon after its reorganization. The lively character of the journals, which in the middle sixteenth century take the place of the older rolls of parliament, can be judged from the extracts under no. 82. Henceforth the procedure of the houses—especially the motions, debates, and speeches in the commons—attain increasing prominence in the annals of the nation. It should, however, be noted that part of the original journals of the Tudor period have not come down to us. All but one of the extracts under no. 82 have been taken from the abstract of the journals made by Sir Simonds D'Ewes in the seventeenth century.

As already stated, no effort has been made to group all documents or parts of documents that deal with local government or social reform. Nos. 86-87 include merely a few illustrative records concerning the militia and the justices of the peace. And to them have been added two famous grants that served as models for the commercial and colonial enterprises of the next century.

From this material reference should be made to the statutes on local justice and administration (notably nos. 73C, 74I, 78D, 81C, H) and to the numerous excerpts from the proceedings of parliament and the acts of the privy council.

In this as in earlier sections it has proved impossible to find room for contemporary writings on political institutions. Indeed, the difficulty becomes doubly apparent·for the Tudor period, when such writings appeared in unprecedented numbers. Among them the most famous are Sir Thomas More's *Utopia*, Sir Thomas Elyot's *The Governour*, Sir Thomas Smith's *De Republica Anglorum*, and William Lambarde's *Eirenarcha*, the best editions of which are given in the general bibliography. There are two excellent collections of documents for the Tudor period, both edited with useful notes: J. R. Tanner, *Tudor Constitutional Documents*, 1485–1603; and G. R. Elton, *The Tudor Constitution; Documents and Commentary*. These books reproduce in full some of the acts that are here abbreviated. All the great statutes concerning the Church are also printed in Gee and Hardy, *Documents Illustrative of English Church History*. G. R. Elton has written extensively on many aspects of Tudor constitutional history, particularly in his book, *The Tudor Revolution in Government*. Sir John Neale has dealt at length with Elizabeth I and her Parliaments. Valuable comment and bibliographies appear in J. D. Mackie, *The Earlier Tudors*, 1485–1558, J. B. Black, *The Reign of Elizabeth*, 1558–1603, and *English Historical Documents, V.*, 1485–1558, editor, C. H. Williams. The standard bibliography is Conyers Read, *Bibliography of British History. Tudor Period*, second edition.

73. HENRY VII: STATUTES

(A) ACT OF SUCCESSION (1485)

Henry, by the grace of God, king of England and of France and lord of Ireland, at the parliament holden at Westminster the seventh day of November, in the first year of the reign of King Henry VII after the Conquest. To the pleasure of Almighty God, the wealth, prosperity, and surety of this realm of England, to the singular comfort of all the king's subjects of the same and in avoiding of all ambiguities and questions: be it ordained, established, and enacted by authority of this present parliament that the inheritances of the crowns of the realms of England and of France, with all the pre-eminence and dignity royal to the same pertaining, and all other seignories to the king belonging beyond the sea, with the appurtenances thereto in any wise due or pertaining, be, rest, remain, and abide in the most royal person of our now sovereign lord, King Henry VII, and in the heirs of his body lawfully coming, perpetually with the grace of God so to endure, and in none other.

Statutes of the Realm, II, 499: 1 Henry VII, c. 1.

(B) Star Chamber Act (1487)[1]

An act giving the court of star chamber authority to punish divers misdemeanours. The king, our sovereign lord, remembereth how, by unlawful maintenances, giving of liveries, signs, and tokens, and retainders by indenture, promises, oaths, writing, or otherwise, embraceries of his subjects, untrue demeanings of sheriffs in making of panels and other untrue returns, by taking of money by juries, by great riots and unlawful assemblies, the policy and good rule of this realm is almost subdued, and for the none punishment of this inconvenience and by occasion of the premises nothing or little may be found by inquiry; whereby the laws of the land in execution may take little effect, to the increase of murders, robberies, perjuries, and unsureties of all men living, and losses of their lands and goods, to the great displeasure of Almighty God: be it therefore ordained for reformation of the premises by the authority of this parliament that the chancellor and treasurer of England for the time being and keeper of the king's privy seal, or two of them, calling to [them] a bishop and temporal lord of the king's most honourable council and the two chief justices of the king's bench and common pleas for the time being, or other two justices in their absence, upon bill or information put to the said chancellor for the king or any other against any person for any misbehaving afore-rehearsed, have authority to call before them by writ or privy seal the said misdoers, and them and other by their discretions to whom the truth may be known to examine, and such as they find therein defective to punish them after their demerits, after the form and effect of statutes thereof made, in like manner and form as they should and ought to be punished if they were thereof convict after the due order of the law. . . .

Ibid., II, 509 f.: 3 Henry VII, c. 1.

(C) Act concerning Justices of the Peace (1489)[2]

An act for justices of peace for the due execution of their commissions. The king our sovereign lord considereth that, by the negligence

---

[1] Cf. nos. 67B (last paragraph), 70G. See A. F. Pollard, "Council, Star Chamber, and Privy Council under the Tudors," in the *English Historical Review*, XXXVII-XXXVIII.

[2] Cf. no. 62 I.

and misdemeaning, favour, and other inordinate causes of the justice
of peace in every shire of this his realm, the laws and ordinances
made for the politic weal, peace, and good rule of the same, and for
perfect security and restful living of his subjects of the same, be not
duly executed according to the tenor and effect that they were made
and ordained for; wherefore his subjects be grievously hurt and out
of surety of their bodies and goods, to his great displeasure; for to
him is nothing more joyous than to know his subjects to live peaceably under his laws and to increase in wealth and prosperity: and to
avoid such enormities and injuries, so that his said subjects may live
more restful under his peace and laws to their increase, he will that
it be ordained and enacted by the authority of this present parliament
that every justice of the peace within every shire of this his said
realm, within the shire where he is justice of peace, do cause openly
and solemnly to be proclaimed yearly, four times in a year in four
principal sessions, the tenor of this proclamation to this bill annexed;
and that every justice of peace being present at any of the said sessions, if they cause not the said proclamation to be made in form
abovesaid, shall forfeit to our said sovereign lord at every time 20*s*.

. . . And his grace considereth that a great part of the wealth and
prosperity of this land standeth in that, that his subjects may live in
surety under his peace in their bodies and goods; and that the husbandry of this land may increase and be upholden, which must be
had by due execution of the said laws and ordinances: [wherefore he]
chargeth and commandeth all the justices of the peace . . . to endeavour them to execute . . . the said laws and ordinances ordained
for subduing of the premises, as they will stand in the love and favour
of his grace, and in avoiding of the pains that be ordained if they do
the contrary. . . . And over this, he chargeth and commandeth all
manner of men, as well the poor as the rich (which be to him all one
in due ministration of justice) that is hurt or grieved in anything that
the said justice of peace may hear or determine or execute in any
wise, that he [who is] so grieved make his complaint to the justice of
peace that next dwelleth unto him, or to any of his fellows, and desire
a remedy. And if he then have no remedy, if it be nigh such time as
his justices of assizes come into that shire, that then he so grieved
show his complaint to the same justices. And if he then have no
remedy, or if the complaint be made long afore the coming of the
justices of assize, then he so grieved [may] come to the king's highness, or to his chancellor for the time being, and show his grief. And
his said highness then shall send for the said justices to know the
cause why his said subjects be not eased and his laws executed;
whereupon, if he find any of them in default of executing of his laws
in these premises according to this his high commandment, he shall do
him so offending to be put out of the commission, and further to be
punished according to his demerits. And over that, his said highness
shall not let for any favour, affection, cost, charge, nor none other
cause, but that he shall see his laws to have plain and due execution.

and his subjects to live in surety of their lands, bodies, and goods, according to his said laws, and the said mischiefs to be avoided, that his said subjects may increase in wealth and prosperity to the pleasure of God.

Ibid., II, 536 f.: 4 Henry VII, c. 12.

(D) POYNING'S LAW (1494)

An act that no parliament be holden in this land [of Ireland] until the acts be certified into England. . . . Item, at the request of the commons of the land of Ireland, be it ordained, enacted, and established that . . . no parliament be holden hereafter in the said land, but at such season as the king's lieutenant and council there first do certify [to] the king, under the great seal of that land, the causes and considerations, and all such acts as them seemeth should pass in the same parliament; and [after] such causes, considerations, and acts affirmed by the king and his council to be good and expedient for that land, and his licence thereupon, as well in affirmation of the said causes and acts, as to summon the said parliament under his great seal of England [are] had and obtained . . . , a parliament [is] to be had and holden after the form and effect above rehearsed. And if any parliament be holden in that land hereafter contrary to the form and provision aforesaid, it [shall] be deemed void and of none effect in law.

Statutes at Large, Ireland, I, 44: 10 Henry VII, c. 4.

(E) STATUTE OF TREASON (1495)[3]

An act that no person going with the king to the wars shall be attaint of treason. The king our sovereign lord, calling to his remembrance the duty of allegiance of his subjects of this his realm, and that they by reason of the same are bounden to serve their prince and sovereign lord for the time being in his wars for the defence of him and the land against every rebellion, power, and might reared against him, and with him to enter and abide in service in battle if the case so require; and . . . that it is not reasonable but against all laws, reason, and good conscience that the said subjects going with their sovereign lord in wars attending upon him in his person, or being in other places by his commandment within this land or without, anything should lose or forfeit for doing their true duty and service of allegiance: it be therefore ordained, enacted, and established by the king our sovereign lord, by advice and assent of the lords spiritual and temporal and commons in this present parliament assembled, and by authority of the same, that from henceforth no manner of person nor persons, whatsoever he or they be, that attend upon the king and sovereign lord of this land for the time being in his person, and do him true and faithful service of allegiance in the same, or be in other places by his commandment, in his wars within this land or without, that for the same

---

[3] Cf. no. 62F.

deed and true service of allegiance he or they be in no wise convict
or attaint of high treason nor of other offences for that cause by act
of parliament or otherwise by any process of law, whereby he or any
of them shall . . . forfeit life, lands, tenements, rents, possessions,
hereditaments, goods, chattels, or any other things, but to be for that
deed and service utterly discharged of any vexation, trouble, or loss;
and if any act or acts or other process of the law hereafter thereupon
for the same happen to be made contrary to this ordinance, that then
that act or acts or other processes of the law, whatsoever they shall
be, stand and be utterly void.

Provided alway that no person nor persons shall take any benefit of
advantage by this act which shall hereafter decline from his or their
said allegiance.

Statutes of the Realm, II, 568: 11 Henry VII, c. 1.

(F) Statute of Liveries (1504)

De retentionibus illicitis. The king our sovereign lord calleth to
his remembrance that, where before this time divers statutes for
punishment of such persons that give or receive liveries, or that retain
any person or persons or be retained with any person or persons . . . ,
have been made and established . . . ,[4] and little . . . is or hath been
done for the punishment of the offenders in that behalf: wherefore
our sovereign lord the king, by the advice of the lords spiritual and
temporal and of his commons of his realm in this parliament being,
and by the authority of the same, hath ordained, stablished, and enacted that all his [such] statutes and ordinances afore this time made
. . . be . . . put in due execution. And over that . . . , the king ordaineth, stablisheth, and enacteth, by the said authority, that no person, of what estate or degree or condition he be . . . , privily or
openly give any livery or sign or retain any person, other than such
as he giveth household wages unto without fraud or colour, or that
he be his manual servant or his officer or man learned in the one law
or in the other,[5] by any writing, oath, promise, livery, sign, badge,
token, or in any other manner . . . unlawfully retain; and if any do
the contrary, that then he run and fall in the pain and forfeiture for
every such livery and sign, badge, or token, 100s., and the taker and
accepter of every such livery, badge, token, or sign [is] to forfeit
and pay for every such livery and sign, badge or token, so accepted,
100s. . . .

Moreover, the king, our sovereign lord, by the advice, assent, and
authority aforesaid, hath ordained, stablished, and enacted that every
person that will sue or complain before the chancellor of England or
the keeper of the king's great seal in the star chamber, or before the
king in his bench, or before the king and his council attending upon
his most royal person wheresoever he be—so that there be three of

---

[4] Cf. no. 64c.

[5] That is to say, the civil or the canon law.

the same council at the least, of the which two shall be lords spiritual or temporal—against any person or persons offending or doing against the form of this ordinance or any other of the premises, be admitted by their discretion to give information . . . ; and that upon the same all such persons be called by writ, subpoena, privy seal, or otherwise, and the said chancellor [etc.] . . . [are] to have power to examine all persons defendants . . . as well by oath as otherwise, and to adjudge him or them convict or attaint, as well by such examination as otherwise in such penalties . . . as the case shall require. . . . And also the same party, plaintiff, or informer shall have such reasonable reward of that that by his complaint shall grow to the king as shall be thought reasonable by the discretion of the said chancellor [etc.] . . .

And also it is enacted by the said authority that the said chancellor [etc.] . . . have full authority and power by this statute to . . . send by writ, subpoena, privy seal, warrant, or otherwise by their discretion, for any person or persons offending or doing contrary to the premises, without any suit or information made or put before them or any of them; and the same person or persons to examine by oath or otherwise by their discretions, and to adjudge all such persons as shall be found guilty in the premises by verdict, confession, examination, proofs, or otherwise, in the said forfeitures and pains as the case shall require, as though they were condemned therein after the course of the common law; and to commit such offenders to ward, and to award execution accordingly. . . .

Ibid., II, 658 f.: 19 Henry VII, c. 14.

74. HENRY VIII: STATUTES

(A) Act concerning the Court of Star Chamber (1529)

An act that the president of the king's council shall be associate with the chancellor and treasurer of England and the keeper of the king's privy seal. Where . . . , in the same good and profitable statute[1] the president of the king's most honourable council for the time being attending upon his most noble and royal person is omitted, and not named . . . to be one of the said persons that should have authority to call before them such misdoers so offending the king's laws in any of the premises as is before rehearsed: be it therefore . . . enacted that from henceforth the chancellor, treasurer of England, and the president of the king's most honourable council attending upon his most honourable person for the time being, and the keeper of the king's privy seal, or two of them, calling unto them one bishop and one temporal lord of the king's most honourable council and the two chief justices of the king's bench and the common pleas for the time being, or other two of the king's justices in their absence, upon any bill or information hereafter to be put in . . . , for any misbehaving before rehearsed . . . , have full power and authority to call be-

---

[1] 3 Henry VII, c. 1 (no. 73B).

fore them by writ of privy seal such misdoers, and them and other by
their discretion by whom the truth may be known to examine; and
such as they shall find defective to punish them after their demerits
after the form and effect of the said former statute, and of all other
statutes thereof tofore made and not repealed nor expired, in like
manner and form as they should and ought to be punished if they
were thereof convicted after the due order in the king's laws. . . .

Ibid., III, 304: 21 Henry VIII, c. 20.

(B) Act in Restraint of Appeals (1533)

An act that the appeals in such cases as have been used to be
pursued to the see of Rome shall not be from henceforth had nor
used but within this realm. Where, by divers sundry old authentic
histories and chronicles, it is manifestly declared and expressed that
this realm of England is an empire, and so hath been accepted in the
world, governed by one supreme head and king having the dignity
and royal estate of the imperial crown of the same, unto whom a
body politic, compact of all sorts and degrees of people divided in
terms and by names of spiritualty and temporalty, be bounden and
owe to bear next to God a natural and humble obedience (he being
also institute and furnished by the goodness and sufferance of Almighty God with plenary, whole, and entire power, pre-eminence,
authority, prerogative, and jurisdiction to render and yield justice
and final determination to all manner of folk residents or subjects
within this his realm, in all causes, matters, debates, and contentions
happening to occur, insurge, or begin within the limits thereof, without restraint or provocation to any foreign princes or potentates of
the world . . .); and whereas the king his most noble progenitors,
and the nobility and commons of this said realm, at divers and sundry
parliaments as well in the time of King Edward I, Edward III, Richard II, Henry IV, and other noble kings of this realm, made sundry
ordinances, laws, statutes, and provisions for the entire and sure conservation of the prerogatives, liberties, and pre-eminences of the said
imperial crown of this realm, and of the jurisdictions spiritual and
temporal of the same, to keep it from the annoyance as well of the
see of Rome as from the authority of other foreign potentates at-
tempting the diminution or violation thereof, as often and from time
to time as any such annoyance or attempt might be known or espied;
and [whereas,] notwithstanding the said good statutes and ordinances
. . . , divers and sundry inconveniences and dangers not provided
for plainly by the said former acts . . . have risen and sprung by
reason of appeals sued out of this realm to the see of Rome, in causes
testamentary, causes of matrimony and divorces, right of tithes, oblations, and obventions . . . : in consideration whereof, the king's highness, his nobles, and commons, considering the great enormities,
dangers, long delays, and hurts that as well to his highness as to his
said nobles, subjects, commons, and residents of this his realm in the

said causes . . . do daily ensue, doth therefore by his royal assent, and by the assent of the lords spiritual and temporal and the commons in this present parliament assembled and by authority of the same, enact, establish, and ordain that all causes testamentary, causes of matrimony and divorces, rights of tithes, oblations, and obventions . . . , whether they concern the king our sovereign lord, his heirs, or successors, or any other subjects or residents within the same of what degree soever they be, shall be from henceforth heard . . . and definitively adjudged and determined within the king's jurisdiction and authority and not elsewhere. . . .

And it is further enacted . . . that, if any person or persons . . . do attempt, move, purchase, or procure from or to the see of Rome, or from or to any other foreign court or courts out of this realm, any manner foreign process, inhibitions, appeals, sentences, summons, citations, suspensions, interdictions, excommunications, restraints, or judgments, of what nature, kind, or quality soever they be, or execute any of the same process, or do any act or acts to the let, impediment, hindrance, or derogation of any process, sentence, judgment, or determination had, made, done, or hereafter to be had, done, or made in any courts of this realm or the king's said dominions or marches of the same for any of the causes aforesaid . . . , that then every person or persons so doing . . . , being convict of the same, for every such default shall incur and run in the same pains, penalties, and forfeitures ordained and provided by the Statute of Provision and Praemunire made in the sixteenth year of the reign of . . . King Richard II. . . .[2]

And furthermore, in eschewing the said great enormities, inquietations, delays, charges, and expenses hereafter to be sustained in pursuing of such appeals and foreign process . . . [they] do therefore . . . ordain and enact that, in such cases where heretofore any of the king's subjects or residents have used to pursue, provoke, or procure any appeal to the see of Rome . . . , they . . . shall from henceforth take, have, and use their appeals within this realm and not elsewhere, in manner and form as hereafter ensueth and not otherwise: that is to say, first from the archdeacon or his official, if the matter or cause be there begun, to the bishop diocesan of the said see . . . ; and likewise, if it be commenced before the bishop diocesan or his commissary, from the bishop diocesan or his commissary, within fifteen days next ensuing the judgment or sentence thereof there given, to the archbishop of the province of Canterbury, if it be within his province, and if it be within the province of York, then to the archbishop of York; and so likewise to all other archbishops in other the king's dominions as the case by the order of justice shall require, and there to be definitively and finally ordered, decreed, and adjudged according to justice, without any other appellation or provocation to any other person or persons, court or courts. And if the matter or contention

---

[2] No. 64F.

for any of the causes aforesaid be or shall be commenced . . . before the archdeacon of any archbishop or his commissary, then the party grieved shall or may take his appeal, within fifteen days next after judgment or sentence there given, to the court of the arches or audience of the same archbishop or archbishops, and from the said court of the arches or audience, within fifteen days then next ensuing after judgment or sentence there given, to the archbishop of the same province, there to be definitively and finally determined without any other or further process or appeal thereupon to be had or sued. . . .

And in . . . any cause, matter, or contention . . . which hath, doth, shall, or may touch the king, his heirs, or successors, kings of this realm . . . , the party grieved . . . shall or may appeal . . . to the spiritual prelates and other abbots and priors of the upper house assembled and convocate by the king's writ in the convocation being or next ensuing within the province or provinces where the same matter of contention is or shall be begun; so that every such appeal be taken by the party grieved within fifteen days next after the judgment or sentence thereupon given or to be given. And . . . whatsoever be done or shall be done and affirmed, determined, decreed, and adjudged by the foresaid prelates, abbots, and priors of the upper house of the said convocation as is aforesaid, appertaining, concerning, or belonging to the king, his heirs, or successors, in any of these foresaid causes of appeals, shall stand and be taken for a final decree, sentence, judgment, definition, and determination, and the same matter so determined never after to come in question and debate, to be examined in any other court or courts. . . .

Ibid., III, 427 f.: 24 Henry VIII, c. 12.

(C) Act for the Submission of the Clergy and Restraint of Appeals (1534)

. . . Be it therefore now enacted by authority of this present parliament, according to the said submission and petition of the said clergy, that [neither] they nor any of them from henceforth shall presume to attempt, allege, claim, or put in ure[3] any constitutions or ordinances, provincial or synodal, or any other canons; nor shall enact, promulge, or execute any such canons, constitutions, or ordinance provincial, by whatsoever name or names they may be called, in their convocations in time coming (which alway shall be assembled by authority of the king's writ), unless the same clergy may have the king's most royal assent and licence . . . , upon pain . . . to suffer imprisonment and make fine at the king's will. . . . Provided alway that no canons, constitutions, or ordinance shall be made or put in execution within this realm by authority of the convocation of the clergy which shall be contrariant or repugnant to the king's prerogative royal or the customs, laws, or statutes of this realm—anything contained in this act to the contrary hereof notwithstanding. . . .

[3] Practice.

And be it further enacted by authority aforesaid that, from the feast of Easter . . . 1534, no manner of appeals shall be had, provoked, or made out of this realm . . . to the bishop of Rome . . . , but that all manner of appeals . . . shall be made and had . . . after such manner, form, and condition as is limited for appeals to be had . . . in causes of matrimony, tithes, oblations, and obventions by a statute thereof made and established since the beginning of this present parliament. . . .[4]

And for lack of justice at or in any the courts of the archbishops of this realm, or in any the king's dominions, it shall be lawful to the parties grieved to appeal to the king's majesty in the king's court of chancery; and that, upon every such appeal, a commission shall be directed under the great seal to such persons as shall be named by the king's highness, his heirs, or successors, like as in case of appeal from the admiral's court, to hear and definitively determine such appeals and the causes concerning the same. . . .

Ibid., III, 460 f.: 25 Henry VIII, c. 19.

(D) Act concerning Ecclesiastical Appointments and Absolute Restraint of Annates (1534).

An act restraining the payment of annates, etc. . . . And forasmuch as in the said act[5] it is not plainly and certainly expressed in what manner and fashion archbishops and bishops shall be elected, presented, invested, and consecrated within this realm and in all other the king's dominions: be it now therefore enacted . . . that the said act and everything therein contained shall be and stand in strength, virtue, and effect; except only that no person nor persons hereafter shall be presented, nominated, or commended to the said bishop of Rome, otherwise called the pope, or to the see of Rome, to or for the dignity or office of any archbishop or bishop within this realm or in any other the king's dominions, nor shall send nor procure there for any manner of bulls, briefs, palls, or other things requisite for an archbishop or bishop, nor shall pay any sums of money for annates, first fruits, or otherwise, for expedition of any such bulls, briefs, or palls; but that by the authority of this act such presenting, nominating, or commending to the said bishop of Rome or to the see of Rome, and such bulls, briefs, palls, annates, first fruits, and every other sums of money heretofore limited, accustomed, or used to be paid at the said see of Rome for procuration or expedition of any such bulls, briefs, or palls, or other thing concerning the same, shall utterly cease and no longer be used within this realm or within any the king's dominions—anything contained in the said act aforementioned, or any use, custom, or prescription to the contrary thereof notwithstanding.

---

[4] The preceding document.

[5] 23 Henry VIII, c. 20, which had provisionally restrained the payment of annates.

And furthermore be it ordained and established by the authority aforesaid that, at every avoidance of any archbishopric or bishopric within this realm or in any other the king's dominions, the king our sovereign lord, his heirs, and successors, may grant unto the prior and convent, or the dean and chapter of the cathedral churches or monasteries where the see of such archbishopric or bishopric shall happen to be void, a licence under the great seal, as of old time hath been accustomed, to proceed to election of an archbishop or bishop of the see so being void, with a letter missive containing the name of the person which they shall elect and choose; by virtue of which licence the said dean and chapter, or prior and convent, to whom any such licence and letters missives shall be directed, shall with all speed and celerity in due form elect and choose the said person named in the said letters missives to the dignity and office of the archbishopric or bishopric so being void, and none other; and if they do defer or delay their election above twelve days next after such licence and letters missives to them delivered, that then for every such default the king's highness, his heirs, and successors, at their liberty and pleasure shall nominate and present, by their letters patents under their great seal, such a person to the said office and dignity so being void as they shall think able and convenient for the same. . . .

And be it further enacted by the authority aforesaid that, if the prior and convent of any monastery, or dean and chapter of any cathedral church, where the see of any archbishop or bishop is within the king's dominions, after such licence as is afore rehearsed shall be delivered to them, proceed not to election and signify the same according to the tenor of this act within the space of twenty days next after such licence shall come to their hands, or else . . . , after any such election, nomination, or presentation shall be signified unto them by the king's letters patents, shall refuse and do not confirm, invest, and consecrate, with all due circumstance as is aforesaid, every such person as shall be so elected, nominate, or presented . . . within twenty days next after the king's letters patents of such signification or presentation shall come to their hands . . . , that then every . . . person . . . so offending . . . shall run into the dangers, pains, and penalties of the Statute of the Provision and Praemunire made in the twenty-fifth year of the reign of King Edward III and in the sixteenth year of King Richard II.[6]

Ibid., III, 462 f.: 25 Henry VIII, c. 20.

(E) ACT CONCERNING PETER'S PENCE AND DISPENSATIONS (1534)

An act for the exoneration from exactions paid to the see of Rome. Most humbly beseech your most royal majesty your obedient and faithful subjects the commons of this your present parliament, assembled by your most dread commandment, that, where your subjects of this your realm, and of other countries and dominions being under

---

[6] No. 64F.

your obeisance, by many years past have been and yet be greatly decayed and impoverished by such intolerable exactions of great sums of money as have been claimed and taken . . . out of this your realm, and other your said countries and dominions, by the bishop of Rome called the pope . . . , pretending . . . that he hath full power to dispense with all human laws, uses, and customs of all realms in all causes which be called spiritual (which matter hath been usurped and practised by him and his predecessors by many years in great derogation of your imperial crown and authority royal, contrary to right and conscience, for where this your grace's realm, recognizing no superior under God but only your grace, hath been and is free from subjection to any man's laws, but only to such as have been devised, made, and ordained within this realm for the wealth of the same, or to such other as by sufferance of your grace and your progenitors the people of this your realm have taken at their free liberty by their own consent to be used amongst them, and have bound themselves by long use and custom to the observance of the same) . . . ; [and whereas], therefore, . . . your royal majesty and your lords spiritual and temporal and commons, representing the whole state of your realm in this your most high court of parliament, have full power and authority not only to dispense but also to authorize some elect person or persons to dispense with those and all other human laws of this your realm and with every one of them, as the quality of the persons and matter shall require, and also the said laws and every of them to abrogate, annul, amplify, or diminish, as it shall be seen unto your majesty and the nobles and commons of your realm present in your parliament meet and convenient for the wealth of your realm . . . :—

It may therefore please your most noble majesty . . . , forasmuch as your majesty is supreme head of the Church of England, as the prelates and clergy of your realm representing the said Church in their synods and convocations have recognized, in whom consisteth full power and authority upon all such laws as have been made and used within this realm, to ordain and enact, by the assent of your lords spiritual and temporal and the commons in this your present parliament assembled, and by authority of the same, that no person or persons of this your realm or of any other your dominions shall from henceforth pay any pensions, censes, portions, Peter pence, or any other impositions to the use of the said bishop or of the see of Rome . . . ; but that all such pensions [etc.] . . . shall from henceforth clearly surcease and never more be levied, taken, perceived, nor paid to any person or persons in any manner of wise—any constitution, use, prescription, or custom to the contrary thereof notwithstanding. . . .

Provided always that [neither] this act nor any thing or things therein contained shall be hereafter interpreted or expounded that your grace, your nobles, and subjects, intend by the same to decline or vary from the congregation of Christ's Church in any things concerning the very articles of the catholic faith of Christendom, or in any other things declared by Holy Scripture and the word of God necessary for your and their salvations; but only to make an ordinance by policies necessary and convenient to repress vice and for good conservation of this realm in peace, unity, and tranquillity from ravin and spoil, ensuing much the old ancient customs of this realm in that behalf, not minding to seek for any reliefs, succours, or remedies for any worldly things or human laws in any cause of necessity but within this realm at the hands of your highness, your heirs, and successors, kings of this realm, which have and ought to have an imperial power and authority in the same and not [be] obliged in any worldly causes to any other superior. . . .

Ibid., III, 464 f.: 25 Henry VIII, c. 21.

(F) First Act of Succession (1534)

An act for the establishment of the king's succession. . . . Your said most humble and obedient subjects, the nobles and commons of this realm . . . , do . . . most humbly beseech your highness . . . that it may be enacted . . . that the marriage heretofore solemnized between your highness and the lady Katherine, being before lawful wife to Prince Arthur your elder brother, which by him was carnally known (as doth duly appear by sufficient proof in a lawful process had and made before Thomas, by the sufferance of God now archbishop of Canterbury and metropolitan and primate of all this realm), shall be by authority of this present parliament definitively, clearly, and absolutely declared, deemed, and adjudged to be against the laws of Almighty God, and also accepted, reputed, and taken of no value nor effect, but utterly void and annulled . . . ; and that the lawful matrimony had and solemnized between your highness and your most dear and entirely beloved wife, Queen Anne, shall be established and taken for undoubtful, true, sincere, and perfect ever hereafter. . . .

And also be it enacted by authority aforesaid that all the issue had and procreate, or hereafter to be had and procreate, between your highness and your said most dearly and entirely beloved wife Queen Anne shall be your lawful children, and be inheritable and inherit, according to the course of inheritance and laws of this realm, the imperial crown of the same, with all dignities, honours, pre-eminences, prerogatives, authorities, and jurisdictions to the same annexed or belonging, in as large and ample manner as your highness to this present time hath the same as king of this realm. . . .[7]

And be it further enacted by authority aforesaid that . . . proclamations shall be made in all shires within this realm of the tenor and contents of this act. And if any person or persons . . . , subject or resident within this realm, or elsewhere within any the king's dominions . . . , by writing or imprinting or by any exterior act or deed maliciously procure or do, or cause to be procured or done, any thing or things to the peril of your most royal person, or maliciously give

---

[7] The king's heirs are enumerated in exact order of succession: first the heirs male and then the heirs female, beginning with Elizabeth.

occasion by writing, print, deed, or act whereby your highness might be disturbed or interrupted of the crown of this realm, or by writing, print, deed, or act procure or do, or cause to be procured or done, any thing or things to the prejudice, slander, disturbance, or derogation of the said lawful matrimony solemnized between your majesty and the said Queen Anne, or to the peril, slander, or disherison of any the issues and heirs of your highness being limited by this act to inherit and to be inheritable to the crown of this realm in such form as is aforesaid—whereby any such issues or heirs of your highness might be destroyed, disturbed, or interrupted in body or title of inheritance to the crown of this realm as to them is limited in this act in form above rehearsed—that then every such person and persons, of what estate, degree, or condition they be of, subject or resident within this realm, and their aiders, counsellors, maintainers, and abettors, and every of them, for every such offence shall be adjudged high traitors, and every offence shall be adjudged high treason, and the offender and their aiders [etc.] . . . , being lawfully convict of such offence by presentment, verdict, confession, or process according to the laws and customs of this realm, shall suffer pains of death as in cases of high treason. . . .

And be it further enacted by authority aforesaid that, if any person or persons . . . , by any words without writing, or any exterior deed or act, maliciously and obstinately publish, divulge, or utter any thing or things to the peril of your highness, or to the slander or prejudice of the said matrimony solemnized between your highness and the said Queen Anne, or to the slander or disherison of the issue and heirs of your body begotten and to be gotten of the said Queen Anne, or any other your lawful heirs which shall be inheritable to the crown of this realm, as is afore limited by this act, that then every such offence shall be taken and adjudged for misprision of treason. . . .

Ibid., III, 471 f.: 25 Henry VIII, c. 22.

(G) SUPREMACY ACT (1534)

An act concerning the king's highness to be supreme head of the Church of England and to have authority to reform and redress all errors, heresies, and abuses in the same. Albeit the king's majesty justly and rightfully is and ought to be the supreme head of the Church of England, and so is recognized by the clergy of this realm in their convocations; yet, nevertheless, for corroboration and confirmation thereof, and for increase of virtue in Christ's religion within this realm of England, and to repress and extirp all errors, heresies, and other enormities and abuses heretofore used in the same, be it enacted by authority of this present parliament that the king, our sovereign lord, his heirs, and successors, kings of this realm, shall be taken, accepted, and reputed the only supreme head in earth of the Church of England called *Anglicana Ecclesia,* and shall have and enjoy, annexed and united to the imperial crown of this realm, as well the title and style thereof as all honours, dignities, pre-eminences, jurisdictions, privileges, authorities, immunities, profits, and commodities to the said dignity of supreme head of the same Church belonging and appertaining; and that our said sovereign lord, his heirs, and successors, kings of this realm, shall have full power and authority from time to time to visit, repress, redress, reform, order, correct, restrain, and amend all such errors, heresies, abuses, offences, contempts, and enormities, whatsoever they be, which by any manner spiritual authority or jurisdiction ought or may lawfully be reformed, repressed, ordered, redressed, corrected, restrained, or amended, most to the pleasure of Almighty God, the increase of virtue in Christ's religion, and for the conservation of the peace, unity, and tranquillity of this realm—any usage, custom, foreign laws, foreign authority, prescription, or any other thing or things to the contrary hereof notwithstanding.

Ibid., III, 492: 26 Henry VIII, c. 1.

(H) STATUTE OF USES (1536)[8]

Where, by the common laws of this realm, lands, tenements, and hereditaments be not devisable by testament, nor ought to be transferred from one to another but by solemn livery and seisin . . . , yet, nevertheless, divers and sundry imaginations, subtle inventions, and practices have been used whereby the hereditaments of this realm have been conveyed from one to another by fraudulent feoffments, fines, recoveries, and other assurances craftily made to secret uses, intents, and trusts, and also by wills and testaments sometime made by . . . words, sometime by signs and tokens, and sometime by writing . . . ; for the extirping and extinguishment of all such . . . , and to the intent that the king's highness or any other his subjects of this realm shall not in any wise hereafter . . . be deceived, damaged, or hurt by reason of such trusts, uses, or confidences . . . . : it may please the king's most royal majesty that it may be enacted by his highness, by the assent of the lords spiritual and temporal and the commons in this present parliament assembled, and by authority of the same . . . , that, where any person or persons stand or be seised or at any time hereafter shall happen to be seised of and in any honours, castles, manors, lands, tenements, rents, services, reversions, remainders, or other hereditaments, to the use, confidence, or trust of any other person or persons, or of any body politic, by reason of any bargain, sale, feoffment, fine, recovery, covenant, contract, agreement, will, or otherwise . . . , in every such case all and every such person and persons and bodies politic . . . shall from henceforth stand and be seised, deemed, and adjudged in lawful seisin, estate, and posses-

---

[8] See no. 64E; and for comment on the law of uses, Holdsworth, *History of English Law*, IV, 449-73.

sion of and in the same honours [etc.] . . . to all intents, constructions, and purposes in the law . . . ; and that the estate, right, title, and possession that was in such person or persons that were or shall be hereafter seised of any lands, tenements, or hereditaments to the use, confidence, or trust of any such person or persons, or of any body politic, be from henceforth clearly deemed and adjudged to be in him or them that have or hereafter shall have such use, confidence, or trust. . . .[9]

Ibid., III, 539 f.: 27 Henry VIII, c. 10.

(I) BEGGARS ACT (1536)

An act for punishment of sturdy vagabonds and beggars. . . . And forasmuch as it was not provided in the said act[10] how and in what wise the said poor people and sturdy vagabonds should be ordered at their repair and at their coming into their countries, nor how the inhabitants of every hundred should be charged for the relief of the same poor people, nor yet for the setting and keeping in work and labour of the aforesaid valiant vagabonds at their said repair into every hundred of this realm: it is therefore now ordained and established and enacted . . . that all the governors and ministers of . . . cities, shires, towns, hundreds, wapentakes, lathes, rapes, ridings, tithings, hamlets, and parishes, as well within liberties as without, shall not only succour, find, and keep all and every of the same poor people by way of voluntary and charitable alms . . . , in such wise as none of them of very necessity shall be compelled to wander idly and go openly in begging to ask alms in any of the same cities, shires, towns, and parishes, but also to cause and to compel all and every the said sturdy vagabonds and valiant beggars to be set and kept to continual labour, in such wise as by their said labours they and every of them may get their own livings with the continual labour of their own hands. . . .

Item, it is ordained and enacted . . . that all and every the mayors, governors, and head officers of every city, borough, and town corporate and the churchwardens or two others of every parish of this realm shall in good and charitable wise take such discreet and convenient order, by gathering and procuring of such charitable and voluntary alms of the good Christian people within the same with boxes every Sunday, holy day, and other festival day or otherwise among themselves, in such good and discreet wise as the poor, impotent, lame, feeble, sick, and diseased people, being not able to work, may be provided, holpen, and relieved; so that in no wise they nor none of them be suffered to go openly in begging, and that such as be lusty, or

---

[9] Other articles make specific application of this principle and establish a number of exceptions.

[10] 22 Henry VIII, c. 12.

having their limbs strong enough to labour, may be daily kept in continual labour, whereby every one of them may get their own substance and living with their own hands. . . .

And for the avoiding of all such inconveniences and infections as oftentime have and daily do chance amongst the people by common and open doles, and that most commonly unto such doles many persons do resort which have no need of the same, it is therefore enacted . . . that no manner of person or persons shall make or cause to be made any such common or open doles, or shall give any ready money in alms, otherwise than to the common boxes and common gatherings . . . , to and for the putting in . . . due execution . . . this present act, upon pain to . . . forfeit ten times the value of all such ready money as shall be given in alms contrary to the tenor and purport of the same; and that every person or persons of this realm, bodies politic corporate, and others that be bound or charged yearly, monthly, or weekly to give or to distribute any ready money, bread, victual, or other sustentation to poor people in any place within this realm, shall . . . give and distribute the same money or the value of all such bread, victual, or sustentation unto such common boxes, to the intent the same may be employed towards the relieving of the said poor, needy, sick, sore, and indigent persons, and also towards the setting in work of the said sturdy and idle vagabonds and valiant beggars. . . .

Ibid., III, 558 f.: 27 Henry VIII, c. 25.

(J) Act for the Government of Wales (1536)

An act for laws and justice to be ministered in Wales in like form as it is in this realm. Albeit the dominion, principality, and country of Wales justly and righteously is and ever hath been incorporated, annexed, united, and subject to and under the imperial crown of this realm as a very member and joint of the same, wherefore the king's most royal majesty of . . . very right is very head, king, lord, and ruler; yet, notwithstanding, because that in the same country, principality, and dominion divers rights, usages, laws, and customs be far discrepant from the laws and customs of this realm, and also because that the people of the same dominion have and do daily use a speech nothing like nor consonant to the natural mother tongue used within this realm, some rude and ignorant people have made distinction and diversity between the king's subjects of this realm and his subjects of the said dominion . . . of Wales, whereby great discord . . . and sedition hath grown between his said subjects: his highness, therefore, of a singular zeal, love, and favour that he beareth towards his subjects of his said dominion of Wales, minding and intending to reduce them to the perfect order, notice, and knowledge of his laws of this his realm, and utterly to extirp all and singular the sinister uses and customs differing from the same, and to bring his said subjects of this his realm and of his said dominion of Wales to an amicable concord and unity, hath by the deliberate advice, consent, and agreement of the lords spiritual and temporal and the commons in this present parliament assembled, and by the authority of the same . . . , established that his said country or dominion of Wales shall be, stand, and continue forever from henceforth incorporated, united, and annexed to and with this his realm of England; and that all and singular person and persons born and to be born in the said . . . dominion of Wales shall have, enjoy, and inherit all and singular freedoms, liberties, rights, privileges, and laws within this realm and other the king's dominions, as other the king's subjects naturally born within the same have, enjoy, and inherit; and that all and singular person and persons inheritable to any manors, lands, tenements, rents, reversions, services, or other hereditaments which shall descend after the feast of All Saints next coming within the said . . . dominion of Wales, or within any particular lordship part or parcel of the said . . . dominion of Wales, shall forever from and after the said feast of All Saints inherit and be inheritable to the same manors [etc.] . . . after the English tenure, without division or partition, and after the form of the laws of this realm of England, and not after any tenure nor after the form of any Welsh laws or customs; and that the laws, ordinances, and statutes of this realm of England forever, and none other laws . . . , from and after the said feast of All Saints . . . , shall be had, used, practised, and executed in the said . . . dominion of Wales and every part thereof in like manner, form, and order as they are and shall be . . . executed in this realm and in such like manner and form as hereafter by this act shall be further established and ordained. . . .[11]

Also be it enacted . . . that all justices, commissioners, sheriffs, coroners . . . , and their lieutenants, and all other officers and ministers of the laws, shall proclaim and keep the sessions, courts, hundreds, leets, sheriff's courts, and all other courts in the English tongue, and all oaths of officers, juries, and inquests, and all other affidavits, verdicts, and wagers of law to be given and done in the English tongue; and also that from henceforth no person or persons that use the Welsh speech or language shall have or enjoy any manner office or fees within the realm of England, Wales, or other the king's dominions, upon pain of forfeiting the same offices or fees, unless he or they use and exercise the speech or language of English. . . .[12]

Ibid., III, 563 f.: 27 Henry VIII, c. 26.

---

[11] The next fifteen sections describe the organization of counties, lordships, towns, parishes, and the like in the different parts of Wales.

[12] Section 22 provides for the representation of Welsh counties and boroughs in the English house of commons, allotting two knights to the county of Monmouth, one knight to each of the other counties, and one burgess to each of the county towns except Merioneth.

(K) Statute of Proclamations (1539)[13]

An act that proclamations made by the king shall be obeyed. Forasmuch as the king's most royal majesty, for divers considerations, by the advice of his council hath heretofore set forth divers and sundry his grace's proclamations, as well for and concerning divers and sundry articles of Christ's religion as for an unity and concord to be had amongst the loving and obedient subjects of this his realm and other his dominions, and also concerning the advancement of his commonwealth and good quiet of his people (which nevertheless divers and many froward, wilful, and obstinate persons have wilfully contemned and broken, not considering what a king by his royal power may do, and for lack of a direct statute and law to coerce offenders to obey the said proclamations . . .) ; considering also that sudden causes and occasions fortune many times which do require speedy remedies, and that by abiding for a parliament in the meantime might happen great prejudice to ensue to the realm ; and weighing also that his majesty, which by the kingly and regal power given him by God may do many things in such cases, should not be driven to extend the liberty and supremacy of his regal power and dignity by wilfulness of froward subjects : it is therefore thought in manner more than necessary that the king's highness of this realm for the time being, with the advice of his honourable council, should make and set forth proclamations for the good and politic order and governance of this his realm of England, Wales, and other his dominions, from time to time for the defence of his regal dignity and the advancement of his commonwealth and good quiet of his people, as the cases of necessity shall require ; and that an ordinary law should be provided, by the assent of his majesty and parliament, for the due punishment, correction, and reformation of such offences and disobediences. Be it therefore enacted . . . that always the king for the time being, with the advice of his honourable council, whose names hereafter followeth, or with the advice of the more part of them, may set forth at all times by authority of this act his proclamations, under such penalties and pains and of such sort as to his highness and his said honourable council or the more part of them shall see [m] necessary and requisite ; and that those same shall be obeyed, observed, and kept as though they were made by act of parliament for the time in them limited, unless the king's highness dispense with them or any of them under his great seal.

Provided always that the words, meaning, and intent of this act be not understood, interpretate, construed, or extended that by virtue of it any of the king's liege people . . . should have any of his or their inheritances, lawful possessions, offices, liberties, privileges, fran-

---

[13] Repealed immediately after the death of Henry VIII as a bid for popularity on the part of Edward VI's council. On the significance of the statute, see E. R. Adair, in the *English Historical Review*, XXXII, 34 f. ; also Pickthorn, *Early Tudor Government, Henry VIII*, pp. 414 f.

chises, goods, or chattels taken from them . . . , nor by virtue of the said act suffer any pains of death, other than shall be hereafter in this act declared; nor that, by any proclamation to be made by virtue of this act, any acts, common laws, standing at this present time in strength and force, nor yet any lawful or laudable customs of this realm . . . shall be infringed, broken, or subverted; and specially all those acts standing this hour in force which have been made in the king's highness's time; but that every such person . . . shall stand and be in the same state and condition, to every respect and purpose, as if this act or proviso had never been had or made . . . , except such persons which shall offend any proclamation to be made by the king's highness, his heirs, or successors, for and concerning any kind of heresies against Christian religion. . . .

And be it further enacted . . . that, if any person or persons . . . at any time hereafter do wilfully offend and break, or obstinately not observe and keep, any such proclamation . . . , then all and every such offender or offenders—being thereof . . . convicted by confession or lawful witness and proofs before the archbishop of Canterbury, metropolitan, the chancellor of England, the lord treasurer of England, the president of the king's most honourable council, the lord privy seal, the great chamberlain of England, [the] lord admiral, [the] lord steward or grand master, [the] lord chamberlain of the king's most honourable household, two other bishops being of the king's council (such as his grace shall appoint for the same), the secretary, the treasurer, and [the] controller of the king's most honourable household, the master of the horse, the two chief judges, and the master of the rolls for the time being, the chancellor of the augmentations, the chancellor of the duchy, the chief baron of the exchequer, the two general surveyors, the chancellor of the exchequer, the under-treasurer of the same, the treasurer of the king's chamber for the time being, in the star chamber at Westminster or elsewhere, or at least before the half of the number afore rehearsed, of which number the lord chancellor, the lord treasurer, the lord president of the king's most honourable council, the lord privy seal, the chamberlain of England, the lord admiral, the two chief judges for the time being, or two of them, shall be two—shall lose and pay such penalties, forfeitures of sums of money . . . , and also suffer such imprisonment of his body, as shall be expressed, mentioned, and declared in any such proclamation. . . .

Ibid., III, 726 f.: 31 Henry VIII, c. 8.

(L) Act Dissolving the Greater Monasteries (1539)

An act for dissolution of abbeys. Where divers and sundry abbots, priors, abbesses, prioresses, and other ecclesiastical governors and governesses of divers monasteries, abbacies, priories, nunneries, colleges, hospitals, houses of friars, and other religious and ecclesiastical houses and places within this our sovereign lord the king's realm of England and Wales, of their own free and voluntary minds, good wills, and assents, without constraint, coercion, or compulsion of any manner of person or persons, since the fourth day of February, the twenty-seventh year of the reign of our now most dread sovereign lord, by the due order and course of the common laws of this his realm of England, and by their sufficient writings of record under their convent and common seals, have severally given, granted, and by the same their writings severally confirmed all their said monasteries [etc.] . . . , and all their sites, circuits, and precincts of the same, and all and singular their manors, lordships, granges, meses, lands, tenements, meadows, pastures, rents, reversions, services, woods, tithes, pensions, portions, churches, chapels, advowsons, patronage, annuities, rights, entries, conditions, commons, leets, courts, liberties, privileges, and franchises, appertaining or in any wise belonging to any such monastery [etc.] . . . , to have and to hold all the said monasteries [etc.] . . . , and all other the premises, to our said sovereign lord, his heirs and successors, forever; and the same their said monasteries [etc.] . . . , and other the premises, voluntarily, as is aforesaid, have renounced, left, and forsaken . . . : be it therefore enacted . . . that the king, our sovereign lord, shall have, hold, possess, and enjoy to him, his heirs, and successors, forever all and singular such late monasteries [etc.] . . . , which since the said fourth day of February . . . have been dissolved . . . , or by any other mean come to his highness; and by the same authority and in like manner shall have, hold, possess, and enjoy all the . . . hereditaments which appertained or belonged to the said late monasteries [etc.] . . . in as large and ample manner and form as the late abbots, priors, abbesses, prioresses, and other ecclesiastical governors and governesses of such late monasteries [etc.] . . . had, held, or occupied . . . their said late monasteries [etc.] . . . at the time of the said dissolution . . . , or by any other manner of mean coming of the same to the king's highness since the fourth day of February above specified.

And it is further enacted by the authority abovesaid that, not only all the said late monasteries [etc.] . . . , but also all other monasteries [etc.] . . . which hereafter shall happen to be dissolved . . . , and also all the . . . hereditaments, whatsoever they be, belonging or appertaining to the same or any of them, whensoever and as soon as they shall be dissolved . . . , shall be vested, deemed, and adjudged by authority of this present parliament in the very actual and real seisin and possession of the king our sovereign lord, his heirs, and successors, forever. . . .

And be it also enacted by authority aforesaid that all the said late monasteries [etc.] . . . which be dissolved . . . , except such thereof as be come to the king's hands by attainder or attainders of treason, and all the said monasteries [etc.] . . . which hereafter shall happen to be dissolved . . . , and all . . . hereditaments, whatsoever they be, belonging to the same or to any of them, except such thereof which shall happen to come to the king's highness by attainder or attainders of treason, shall be in the order, survey, and governance of our said sovereign lord the king's court of augmentations of the revenues of his crown. . . .

Ibid., III, 733 f.: 31 Henry VIII, c. 13.

(M) Statute of the Six Articles (1539)

An act abolishing diversity in opinions. Where the king's most excellent majesty is by God's law supreme head immediately under Him of this whole Church and Congregation of England, intending the conservation of the same Church and Congregation in a true, sincere, and uniform doctrine of Christ's religion . . . , and . . . hath therefore caused and commanded this his most high court of parliament, for sundry and many urgent causes and considerations, to be at this time summoned, and also a synod and convocation of all the archbishops, bishops, and other learned men of the clergy of this his realm to be in like manner assembled; and forasmuch as in the said parliament, synod, and convocation there were certain articles, matters, and questions proponed and set forth touching Christian religion . . . : whereupon, after a great and long deliberate and advised disputation and consultation had and made concerning the said articles, as well by the consent of the king's highness as by the assent of the lords spiritual and temporal and other learned men of his clergy in their convocation, and by the consent of the commons in this present parliament assembled, it was and is finally resolved, accorded, and agreed in manner and form following—that is to say, first, that in the most blessed sacrament of the altar, by the strength and efficacy of Christ's mighty word, it being spoken by the priest, is present really, under the form of bread and wine, the natural body and blood of our Saviour Jesu Christ, conceived of the Virgin Mary, and that after the consecration there remaineth no substance of bread and wine, nor any other substance but the substance of Christ, God and man; secondly, that communion in both kinds is not necessary *ad salutem* by the law of God to all persons, and that it is to be believed and not doubted of but that in the flesh under form of bread is the very blood, and with the blood under form of wine is the very flesh, as well apart as though they were both together; thirdly, that priests, after the order of priesthood received as afore, may not marry by the law of God; fourthly, that vows of chastity or widowhood by man or woman made to God advisedly ought to be observed by the law of God, and that it exempteth them from other liberties of Christian people which without that they might enjoy; fifthly, that it is meet and necessary that private masses be continued and admitted in this the king's English Church and Congregation, as whereby good Christian people ordering themselves accordingly do receive both godly and goodly consolations and benefits, and it is agreeable also to God's law; sixthly, that auricular confession is expedient and necessary to be retained and continued, used, and frequented, in the Church of God. . . .

And be it further enacted . . . that, if any person or persons . . . contemn or contemptuously refuse, deny, or abstain to be confessed at the time commonly accustomed within this realm and Church of England, or contemn or contemptuously refuse, deny, or abstain to receive the holy and blessed sacrament abovesaid at the time commonly used and accustomed for the same, that then every such offender . . . shall suffer such imprisonment and make such fine and ransom to the king our sovereign lord and his heirs as by his highness or by his or their council shall be ordered and adjudged in that behalf; and if any such offender . . . do eftsoons[14] . . . refuse . . . to be confessed or to be communicate . . . , that then every such offence shall be deemed and adjudged felony, and the offender . . . shall suffer pains of death, and lose and forfeit all his . . . goods, lands, and tenements, as in cases of felony. . . .

Ibid., III, 739 f.: 31 Henry VIII, c. 14.

(N) THIRD ACT OF SUCCESSION (1543)[15]

An act concerning the establishment of the king's majesty's succession in the imperial crown of the realm. . . . Forasmuch as our said most dread sovereign lord the king, upon good and just grounds and causes, intendeth by God's grace to make a voyage royal in his majesty's most royal person into the realm of France against his ancient enemy the French king, his highness, most prudently and wisely considering and calling to his remembrance how this realm standeth at this present time in the case of succession . . . , recognizing and knowledging also that it is the only pleasure and will of Almighty God how long his highness or his said entirely beloved son Prince Edward shall live, and whether the said prince shall have heirs of his body lawfully begotten or not, or whether his highness shall have heirs begotten and procreated between his majesty and his said most dear and entirely beloved wife, Queen Katherine that now is, or any lawful heirs and issues hereafter of his own body begotten by any other his lawful wife; and albeit that the king's most excellent majesty, for default of such heirs as be inheritable by the said act, might . . . give and dispose the said imperial crown and other the premises by his letters patents under his great seal, or by his last will in writing signed with his most gracious hand, to any person or persons of such estate therein as should please his highness to limit and appoint; yet to the intent that his majesty's disposition and mind therein should be openly declared and manifestly known and notified as well to the lords spiritual and temporal

---

[14] Again.

[15] A second Act of Succession (1536), necessitated by the king's marriage to Jane Seymour, had included additional provisions, some of which are here rehearsed.

as to all other his loving and obedient subjects of this his realm, to the intent that their assent and consent might appear to concur with thus far as followeth of his majesty's declaration in this behalf: his majesty therefore thinketh convenient, afore his departure beyond the seas, that it be enacted . . . that, in case it shall happen to the king's majesty and the said excellent prince, his yet only son . . . and heir apparent, to decease without heir of either of their bodies lawfully begotten (as God defend!) . . . , that then the said imperial crown and all other the premises shall be to the lady Mary, the king's highness's daughter and to the heirs of the body of the same lady Mary lawfully begotten, with such conditions as by his highness shall be limited by his letters patents under his great seal, or by his majesty's last will in writing signed with his gracious hand; and for default of such issue, the said imperial crown and other the premises shall be to the lady Elizabeth, the king's second daughter, and to the heirs of the body of the said lady Elizabeth lawfully begotten, with such conditions [etc.] . . .[16]

Ibid., III, 955: 35 Henry VIII, c. 1.

[16] In default of the heirs mentioned, the king might determine the succession by his letters patent or will, as provided in the act of 1536 (cf. no. 76).

75. ORDER FOR THE COUNCIL OF THE NORTH (1545)[1]

His majesty, much desiring the quietness and good governance of the people there, and for speedy and indifferent administration of justice to be had between party and party, intendeth to continue his right honourable council called the King's Council in the North Parts. And his highness, knowing the approved truth, wisdom, and experience of the said archbishop of York, with his assured discretion and dexterity in executing of justice, hath first appointed him to be president of the said council so established, and by these presents do give unto him the name and title of lord president of the said council; and with the said name, power and authority to call all such others as shall be named of the said council, at this time or hereafter, together, at all such seasons as he shall think the same expedient; and otherwise by his letters, when they shall be absent, to appoint them and every of them to do such things for the advancement of justice and for the repression and punishment of malefactors as, by the advice of such part of the said council as then shall be present with him, he shall think meet for the furtherance of his grace's affairs and the due administration of justice between his highness's subjects. And further, his majesty by these presents giveth unto the said lord president, in all counsel where things shall be debated at length for the bringing out of the most perfect sentence—which his majesty's pleasure is shall be observed in all cases where the same shall be such as may abide advisement and consultation—a voice negative, to the intent nothing shall pass but by his express

[1] See especially R. R. Reid, *The King's Council in the North.*

commandment, consent, and order. And his highness also willeth
and commandeth that all and every of the said councillors to be
hereafter named shall exhibit to the said lord president as much
honour, obedience, and reverent behaviour in all things (kneeling
only excepted) as they would exhibit unto his own person if he
were there present amongst them; and in like sort receive and execute
all his precepts and commandments to be addressed unto them or any
of them, for any matter touching his majesty or any process or thing
to be done or served in his grace's name.

And to the intent the said president, being thus established as head
and director of such council as his highness hath erected and established there for the purposes abovesaid, may be furnished with such
assistants and members as be of wisdom, experience, gravity, and
truth, meet to have the name of his grace's councillors, his majesty
upon good advisement and deliberation hath elected and chosen these
persons whose names ensue hereafter to be his councillors joined in
the said council in the north parts with the said president. . . .[2]

His majesty ordaineth that [ten of these] . . . shall give their
attendance at their own pleasure; that is to say, go and come when
their will is, unless they shall be otherwise by the said president appointed, saving only at four general sittings, where every of the
said council shall be present unless they have some just necessary
impediment to the contrary. And because it shall be convenient that
a number shall be continually abiding with the said president, to
whom he may commit the charge and hearing of such matters as shall
be exhibited unto him for the more expedition of the same, by these
presents his highness doth also ordain that [four of the sixteen] . . .
shall give their continual attendance upon the said president, or at the
least two of them; so as none of this number appointed to give his
continual attendance shall in any wise depart at any time from the
said president without his special licence, and the same not to extend above six weeks at one season. . . .[3]

And to furnish the said president and council in all things with
authority sufficient and ready to execute justice, as well in causes
criminal as in matters of controversy between party and party, his
majesty hath commanded two commissions to be made out under his
great seal of England, by virtue whereof they shall have full power
and authority in either case to proceed as the matter occurrent shall
require. And for the more speedy expedition to be used in all cases
of justice, his majesty's pleasure is that the said president and council
shall cause every complainant and defendant that shall have to do
before them to put their whole matter in their bill of complaint and
answer, without replication, rejoinder, or other delay to be had or used
therein. . . . To which president and council the king's majesty
by these presents doth give full power and authority, as well to

---

[2] Sixteen men are named.
[3] Salaries, lodgings, and servants are assigned to the councillors.

punish such persons as in anything shall neglect or contemn their commandments, as all other that shall speak any seditious words, invent rumours, or commit any such offences, not being treason, whereof any inconvenience might grow, by pillory, cutting their ears, wearing of papers, or otherwise at their discretions; and to poor suitors having no money, at their discretions to appoint counsel and other requisites without paying of any money for the same. And likewise his highness giveth full power and authority to the said president and council being with him, to cess fines of all persons that shall be convict of any riots, how many soever they be in number, unless the matter of such riot shall be thought unto them of such importance as the same shall be meet to be signified unto his majesty, and punished in such sort, by the order of his council attendant upon his person, as the same may be noted for an example to others, and semblably, his grace giveth full power and authority unto them by their discretions to award costs and damages, as well to the plaintiff as to the defendants, and execution of their decrees; all which decrees the said secretary shall be bounden, incontinently upon the promulgation of every of the same, to write or cause to be written fair in a book, which book shall remain in the hands and custody of the said president. . . .

And if it shall chance that the said president and council shall be variant in opinion, either in law or for any order to be taken upon any fact, that like as if the case be not of very great importance, that part wherein shall be the greater number of the councillors appointed to give continual attendance shall determine, or else, if they be of like number, that part whereunto the president shall consent and lean, who in all causes as is aforesaid shall ever have a voice negative; so being the case of great importance, if the question be of the law, the said president and council shall signify the case to the judges at Westminster, who shall with diligence advertise them again of their opinions in it. And if it be an order to be taken upon the fact, the said president and council shall in that case advertise the king's majesty, or his council attendant upon his person, upon the same; whereupon they shall have knowledge how to use themselves in that behalf. . . .

State Papers, Henry VIII, V, 402 f.

76. WILL OF HENRY VIII (1546)[1]

Henry R. In the name of God and of the glorious and blessed Virgin, our Lady Saint Mary, and of all the holy company of heaven, we, Henry, by the grace of God king of England, France, and Ireland, Defender of the Faith, and in earth immediately under God the supreme head of the Church of England and Ireland, of that name

---

[1] On the authenticity of this document, see Pollard, *Protector Somerset*, pp. 3 f.

the eighth, calling to our remembrance the great gifts and benefits of Almighty God given to us in this transitory life, give unto Him our most lowly and humble thanks, acknowledging ourself insufficient in any part to deserve or recompense the same, but fear that we have not worthily received the same. . . .

We will by these presents that, immediately after our departure out of this present life, our said son Edward shall have and enjoy the said imperial crown and realm of England and Ireland, our title to France, with all dignities, honours, pre-eminences, prerogatives, authorities, and jurisdictions, lands and possessions, to the same annexed or belonging to him and to his heirs of his body lawfully begotten.

And for default of such issue of our said son Prince Edward's body lawfully begotten, we will the said imperial crown and other the premises, after our two deceases, shall wholly remain and come to the heirs of our body lawfully begotten of the body of our entirely beloved wife, Queen Katherine, that now is, or of any other our lawful wife that we shall hereafter marry. And for lack of such issue and heirs . . . , the said imperial crown and all other the premises shall wholly remain and come to our said daughter Mary and the heirs of her body lawfully begotten; upon condition that our said daughter Mary, after our decease, shall not marry nor take any person to her husband without the assent and consent of the privy councillors and others appointed by us to our dearest son Prince Edward aforesaid to be of council. . . . We will that, after our decease, and for default of issue of . . . our daughter Mary, the said imperial crown and other the premises shall wholly remain and come to our said daughter Elizabeth and to the heirs of her body lawfully begotten; upon condition [etc.] . . .[2]

Also we, being now at this time (thanks be to Almighty God!) of perfect memory, do constitute and ordain these personages following our executors and performers of this our last will and testament. . . .[3] And all these we will to be our executors and councillors of the privy council with our said son Prince Edward, in all matters concerning both his private affairs and public affairs of the realm. . . . Whom we ordain, name, and appoint, and by these presents signed with our hand do make and constitute of privy council with our said son; and will that they have the government of our most dear son Prince Edward and of all our realms, dominions, and subjects, and of all the affairs public and private, until he shall have fully completed the eighteenth year of his age. . . .

Rymer, Foedera, XV, 110-15.

---

[2] Here follow similar provisions establishing the succession to the crown in favour of his nieces, Frances and Eleanor; and, should they have no lawful issue, in favour of "the next rightful heirs."

[3] The archbishop of Canterbury, the lord chancellor, and fourteen others.

77. EDWARD VI: STATUTES

(A) First Act of Uniformity (1549)

An act for the uniformity of service and administration of the sacraments throughout the realm. Where of long time there hath been had in this realm of England and Wales divers forms of common prayer . . . , and besides the same now of late much more divers and sundry forms and fashions have been used in the cathedral and parish churches of England and Wales, as well concerning the matins or morning prayer and the evensong, as also concerning the holy communion commonly called the mass, with divers and sundry rites and ceremonies concerning the same, and in the administration of other sacraments of the Church; and as the doers and executors of the said rites and ceremonies in other form than of late years they have been used were pleased therewith, so other not using the same rites and ceremonies were thereby greatly offended; and albeit the king's majesty, with the advice of his most entirely beloved uncle, the lord protector and other of his highness's council, hath heretofore divers times essayed to stay innovations or new rites concerning the premises, yet the same hath not had such good success as his highness required in that behalf: whereupon his highness by the most prudent advice aforesaid, being pleased to bear with the frailty and weakness of his subjects in that behalf, of his great clemency hath not been only content to abstain from punishment of those that have offended in that behalf—for that his highness taketh that they did it of a good zeal—but also to the intent a uniform, quiet, and godly order should be had concerning the premises, hath appointed the archbishop of Canterbury and certain of the most learned and discreet bishops and other learned men of this realm to consider and ponder the premises, and thereupon, having as well eye and respect to the most sincere and pure Christian religion taught by the Scripture as to the usages in the primitive Church, should draw and make one convenient and meet order, rite, and fashion of common and open prayer and administration of the sacraments, to be had and used in his majesty's realm of England and in Wales. The which at this time, by the aid of the Holy Ghost, with one uniform agreement is of them concluded, set forth, and delivered to his highness, to his great comfort and quietness of mind, in a book entitled The Book of the Common Prayer and Administration of the Sacraments and other Rites and Ceremonies of the Church after the Use of the Church of England: wherefore the lords spiritual and temporal and the commons in this present parliament assembled . . . do give to his highness most hearty and lowly thanks for the same, and humbly pray that it may be ordained and enacted by his majesty, with the assent of the lords and commons in this present parliament assembled and by the authority of the same . . . , that all and singular ministers in any cathedral or parish church, or other place within this realm of England, Wales, Calais, and marches of the same, or other the king's dominions, shall from and after the feast of Pentecost next coming be bounden to say and use the matins, even-song, celebration of the Lord's Supper commonly called the mass, and administration of each of the sacraments, and all their common and open prayer, in such order and form as is mentioned in the said book and none other or otherwise.

And albeit that the same be so godly and good that they give oc-casion to every honest and conformable man most willingly to em-brace them, yet lest any obstinate person who willingly would disturb so godly order and quiet in this realm should not go unpunished . . . , [be it] ordained and enacted by the authority aforesaid that, if any manner of parson, vicar, or other whatsoever minister that ought or should sing or say common prayer mentioned in the said book or minister the sacraments, shall after the said feast of Pente-cost next coming refuse to use the said common prayers or to minister the sacraments in such cathedral or parish church or other places as he should use or minister the same . . . , [he] shall lose and forfeit to the king's highness, his heirs, and successors, for his first offence the profit of such one of his spiritual benefices or promotions as it shall please the king's highness to assign or appoint coming and arising in one whole year next after his conviction; and also that the same person so convicted shall for the same offence suffer im-prisonment by the space of six months without bail or mainprise. . . .

And it is ordained and enacted by the authority abovesaid that, if any person or persons whatsoever, after the said feast of Pentecost next coming, shall in any interludes, plays, songs, rhymes, or by other open words, declare or speak anything in the derogation, de-praving, or despising of the same book or of anything therein con-tained or any part thereof . . . , then every person being thereof law-fully convicted in form abovesaid shall forfeit to the king our sover-eign lord, his heirs, and successors, for the first offence £10. . . .

Provided always that it shall be lawful to any man that under-standeth the Greek, Latin, and Hebrew tongue, or other strange tongue, to say and have the said prayers heretofore specified of matins and evensong in Latin or any such other tongue, saying the same privately as they do understand; and for the further encouraging of learning in the tongues in the universities of Cambridge and Ox-ford, to use and exercise in their common and open prayer in their chapels, being no parish churches or other places of prayer, the matins, evensong, litany, and all other prayers, the holy communion commonly called the mass excepted, prescribed in the said book . . . in Greek, Latin, or Hebrew—anything in this present act to the con-trary notwithstanding. . . .

Statutes of the Realm, IV, 37　: 2-3 Edward VI, c. 1.

(B) SECOND ACT OF UNIFORMITY (1552)

An act for the uniformity of common prayer and administration of the sacraments. . . . Be it enacted . . . that, from and after the feast of All Saints next coming, all and every person and persons inhabiting within this realm or any other the king's majesty's dominions, shall diligently and faithfully, having no lawful or reasonable excuse to be absent, endeavour themselves to resort to their parish church or chapel accustomed, or upon reasonable let thereof to some usual place where common prayer and such service of God shall be used in such time of let, upon every Sunday and other days ordained and used to be kept as holy days, and then and there to abide orderly and soberly during the time of the common prayer, preachings, or other service of God there to be used and ministered; upon pain of punishment by the censures of the Church.

And for the due execution hereof the king's most excellent majesty, the lords temporal, and all the commons in this present parliament assembled doth in God's name earnestly require and charge all the archbishops, bishops, and other ordinaries[1] that they shall endeavour themselves to the uttermost of their knowledge that the due and true execution hereof may be had throughout their dioceses and charges, as they will answer before God for such evils and plagues wherewith Almighty God may justly punish His people for neglecting this good and wholesome law. . . .

And because there hath arisen in the use and exercise of the foresaid common service in the Church heretofore set forth divers doubts for the fashion and manner of the ministration of the same, rather by the curiosity of the minister, and mistakers, than of any other worthy cause: therefore, as well for the more plain and manifest explanation hereof as for the more perfection of the said order of common service, in some places where it is necessary to make the same prayers and fashion of service more earnest and fit to stir Christian people to the true honouring of Almighty God, the king's most excellent majesty, with the assent of the lords and commons in this present parliament assembled and by the authority of the same, hath caused the foresaid order of common service entitled The Book of Common Prayer to be faithfully and godly perused, explained, and made fully perfect; and by the foresaid authority hath annexed and joined it so explained and perfected to this present statute, adding also a form and manner of making and consecrating archbishops, bishops, priests, and deacons, to be of like force, authority, and value as the same like foresaid book entitled The Book of Common Prayer was before, and to be accepted, received, used, and esteemed in like sort and manner, and with the same clauses of provisions and exceptions to all intents, constructions, and purposes, as by the act of parliament made in the second year of the king's majesty's reign was ordained and limited, expressed and appointed, for the uniformity of service and administration of the sacraments throughout the realm. . . .

Ibid., IV. 130: 5-6 Edward VI, c. 1.

---

[1] Persons possessing jurisdiction in their own right.

78. MARY: STATUTES

(A) First Statute of Repeal (1553)

An act for the repeal of certain statutes made in the time of the reign of King Edward VI. Forasmuch as, by divers and several acts hereafter mentioned, as well the divine service and good administration of the sacraments as divers other matters of religion which we and our forefathers found in this Church of England, to us left by the authority of the Catholic Church, be partly altered and in some part taken from us; and in place thereof new things imagined and set forth by the said acts, such as a few of singularity have of themselves devised; whereof hath ensued amongst us in very short time numbers of divers and strange opinions and diversities of sects, and thereby grown great unquietness and much discord, to the great disturbance of the commonwealth of this realm, and in very short time like to grow to extreme peril and utter confusion of the same, unless some remedy be in that behalf provided, which thing all true, loving, and obedient subjects ought and are bounden to foresee and provide to the uttermost of their power . . . : [nine ecclesiastical statutes of Edward VI's reign are totally repealed].

And be it further enacted by the authority aforesaid that all such divine service and administration of sacraments as were most commonly used in the realm of England in the last year of the reign of our late sovereign lord, King Henry VIII, shall be . . . used and frequented through the whole realm of England and all other the queen's majesty's dominions; and that no other kind nor order of divine service nor administration of sacraments be after the said 20th day of December used or ministered in any other manner, form, or degree within the said realm of England or other the queen's dominions than was most commonly used, ministered, and frequented in the said last year of the reign of the said late King Henry VIII. . . .

Ibid., IV, 202: 1 Mary, st. 2, c. 2.

(B) Act concerning the Regal Power (1554)

An act declaring that the regal power of this realm is in the queen's majesty as fully and absolutely as ever it was in any of her most noble progenitors, kings of this realm. Forasmuch as the imperial crown of this realm, with all dignities, honours, prerogatives, authorities, jurisdictions, and pre-eminences thereunto annexed, united, and belonging, by the divine providence of Almighty God is most lawfully, justly, and rightfully descended and come unto the queen's highness that now is, being the very true and undoubted heir and inheritrix thereof, and invested in her most royal person, according unto the laws of this realm . . . : be it declared and enacted by the authority of this present parliament that the law of this realm is and ever hath been, and ought to be understood, that the kingly or regal office of the realm, and all dignities [etc.] . . . thereunto annexed, united, or belonging, being invested either in

male or female, are and be and ought to be as fully, wholly, absolutely, and entirely deemed, judged, accepted, invested, and taken
in the one as in the other; so that what or whensoever statute or law
doth limit and appoint that the king of this realm may or shall have,
execute, and do anything as king, or doth give any profit or com-
modity to the king, or doth limit or appoint any pains or punishment for the correction of offenders or transgressors against the
regality and dignity of the king or of the crown, the same the queen
. . . may by the same authority and power likewise have, exercise,
execute, punish, correct, and do, to all intents, constructions, and
purposes, without doubt, ambiguity, scruple, or question—any custom, use, or scruple, or any other thing whatsoever to be made to the
contrary notwithstanding.

Ibid., IV, 222: 1 Mary, st. 3, c. 1.

(C) SECOND STATUTE OF REPEAL (1555)

An act repealing all statutes, articles, and provisions made against
the see apostolic of Rome since the twentieth year of King Henry
VIII, and also for the establishment of all spiritual and ecclesiastical
possessions and hereditaments conveyed to the laity. Whereas, since
the twentieth year of King Henry VIII of famous memory, father
unto your majesty, our most natural sovereign and gracious lady and
queen, much false and erroneous doctrine hath been taught, preached,
and written . . . , by reason whereof as well the spiritualty as the
temporalty of your highness's realms and dominions have swerved
from the obedience of the see apostolic and declined from the unity
of Christ's Church, and so have continued until such time as, your
majesty being first raised up by God and set in the seat royal over
us and then by His divine and gracious providence knit in marriage
with the most noble and virtuous prince, the king our sovereign lord
your husband, the pope's holiness and the see apostolic sent hither
unto your majesties . . . and to the whole realm the most reverend
father in God, the lord cardinal Pole, legate *de latere*, to call us
home again into the right way . . . ; and we . . . , seeing by the
goodness of God our own errors, have acknowledged the same unto
the said most reverend father, and by him have been . . . received
and embraced into the unity and bosom of Christ's Church . . . ,
upon our humble submission and promise . . . to repeal and abrogate
such acts and statutes as had been made in parliament since the said
twentieth year of the said King Henry VIII against the supremacy of
the see apostolic . . . : [therefore, all such statutes are hereby re-
pealed].

And finally, where certain acts and statutes have been made in the
time of the late schism concerning the lands and hereditaments of
archbishoprics and bishoprics, the suppression and dissolution of
monasteries, abbeys, priories, chantries, colleges, and all other the
goods and chattels of religious houses; since the which time the

right and dominion of certain lands and hereditaments, goods and chattels, belonging to the same be dispersed abroad and come to the hands and possessions of divers and sundry persons who by gift, purchase, exchange, and other means, according to the order of the laws and statutes of this realm for the time being, have the same: for the avoiding of all scruples that might grow by any the occasions aforesaid or by any other ways or means whatsoever, it may please your majesties to be intercessors and mediators to the said most reverend father, Cardinal Pole, that all such causes and quarrels as by pretence of the said schism or by any other occasion or mean whatsoever might be moved, by the pope's holiness or see apostolic or by any other jurisdiction ecclesiastical, may be utterly removed and taken away; so as all persons having sufficient conveyance of the said lands and hereditaments, goods and chattels, as is aforesaid by the common laws, acts, or statutes of this realm, may without scruple of conscience enjoy them, without impeachment or trouble by pretence of any general council, canons, or ecclesiastical laws, and clear from all dangers of the censures of the Church. . . .

Ibid., IV, 246 f.: 1-2 Philip & Mary, c. 8.

(D) Highways Act (1555)

An act for the amending of highways. For amending of highways, being now both very noisome and tedious to travel in and dangerous to all passengers and carriages, be it enacted . . . that the constables and churchwardens of every parish within this realm shall yearly, upon the Tuesday or Wednesday in Easter Week, call together a number of the parochians[1] and shall then elect and choose two honest persons of the parish to be surveyors and orderers for one year of the works for amendment of the highways in their parish leading to any market town, the which persons shall have authority by virtue hereof to order and direct the persons and carriages that shall be appointed for those works by their discretions; and the said persons so named shall take upon them the execution of their said offices upon pain of every of them making default to forfeit 20s. And the said constables and churchwardens shall then also name and appoint four days for the amending of the said ways before the feast of the Nativity of St. John Baptist then next following, and shall openly in the church, the next Sunday after Easter, give knowledge of the same four days; and upon the said days the parochians shall endeavour themselves to the amending of the said ways, and shall be chargeable thereunto as followeth: that is to say, every person, for every ploughland in tillage or pasture that he or she shall occupy in the same parish, and every other person keeping there a draught or plough, shall find and send, at every day and place to be appointed for the amending of the ways in that parish as is aforesaid, one wain or cart furnished after the custom of the country with oxen, horses,

---

[1] Parishioners.

or other cattle, and all other necessaries meet to carry things convenient for that purpose, and also two able men with the same, upon pain of every draught making default 10*s*.; and every other householder, and also every cottager and labourer of that parish able to labour and being no hired servant by the year, shall by themselves, or one sufficient labourer for every of them, upon every of the said four days work and travail in the amendment of the said highways, upon pain of every person making default to lose for every day 12*d*. And if the carriages of the parish, or any of them, shall not be thought needful by the supervisors to be occupied upon any of the said days . . . , then every such person that should have sent any such carriage shall send to the said work for every carriage so spared two able men there to labour for that day, upon pain to lose for every man not so sent to the said work 12*d*. And every person and carriage abovesaid shall have and bring with them such shovels, spades, picks, mattocks, and other tools and instruments as they do make their own ditches and fences withal, and such as be necessary for their said work; and all the said persons and carriages shall do and keep their work, as they shall be appointed by the said supervisors or one of them, eight hours of every of the said days, unless they shall be otherways licensed by the said supervisors or one of them. . . .

Ibid., IV, 284 f.: 2-3 Philip & Mary, c. 8

79. PROCEEDINGS OF THE PRIVY COUNCIL (1526-57)

(A) Regulations for the Council (1526)

. . . To the intent that as well matters of justice and complaints touching the griefs of the king's subjects and disorder of his realm and otherwise . . . as also other great occurrences concerning his own particular affairs may be the better ordered and with his grace more ripely debated, digested, and resolved from time to time, as the case shall require; it is ordered and appointed by his highness, that a good number of honourable, virtuous, sad, wise, expert, and discreet persons of his council shall give their attendance upon his most royal person, whose names hereafter follow: that is to say, the lord cardinal, chancellor of England; the duke of Norfolk, treasurer of England; the bishop of London, keeper of the king's privy seal; the duke of Suffolk, marshal of England; the marquess Dorset; the marquess Exeter; the earl of Shrewsbury, steward of the king's household; the lord chamberlain; the bishop of Bath; the bishop of Lincoln; Lord Sandys; Sir William Fitz-William, treasurer of the king's household; Sir Henry Guilford, comptroller; the secretary; Sir Thomas More, chancellor of the duchy; the dean of the king's chapel; Sir Henry Wyat, treasurer of the king's chamber; the vice-chamberlain; the captain of the guard; Doctor Wolman.

And forasmuch as the said lord cardinal, the lord treasurer of England, lord privy seal, lord steward, and divers other lords and personages before mentioned, by reason of their attendance at the terms for administration of justice and exercising of their offices and other reasonable impediments, shall many seasons fortune to be absent from the king's court, and specially in term times; to the intent the king's highness shall not be at any season unfurnished of an honourable presence of councillors about his grace, with whom his highness may confer upon the premises, at his pleasure: it is ordered that the persons hereafter mentioned shall give their continual attendance in the causes of his said council, unto what place soever his highness shall resort—that is to say, the lord chamberlain, the bishop of Bath, the treasurer and comptroller of the king's household, the secretary, the chancellor of the duchy of Lancaster, the dean of the king's chapel, the vice-chamberlain, the captain of the guard; and (for ordering of poor men's complaints and causes) Doctor Wolman.

And because . . . it may chance some of these aforenamed persons to be absent for some reasonable cause; be it always provided and foreseen that either the bishop of Bath, the secretary, Sir Thomas More, and the dean of the chapel, or two of them at the least, always be present, except the king's grace give licence to any of them of the contrary. Which said councillors, so appointed for continual attendance, shall apply themselves effectually, diligently, uprightly, and justly in the premises; being every day, in the forenoon by ten of the clock at the furthest and at afternoon by two of the clock, in the king's dining-chamber, or in such other place as shall fortune to be appointed for the council chamber, there to be in readiness, not only in case the king's pleasure shall be to commune or confer with them upon any cause or matter, but also for hearing and direction of poor men's complaints on matters of justice; which direction well observed, the king's highness shall always be furnished of an honourable presence of councillors about his grace, as to his high honour doth appertain.

Nicolas, *Proceedings of the Privy Council,* VII, v-viii.

(B) Letters of the Council (1547)

[24 March.] Letters to my lord Wharton: that, being advertised by his letters of a late raid of the Scots . . . , the lords here thought good . . . to require him that, by one letter apart, he should inform them of the very certainty of their number and damage done by them at that time as truly as he himself was instructed therein; and by another letter to enlarge the matter, describing their number to have been upon seven hundred, and that they burned three or four villages on our borders, took notable Grays,[1] prisoners, and cattle away, with such other aggravations of that their raid as his wisdom in that behalf could set forth.

---

[1] Presumably men by that name.

[28 August.] To Sir Thomas Chenye, lord warden of the Cinque Ports: to recommend Sir John Baker so to those that have the naming of knights of the shire as at the next parliament he may be made knight of the shire of Kent accordingly.

[28 September.] To the sheriff of Kent: that, where the lords wrote to him afore to the end to make his friends for the election of Sir John Baker to be knight of the shire, understanding that he did abuse towards those of the shire their request into a commandment, their lordships advertise him that, as they meant not nor mean to deprive the shire by any their commandment of their liberty of election whom they should think meet, so nevertheless if they would in satisfaction of their lordship's request grant their voices to Mr. Baker, they would take it thankfully. A like letter written to the lord warden of the Cinque Ports with this addition, that, being informed he should abuse their request to menace them of the shire of Kent, as they would not believe it, so they advised him to use things in such sort as the shire might have free election.

Acts of the Privy Council, N.S., II, 461, 516, 518 f.

(C) MINUTES OF 28-29 APRIL 1550

At the star chamber. The lord chancellor, the lord high treasurer, the lord privy seal, the bishop of Ely, the lord Paget, the lord Mountague, Sir John Baker, Sir John Gage, Sir Edward North. . . .

Complaint was made by certain clothiers that the Merchants Adventurers by agreement had set such a price upon their cloths that, without the loss of 20s. in a piece, they could not utter them; for the more perfect knowledge whereof all manner of clothiers that then were in London appeared in the star chamber by commandment, where the more part denied to be privy or of counsel with the said complaint, finding great fault with the multitude of clothiers lately increased in the realm, affirming that, as long as every man that would had liberty to be a clothier, as they have now, it was impossible to have good cloth made in the realm. For he that is not bred up in that faculty must trust his factors, and so is commonly deceived; and now the good making is decayed, the cloths are out of estimation, by reason whereof the prices must also decay. Wherefore it was concluded that some device should be had for a law that none should meddle with cloth-making but such as have been apprentices to the occupation.

For the clothiers' matter the Merchants Adventurers were called before the council, for whom the mayor of London with certain of the chiefest of the company appeared, and to the complaint of the clothiers answered that they agreed not together to hinder the clothiers' prices; but the truth is that there lie at Antwerp such a number of our cloths unsold, that till they were uttered these here would not well be bought, which, together with the naughtiness of the making, hindered the prices; and besides that it was commonly not used to ship any between Easter and Whitsuntide.

Further divers reasons were made by them touching the decay of our money by exchange, with other devices touching the commonwealth, which they were commanded to put in writing. . . .

Upon a letter received from the mayor and citizens of Newcastle, declaring the restraint made for uttering of coal into strange parts, and desiring now to know whether they might sell any to such Frenchmen as were already come thither for them: it was agreed that for the present time, to the intent we should not seem uncourteous to the French upon the conclusion of this peace,[2] they therefore that were there might carry coals away; nevertheless, forasmuch as the price of coal is wonderfully increased within the realm, and will daily be dearer if strangers may carry it oversea, therefore the restraint shall continue, and warning be given to the Frenchmen that be there now to come no more, and to warn their countrymen not to lose their travail; with further commandment to the mayor and his brethren to write the names of the carriers and the quantity of the coal that should be sent to Calais or Dover, that if it be transported otherwise the parties may be punished, for the more surety whereof they that do ship it shall at their return bring a testimony in writing where and how they have delivered it. . . .

Ibid., III, 19 f.

(D) REPORT TO THE COUNCIL ON PRINCESS MARY (1551)[3]

First having received commandment and instructions from the king's majesty, we repaired to the said Lady Mary's house . . . , where shortly after our coming I, the lord chancellor, delivered his majesty's letters unto her, which she received upon her knees, saying that, for the honour of the king's majesty's hand wherewith the said letters were signed, she would kiss the letter, and not for the matter contained within them. "For the matter," said she, "I take to proceed not from his majesty but from you of the council." In reading of the letter, which she did read secretly to herself, she said these words in our hearing: "Ah! Good Master Cecil took much pain here." . . . We told her . . . that the king's majesty's pleasure was we should give straight charge to her chaplains that none of them should presume to say any mass or other divine service than is set forth by the laws of the realm. . . . Hereunto her answer was this: first, she protested that to the king's majesty she was, is, and ever will be his majesty's most humble and most obedient subject and poor sister, and would most willingly obey all his commandments in anything, her conscience saved; yea, and would willingly and gladly suf-

---

[2] Signed 24 March 1550.

[3] Made by commissioners who had been sent by the council to warn her to obey the law concerning religious usages.

fer death to do his majesty good. But rather than she would agree to use any other service than was used at the death of the late king her father, she would lay her head on a block and suffer death. "But," said she, "I am unworthy to suffer death in so good a quarrel. When the king's majesty," said she, "shall come to such years that he may be able to judge these things himself, his majesty shall find me ready to obey his orders in religion; but now in these years, although he, good sweet king, had more knowledge than any other of his years, yet is it not possible that he can be a judge in these things. . . ."

Finally, when we had said and done as is aforesaid and were gone out of the house, tarrying there for one of her chaplains who was not with the rest when we gave the charge aforesaid unto them, the lady Mary's grace sent to us to speak with her one word at a window. When we were come into the court, notwithstanding that we offered to come up to her chamber, she would needs speak out of the window, and prayed us to speak to the lords of the council that her comptroller might shortly return. "For," said she, "since his departing I take the account myself of my expenses and learn how many loaves of bread be made out of a bushel of wheat, and I wis my father and my mother never brought me up with baking and brewing; and, to be plain with you, I am weary with my office, and therefore, if my lords will send my officer home, they shall so give me pleasure. . . . And I pray God to send you to do well in your souls, and your bodies, too, for some of you have but weak bodies."

Ibid., III, 347 f.

(E) LETTERS OF THE COUNCIL (1552-53)

[19 January 1552.] A letter to the sheriff of Essex and Hertfordshire: to elect a new knight of that shire in lieu of Sir Henry Parker, deceased, at the next county day; and to use the matter in such sort as Mr. Sadlier may be elected and returned, for that he seemeth most fittest of any other person thereabouts.

[31 December 1552.] A letter to Thomas Gresham: to take order for the sending over of the king's majesty fustians by piecemeal by forty or fifty bales at once; so as thereby the matter may be so warily and circumspectly handled as the prices of the same fustians may be in any wise furthered to the king's majesty's best advantage.

[15 March 1553.] A letter to the lord treasurer: to suffer Thomas Galiard to transport beyond the seas 200,000 pair of old shoes; providing that under colour thereof he do convey beyond the seas nothing prohibited to be carried out of the realm.

Ibid., III, 459; IV, 199, 236.

(F) COMMITTEES OF THE COUNCIL (1554)

The names of all such as be appointed for the purposes following. To call in debts and provide for money: my lord chancellor, my lord Paget, my lord chamberlain, Mr. Comptroller. To give order for supply of all wants at Calais, Guisnes, and all other pieces of those marches; to give like order for Berwick and other places upon the borders of the north; to give like order for Ireland, Portsmouth, the Isle of Wight, and the islands: my lord treasurer, my lord steward, my lord privy seal, my lord of Sussex, my lord of Pembroke, Sir John Bourne, master of the horse, Sir Richard Southwell, Sir Thomas Cornewalles. To give order for the ships and to appoint captains and others to serve in them: my lord admiral. To give order for victuals necessary to be sent to Calais, Berwick, etc.: Mr. Comptroller, Sir Thomas Cornewalles, Sir William Drury. To consider what laws shall be established in this parliament and to name men that shall make the books thereof: my lord chancellor, my lord treasurer, my lord of Durham, my lord Paget, Mr. Petre, Mr. Baker, Mr. Hare. To appoint men to continue in the examination of the prisoners: [left blank]. To consider what lands shall be sold and who shall be in commission for that purpose: [left blank]. To moderate the excessive charges: my lord steward, etc., for the household; my lord chamberlain, etc., for the chamber. To consider the patents and annuities payable in sundry places, so as the same may be paid all in one place: my lord chancellor, my lord treasurer, my lord steward, Mr. Baker, my lord Paget, Mr. Petre. To appoint a council to attend and remain at London: my lord Riche, Mr. Peckham, the master of the rolls, Sir Thomas Pope, Sir John Mordant, the lieutenant of the Tower.

Ibid., IV, 397 f.

(G) Letters of the Council (1555-57)

[3 May 1555.] A letter to George Colte and Thomas Danyell: to make search for John Barnarde and John Walshe, who have used to repair to Sudbury and, carrying the bones of one Pygott that was burned about them, do show the same to the people as relics and persuade them to stand in their error; and upon their apprehension to examine them and, if they be found faulty herein, to commit them to ward; and further to order them according to the laws, and to signify their doings hither.

[29 June 1555.] Several letters to the sheriffs of Kent, Bucks, Berks, and Oxon: to make search for one Francis Baringden, who is thought to lurk in those counties with the wife of one Fallowfelde, merchant of London, whom he hath enticed from her husband; and to apprehend them both and to commit them to ward, and to signify what they shall have done herein hither.

[7 January 1556.] A letter to the mayor and aldermen of the city of Coventry: to cause some Catholic and grave man to be chosen to their mayor for this year coming; and for that the queen's majesty is advertised that John Fitzherbert, Richard Whestler, and one Colman, of the said city, are Catholic and honest persons, they are required to give their voices to one of them to be mayor.

[14 January 1556.] A letter to the lord mayor and sheriffs of London: to give substantial order that, when any obstinate man condemned by order of the laws shall be delivered to be punished for heresy, that there be a good number of officers and other men appointed to be at the execution, who may be charged to see such as shall misuse themselves, either by comforting, aiding, or praising the offenders, or otherwise use themselves to the ill example of others, to be apprehended and committed to ward; and besides to give commandment that no householder suffer any of his apprentices or other servants to be abroad, other than such as their masters will answer for. . . .

[27 June 1557.] A letter to John Fuller, mayor of Canterbury: of thanks for his diligence in the apprehending and committing of the players to ward, whom they are willed to keep so until they shall receive further order from hence; and in the mean[time] their lewd play book is committed to the consideration of the king and queen majesty's learned counsel, who are willed to declare what the same weigheth unto in the law, whereupon they shall receive further order from hence touching the said players.

[18 October 1557.] A letter to the master of the horse, the lord chief justice of the king's bench, Sir Richard Southwell, and Mr. Newdigate: to call before them one Newport and his man, remaining presently in Newgate, and one Cowley, remaining in the king's bench, and to examine them by the best means and ways they can touching certain counterfeit crowns taken with the said Newport, and to put them to the torture if they shall think so convenient.

Ibid., V, 120, 154, 218, 224; VI, 110, 187.

80. RECORDS OF CASES IN STAR CHAMBER (1505-53)[1]

(A) THE BISHOP OF WORCESTER v. THOMASYN AND OTHERS (1505)

To the king our sovereign lord. Humbly showeth unto your highness your faithful chaplain and continual orator Sylvester, bishop of Worcester, that, where at a law-day and court holden for your suppliant at Stratford-upon-Avon, in your county of Warwick, election was made, by the twelve men sworn at the same law-day and court, of two constables for the conservation of your peace within the precinct of the same town, and of a bailiff, there to be for the year following . . . : one Thomas Thomasyn, of the said town yeoman, which of his own presumptuous mind would have been bailiff there for this year, not pleased with the said election, assembled with one Richard Bentley and John Staffordshire of the same, yeoman, and

---

[1] Cf. nos. 73B, 74A; and on the general character of these records, see Leadam's introduction to *Select Cases in Star Chamber*, vol. I.

other misruled persons to the number of twelve, with bills, clubs, stones, and swords, came riotously to the house where the said law-day and court was held; and then and there would have slain one John Elys, deputy steward, sitting and keeping the said court; and there with exclamation said that William Cottoun, which was elected bailiff as is aforesaid, should not be bailiff there, whosoever should say nay; and with assaults and exclamations riotously kept the said deputy steward, bailiff, and twelve men till it was past ten of the clock in the night, to the great disturbance of your peace and in contempt of your highness, and of your laws, to the perilous example of misdoers unless they may have due punishment therefor. . . .

This is the answer of Thomas Thomas[yn], Richard Bentley, and John Staffordshire to the bill of complaint of Sylvester, bishop of Worcester. They say that, at the said law-day held at the town of Stratford-upon-Avon . . . , such twelve men that there should be sworn have been used out of time of mind to be twelve of the most substantial and honest persons of the same town, to the intent that they should choose substantial men and men of honest conversation to be constables and bailiffs of the same town for the year ensuing; and one John Elys, being steward deputy of the same town, to the intent that he would make bailiffs and constables of the said town such as him should please, caused the jury to be made of the most silliest and simplest persons of the said town—and some of them were but men's servants—and left the substantial men out of the same jury; and after the said jury was sworn, they could not agree upon one of the bailiffs; and, they so being not agreed, the said John Elys proclaimed bailiffs and constables at large in the said town such as him pleased, as though the same jurors had been fully agreed upon the same, without the assent or agreement of the said twelve men and before any verdict by them given; and then Richard Bentley and John Staffordshire came to the said John Elys and showed him that they did not well to proclaim the said officers before the said jury were agreed upon them, but advised him to put the said jury in a house until they were agreed. And the said Thomas Thomas[yn] says that, in the morning of the same day out of the court and long before the court began, the same John Elys and the said Thomas Thomas[yn] fell at words for an entry made by the said John Elys in the name of the said bishop into certain lands of Thomas and his wife, by occasion whereof the same John Elys was about to draw his knife at the said Thomas Thomas[yn]. . . .

Leadam, Select Cases in Star Chamber, I, 230 f.

(B) Mulsho v. the Inhabitants of Thingden (1529)

To the king our sovereign lord. In full humble wise showeth unto your highness your faithful subject, John Mulsho of Thingden in the county of Northampton, esquire, that, where the same John Mulsho was and is seised of . . . the manor of Thingden . . . in the

said county of Northampton . . . in his demesne as of fee, and
so . . . hath inhabited himself in the said town of Thingden, using
there great husbandry, sometimes with four ploughs and sometimes
with three and with two at the least, and yet doth: the said John
Mulsho, being lord of the said manor as is before said, having no
several grass there to maintain his . . . beasts necessary and convenient for the maintenance there of the said husbandry . . . , lawfully improved and enclosed twenty-six acres of lea ground in Thingden aforesaid, being not ploughed many years before, and fourteen
acres of arable ground, all which arable ground and leas were parcel
of the demesne of the manor belonging to the said John Mulsho, with
ditches and hedges quickset with oak, ash, elm, willow, sallow, maple,
crab tree, and thorn, to the intent he would have increase of wood
there for necessary fuel for his house, because the said town of
Thingden is six or seven miles from any forest or great wood. Which
enclosure was in several closes divided, and no house of husbandry
[was] by the same decayed, and the freeholders, tenants, and inhabitants of the town, notwithstanding the said enclosure, had and
yet have sufficient common pasture for all their cattle in the residue
of the field of Thingden aforesaid after rate and quantity of their
tenures. All which closes the said John Mulsho hath peaceably kept in
severalty without let . . . , till now of late that by the sinister labour
of the tenants-at-will and copyholders of the said John Mulsho of
Thingden and other inhabitants of the same town made to Thomas,
lord cardinal, late chancellor of England . . . , who in the king's
name granted a writ out of the chancery to Sir William Fitz-William,
knight . . . , sheriff of the county of Northampton, commanding
him . . . to take the power of the said county with him to throw
down the said hedges and ditches about the said closes made by the
said John Mulsho, without calling the said John Mulsho by any
ordinary process to make answer to the same . . . ; whereupon the
said Sir William Fitz-William . . . , taking with him the power
of the same county, hath thrown down the said hedges and ditches
. . . to the great decay of the husbandry of the said John Mulsho
and to his utter undoing. . . . And the said tenants and inhabitants of
the said town of Thingden, not contented with the throwing down
of the said ditches and hedges and destroying of the wood . . . ,
riotously assembled themselves and with force and arms hewed and
cut up the gate-posts and supports of the gates that belonged to the
said closes whereof the said hedges and ditches were thrown down as
is aforesaid. And after the sheriff with the power of the shire were
departed from thence, and had executed and done as much as the
king's writ had commanded them . . . , divers . . . riotous persons
to the number of three score . . . riotously assembled themselves
. . . with force and arms, that is to say, with bills, hatchets, clubs,
piked staves, pitchforks, shovels, and spades, riotously dug up the
roots of all such willows . . . and of all other trees which the said
John Mulsho had there set for the increase of wood necessary for fuel

for his house, and so daily continued riotously by the space of eight days together, with knelling of bells, hooting, and shouting in most riotous manner that the like thereof hath not been seen in these parts. . . .

Ibid., II, 38 f.

(C) Broke v. Spyttull (1534)

To the king our sovereign lord. Whereas your subject Ralph Broke, gentleman, 8th December in this 26th year of your reign, came to a certain pasture . . . belonging to John Broke, father of your beseecher, called the Newe Rudding, to see to such cattle as he then had in the same . . . : at which time Hugh Spyttull of the Mere in the said county, husbandman; Sir William Spyttull of Enfield in the said county, priest; Richard Humphrey Taylor, other wise Wilcox; John Taylor, otherwise Wilcox; Thomas Spyttull, John Watkes, William Tyrry, and Thomas Kyrkham came to him, by the procurement of Hugh, Humphrey Spyttull, and John Spyttull, in forcible manner and riotously assaulted your subject and Michael Broke, his brother, and Thomas Bailey, then in his company, and sore threatened them, by means of which fear your subjects suffered the said riotous persons to approach nigh to them. And the said persons beat the said Ralph to the ground and sore wounded him, and Thomas Bailey by hard means escaped and came to the town called the Mere and raised hue and cry that his master and Michael his brother were in point to be slain. . . . Whereupon Sir Thomas Dasshefen, priest, Nicholas Moseley, John Dasshefen, and others, minding to keep the peace, came to the said assault. Then the said misdemeaned persons, perceiving that company, kept your said subject in their ward, and feigned that the said Ralph, Michael, and Thomas came to break their hedges about a ground called Small Heath, otherwise Clareheys. Wherefore they said they would justify the beating of them, and imprison them till they found surety that they would break no hedges; where of truth your subjects broke no hedges, although the said Clareheys ought to lie in common to the townships of Lutley and the Mere, [and was] lately enclosed by the said Hugh Spyttull and others, contrary to right. Of which assault the said misdemeaned persons have been, before the justices of the peace in county Stafford, indicted. In consideration whereof, please your highness to grant your writ of *subpoena* to the said persons, commanding them to appear before you, etc. . . .

To our sovereign lord the king. We, Walter Wrottesley, esquire, and John Gravenour, gentleman, commissioners assigned by your writ of *dedimus potestatem* directed to us to hear and examine witnesses concerning the matter in variance in the books hereunto annexed contained, between Ralph Broke and others, plaintiffs, and Hugh Spyttull and others, defendants, certify your highness that we, by force of your writ, the Monday after the feast of St. John the Baptist last, sat at Tresull and called before us the said parties; and the plaintiffs brought before us divers persons hereunder named, who, then examined, deposed as hereunto annexed appears:—

Thomas Lea of the Woo, gentleman, aged 28 years. He saw Ralph Broke's head broken. He saw no hedges broken nor moved. He examined John Watkes, one of the parties with Spyttull, who said he saw not the said Broke within the said Clareheys. The said Thomas Bailey made hue and cry at the Mere, and Sir Thomas Dasshefen, John Dasshefen, Lewes Clare, and Nicholas Moseley came to the rescue. Clareheys is a mile from Enfield. The said Ralph and others say that they were led thither against their wills. On the night of the affray there was no hedge or ditch broken. He saw them as whole as they were the morning before.

William Byllyngesley of Ludston, aged 49 years. . . . On the Wednesday before the fray in Hampton the said Hugh Spyttull and Ralph Broke quarrelled. Further, for forty years past he knew Clareheys lie common, and never knew it enclosed till William Bulwardyn enclosed it and held it sometimes closed and sometimes open for three years or thereabouts.

Thomas Woorwood of Morff, gentleman, aged 88 years. He has known Clareheys lie open for eighty years past until, about sixteen or seventeen years since, William Bulwardyn enclosed it. . . .

Thomas Dasshefen of Enfield, aged 47 years, says that there were nine persons at the said affray, and Hugh Spyttull and Sir William Spyttull had bows and arrows, and the others had staves; and that Ralph Broke had his head broken. . . .

Nicholas Moseley of the Mere, aged 43 years, says that William Tyrry, being at the affray and therefore indicted of riot, said that Ralph Broke had no cause to indict him; for when he, the said William, had the said Ralph by one arm and Humphrey Taylor had him by the other, if he had not pulled the said Ralph back, Richard Spyttull would have slain him. At the same assault they did hit by command of Humphrey Spyttull. Thomas Bailey made hue and cry at the township of the Mere, by reason whereof this deponent, Sir Thomas Dasshefen, and Sir John Dasshefen came to the house of Beves Clares in the Mere, where the said Ralph and Michael were in custody. . . .

Collections for a History of Staffordshire, 1912, pp. 71 f.

(D) PETYT v. JOBBER AND OTHERS (1540-41)

To the king our sovereign lord: your orator, John Petyt, of Chebsey, county Stafford, gentleman. Whereas your orator, 8th May last, was at Chebsey, John Jobber, husbandman [and thirteen others] . . . , with force and arms made assault on your said orator; may it please you to grant your writs of *subpoena* to be directed to them, to appear before you to answer the premises.

The answer of John Jobber, William Palmer, and Robert Stedeman to the bill of complaint of John Petyt. The said bill of complaint is untrue. . . . The town of Chebsey, wherein the pretended offences are supposed to be done, is held of the honour of Tutbury, parcel of the duchy of Lancaster, and all riots there done are determinable before the chancellor of the said duchy. There is a custom in the manor of Chebsey that, if any beasts and cattle or other distress have been taken for any cause . . . , the same distress be impounded in the same manor; and if the takers thereof have been about to drive the same to any other place, the tenants thereof have been used to resist the same. Further, the defendants say that the plaintiff, John Hille of the Pype, John Petyt the younger, and John Bradley, arrayed in forcible manner, with other gentlemen of county Stafford, took and distrained four oxen of Robert Stedeman and would have driven them out of the lordship, whereupon the defendants resisted the same, which is the riot supposed by the plaintiff's bill.

Ibid., p. 140.

(E) GERARD v. DODD (1547-53)

To the king our most dread sovereign lord: your subject, Sir Thomas Gerard, knight, and William Hunt, servant to your said suppliant. Whereas your subject and all his ancestors have been seised by lawful title of descent of the manor of Bromley in the parish of Ecclessall, county Stafford, parcel of which manor is wood called Willibrydge Parke, in which wood for a long time there have eyried sparrowhawks by the space of sixty years last, and this present year the said hawk eyried there and had five young hawks, and your said subject commanded his said servant to make him a cabin in the said wood to keep and watch the said hawks there: so it is that John Dodd of Clorley, county Salop, esquire, enticed Robert Parkes, yeoman, his household servant; Thomas Taylor of Pyxley, county Salop, bailiff to the said John Dodd; and Richard Emys, otherwise Enys, of Drayton in Hales, county Salop, shearman; to convey away the said hawks. By force whereof, 27th June last, they assembled in riotous manner at the said woodside and entered the said wood with vizors upon their faces, hoods upon their heads, and otherwise disguised, one hour after sunrise, and made assault on the said William Hunt, then being within his cabin, and after took him and bound him to a tree, and after, with like force, took away five young hawks out of the nest of the said sparrowhawk and conveyed them to the house of John Dodd, to the loss of your suppliant and the utter undoing of William Hunt, who has consumed all he has in surgery and, by reason of his beating, is not able to serve again. In consideration whereof, please your highness to grant your writ of *subpoena* to be directed to the said John Dodd and Robert Parkes, commanding them to appear before you to make answer to the premises.

The answer of John Dodd, esquire. The said bill is uncertain. . . .

If it were true, as it is not, it is determinable at the common law. As to the riot, entry, etc., he is not guilty. . . .

The answer of Robert Parkes. As to any riot . . . or other misdemeanours in the said surmised bill alleged, he is not guilty.

Ibid., p. 180.

(F) THE KING V. A JURY OF LICHFIELD (1551-53)

The answer of John Pyllysworth [and ten others]. The said Rowlande Orme and William Fowler do, and at the time of the said verdict did, dwell two miles out of the city of Lichfield, and never dwelt there; and the rest of the defendants do, and at the time of the making of the said verdict did, dwell within the said town. The said Harry Oliver was indicted in the said town before the coroner there for murdering the said John Wescote, and was arraigned before the bailiff and recorder of the town at the said jail-delivery held within the said city, whereunto he pleaded not guilty; which they know to be true, because the said indictment was read to them when they, with the said Raufe Bagnolde, were sworn to try the said Harry. At the time of the said jail-delivery they came to the place where it was held, not thinking to be sworn to try the said Harry, and they, with the said Raufe Bagnolde, were sworn before the said justices to try the said Harry. Proclamation was made that, if any man would give evidence against the same prisoner, that he should come forth and be heard; but, notwithstanding, no man came to give any evidence, and so the said defendants with Raufe Bagnolde went to commune together of their verdict. And as they were going from the bar, one said that he could give evidence concerning the same matter. The recorder of the town asked him if he was not of another jury for life and death, and he said yes; so he could not be sworn to give any evidence. Therefore the said defendants had no evidences given them to find the said Harry guilty. They made their verdict plainly, without favour, and found the said Harry not guilty of the said murder; without that, that they were corrupted by John Ferrers and William Wescote and other their friends to acquit the said Harry, or that they had knowledge themselves how the said murder was committed, or that they found their verdict contrary to their conscience and knowledge. . . .

William Corpson, of Lichfield, spurrier . . . , says that John Wescote was slain in the open street at Lichfield on Ash Wednesday last, being fair day there, and by common report Harry Oliver killed the said Wescote and was indicted for the same, but how many times he knew not. . . . He denies that any labour was made to him to be of the inquest on the trial of the said Harry; nor any sum of money given to him or promised by any person to be favourable to the said Harry Oliver at his arraignment. . . . The said Wescote was slain indeed, and no other person but Harry Oliver was accused of his death and therefore he thinks the said Harry Oliver killed him; but how he knows not, nor had any evidence given thereof. . . .[2]

Ibid., pp. 194 f.

[2] Five other jurymen, being interrogated, say the same.

81. ELIZABETH: STATUTES

(A) Act of Supremacy (1559)

An act restoring to the crown the ancient jurisdiction over the state ecclesiastical and spiritual and abolishing all foreign power repugnant to the same. Most humbly beseech your most excellent majesty your faithful and obedient subjects, the lords spiritual and temporal and the commons in this your present parliament assembled, that, where in time of the reign of your most dear father of worthy memory, King Henry VIII, divers good laws and statutes were made and established, as well for the utter extinguishment and putting away of all usurped and foreign powers and authorities out of this your realm and other your highness's dominions and countries, as also for the restoring and uniting to the imperial crown of this realm the ancient jurisdictions, authorities, superiorities, and pre-eminences to the same of right belonging and appertaining; by reason whereof we, your most humble and obedient subjects, from the five-and-twentieth year of the reign of your said dear father, were continually kept in good order, and were disburdened of divers great and intolerable charges and exactions before that time unlawfully taken and exacted by such foreign power and authority as before that was usurped, until such time as all the said good laws . . . in the first and second years of the reigns of the late King Philip and Queen Mary . . . were . . . repealed . . . ;[1] by reason of which act of repeal your said humble subjects were eftsoons brought under an usurped foreign power and authority, and yet do remain in that bondage, to the intolerable charges of your loving subjects, if some redress by the authority of this your high court of parliament with the assent of your highness be not had and provided: may it therefore please your highness, for the repressing of the said usurped foreign power and the restoring of the rights, jurisdictions, and pre-eminences appertaining to the imperial crown of this your realm, that it may be enacted by the authority of this present parliament that the said act . . . and all and every branch, clauses, and articles therein contained, other than such branches, clauses, and sentences as hereafter shall be excepted, may from the last day of this session of parliament, by authority of this present parliament, be repealed, and shall from thenceforth be utterly void and of none effect. . . .[2]

And to the intent that all usurped and foreign power and authority,

[1] No. 78c.
[2] The following three sections revive Henry VIII's statutes declaring the supremacy of the crown in ecclesiastical affairs.

spiritual and temporal, may forever be clearly extinguished and never to be used nor obeyed within this realm or any other your majesty's dominions or countries, may it please your highness that it may be further enacted by the authority aforesaid that no foreign prince, person, prelate, state, or potentate, spiritual or temporal, shall at any time after the last day of this session of parliament use, enjoy, or exercise any manner of power, jurisdiction, superiority, authority, pre-eminence, or privilege, spiritual or ecclesiastical, within this realm or within any other your majesty's dominions or countries that now be or hereafter shall be, but from thenceforth the same shall be clearly abolished out of this realm and all other your highness's dominions forever, any statute, ordinance, custom, constitutions, or any other matter or cause whatsoever to the contrary in any wise notwithstanding . . . ; and that your highness, your heirs, and successors, kings or queens of this realm, shall have full power and authority . . . to exercise . . . all manner of jurisdictions, privileges, and pre-eminences in any wise touching or concerning any spiritual or ecclesiastical jurisdiction within these your realms. . . .

And for the better observation and maintenance of this act, may it please your highness that it may be further enacted by the authority aforesaid that all and every archbishop, bishop, and all and every other ecclesiastical person and other ecclesiastical officer and minister, of what estate, dignity, pre-eminence, or degree soever he or they be or shall be, and all and every temporal judge, justicer, mayor, and other lay or temporal officer and minister, and every other person having your highness's fee or wages within this realm or any your highness's dominions shall make, take, and receive a corporal oath upon the Evangelist, before such person or persons as shall please your highness, your heirs or successors, under the great seal of England to assign and name to accept and take the same, according to the tenor and effect hereafter following, that is to say—

"I, A. B., do utterly testify and declare in my conscience that the queen's highness is the only supreme governor of this realm and of all other her highness's dominions and countries, as well in all spiritual or ecclesiastical things or causes as temporal, and that no foreign prince, person, prelate, state, or potentate hath or ought to have any jurisdiction, power, superiority, pre-eminence, or authority, ecclesiastical or spiritual, within this realm; and therefore I do utterly renounce and forsake all foreign jurisdictions, powers, superiorities, and authorities, and do promise that from henceforth I shall bear faith and true allegiance to the queen's highness, her heirs, and lawful successors, and to my power shall assist and defend all jurisdictions, pre-eminences, privileges, and authorities granted or belonging to the queen's highness, her heirs, and successors, or united or annexed to the imperial crown of this realm: so help me God and by the contents of this Book." . . .[3]

---

[3] Persons refusing to take this oath were to be debarred from offices in church and state.

And for the more sure observation of this act and the utter extinguishment of all foreign and usurped power and authority, may it please your highness that it may be further enacted by the authority aforesaid that, if any person or persons dwelling or inhabiting within this your realm or in any other your highness's realms or dominions . . . , shall by writing, printing, teaching, preaching, express words, deed, or act, advisedly, maliciously, and directly affirm, hold, stand with, set forth, maintain, or defend the authority, pre-eminence, power, or jurisdiction, spiritual or ecclesiastical, of any foreign prince, prelate, person, state, or potentate whatsoever, heretofore claimed, used, or usurped within this realm or any dominion or country being within or under the power, dominion, or obeisance of your highness, or shall advisedly, maliciously, or directly put in ure or execute anything for the extolling, advancement, setting forth, maintenance, or defence of any such pretended or usurped jurisdiction, power, pre-eminence, or authority, or any part thereof, that then every such person and persons so doing and offending, their abettors, aiders, procurers, and counsellors, being thereof lawfully convicted and attainted according to the due order and course of the common laws of this realm [shall suffer specified penalties, culminating in punishment for high treason on the third offence]. . . .

Provided always, and be it enacted by the authority aforesaid, that such person or persons to whom your highness, your heirs, or successors, shall hereafter by letters patents under the great seal of England give authority to have or execute any jurisdiction, power, or authority spiritual, or to visit, reform, order, or correct any errors, heresies, schisms, abuses, or enormities by virtue of this act, shall not in any wise have authority or power to order, determine, or adjudge any matter or cause to be heresy but only such as heretofore have been determined, ordered, or adjudged to be heresy by the authority of the canonical Scriptures, or by the first four general councils or any of them, or by any other general council wherein the same was declared heresy by the express and plain words of the said canonical Scriptures, or such as hereafter shall be ordered, judged, or determined to be heresy by the high court of parliament of this realm, with the assent of the clergy in their convocation—anything in this act contained to the contrary notwithstanding. . . .

Statutes of the Realm, IV, 350 f.: 1 Elizabeth, c. 1.

(B) ACT OF UNIFORMITY (1559)

An act for the uniformity of common prayer and divine service in the Church, and the administration of the sacraments. . . . And further be it enacted . . .[4] that all and singular ministers in any cathedral or parish church or other place within this realm of England, Wales, and the marches of the same, or other the queen's dominions, shall, from and after the feast of the Nativity of St. John Baptist next

---

[4] The first section repeals Mary's statute of 1553 (no. 78A).

coming, be bounden to say and use the matins, evensong, celebration of the Lord's Supper and administration of each of the sacraments, and all their common and open prayer, in such order and form as is mentioned in the . . . book so authorized by parliament in the . . . fifth and sixth year of the reign of King Edward VI,[5] with one alteration or addition of certain lessons to be used on every Sunday in the year, and the form of the litany altered and corrected, and two sentences only added in the delivery of the sacrament to the communicants, and none other or otherwise; and that, if any manner of parson, vicar, or other whatsoever minister that ought or should sing or say common prayer mentioned in the said book or minister the sacraments . . . refuse to use the said common prayers or to minister the sacraments . . . in such order and form as they be mentioned and set forth in the said book, or shall wilfully or obstinately . . . use any other rite, ceremony, order, form, or manner of celebrating of the Lord's Supper openly or privily, or matins, evensong, administration of the sacraments, or other open prayers, than is mentioned and set forth in the said book . . . , or shall preach, declare, or speak anything in the derogation or depraving of the said book or anything therein contained, or of any part thereof, and shall be thereof lawfully convicted according to the laws of this realm by verdict of twelve men, or by his own confession, or by the notorious evidence of the fact . . . , [he shall suffer fine or imprisonment—life imprisonment for the third offence].

And it is ordained and enacted by the authority abovesaid that, if any person or persons whatsoever after the said feast . . . shall in any interludes, plays, songs, rhymes, or by other open words, declare or speak anything in the derogation, depraving, or despising of the same book, or of anything therein contained, or any part thereof, or shall by open fact, deed, or by open threatenings, compel or cause or otherwise procure or maintain any parson, vicar, or other minister in any cathedral or parish church or in chapel or in any other place to sing or say any common or open prayer or to minister any sacrament otherwise or in any other manner and form than is mentioned in the said book, or that by any of the said means shall unlawfully interrupt or let any parson, vicar, or other minister in any cathedral or parish church, chapel, or any other place to sing or say common and open prayer, or to minister the sacraments or any of them, in such manner and form as is mentioned in the said book, that then every such person, being thereof lawfully convicted in form abovesaid . . . , [shall suffer fine or imprisonment—life imprisonment for the third offence].

And . . . from and after the said feast . . . all and every person and persons inhabiting within this realm or any other the queen's majesty's dominions shall diligently and faithfully, having no lawful or reasonable excuse to be absent, **endeavour themselves to resort to**

[5] No. 7/B.

their parish church or chapel accustomed, or upon reasonable let
thereof, to some usual place where common prayer and such service
of God shall be used in such time of let, upon every Sunday and
other days ordained and used to be kept as holy days; and then and
there . . . abide orderly and soberly during the time of the common
prayer, preachings, or other service of God there to be used and
ministered, upon pain of punishment by the censures of the Church,
and also upon pain that every person so offending shall forfeit for
every such offence 12d., to be levied by the churchwardens of the
parish where such offence shall be done, to the use of the poor of the
same parish. . . .

Provided always, and be it enacted, that such ornaments of the
Church and of the ministers thereof shall be retained and be in use
as was in the Church of England by authority of parliament in the
second year of the reign of King Edward VI, until other order shall
be therein taken by the authority of the queen's majesty, with the
advice of her commissioners appointed and authorized under the great
seal of England for causes ecclesiastical or of the metropolitan of
this realm; and also that, if there shall happen any contempt or ir-
reverence to be used in the ceremonies or rites of the Church by the
misusing of the orders appointed in this book, the queen's majesty
may, by the like advice of the said commissioners or metropolitan,
ordain and publish such further ceremonies or rites as may be most
for the advancement of God's glory, the edifying of His Church, and
the due reverence of Christ's holy mysteries and sacraments.

And be it further enacted by the authority aforesaid that all laws,
statutes, and ordinances wherein or whereby any other service, administration of sacraments, or common prayer is limited, established,
or set forth to be used within this realm, or any other the queen's
dominions or countries, shall from henceforth be utterly void and of
none effect.

Ibid., IV, 355 f.: 1 Elizabeth, c. 2.

(C) STATUTE OF ARTIFICERS (1563)

An act containing divers orders for artificers, labourers, etc. Although there remain and stand in force presently a great number of
acts and statutes concerning the retaining, departing, wages, and orders of apprentices, servants, and labourers, as well in husbandry as
in divers other arts, mysteries, and occupations, yet, partly for the
imperfection and contrariety that is found and do appear in sundry
of the said laws, and for the variety and number of them, and chiefly
for that the wages and allowances limited and rated in many of the
said statutes are in divers places too small and not answerable to this
time, respecting the advancement of prices of all things belonging to
the said servants and labourers, the said laws cannot conveniently,
without the great grief and burden of the poor labourer and hired
man, be put in good and due execution; and as the said several acts

and statutes were at the time of the making of them thought to be very good and beneficial for the commonwealth of this realm, as divers of them yet are, so if the substance of as many of the said laws as are meet to be continued shall be digested and reduced into one sole law and statute, and in the same an uniform order prescribed and limited concerning the wages and other orders for apprentices, servants, and labourers, there is good hope that it will come to pass that the same law, being duly executed, should banish idleness, advance husbandry, and yield unto the hired person both in the time of scarcity and in the time of plenty a convenient proportion of wages . . . : be it . . . enacted that no person which shall retain any servant shall put away his or her said servant, and that no person retained according to this statute shall depart from his master, mistress, or dame before the end of his or her term . . . , unless it be for some reasonable and sufficient cause or matter to be allowed before two justices of peace, or one at the least, within the said county, or before the mayor or other chief officer of the city, borough, or town corporate wherein the said master, mistress, or dame inhabiteth, to whom any of the parties grieved shall complain; which said justices or justice, mayor or chief officer, shall have and take upon them or him the hearing and ordering of the matter between the said master, mistress, or dame, and servant according to the equity of the cause. . . .

And for the declaration and limitation what wages servants, labourers, and artificers, either by the year or day or otherwise, shall have and receive, be it enacted . . . that the justices of peace . . . shall yearly, at every general sessions first to be holden and kept after Easter . . . , assemble themselves together; and they so assembled, calling unto them such discreet and grave persons of the said county or of the said city or town corporate as they shall think meet, and conferring together respecting the plenty or scarcity of the time and other circumstances necessary to be considered, shall have authority . . . to limit, rate, and appoint the wages . . . of . . . artificers, handicraftsmen, husbandmen, or any other labourer, servant, or workman . . . , and shall . . . certify the same, engrossed in parchment with the considerations and causes thereof under their hands and seals, into the queen's most honourable court of chancery, whereupon it shall be lawful to the lord chancellor of England . . . , upon declaration thereof to the queen's majesty, her heirs, or successors, or to the lords and others of the privy council for the time being attendant upon their persons, to cause to be printed and sent down . . . into every county, to the sheriff and justices of peace there . . . , ten or twelve proclamations or more, containing in every of them the several rates appointed by the said justices . . . , with commandment by the said proclamations to all persons in the name of the queen's majesty . . . straitly to observe the same, and to all justices, sheriffs, and other officers to see the same duly and severely observed. . . .

Provided always, and be it enacted . . . , that in the time of hay or corn harvest, the justices of peace and every of them, and also the constable or other head officer of every township, upon request and for the avoiding of the loss of any corn, grain, or hay, shall and may cause all such artificers and persons as be meet to labour . . . to serve by the day for the mowing, reaping, shearing, getting, or inning of corn, grain, and hay, according to the skill and quality of the person; and that none of the said persons shall refuse so to do, upon pain to suffer imprisonment in the stocks by the space of two days and one night. . . .

And be it further enacted . . . that two justices of peace, the mayor . . . of any city, borough, or town corporate, and two aldermen . . . shall and may, by virtue hereof, appoint any such woman as is of the age of twelve years and under the age of forty years and unmarried and forth of service, as they shall think meet to serve, to be retained or serve by the year or by the week or day, for such wages and in such reasonable sort and manner as they shall think meet. And if any such woman shall refuse so to serve, then it shall be lawful for the said justices of peace, mayor, or head officers to commit such woman to ward until she shall be bounden to serve as aforesaid.

And be it further enacted that, if any person shall be required by any householder, having and using half a ploughland at the least in tillage, to be an apprentice and to serve in husbandry or in any other kind of art, mystery, or science before expressed, and shall refuse so to do, that then, upon the complaint of such housekeeper made to one justice of peace of the county wherein the said refusal is or shall be made . . . , the said justice or the said mayor . . . shall have power and authority by virtue hereof, if the said person refuse to be bound as an apprentice, to commit him unto ward, there to remain until he be contented and will be bounden to serve as an apprentice should serve, according to the true intent and meaning of this present act.

And if any such master shall misuse or evil intreat his apprentice, or . . . the said apprentice shall have any just cause to complain, or the apprentice do not his duty to his master, then the said master or ·prentice being grieved and having cause to complain shall repair unto one justice of peace within the said county, or to the mayor . . . of the city, town corporate, market town, or other place where the said master dwelleth, who shall by his wisdom and discretion take such order and direction between the said master and his apprentice as the equity of the cause shall require. And if for want of good conformity in the said master, the said justice of peace or . . . mayor . . . cannot compound and agree the matter between him and his apprentice, then the said justice or . . . mayor . . . shall take bond of the said master to appear at the next sessions then to be holden in the said county or . . . town . . . , and, upon his appearance and hearing of the matter before the said justices or the said mayor . . . , if it be thought meet unto them to discharge the said apprentice of his apprenticehood, that then the said justices or four of them at the least . . . , or the said mayor . . . , with the consent of three other of his brethren or men of best reputation within the said . . . town . . . , shall have power . . . , in writing under their hands and seals, to pronounce and declare that they have discharged the said apprentice of his apprenticehood, and the cause thereof; and the said writing, so being made and enrolled by the clerk of the peace or town clerk amongst the records that he keepeth, shall be a sufficient discharge for the said apprentice against his master, his executors, and administrators. . . . And if default shall be found to be in the apprentice, then the said justices or . . . mayor . . . , with the assistants aforesaid, shall cause such due correction and punishment to be ministered unto him as by their wisdom and discretions shall be thought meet. . . .

Ibid., IV, 414 f.: 5 Elizabeth, c. 4.

(D) Treasons Act (1571)[6]

An act whereby certain offences be made treason. . . . Be it enacted, declared, and established . . . that, if any person or persons whatsoever, at any time after the last day of June next coming during the natural life of our most gracious sovereign lady, Queen Elizabeth . . . , shall, within the realm or without, compass, imagine, invent, devise, or intend the death or destruction, or any bodily harm tending to death, destruction, maim, or wounding of the royal person of the same our sovereign lady, Queen Elizabeth; or to deprive or depose her of or from the style, honour, or kingly name of the imperial crown of this realm or of any other realm or dominion to her majesty belonging, or to levy war against her majesty within this realm or without, or to move or to stir any foreigners or strangers with force to invade this realm or the realm of Ireland or any other her majesty's dominions being under her majesty's obeisance, and such compasses, imaginations, inventions, devices, or intentions, or any of them, shall maliciously, advisedly, and expressly utter or declare by any printing, writing, ciphering, speech, words, or sayings; or if any person or persons whatsoever, after the said last day of June, shall maliciously, advisedly, and directly publish, declare, hold opinion, affirm or say by any speech, express words, or sayings that our said sovereign lady, Queen Elizabeth, during her life is not or ought not to be queen of this realm of England and also of the realms of France and Ireland, or that any other person or persons ought of right to be king or queen of the said realms . . . , during her majesty's life, or shall by writing, printing, preaching, speech, express words, or sayings maliciously, advisedly, and directly publish, set forth, and affirm that . . . our said sovereign lady, Queen Elizabeth, is an heretic, schismatic, tyrant, infidel, or an usurper of

[6] Cf. no. 73E. For comment on the treason acts passed between 1495 and 1571, see Tanner, *Tudor Constitutional Documents*, pp. 378-81.

the crown of the said realms or any of them; that then all and every such said offence or offences shall be taken, deemed, and declared, by the authority of this act and parliament, to be high treason; and that as well the principal offender or offenders therein as all and every the abettors, counsellors, and procurers to the same offence or offences, and all and every aiders and comforters of the same offender or offenders . . . shall suffer pains of death and also forfeit unto the queen's majesty, her heirs, and successors, all and singular lands, tenements, and hereditaments, goods, and chattels, as in cases of high treason by the laws and statutes of this realm at this day of right ought to be forfeited and lost. . . .

And be it further enacted that, if any person shall in any wise hold and affirm or maintain that the common laws of this realm not altered by parliament ought not to direct the right of the crown of England; or that our said sovereign lady . . . , with and by the authority of the parliament of England, is not able to make laws and statutes of sufficient force and validity to limit and bind the crown of this realm and the descent, limitation, inheritance, and government thereof; or that this present statute, or any part thereof, or any other statute to be made by the authority of the parliament of England with the royal assent of our said sovereign lady . . . for limiting of the crown, or any statute for recognizing the right of the said crown and realm to be justly and lawfully in the most royal person of our said sovereign lady . . . is not, are not, or shall not or ought not to be forever of good and sufficient force and validity to bind, limit, restrain, and govern all persons . . . whatsoever; every such person, so holding, affirming, or maintaining during the life of the queen's majesty, shall be judged a high traitor, and suffer and forfeit as in cases of high treason is accustomed. . . .

Ibid., IV, 526 f.: 13 Elizabeth, c. 1.

(E) ACT PROHIBITING BULLS FROM ROME (1571)[7]

An act against the bringing in and putting in execution of bulls and other instruments from the see of Rome. Where, in the parliament holden at Westminster in the fifth year of the reign of our sovereign lady the queen's majesty that now is, by one act and statute then and there made . . . it is among other things very well ordained and provided, for the abolishing of the usurped power and jurisdiction of the bishop of Rome and of the see of Rome heretofore unlawfully claimed and usurped within this realm and other the dominions to the queen's majesty belonging, that no person or persons shall hold or stand with to set forth, maintain, defend, or extol the same usurped power, or attribute any manner jurisdiction,

---

[7] Passed in reply to Pius V's bull of the previous year declaring Elizabeth a usurper and freeing her subjects from their allegiance.

authority, or pre-eminence to the same, to be had or used within this realm or any the said dominions, upon pain to incur the danger, penalties, and forfeitures ordained and provided by the Statute of Provision and Praemunire made in the sixteenth year of the reign of King Richard II . . . ; and yet, nevertheless, divers seditious and very evil-disposed people . . . have lately procured and obtained to themselves from the said bishop of Rome and his said see divers bulls and writings, the effect whereof hath been and is to absolve and reconcile all those that will be contented to forsake their due obedience to our most gracious sovereign lady the queen's majesty, and to yield and subject themselves to the said feigned, unlawful, and usurped authority . . . : be it enacted . . . that, if any person or persons, after the first day of July next coming, shall use or put in ure in any place within this realm or in any the queen's dominions any such bull, writing, or instrument . . . of absolution or reconciliation at any time heretofore obtained and gotten, or at any time hereafter to be obtained and gotten, from the said bishop of Rome or any his successors, or from any other person or persons authorized or claiming authority by or from the said bishop of Rome, his predecessors, or successors, or see of Rome; or if any person or persons, after the said first day of July, shall take upon him or them, by colour of any such bull [etc.] . . . , to grant or promise to any person or persons within this realm or any other the queen's majesty's dominions any such absolution or reconciliation by any speech, preaching, teaching, writing, or any other open deed; or if any person or persons within this realm or any the queen's dominions, after the said first day of July, shall willingly receive and take any such absolution or reconciliation; or else if any person or persons have obtained or gotten, since the last day of parliament holden in the first year of the queen's majesty's reign, or after the said first day of July shall obtain or get from the said bishop of Rome or any his successors or see of Rome any manner of bull [etc.] . . . , containing any thing, matter, or cause whatsoever, or shall publish or by any ways or means put in ure any such bull [etc.] . . . ; that then all and every such act and acts, offence and offences, shall be deemed and adjudged by the authority of this act to be high treason, and the offender and offenders therein, their procurers, abettors, and counsellors . . . , shall be deemed and adjudged high traitors to the queen and the realm, and, being thereof lawfully indicted and attainted . . . , shall suffer pains of death, and also lose and forfeit all their lands, tenements, hereditaments, goods, and chattels, as in cases of high treason by the laws of this realm ought to be lost and forfeited. . . .

And be it further enacted by the authority aforesaid that, if any person or persons shall at any time after the said first day of July bring into this realm of England or any the dominions of the same any token or tokens . . . , crosses, pictures, beads, or suchlike vain and superstitious things from the bishop or see of Rome . . . and

. . . shall deliver or offer or cause to be delivered the same or any of them to any subject of this realm, or of any the dominions of the same, to be worn or used in any wise; that then as well the same person and persons so doing as also all and every other person or persons which shall receive and take the same to the intent to use or wear the same, being thereof lawfully convicted and attainted . . . , shall incur into the dangers, penalties, pains, and forfeitures ordained and provided by the Statute of Praemunire and Provision made in the sixteenth year of the reign of King Richard II. . . .

Ibid., IV, 528 f.: 13 Elizabeth, c. 2.

(F) ACT AGAINST SECTARIES (1593)

An act to retain the queen's subjects in obedience. For the preventing and avoiding of such great inconveniences and perils as might happen and grow by the wicked and dangerous practices of seditious sectaries and disloyal persons: be it enacted by the queen's most excellent majesty, and by the lords spiritual and temporal and the commons in this present parliament assembled, and by the authority of the same, that, if any person or persons above the age of sixteen years . . . shall obstinately refuse to repair to some church, chapel, or usual place of common prayer to hear divine service established by her majesty's laws and statutes in that behalf made . . . , [and] shall . . . by printing, writing, or express words or speeches advisedly and purposely practise or go about to move or persuade any of her majesty's subjects . . . to deny, withstand, and impugn her majesty['s] power and authority in causes ecclesiastical, united and annexed to the imperial crown of this realm, or to that end or purpose shall advisedly and maliciously move or persuade any other person whatsoever to forbear or abstain from coming to church to hear divine service, or to receive the communion according to her majesty's laws and statutes aforesaid, or to come to or to be present at any unlawful assemblies, conventicles, or meetings under colour or pretence of any exercise of religion contrary to her majesty's said laws and statutes; or if any person or persons . . . shall . . . willingly join or be present at any such assemblies, conventicles, or meetings . . . ; that then every such person so offending as aforesaid and being thereof lawfully convicted shall be committed to prison, there to remain without bail or mainprise until they shall conform and yield themselves to come to some church, chapel, or usual place of common prayer and hear divine service according to her majesty's laws and statutes aforesaid. . . .[8]

---

[8] The subsequent articles, among other provisions, establish penalties for offenders who refuse to conform, and an oath to be taken by those who submit to the law.

Ibid., IV, 841: 35 Elizabeth, c. 1.

(G) ACT AGAINST PAPISTS (1593)[9]

An act against popish recusants. For the better discovering and avoiding of all such traitorous and most dangerous conspiracies and attempts as are daily devised and practised against our most gracious sovereign lady, the queen's majesty, and the happy estate of this commonweal by sundry wicked and seditious persons, who, terming themselves Catholics and being indeed spies and intelligencers, not only for her majesty's foreign enemies, but also for rebellious and traitorous subjects born within her highness's realms and dominions, and hiding their most detestable and devilish purposes under a false pretext of religion and conscience, do secretly wander and shift from place to place within this realm to corrupt and seduce her majesty's subjects and to stir them to sedition and rebellion: be it ordained and enacted . . . that every person above the age of sixteen years, born within any the queen's majesty's realms or dominions or made denizen, being a popish recusant . . . and having any certain place of dwelling and abode within this realm, shall within forty days next after the end of this session of parliament . . . repair to their place of dwelling where they usually heretofore made their common abode, and shall not any time after pass or remove above five miles from thence. . . .

Provided always, and be it further enacted by the authority aforesaid, that all such persons as . . . aforesaid shall within twenty days next after their coming to any of the said places, as the case shall happen, notify their coming thither and present themselves and deliver their true names in writing to the minister or curate of the same parish and to the constable, headborough, or tithingman of the town; and thereupon the said minister or curate shall presently enter the same into a book to be kept in every parish for that purpose. And afterward the said minister or curate and the said constable, headborough, or tithingman shall certify the same in writing to the justices of the peace of the same county at the next general or quarter sessions to be holden in the said county; and the said justices shall cause the same to be entered by the clerk of the peace in the rolls of the same sessions.

And to the end that the realm be not pestered and overcharged with the multitude of such seditious and dangerous people as is aforesaid, who, having little or no ability to answer or satisfy any competent penalty for their contempt and disobedience of the said laws and statutes and being committed to prison for the same, do live for the most part in better case there than they could if they were abroad at their own liberty . . . : if any such person or persons, being a popish recusant . . . , shall not . . . repair to their place of usual dwelling [etc.] . . . as is aforesaid . . . , and shall not . . . conform themselves to the obedience of the laws and statutes of this realm in coming usually to the church to hear divine

---

[9] An earlier act, 1585, had banished Jesuits and seminary priests.

service, and in making such public confession and submission as hereafter in this act is appointed . . . , such offender . . . shall, upon his . . . corporal oath before any two justices of the peace or coroner of the same county, abjure this realm of England and all other the queen's majesty's dominions forever.

Ibid., IV, 843 f.: 35 Elizabeth, c. 2.

(H) Poor Relief Act (1598)[10]

An act for the relief of the poor. Be it enacted by the authority of this present parliament that the churchwardens of every parish and four substantial householders there . . . , who shall be nominated yearly in Easter week under the hand and seal of two or more justices of the peace in the same county . . . dwelling in or near the same parish, shall be called overseers of the poor of the same parish; and they, or the greater part of them, shall take order from time to time, by and with the consent of two or more such justices of peace, for setting to work of the children of all such whose parents shall not by the said persons be thought able to keep and maintain their children, and also all such persons married or unmarried as, having no means to maintain them, use no ordinary and daily trade of life to get their living by; and also to raise weekly or otherwise, by taxation of every inhabitant and every occupier of lands in the said parish in such competent sum and sums of money as they shall think fit, a convenient stock of flax, hemp, wool, thread, iron, and other necessary ware and stuff to set the poor on work, and also competent sums of money for and towards the necessary relief of the lame, impotent, old, blind, and such other among them being poor and not able to work, and also for the putting out of such children to be apprentices, to be gathered out of the same parish according to the ability of the said parish; and to do and execute all other things, as well for disposing of the said stock as otherwise concerning the premises, as to them shall seem convenient. Which said churchwardens and overseers so to be nominated, or such of them as shall not be let by sickness or other just excuse, to be allowed by such two justices of peace or more, shall meet together at the least once every month in the church of the said parish, upon the Sunday in the afternoon after divine service, there to consider of some good course to be taken and of some meet orders to be set down in the premises; and shall, within four days after the end of their year . . . , make and yield up to such two justices of peace a true and perfect account of all sums of money by them received . . . , upon pain that every one of them absenting them-

---

[10] The provision in this act that local officials should supply the poor with raw materials had appeared in a statute of 1576 to supplement Henry VIII's Beggars Act (no. 74 I). The present statute was re-enacted in 1601 with extension of the tax-paying group and other minor changes. Later poor laws normally cite the revised act.

selves without lawful cause as aforesaid from such monthly meeting for the purpose aforesaid, or being negligent in their office or in the execution of the orders aforesaid, being made by and with the assent of the said justices of peace, to forfeit for every such default 20*s*.

And be it also enacted that, if the said justices of peace do perceive that the inhabitants of any parish are not able to levy among themselves sufficient sums of money for the purposes aforesaid . . . , the said justices shall and may tax, rate, and assess as aforesaid any other [persons] of other parishes, or out of any parish within the hundred where the said parish is . . . , [and] pay such sum and sums of money to the churchwardens and overseers of the said poor parish for the said purposes as the said justices shall think fit, according to the intent of this law. And if the said hundred shall not be thought to the said justices able and fit to relieve the said several parishes not able to provide for themselves as aforesaid, then the justices of peace at their general quarter sessions, or the greater number of them, shall rate and assess as aforesaid . . . other parishes . . . , as in their discretion shall seem fit. . . .

And to the intent that necessary places of habitation may more conveniently be provided for such poor impotent people, be it enacted by the authority aforesaid that it shall and may be lawful for the said churchwardens and overseers, or the greater part of them, by the leave of the lord or lords of the manor whereof any waste or common within their parish is or shall be parcel . . . , to erect, build, and set up . . . in such waste or common, at the general charges of the parish or otherwise of the hundred or county as aforesaid . . . , convenient houses of dwelling for the said impotent poor; and also to place inmates or more families than one in one cottage or house. . . .

And be it further hereby enacted that the mayors, bailiffs, or other head officers of every corporate town within this realm, being justice or justices of peace, shall have the same authority by virtue of this act within the limits and precincts of their corporations, as well out of sessions as at their sessions, as is herein limited, prescribed, and appointed to any of the justices of peace in the county for all the uses and purposes in this act prescribed, and no other justice of peace to enter or meddle there. . . .

And forasmuch as all begging is forbidden by this present act, be it further enacted by the authority aforesaid that the justices of peace of every county or place corporate, or the more part of them, in their general sessions to be holden next after the end of this session of parliament, or in default thereof at the quarter sessions to be holden about the feast of Easter next, shall rate every parish to such a weekly sum of money as they shall think convenient; so as no parish be rated above the sum of sixpence nor under the sum of an halfpenny weekly to be paid, and so as the total sum of such taxation of the parishes in every county amount not above the rate of twopence for every parish in the said county. Which sums so taxed shall be yearly assessed by the agreement of the parishioners within themselves, or in default thereof by the churchwardens and constables of the same parish or the more part of them, or in default of their agreement by the order of such justice or justices of peace as shall dwell in the same parish or, if none be there dwelling, in the parts next adjoining. . . .

Ibid., IV, 896 f.: 39 Elizabeth, c. 3.

82. PROCEEDINGS IN PARLIAMENT (1559-1601)

(A) OPENING OF PARLIAMENT (1559)[1]

[25 January.] The knights, citizens, and burgesses of the house of commons remained sitting in their own house till notice was brought them . . . that her majesty, the lords spiritual and temporal, and the residue were set in the upper house expecting their repair thither. Whereupon they went up immediately unto the said house and . . . Sir Nicholas Bacon, lord keeper . . . , went and stood behind the cloth of estate on the right hand and there spake as followeth, *viz.*: "My lords and masters all, the queen's most excellent majesty, our natural and most gracious sovereign lady, having as you know summoned hither her high court of parliament, hath commanded me to open and declare the chief causes and considerations that moved her highness thereunto. . . . The immediate cause of this summons and assembly be consultations, advice, and contentation. For although divers things that are to be done here in parliament might by means be reformed without parliament, yet the queen's majesty . . . , reposing herself not a little in your fidelities, wisdoms, and discretions, meaneth not at this time to make any resolutions in any matter of weight before it shall be by you sufficiently and fully debated, examined, and considered. Now the matters and causes whereupon you are to consult are chiefly and principally three points. Of those the first is of well-making of laws, for the according and uniting of these people of the realm into an uniform order of religion, to the honour and glory of God, the establishing of the Church, and tranquillity of the realm. The second [is] for the reforming and removing of all enormities and mischiefs that might hurt or hinder the civil orders and policies of this realm. The third and last is advisedly and deeply to weigh and consider the estate and condition of this realm and the losses and decays that have happened of late to the imperial crown thereof; and therefore to advise the best remedies to supply and relieve the same. . . ."

Whereupon, the knights, citizens, and burgesses, departing to their own house, did there take their several places; and, most remaining

---

[1] The following extracts are taken from the journals of the two houses as edited by Sir Simonds D'Ewes. For the sake of preserving the chronological order, a section from the commons' journal is here inserted between two sections of the lords' journal.

silent or speaking very submissively, Mr. Treasurer of the queen's house, standing up uncovered, did first put the house in remembrance of the lord keeper's late speech, and of his declaration of her majesty's pleasure, that they should choose a speaker. And therefore, in humble obedience to her majesty's said pleasure, seeing others remain silent, he thought it his duty to take that occasion to commend to their choice Sir Thomas Gargrave, knight, one of the honourable council in the north parts, a worthy member of the house, and learned in the laws of this realm; by which commendations of his, of the aforesaid worthy member of the house to their consideration, he said he did not intend to debar any other there present from uttering their free opinions and nominating any other whom they thought to be more fitting; and therefore desired them to make known their opinions. Who thereupon did with one consent and voice allow and approve of Mr. Treasurer's nomination, and elected the said Sir Thomas Gargrave to be the prolocutor or speaker of the said house.

The said Sir Thomas Gargrave, being thus elected speaker, after a good pause made, stood up uncovered; and, having in all humility disabled himself, as being unfurnished with that experience and other qualities which were required for the undertaking and undergoing of so great a charge, did conclude with an humble request to the house, to proceed to the new election of some other more able and worthy member amongst them. But, the house still calling upon him to take his place of Mr. Speaker, the before-mentioned Mr. Treasurer and Mr. Comptroller of her majesty's household . . . did rise from their places and, going unto the said Sir Thomas Gargrave unto the place where he sat, did each of them take him, one by the right arm and the other by the left, and led him to the chair at the upper end of the house of commons, and there placed him. Where having sat a while covered, he arose and so, standing bare-headed, he returned his humble thanks unto the whole house for their good opinion of him, promising his best and uttermost endeavour for the faithful discharge of that weighty place to which they had elected him.

[28 January.] The knights, citizens, burgesses, and barons of the house of commons, having notice about one of the clock in the afternoon . . . that her majesty, the lord keeper, and divers lords spiritual and temporal were set in the upper house expecting their attendance, they repaired immediately thither with Sir Thomas Gargrave, knight, their speaker elect. . . . The said Sir Thomas Gargrave was led up to the rail or bar at the lower end of the said house . . . , where, after three reverences made to her majesty, he modestly and submissively excused himself as being unable to undergo the many and great difficulties of that place to which . . . he had been chosen. . . . But, notwithstanding all these reasons and excuses according to the usual form . . . , Sir Nicholas Bacon . . . , by her majesty's commandment . . . , assured him of the queen's acceptance and admission of him. . . .

Upon which speech of the lord keeper's, Sir Thomas Gargrave humbly submitting himself to the undergoing of the charge . . . , made a discreet and submissive answer. . . . Then he proceeded to many hearty prayers and feeling expressions of the good success of the parliament. . . . And lastly he came, according to the usual form, first to desire liberty of access for the house of commons to the queen's majesty's presence upon all urgent and necessary occasions. Secondly . . . , if in anything himself should mistake or misreport or over-slip that which should be committed unto him to declare, that it might, without prejudice to the house, be better declared, and that his unwilling miscarriage therein might be pardoned. Thirdly, that they might have liberty and freedom of speech in whatsoever they treated of, or had occasion to propound and debate in the house. The fourth and last, that all the members of the house, with their servants and necessary attendants, might be exempted from all manner of arrests and suits during the continuance of the parliament and the usual space, both before the beginning and after the ending thereof, as in former times hath always been accustomed. . . .

To which speech of the said speaker the lord keeper, without any long pausing, replied again in manner and form following: . . . "To these petitions the queen's majesty hath commanded me to say unto you that her highness is right well contented to grant them unto you, as largely, as amply, and as liberally as ever they were granted by any her noble progenitors; and to confirm the same with as great an authority. Marry, with these conditions and cautions: first, that your access be void of importunity, and for matters needful, and in time convenient; for the second, that your diligence and carefulness be such, Mr. Speaker, that the defaults in that part be as rare as may be, whereof her majesty doubteth little; for the third, which is for liberty of speech, therewith her highness is right well contented, but so as they be neither unmindful or uncareful of their duties, reverence, and obedience to their sovereign; for the last, great heed would be taken that no evil-disposed person seek of purpose that privilege for the only defrauding of his creditors and for the maintenance of injuries and wrongs. These admonitions being well remembered, her majesty thinketh all the said liberties and privileges well granted. . . ."

D'Ewes, *Journal*, pp. 11-40.

(B) Procedure on a Bill (1559)

[3 February.] . . . The clerk of the said house, having read the title and the bill aforesaid, standing, kissing his hand, delivered the same, with a breviate containing the substance of the bill annexed unto it, unto the speaker; who thereupon, standing up uncovered and reading both the title and the breviate, said, "This is the second reading." And then, having paused a while, and . . . none speaking against the bill, he put the question for the committing thereof, as followeth, *viz.*: "As many as do think fit this bill should be committed say Yea"; and after the affirmative voice given, "As many as shall think the contrary say No." And then . . . the speaker, judging that the affirmative voice was the greatest, did put the house in mind to name committees. And thereupon every one of the house that listed did name such other members of the same, to be of the committee, as they thought fit. . . . And when a convenient number of the committees named were set down by the clerk, then did the speaker move the house to name the time and place when and where they should meet, which the clerk did also doubtless then take a note of, and did also (silence being made in the house) read out of that book or paper (in which he entered them) the committees' names, with the time and place of their meeting. . . .

[7 February.] The clerk of the house, standing up, read the title and the bill aforesaid and, kissing his hand, delivered the same unto the speaker. Who, standing up uncovered, read again the title of the said bill and opened shortly the effects thereof, and then said, "This is the third reading of this bill"; and told them further that with their favour he would now put it to the question for the passing, but paused a while to see if any member of the house would speak unto it. . . . And whether any of the said house spake unto the said bill or not doth not appear. But the speaker, holding the bill in his hand, made the question for the passing of it in this sort, *viz.*: "As many as are of the mind that the bill shall pass say Yea." Which being answered accordingly by the house, or the greatest part of them, the bill passed; and so he delivered it again unto the clerk who, because the bill was originally begun and first passed in the house of commons, wrote within the said bill, on top of it towards the right hand, these words, *viz.*: *Soit baillé aux seigneurs.*[2]

Ibid., pp. 44 f.

(C) Speech of the Lord Keeper on the Administration of Justice (1559)

. . . Is it not great fondness, trow you, for men to use their endeavours to make good laws to govern men's doings and to weed out those that be evil in the commonwealth, and thereupon to bind them fair in books, and to lay them up without seeing to the execution of those laws? Yes, surely. Wherefore ye see that, as there hath been used by you great wisdom and discretion in devising of some, so it is very necessary that like diligence and pains be taken by you and others to see the good execution of all. The effect of which charge consisteth principally in three points: the first in conservation of the queen's peace; the second in administration of justice between subject and subject; and the third in the observation of one uniform order in religion according to the laws now established.

For the first, ye are to foresee all manner of frays, forces, riots, and routs, and the discovering and repealing in time of all manner of

---

[2] Let it be delivered to the lords.

conspiracies, confederacies, and conventicles. And in this part also you are to provide for the swift and speedy appeasing of all manner of tumults, stirs, and uproars, if any happen; and for the diligent searching out and severe punishment of all manner of felonies, burglaries, and all other like enormities—matters, as you know, against the queen's majesty's peace, crown, and dignity. For the well-doing whereof two things are chiefly to be eschewed: the one is slothfulness; the other is uncarefulness. For how can justice banish these enormities, where her ministers be so slothful that they will never creep out of their doors to any courts, sessions, or assizes for the due administration thereof, except they be drawn thereunto with some matters of their own; nor cannot endure to have their ears troubled with the hearing of controversies of their neighbours, for the good appeasing of the same? Or how can the uncareful man that maketh no account of any of the common causes of his country, but respecteth only his private matters and commodities, become a just and diligent searcher out, follower, and corrector of felonies, murders, and suchlike common enemies to the commonwealth? And yet true it is that such careless and slothful men do daily colour and cloak these their faults with the title of quietness. . . .

For the second, you are to provide that all embracers, maintainers, and champerties,[3] which be utter enemies to the due execution of justice between subject and subject, be neither committed by any of you nor, as near as you can, be suffered to be committed by any other—a very behoveful matter to be both carefully and earnestly looked unto, as the root and seed of all justice, and especially if any of these faults light upon any person that hath authority or rule in the country or hath any office of justice to execute among the people. Is it not, trow you, a monstrous disguising to have a justicer a maintainer; to have him, that should by his oath and duty set forth justice and right, against his oath and duty to offer injury and wrong; to have him, that is specially chosen amongst a number by the prince to appease all brablings and controversies, to be a sower and maintainer of strife and sedition, amongst them seeking his reputation and opinion by leading and swaying of juries according to his will—acquitting some for gain, indicting others for malice; bearing with him as his servant, overthrowing the other as his enemy; procuring all questmongers to be of his livery, or otherwise in his danger, that his winks, frowning, and countenance may direct all inquests? Surely, surely, it is true that these be they that be subverters and perverters of all laws and orders; yea, that make daily the laws, that of their own nature be good, to become instruments of mischief. These indeed be they of whom such examples would be made and the founders and maintainers of all enormities. And these be those, whom if you can-

---

[3] A champertor was a man who supported a litigant for a share in the proceeds of the suit.

not reform for their greatness, yet ought you to complain of their villainies. And thus much for the due administration of justice. . . .

Ibid., pp. 33 f.

(D) A Day's Business in the Commons (1563)

[8 March.] On Monday, the 8th day of March, three bills had each of them one reading; of which the first, being the bill that St. Katherine's Church shall be a parish church, and the second, for the repairing and mending of highways, were read the third time and passed the house, and were sent up to the lords by Mr. Comptroller. Mr. Attorney brought from the lords three bills, of which one was the bill for denizens' children. The bill also against the unlawful taking of fish, deer, or hawks was read the third time and passed. *Post Meridiem.* In the afternoon eight bills had each of them one reading; of which one was the bill for the subsidy of the clergy. Richard Parrott, gentleman, burgess for Sandwich, for his sickness was licensed to be absent.

Ibid., p. 87.

(E) Procedure on a Request for Supply (1566)

[17 October.] . . . Sir Edward Rogers, knight, comptroller of her majesty's household, moved the house to have consideration of the queen's majesty's late great and extraordinary expenses, to proportion out some supply accordingly. And thereupon Sir William Cecil, knight, her highness' principal secretary, made an excellent declaration of the queen's great charges in defending New Haven in France, in repairing and increasing the navy and munition, her charges also against John O'Neill in Ireland. And immediately thereupon all the privy council being members of this house, the master of the rolls, and forty others of the house, whose names are omitted through the negligence of the clerk, were nominated and appointed to consider of the rate and payment of some supply and aid to be given to her majesty, and ordered to meet to-morrow in the afternoon, in the star chamber.

Ibid., p. 124.

(F) Debate on Freedom of Speech (1566)[4]

[9 November.] . . . Sir Francis Knolles, knight, her majesty's vice-chamberlain, declared the queen's majesty's express commands to this house that they should no further proceed in their suit, but to satisfy themselves with her highness' promise of marriage. After whom Mr. Secretary Cecil and Mr. Comptroller severally rehearsed the like matter. . . .

[11 November.] . . . Paul Wentworth, a burgess of the house,

---

[4] See J. E. Neale, "The Commons' Privilege of Free Speech in Parliament," in *Tudor Studies,* pp. 257 f.

by way of motion desired to know whether the queen's command and inhibition, that they should no longer dispute of the matter of succession . . . , were not against the liberties and privileges of the said house. And thereupon arose divers arguments, which continued from nine of the clock in the morning till two of the clock in the afternoon. But then, because the time was far spent, all further debate and reasoning was deferred until the next morning. . . .

[12 November.] Mr. Speaker, being sent for to attend upon the queen's majesty at the court, about nine of the clock, sent word to the house where he was, requiring the house to have patience; and at his coming, after ten of the clock, began to show that he had received a special command from her highness to this house, notwithstanding her first commandment, that there should not be further talk of that matter in the house (touching the declaration of a successor, in case that her majesty should die without issue), and if any person thought himself not satisfied, but had further reasons, let him come before the privy council and there show them. . . .

[25 November.] . . . Mr. Speaker, coming from the queen's majesty, declared her highness' pleasure to be that, for her good will to the house, she did revoke her two former commandments, requiring the house no further to proceed at this time in the matter. Which revocation was taken of all the house most joyfully, with most hearty prayer and thanks for the same. . . .

Ibid., pp. 128-30.

(G) Speech of the Queen (1567)

[2 April.] . . . Then the queen, standing up, said (after she had given her royal assent unto nineteen public acts, and thirteen private): "My lords and others the commons of this assembly, although the lord keeper hath, according to order, very well answered in my name, yet as a periphrasis I have a few words further to speak unto you, notwithstanding I have not been used nor love to do it in such open assemblies. Yet now, not to the end to amend his talk, but remembering that commonly princes' own words be better printed in the hearers' memory than those spoken by her command, I mean to say thus much unto you. I have in this assembly found so much dissimulation, where I always professed plainness, that I marvel thereat—yea, two faces under one hood (and the body rotten) being covered with two vizors, succession and liberty, which they determined must be either presently granted, denied, or deferred. In granting whereof, they had their desires; and denying or deferring thereof (those things being so plaudable as indeed to all men they are) they thought to work me that mischief which never foreign enemy could bring to pass, which is the hatred of my commons. But, alas, they began to pierce the vessel before the wine was fined; and began a thing, not foreseeing the end, how by this means I have seen my well-willers from mine enemies, and can, as me seemeth, very well divide the house into four: first, the broachers and workers thereof, who are in the greatest fault; secondly, the speakers, who by eloquent tales persuaded others, are in the next degree; thirdly, the agreers, who, being so light of credit that the eloquence of the tales so overcame them, that they gave more credit thereunto than unto their own wits; and lastly, those that sat still mute and meddled not therewith, but rather wondered, disallowing the matter, who in my opinion are most to be excused.

"But do you think that either I am unmindful of your surety by succession, wherein is all my care, considering I know myself to be mortal? No, I warrant you. Or that I went about to break your liberties? No, it was never in my meaning; but to stay you before you fell into the ditch. For all things have their time. And although perhaps you may have after me one better learned or wiser; yet, I assure you, none more careful over you. And therefore henceforth, whether I live to see the like assembly or no, or whoever it be, yet beware however you prove your prince's patience, as you have now done mine. And now to conclude, all this notwithstanding (not meaning to make a Lent of Christmas), the most part of you may assure yourselves that you depart in your prince's grace." . . .

Ibid., pp. 116 f.

(H) Debate on Freedom of Speech (1571)

[20 April.] . . . Mr. Wentworth, very orderly, in many words remembered the speech of Sir Humphrey Gilbert delivered some days before. He proved his speech (without naming him) to be an injury to the house; he noted his disposition to flatter and fawn on the prince, comparing him to the chameleon, which can change himself into all colours saving white. "Even so," said he, "this reporter can change himself to all fashions but honesty." He showed further the great wrong done to one of the house by a misreport made to the queen (meaning Mr. Bell); he showed his speech to tend to no other end than to inculcate fear into those which should be free. He requested care for the credit of the house and for the maintenance of free speech (the only means of ordinary proceedings), and to preserve the liberties of the house, to reprove liars, inveighing greatly out of the Scriptures and otherwise against liars—as this of David, "Thou, O Lord, shalt destroy liars," etc.

Mr. Treasurer signified his desire to have all things well, saying he could not enter into judgment of any; but he said it was convenient ill speeches should be avoided, and the good meaning of all men to be taken, without wresting or misreporting, and the meaning of all men to be showed in good sort without unseemly words.

Mr. Speaker endeavoured an agreement and unity in the house, making signification that the queen's majesty had in plain words declared unto him that she had good intelligence of the orderly proceeding among us; whereof she had as good liking as ever she had of any parliament since she came unto the crown, and wished we should give her no other cause than to continue the same ; and added further her majesty's pleasure to be to take order for licences, wherein she had been careful, and more careful would be.

Mr. Carleton, with a very good zeal and orderly show of obedience, made signification how that a member of the house was detained from them (meaning Mr. Strickland), by whose commandment or for what cause he knew not. But forasmuch as he was not now a private man, but to supply the room, person, and place of a multitude specially chosen and therefore sent, he thought that neither in regard of the country, which was not to be wronged, nor for the liberty of the house, which was not to be infringed, we should permit him to be detained from us ; but, whatsoever the intendment of this offence might be, that he should be sent for to the bar of that house, there to be heard, and there to answer.

Mr. Treasurer in some case gave advertisement to be wary in our proceedings, and neither to venture further than our assured warrant might stretch nor to hazard our good opinion with her majesty on any doubtful cause. Withal, he wished us not to think worse than there was cause. "For the man," quoth he, "that is meant is neither detained nor misused ; but on considerations is required to expect the queen's pleasure upon certain special points"—wherein he said he durst to assure that the man should neither have cause to dislike or complain, since so much favour was meant unto him as he reasonably could wish. He further said that he was in no sort stayed for any word or speech by him in that place offered, but for the exhibiting of a bill into the house against the prerogative of the queen ; which was not to be tolerated. Nevertheless, the construction of him was rather to have erred in his zeal and bill offered than maliciously to have meant anything contrary to the dignity royal. And lastly, he concluded that oft it had been seen that speeches have been examined and considered of. . . .

Ibid., p. 175.

(I) INTERVENTION BY THE QUEEN (1572)

[22 May.] . . . Upon declaration made unto this house by Mr. Speaker from the queen's majesty, that her highness' pleasure is that from henceforth no bills concerning religion shall be preferred or received into this house, unless the same should be first considered and liked by the clergy ; and further, that her majesty's pleasure is to see the two last bills read in this house touching rites and ceremonies : it is ordered by the house that the same bills shall be delivered unto her majesty by all the privy council that are of this house, Mr. Heneage, and Mr. Doctor Wilson, master of the requests, or by any four of them. . . .

[23 May.] Mr. Treasurer reported to the house the delivery of the two bills of rites and ceremonies to her majesty, together with the humble request of this house, most humbly to beseech her highness not to conceive ill opinion of this house if it so were that her majesty should not like well of the said bills, or of the parties that preferred them; and declared further that her majesty seemed utterly to mislike of the first bill, and of him that brought the same into the house, and that her highness' express will and pleasure was that no preacher or minister should be impeached or indicted, or otherwise molested or troubled, as the preamble of the said bill did purport; adding these comfortable words farther, that her majesty, as defender of the faith, will aid and maintain all good Protestants to the discouraging of all Papists. . . .

Ibid., p. 213 f.

(J) The Case of Peter Wentworth (1576)[5]

[8 February.] . . . Peter Wentworth, esquire, one of the burgesses for the borough of Tregony in the county of Cornwall, was, for unreverent and undutiful words uttered by him in this house of our sovereign lady the queen's majesty, sequestered, that the house might proceed to conference and consideration of his said speech [which in part follows] :—

"Mr. Speaker, I find written in a little volume these words in effect: 'Sweet is the name of liberty, but the thing itself a value beyond all inestimable treasure.' So much the more it behooveth us to take care lest we, contenting ourselves with the sweetness of the name, lose and forgo the thing, being of greatest value that can come unto this noble realm. The inestimable treasure is the use of it in this house. . . .

"I was never of parliament but the last, and the last session [of this parliament] ; at both which times I saw the liberty of free speech, the which is the only salve to heal all the sores of this commonwealth, so much and so many ways infringed, and so many abuses offered to this honourable council, as hath much grieved me even of very conscience and love to my prince and state. Wherefore, to avoid the like, I do think it expedient to open the commodities that grow to the prince and whole state by free speech used in this place—at the least so much as my simple wit can gather of it, the which is very little in respect of that that wise heads can say therein; and so it is of the more force.

"First, all matters that concern God's honour through free speech, shall be propagated here and set forward, and all things that do hinder it removed, repulsed, and taken away.

"Next, there is nothing commodious, profitable, or any way beneficial for the prince or state, but faithful and loving subjects will offer it in this place.

"Thirdly, all things discommodious, perilous, or hurtful to the

---

[5] See J. E. Neale, "Peter Wentworth," in the *English Historical Review,* XXXIX, 36 f., 175 f.

prince or state shall be prevented—even so much as seemeth good to our merciful God to put into our minds, the which no doubt shall be sufficient if we do earnestly call upon Him and fear Him; for Solomon saith, 'The fear of God is the beginning of wisdom.' Wisdom, saith he, breatheth life into her children, receiveth them that seek her, and will go beside them in the way of righteousness; so that our minds shall be directed to all good, needful, and necessary things, if we call upon God with faithful hearts.

"Fourthly, if the envious do offer anything hurtful or perilous to the prince or state in this place, what incommodity doth grow thereby? Verily I think none. Nay, will you have me to say my simple opinion therein, much good cometh thereof. How forsooth? For by the darkness of the night the brightness of the sun showeth more excellent and clear. And how can truth appear and conquer until falsehood and all subtleties that should shadow and darken it be found out? For it is offered in this place a piece of fine needlework unto them that are most skilful therein; for there cannot be a false stitch (God aiding us) but will be found out.

"Fifthly, this good cometh thereof: a wicked purpose may the easier be prevented when it is known.

"Sixthly, an evil man can do the less harm when it is known.

"Seventhly, sometime it happeneth that a good man will in this place (for argument sake) prefer an evil cause, both for that he would have a doubtful truth to be opened and manifested, and also the evil prevented; so that to this point I conclude that in this house, which is termed a place of free speech, there is nothing so necessary for the preservation of the prince and state as free speech. And without, it is a scorn and mockery to call it a parliament house; for in truth it is none, but a very school of flattery and dissimulation, and so a fit place to serve the devil and his angels in, and not to glorify God and benefit the commonwealth. . . .

"Now to the impediments thereof. . . . Amongst other, Mr. Speaker, two things do great hurt in this place, of the which I do mean to speak. The one is a rumour which runneth about the house, and this it is: 'Take heed what you do; the queen's majesty liketh not such a matter; whosoever prefereth it, she will be offended with him'—(or the contrary) 'Her majesty liketh of such a matter; whosoever speaketh against it she will be much offended with him.' The other: sometimes a message is brought into the house either of commanding or inhibiting, very injurious to the freedom of speech and consultation. I would to God, Mr. Speaker, that these two were buried in hell—I mean rumours and messages; for wicked undoubtedly they are. The reason is the devil was the first author of them, from whom proceedeth nothing but wickedness. Now I will set down reasons to prove them wicked. . . .

"The queen's majesty is the head of the law and must of necessity maintain the law; for by the law her majesty is made justly our queen and by it she is most chiefly maintained. Hereunto agreeth the most excellent words of Bracton, who saith, 'The king hath no peer nor equal in his kingdom.' He hath no equal, for otherwise he might lose his authority of commanding, sithence that an equal hath no rule of commandment over his equal. The king ought not to be under man, but under God and under the law, because the law maketh him a king. Let the king therefore attribute that to the law which the law attributeth unto him: that is, dominion and power; for he is not a king in whom will and not the law doth rule. And therefore he ought to be under the law. . . ."

Upon this speech, the house, out of a reverend regard of her majesty's honour, stopped his further proceeding before he had fully finished his speech. . . . Mr. Wentworth being sequestered the house as aforesaid for his said speech, it was agreed and ordered by the house upon the question, after sundry motions and disputations had therein, that he should presently be committed to the serjeant's ward as prisoner and, so remaining, should be examined upon his said speech, for the extenuating of his fault therein, by all the privy council being of this house, the master of the requests, the captain of the guard, Mr. Treasurer of the Chamber, the master of the jewelhouse, the master of the wardrobe, Mr. Lieutenant of the Tower, Sir Thomas Scott, Sir Rowland Hayward, Mr. Attorney of the Duchy, Mr. Henry Knolles the elder, Mr. Sampoole, Mr. Randall, Mr. Birched, Mr. Marsh—who were appointed to meet this afternoon between two and three of the clock at the star chamber, and to make report at this house to-morrow next. . . .

Committee . . . : "Here you have uttered certain rumours of the queen's majesty. Where and of whom heard you them?"
Wentworth: "If your honours ask me as councillors to her majesty, you shall pardon me: I will make you no answer. I will do no such injury to the place from whence I came; for I am now no private person. I am a public, and a councillor to the whole state in that place where it is lawful for me to speak my mind freely, and not for you as councillors to call me to account for anything that I do speak in the house. And therefore, if you ask me as councillors to her majesty, you shall pardon me: I will make no answer. But if you ask me as committees from the house, I will make you the best answer I can."
Committee: "We ask you as committees from the house."
Wentworth: "I will then answer you. . . ."

[9 February.] This day Mr. Treasurer, in the name of all the committees yesterday appointed for the examination of Peter Wentworth, burgess for Tregony, declared that all the said committees did meet yesterday in the afternoon in the star chamber according to their commission; and there, examining the said Peter Wentworth touching the violent and wicked words yesterday pronounced by him in this house touching the queen's majesty, made a collection of the same words, which words, so collected, the said Peter Wentworth did acknowledge and confess. And then did the said Mr.

Treasurer read unto the house the said note of collection. Which being read, he declared further that the said Peter Wentworth, being examined what he could say for the extenuating of his said fault and offence, could neither say anything at all to that purpose, neither yet did charge any other person as author of his said speech; but did take all the burden thereof unto himself. And so the said Mr. Treasurer thereupon moved for his punishment and imprisonment in the Tower as the house should think good and consider of. Whereupon, after sundry disputations and speeches, it was ordered upon the question that the said Peter Wentworth should be committed close prisoner to the Tower for his said offence, there to remain until such time as this house should have further consideration of him. And thereupon, immediately, the said Peter Wentworth, being brought to the bar by the serjeant, received his said judgment accordingly by the mouth of Mr. Speaker in form above-recited. And so Mr. Lieutenant of the Tower was presently charged with the custody of the said Peter Wentworth. But the said Peter Wentworth was shortly, by the queen's special favour, restored again to his liberty and place in the house. . . .

Ibid., pp. 236-44.

(K) THE CASE OF ARTHUR HALL (1581)[6]

[4 February.] . . . Upon a motion made to this house by Mr. Norton, in which he declared that some person of late had caused a book to be set forth in print (not only greatly reproachful against some particular good members of this house of great credit, but also very much slanderous and derogatory to the general authority, power, and state of this house, and prejudicial to the validity of the proceedings of the same in making and establishing of laws: charging this house with drunkenness, as accompanied in their councils with Bacchus; and then also with choler, as those which had never failed to Anticyra; and the proceedings of this house to be *opera tenebrarum*) and further that, by the circumstance of the residue of the discourse of the said book, he conjectured the same to be done and procured by Mr. Arthur Hall, one of this house; and so prayed thereupon the said Mr. Hall might be called by this house to answer, and the matter further to be duly examined as the weight thereof, in due consideration of the gravity and wisdom of this house and of the authority, state, and liberty of the same, requireth: it is resolved that the said Mr. Hall be forthwith sent for by the serjeant-at-arms attending upon this house, to make his appearance here in that behalf accordingly.

And then immediately Mr. Secretary Wilson did thereupon signify unto this house that the said Mr. Hall had, upon his examination therein before the lords of the council, heretofore confessed in the hearing of the said Mr. Secretary that he did cause the said

---

[6] See H. Wright, *Arthur Hall*.

book to be printed indeed. Upon relation whereof, and after some speech then also uttered unto this house by Mr. Chancellor of the Exchequer, of the dangerous and lewd contents of the book, the serjeant was forthwith, by order of this house, sent to apprehend the said Arthur Hall, and presently assisted for that purpose with Sir Thomas Scott and Sir Thomas Browne, by the appointment of this house. . . .

[14 February.] Mr. Vice-Chamberlain, for himself and the residue of the committees appointed to examine Mr. Hall, the printer, the scrivener, and all other persons privy to the setting forth and publishing of the book, declared that they had charged the said Mr. Hall with contempt against this house the last session. . . . Unto all which things . . . the said Mr. Hall could make no reasonable answer or denial. . . .

Mr. Hall was brought to the bar, where, after some reverence done by him (though not yet in such humble and lowly wise as the state of one in that place to be charged and accused requireth), whereof being admonished by Mr. Speaker and further by him charged with sundry of the said parts collected out of the said book, he submitted himself to the house, refusing to make any answer or defence at all in the matter; but, acknowledging his error, prayed pardon of the whole house with all his heart; and, that done, was sequestered.

After which, upon sundry motions and arguments had touching the quality and nature of his faults, and of some proportionable forms of punishment for the same (as imprisonment, fine, banishment from the fellowship of this house, and an utter condemnation and retraction of the said book), it was upon the question resolved by the whole house, without any one negative voice, that he should be committed to prison. And upon another question [it was] likewise resolved that he should be committed to the prison of the Tower, as the prison proper to this house. And upon another question it was in like manner resolved that he should remain in the said prison of the Tower by the space of six months, and so much longer as until himself should willingly make a retractation of the said book to the satisfaction of this house, or of such order as this house shall take for the same during the continuance of this present parliament. And upon another question it was also in like manner resolved that a fine should be assessed by this house, to the queen's majesty's use, upon the said Mr. Hall for his said offence. And upon another question it was also resolved in like manner that the said fine should be 500m. And upon another question also it was likewise resolved that the said Mr. Hall should presently be severed and cut off from being a member of this house any more during the continuance of this present parliament; and that Mr. Speaker, by authority of this house, should direct a warrant from this house to the clerk of the crown-office in the chancery for awarding of the queen's majesty's writ to the sheriff of the said county of Lincoln, for a new burgess to be returned into this present parliament for the said borough of Grantham in lieu and stead of the said Arthur Hall, so as before disabled any longer to be a member of this house. . . .

Ibid., pp. 291 f.

(L) PETER WENTWORTH'S QUESTIONS ON FREE SPEECH (1587)

On Wednesday, the first day of March, Mr. Wentworth delivered unto Mr. Speaker certain articles which contained questions touching the liberties of the house . . . :—

Whether this council be not a place for any member of the same here assembled, freely and without controlment of any person or danger of laws, by bill or speech to utter any of the griefs of this commonwealth whatsoever touching the service of God, the safety of the prince, and this noble realm. Whether that great honour may be done unto God, and benefit and service unto the prince and state without free speech in this council which may be done with it. Whether there be any council which can make, add to, or diminish from the laws of the realm, but only this council of parliament. Whether it be not against the orders of this council to make any secret or matter of weight, which is here in hand, known to the prince or any other, concerning the high service of God, prince, or state, without the consent of the house. Whether the speaker or any other may interrupt any member of this council in his speech used in this house, tending to any of the forenamed high services. Whether the speaker may rise when he will, any matter being propounded, without consent of the house or not. Whether the speaker may overrule the house in any matter or cause there in question, or whether he is to be ruled or overruled in any matter or not. Whether the prince and state can continue, stand, and be maintained without this council of parliament, not altering the government of the state.

At the end, lastly, of the said speech and questions is set down this short note or memorial ensuing; by which it may be perceived both what Serjeant Puckering, the speaker, did with the said questions after he had received them, and what became also of this business. . . . These questions Mr. Puckering pocketed up and showed Sir Thomas Heneage, who so handled the matter that Mr. Wentworth went to the Tower and the questions [were] not at all moved. . . .

Ibid., p. 411.

(M) SPEECH OF THE LORD KEEPER ON THE PRIVILEGES OF THE COMMONS (1593)

. . . Her gracious majesty is well pleased to grant them so far as they be grantable. She saith there be two things in a man most behoveful if they be well used, and most deadly if they be ill used: wit and tongue, they are those. They be most happy possessions and needful helps, and all as they be placed. Having therefore especial care that that may never hurt you, which she by her grant doth yield you, she wills you take good heed in what sort she permits it. She would be sorry that folly past should by new redouble the faults, and chargeth you, Mr. Speaker, if any shall deliver to you any bill that passeth the reach of a subject's brain to mention, that same you receive not, but with purpose to show it where it best becometh you. Next, if any speech undecent or matter unfit for that place be used, remember them of this lesson: your petitions . . . must be ruled, and that thus her majesty granteth you liberal but not licentious speech; liberty therefore, but with due limitation. For even as there can be no good consultation where all freedom of advice is barred, so will there be no good conclusion where every man speak what he listeth, without fit observation of persons, matters, times, places, and other needful circumstances. It shall be meet, therefore, that each man of you contain his speech within the bounds of loyalty and good discretion, being assured that, as the contrary is punishable in all men, so most of all in them that take upon them to be counsellors and procurators of the commonwealth. For liberty of speech her majesty commandeth me to tell you that, to say yea or no to bills, God forbid that any man should be restrained or afraid to answer according to his best liking, with some short declaration of his reason therein, and therein to have a free voice, which is the very true liberty of the house; not, as some suppose, to speak there of all causes as him listeth, and to frame a form of religion or a state of government as to their idle brains shall seem meetest. She saith no king fit for his state will suffer such absurdities; and, though she hopeth no man here longeth so much for his ruin as that he mindeth to make such a peril to his own safety, yet, that you may better follow what she wisheth, she makes of her goodness you the partakers of her intent and meaning.

English Historical Review, XXXI, 136.

(N) Speech of Serjeant Heyle (1601)

[9 November.] . . . Then Serjeant Heyle stood up and made a motion, saying: "Mr. Speaker, I marvel much that the house will stand upon granting of a subsidy, or the time of payment, when all we have is her majesty's; and she may lawfully at her pleasure take it from us. Yea, she hath as much right to all our lands and goods as to any revenue of her crown." At which all the house hemmed and laughed and talked. "Well," quoth Serjeant Heyle, "all your hemming shall not put me out of countenance." So Mr. Speaker stood up and said, "It is a great disorder that this should be used; for it is the ancient use of every man to be silent when any one speaketh, and he that is speaking should be suffered to deliver his mind without interruption." So the said serjeant proceeded and, when he had spoken a little while, the house hemmed again; and so he sat down. In his latter speech he said he could prove his former position by precedent in the times of Henry III, King John, King Stephen; which was the occasion of their hemming. . . .

D'Ewes, *Journal*, p. 633.

(O) SPEECHES BY SIR ROBERT CECIL (1601)

[24 November.] . . . Upon some loud confusion in the house touching some private murmur of monopolies, Mr. Secretary Cecil said: "The duty I owe and the zeal to extinguish monopolies makes me to speak now, and to satisfy their opinions that think there shall be no redress of these monopolies. Order is attended with these two handmaids, gravity and zeal; but zeal with discretion. I have been (though unworthy) a member of this house in six or seven parliaments; yet never did I see the house in so great confusion. I believe there never was in any parliament a more tender point handled than the liberty of the subject; that, when any is discussing this point, he should be cried and coughed down—this is more fit for a grammar school than a court of parliament. I have been a councillor of state this twelve years; yet did I never know it subject to construction of levity and disorder. Much more ought we to be regardful in so great and grave an assembly. Why, we have had speeches upon speeches, without either order or discretion. One would have had us proceed by bill and see if the queen would have denied it; another, that the patents should be brought here before us and cancelled—and this were bravely done! Others would have us to proceed by way of petition, which course doubtless is best; but for the first, and especially for the second, it is so ridiculous, that I think we should have as bad success as the devil himself would have wished in so good a cause. Why, if idle courses had been followed, we should have gone forsooth to the queen with a petition to have repealed a patent of monopoly of tobacco pipes (which Mr. Wingfield's note had) and I know not how many conceits. But I wish every man to rest satisfied till the committees have brought in their resolutions according to your commandments." . . .

[25 November.] . . . Mr. Secretary Cecil stood up and said: "I fear we are not secret within ourselves. Then must I needs give you this for a future caution: that whatsoever is subject to public expectation cannot be good, while the parliament matters are ordinary talk in the street. I have heard myself, being in my coach, these words spoken aloud: 'God prosper those that further the overthrow of these monopolies! God send the prerogative touch not our liberty!' I will not wrong any so much as to imagine he was of this assembly. Yet let me give you this note: that the time was never more apt to disorder and make ill interpretation of good meaning. I think those persons would be glad that all sovereignty were converted into popularity. We, being here, are but the popular branch, and our liberty [is] the liberty of the subject. And the world is apt to slander most especially the ministers of government. . . ."

Ibid., pp. 651, 653.

(P) SPEECH OF THE QUEEN (1601)

[30 November.] In the afternoon, about three of the clock, some sevenscore of the house met at the great chamber before the council chamber in Whitehall. At length the queen came into the council chamber where, sitting under the cloth of state at the upper end, the speaker with all the company came in and, after three low reverences made, he spake to this effect. . . . And, after three low reverences made, he with the rest kneeled down, and her majesty began thus to answer herself, *viz.*: "Mr. Speaker, we have heard your declaration and perceive your care of our state by falling into the consideration of a grateful acknowledgment of such benefits as you have received; and that your coming is to present thanks unto us, which I accept with no less joy than your loves can have desire to offer such a present. I do assure you that there is no prince that loveth his subjects better, or whose love can countervail our love. There is no jewel, be it of never so rich a prize, which I prefer before this jewel; I mean your love. For I do more esteem it than any treasure or riches; for that we know how to prize, but love and thanks I count inestimable. And though God hath raised me high, yet this I count the glory of my crown, that I have reigned with your loves. This makes me that I do not so much rejoice that God hath made me to be a queen, as to be a queen over so thankful a people. Therefore I have cause to wish nothing more than to content the subject, and that is a duty which I owe. Neither do I desire to live longer days than that I may see your prosperity, and that's my only desire. And as I am that person that still, yet under God, hath delivered you, so I trust, by the almighty power of God, that I still shall be His instrument to preserve you from envy, peril, dishonour, shame, tyranny, and oppression; partly by means of your intended helps, which we take very acceptably, because it manifesteth the largeness of your loves and loyalties unto your sovereign. Of myself I must say this: I never was any greedy, scraping grasper, nor a strait fast-holding prince, nor yet a waster. My heart was never set on worldly goods, but only for my subjects' good. What you do bestow on me, I will not hoard it up, but receive it to bestow on you again. Yea, mine own properties I count yours to be expended for your good. Therefore render unto them from me I beseech you, Mr. Speaker, such thanks as you imagine my heart yieldeth, but my tongue cannot express."

Note that all this while they kneeled. Whereupon her majesty said, "Mr. Speaker, I would wish you and the rest to stand up, for I shall yet trouble you with longer speech." So they all stood up and she went on in her speech, saying: ". . . I know the title of a king is a glorious title; but assure yourself that the shining glory of princely authority hath not so dazzled the eyes of our understanding but that we will know and remember that we also are to yield an account of our actions before the Great Judge. To be a king and wear a crown is more glorious to them that see it, than it is pleasure to them that bear it. For myself, I was never so much enticed with the glorious name of a king, or royal authority of a queen, as delighted that God hath made me this instrument to maintain His truth and glory, and to defend this kingdom, as I said, from peril, dishonour, tyranny, and oppression. There will never queen sit in my seat with more zeal to my country, care to my subjects, and that will sooner with willingness yield and venture her life for your good and safety than myself. And though you have had and may have many princes more mighty and wise sitting in this seat, yet you never had or shall have any that will be more careful and loving. . . . And so I commit you all to your best fortunes and further counsels. And I pray you, Mr. Comptroller, Mr. Secretary, and you of my council, that, before these gentlemen depart into their countries, you bring them all to kiss my hand."

Ibid., pp. 659 f.

83. RECORDS CONCERNING THE COUNCIL (1558-1600)

(A) PROCEEDINGS ON A CASE IN LONDON (1558-59)

[3 December.] Where the chief justice of the king's bench did of late make out an attachment against the judge of the admiralty, upon pretence that he had intermeddled in his jurisdiction in a matter depending between one Adam Wyntropp of London and John Combes, a Frenchman: it was this day ordered by my lords of the council, upon the hearing of both the said judges and what either of them could allege for himself, that as well the process awarded out against the said judge of the admiralty as the said matter in controversy between the said Wyntropp and Combes shall be stayed until their lordships, upon consideration of what hath been alleged on both sides for the maintenance of their several jurisdictions, shall take some further order therein; for the better doing whereof they were commanded to bring to my said lords of the council a note in writing of the cases wherein they have or may contend for their said jurisdictions, so as thereupon their lordships may determine some stay and order between them according to equity and justice. The said Wyntropp, being this day brought before my lords, was commanded that he shall not any further proceed in the matter between Combes and him until their lordships shall take further order therein, upon pain of double the sums of the action that is taken against him.

[27 February.] A letter to Alderman Marten, Thomas Hunt, Thomas Huett, William Holland, and Edward Castelin of London, merchants; with a supplication enclosed and exhibited unto the lords of the council containing matter of variance of long depending between one Adam Wyntropp and one John Combes, Frenchman: by which letter the said alderman and the others are authorized to call the parties before them from time to time and to hear and determine all matters of controversy between them, and to take such final order in the same as may both be agreeable to equity and the good quiet also of the parties hereafter, wherein they be required to travail and take some pains and to certify thereupon what they shall have done in the premises.

Acts of the Privy Council, N. S., VII, 12, 62.

(B) COMMITTEES OF THE COUNCIL (1558)

[23 December.] For care of the north parts towards Scotland and Berwick: the earl of Arundel, the earl of Shrewsbury, the earl of Bedford, the earl of Pembroke, the lord admiral, Sir Ambrose Cave. To survey the office of the treasurer of the chamber and to assign order of payment: the lord chamberlain, Mr. Comptroller, Mr. Secretary, Sir Walter Mildmay. For Portsmouth and the Isle of Wight: marquess of Winchester, the earl of Arundel, the earl of Pembroke, the lord admiral, the captain of Portsmouth, Richard Wurseley, Peter Smith. For consideration of all things necessary for the parliaments: the lord great seal, the judges, the serjeants-at-law, Mr. Attorney, Mr. Solicitor, Sir Thomas Smith, Mr. Goodericke. To understand what lands have been granted from the crown in the late queen's time: the marquess of Winchester, the lord great seal, the lord Rich, the lord North, Mr. Mildmay.

Ibid., VII, 27 f.

(C) LETTERS ON JUDICIAL MATTERS (1559-66)

[15 March 1559.] A letter to the lieutenant of the Tower: that, where there remaineth in his custody the bodies of one Pytt and Nycholles, for the robbing of a widow called Bate in Saint Ellyn's in London, he is required to call the knight marshal unto him in this matter; and, upon examination of the parties, if they shall obstinately persist in the denial of their fact,[1] he is willed to cause them to be brought to the rack and to feel the smart thereof as they by their discretions shall think good for the better bolting out of the truth of this matter.

[25 February 1565.] A letter to Sir John Rogers, knight, George Rogers, Thomas Morton, Robert Coker, John Lewsten, esquires, or to two of them: to cause one Agnes Mondaye, of the county of Dorset, to be apprehended and committed to ward, to be further ordered according to the quality of her fault; and further to make search in her house or other resorting places for all such things as they think may tend to witchcraft, and to advertise hither what they

---

[1] Deed.

shall do herein—which Agnes, besides many other devilish parts, hath of late bewitched one Mistress Chettell that she hath been in peril of her life.

[16 March 1565.] A letter to the commissioners in Cornwall: that they should proceed to the execution of three pirates indicted of piracy, unless by the justices of assize it should be thought otherwise good; and also to send up the twelve men that acquitted one Akers, being indicted also of piracy, and with them their bonds and evidences against the said Akers, to the end the matter shall be heard the first day of the next term in the star chamber.

[20 October 1566.] A letter to the judge of the admiralty, signifying unto him that the queen's majesty, upon information given to her highness that John Hawkins of Plymouth hath prepared a ship to be sent into the king of Spain's Indias, did give order that the said ship should be stayed and the said Hawkins commanded to repair hither to answer his doings in this behalf. Forasmuch as the said Hawkins, being now come hither for that purpose, hath affirmed that he meaneth not to send any ship of his, or by his setting forth, to any of those places that are suspected, the said judge is willed to take sufficient bonds of him, not only that he shall forbear to send any ship or ships to any of those ports of the Indias which are privileged to any person or persons by the king of Spain, but also that neither he nor any other that shall go in any ship of his, or of his setting forth, shall rob, spoil, or evil-handle any of the queen's majesty's subjects, allies, confederates, or friends; and thereupon to signify hither what he shall have done herein, to the end order may be taken to cause his said ship to be set at liberty.

Ibid., VII, 66, 200, 206, 315.

(D) Memorandum on the Statute of Artificers (1565)[2]

[8 July.] Where, according to the statute made in the fifth year of the queen's majesty's reign for the limiting and appointing of wages for artificers, husbandmen, and any other labourer, servant, or workman, it was ordered that the justices of each county of this realm should yearly certify before the twelfth of July, under their hands and seals, what they thought meet to be allowed unto every of them, with the causes and considerations thereof, into the chancery; and that thereupon the lord chancellor or lord keeper should make declaration of the same to the queen's majesty or her highness's privy council, and so cause it to be published by print, as in the said statute more at large appeareth: this day the lord keeper of the great seal showed unto their lordships such certificates as he hath received in this matter, which his lordship was by their lordships desired to

---

[2] No. 81c.

cause to be imprinted and sent abroad according to the tenor of the said act.

Ibid., VII, 230.

(E) Memorandum on Appeals from Jersey (1572)

[13 May.] Where certain petitions have been exhibited to my lords of the council by . . . one of the jurats and justices [of the isle of Jersey] . . . for the reformation of certain inconveniences arising in some point of the laws of that isle, and the manner of prosecuting the same . . . , it was commanded by my said lords that an order touching those petitions and for reformation in those cases to be had should be written down in the council book in manner and form following . . . : first, that no appeal be admitted . . . from any sentence or judgment in any matter . . . not exceeding the value . . . of £7 sterling . . . ; that no appeal in any cause . . . be permitted . . . before the same . . . be fully examined and ended by definitive sentence . . . ; that every appeal shall be prosecuted within three months next ensuing the sentence or judgment given therein, except there be just cause of . . . impediment . . . ; [but] no appeal be hereafter received without the copy as well of the sentence or judgment as also of the whole process of the cause closed together under the seal of the isle; and, that there may be no let to the appellant in having thereof, it is ordered by the said lords that the bailiff and jurats of the isle from whom the appeal shall be made, shall, upon request made to them, deliver . . . to the said party appellant the said copy within eight days after such request.

Ibid., VIII, 75 f.

(F) Oath of the Clerk of the Council (1572)[3]

The oath of Robert Beale, esquire, to be one of the clerks of the privy council. You shall swear to be a true and faithful servant unto the queen's majesty as one of the clerks of her highness's privy council. You shall not know or understand of any manner thing to be attempted, done, or spoken against her majesty's person, honour, crown, or dignity royal, but you shall let or withstand the same to the uttermost of your power, and either do or cause it to be revealed either to her majesty's self or to her privy council. You shall keep secret all matters committed and revealed unto you, or that shall be treated of secret in council, and if any of the same treaties or counsels shall touch any of the same counsellors, you shall not reveal the same unto him, but shall keep the same until such time as, by consent of her majesty or the council, publication shall be made thereof. You shall to your uttermost bear faith and true allegiance to the queen's majesty, her heirs and lawful successors, and shall assist and defend all jurisdictions, pre-eminences, and authorities granted to her majesty and annexed to her crown [against] all foreign princes, persons, prel-

---

[3] This is virtually the same as the privy councillor's oath of office; cf. no. 53.

ates, or potentates, etc., by act of parliament or otherwise; and generally in all things you shall do as a faithful and true servant and subject ought to do to her majesty. So help you God and the holy contents of this Book.

Ibid., VIII, 78 f.

(G) MISCELLANEOUS LETTERS (1573-93)

[7 June 1573.] A letter to the justices of assizes in the county of Kent: to make an agreement betwixt Antony Parkehurst and his father that meaneth to disinherit him, or to return in whom the fault is.

[24 October 1576.] A letter to Sir Henry Nevill, knight, Richard Ward, esquire, cofferer of her majesty's household, and Richard Lovelace, esquire: to examine a complaint exhibited by one Humphrey Kerry of London, merchant, that, being robbed in a thicket near Maidenhead, hue and cry being raised and followed to the said town, they made not such pursuit after the offenders as by law they were bound; and if upon examination of the matter any default shall appear in the officers, to commit them until they should hear further; and besides, the information being true, to advise how the said Kerry might be recompensed for his losses according to law.

[25 October 1576.] A letter to the customers, comptrollers, and searchers, and other officers of the port of London: to release certain of Holland ordinarily bringing in victuals for the provision of the city of London, who were stayed by them, and that also they may be permitted to pass and repass to and fro from time to time as they shall have occasion for the bringing in of any such victuals; and because the same is a great relief to the poor people of London, they shall from henceforth freely suffer all such as trade hither with victuals to come and return until they shall be further directed from the lords in that behalf.

[6 March 1577.] A letter to the lord president in the north, signifying unto him that, where this last year there was a voyage taken in hand by Martin Frobisher for discovery of some parts of the world unknown, wherein there is great likelihood that the continuance thereof will be beneficial both to the whole realm and particularly to such as are venturers in the same, and for that some encouragement might be given for the following thereof, her majesty is pleased to contribute largely towards such charges as are now to be employed. Wherefore their lordships, understanding that divers merchants in the city of York, towns of Newcastle, Hull, and other places under his lordship's jurisdiction would also be willing to venture somewhat in the said voyage, so as they might be assured of her majesty's and their lordships' good liking . . . , his lordship would signify to the inhabitants thereabouts that, if any merchant or others shall be willing to contribute and adventure any portion of money in this matter at this time, he shall rateably be admitted to the profit thereof as others are. Only their lordships require of them that some expedition be made in the certifying of the names and abilities of such persons as shall be found willing to contribute anything, to the intent the voyage now shortly intended might neither be hindered nor they anywise disappointed. And what shall be done herein their lordships desire to be advertised. The like letter to the mayor and his brethren of the city of Bristol.

[6 March 1577.] A letter to the commissioners for the restraint of grain in the county of Essex, requiring them to suffer Walter Persons and Henry Pometell, bakers . . . , to transport out of the said county eighty quarters of wheat which they have already bargained for . . . , which said wheat is to be employed in biscuit necessary for the furniture of certain barks of Martin Frobisher and others now intending a voyage to the seas; and that bonds be taken of the said bakers or their factors that they shall return certificates from the customer of London that the said wheat hath been brought to London and employed as aforesaid.

[26 February 1579.] To the lord mayor of London: that, whereas their lordships were informed that one Beton, a surgeon, entertained in a ship called *The Thomas of Ipswich* in a voyage towards the northwest, had entered an action before him against Thomas Bonham, owner of the said ship, and that the mariners of the said ship intend to do the like, and that the misdemeanours of the said mariners in the said voyage hath been such as they rather deserve punishment than wages; and, the matter not yet examined and determined, their lordships pray him to give order that all suit in any of his courts may be forborne, as well of the said Beton as of all others for this cause, until the matter may be farther considered and ordered according to right.

[19 February 1581.] A letter unto Barnard Randall, Thomas Gardner, and the constable: that, where it pleased the queen's majesty for certain good considerations to grant unto Jacomo Vertolini under the great seal of England a privilege to erect a glass-house and to make drinking glasses, prohibiting thereby that no person whatsoever should to the prejudice of his said grant make and erect any glass-houses and make glasses of that kind within the realm; forasmuch as complaint is made unto their lordships by the said Jacomo that one Sebastian Orlandini and one John Smith have very lately set up a furnace at the gunpowder mill by Ratcliffe intending to make glasses . . . , they are therefore required forthwith, upon the receipt hereof, to repair unto the said gunpowder mill and there, by virtue of these their lordships' letters, to cause the said furnace to be presently defaced in their own presence before they do depart from the place, and to enjoin them both in her majesty's name that they forbear to attempt the like hereafter, upon pain to receive such punish-

ment for their contempt as by her majesty's said grant is prescribed. . . .

[29 July 1593.] A letter to the vice-chancellor of Cambridge:
whereas the two universities of Cambridge and Oxford are the
nurseries to bring up youth in the knowledge and fear of God and in
all manner of good learning and virtuous education, whereby after
they may serve their prince and country in divers callings; for which
respect a special care is to be had of those two universities that all
means may be used to further the bringing up of the youth that are
bestowed there in all good learning, civil education, and honest manners, whereby the state and commonwealth may receive hereafter
great good . . . : we therefore as councillors of estate to her
majesty, amongst other things concerning the good government of this
realm, cannot but have a more especial regard of these principal
places, being the fountains from whence learning and education doth
flow and so is derived into all other parts of the realm. And for that
cause, understanding that common players do ordinarily resort to
the university of Cambridge, there to recite interludes and plays,
some of them being full of lewd example and most of vanity, besides
the gathering together of multitudes of people whereby is great occasion also of divers other inconveniences, we have thought good to
require you, the vice-chancellor, with the assistance of the heads of
the colleges, to take special order that hereafter there may no plays
or interludes of common players be used . . . , either in the university or in any place within the compass of five miles . . . , nor
any shows of unlawful games that are forbidden by the statutes of
this realm. . . .

The like letter to vice-chancellor and heads of the houses and several colleges in Oxford.

Ibid., VIII, 111; IX, 218 f., 302 f.; XI, 59; XII, 336; XXIV, 427 f.

(H) Instructions to Local Government Officials (1598)[4]

[25 March.] A minute of letters directed unto the high sheriff and
justices of the peace in the several counties of the realm. . . . Although we doubt not but the justices of the assize in their several
circuits have had special regard . . . to admonish you and other
justices at the last assizes to have extraordinary care for the due execution of divers good statutes yet in force, and especially of those
lately made this last parliament for the good and benefit of the whole
state of the realm concerning the relief of poor people, maimed
soldiers, the punishment of vagabonds and rogues, and maintenance
of tillage, the care whereof is specially recommended to you by the
said statutes: nevertheless, considering the remissness that hath been
used generally by the justices of the peace in many parts of the realm
and the great good that may ensue by the due execution of so good

[4] Cf. nos. 73c, 741, 81h, 82c.

and necessary laws, her majesty . . . hath commanded us very earnestly . . . to recommend unto your better and more due regard that which belongeth to your duties and the law requireth of you. . . .

To which end it is thought meet that at the next general sessions after Easter you do assemble together and take special order amongst yourselves for one strict and uniform course to be holden for the due observing . . . of the same laws and statutes; and further that you do from thenceforth, from time to time so often as it shall be found requisite . . . , assemble within your several limits to take account of the constables and other under-officers of their proceedings to be informed of those abuses that are to be reformed. . . . Which service if you shall effect according to the trust reposed in you, and with that care which public officers ought to use, and according to her majesty's most earnest desire, yourselves and the whole country shall be partakers of the benefit of the same and her majesty receive that satisfaction which she looketh for. But if you shall neglect the same, her majesty cannot but account you to be unmeet and unworthy for the authority and places which you hold under her. And because her majesty hath had report diversely made unto her that, although there are a great number commonly in every county of the realm by common made justices of the peace, whereof some sort of them do not give their attendance but at times when they have special causes of their own or their friends to treat upon, her majesty, meaning to be more certainly informed of that abuse, commandeth you that shall be present at these sessions next after Easter to certify unto her council who shall they be that should be present to attend the service, so as thereby it may be understood who shall be absent, and they to answer thereunto; whereby her majesty shall be pleased with your service and shall enter into consideration how to reform the negligence of the others. . . .

Ibid., XXVIII, 388 f.

(I) John Herbert's Memorandum (1600)

Titles of matters whereof I am charged to have regard as a councillor and secretary: first, to inform myself of all treaties with foreign princes . . . , to be acquainted with the particular actions and negotiations of ambassadors to her majesty and from her; to inform myself of the power and form of proceeding at the council of the marches in Wales and the council in the north, and to understand the manner of the warden's government; to be well informed of the state of Ireland, both the yearly charge of the army and the extraordinary, the state of revenue there and the state of the undertakers, the charge of the Low Country wars, the charges of the French king, the state of their debts to the queen, what the assurances are and where they are; to oversee the order of the councilbook and muster-book of the realm; to have the custody of letters from foreign princes to the queen and answers made to them; to have care to the intelligences abroad.

Memorandum, that all causes to be treated on in council and re-solved are either only for her majesty or betwixt party and party or betwixt some party, either subject or stranger, and the queen's maj-esty. The first doth handle principally questions and consultations of state growing from foreign advertisements or some extraordinary accidents within the realm. The second, between party and party, are very seldom heard particularly, but rather ended by overruling an obstinate person who is made to acknowledge his fault; or else the parties are remitted to some court of justice or equity, or recom-mended by some letters to some justices in the country to compound the differences either by consent of the parties or by direction; or if the cause be great, then to write letters to some principal persons, to have some circumstances better understood and examined con-cerning matter of fact whereof the council cannot be so well informed when they have only the suggestions of one party against another, upon which report it often happeneth that quarrels and differences are taken up by the council when it appears clearly who is in default. When there is anything in question wherein the queen is a party, it is commonly either by the breach of peace or for some other title. If there be breach of peace, the lords do either punish the offender by commitment or do refer the matter to be further proceeded in the star chamber, where great riots and contempts are punished. If it be matter of title, then the lords refer it to the queen's learned counsel and recommend the same to the judges' care. If there be some suits to the queen of poor men, then do the lords endorse their peti-tions with their opinions and recommend the dispatch to the secretary or for the poorer sort to the master of the requests.

Prothero, Constitutional Documents, pp. 166 f.

84. COMMISSION FOR ECCLESIASTICAL CAUSES (1559)[1]

Elizabeth, by the grace of God, etc., to the reverend father in God, Mathew Parker, nominated bishop of Canterbury; and Edmond Grindall, nominated bishop of London; and to our right trusted and right well-beloved councillors, Francis Knowles, our vice-chamberlain and Ambrose Cave, knights; and to our trusty and well-beloved An-thony Cooke and Thomas Smyth, knights; William Bill, our almoner; Walter Haddon and Thomas Sackford, masters of our requests; Rowland Hill and William Chester, knights; Randoll Cholmely and John Southcote, serjeants-at-the-law; William May, doctor of law; Francis Cave, Richard Gooderick, and Gilbert Gerrard, esquires; Robert Weston and Thomas Huick, doctors of law; greeting.

Where, at our parliament holden at Westminster the 25th day of January and there continued and kept until the 8th of May then next following, amongst other things there was two acts and statutes made and established . . . ; and where divers seditious and slanderous

---

[1] This is but one of many such commissions that were issued; see R. G. Usher, *The Rise and Fall of the High Commission.*

persons do not cease daily to invent and set forth false rumours, tales, and seditious slanders, not only against us and the said good laws and statutes, but also have set forth divers seditious books within this our realm of England, meaning thereby to move and procure strife, division, and dissension amongst our loving and obedient subjects, much to the disquieting of us and our people : wherefore we, earnestly minding to have the same acts before mentioned to be duly put in execution, and such persons as shall hereafter offend in anything contrary to the tenor and effect of the said several statutes to be condignly punished, and having especial trust and confidence in your wisdoms and discretions, have authorized, assigned, and appointed you to be our commissioners ;[2] and by these presents do give our full power and authority to you, or six of you . . . , from time to time hereafter during our pleasure to inquire, as well by the oaths of twelve good and lawful men as also by witnesses and all other ways and means ye can devise, for all offences, misdoers, and misdemeanours done and committed and hereafter to be committed or done contrary to the tenor and effect of the said several acts and statutes and either of them, and also of all and singular heretical opinions, seditious books, contempts, conspiracies, false rumours, tales, seditions, misbehaviours, slanderous words or showings, published, invented or set forth . . . by any person or persons against us or contrary or against any the laws or statutes of this our realm, or against the quiet governance and rule of our people and subjects in any . . . place or places within this our realm of England, and of all and every of the coadjutors, counsellors, comforters, procurers, and abettors of every such offender.

And further, we do give power and authority to you, or six of you . . . , from time to time hereafter during our pleasure, as well to hear and determine all the premises as also to inquire, hear, and determine all and singular enormities, disturbances, and misbehaviours done and committed . . . in any church or chapel, or against any divine service, or the minister or ministers of the same, contrary to the laws and statutes of this realm; and also to inquire of, search out, and to order, correct, and reform all such persons as hereafter shall or will obstinately absent themselves from church and such divine service as by the laws and statutes of this realm is appointed to be had and used.

And also we do give and grant full power and authority unto you, and six of you . . . , from time to time and at all times during our pleasure to visit, reform, redress, order, correct, and amend in all places within this our realm of England all such errors, heresies, crimes, abuses, offences, contempts, and enormities spiritual and ecclesiastical wheresoever, which by any spiritual or ecclesiastical power, authority, or jurisdiction can or may lawfully be reformed, ordered, redressed, corrected, restrained, or amended, to the pleasure of Al-

---

[2] Cf. no. 85B. The two statutes referred to are no. 81A, B.

mighty God, the increase of virtue, and the conservation of the peace and unity of this our realm, and according to the authority and power limited, given, and appointed by any laws or statutes of this realm.

And also that you, or six of you . . . , shall likewise have full power and authority from time to time to inquire of and search out all masterless men, quarrellers, vagrant and suspect persons within our city of London, and ten miles compass about the same city, and of all assaults and affrays done and committed within the same city and compass aforesaid.

And also we give full power and authority unto you, and six of you . . . , summarily to hear and finally determine, according to your discretions and by the laws of this realm, all causes and complaints of all them, which in respect of religion, or for lawful matrimony contracted and allowed by the same, were injuriously deprived, de-- frauded, or spoiled of their lands, goods, possessions, rights, digni-- ties, livings, offices, spiritual or temporal; and them so deprived, as before, to restore into their said livings and to put them in possession, amoving the usurpers in convenient speed, as it shall seem to your discretions good. . . .

And further we do give power and authority unto you, and six of you . . . , not only to hear and determine the same and all other offences and matters before mentioned and rehearsed, but also all other notorious and manifest adulteries, fornications, and ecclesiasti- cal crimes and offences within this our realm, according to your wis- doms, consciences, and discretions; willing and commanding you, or six of you . . . , to use and devise all such politic ways and means for the trial and searching out of all the premises as . . . shall be thought most expedient and necessary. And upon due proof had, and the offence or offences before specified, or any of them, sufficiently proved against any person or persons by confession of the party, or by lawful witnesses, or by any due mean . . . , then you or six of you, as aforesaid, shall have full power and authority to award such punishment to every offender by fine, imprisonment, or otherwise, by all or any of the ways aforesaid, and to take such order for the re- dress of the same, as to your wisdoms and discretions [shall be thought meet and convenient].

[And further we do give full power and authority unto you,] or six of you . . . , to call before you . . . all and every offender or offenders, and such as [to] you . . . shall seem to be suspect per- sons in any of the premises; and also all such witnesses as you . . . shall think [meet] to be called before you or six of you as aforesaid and them and every of them to examine upon their corporal oath for the better trial and opening of the premises or any part thereof.

And if you or six of you, as aforesaid, shall find any person or persons obstinate or disobedient either in their [appearance] before you . . . at your calling or commandment, or else not accomplishing or not obeying your order, decrees, and commandments in anything touching the premises or any part thereof . . . , then you . . . shall have full power and authority to commit the same person or persons so offending to ward, there to remain until he or they shall be by you . . . enlarged and delivered. . . .

And more, we will and command all and singular justices of the peace, mayors, sheriffs, bailiffs, constables, and other our officers, ministers, and faithful subjects, to be aiding, helping, and assisting and at your commandment in the due execution hereof, as they tender our pleasure, and will answer to the contrary at their utmost perils. . . .

Ibid., pp. 227 f.

85. ACTS CONCERNING PRINTING (1530-85)

(A) PROCLAMATION AGAINST ERRONEOUS BOOKS (1530)

The king, our most dread sovereign lord, studying and providing daily for the weal, benefice, and honour of this his most noble realm, well and evidently perceiveth that, partly through the malicious suggestions of our ghostly enemy, partly by the evil and perverse inclination . . . of sundry persons, divers heresies and erroneous opinions have been late sown and spread among his subjects of this his said realm by blasphemous and pestiferous English books, printed in other regions and sent into this realm to the intent as well to pervert and withdraw the people from the catholic and true faith of Christ, as also to stir and incense them to sedition and disobedience against their princes, sovereigns, and heads, as also to cause them to condemn and neglect all good laws, customs, and virtuous manners, to the final subversion and desolation of this noble realm . . . : whereupon the king's highness . . . hath invited and called to him the primates of this his grace's realm, and also a sufficient number of discreet . . . and well-learned personages in divinity . . . , giving unto them liberty to speak . . . their . . . determinations concerning as well the approbation or rejecting of such books as be in any part suspected as also the admission and divulgation of the Old and New Testament translated into English.

Whereupon his highness in his own royal person, calling to him the said primates and divines, hath seriously . . . discussed the premises and finally by all their free assents . . . determined that these books ensuing . . .[1] and divers other books made in the English tongue . . . do contain in them pestiferous errors and blasphemies, and for that cause shall from henceforth be reputed and taken of all men for books of heresy. . . . The king's said highness therefore straitly chargeth . . . all and every his subjects . . . that they from henceforth do not buy, receive, or have any of the books before named, or any other book being in the English tongue and printed beyond the sea of what matter soever it be, or any copy written [and] drawn out of the same, or the same books in the French or Dutch

---

[1] Five books are named.

tongue. . . . [Offenders against this proclamation are to be brought] to the king's highness and his most honourable council, where they shall be corrected and punished for their contempt and disobedience to the terrible example of other like transgressors.

Moreover, his highness commandeth that no manner of person or persons take upon him or them to print any book or books in the English tongue concerning Holy Scripture, not before this time printed within this his realm, until such time as the same book or books be examined and approved by the ordinary of the diocese, where the said books shall be printed; and that the printer thereof, upon every of the said books being so examined, do set the name of the examiner or examiners, with also his own name upon the said books, as he will answer to the king's highness at his uttermost peril. . . .

If it shall hereafter appear to the king's highness that his said people do utterly abandon and forsake all perverse, erroneous, and seditious opinions, with the New Testament and the Old corruptly translated into the English tongue now being in print, and that the same books and all other books of heresy . . . be clearly exterminated and exiled out of this realm of England forever, his highness intendeth to provide that the Holy Scripture shall be by great and learned and catholic persons translated into the English tongue, if it shall then seem to his grace convenient to be. . . .

Wilkins, *Concilia,* III, 740.

(B) DECREE IN STAR CHAMBER CONCERNING BOOKS (1566)

I. That no person should print, or cause to be printed, or bring or procure to be brought into the realm printed, any book against the force and meaning of any ordinance, prohibition, or commandment, contained in any the statutes or laws of this realm, or in any injunctions, letters patents, or ordinances passed or set forth, or to be passed or set forth, by the queen's grant, commission, or authority.

II. That whosoever should offend against the said ordinances should forfeit all such books and copies; and from thenceforth should never use or exercise, or take benefit by any using or exercising, the feat of printing, and to sustain three months' imprisonment without bail or mainprise.

III. That no person should sell or put to sale, bind, stitch, or sew any such books or copies, upon pain to forfeit all such books and copies, and for every book 20*s.*

IV. That all books so forfeited should be brought into Stationers' Hall; and there one moiety of the money forfeited to be reserved to the queen's use, and the other moiety to be delivered to him or them that should first seize the books or make complaint thereof to the warden of the said company; and all the books so to be forfeited to be destroyed or made waste paper.

V. That it should be lawful for the wardens of the company for the time being or any two of the said company thereto deputed by the said wardens, as well in any ports or other suspected places to open and view all packs, dryfats, maunds,[2] and other things wherein books or paper shall be contained, brought into this realm, and make search in all work-houses, shops, warehouses, and other places of printers, booksellers, and such as bring books into the realm to be sold, or where they have reasonable cause of suspicion; and all books to be found against the said ordinances to seize and carry to the Hall to the uses abovesaid, and to bring the persons offending before the queen's commissioners in causes ecclesiastical.

VI. Every stationer, printer, bookseller, merchant, using any trade of book-printing, binding, selling, or bringing into the realm, should, before the commissioners or before any other persons thereto to be assigned by the queen's privy council, enter into several recognizances of reasonable sums of money to her majesty, with sureties or without, as to the commissioners should be thought expedient, that he should truly observe all the said ordinances, well and truly yield and pay all such forfeitures, and in no point be resisting but in all things aiding to the said wardens and their deputies for the true execution of the premises.

Upon the consideration before expressed and upon the motion of the commissioners, we of the privy council have agreed this to be observed and kept upon the pains therein contained. At the star chamber.

Strype, *Life of Parker,* I, 442 f.

(C) Decree in Star Chamber concerning Printers (1585)

Imprimis, that every printer and other person . . . which at this time present hath erected . . . any printing-press, roll, or other instrument for imprinting of books, charts, ballads, portraitures, paper called damask paper, or any such things or matters whatsoever, shall bring a true note or certificate of the said presses . . . already erected, within ten days next coming after the publication hereof, and of the said presses . . . hereafter to be erected or set up from time to time, within ten days next after the erecting or setting up thereof, unto the master and wardens of the Company of Stationers of the city of London for the time being; upon pain that every person failing or offending herein shall have all and every the said presses . . . utterly defaced and made unserviceable for imprinting forever, and shall also suffer twelve months' imprisonment. . . .

Item, that no printer of books nor any other person or persons whatsoever shall set up, keep, or maintain any press or presses . . . , but only in the city of London or the suburbs thereof (except one press in the university of Cambridge and one other press in the university of Oxford and no more); and that no person shall hereafter

---

[2] Wooden and wicker containers.

erect, set up, or maintain in any secret or obscure corner or place any such press . . . , but that the same shall be in such open place or places in his or their houses as the wardens of the said company of stationers for the time being, or such other person or persons as by the said wardens shall be thereunto appointed, may from time to time have ready access unto to search for and view the same. And that no printer . . . shall at any time hereafter withstand or make resistance to . . . any such view or search, nor deny, to keep secret, any such press. . . .

Item, that no person or persons shall imprint or cause to be imprinted or suffer by any means to his knowledge his press, letters, or other instruments to be occupied in printing of any book, work, copy, matter, or thing whatsoever except the same . . . hath been heretofore allowed, or . . . be first seen and perused by the archbishop of Canterbury and bishop of London for the time being, or one of them. . . .

Item, that it shall be lawful to or for the said wardens for the time being, or any two by them appointed . . . , to enter into any house, workhouse, warehouse, shop, or other place or places, and to seize, take, and carry away all presses, letters, and all other printing instruments set up, used, or employed contrary to the true meaning hereof, to be defaced and made unserviceable. . . .

Strype, Life of Whitgift, III, 160 f.

86. LOCAL JUDICIAL RECORDS (1553-96)[1]

(A) OATH OF OFFICE OF A JUSTICE OF THE PEACE

Ye shall swear that, as justices of the peace in the county of Kent, in all articles in the queen's commission to you directed ye shall do equal right to the poor and to the rich after your cunning, wit, and power, and after the laws and customs of the realm and the statutes thereof made; and ye shall not be of counsel with any quarrel hanging before you; and that ye hold your sessions after the form of statutes thereof made; and the issues, fines, and amercements that shall happen to be made, and all forfeitures which shall fall before you, ye shall cause to be entered without any concealment or embezzling and truly send them to the queen's exchequer. Ye shall not let for gift or other cause, but well and truly ye shall do your office of justice of the peace in that behalf; and that you take nothing for your office of justice of the peace to be done, but of the queen, and fees accustomed, and costs limited by the statute; and ye shall not direct nor cause to be directed any warrant by you to be made to the parties, but ye shall direct them to the bailiffs of the said county or other the queen's officers or ministers, or other indifferent persons,

---

[1] For other documents dealing with the justices of the peace and their activities, see nos. 73c; 81c, f, g, h; 82c; 83h.

to do execution thereof. So help you God and by the contents of this Book.

Lambarde, *Eirenarcha,* p. 59.

(B) PERSONS SUMMONED TO THE STAFFORDSHIRE QUARTER SESSIONS (October, 1585)

[Justices]

Thos. Bromley, knt., lord chancellor
Wm. Lord Burghley, lord treasurer
George, earl of Shrewsbury
Robt., earl of Leicester, master of the horse
Wm., bishop of Coventry and Lichfield
Edward, Lord Stafford
Edward, Lord Dudley
Jas. Crofte, knt., controller of the household
Gilbert Gerrard, knt., master of the rolls
Francis Wyndham, one of the justices of the bench
Edward Flowerdew one of the barons of the exchequer

John Littleton, knt.	Humphrey Ferrers, esq.
Walter Aston, knt.	John Chetwin, esq.
Ralph Egerton, knt.	John Bowes, esq.
Thos. Trentham, esq.	Walter Leveson, esq.
Walter Harecourte, esq.	Ric. Bagott, esq.
Ralph Sneid, esq.	John Grey, esq.
Thos. Grasley, esq.	Henry Griffin, esq.
Wm. Bassett, esq.	Thos. Lane, esq.
Edward Aston, esq.	Thos. Rudyer, esq.
Edward Littleton, esq.	Ric. Crompton, esq.
Ralph Aderley, esq.	Thos. Waringes, esq.
Robt. Stanford, esq.	Wm. Madder. esq.

Coroners

Wm. Greene, gent.
John Jarvice, gent.
George Warner, gent.

Chief Constables

Thos. Corbett, gent. ⎫
Hugh Fodon, gent. ⎬ chief constables of Pirehill Hundred
Humphrey Minors, gent., Offlow Hundred
Thos. Warner, gent., Tottmonslow Hundred
Ric. Mills, gent., Cutleston Hundred
Thos. Rickthorne, gent., Seisdon Hundred

Bailiffs of the Liberties

Robt. Whytall, liberty of the duchy of Lancaster
Thos. Ayre, liberty of Robt., earl of Essex, of Lichfield
Robt. Persall, gent., liberty of Wm., bishop of Coventry and Lichfield

Bailiffs of the Hundreds

Wm. Pedley, Tottmonslow Hundred
John Marten, Pirehill Hundred
Thos. Harpur, Seisdon Hundred
Wm. Bennett, Offlow Hundred
Ric. Suker, Cudleston

Bailiffs Itinerant

Thurston Garter
Geoffrey Lightwood
Ric. Chauner
Jas. Arendale
John More
Robt. Burges
John Grene
Robt. Mole[2]

Collections for a History of Staffordshire, 1929, pp. 105 f.

(C) STAFFORDSHIRE QUARTER SESSIONS ROLLS (1587–96)

[1587. Writ of restitution] tested by Robert, earl of Essex, at
Uttoxeter, 26 July . . . : that, whereas by inquisition . . . at Uttoxeter . . . before Richard Bagot, Ralph Adderly, and Philip
Okeover esquire, justices of the peace, it was presented by twelve
jurors that George Partridge [and four others] . . . have entered
a messuage and close called Ridware Park, the free tenement of
Thomas Fitzherbert, knight . . . , and as yet hold him out of it,
contrary to the form of the statute of 8 Henry VI, the sheriff is
ordered to make reseisin of the premises and restore to Thomas his
former possession. [Return by the sheriff]: 29 July . . . I have
made reseisin of the premises and restored to Thomas Fitzherbert
his former possession. . . .

[1589] Before Edward Leghe, esquire, J. P., 15 February . . . :
Richard Painter of Wolverhampton, husbandman, to appear at the
next general sessions after Easter; sureties, the said Richard £5.
John Creswell of Wolverhampton, gentleman, £5. . . .

Before Richard Crompton esquire, J. P., 17 January: John Lebarne
of the city of Lichfield, labourer, to appear at the next general sessions after Easter and in the meantime to keep the peace against
James Toye of Walton, county Derby, husbandman; sureties, the
said John, £20, Thomas Hardyne of the city of Lichfield, shoemaker, £10, John Smabrydge of the same, dyer, £10. [Added in
another hand:] Discharged by the court because agreed. . . .

10 March . . . , Richard Prichard of Fradswell and William Emery

---

[2] Of the persons summoned, there appeared three justices, two coroners, three
chief constables, two bailiffs of the liberties, five bailiffs of the hundreds, and
six bailiffs itinerant.

of the same, to appear at the next general sessions after Easter and to keep the peace; surety, each man for the other £10. . . .

[1591. Articles] exhibited to the justices by Richard Aukers and Thomas Collye, constables of the town of Wolverhampton, against John Greene of the same, 13 April. . . . First, the said John Green is a common drunkard, a common brawler, quarreller, and breaker of her majesty's peace. Item, he keepeth common ale-selling and usually lodgeth and receiveth persons of ill behaviour, etc. Item, where about Easter last there was a stranger apprehended at Wolverhampton by one Mr. Richards upon suspicion for stealing an old cloak off a hedge; and where thereupon, for the better examination of that fact, the said Aukers went with the said stranger and a servant of the said Mr. Richards to Mr. John Grey, one of the justices of the peace for the said county; and where upon examination of the said stranger it pleased Mr. Grey, for that no person would directly charge the said stranger with the said felony, to remit him: the said Greene at Wolverhampton aforesaid repaired to the said Aukers, most spitefully reviling him and most undutifully exclaiming against the said Mr. Grey, calling the said Mr. Grey villain and false knave, affirming openly it were a good deed he were hanged; whereupon the said constable, willing the said Greene to satisfy himself and not to give out such unseemly speeches, he thereupon reviled most impudently the said constable.

Item, where thereupon the said constable that evening, seeing the unruliness of the said Greene and the violent assaulting of him, the said constable, did therefore put him into the stocks; the said Greene in the night-time with force [did] break open the said stocks, cut them in pieces and took away the ironwork thereof, and, not so satisfied, then and in the night-time came to the door of the dwelling-house of the said constable bragging he was out of the stocks and . . . calling for a fresh pair of stocks. Item, the said Greene hath of late threatened to set fire in the house of the said constable and . . . to kill the said constable with his dagger. Item, the said Greene hath of late threatened to set fire in the house of one Mr. Wats. . . . Item . . . , being for these misdemeanours committed by the said Mr. Grey to the jail at Stafford, the said Greene hath procured himself out of prison by what mean is not known; and upon his return to Wolverhampton upon Easter even, got into his hat upon the one side a feather and upon [the] other side the *mittimus* by which [he] was committed by the said Mr. Grey . . . , and the same openly did wear in his said hat. . . .

Item, upon Easter day the said Greene, coming into the church . . . with the said feather in his hat, seeing the said constable there, in derision . . . made very low obeisance to the said constable . . . ; so looking over his shoulder went out of the church and, putting on a blue coat, [made] the like obeisance in derision of the said constable and his said office. The premises considered, ready all to be proved to your worships, it would please you to take such order that not only the said Greene may be punished for the said misdemeanours and ordered to re-edify the said stocks, but also that he might be bound to his good behaviour hereafter; whereby the said inhabitants may stand more secure from such the violent and unlawful purposes of the said Greene. . . .

[Information] of William Kinge of Lowborowe, county Leicester, draper, against Francis Hilton, servant of the said William, taken 2 December 1596 before Richard Bagot, esq., J. P.: who saith that, Monday the 29th of November last, he sent one Richard Evenson, his son-in-law, to Shrewsbury to buy clothes, accompanied with the said Francis Hilton, and delivered unto the said Richard £30 in money to pay for the said clothes; which money was carried in a bag of malt containing a bushel or thereabouts for more safety. And the said Richard and Francis, travelling together as far as Norton by Cannocke in the county of Stafford, [did] there lodge all night. And Francis Hilton, rising in the morning before the said Richard, took the said £30 out of the said bag, to which the said Richard afterwards coming . . . , missed the same, together with the said party. Whereupon he caused the constable there to be sent for, who, after examination of the matter, raised the said town and sent both horsemen and footmen with billets to every constable for the attaching the said party, who was apprehended at Haywood the next day following; upon whom the most part of the money was found, *viz.*, £29 or thereabouts.

Ibid., 1929, 196, 334 f.; 1930, 110 f.; 1932, 244 f.

(D) ROLLS OF BOROUGH SESSIONS AT NOTTINGHAM (1553-88)

[Presentments of the Mickletorn jury, 27 April 1553.] . . . We present George Taylor (12*d.*) for staking of willows in the Lene, and so letteth the course of the water. We present the schoolmaster that should teach the free school, for there hath been divers men before us and hath complained of him; wherefore we desire you to have him changed. We present Bartholmew Chettel (3*s.* 4*d.*) as a man not worthy to have the office [of common pavior] which he hath, for misbehaving of himself in taking of excess toll, and for because he doth not call of the chamberlains for sand and stone, considering so greatly as this town doth go in decay for fault of paving and by his negligence. . . . We present the cow pasture for the overlying of it; wherefore we desire you that there may be a certainty how many shall be taken in. And we think the number of five score is sufficient, and no burgess to have above two. . . . If any such default be taken, to pay 3*s.* 4*d.* . . .

[Presentments by the constables of the town of Nottingham, 8 October 1566.] We present Robert Parke (8*d.*) for brewing and tippling, being not bound. We present Master Caterne's daughter (4*d.*) and Charles Overay wife (4*d.*), for buying butter and eggs

without the Chapel Bar. We present Richard Bredun (4*d*.), Robert
Rede (4*d*.), John Freeman (4*d*.) for digging down the common
ditch unto the Wishing Stairs for getting of worms. . . .

[Presentments by the constables of the town of Nottingham, 20
July 1573.] We present Edward Backhouse for selling of fruit . . .
to men's apprentices . . . ; which we think is not convenient. We
present Robert Allyng (40*d*.) for lodging of vagabonds contrary
to the constables' mind. We present Mistress Cockyng, widow, for
calling the constables knaves and villains when they come for post-
horses. . . .

[Presentments of the Mickletorn jury, 28 October 1579.] . . . We
present to have an usher for the free school, a thing very needful
for this town, and to give him £10 a year to have a good one; it will
be a credit to have a good master and a good usher in one school.
We present that the burgesses may hear the end and reckoning of any
subsidy when any is; also that they may hear the accounts both of
the bridgemasters and the wardens of the free school. We present
that the Red Book[3] may be openly read at every sessions in the
hearing of the burgesses, or at the least such things as shall be most
needful, that burgesses may the better discharge their oath and their
duty for the common weal of this town. We present to have two sworn
men to view the market every Saturday, for the countrymen buy
both barley and other corn great store; and they should bring to
the market to sell as much of other corn as they buy, or else let
the advantage of the statute to be shown upon such offenders, for they
hurt our market very sore. . . .

Master Mayor, we request you and your brethren that, according
as we have a grant for two fairs in the year by our charter, that
there may be some building made on the Timber Hill with the town's
money and in short time (by good provision made, the town may
reap a great rent for the same and other places as well), and that
the continuance of the fair may be proclaimed in every market and
fair three months before the fair.

[Presentments of the Mickletorn jury, 22 April 1588.] . . . We
have thought good, forasmuch as we have a most godly exercise
of preaching on the Friday once a week, and lest the same should
decay amongst us through our negligence, in not coming as we
ought to do, and specially of the chiefest of our town . . . , it shall
be very good not only for yourself, Master Mayor, with the rest
of your brethren, but also that the whole council, with the clothing[4]
of this town, most reverently to observe the same by some special
order set down by you and that the same be duly kept. We present
William Hodgkinson for setting part of his house on the common
ground in the Holmes (12*d*.). We present the free school to lack

---

[3] The official record of the by-laws.

[4] Livery company.

repairs, and that the school is greatly annoyed for lack of casements. We present the new bridge to lack a rail. We present the Long Butts to be in decay.

Stevenson, Records of the Borough of Nottingham, IV, 105-223.

87. RECORDS CONCERNING THE MILITIA (1539-77)

(A) COMMISSION OF A LORD LIEUTENANT (1576)[1]

Elizabeth, by the grace of God of England, France, and Ireland queen . . . , to our trusty and well-beloved councillor, Sir Christopher Hatton, knight, our vice-chamberlain, greeting. Know ye that, for the great and singular trust . . . we have in your approved fidelity . . . , we have assigned . . . you to be our lieutenant within our county of Northampton and all corporate and privileged places within the limits . . . of the same county, as well within liberties as without. And [we] do by these presents give full power and authority unto you that you from time to time may levy, gather, or call together all . . . our subjects . . . dwelling . . . within our said county . . . , meet and apt for the wars; and them to try, array, and put in readiness, and them also . . . , after their abilities . . . , sufficiently to cause to be armed and weaponed; and to take the musters of them from time to time in places most meet for that purpose after your good discretion: and also the same our subjects, so arrayed, tried, and armed, as well men-of-arms as other horsemen, archers, and footmen . . . meet and apt for the wars, to conduct and lead, as well against all . . . enemies as also against all . . . rebels, traitors, and other offenders and their adherents . . . , from time to time so often as need shall require by your discretion; and with the said enemies . . . to fight, and them to invade, resist, repress, and subdue, slay, kill, and put to execution of death by all ways and means . . . ; and to . . . execute and use against the said enemies . . . , as necessity shall require by your discretion, the law called the martial law. . . . And further we give you full power and authority, for the execution of this our commission, to appoint and assign in our said county . . . muster masters and one provost marshal. Which provost marshal shall execute and use the martial law, in case of any invasion or rebellion, in conducting any numbers of men of war against the said invaders, traitors, or rebels. . . . And forasmuch as it may be there shall be instant cause, as now there is, for you to be attendant upon our person, or to be otherwise employed in our service, whereby this our service of lieutenancy committed to your fidelity cannot be by you in person exccuted in such force as we have appointed the same: therefore we give unto you . . . authority to appoint, assign, and constitute by your writing, under your hand and seal, our trusty and well-beloved Sir John Spencer,

---

[1] Less elaborate commissions of this kind had been issued since the reign of Edward VI. For an excellent discussion of the subject, see Miss Thomson's work cited below.

knight, Sir Richard Knightley, knight, and Sir Edward Montague, knight, to be your deputies in this said service in our said county of Northampton. . . . And by this . . . commission we give unto the said [Spencer, Knightley, and Montague] . . . , or any two of them, full power of authority in your absence to do and execute in our said county of Northampton . . . every thing and things before by this our commission assigned and appointed by you to be done and executed. . . . And further we will and command . . . our justices of the peace, mayors, sheriffs, bailiffs, constables, headboroughs, and all other our officers, ministers, and subjects, meet and apt for the wars within our said county of Northampton . . . , that they and every one of them, with their power and servants, from time to time shall be attendant, aiding, and assisting, counselling, helping, and at the commandment as well of you as of your said deputies . . . , as they and every of them tender our pleasure and will answer for the contrary at their uttermost perils.

Thomson, Lords Lieutenants in the Sixteenth Century, pp. 153 f.

(B) Instructions for General Musters (1572)

Instructins . . . for general musters and training of all manner of persons able for the wars to serve as well on horseback as on foot. The principal intent of the queen's majesty . . . is to have perfect knowledge of the numbers, qualities, abilities, and sufficiency of all her subjects in that county . . . , from the age of sixteen years upward, that may be found able to bear armour or to use weapon on horseback or on foot; and out of that . . . number, being viewed, mustered, and registered, to have a . . . sufficient number of the most able to be chosen and collected, to be by the reasonable charge of the inhabitants in every shire tried, armed, and weaponed, and so consequently taught and trained . . . for the service and defence of her majesty, her crown, and realm against all attempts both inward and outward. . . .

Articles of the instructions to the commissioners. It is necessary that, by your precept to the constable of the hundreds or other officers thereto requisite . . . , all able persons from sixteen upwards which are within the limits of this your commission in any parish, hamlet, or village, be summoned to appear at days and places certain and meet for the musters; so none, being able of any degree, be forborne to be warned and called to the same general musters. . . . And therefore it shall be well done to command in your precept that the names and surnames of all persons in every parish . . . , able to bear armour or to use weapons . . . , be immediately collected and put in writing . . . ; naming in the said writing or note every householder by himself, with his sons, servants, apprentices, journeymen, or any other sojourners or indwellers remaining in their houses . . . ; and that the said householders be charged to bring all the said persons by name with their armour and weapons at such several times and places as shall be thereto limited. And so, after the return to the commissioners of the said writing containing their names, the said commissioners shall call for the persons and proceed to the musters of them, and register the names of such as shall appear with notes of their armours and weapons. And when some shall not have armour or weapons meet there, it shall be noted to what kind of service for the wars every of the said persons shall seem meet; wherein is meant not to omit to note what number of them may serve for labourers or pioneers, and who are also carpenters, smiths, or suchlike artificers, so as there may be some use had of their abilities for service of their country as cause shall require. . . .

Item, the commissioners shall upon the first musters consider particularly all the imperfections in the persons appearing, and in the armours, weapons, and suchlike, and shall give particular instructions and charge how to remedy the same . . . , and shall appoint certain persons . . . to see to and give order for the reformation thereof against the time of the next musters.

Item, where always of very ancient time there hath been and still are a number certain of soldiers furnished of armour and weapons to be found of the common charge of every town or parish, over and besides such particular persons as are by the late statutes chargeable by reason of their own private possessions or goods to find soldiers, armour, and weapons: the commissioners shall do well, upon the registering of the general musters, to cause special entries to be made apart of the numbers found by the parishes in the musterbooks distinct from the others. . . .

Item, because the training and exercise of a multitude of people in their armour and weapons, and namely archers and harquebusiers, may seem costly and chargeable, and that it shall not seem necessary in many places to have the whole numbers of the able people to be armed and weaponed: therefore [the commissioners] . . . shall therein use their discretions . . . , and shall consider and determine what were or may be a convenient number in every part of the shire to be collected out of the total number, meet to be sorted in bands, and to be trained and exercised in such sort as may . . . reasonably be borne by a common charge of the whole country. . . .

And because, in the choice of the numbers to be trained and exercised, divers of the soldiers inhabiting in many towns shall be forborne and not appointed to be of the trained number, and yet the service of the persons chosen and trained doth appertain to the weal of the whole shire; there shall be consideration had, in the collection of the charges to maintain the said training and exercise, that every town and parish of the shire and inhabitants thereof be rateably charged without burdening some more than other. . . .

Grose, *Military Antiquities,* I, 79 f.

(C) CERTIFICATE OF MUSTER MASTERS (1539)

This is the certificate of Sir George Gresley, knight, John Vernon and William Wyrley, esquires, three of the king's commissioners . . . appointed for the trial and the view of all persons armed within the hundred of Ofelaw in the county of Stafford, above sixteen years, as well horsemen, footmen, bowmen, and billmen within the said hundred, whose names with their surnames and their weapons severally appeareth; and have given monition to every of them . . . to be ready with their horse and harness, and to have their harness according to the king's statute thereof made. In witness we have subscribed our names and set to our seals the 27th day of April, 1539. . . .[2]

Elford and Hasulhowre

Richard Huddilston—horse, harness, bill; able
John Hervy—harness, without a horse, a bill; able
Richard Wryght ⎫
Rauf Massye ⎪
Petur Foleshist ⎪
John Janens ⎬ —bowmen, able; without horse or harness
John Melburne ⎪
Thomas Smyth ⎪
Alexander Hodson ⎭
Philipp Wright—a bowman, not able

Collections for a History of Staffordshire, 1901, p. 217.

(D) INSTRUCTIONS FOR TRAINING MEN IN LANCASHIRE (1577)

To our very good lords, the earl of Derby and Lord Mounteagle, and to the rest of the commissioners appointed in the fifteenth year of her majesty's reign for the taking of the general musters in the county of Lancashire: after our hearty commendations. Whereas it pleased the queen's majesty . . . to direct her commission . . . unto you for the taking of views and musters of her loving subjects of the county of Lancashire . . . , we would have wished that you had set them down in writing more particularly, according to such direction as was contained in the said instruction. For want whereof we are first to require you . . . you would certify your former musterings somewhat more orderly, according to a schedule which we send you herewith enclosed . . . ; and further, forasmuch upon some considerations . . . it is thought requisite that out of the total number then mustered in that county the number of three hundred should be selected and trained, the same number being so small it is not doubted but the country is very well able to bear the charges of the training (for which cause both her majesty and we assure ourselves that as heretofore you have showed yourselves very forward in executing her majesty's commandment tending to so good an

---

[2] A list similar to the one following is given for each township within the hundred.

end), so now also in respect of some small charges or pains, which the country is to be at, you will not fail to employ your best endeavours for the executing thereof as appertaineth to good and dutiful subjects. And yet our meaning is not, by this present preparation of this small number of shot,[3] but that also . . . all the rest of the serviceable men which were before mustered . . . otherwise to supply and continue in readiness, so as they may be ready to be mustered, as you shall have further commission; by which is meant that the footmen shall be mustered about the month of May and the horsemen about July, whereof we require you to have some consideration in giving warning now aforehand. . . . And so we bid you heartily farewell. Westminster [20 March 1577]. Your loving friends: William Burleigh, Robert Leicester, Francis Bedford, Francis Knowles, Ambrose Warwick, Thomas Sussex, James Crofte, Francis Walsingham.

J. Harland, Lancashire Lieutenancy, I, 91 f.

---

[3] Men armed with bows or firearms.

88. GRANTS FOR TRADE AND COLONIES (1578-1601)

(A) LETTERS PATENT TO SIR HUMPHREY GILBERT (1578)

Elizabeth, by the grace of God, queen of England, etc. . . . Know ye that . . . we have given and granted . . . , for us, our heirs, and successors . . . , to our trusty and well-beloved servant, Sir Humphrey Gilbert of Compton . . . , and to his heirs and assigns forever, free liberty and licence . . . at all times forever hereafter to discover, find, search out, and view such remote, heathen, and barbarous lands, countries, and territories, not actually possessed of any Christian prince or people, as to him . . . shall seem good; and the same to have . . . and enjoy to him, his heirs and assigns forever, with all commodities, jurisdictions, and royalties both by sea and land; and the said Sir Humphrey, and all such as from time to time by licence of us [etc.] shall go and travel thither, to inhabit or remain there, to build and fortify at the discretion of the said Sir Humphrey [etc.] . . .

And further that he, the said Humphrey [etc.] . . . , shall have . . . and enjoy to him [etc.] . . . all the soil of all such lands, countries, and territories so to be discovered or possessed as aforesaid . . . , to be had or used with full power to dispose thereof, and of every part thereof in fee simple or otherwise according to the order of the laws of England, as near as the same conveniently may be . . . ; paying unto us for all services, duties, and demands the fifth part of all the ore of gold and silver that . . . shall be there gotten. . . .

And for uniting in more perfect league and amity of such countries, lands, and territories so to be possessed and inhabited as aforesaid with our realms of England and Ireland, and for the better encouragement of men to this enterprise, we do by these presents grant and declare that all such countries, so hereafter to be possessed and inhabited as aforesaid, from thenceforth shall be of the allegiance of us, our heirs, and successors, and we do grant to the said Sir Humphrey [etc.] . . . , and to all and every other person and persons being of our allegiance . . . that with the assent of the said Sir Humphrey [etc.] . . . shall now in this voyage for discovery, or in the second journey for conquest, hereafter travel to such lands . . . as aforesaid . . . , that they . . . shall and may have . . . all the privileges of free denizens and persons native of England and within our allegiance. . . .

And forasmuch as, upon the . . . inhabiting of such remote lands . . . , it shall be necessary for the safety of all men . . . to determine to live together in Christian peace and civil quietness each with other . . . , we . . . are likewise pleased . . . [to] grant to the said Sir Humphrey [etc.] . . . that he and they . . . may from time to time . . . within the said mentioned remote lands . . . have full and mere power and authority to correct, punish, pardon, govern, and rule by their . . . good discretions and policies, as well in causes capital or criminal as civil . . . , all such our subjects and others as shall . . . hereafter adventure themselves in the said . . . voyages . . . or . . . inhabit any such lands . . . , according to such statutes, laws, and ordinances as shall be by him, the said Sir Humphrey [etc.] . . . , devised or established for the better government of the said people . . . ; so always that the said statutes [etc.] . . . may be, as near as conveniently may, agreeable to the form of the laws and policy of England, and also that they be not against the true Christian faith or religion now professed in the Church of England. . . .

Hakluyt, Principal Navigations, VIII, 17 f.

(B) CHARTER TO THE EAST INDIA COMPANY (1601)

Elizabeth, by the grace of God, etc. . . . Whereas our most dear and loving cousin, George, earl of Cumberland, and our well-beloved subjects, Sir John Hart, of London, knight, [and 217 others] have . . . been petitioners unto us for our royal assent and licence to be granted unto them, that they, at their own adventures, costs, and charges . . . , might adventure and set forth one or more voyages, with convenient number of ships and pinnaces, by way of traffic and merchandise to the East Indies, in the countries and parts of Asia and Africa, and to as many of the islands, ports, cities, towns and places thereabouts as where trade and traffic may by all likelihood be . . . had; divers of which countries and many of the islands, cities and ports thereof, have long since been discovered by others of our subjects, albeit not frequented in trade of merchandise: know ye therefore that we, greatly tendering the honour of our nation, the wealth of our people, and the encouragement of them and others of our loving subjects in their good enterprises, for the increase of our navigation and the advancement of lawful traffic to the benefit of

our commonwealth, have . . . granted . . . unto our said loving subjects . . . that they . . . from henceforth be . . . one body corporate and politic, in deed and in name, by the name of the Governor
and Company of Merchants of London Trading into the East Indies
. . . ; and that by the same name . . . they shall have succession ;
and that they and their successors . . . shall be at all times hereafter
. . . capable in law to have . . . and retain lands, rents, privileges,
liberties, jurisdictions, franchises, and hereditaments of whatsoever
kind . . . , and also to give . . . and dispose lands, tenements, and
hereditaments, and to do and execute all . . . other things, by the
same name, that to them shall appertain to do; and that they and
their successors . . . may plead and be impleaded . . . in whatsoever courts and places . . . in all . . . actions . . . , causes, and demands whatsoever. . . .

And . . . we do ordain that there shall be from henceforth one
of the same company . . . , which shall be called the governor of the
said company; and that there shall be from henceforth twenty-four of
the said company . . . , which shall be called the committee of the
said company, who, together with the governor . . . , shall have the
direction of the voyages of or for the said company, and the provision of the shipping and merchandises thereto belonging, and also
the sale of all merchandises returned in the voyages . . . , and the
managing and handling of all other things belonging to the said
company. And for the better execution of this our will and grant
in this behalf, we have assigned . . . and make the said Thomas
Smith, alderman of London, to be the first and present governor of
the said company . . . ; and also we have assigned . . . and make
the said Paul Banning [and twenty-three others] to be the twenty-
four first and present committees of the said company. . . .

And further we will . . . that it shall . . . be lawful to and for
the said governor and company . . . present at any public assembly,
commonly called the court, holden for the said company . . . to elect
. . . one of the said company to be deputy to the said governor. . . .
And further we will and grant . . . unto the said governor and
company . . . that they . . . shall . . . have authority and power
yearly . . . to elect and nominate one of the said company which
shall be governor . . . for one whole year. . . .[1]

And further we . . . grant unto the said governor and company
. . . that they . . . and all the sons of them . . . , at their several
ages of one-and-twenty years or upwards, and further all such the
apprentices, factors, and servants of them . . . , which hereafter
shall be employed by the said governor and company . . . , may, by
the space of fifteen years . . . , freely traffic and use the trade of
merchandise by seas, in and by such ways and passages . . . as they
shall esteem and take to be fittest, into and from the said East Indies,
in the countries and parts of Asia and Africa . . . in such

---

[1] Members of the committee were also to be annually elected.

order . . . as shall be from time to time at any public assembly or court held by or for the said governor and company . . . limited and agreed, and not otherwise . . . ; so always the same trade be not undertaken nor addressed to any country . . . or place already in the lawful and actual possession of any such Christian prince or state as at this present is or at any time hereafter shall be in league or amity with us, our heirs, or successors, and who doth not or will not accept of such trade, but doth overtly declare . . . the same to be utterly against his or their goodwill and liking.

And further . . . we do grant . . . that it shall and may be lawful to and for the said governor and company . . . to hold court for the said company and the affairs thereof; and that also it shall and may be lawful to and for them . . . to make, ordain, and constitute such and so many reasonable laws . . . as to them . . . shall seem necessary and convenient for the good government of the same company and of all factors, masters, mariners, and other officers employed or to be employed in any of their voyages . . . ; so always as the said laws . . . be reasonable and not contrary to the laws, statutes, or customs of this our realm. . . .

And we . . . grant to the said governor and company . . . that the said East Indies . . . shall not be visited . . . by any of the subjects of us . . . during the said term of fifteen years, contrary to the true meaning of these presents. And by virtue of our prerogative royal, which we will not in that behalf have argued or brought in question, we straitly charge . . . all the subjects of us . . . that none of them, directly or indirectly, do visit . . . or trade . . . into or from any of the said East Indies, or into or from any the . . . places aforesaid, other than the said governor and company . . . , unless it be by . . . licence and agreement of the said governor. . . .[2]

Charters Granted to the East India Company, pp. 3 f.

---

[2] Other articles provide penalties and allow for the revocation or continuance of the charter.

SECTION
VIII

THE EARLY STUARTS

THE period from 1603 to 1642, though little more than a third of a century, is here represented by another long series of documents. The reason, of course, is the extraordinary interest of the constitutional struggle under James I and Charles I. And since the struggle was from the beginning concentrated in parliament, it has seemed best to arrange the pertinent materials according to certain convenient divisions of parliamentary history. In this way the various letters and speeches of the kings, as well as the formal resolutions, debates, and other proceedings of parliament, have been kept together in chronological order.

As in previous sections, a number of judicial records have been included for illustrative purposes—especially the reports of ordinary business in the courts of star chamber and high commission. But most of the cases under nos. 91 and 94 have a greater significance: they raised problems concerning the fundamentals of English government. Frequently the judgments by which they were concluded became political issues of first magnitude. Judges of the king's central courts now began to rival his ministers and generals in public fame.

The remaining documents in the present section require few words of comment. No. 97 is particularly valuable for its statement of the doctrine of divine right as officially set forth by some of the clergy. Under no. 98 a series of typical records from the counties show how, despite the rising conflict between crown and parliament, English local government continued its normal routine and constantly extended its activity. Lastly, in the three documents given under no. 99, may be seen the precedents set by the early Stuarts in colonial organization.

The constitutional developments of these momentous years cannot be explained in a short introductory note, but a word may be said with regard to certain important features of parliamentary history. With the first session in 1604, controversy between the king and his critics suddenly became acute. In Elizabeth's reign only a few members of the commons had been given to political agitation, and they had often been opposed by a majority of their fellows. Most argument concerning crown and parliament had then been couched in general terms. In 1604 the champions of parliamentary rights led a strong party in the commons and formulated a detailed programme. Under their guidance, the house drew up the Apology of the Commons, setting forth in large measure the issues that dominated the ensuing struggle. As controversy proceeded, those who spoke for the commons gradually strengthened the position of the house. They gave close attention to parliamentary procedure and marshalled legal precedents to vindicate their privileges and lawful powers—as may be seen by comparing the Apology with the Petition of Right. To refute their arguments, the king elaborated a more cogent statement of the monarchical cause, matching their proofs with his own. During the sessions of 1606-11 and 1621-29 the issues dividing the two camps thus came to be more sharply defined. If this development were to be fully illustrated, the whole series of parliamentary records would have to be drawn upon. For present purposes, however, examples of procedure have been taken from the years 1604-11, when many new practices came into use.

Before 1640 the struggle between king and parliament brought little change in the structure of English government, but with the opening of the Long Parliament the way was cleared for swift legislative action. The new laws (no. 96A-I) struck down the prerogative courts, set further limits to the king's fiscal rights, and assured the regular calling of parliament. This constitutional reform, one of the greatest in English history, was effected in the year 1641 and had the general support of the English public. A considerable party, however, made two additional demands: reorganization of the English Church according to Puritan principles, and extension of parliamentary control over the executive government. These demands (here reflected in no. 96J-P) led to the outbreak of civil war in the summer of 1642.

The great interest of the educated classes in constitutional problems under the early Stuarts had expression in two significant ways: the assiduous reporting of debates by ordinary members of parliament, and the historical study of English institutions. The first is best presented to the reader in the diaries edited by

W. Notestein and his associates;[1] the second in the works of Sir Edward Coke, Sir Simonds D'Ewes, and John Selden.

Three collections of documents deal with the early Stuart period and provide comment on constitutional issues; they are J. P. Kenyon, *The Stuart Constitution; Documents and Commentary,* J. R. Tanner, *Constitutional Documents of the Reign of James I,* and S. R. Gardiner, *Constitutional Documents of the Puritan Revolution,* 1625–1660. For general discussion the student should read appropriate sections in C. Hill, *The Century of Revolution,* 1603–1714; G. Davies, *The Early Stuarts,* 1603–1660; M. A. Judson, *The Crisis of the Constitution;* and S. R. Gardiner, *History of England,* 1603–1642. The fundamentals of English constitutional law—a subject given prominence in this and the following sections—will be found clearly presented in A. V. Dicey, *The Law of the Constitution;* and in W. R. Anson, *The Law and Custom of the Constitution.* An important interpretative work is J. G. A. Pocock, *The Ancient Constitution and the Feudal Law: A Study in English Historical Thought in the Seventeenth Century.* The standard bibliography for Stuart history is G. Davies, *Bibliography of British History; Stuart Period,* 1603–1714.

---

[1] *Commons Debates, 1621,* edited by W. Notestein, F. H. Relf, and H. Simpson; *Common Debates for 1629,* edited by W. Notestein and F. H. Relf; *The Journal of Sir Simonds D'Ewes,* edited by W. Notestein. See also his "Winning of the Initiative by the House of Commons," in *Proceedings of the British Academy,* 1924.

89. RECORDS OF PARLIAMENT AND TAXES (1604-22)

(A) James I: Proclamation concerning Elections (1604)

. . . We do hereby straitly charge and admonish all persons interested in the choice of knights for the shires, first, that the knights for the county be selected out of the principal knights or gentlemen of sufficient ability within that county wherein they are chosen; and, for the burgesses, that choice be made of men of sufficiency and discretion without any partial respects or factious combination. . . . Next and above all things, considering that one of the main pillars of this estate is the preservation of unity in the profession of sincere religion of Almighty God, we do also admonish that there be great care taken to avoid the choice of any persons either noted for their superstitious blindness one way, or for their turbulent humours other ways; because their disorderly and unquiet spirits will disturb all the discreet and modest proceeding in that greatest and gravest council. Further, we do command that an express care be had that there be not chosen any persons bankrupts or outlawed, but men of known good behaviour and sufficient livelihood, and such as are not only taxed to the payment of subsidies and other like charges, but also have ordinarily paid and satisfied the same . . . ; next, that all sheriffs be charged that they do not direct any precept for electing and returning of any burgesses to or for any ancient borough-town within their counties being so utterly ruined and decayed that there are not sufficient residents to make such choice, and of whom lawful election may be made; also to charge all cities and boroughs and the inhabitants of the same, that none of them seal any blanks, referring or leaving to any others to insert the names of any citizens or burgesses to serve for any such city or borough, [but that they] do make open and free election according to the law, and set down the names of the persons whom they choose before they seal the certificate. Furthermore, we notify by these presents that all returns and certificates of knights, citizens, and burgesses ought and are to be brought to the chancery, and there to be filed of record. And if any shall be found to be made contrary to this proclamation, the same is to be rejected as unlawful and insufficient, and the city or borough to be fined for the same; and if it be found that they have committed any gross or wilful default and contempt in their election, return, or certificate, that then their liberties according to the law are to be seized into our hands as forfeited. And if any person take upon him the place of a knight, citizen, or burgess, not being duly elected, returned, and sworn according to the laws and statutes in that behalf provided, and according to the purport, effect, and true meaning of this our proclamation, then every person so offending [is] to be fined and imprisoned for the same. . . .

Given at our honour of Hampton Court, the 11th day of January.

Rymer, *Foedera*, XVI, 561 f.

(B) Early Proceedings of the Commons (1604)

[22 March.] . . . Mr. Speaker with all submissive reverence to his majesty taking leave, he with the commons departed to their usual place. And there being assembled, the first motion was made by Sir William Fleetwood, one of the knights returned for the county of Buckingham on the behalf of Sir Francis Goodwin, knight, who, upon the first writ of summons directed to the sheriff of Buckingham, was elected the first knight for that shire; but, the return of his election being made, it was refused by the clerk of the crown, *quia utlagatus*,[1] and because Sir John Fortescue, upon a second writ, was elected and entered in that place. His desire was that this return might be examined and Sir Francis Goodwin received as a member of the house. The house gave way to the motion; and, for a more deliberate and judicial proceeding in a case of privilege so important to the house, ordered that the serjeant, the proper officer of the house,

---

[1] Because he had been outlawed; see below, p. 410.

should give warning to the clerk of the crown to appear at the bar
at eight o'clock the next morning, and to bring with him all the
writs of summons, indentures, and returns of elections for the
county of Buckingham made and returned for this parliament; and
to give warning also to Sir Francis Goodwin to attend in person,
whom their pleasure was to hear . . . deliver the state of his own
cause and the manner and reasons of the proceeding in the election
of the knights of the shire for that county.

This, being a motion tending to matter of privilege, was seconded
with another by Mr. Serjeant Shirley, touching an arrest made the
15th of March last, the day of his majesty's solemn entrance through
London, and four days before the sitting of the parliament, upon the
body of Sir Thomas Shirley, elected one of the burgesses for the
borough of Steyning in the county of Sussex, at the suit of one
Giles Sympson, a goldsmith, dwelling in Lombard Street, London,
by one William Watkins, a serjeant-at-mace and Thomas Aram, his
yeoman. And [it was] prayed that the body of the said Sir Thomas
might be freed according to the known privilege of the house. Hereupon the house, in affirmation of their own privilege, assented, and
ordered that a warrant, according to the ancient form, should be directed under the hand of Mr. Speaker to the clerk of the crown, for
the granting of a writ of *habeas corpus* to bring the body of the said
Sir Thomas into the house upon Tuesday next at eight o'clock in the
morning. . . .

Sir George Moore, allowing these grave and advised resolutions
in point of privilege, for the better advancement thereof and for
a more deliberate and due proceeding in these and the like cases
best beseeming the gravity and honour of that assembly, moved that
a select committee might be appointed to consider of all cases of
returns and privileges during the time of parliament. This is an
usual motion in the beginning of every parliament.

[23 March.] This day may be called *dies juridicus*, the first day
of business; the other were but of form and ceremony, yet ever
usual and necessary in respect of the magnificence and state of such
an assembly. *Principium a Deo:* the beginning was with prayers to
God for good success; and such prayers as have been ordinary in
former parliaments in the reign of the late queen, and are placed in
the front of the Book of Common Prayer, were read by the clerk
of the house, to whose place that service anciently appertains. And
one other special prayer, fitly conceived for that time and purpose,
was read by Mr. Speaker; which was voluntary and not of duty or
necessity, though heretofore of late time the like hath been done by
other speakers. . . .

After prayers ended and the house settled, with expectation of
what should be propounded for the weal of the common subject;
Sir Robert Wroth, one of the knights of the shire returned for the
county of Essex, moved that matters of most importance might first

be handled; and to that purpose offered to the consideration of the house these particulars: *viz.,* (1) confirmation of the Book of Common Prayer; (2) the wardship of men's children, as a burden and servitude to the subjects of this kingdom; (3) the general abuse and grievance of purveyors, and cart-takers, etc.; (4) particular and private patents, commonly called monopolies; (5) dispensations in penal statutes; (6) transportation of ordnance; (7) the writ of *quo titulo ingressi,* etc., abuses of the exchequer, etc.

This motion for the time passed with silence; and Sir Edward Montague, one of the knights for Northamptonshire, proceedeth in another; expressing three main grievances of his country and praying some care to be had of remedy for them: *viz.,* the burden, vexation, and charge of commissaries' courts; (2) the suspension of some learned and grave ministers for matters of ceremony and for preaching against popish doctrine; (3) depopulations by enclosure.

Sir Thomas Crompton, doctor of the civil law, and the king's advocate, being one of the burgesses returned for the university of Oxford by virtue of a new charter granted by his majesty that now is, with some length of speech examined the circumstances and approveth the general purpose of the former motion.

Another learned and good member of the house, taking occasion as well from Sir Thomas Shirley's case, opened the last sitting-day, as from the course begun in these foresaid motions, prayeth generally a consideration of the honour and privilege of this house; which, he said, ought to be kept sacred and inviolable. And thereof a true member of the body ought to be sensible and careful; but unnatural and strange members could not be so tender of the welfare of the whole. And therefore it were fit to examine whether every one here did hold his place by a lawful and just election and return, and were a true member of the body; that, if any were found otherwise, he might be cut off and dismissed, as incompatible for the service of this so honourable and well-compounded an assembly.

A third grave person, and an ancient parliament-man, remembereth and alloweth the motions made by Sir Robert Wroth and Sir Edward Montague; but moveth that nothing might be offered in a general and vanishing speech, without a bill ready framed and exhibited to the house by the mover.

Hereupon the motion was continued that a select committee might be named for the consideration of the particulars mentioned by Sir Robert Wroth; and to that purpose were called and set down by name. . . .[2] And the same committees [are] to make report of their proceeding in all or any of these from time to time, as they shall find fit or as the house shall direct them. And for their first meeting [they] are appointed to assemble themselves the same day at two o'clock in the afternoon in the exchequer chamber.

For the three grievances opened by Sir Edward Montague, were

---

[2] Forty-seven members of the house.

named. . . .[3] And [they] were appointed to meet on Monday following . . . at two o'clock in the afternoon in the star chamber. . . .

Journals of the Commons, I, 149-51.

(C) THE CASE OF SIR FRANCIS GOODWIN (1604)

[23 March.] . . . Sir George Coppyn, knight, clerk of the crown in the chancery, this day, according to former order, being attended by the serjeant of the house with his mace, appeared at the bar and produced all the writs of summons, indentures, and returns made of the knights for Buckinghamshire for this parliament; which were severally read by the clerk of the house. And then the clerk of the crown [was] commanded to retire to the door; and after, Sir Francis Goodwin himself, whom it specially concerned, attending to know the pleasure of the house, was called in. . . .

In this meantime the whole case was at large opened and argued *pro et contra* by sundry learned and grave members of the house, and after much dispute the question was agreed upon and made, whether Sir Francis Goodwin were lawfully elected and returned one of the knights for Buckinghamshire and ought to be admitted and received as a member of this house. Upon this question it was resolved in the affirmative, that he was lawfully elected and returned and *de jure* ought to be received. Hereupon the clerk of the crown was commanded to file the first indenture of return, and order was given that Sir Francis should presently take the oath of supremacy usual and his place in the house; which he did accordingly. . . .

[29 March.] . . . Mr. Speaker relateth what he had delivered to the king by warrant from the house the day before touching their proceeding in Sir Francis Goodwin's case, and his majesty's answer. . . . He said he first delivered (1) the manner and the matter; (2) then such precedents as had been vouched and stood upon; (3) he opened the body of the law for election. . . . For the matter of outlawry . . . , Sir Francis has since been chosen, admitted, and served as a member of this house in . . . several parliaments. . . . The outlawry remained in the hustings; so, as the law could not take notice of it, neither was it pleadable. . . .

His majesty answered he was loath he should be forced to alter his tune, and that he should now change it into matter of grief by way of contestation. He did sample it to the murmur and contradiction of the people of Israel. He did not attribute the cause of his grief to any purpose in the house to offend him, but only to a mistaking of the law. For matters of fact, he answered them all particularly that, for his part, he was indifferent which of them were chosen, Sir John or Sir Francis; that they could suspect no special affection in him, because this was a counsellor not brought in by himself. That he had no purpose to impeach their privilege; but, since

---

[3] All privy councillors in the house and fifty-nine others.

they derived all matters of privilege from him, and by his grant, he expected they should not be turned against him. [He said] that there was no precedent did suit this case fully; precedents in the times of minors, of tyrants, of women, of simple kings, [were] not to be credited, because [such were] for some private ends. By the law, this house ought not to meddle with returns, being all made into the chancery; and are to be corrected or reformed by that court only into which they are returned. [In] 35 Henry VI it was the resolution of all the judges that matter of outlawry was a sufficient cause of dismission of any member out of the house; that the judges have now resolved that Sir Francis Goodwin standeth outlawed according to the laws of this land. In conclusion, it was his majesty's special charge unto us that, first, the course already taken should be truly reported; (2) that we should debate the matter and resolve amongst ourselves; (3) that we should admit of conference with the judges; (4) that we should make report of all the proceedings unto the council. . . .

[30 March.] . . . Upon the conclusion of this debate . . . ,[4] the house proceeded to question. . . . First question: whether the house was resolved in the matter. And the question was answered by general voice that the whole house was resolved. Second question: whether the reasons of their proceeding shall be set down in writing. Resolved that they shall be set down in writing; and ordered further that a committee should be named for that purpose. . . . The committees were instantly named, *viz*. . . .

The house being resolved upon the question that the reasons of their precedent resolution touching the return, admittance, and retaining of Sir Francis Goodwin as a member of this house should be set down in writing, these committees were specially appointed to perform that service; and have warrant from the house to send for any officer, to view and search any record or other thing of that kind which may help their knowledge or memory in this particular service. And, having deliberately by general consent set down all such reasons, they are to bring them in writing into the house, there to be read and approved, as shall be thought fit.

[2 April.] . . . It was then moved that committees might be named to take the examination of the sheriff of Buckinghamshire, who was by former order sent for and now come. . . . The examination was presently taken by these committees and returned in this form:—
Interrogation 1: Why he removed the county [court] from Aylesbury to Brickhill. He saith it was by reason of the plague being at Aylesbury, the county [court] being the 25th of January, at which time three were dead of the plague there. This was [the] only motive of removing his county [court]. Interrogation 2: Whether he

---

[4] The house had debated the case of Goodwin since the speaker's report on the previous day.

were present at the first election. Saith he was present, and was as faithful to wish the second place to Sir Francis Goodwin as the first to Sir John Fortescue; sent Sir Francis Goodwin word before the election he should not need to bring any freeholders, for the election, he thought, would be without scruple for them both: first to Sir John, second to Sir Francis. About eight of the clock he came to Brickhill [and] was then told by Sir George Throckmorton and others that the first voice would be given for Sir Francis. He answered he hoped it would not be so and desired every gentleman to deal with his freeholders. After eight of the clock [he] went to the election, a great number there being children never at the county [court]. After the writ read, he first intimated the points of the proclamation; then jointly propounded Sir John Fortescue and Sir Francis Goodwin. The freeholders cried first, "A Goodwin! A Goodwin!" Every justice of peace on the bench said, "A Fortescue! A Fortescue!"; and came down from the bench before they named any for a second place and desired the freeholders to name Sir John Fortescue for the first. Sir Francis Goodwin, being in a chamber near, was sent for by the sheriff and justices; and he came down and earnestly persuaded with the freeholders, saying Sir John was his good friend; had been his father's; and that they would not do Sir John that injury. Notwithstanding, the freeholders would not desist, but still cried, "A Goodwin! A Goodwin!": some crying, "A Fortescue!" to the number of sixty or thereabouts; the other, for Sir Francis Goodwin, being about two or three hundred. And Sir Francis Goodwin, to his thinking, dealt very plainly and earnestly in this matter for Sir John Fortescue; for that Sir Francis Goodwin did so earnestly protest it unto him. . . .

[3 April.] . . . The reasons of the proceeding of the house in Sir Francis Goodwin's case penned by the committee were, according to former order, brought in by Mr. Francis Moore and read by the clerk, directed in form of a petition:—

To the king's most excellent majesty: The humble answer of the commons house of parliament to his majesty's objections in Sir Francis Goodwin's case. . . . There were objected against us by your majesty and your reverend judges four things to impeach our proceedings in receiving Francis Goodwin, knight, into our house. . . . The first [was] that we assumed to ourselves power of examining of the elections and returns of knights and burgesses, which belonged to your majesty's chancery and not to us. . . . Our humble answer is that until the seventh year of King Henry IV all parliament writs were returnable into the parliament. . . . In which year a statute was made that thenceforth every parliament writ . . . should have this clause. . . . By this, although the form of the writ be somewhat altered, yet the power of parliament to examine and determine of elections remaineth; for so the statute hath been always expounded . . . to this day. . . . And also the commons, in the beginning of every parliament, have ever used to appoint special committees all the parliament time for examining controversies concerning elections and returns of knights and burgesses; during which time the writs and indentures remain with the clerk of the crown, and after the parliament ended, and not before, are delivered to the clerk of the petty bag in chancery, to be kept there. Which is warranted by reason and precedents; reason, for that it is fit that the returns should be in that place examined, where the appearance and service of the writ is appointed. The appearance and service is in parliament; therefore the return [is] examinable in parliament. . . .[5]

[5 April.] Mr. Speaker excuseth his absence, by reason he was commanded to attend upon his majesty, and bringeth message from his majesty to this effect: that the king had received a parchment from the house. Whether it were an absolute resolution or reason to give him satisfaction he knew not; he thought it was rather intended for his satisfaction. His majesty protested, by that love he bare to the house, as his loving and loyal subjects, and by the faith he did ever owe to God, he had as great a desire to maintain their privileges as ever any prince had, or as they themselves. He had seen and considered of the manner and the matter; he had heard his judges and council; and . . . he was now distracted in judgment. Therefore, for his further satisfaction, he desired and commanded, as an absolute king, that there might be a conference between the house and the judges; and that, for that purpose, there might be a select committee of grave and learned persons out of the house; that his council might be present, not as umpires to determine, but to report indifferently on both sides.

Upon this unexpected message, there grew some amazement and silence; but at last one stood up and said: "The prince's command is like a thunderbolt; his command upon our allegiance like the roaring of a lion. To his command there is no contradiction; but how, or in what manner, we should now proceed to perform obedience, that will be the question." Another answered: "Let us petition to his majesty that he will be pleased to be present, to hear, moderate, and judge the case himself." Whereupon Mr. Speaker proceeded to this question: . . . whether to confer with the judges in the presence of the king and council. Which was resolved in the affirmative, and a select committee [was] presently named for the conference. . . .

These committees were selected and appointed to confer with the judges of the law touching the reasons of proceeding in Sir Francis Goodwin's case set down in writing and delivered to his majesty, in the presence of the lords of his majesty's council, according to his highness' pleasure, signified by Mr. Speaker this day to the house. It was further resolved and ordered by the house, upon the motion to that end by Mr. Lawrence Hyde, that the foresaid committees should

---

[5] The address then cites precedents and continues the argument to meet the other objections raised by the king.

insist upon the fortification and explaining of the reasons and answers delivered unto his majesty, and not proceed to any other argument or answer, what occasion soever moved in the time of that debate. . . .

[11 April.] . . . Sir Francis Bacon . . . reporteth what had passed in conference in the presence of his majesty and his council. The king said . . . that our privileges were not in question. . . . He granted it was a court of record and a judge of returns. He moved that neither Sir John Fortescue nor Sir Francis Goodwin might have place. . . .

Upon this report, a motion was made that it might be done by way of warrant. . . . Question: whether Sir John Fortescue and Sir Francis Goodwin shall both be secluded and a warrant for a new writ directed. And upon the question [it was] resolved that a writ should issue for a new choice, and a warrant [was] directed accordingly. . . .

Ibid., I, 151-68.

(D) The Case of Sir Thomas Shirley (1604)

[27 March.] This day the writ of *habeas corpus*, formerly awarded by order of the house, for the bringing in of the body of Sir Thomas Shirley, one of the members of the house and prisoner in the Fleet, was returned by the warden of the Fleet. The prisoner himself [was] brought to the bar; and Simpson, the goldsmith, and Watkins, the serjeant-at-mace, as delinquents, [were] brought in by the serjeant of the house. The writ and return was read by the clerk. . . .

Mr. Speaker proposed divers questions to be answered by the said offenders by whose relation it was averred that the writ of execution was taken forth the 30th of January [and] was delivered to the serjeant the 11th of February, before Sir Thomas was elected burgess; that Simpson and the serjeant, in the interim before the arrest, had no conference or privity one with the other; that the serjeant knew nothing at all of Sir Thomas his election, but understood by his majesty's proclamation that no person outlawed for treason, felony, debt, or any other trespass ought to be admitted a member of the parliament, and was thereupon induced to think that Sir Thomas Shirley, standing outlawed, should not be elected or admitted a burgess; which if he had known or suspected, he would have been very careful not to have given offence to this honourable house by any such arrest.

To this Sir Thomas was admitted to answer, who affirmed that the arrest was made the 15th day of March, the day of his majesty's first and solemn entrance through London; at what time he was going by commandment to wait upon his majesty; whereof, upon the first offer to touch him, he wished the serjeant to take knowledge, as also that he was elected a burgess for the borough of Steyning in the county of Sussex to serve at this present parliament; that, notwithstanding, they persisted in the arrest and carried his body to the prison of the Compter. . . .

And the whole case, after long dispute, [was] summarily considered in three particulars: *viz.*, first, privilege to a member; (2) interest reserved to a stranger; (3) punishment of the offender. Which being the grounds of all the subsequent arguments in this case, the dispute ended for this day; with caution that the house should so proceed as they gave not way and encouragement to others to practise to be arrested upon execution with a purpose, by pretence of privilege, to discharge the debt; and a motion that a special committee might be named for the consideration of all the questions and doubts in this case. . . .

[16 April.] Moved that a bill might be drawn in the matter of Sir Thomas Shirley, wherein was to be considered only two things: justice of privilege and justice to the party. For better information of the house and direction to the committees, certain ancient precedents of petitions to the kings of this realm, with answer and assent from the said kings in the very point of privilege, and of arrest upon execution, taken out of the parliament records in the Tower, upon this occasion were produced and read in the house, in number three, as followeth. . . .[6]

After these precedents read, and some consideration had what was to be done, the house agreed upon three questions: (1) whether Sir Thomas Shirley shall have privilege; (2) whether presently or [to] be deferred till further order; (3) whether we shall be petitioners to his majesty, according to former precedents, for some course of securing the debt to the party and saving harmless the warden of the Fleet. These questions, being severally put, were all resolved in the affirmative; and so left for this day. . . .[7]

Ibid., I, 155-75.

(E) Notes concerning Procedure in the Commons (1604-07)

[26 March 1604.] . . . Note that committees, being once named and a place appointed for their meeting by the house, may from time to time, until the report of their proceedings be made, adjourn and alter their place and time of meeting and select such sub-committees from amongst themselves as they shall find cause, for any particular purpose or service, to be assigned by themselves or the house upon their report. . . .

Note, as an ancient rule of the house, that upon any conference the number of the commons named for the said conference are always double to those of the lords; and the place and time of meeting [are] appointed by the lords. . . .

[14 April 1604.] . . . In the matter formerly proposed touching

---

[6] The commons cite Larke's case (no. 67c) and two later instances.
[7] Cf. no. 90c.

the abuses of purveyors, it was now argued whether it were fittest to proceed by way of petition to his majesty or by bill, by Mr. Martin, Mr. Hoskins, and Mr. Hyde, and, lastly, by Sir Henry Jenkins, who was observed to mistake the question and therefore, to prevent the idle expense of time, was interrupted by Mr. Speaker. And thereupon a rule [was] conceived that, if any man speak impertinently or besides the question in hand, it stands with the orders of the house for Mr. Speaker to interrupt him and to know the pleasure of the house, whether they will further hear him. . . .

[27 April 1604.] Sir Francis Bacon reporteth from the committee touching the union[8] that they had digested their resolutions into heads and assigned several parts to several persons of several qualities as they conceived fit . . . :—

Matter of generality or common reason, two parts: (1) that there is no cause of change, Sir Francis Bacon; (2) that there is no precedent of like change, Sir Edwin Sandys.

Matter of estate inward and of law: Mr. Serjeant Hobart, Serjeant Dodridge, Serjeant Tanfield, Mr. Attorney of the Wards.

Matter of estate foreign or matter of intercourse: Sir Henry Nevill, Sir Richard Spencer, Sir John Hollis, Sir Arthur Atye, Sir Christopher Perkins, Sir Lewis Lewknor, Sir George Carey, master of the chancery.

Matter of honour and reputation: Sir Francis Hastings, Sir Maurice Berkley, Sir George Moore, Sir Herbert Crofts, Mr. Martin, Mr. Yelverton, Sir John Savill, Sir Robert Wingfield, Sir Oliver St. John, Sir Robert Wroth, Mr. Crewe, Sir Edward Hobby, Mr. Hyde. . . .

[12 May 1604.] . . . The commissioners for the union [were] named by the house and a several question [was] put upon every name. Privy councillors, two: Sir John Stanhope, knight, vice-chamberlain to the king; Sir John Harbert, second secretary to his majesty. Common lawyers, four: Sir Francis Bacon, one of his majesty's counsel learned; Sir Thomas Hesketh, knight, attorney of the wards; Sir Lawrence Tanfield, knight, serjeant-at-law; Sir Henry Hobart, knight, serjeant-at-law. Civilians, two: Sir John Bennett, knight, doctor of the laws; Sir Daniel Dun, knight, doctor of the laws. Merchants, four: Sir Henry Billingsley, Mr. Robert Askwith, Mr. Thomas James, Mr. Henry Chapman. Ambassadors, two: Sir Edward Stafford, Sir Henry Nevill. Gentlemen of several qualities and parts of the kingdom, [sixteen]. . . .

[19 May 1604.] . . . A motion [was] made that there might be a special place built and assigned for the keeping of the register and records and papers of the house, etc.; and for the clerk and his servants to attend and write in for the service of the house. The lord

[8] The proposed union of England and Scotland, vainly urged by James I during these years.

treasurer [was] to be moved in this. For this purpose a warrant was conceived in this form:—

. . . Whereas it is thought fit and so ordered by the commons house of parliament that all acts, resolutions, and judgments of the house, which are there entered and registered by their common servant, the clerk, should be written and engrossed in one fair register book, and that to be kept by the clerk for the use and direction of the said house; as also that all bills, whether passed or rejected, papers, notes, and other entries and proceedings of the house be preserved and kept in safety: it is required, on the behalf of the said house, that a room or place be provided near at hand with convenient presses and shelves, for the disposing and preserving of the said register, papers, and entries, and for the clerk and his servants to attend upon all occasions for the service of the said house; and this to be performed before the next session of this present parliament. Ed. Phelipps, speaker.

[8 June 1604.] . . . Concluded and resolved, upon a double question, (1) that the great committee [for matters of religion] shall select a sub-committee amongst themselves to search, view, and consider of all such precedents as have warranted or may warrant this house to intermeddle with matters ecclesiastical; (2) to consider of the frame of a petition to be exhibited to his majesty for dispensation, with some learned and faithful ministers, in matters indifferent and of ceremony. And if they shall not think it meet to be done by way of petition, to report their opinion to the house. . . .

[26 June 1607.] . . . The amendments and provisions annexed to the bill of hostile laws sent down from the lords were secondly read and committed to the great committee named upon the second reading of the bill itself in this house. And [it was] moved that Mr. Speaker might depart, and the committee being compounded of the whole house . . . might, for saving of time, presently enter into consideration of their charge. Which, after some dispute whether it were fit or no, being without precedent, seldom moved, and carrying with it no decorum in respect of Mr. Speaker's ordinary and necessary attendance upon the house till eleven o'clock, grew to a question, *viz.*, whether the committee should now sit or in the afternoon. And [it was] resolved upon question they should meet in the afternoon and not now. . . .[9]

Ibid., I, 153, 154, 171, 188, 208, 215, 387.

---

[9] Robert Bowyer's diary (edited by D. H. Willson, pp. 350 f.) gives the following version of these proceedings: "Mr. Speaker did put the house in mind that there is but three courses: 'Either,' said he, 'you must be pleased to dispute it, or to commit it, or to put it to the question.' Whereupon it was committed, the whole house to be committees in this place this afternoon, but not upon a question. Sir William Stroude moved that, being but ten of the clock, the speaker might depart and the house presently to proceed by committee. Of this point divers opinions arose, whereupon the question was made whether now

(F) MESSAGE OF JAMES I TO THE COMMONS (5 JUNE 1604)

. . . Mr. Speaker delivereth from the king a message, of three parts: the motives of his majesty's unkindness; matter of his relation to us; of his princely satisfaction. When he looked into the gravity and judgment of this house, and of the long continuance of the parliament—[that] so few matters of weight [had been] passed and that matter of privilege had taken much time (which, notwithstanding, he was as careful to preserve as we ourselves)—he was moved with jealousy that there was not such proceeding as, in love, he expected. This [was] the cause of [his] unkindness . . . ; we should not think this declaration to us was any condemnation of our ingratitude or forgetfulness of him, but by way of commemoration and admonition, as a father to his children. Neither did he tax us, but only [did] remember us of expedition omitted and desired. Lastly . . . , he is resolved we have not denied anything which is fit to be granted. . . . He had divers arguments of our good affections: (1) our doubt of his displeasure; (2) our desire to give him satisfaction, which he accepteth as a thing done because desired by us; (3) he observeth the difference of our proceeding, sithence his speech unto us, with greater expedition in those things desired to be effected by him than before. He giveth us thanks and wisheth we would not trouble ourselves with giving him satisfaction. And he giveth what time we desire for finishing the matters of importance depending. . . .

Ibid., I, 232 f.

(G) THE APOLOGY OF THE COMMONS (20 JUNE 1604)

The form of apology and satisfaction to be presented to his majesty, penned and agreed by a former select committee, was now reported and delivered into the house by Sir Thomas Ridgeway, one of the committees. . . .

To the king's most excellent majesty: from the house of commons assembled in parliament. Most gracious sovereign, we cannot but with much joy and thankfulness of mind acknowledge your majesty's great graciousness in declaring lately unto us, by the mouth of our speaker, that you rested now satisfied with our doings. Which satisfaction . . . yet proceeding merely from your majesty's most gracious disposition and not from any justification which on our behalf hath been made, we . . . could not . . . but tender in humble sort this further satisfaction. . . . With these minds, dread sovereign, your commons of England, represented now in us their knights, citizens, and burgesses, do come with this humble declaration to your

or in the afternoon. . . . It was put to the question and, the voices being doubtful and the question put again, the No prevailed. . . . After dinner members assembled in the house. The voice, as I and others conceived, was for Mr. Fuller to take the chair and some on Mr. Attorney. Mr. Fuller modestly refusing . . . , Mr. Attorney offered himself to it. . . ."

highness and in great assurance of your most gracious disposition, that your majesty with benignity of mind correspondent to our dutifulness, will be pleased to peruse it.

We know, and with great thankfulness to God acknowledge, that He hath given us a king of such understanding and wisdom as is rare to find in any prince in the world. Howbeit, seeing no human wisdom, how great soever, can pierce into the particularities of the rights and customs of people, or of the sayings and doings of particular persons, but by tract of experience and faithful report of such as know them . . . , what grief, what anguish of mind hath it been unto us at some times in presence to hear and see, in other things to find and feel by effect, your gracious majesty, to the extreme prejudice of this house of the commons, thereof so greatly wronged by information. . . ! We have been constrained, as well in duty to your royal majesty, whom with faithful hearts we serve, as to our dear country, for which we serve in this parliament . . . , freely to disclose unto your majesty the truth of such matters concerning your subjects, the commons, as heretofore by misinformation have been suppressed or perverted. Wherein . . . we shall reduce these misinformations to three principal heads: first, touching the cause of the joyful receiving of your majesty into this your kingdom; secondly, concerning the liberties and rights of your subjects of England and the privileges of this house; thirdly, touching the several actions and speeches passed in the house.

It has been told us to our faces by some of no small place, and the same spoken also in the presence of your majesty, that, on the 24th of March was twelvemonth,[10] we stood in so great fear that we would have given half we were worth for the security wherein we now stand. . . . We contrariwise most truly protest the contrary, that we stood not at that time, nor of many a day before, in any doubt or fear at all. We . . . , standing clear in our own consciences touching your majesty's right, were both resolute with our lives and all other abilities to have maintained the same against all the world. . . . But the true cause of our extraordinary great cheerfulness and joy in performing that day's duty was the great and extraordinary love which we bare towards your majesty's most royal and renowned person and a longing thirst to enjoy the happy fruits of your most wise, religious, just, virtuous, and gracious heart. Whereof not rumours, but your majesty's own writings, had given us a strong and undoubted assurance. . . .

Now concerning the ancient right of the subjects of this realm, chiefly consisting in the privileges of this house of the parliament, the misinformation openly delivered to your majesty hath been in three things: first, that we hold not our privileges of right, but of grace only, renewed every parliament by way of donative upon petition, and so to be limited; secondly, that we are no court of record,

---

[10] The day of Elizabeth's death.

nor yet a court that can command view of records, but that our proceedings here are only to acts and memorials, and that the attendance with the records is courtesy, not duty; and, lastly, that the examination of the returns of writs for knights and burgesses is without our compass, and due to the chancery. Against which assertions . . . , tending directly and apparently to the utter overthrow of the very fundamental privileges of our house—and therein of the rights and liberties of the whole commons of your realm of England, which they and their ancestors from time immemorial have undoubtedly enjoyed under your majesty's noble progenitors—we, the knights, citizens, and burgesses in the house of commons assembled in parliament, and in the name of the whole commons of the realm of England, with uniform consent for ourselves and our posterities, do expressly protest, as being derogatory in the highest degree to the true dignity, liberty, and authority of your majesty's high courts of parliament, and consequently to the right of all your majesty's said subjects, and the whole body of this your kingdom; and desire that this our protestation may be recorded to all posterity. And contrariwise . . . , we most truly avouch that our privileges and liberties are our rights and due inheritance no less than our very lands and goods; that they cannot be withheld from us, denied, or impaired, but with apparent wrong to the whole state of the realm; and that our making of request in the entrance of parliament to enjoy our privileges is an act only of manners and doth not weaken our right, no more than our suing to the king for our lands by petition. . . .

From these misinformed positions . . . the greatest part of our troubles, distrust, and jealousy have arisen; having apparently found that in this first parliament of the happy reign of your majesty the privileges of our house, and therein the liberties and stability of the whole kingdom, have been more universally and dangerously impugned than ever, as we suppose, since the beginnings of parliaments. For although it may be true that in the latter times of Queen Elizabeth some one privilege now and then were by some particular act attempted against . . . , yet was not the same ever by so public speech nor by positions in general denounced against our privileges. Besides that in regard to her sex and age which we had great cause to tender, and much more upon care to avoid all trouble, which by wicked practice might have been drawn to impeach the quiet of your majesty's right in the succession, those actions were then passed over, which we hoped, in succeeding times of freer access to your highness' so renowned grace and justice, to redress, restore, and rectify. Whereas, contrariwise, in this parliament . . . , by reason of those misinformations, not only privileges but the whole freedom of the parliament and realm have from time to time, upon all occasions, been mainly hewed at; the freedom of our persons in election hath been impeached; the freedom of our speech prejudiced by often reproofs; thirdly, particular persons noted with taunt and disgrace, who have spoken their consciences in matters proposed to the house, but with all due respect and reverence to your majesty. . . .

What cause we, your poor commons, have to watch over our privileges is manifest in itself to all men. The prerogatives of princes may easily and do daily grow; the privileges of the subject are for the most part at an everlasting stand. They may be by good providence and care preserved; but, being once lost, are not recovered but with much disquiet. If good kings were immortal as well as kingdoms, to strive so for privilege were vanity perhaps and folly. But, seeing the same God, who in His great mercy hath given us a most wise king and religious, doth also sometimes permit hypocrites and tyrants in His displeasure and for sins of people, from hence hath the desire of rights, liberties, and privileges, both for nobles and commons, had his just original; by which an harmonical and stable state is framed, each member under the head enjoying that right, and performing that duty, which for the honour of the head and happiness of the whole is requisite. Thus much touching the wrong done to your majesty by misinformation touching our privileges. The last kind of misinformation made to your majesty hath been touching the actions and speeches of particular persons used in the house. . . . It is very clear unto us, by the effect, that divers things spoken in the house have been perverted and very untruly reported to your majesty. . . .

And now, most gracious sovereign, these necessary grounds of our cause and defence being truly laid . . . , the justification of . . . particulars we trust will be plain and expedite. . . .

1. The gentleman usher's fault in depriving by his unaccustomed neglect a great part of our house from hearing your majesty's speech the first day of the parliament we could not . . . but complain of in decent sort among ourselves, and further we proceeded not. Your majesty's extraordinary great grace and favour, in rehearsing the day following your former admirable speech, did give us content with abundant increase of joy.

2. The yeomen of the guard's words were very opprobrious, and howsoever they might have been not unfitly applied to the peasants of France or boors of Germany, yet could they not be other than very reproachful and injurious to the great dignities and honour of the commons of this realm, who contain not only the citizens, burgesses, and yeomanry, but also the whole inferior nobility of the kingdom, and knights, esquires, and gentlemen; many of which are come immediately out of the most noble families, and some other of their worth advanced to high honour of your majesty's privy council, and otherwise have been employed in very honourable service. In sum, the sole persons of the higher nobility excepted, they contain the whole flower and power of your kingdom; with their bodies your wars, with their purses your treasures, are upheld and supplied. Their hearts are the strength and stability of your royal seat. All these, amounting to many millions of people, are representatively

present in us of the house of commons. The wrong done to us doth redound to the whole land and will so be construed. We could not therefore do less in duty to the realm than to advertise such a delinquent of the unseemliness of this fault; neither yet could we do more in duty to your majesty than upon his acknowledgment thereof to remit it.

3. The right of the liberty of the commons of England in parliament consisteth chiefly in these three things: first, that the shires, cities, and boroughs of England . . . have free choice of such persons as they shall put in trust to represent them; secondly, that the persons chosen during the time of the parliament, as also of their access and recess, be free from restraint, arrest, and imprisonment; thirdly, that in parliament they may speak freely their consciences without check or controlment, doing the same with due reverence to the sovereign court of parliament—that is, to your majesty and to both the houses, who all in this case make but one politic body, whereof your highness is the head. . . .

7. For matter of religion, it will appear by examination of truth and right that your majesty should be misinformed, if any man should deliver that the kings of England have any absolute power in themselves, either to alter religion (which God forfend should be in the power of any mortal man whatsoever!) or to make any laws concerning the same, otherwise than in temporal causes by consent of parliament. We have and shall at all times by our oaths acknowledge that your majesty is sovereign lord and supreme governor in both. Touching our own desires and proceedings therein, they have not been a little misconceived and misreported. We have not come in any Puritan or Brownist spirit to introduce their purity, or to work the subversion of the state ecclesiastical, as now it stands—things so far and so clear from our meaning as that, with uniform consent in the beginning of this parliament, we committed to the Tower a man who out of that humour had, in a petition exhibited to our house, slandered the bishops. But according to the tenor of your majesty's writ of summons directed to the counties from which we came, and according to the ancient and long-continued use of parliaments, as by many records from time to time appeareth, we came with another spirit, even the spirit of peace. We disputed not of matters of faith and doctrine; our desire was peace only, and our device of unity: how this lamentable and long-lasting dissension amongst the ministers (from which both atheism, sects, and ill life have received such encouragement and so dangerous increase) might at length, before help come too late, be extinguished. And for the ways of this peace, we are not addicted at all to our own inventions, but ready to embrace any fit way that may be offered. Neither desire we so much that any man, in regard of weakness of conscience, may be exempted after parliament from obedience to laws established, as that in this parliament such laws may be enacted as, by relinquishment of some few ceremonies of small importance, or by any way better,

a perpetual uniformity may be enjoined and observed. Our desire has been also to reform certain abuses crept into the ecclesiastical state, even as into the temporal; and, lastly, that the land might be furnished with a learned, religious, and godly ministry, for the maintenance of whom we would have granted no small contribution, if in these, as we trust, just and religious desires we had found that correspondency from other which was expected. . . .

9. . . . A general, extreme, unjust, crying oppression is in the cart-takers and purveyors. . . .[11] We have not in this parliament sought anything against them but execution of those laws which are in force already. We demand but that justice which our princes are sworn neither to deny, delay, nor sell.[12] That we sought into the accounts of your majesty's expense was not our presumption, but upon motion from the lords of your majesty's council and offer from your officers of your highness' household; and that upon a demand of a perpetual yearly revenue in lieu of the taking away of these oppressions—unto which composition neither knew we well how to yield, being only for justice and due right, which is unsalable, neither yet durst we impose it by law upon the people, without first acquainting them, and having their counsel unto it. But if your majesty might be pleased in your gracious favour to treat of composition with us for some grievance which is by law and just, how ready should we be to take that occasion and colour to supply your majesty's desire concerning these also, we hold for unjust, should appear, we nothing doubt, to your majesty's full satisfaction.

10. And therefore we come, lastly, to the matter of wards, and such other just burdens (for so we acknowledge them) as to the tenures of [in] capite and knight's service are incident. We cannot forget (for how were it possible?) how your majesty, in a former most gracious speech in your gallery at Whitehall, advised us for unjust burdens to proceed against them by bill; but for such as were just, if we desired any ease, that we should come to yourself by way of petition, with tender of such countervailable composition in profit as for the supporting of your royal estate was requisite. According unto which your majesty's most favourable grant and direction, we prepared a petition to your most excellent majesty for leave to treat with your highness touching a perpetual composition, to be raised by yearly revenue out of the lands of your subjects for wardships and other burdens depending upon them or springing with them. Wherein we first entered into this dutiful consideration, that this prerogative of the crown, which we desire to compound for, was a matter of mere profit and not of any honour at all or princely dignity. . . . Our sayings have always been that this burden was just, that the remitting thereof must come from your majesty's grace, and that the denying of the suit were no wrong unto us. . . .

[11] Cf. no. 62J.
[12] Art. 40 of Magna Carta (above, p. 121).

There remaineth . . . yet one part more of our duty at this present. . . . Let your majesty be pleased to receive public information from your commons in parliament as well of the abuses in the church as in the civil estate and government; for private informations pass often by practice. The voice of the people in things of their knowledge is said to be as the voice of God. And if your majesty shall vouchsafe at your best pleasure and leisure to enter into gracious consideration of our petitions, for ease of those burdens under which your whole people have long time mourned, hoping for relief by your majesty, then may you be assured to be possessed of their hearts; and, if of their hearts, then of all they can do or have. And we, your majesty's most humble and loyal subjects, whose ancestors have with great loyalty, readiness, and joyfulness, served your famous progenitors, kings and queens of this realm, shall with like loyalty and joy, both we and our posterity serve your majesty and your most royal issue forever with our lives, lands, and goods, and all other our abilities; and by all means endeavour to procure your majesty's honour with all plenty, tranquillity, joy, and felicity.[13]

Ibid., I, 243.

(H) James I: Levy of Impositions (1608)[14]

James, by the grace of God king . . . , to our right trusty and right well-beloved councillor, Robert, earl of Salisbury, our high treasurer of England, greeting. It is well known unto all men of judgment . . . that the care imposed upon princes to provide for the . . . welfare of their subjects is accompanied with so heavy a charge as all the circumstances belonging thereunto can hardly fall under the conceit of any other than of those who are acquainted with the carriage of public affairs. And therefore this special power and prerogative, amongst many others, hath both by men of understanding in all ages and by the laws of all nations been yielded and acknowledged to be proper and inherent in the persons of princes, that they may according to their several occasions raise to themselves such fit and competent means by levying of customs and impositions upon merchandises transported out of their kingdoms or brought into their dominions, either by the subjects born under their allegiance or by strangers . . . , as to their wisdoms and discretions may seem convenient, without prejudice of trade and commerce, sufficiently to supply and sustain the great . . . expense incident unto them in the maintenance of their crowns and dignities. So we at this time, out of many . . . weighty considerations, as well for the exonerating of

---

[13] The official journal contains only the beginning of this document; the rest of the preceding version has been transcribed from *State Papers Domestic, James I*, viii, fol. 60 f. For evidence that the Apology was actually presented to the king, see Notestein, Relf, and Simpson, *Commons Debates, 1621*, V, 433.

[14] This was a general order issued by the king as the result of his victory in Bates' case (no. 91A).

the crown of divers just . . . debts as for the supply of many other our . . . important occasions known to us and our council, and now particularly for the service of Ireland . . . , have been forced to resort to some such course of raising profit upon merchandise passing outward and inward as in former times hath been usual, not only by our progenitors, kings and princes of this realm, but also often in practice among other nations. . . . And although we have resolved to lay some kind of impositions both upon many foreign merchandises brought into this our realm and also upon divers native commodities and merchandises . . . , yet, to the intent it may appear what care we have in all things of this nature to avoid the least inconvenience or grievance that may arise to our people, we have . . . given special charge in the levying of the same to . . . exempt all such merchandises as are requisite for the food and sustenance of our people, or which contain matter of munition necessary for the defence of our realms . . . , or any other . . . materials fit . . . for the maintenance and enlargement of trade and navigation. . . .

Know ye therefore that, for the considerations aforesaid . . . , we have . . . ordained . . . that there shall be forever, from and after the 29th day of September next ensuing . . . , levied, taken, and received by way of imposition now newly set, over and besides the customs, subsidies, and other duties heretofore due and payable unto us, upon all merchandises . . . which . . . shall be either brought from any part beyond the seas unto this our realm . . . or which shall be transported . . . forth of the same . . . , just so much for the said new imposition as hath been and is now answered and paid unto us for the subsidy of the said merchandises, and neither more nor less . . . ; excepting such merchandises only as in a schedule hereunto annexed are expressed, which are either altogether . . . exempted from payment of any of the said new impositions or else are appointed . . . to pay the same in such proportion as is either more or less than the subsidy payable for the same, as in the said schedule is more plainly . . . expressed. Wherefore we do . . . command you that forthwith . . . you give order . . . unto all customers or collectors . . . and other our officers and ministers of all our ports . . . that they shall . . . take of all Englishmen, aliens . . . , and all persons . . . which shall bring into this our realm . . . or . . . carry forth . . . of the same . . . any goods, wares or merchandises . . . so much for and by way of the said new imposition as hath been and now is answered and paid unto us for the subsidy of the said merchandises. . . .

Prothero, Constitutional Documents, pp. 353 f.

(I) Address of the Commons to James I (1610)

Most gracious sovereign: Whereas your majesty's most humble subjects, the commons assembled in parliament, have received, first by message and since by speech from your majesty, a commandment of restraint from debating in parliament your majesty's right of imposing upon your subjects' goods exported or imported out of or into this realm; yet allowing us to examine the grievance of those impositions in regard of quantity, time, and other circumstances of disproportion thereto incident: we your said humble subjects, nothing doubting but that your majesty had no intent by that commandment to infringe the ancient and fundamental right of the liberty of the parliament in point of exact discussing of all matters concerning them and their possessions, goods, and rights whatsoever (which yet we cannot but conceive to be done, in effect, by this commandment), do with all humble duty make this remonstrance to your majesty:—

First, we hold it an ancient, general, and undoubted right of parliament to debate freely all matters which do properly concern the subject and his right or state; which freedom of debate being once foreclosed, the essence of the liberty of parliament is withal dissolved.

And whereas, in this case, the subjects' right on the one side and your majesty's prerogative on the other cannot possibly be severed in debate of either: we allege that your majesty's prerogatives of that kind, concerning directly the subjects' right and interest, are daily handled and discussed in all courts at Westminster, and have been ever freely debated upon all fit occasions both in this and all former parliaments without restraint; which being forbidden, it is impossible for the subject either to know or to maintain his right and propriety to his own lands and goods, though never so just and manifest.

It may farther please your most excellent majesty to understand that we have no mind to impugn, but a desire to inform ourselves of, your highness' prerogative in that point, which, if ever, is now most necessary to be known; and though it were to no other purpose, yet to satisfy the generality of your majesty's subjects, who, finding themselves much grieved by these new impositions, do languish in much sorrow and discomfort.

These reasons, dread sovereign, being the proper reasons of parliament, do plead for the upholding of this our ancient right and liberty. Howbeit, seeing it hath pleased your majesty to insist upon that judgment in the exchequer[15] as being direction sufficient for us without further examination, upon great desire of leaving your majesty unsatisfied in no one point of our intents and proceedings, we profess, touching that judgment, that we neither do nor will take upon us to reverse it; but our desire is to know the reasons whereupon the same was grounded, and the rather for that a general conceit is had that the reasons of that judgment may be extended much farther, even to the utter ruin of the ancient liberty of this kingdom, and of your subjects' right of propriety of their lands and goods. . . .

We therefore, your highness' loyal and dutiful commons, not

---

[15] Bates' case (no. 91A).

swerving from the approved steps of our ancestors, most humbly and instantly beseech your gracious majesty that, without offence to the same, we may, according to the undoubted right and liberty of parliament, proceed in our intended course of a full examination of these new impositions. . . .[16]

Journals of the Commons, I, 431 f.

(J) Letter of James I to the Commons (1621)

Mr. Speaker: We have heard by divers reports, to our great grief, that our distance from the houses of parliament, caused by our indisposition of health, hath emboldened some fiery and popular spirits of some of the house of commons to argue and debate publicly of the matters far above their reach and capacity, tending to our high dishonour and breach of prerogative royal. These are therefore to command you to make known, in our name, unto the house that none therein shall presume henceforth to meddle with anything concerning our government or deep matters of state; and, namely, not to deal with our dearest son's match with the daughter of Spain, nor to touch the honour of that king or any other our friends and confederates, and also not to meddle with any man's particulars which have their due motion in our ordinary courts of justice. And whereas we hear they have sent a message to Sir Edward[17] Sandys to know the reasons of his late restraint, you shall in our name resolve them that it was not for any misdemeanour of his in parliament. But, to put them out of doubt of any question of that nature that may arise among them hereafter, you shall resolve them, in our name, that we think ourself very free and able to punish any man's misdemeanours in parliament, as well during their sitting as after—which we mean not to spare hereafter upon any occasion of any man's insolent behaviour there that shall be ministered unto us. And if they have already touched any of these points, which we have forbidden, in any petition of theirs which is to be sent unto us, it is our pleasure that you shall tell them that, except they reform it before it come to our hands, we will not deign the hearing nor answering of it.

Rushworth, Historical Collections, I, 43 f.

(K) Debates in the Commons on Privilege (1621)

. . . Here again, the speaker going out of the chair, the grand committee falleth into debate of the privileges of the house. Mr.

---

[16] No clear statement of the royal reply to this petition is contained in the official journal of the house, but a private diary of the period (Gardiner, *Parliamentary Debates in 1610,* pp. 41 f.) gives the following report: ". . . For our petition, he granted it as we had set it down ourselves, but he put us in mind to observe three things therein contained: (1) not to impugn his prerogative; (2) to seek his content and satisfaction; (3) to endeavour to unite and confirm his subjects' hearts unto him—protesting that he never meant to abridge us of any liberties appertaining unto us, which he hoped we would not abuse."

[17] A mistake for Edwin.

Alford would have a select committee appointed to consider of the points of such of our privileges as are impeached, and to draw a protestation for the same privileges in particular and also of all the rest in general. Mr. Thomas Crewe saith that, though the calling of a parliament and the continuing, prorogation, and dissolving of it be in the king's sole power, yet, when we are called, we are without limitation to deal in what business ourselves think best; for otherwise shall we not be able to do their business for whom we come hither, which is that of the country. He would not have this committee to insist so much on particulars as on the generality of our privileges. Sir Edward Coke would not have us here at this time, in the handling and debating of our privileges, to meddle with war or marriage; and would have a sub-committee appointed for this; and this sub-committee shall consider of all those matters which are mentioned in the writ of parliament, and also of our liberty of speech and of our power to punish those that speak too lavishly, and of our power to meddle and debate of what we shall of ourselves think fit.

The heads to be considered of by the sub-committee for privileges: (1) concerning freedom of speech; and therein to treat *de arduis et urgentibus negotiis regni* according to the writ of summons, whether it be concerning the king or otherwise; (2) touching the liberty of this house to punish the misdemeanours of any parliament-man in parliament for things whereof this house hath cognizance, whether he ought not to be censured here by the house only; (3) whether, when we receive commandment from the king, the house shall thereon desist, and not proceed notwithstanding such command in any business; (4) whether our privileges be not our right and inheritance; (5) that the sub-committee shall consider of anything else incident to the liberty of the house; (6) that the sub-committee shall consider whether it be not fit for us to make an expression here in the house, that it is an ancient privilege of parliament that no member of this house shall presume to acquaint the king with any business in debate here but by order from the whole house or from the speaker.

It is ordered at this grand committee that a sub-committee shall reduce all these heads which have been propounded into the form of a protestation; and that they shall render an account and their reasons of such things as they shall think not fit to be reduced into a protestation. And the sub-committee is appointed accordingly, and is to sit this afternoon in the committee chamber.

The speaker being in the chair, it is ordered that the speaker shall attend here at four of the clock this afternoon; that, the sub-committee having drawn the foresaid heads into the form of a protestation and made a report thereof to the grand committee, the house may, if occasion be, confirm the protestation; because otherwise it may be the king will command the house to be adjourned before such protestation be made in the house, and so may we endanger the validity of our privileges and liberties in those points wherein they have seemed to be impeached at this our meeting, *viz.*, in those heads before ordered to be considered of by the sub-committee. . . .

The sub-committee bring the draught of a protestation of the grand committee, which containeth as followeth:—

The commons, now assembled in parliament, being justly occasioned thereunto, concerning sundry liberties, franchises, and privileges of parliament amongst others not herein mentioned, do make this protestation following: That the liberties, franchises, privileges and jurisdictions of parliament are the ancient and undoubted birthright and inheritance of the subjects of England; and that the arduous and urgent affairs concerning the king, state, and the defence of the realm, and of the Church of England, and the making and maintenance of laws, and redress of mischiefs and grievances, which daily happen within this realm, are proper subjects and matter of counsel and debate in parliament; and that in the handling and proceeding of those businesses every member of the house hath and of right ought to have freedom of speech to propound, treat, reason, and bring to conclusion the same; that the commons in parliament have like liberty and freedom to treat of those matters in such order as in their judgments shall seem fittest; and that every such member of the said house hath like freedom from all impeachment, imprisonment, and molestation (other than by the censure of the house itself) for or concerning any bill, speaking, reasoning, or declaring of any matter or matters touching the parliament or parliament business; and that, if any of the said members be complained of and questioned for anything said or done in parliament, the same is to be showed to the king by the advice and assent of all the commons assembled in parliament before the king give credence to any private information.

The speaker being in the chair, it is ordered, by question in the house, that this protestation shall be here entered forthwith in the book of the house, and there to remain as of record. And accordingly it was here entered, sitting the house, between five and six of the clock at night by candle-light.[18]

Nicholas, *Proceedings in the Commons in 1620 and 1621*, II, 357 f.

(L) THE KING'S DISSOLUTION OF PARLIAMENT (1622)

Albeit the assembling, continuing, and dissolving of parliaments be a prerogative so peculiarly belonging to our imperial crown, and the times and seasons thereof so absolutely in our own power, that we need not give account thereof unto any; yet, according to our continual custom to make our good subjects acquainted with the reasons of all our public resolutions and actions, we have thought it expedient at this time to declare, not only our pleasure and resolution therein, grounded upon mature deliberation with the advice and

---

[18] In the margin of the journal, where this entry had been made, is the memorandum: "King James in council with his own hand rent out this protestation" (*Journals of the Commons*, I, 668, note a).

uniform consent of our whole privy council, but therewith also to note some especial proceedings moving us to this resolution. . . .

This parliament was by us called, as for making good . . . laws, so more especially, in this time of miserable distraction throughout Christendom, for the better settling of peace and religion and restoring our children to their ancient and lawful patrimony. . . . This parliament, beginning in January last, proceeded some months with such harmony between us and our people as cannot be paralleled by any former time; for, as the house of commons at the first, both in the manner of their supply and otherwise, showed greater love and more respect than ever any house of commons did to us or, as we think, to any king before us, so we upon all their complaints have afforded them such memorable and rare examples of justice as many ages past cannot show the like. . . . And although, after their first recess at Easter, we found that they misspent a great deal of time . . . , yet we gave them time and scope for their parliamentary proceedings and prolonged the session to an unusual length. . . .

But, during the time of this long recess having to our great charges mediated with the emperor by the means of our ambassador, the lord Digby, and having found those hopes to fail . . . , we, in confidence of the assistance of our people thus freely promised and protested in parliament, did . . . reassemble our parliament the 20th day of November last, and made known unto them the true state and necessity of our children's affairs. . . . Wherein, howbeit we are well satisfied of the good inclination of most part of our house of commons, testified by their ready assent to the speedy payment of a subsidy newly to be granted; yet, upon this occasion, some particular members of that house took such inordinate liberty, not only to treat of our high prerogatives and of sundry things that, without our special direction, were no fit subjects to be treated of in parliament, but also to speak with less respect of foreign princes, our allies, than was fit for any subject to do of any anointed king, though in enmity and hostility with us. And when, upon this occasion, we used some reprehension towards those miscarriages, requiring them not to proceed but in such things as were within the capacity of that house according to the continual custom of our predecessors; then, by the means of some evil-affected and discontented persons, such heat and distemper was raised in the house that, albeit themselves had sued unto us for a session and for a general pardon, unto both which at their earnest suit we assented, yet after this fire kindled they rejected both and, setting apart all businesses of . . . weight, notwithstanding our . . . earnest pressing them to go forward, they either sat as silent or spent the time in disputing of privileges, descanting upon the words and syllables of our letters and messages. . . . And notwithstanding the sincerity of our protestations not to invade their privileges, yet, by persuasion of such as had been the cause of all these distempers, they fall to carve for themselves and, pretending causelessly to be occasioned thereunto, in an unseasonable hour of the day and a very thin house, contrary to their own customs in all matters of weight, conclude and enter a protestation for their liberties, in such ambiguous and general words as might serve for future times to invade most of our . . . prerogative annexed to our imperial crown; whereof, not only in the times of other our progenitors but in the blessed reign of our late predecessor, that renowned queen, Elizabeth, we found our crown actually possessed—an usurpation that the majesty of a king can no means endure. By all which may appear that, howsoever in the general proceedings of that house there are many footsteps of . . . well-affected duty towards us, yet some ill-tempered spirits have sowed tares among the corn, and thereby frustrated the hope of that plentiful . . . harvest which might have multiplied the wealth and welfare of this whole land, and by their cunning diversions have imposed upon us a necessity of discontinuing this present parliament without putting unto it the name or period of a session.

And therefore, whereas the said assembly of parliament was by our commission adjourned until the 8th day of February now next ensuing, we, minding not to continue the same any longer . . . , have thought fit to signify this our resolution, with the reasons thereof, unto all our subjects inhabiting in all parts of this realm; willing and requiring the said prelates, noblemen, and states, and also the said knights, citizens, and burgesses, and all others to whom in this case it shall appertain, that they forbear to attend at the day and place prefixed by the said adjournment. . . . And albeit we are at this time enforced to break off this convention of parliament, yet our will and desire is that all our subjects should take notice, for avoiding of all sinister suspicions and jealousies, that our . . . full resolution is to govern our people in the same manner as our progenitors and predecessors, kings and queens of this realm, of best government, have heretofore done . . . ; and that we shall be as glad to lay hold on the first occasion in . . . convenient time, which we hope shall not be long, to . . . assemble our parliament with confidence of the . . . hearty love . . . of our subjects, as either we or any of our progenitors have at any time heretofore.

Rymer, Foedera, XVII, 344.

90. JAMES I: STATUTES

(A) Succession Act (1604)

A most joyful and just recognition of the immediate, lawful, and undoubted succession, descent, and right of the crown. . . . We . . . , your most humble and loyal subjects, the lords spiritual and temporal and the commons in this present parliament assembled, do from the bottom of our hearts yield to the divine majesty all humble thanks and praises . . . , and in most humble and lowly manner do beseech your most excellent majesty that, as a memorial to all posterities amongst the records of your high court of parliament forever to endure, of our loyalty, obedience, and hearty and humble affection, it may be published and declared in this high court of parliament, and enacted by authority of the same, that we, being bounden thereunto both by the laws of God and man, do recognize and acknowledge, and thereby express our unspeakable joys, that immediately upon the dissolution and decease of Elizabeth, late queen of England, the imperial crown of the realm of England, and of all the kingdoms, dominions, and rights belonging to the same, did, by inherent birthright and lawful and undoubted succession, descend and come to your most excellent majesty, as being lineally, justly, and lawfully next and sole heir of the blood royal of this realm as is aforesaid; and that, by the goodness of God Almighty and lawful right of descent, under one imperial crown, your majesty is of the realms and kingdoms of England, Scotland, France, and Ireland the most potent and mighty king. . . .

Statutes of the Realm, IV, 1017 f.: 1 James I, c. 1.

(B) ACT TO EXPLAIN THE STATUTE OF ARTIFICERS (1604)[1]

An act . . . for the explanation of the statute . . . concerning labourers. . . . Whereas the said act hath not, according to the true meaning thereof, been duly put in execution . . . , by reason that ambiguity and question have risen and been made whether the rating of all manner of artificers . . . , other than such as by some statute and law have been rated or else such as did work about husbandry, should or might be rated by the said law: forasmuch as the said law hath been found beneficial for the commonwealth, be it enacted by authority of this present parliament that the said statute, and the authority by the same statute given to any person or persons for assessing and rating of wages . . . , shall be expounded and construed, and shall by force of this act give authority to all persons having any such authority to rate wages of any labourers, weavers, spinsters, and workmen or workwomen whatsoever, either working by the day, week, month, year, or taking any work at any person or persons' hand whatsoever, to be done in great or otherwise. . . .

And furthermore be it enacted . . . that, if any clothier or other shall refuse to obey the said order, rate, or assessment of wages as aforesaid, and shall not pay so much or so great wages to their weavers, spinsters, workmen, or workwomen as shall be so set down, rated, and appointed . . . , that then every clothier and other . . . persons so offending shall forfeit . . . for every such offence, to the party aggrieved, 10s.; and that, if the . . . offence and offences of not paying so much or so great wages to their . . . workmen, workwomen, and others shall be confessed by the offender, or . . . the same shall be proved by two sufficient and lawful witnesses before the justices of peace in their quarter sessions . . . , the justices

[1] No. 81c.

of assize in their sessions, or before any two justices of the peace . . . ,
then every such person shall forthwith stand and be in law convicted
thereof. . . .

Provided, nevertheless, . . . that no clothier, being a justice of
peace in any precinct or liberty, shall be any rater of any wages
for any weaver, tucker, spinster, or other artisan that dependeth
upon the making of cloth; and in case there be not above the number
of two justices of peace within such precinct or liberty but such
as are clothiers, that in such case the same wages shall be rated
and assessed by the major part of the common council of such precinct
or liberty, and such justice or justices of peace, if any there be, as
are not clothiers.

Ibid., IV, 1022 f.: 1 James I, c. 6.

(C) GENERAL ACT IN SHIRLEY'S CASE (1604)[2]

An act for new executions to be sued against any which shall
hereafter be delivered out of execution by privilege of parliament,
and for discharge of them out of whose custody such persons shall
be delivered. Forasmuch as heretofore doubt hath been made, if any
person being arrested in execution and by privilege of either of the
houses of parliament set at liberty, whether the party at whose suit
such execution was pursued be forever after barred and disabled
to sue forth a new writ of execution in that case: for the avoiding
of all further doubt and trouble which in like cases may hereafter
ensue, be it enacted by the king's most excellent majesty, by the
lords spiritual and temporal, and by the commons in this present
parliament assembled that from henceforth the party at or by whose
suit such writ of execution was pursued, his executors, or administrators, after such time as the privilege of that session of parliament
in which such privilege shall be so granted shall cease, may sue forth
and execute a new writ or writs of execution in such manner and
form as by the law of this realm he or they might have done if no
such former execution had been taken forth and served; and that
from henceforth no sheriff, bailiff, or other officer, from whose arrest
or custody any such person so arrested in execution shall be delivered
by any such privilege, shall be charged or chargeable with or by
any action whatsoever for delivering out of execution any such privileged person so as is aforesaid by such privilege of parliament set
at liberty—any law, custom, or privilege heretofore to the contrary
notwithstanding. Provided always that this act or anything therein
contained shall not extend to the diminishing of any punishment
to be hereafter by censure in parliament inflicted upon any person
which hereafter shall make or procure to be made any such arrest
as is aforesaid.

Ibid., IV, 1029: 1-2 James I, c. 13.

---

[2] Cf. no. 89D.

(D) Statute of Monopolies (1624)

An act concerning monopolies and dispensations with penal laws and the forfeiture thereof. Forasmuch as your most excellent majesty, in your royal judgment and of your blessed disposition to the weal and quiet of your subjects, did, in the year of our Lord God 1610, publish in print to the whole realm and to all posterity that all grants of monopolies and of the benefit of any penal laws, or of power to dispense with the law or to compound for the forfeiture, are contrary to your majesty's laws, which your majesty's declaration is truly consonant and agreeable to the ancient and fundamental laws of this your realm; and whereas your majesty was further graciously pleased expressly to command that no suitor should presume to move your majesty for matters of that nature; yet, nevertheless, upon misinformations and untrue pretences of public good, many such grants have been unduly obtained and unlawfully put in execution, to the great grievance and inconvenience of your majesty's subjects, contrary to the laws of this your realm and contrary to your majesty's royal and blessed intention so published as aforesaid: for avoiding whereof and preventing of the like in time to come, may it please your most excellent majesty . . . that it may be declared and enacted, and be it declared and enacted . . . , that all monopolies and all commissions, grants, licences, charters and letters patents . . . to any person . . . , bodies politic or corporate whatsoever . . . , for the sole buying, selling, making, working, or using of anything within this realm or the dominion of Wales, or of any other monopolies, or of power . . . to dispense with any others, or to give licence or toleration to do . . . anything against the tenor . . . of any law or statute . . . , and all proclamations, inhibitions, restraints, warrants of assistance, and all other . . . things whatsoever any way tending to the instituting . . . or countenancing of the same . . . , are altogether contrary to the laws of this realm, and so are and shall be utterly void and of none effect. . . .

And be it further . . . enacted . . . that all monopolies and all such commissions, grants . . . , and all other . . . things tending as aforesaid . . . ought to be and shall be forever hereafter . . . tried and determined . . . according to the common laws of this realm, and not otherwise. . . .

Provided nevertheless . . . that any declaration before mentioned shall not extend to any letters patents and grants of privilege for the term of one-and-twenty years or under, heretofore made of the sole working or making of any manner of new manufacture within this realm to the first and true inventor or inventors of such manufactures, which others, at the time of the making of such letters patents and grants, did not use, so they be not contrary to the law, nor mischievous to the state by raising of the prices of commodities at home or hurt of trade, or generally inconvenient; but that the same shall be of such force as they were or should be if this act had not been made. . . .

Provided also, and be it . . . enacted, that any declaration before mentioned shall not extend to any letters patents and grants of privilege for the term of fourteen years or under, hereafter to be made, of the sole working or making of any manner of new manufactures within this realm, to the true and first inventor and inventors of such manufactures. . . .

Ibid., IV, 1212 f.: 21-22 James I, c. 3.

91. RECORDS OF JUDICIAL CASES (1606-21)

(A) Bates' Case (1606)[1]

Clark: . . . It seemeth to me strange that any subjects would contend with the king in this high point of prerogative; but such is the king's grace that he had showed his intent to be that this matter shall be disputed and adjudged by us according to the ancient law and custom of the realm. And because that the judgment of this matter cannot be well directed by any learning delivered in our books of law, the best directions herein are precedents of antiquity and the course of this court, wherein all actions of this nature are to be judged; and the acts of parliament recited in arguments of this case prove nothing to the purpose. . . . The precedents of every court ought to be a direction to that court to judge of matters which are aptly determinable therein: as in the king's bench for matters of the crown, in the common pleas for matters of inheritance and civil contracts, and in the exchequer for matters of the king's prerogative, his revenue and government. And as it is not a kingdom without subjects and government, so he is not a king without revenues; for without them he cannot preserve his dominions in peace, he cannot maintain war, nor reward his servants according to the state and honour of a king. And the revenue of the crown is the very essential part of the crown; and he who rendeth that from the king pulleth also the crown from his head, for it cannot be separated from the crown. And such great prerogatives of the crown, without which it cannot be, ought not to be disputed; and in these cases of prerogative the judgment shall not be according to the rules of the common law, but according to the precedents of this court, wherein these matters are disputable and determinable. . . .[2]

And so much for precedents. And now for statutes. The statute of Magna Carta, c. 30 . . . , was objected—that thereby all merchants

---

[1] In 1606 John Bates, a merchant trading with the Levant, refused to pay a custom of 5*s*. a hundredweight imposed by James I in addition to the poundage of 2*s*. 6*d*. established by parliament (cf. no. 89H). For this refusal Bates was brought to trial before the court of the exchequer, which, after lengthy arguments on both sides, upheld the legality of the king's imposition. The following extracts are from the opinions of Baron Clark and Chief Baron Fleming.

[2] Here Clark cites a number of precedents for the king's laying of impositions.

may have safe, etc., to buy and sell without ill toltes—but there is a saving, *viz.,* by the ancient and old customs. The statute of Articuli super Cartas, c. 2, hath a saving in the end of it . . . [regarding] ancient prises due and accustomed.[3] So are all the other statutes of purveyors. The statute of . . . 45 Edward III, c. 4,[4] which has been so much urged—that no new imposition shall be imposed upon wool-fells, wool, or leather, but only the custom and subsidy granted to the king—this extends only to the king himself and shall not bind his successors; for it is a principal part of the crown of England, which the king cannot diminish. . . . As to that which was objected, that the defendant had paid poundage granted by the statute . . . , that is nothing to this purpose, for that is a subsidy and not a custom. For when any imposition is granted by parliament, it is only a subsidy and not a custom, for the nature thereof is changed. . . .

The writ of *ne exeat regnum* comprehends a prohibition to him to whom it is directed, that he shall not go beyond the seas; and this may be directed at the king's pleasure to any man who is his subject. And so, consequently, may he prohibit all merchants. And as he may prohibit the persons, so may he the goods of any man, *viz.,* that he shall export or import at his pleasure. And if the king may generally inhibit that such goods shall not be imported, then by the same reason may he prohibit them upon condition . . . , that, if they import such goods, that then they shall pay, etc. . . .

And so, for all these reasons, judgment shall be given for the king.

Fleming, Chief Baron: . . . The state of the question is touching a new custom. The impositions or customs are duties or sums of money newly imposed by the king without parliament upon merchandise for the augmentation of his revenues. . . . To the king is committed the government of the realm and his people. . . . The king's power is double, ordinary and absolute; and they have several laws and ends. That of the ordinary is for the profit of particular subjects—for the execution of civil justice . . . , and this is exercised by equity and justice in ordinary courts, and by the civilians is nominated *ius privatum,* and with us common law. And these laws cannot be changed without parliament . . . The absolute power of the king is not that which is converted or executed to private use, to the benefit of any particular person, but is only that which is applied to the general benefit of the people . . . , as the people is the body and the king the head. And this power . . . is most properly named policy and government. And as the constitution of this body varieth with the time, so varieth this absolute law according to the wisdom of the king for the common good. . . .

The matter in question is material matter of state and ought to be ruled by the rules of policy. And if it be so, the king hath done well to execute his extraordinary power. All customs, be they old or new,

---

[3] Nos. 44, 51A.

[4] A re-enactment of no. 62J.

are no other but the effects and issues of trades and commerce with foreign nations. But all commerce and affairs with foreigners, all wars and peace, all acceptance and admitting for current foreign coin, all parties and treaties whatsoever, are made by the absolute power of the king; and he who hath power of causes hath power also of effects. . . . It is said that an imposition may not be upon a subject without parliament. . . . It is not here the question if the king may impose upon the subject or his goods. But the impost here is not upon a subject; but here it is upon Bates as upon a merchant who imports goods within this land charged before by the king. And at the time when the impost was imposed upon them they were the goods of the Venetians, and not the goods of a subject nor within the land. . . .

And whereas it is said that, if the king may impose, he may impose any quantity what he pleases, true it is that this is to be referred to the wisdom of the king, who guideth all under God by his wisdom, and this is not to be disputed by a subject. . . . To prove the power of the king by precedents of antiquity in a case of this nature may easily be done. And if it were lawful in ancient times it is lawful now; for the authority of the king is not diminished, and the crown hath the same attributes that then it had. . . .

All these statutes[5] prove expressly that the king had power to increase the impost, and that upon commodities of the land; and that he continually used this power notwithstanding all acts of parliament against it. And so much for commodities of this land. But for foreign commodities it appears by no act of parliament or other precedent that ever any petition or suit was made to abate the impost of foreign commodities, but of them the impost was paid without denial. . . . Wherefore I think that the king ought to have judgment. . . .

Howell, State Trials, II, 382-94.

(B) The Question of Prohibitions (1607)[6]

. . . Upon complaint made to him by Bancroft, archbishop of Canterbury concerning prohibitions, the king was informed that, when the question was made of what matters the ecclesiastical judges have cognizance, either upon the exposition of the statutes concerning tithes or any other thing ecclesiastical, or upon the statute of 1 Elizabeth concerning the high commission, or in any other case in which there is not express authority in law, the king himself may decide it in his royal person; and that the judges are but the delegates of the king, and that the king may take what causes he shall please to determine from the determination of the judges and may determine them himself. And the archbishop said that this was clear in

---

[5] A long list of acts under Edward I, Edward III, and Richard II.

[6] The question arose through complaints by the archbishop of Canterbury that the ecclesiastical courts were being unjustly interfered with through writs of prohibition (see above, no. 33 1). Coke, as chief justice of the king's bench, warmly defended the common law practice, as appears from the following excerpt from his reports.

divinity, that such authority belongs to the king by the word of God in the Scripture. To which it was answered by me, in the presence and with the clear consent of all the judges of England and barons of the exchequer, that the king in his own person cannot adjudge any case, either criminal . . . or betwixt party and party . . .; but this ought to be determined and adjudged in some court of justice according to the law and custom of England. . . .

Then the king said that he thought the law was founded upon reason, and that he and others had reason as well as the judges. To which it was answered by me that true it was that God had endowed his majesty with excellent science and great endowments of nature; but his majesty was not learned in the laws of his realm of England, and causes which concern the life or inheritance or goods or fortunes of his subjects are not to be decided by natural reason, but by the artificial reason and judgment of law—which law is an act which requires long study and experience, before that a man can attain to the cognizance of it—and that the law was the golden metwand and measure to try the causes of the subjects, and which protected his majesty in safety and peace. With which the king was greatly offended, and said that then he should be under the law—which was treason to affirm, as he said. To whom I said that Bracton saith *quod rex non debet esse sub homine, sed sub Deo et lege*.[7]

Coke, Reports, XII, 64.

(C) THE CASE OF THE POSTNATI (1608)[8]

[Chief Justice Coke:] . . . There is a diversity between a conquest of a kingdom of a Christian king and the conquest of a kingdom of an infidel. For, if a king come to a Christian kingdom by conquest . . . , he may at his pleasure alter and change the laws of that kingdom; but, until he doth make an alteration of those laws, the ancient laws of that kingdom remain. . . . But if a Christian king should conquer a kingdom of an infidel and bring them under his subjection, there *ipso facto* the laws of the infidel are abrogated; for that they be, not only against Christianity, but against the law of God and of nature contained in the Decalogue. . . . But if a king

---

[7] That the king ought not to be under man, but under God and the law.

[8] The origin of this case was an assize of *novel disseisin* (see no. 33B) sought by the guardians of Robert Calvin against Richard and Nicholas Smith regarding a certain freehold in London. The defendants argued that they were not bound to reply in such action, because Robert Calvin was an alien, having been born in Scotland in the year 1606. The question raised was therefore whether a Scot born after (*postnatus*) the accession of James I to the English throne was entitled to bring suit in an English court concerning English lands. As the question was a new one, which came to involve actions both in common law and equity, the case was transferred to the court of exchequer chamber to be argued by all judges of the central courts. The following extracts are from, first, the report of Coke, chief justice of the common pleas, and, secondly, the opinion of Lord Chancellor Ellesmere.

hath a kingdom by title of descent, there seeing by the laws of that kingdom he doth inherit the kingdom, he cannot change those laws of himself without consent of parliament. Also, if a king hath a Christian kingdom by conquest, as Henry II had Ireland—after John had given unto them, being under his obedience and subjection, the laws of England for the government of that country, no succeeding king could alter the same without parliament. And in that case, while the realm of England and that of Ireland were governed by several laws, any that was born in Ireland was no alien to the realm of England. . . .[9]

Whosoever are born under one natural ligeance and obedience, due by the law of nature to one sovereign, are natural-born subjects. . . . Whosoever is born within the king's power or protection is no alien. .. . . Whatsoever is due by the law or constitution of man may be altered, but natural ligeance or obedience to the sovereign cannot be altered. . . . Lastly, whosoever at his birth cannot be an alien to the king of England cannot be an alien to any of his subjects of England. . . .

The judgment in the said case, as entered on record, etc. Whereupon all and singular the premises being seen, and by the court of the lord the now king here diligently inspected and examined, and mature deliberation being had thereof; for that it appears to the court of the lord the now king here that the aforesaid plea of the said Richard Smith and Nicholas Smith, above pleaded, is not sufficient in law to bar the said Robert Calvin from having an answer to his aforesaid writ: therefore it is considered by the court of the lord the now king here that the aforesaid Richard Smith and Nicholas Smith to the writ of the said Robert do further answer.

[Lord Chancellor Ellesmere:] . . . King James hath now the kingdoms of England, Scotland, and Ireland, and the isles of Guernsey and Jersey by descent. All these be his dominions and under his subjection and obedience. . . . If at this time subjects born in Ireland or Guernsey and Jersey be no aliens, but capable of lands in England, then, by an analogical interpretation, why should not subjects born in Scotland be at this time in like degree? . . . [10]

In this new learning there is one part of it so strange and of so dangerous consequent as I may not let it pass: *viz.*, that the king is as a king divided in himself, and so as two kings of two several kingdoms; and that there be several allegiances and several subjec-

---

[9] Coke goes on to discuss at great length the precedents earlier set in connection with Guienne, Normandy, the Isle of Man, and other non-English possessions of the English king. Then follow his conclusions drawn alike from history and natural reason.

[10] The chancellor here reviews the matter of historical precedent, only to agree with the opinions already delivered by Coke and other judges. Then, coming to the objections raised by the attorneys for the defence, he continues with the argument that follows.

tions due unto him respectively in regard of his several kingdoms, the one not participating with the other. This is a dangerous distinction between the king and the crown, and between the king and the kingdom. It reacheth too far; I wish every good subject to beware of it. . . . Upon this subtle and dangerous distinction of faith and allegiance due to the king and of faith and allegiance due to the crown and to the kingdom—which is the only basis and fundamental main reason to disable the plaintiff and all *postnati*—there follow too many gross and foul absurdities; whereof I will touch some few, and so conclude that in law and reason this subtle but absurd and dangerous distinction ought not to be allowed. This bond of allegiance whereof we dispute is *vinculum fidei*; it bindeth the soul and conscience of every subject severally and respectively to be faithful and obedient to the king. And, as a soul or conscience cannot be framed by policy, so faith and allegiance cannot be framed by policy, nor put into a politic body. An oath must be sworn by a natural body; homage and fealty must be done by a natural body, a politic body cannot do it. Now then, since there is but one king and sovereign, to whom this faith and allegiance is due by all his subjects of England and Scotland, can any human policy divide this one king and make him two kings? . . .

I said there was another general rule for expounding of laws, which I reserved to be last spoken of. I will now but touch it; for I will not stand to examine by human reasons whether kings were before laws or laws before kings, nor how kings were first ordained, nor whether the kings or the people did first make laws, nor the several constitutions and frames of states and commonweals, nor what Plato or Aristotle have written of this argument. . . . They were born and lived in Greece, and in popular states; they were enemies, or at least mislikers, of all monarchies . . . ; they accounted all the world barbarous but their own country of Greece; their opinions, therefore, are no canons to give laws to kings and kingdoms, no more than Sir Thomas More's *Utopia* or such pamphlets as we have at every mart. . . .

If this question seem difficult—that neither direct law, nor examples and precedents, nor application of like cases, nor discourse or reason, nor the grave opinion of the learned and reverend judges can resolve it—here is a true and certain rule how, both by the civil law and the ancient common law of England, it may and ought to be decided: that is by sentence of the most religious, learned, and judicious king that ever this kingdom or island had. But this case is so clear as this needeth not at all. And in this I would not be misunderstood, as though I spake of making of new laws or of altering the laws now standing. I mean not so; but I speak only of interpretation of the law in new questions and doubts, as now in this present case. Neither do I mean hereby to derogate anything from the high court of parliament—far be it from my thought! . . . But certain it is it hath been the wisdom of the kings of this realm to reserve in themselves that supreme power to call their nobles, clergy, and commons together, when they saw great and urgent causes, and by that great council to make edicts and statutes for the weal of their people and safety of the kingdom and state. . . .

Thus I have here delivered my concurrence in opinion with my lords the judges, and the reasons that induce and satisfy my conscience that Robert Calvin, and all the *postnati* in Scotland are in reason and by the common law of England natural-born subjects . . . of the king of England, and enabled to purchase and have freehold and inheritance of lands in England and to bring real actions for the same in England. . . .

Howell, *State Trials,* II, 638-96.

(D) The Question of Royal Proclamations (1610)[11]

. . . The lord chancellor said that every precedent had first a commencement and that he would advise the judges to maintain the power and prerogative of the king, and in cases in which there is no authority and precedent to leave it to the king to order in it, according to his wisdom and for the good of his subjects, or otherwise the king would be no more than the duke of Venice; and that the king was so much restrained in his prerogative that it was to be feared the bonds would be broken. And the lord privy seal said that the physician was not always bound to a precedent, but to apply his medicine according to the quality of the disease. And all concluded that it should be necessary at that time to confirm the king's prerogative with our opinions, although that there were not any former precedent or authority in law; for every precedent ought to have a commencement. To which I answered that true it is that every precedent hath a commencement; but, when authority and precedent is wanting, there is need of great consideration before that anything of novelty shall be established, and to provide that this be not against the law of the land. For I said that the king cannot change any part of the common law, nor create any offence by his proclamation which was not an offence before, without parliament. . . .

It was resolved by the two chief justices, chief baron, and Baron Altham, upon conference betwixt the lords of the privy council and them, that the king by his proclamation cannot create any offence which was not an offence before; for then he may alter the law of the land by his proclamation in a high point. For, if he may create an offence where none is, upon that ensues fine and imprisonment. Also the law of England is divided into three parts: common law, statute law, and custom. But the king's proclamation is none of them. . . . Also it was resolved that the king hath no prerogative but that which the law of the land allows him. But the king, for prevention of offences, may by proclamation admonish his subjects

---

[11] Cf. no. 74K.

that they keep the laws and do not offend them, upon punishment to be inflicted by the law, etc. . . .

Coke, Reports, XII, 74 f.

(E) Council Proceedings on a Judgment in Chancery (1613)

The lords having this day heard Sir Henry Billingsley, knight, and Edmund Mathewes, esquire, between whom a controversy hath long depended in the high court of chancery concerning great sums of money due by Mathewes unto the said Billingsley, to the payment whereof sundry his lands and possessions were liable, which the said Billingsley did humbly desire he might, with their lordships' favours, dispose of towards his own satisfaction, according to a solemn decree in chancery given on his behalf; their lordships being nevertheless favourably inclined for Mr. Mathewes' relief . . . , being a gentleman of a good house, and whose distressed estate doth move them to compassion to make some such agreement betwixt them as that the land might be sold to the best advantage and Sir Henry Billingsley satisfied his debt with the moneys arising thereupon, the residue (if any be) to remain unto Mr. Mathewes, provided that the same might be accomplished in such convenient time as Sir Henry Billingsley his estate and occasion might well suffer without much prejudice; and finding the same not possible to be effected by any overtures or motions which their lordships could make unto them, as was desired, the cause is dismissed from this table and Sir Henry Billingsley left unto the validity of his decree and conveyances, to make such use thereof as he shall see cause, and in the meantime Mr. Mathewes required, neither by himself or any other on his behalf, to importune the lords or any of them with further petitions.

Acts of the Privy Council, 1613-1614, p. 87.

(F) The Question of Commendams (1616)[12]

His majesty and the lords [of the council] thought good to ask the judges severally their opinion, the question being put in this manner: whether, if at any time in a case depending before the judges which his majesty conceived to concern him either in power or profit, and thereupon required to consult with them and that they should stay proceedings in the meantime, they ought not to stay accordingly. They all (the lord chief justice only except) yielded that

---

[12] During the course of a trial in the common pleas the question arose whether the king had the right to present a man to an ecclesiastical living *in commendam*—that is to say, to make a temporary appointment. James, wishing to delay the judgment in order to have a preliminary discussion of the problem, caused Bacon, his attorney general, to summon the judges before him for that purpose. At the instance of Coke, now chief justice of the king's bench, they replied that they were bound by oath not to delay a case and that the summons of the attorney general was illegal. But the king compelled them to appear before him in the council and, on bended knees, to listen to his arguments. Whereupon proceedings continued as described in the following account.

they would, and acknowledged it to be their duty so to do. Only the lord chief justice of the king's bench said for answer that when that case should be, he would do that should be fit for a judge to do. And the lord chief justice of the common pleas, who had assented with the rest, added that he would ever trust the justness of his majesty's commandment.

After this was put to a point, his majesty thought fit, in respect of the further day of argument appointed the Saturday following for the *commendams*, to know from his judges what he might expect from them concerning the same. Whereupon, the lord [archbishop] of Canterbury breaking the case into some questions, his majesty did require his judges to deal plainly with him, whether they meant in their argument to touch the general power of granting *commendams*, yea or no. Whereupon all his said judges did promise and assure his majesty that in the argument of the said case of *commendams* they would speak nothing which should weaken or draw into doubt his majesty's prerogative for the granting of them; but intended particularly to insist upon the point of the lapse and other individual points of this case, which they conceive to be of a form differing from all other *commendams* which have been practised. The judges also went further, and did promise his majesty that they would not only abstain from speaking anything to weaken his majesty's prerogative of *commendams*, but would directly and in plain terms affirm the same and correct the erroneous and bold speeches which had been used at the bar in derogation thereof. Also, all the judges did in general acknowledge and profess with great forwardness that it was their duty, if any counsellor at the bar presumed at any time to call in question his majesty's high prerogatives and regalities, that they ought to reprehend them and silence them; and promised so to do hereafter.

Ibid., 1615-1616, pp. 607 f.

(G) Council Proceedings against Sir Edward Coke (1616)

Sir Edward Coke, knight, chief justice of the king's bench, presenting himself this day at this board upon his knees, Mr. Secretary Winwood signified unto him that their lordships had made report to his majesty of that which passed on Wednesday last at Whitehall, where he was charged by his majesty's solicitor with certain things wherein his majesty was much unsatisfied. . . . Which being delivered in writing and in his princely judgment duly weighed and considered of, his majesty was no way satisfied with his answers to any of those three points, wherewith he stood charged (*viz.*, neither in that which he made concerning the bond and defeasance upon the installment of a debt of Sir Christopher Hatton, late lord chancellor of England; nor yet in that which he maketh concerning his speeches of high contempt, uttered as he sat in the seat of justice, concerning the overthrow of the common law; nor, lastly, in the answer he offereth to excuse his uncivil and indiscreet carriage before his majesty, assisted with his privy council and his judges), but that the charge lieth still upon him, notwithstanding anything contained in his said answers.

Nevertheless, such is his majesty's clemency and goodness as he is pleased not to proceed heavily against him, but rather to look upon the merit of his former services, and accordingly hath decreed: first, that he be sequestered from the council table until his majesty's pleasure be further known; secondly, that he do forbear to ride this summer's circuit as justice of assize; lastly, that during this vacation . . . he take into his consideration and review his book of reports, wherein (as his majesty is informed) there be many exorbitant and extravagant opinions set down and published for positive and good law. And if, in the review and reading thereof, he find anything fit to be altered or amended, the correcting thereof is left to his discretion. Amongst other things, his majesty was not well pleased with the title of those books, wherein he styled himself lord chief justice of England. whereas he could challenge no more than chief justice of the king's bench. And having corrected what in his discretion he found meet in those reports, his majesty's pleasure was that he should bring the same privately to himself, that he might consider thereof as in his princely judgment should be found expedient. . . .

Hereunto the lord chief justice made answer that he did in all humility prostrate himself to his majesty's good pleasure; that he acknowledged the decree to be just. . . .

Ibid., 1615-1616, pp. 648-50.

(H) PIGG v. CALEY (1618)[13]

Pigg brought an action of trespass against Caley for taking his horse, etc. Caley said that he is seised of the manor of D. to which Pigg is a villein regardant; and that and all those, etc., have been seised of the plaintiff and his ancestors. The plaintiff said that he is free, etc.; *absque hoc*, that the defendant, etc., were seised of the plaintiff, etc., as of villein regardant. And the issue is found for the plaintiff. And upon motion in arrest of judgment, it is ruled that the traverse is well taken. . . .

Noy, *Reports*, p. 27.

(I) IMPEACHMENT OF FRANCIS BACON (1621)[14]

[15 March.] Sir Robert Phillips reporteth from the committee for

---

[13] This brief report of an action before the king's bench is included here because it is the last recorded trial concerning villeinage in an English court. Caley's argument was that Pigg, being his villein attached to his manor, had no right to sue him for trespass. Such status was denied (the implication of the *absque hoc*) by Pigg. And since the jury rendered a verdict in his favour, his action was allowed to stand. See Holdsworth, *History of English Law*, III, 502 f.

[14] Only the crucial points in this famous trial are given here: the formal accusation as shown from the commons journals, supplemented by the contemporary notes of Edward Nicholas, and the final judgment delivered by the lords, as recorded in the journals of that house.

courts of justice three parts: person against whom, the matter, and opinion of the committee—with desire of further direction.

The person, the lord chancellor . . . ; the matter, corruption; the parties accusing, Awbrey and Egerton. Awbrey complaineth that, wearied in his cause in chancery, he was advised by his counsel, to expedite his business, to present the lord chancellor with £100. He got at use £100; goeth with Sir George Hastings and Mr. Jenkyns to York House. There they two went [in], and returned to him with thanks from my lord and hopes of better success in his cause than formerly. . . . The next, Edward Egerton, [declares] that, having many suits, he first presented my lord with a basin and ewer of £52 . . . ; that he sold tithes, raised £400, carried it to White-hall to my lord chancellor's lodging, called for Sir George and Sir Richard Yong, and by them sent in this gold in a purse . . . to my lord, who started at it, saying it was too much; that thanks [were] returned to him from my lord. . . .

Journals of the Commons, I, 554.

[19 March.] Sir Robert Phillips reporteth that he acquainted their lordships from this house that we have received a complaint and information against some noble lord of that house, and that therefore we of this house desire a conference with their lordships to acquaint them with the particulars of the complaint and the circumstances; that their lordships have appointed the conference for this afternoon, at two of the clock, the number to be the whole house.

The heads and circumstances of the accusation against the lord chancellor [by Awbrey and Egerton] are set down in writing and are read here in the house; but are to be delivered by word of mouth by Sir Robert Phillips this afternoon at a conference with the lords. . . .

Nicholas, Proceedings in the Commons, I, 194 f.

[20 March.] The lord treasurer reported the conference yesterday with the commons. At which conference was delivered the desire of the commons to inform their lordships of the great abuses of the courts of justice. . . . The lord chancellor is accused of great bribery and corruption committed by him in this eminent place, whereof two cases were alleged: the one concerning Christopher Awbrey, the other concerning Edward Egerton. . . .

[24 April.] . . . Their lordships resolved that the lord chancellor should be charged particularly with the briberies and corruptions complained of against him and that his lordship should make a particular answer thereunto. . . . Memorandum that, during the time the whole house was a committee, the collections of corruptions charged upon the lord chancellor and the proofs thereof made by the three committees . . . was read by Mr. Attorney General. . . . Here followeth the said collection. . . .[15]

[30 April.] . . . The lord chief justice . . . signified that he had received from the lord chancellor a paper roll sealed up, which was

---

[15] Twenty-three instances of corrupt practices are enumerated.

delivered to the clerk, and, being opened and found directed to their lordships, it was . . . read; which follows in these words: "To the right honourable the lords spiritual and temporal in the high court of parliament assembled: the confession and humble submission of me, the lord chancellor. Upon advised consideration of the charge, descending into my own conscience and calling my memory to account, so far as I am able, I do plainly and ingenuously confess that I am guilty of corruption and do renounce all defence, and put myself upon the grace and mercy of your lordships. The particulars I declare and confess to be as followeth. . . ."

[3 May.] . . . It was put to the question whether the lord chancellor be guilty of the matters wherewith he is charged or no, and it was agreed by all . . . that he was thereof guilty. . . .

The lords, having agreed upon the sentence to be given against the lord chancellor, did send a message to the house of commons . . . , that the lords are ready to give judgment against the lord viscount St. Albans, lord chancellor, if they with their speaker will come to demand it. In the meantime the lords put on their robes and, answer being returned of this message, the commons come. The speaker came to the bar and, making three low obeisances, said: "The knights, citizens, and burgesses of the commons' house of parliament have made complaint unto your lordships of many exorbitant offences of bribery and corruption committed by the lord chancellor. We understand that your lordships are ready to give judgment upon him for the same. Wherefore I, their speaker, in their name do humbly demand and pray judgment against him, the lord chancellor, as the nature of his offence and demerits do require."

The lord chief justice answered: "Mr. Speaker, upon the complaint of the commons against the lord viscount St. Albans, lord chancellor, this high court hath thereby, and by his own confession, found him guilty of the crimes and corruptions complained of by the commons and of sundry other crimes and corruptions of like nature. And therefore this high court (having first summoned him to attend, and having received his excuse of not attending by reason of infirmity and sickness; which he protested was not feigned or else he would most willingly have attended), doth nevertheless think fit to proceed to judgment. And therefore this high court doth adjudge: (1) that the lord viscount St. Albans, lord chancellor of England, shall undergo fine and ransom of £40,000; (2) that he shall be imprisoned in the Tower during the king's pleasure; (3) that he shall forever be incapable of any office, place, or employment in the state or commonwealth; (4) that he shall never sit in parliament nor come within the verge of the court. This is the judgment and resolution of this high court."

The prince his highness was entreated by the house that, accompanied with divers of the lords of this house, he would be pleased to present this sentence given against the late lord chancellor unto his majesty. His highness was pleased to yield unto this request. . . .

Journals of the Lords, III, 53-106.

92. RECORDS CONCERNING PARLIAMENT (1626-29)

(A) Letter of Charles I to the Commons (1626)

Trusty and well-beloved, we greet you well. Our house of commons cannot forget how often and how earnestly we have called upon them for the speeding of that aid which they intended unto us for our great and weighty affairs concerning the safety and honour of us and our kingdoms; and now, the time being so far spent that, unless it be presently concluded, it can neither bring us money nor credit by the time which themselves have prefixed—which is the last of this month—and being further deferred would be of little use. We being daily advertised from all parts of the great preparations of the enemy, ready to assail us, we hold it necessary by these our letters to give them our last and final admonition, and to let them know that we shall account all further delays and excuses to be express denials. And therefore we will and require you to signify unto them that we do expect that they forthwith bring forth their bill of subsidy to be passed without delay or condition, so as it may fully pass that house by the end of the next week at the furthest—which if they do not, it will force us to take other resolutions. But let them know that, if they finish this according to our desire, that we are resolved to let them sit together for the dispatch of their other affairs and, after their recess, to bring them together again the next winter. And if by their denial or delay anything of ill consequence shall fall out either at home or abroad, we may call God and man to witness that we have done our part to prevent it by calling our people together to advise with us, by opening the weight of our occasions unto them, and by requiring their timely help and assistance in those actions wherein we stand engaged by their own counsels. And we will and command you that this letter be publicly read in the house. [9 June, 1626.]

Ibid., III, 670.

(B) Charles I: Ordinance for Levying Customs (1626)[1]

Charles, by the grace of God king of England, Scotland, France, and Ireland, defender of the faith, etc., to our lord treasurer of England . . . , the commissioners of our treasury . . . , to our chancellor and under-treasurer of our exchequer . . . , to our chief baron and the rest of the barons of our exchequer . . . , to the customers, comptrollers, searchers, and all other the officers and ministers of our ports or belonging to our customs . . . , and to all other our officers, ministers, and loving subjects . . . to whom these presents shall come greeting.

Whereas the lords and others of our privy council have taken into their serious consideration the present state of our revenue arising by

---

[1] In the previous year the commons had drawn up a bill giving Charles tunnage and poundage for one year—instead of for life as had been customary for over a century (see above, p. 273, n. 1). But parliament was dissolved before the bill was passed by the lords, and no agreement on the matter was reached by the parliament of 1626.

customs, subsidy, and impost upon goods and merchandise to be exported and imported out of and into this our realm of England and dominion of Wales and port and town of Berwick, and, finding that it hath been constantly continued for many ages, and is now a principal part of the revenue of our crown and is of necessity to be so continued for the supportation thereof—which in the two last parliaments hath been thought upon, but could not there be settled by authority of parliament as from time to time by many ages and descents past it hath been, by reason of the dissolution of those parliaments before those things which were there treated of could be perfected—have therefore. . . specially ordered that all those duties upon goods and merchandises, called by the several names of customs, subsidy, and imposts, should be levied, collected, and received for our use in such manner and form as the same were levied, collected, and received in the time of our late dear father, King James of blessed memory . . . ; and forasmuch as, through the want of a parliamentary course to settle the payment of those duties, many inconveniences may arise which would tend to the impairing of our revenue of that nature, if in convenient time some settled course should not be taken for the prevention thereof :—

Know ye therefore that we . . . , by the advice of the lords and others of our privy council, do by these presents declare our will and pleasure to be that all those duties upon goods and merchandises . . . shall be levied, collected, and received in such manner and form as the same were levied, collected, and received at the time of the decease of our said late father. . . . And if any person or persons whatsoever shall refuse or neglect to pay the duties, customs, subsidies, or imposts aforesaid . . . , we do further grant by these presents unto the lords and others of our privy council . . . , or unto the lord treasurer of England or chancellor of our exchequer . . . , full power and authority to commit all and every such person and persons to prison. . . .

And for the better execution of this our will and pleasure herein, and to the end that all our officers and subjects may take notice hereof, our will and pleasure is that these our letters patents shall be transcribed and several copies thereof made and sent into every part of this realm. . . .

Witness ourself at Westminster, the 26th day of July.

Rymer, *Foedera,* XVIII, 737 f.

(C) Proceedings on the Arrest of Certain Lords (1626)

[14 March.] . . . The earl of Arundel, being committed by the king to the Tower, sitting the parliament, the house was moved to take the same into their consideration and so to proceed therein as they might give no just offence unto his majesty and yet preserve the privilege of parliament. The lord keeper thereupon signified to the house that he was commanded to deliver this message from his majesty unto their lordships : *viz.,* that the earl of Arundel was restrained for a misdemeanour which was personal unto his majesty and lay in the proper knowledge of his majesty and had no relation to matters of parliament. . . .

[30 March.] . . . The petition of the earl of Bristol for his writ of summons being referred to the lords' committees for privileges, etc., the earl of Hertford reported the same, on this manner, *viz.*: "My lords, whereas the earl of Bristol hath preferred a petition unto this house, thereby signifying that his writ of summons is withheld from him . . . , this petition being referred unto the committee for privileges, and after diligent search no precedent being found that any writ of summons hath been detained from any peer that is capable of sitting in the house of parliament; and considering withal how far it may trench into the right of every member of this house, whether sitting by ancient right of inheritance or by patent, to have their writs detained: the lords' committees are all of opinion that it will be necessary for this house humbly to beseech his majesty that a writ of summons may be sent to this petitioner, and to such other lords to whom no writ of summons hath been directed for this parliament, excepting such as are made incapable to sit in parliament by judgment of parliament or any other legal judgment." Whereupon the duke of Buckingham signified unto the house that, upon the earl of Bristol's petition, the king had sent him his writ of summons. . . .

[19 April.] The lord president reported the petition of the earl of Bristol . . . : "To the right honourable the lords of the higher house of parliament, the humble petition of John, earl of Bristol, humbly showing unto your lordships that he hath lately received his writ of parliament . . . , but jointly with it a letter from my lord keeper, commanding him in his majesty's name to forbear his personal attendance. And although he shall ever obey the least intimation of his majesty's pleasure, yet he most humbly offereth to your lordships' wise considerations . . . how far this may trench upon the liberty and safety of the peers." . . .

The lord president also reported the remonstrance and petition of the peers concerning the claim of their privileges from arrests and imprisonments. . . . May it please your majesty: we, the peers of this your realm assembled in parliament, finding the earl of Arundel absent from his place . . . [therefore called for] his presence. . . . But hereupon a message was delivered unto us from your majesty by the lord keeper, that the earl of Arundel was restrained for a misdemeanour which was personal to your majesty and lay in the proper knowledge of your majesty and had no relation to matter of parliament. This message occasioned us to inquire into the acts of our ancestors . . . ; and, after diligent search both of all [hi]stories, statutes, and records that might inform us in this case, we find it to be an undoubted right and constant privilege of parliament that no lord of parliament, sitting the parliament, or within the usual times of privilege of parliament, is to be imprisoned or restrained without sentence or order of the house, unless it be for treason or felony or for refusing to give surety for the peace. . . . Wherefore we, your majesty's loyal subjects and servants, the whole body of the peers now assembled in parliament, most humbly beseech your majesty that the earl of Arundel, a member of this body, may presently be admitted, with your gracious favour, to come, sit, and serve your majesty and the commonwealth in the great affairs of this parliament. . . .

This remonstrance and petition being read, it was generally approved of by the whole house, and agreed to be presented unto his majesty by the whole house. . . .[2]

Journals of the Lords, III, 526-64.

(D) PETITION OF RIGHT (1628)

The petition exhibited to his majesty by the lords spiritual and temporal, and commons in this present parliament assembled, concerning divers rights and liberties of the subjects, with the king's majesty's royal answer thereunto in full parliament.

To the king's most excellent majesty: Humbly show unto our sovereign lord the king the lords spiritual and temporal, and commons in parliament assembled, that, whereas it is declared and enacted by a statute made in the time of the reign of King Edward the First, commonly called *Statutum de Tallagio non Concedendo*,[3] that no tallage or aid should be laid or levied by the king or his heirs in this realm without the goodwill and assent of the archbishops, bishops, earls, barons, knights, burgesses, and other the freemen of the commonalty of this realm; and, by authority of parliament holden in the five-and-twentieth year of the reign of King Edward III, it is declared and enacted that from thenceforth no person should be compelled to make any loans to the king against his will, because such loans were against reason and the franchise of the land; and by other laws of this realm it is provided that none should be charged by any charge or imposition, called a benevolence,[4] or by such like charge; by which the statutes before mentioned, and other the good laws and statutes of this realm, your subjects have inherited this freedom, that they should not be compelled to contribute to any tax, tallage, aid, or other like charge not set by common consent in parliament: yet, nevertheless, of late divers commissions directed to sundry commissioners in several counties with instructions have issued, by means whereof your people have been in divers places assembled and required to lend certain sums of money unto your majesty; and many of them, upon their refusal so to do, have had an oath administered

[2] Eventually Bristol was permitted to return to the house, where charges were brought against him by the king. In the case of Arundel, however, the king delayed a specific answer until the parliament was dissolved in June. Both peers occupied their regular places in the next parliament.

[3] See above, p. 165, n. 1.

[4] Cf. no. 69H.

unto them, not warrantable by the laws or statutes of this realm, and have been constrained to become bound to make appearance and give attendance before your privy council and in other places; and others of them have been therefor imprisoned, confined, and sundry other ways molested and disquieted; and divers other charges have been laid and levied upon your people in several counties by lord lieutenants, deputy lieutenants, commissioners for musters, justices of peace, and others, by command or direction from your majesty or your privy council, against the laws and free customs of the realm.

And where also, by the statute called the Great Charter of the Liberties of England, it is declared and enacted that no freeman may be taken or imprisoned, or be disseised of his freehold or liberties or his free customs, or be outlawed or exiled or in any manner destroyed, but by the lawful judgment of his peers or by the law of the land; and in the eight-and-twentieth year of the reign of King Edward III it was declared and enacted by authority of parliament that no man, of what estate or condition that he be, should be put out of his land or tenements, nor taken, nor imprisoned, nor disherited, nor put to death, without being brought to answer by due process of law: nevertheless, against the tenor of the said statutes and other the good laws and statutes of your realm to that end provided, divers of your subjects have of late been imprisoned without any cause showed; and when for their deliverance they were brought before your justices by your majesty's writs of *habeas corpus*, there to undergo and receive as the court should order, and their keepers commanded to certify the causes of their detainer, no cause was certified, but that they were detained by your majesty's special command, signified by the lords of your privy council; and yet were returned back to several prisons, without being charged with anything to which they might make answer according to the law.

And whereas of late great companies of soldiers and mariners have been dispersed into divers counties of the realm, and the inhabitants against their wills have been compelled to receive them into their houses, and there to suffer them to sojourn, against the laws and customs of this realm, and to the great grievance and vexation of the people: and whereas also, by authority of parliament in the five-and-twentieth year of the reign of King Edward III, it is declared and enacted that no man should be forejudged of life or limb against the form of the Great Charter and the law of the land; and, by the said Great Charter and other the laws and statutes of this your realm, no man ought to be adjudged to death but by the laws established in this your realm, either by the customs of the same realm or by acts of parliament; and whereas no offender of what kind soever is exempted from the proceedings to be used, and punishments to be inflicted by the laws and statutes of this your realm: nevertheless of late divers commissions under your majesty's great seal have issued forth, by which certain persons have been assigned and appointed commissioners, with power and authority to proceed within the land according to the justice of martial law against such soldiers or mariners. or other dissolute persons joining with them, as should commit any murder, robbery, felony, mutiny, or other outrage or misdemeanour whatsoever, and by such summary course and order as is agreeable to martial law and as is used in armies in time of war, to proceed to the trial and condemnation of such offenders, and them to cause to be executed and put to death according to the law martial; by pretext whereof some of your majesty's subjects have been by some of the said commissioners put to death, when and where, if by the laws and statutes of the land they had deserved death, by the same laws and statutes also they might, and by no other ought to have been, adjudged and executed; and also sundry grievous offenders, by colour thereof claiming an exemption, have escaped the punishments due to them by the laws and statutes of this your realm, by reason that divers of your officers and ministers of justice have unjustly refused or forborne to proceed against such offenders according to the same laws and statutes, upon pretence that the said offenders were punishable only by martial law and by authority of such commissions as aforesaid; which commissions and all other of like nature are wholly and directly contrary to the said laws and statutes of this your realm.

They do therefore humbly pray your most excellent majesty that no man hereafter be compelled to make or yield any gift, loan, benevolence, tax, or such like charge without common consent by act of parliament; and that none be called to make answer, or take such oath, or to give attendance, or be confined, or otherwise molested or disquieted concerning the same, or for refusal thereof; and that no freeman, in any such manner as is before mentioned, be imprisoned or detained; and that your majesty would be pleased to remove the said soldiers and mariners; and that your people may not be so burdened in time to come; and that the foresaid commissions for proceeding by martial law may be revoked and annulled; and that hereafter no commissions of like nature may issue forth to any person or persons whatsoever, to be executed as aforesaid, lest by colour of them any of your majesty's subjects be destroyed or put to death, contrary to the laws and franchise of the land (all of which they most humbly pray of your most excellent majesty as their rights and liberties according to the laws and statutes of this realm) ; and that your majesty would also vouchsafe and declare that the awards, doings, and proceedings to the prejudice of your people in any of the premises shall not be drawn hereafter into consequence or example; and that your majesty would be also graciously pleased, for the further comfort and safety of your people, to declare your royal will and pleasure that in the things aforesaid all your officers and ministers shall serve you according to the laws and statutes of this realm, as they tender the honour of your majesty and the prosperity of this kingdom.

Statutes of the Realm, V, 23 f.

(E) PROCEEDINGS ON THE PETITION OF RIGHT (1628)

[2 June.] His majesty, being seated on his royal throne, delivered unto the clerk of parliament his answer unto the Petition of Right, exhibited by the lords and commons this parliament. The commons, with their speaker, came. His majesty made a short speech unto the lords and commons. The lord keeper then conferred with his majesty and declared unto the lords and commons. . . . The lord keeper having ended his speech, the clerk of the crown read the Petition of Right . . . , and the clerk of the parliament the king's answer, *in haec verba, viz.*: "The king willeth that right be done according to the laws and customs of the realm; and that the statutes be put in due execution, that his subjects may have no cause to complain of any wrongs or oppressions, contrary to their just rights and liberties, to the preservation whereof he holds himself . . . as well obliged as of his prerogative. . . ."

[7 June.] The king's majesty being placed in his royal throne, the lords in their robes, and the commons with their speaker present; the lord keeper, standing in his place as a peer, spoke as followeth, *viz.*: "May it please your most excellent majesty, the lords spiritual and temporal and commons assembled in parliament, taking into their considerations that the good intelligence betwixt your majesty and your people doth much depend upon your majesty's answer unto their Petition of Right, formerly presented with an unanimous consent unto your majesty, do now become most humble suitors unto your majesty that you will be pleased to give a clear and satisfactory answer thereunto in full parliament."

This being spoken by the lord keeper, his majesty said: "The answer I have already given you was made with so good deliberation, and approved by the judgment of so many wise men, that I could not have imagined but that it should have given you full satisfaction; but, to avoid all ambiguous interpretations and to show you that there is no doubleness in my meaning, I am willing to please you in words as well as in the substance. Read your petition, and you shall have such an answer as I am sure will please you."

Then the clerk of the crown read the said Petition of Right. And the clerk of the parliament read and pronounced the king's answer, *viz.*: "Soit droit fait come est désiré."[5]

[26 June.] His majesty being placed in his royal throne, the commons were sent for, to hear his royal answer to the bills. The commons being come, his majesty made this speech, *viz.*: "My lords and gentlemen, it may seem strange that I come so suddenly to end this session. Wherefore, before I give my assent to the bills, I will tell you the cause; though I must avow that I owe an account of my actions to none but to God alone. It is known to every one that a

---

[5] "Let right be done as is desired." On the significance of this whole proceeding, see F. H. Relf, *The Petition of Right.*

while ago the house of commons gave me a remonstrance—how acceptable every man may judge. And for the merit of it, I will not call that in question; for I am sure no wise man can justify it. Now, since I am certainly informed that a second remonstrance is preparing for me, to take away my profit of tunnage and poundage—one of the chief maintenances of the crown—by alleging that I have given away my right thereof by my answer to your petition, this is so prejudicial unto me that I am forced to end this session some few hours before I meant it, being willing not to receive any more remonstrances to which I must give an harsh answer. And since I see that even the house of commons begins already to make false constructions of what I granted in your petition; lest it might be worse interpreted in the country, I will now make a declaration concerning the true meaning thereof. The profession of both houses, in time of hammering this petition, was by no ways to entrench upon my prerogative, saying they had neither intention or power to hurt it. Therefore it must needs be conceived that I have granted no new, but only confirmed the ancient, liberties of my subjects. Yet, to show the clearness of my intentions, that I neither repent nor mean to recede from anything I have promised you, I do here declare that those things which have been done—whereby men had some cause to suspect the liberty of the subjects to be trenched upon, which indeed was the first and true ground of the petition—shall not hereafter be drawn into example for your prejudice; and in time to come—in the word of a king—you shall not have the like cause to complain. But as for tunnage and poundage, it is a thing I cannot want and was never intended by you to ask, never meant, I am sure, by me to grant. To conclude, I command you all that are here to take notice of what I have spoken at this time, to be the true intent and meaning of what I granted you in your petition. But you, my lords the judges . . . , to you only under me belongs the interpretation of the laws; for none of the house of commons, joint or separate, what new doctrine soever may be raised, have any power either to make or declare a law without my consent."

Journals of the Lords, III, 835-79.

(F) Resolutions of the Commons (1629)[6]

(1) Whosoever shall bring in innovation of religion, or by favour or countenance seek to extend or introduce popery or Arminianism, or other opinion disagreeing from the true and orthodox church, shall be reputed a capital enemy to this kingdom and commonwealth.

(2) Whosoever shall counsel or advise the taking and levying of the subsidies of tunnage and poundage, not being granted by parliament, or shall be an actor or instrument therein, shall be likewise reputed an innovator in the government, and a capital enemy to the kingdom and commonwealth.

---

[6] Passed while the speaker was held in his chair and the king waited to dissolve parliament.

(3) If any merchant or person whatsoever shall voluntarily yield or pay the said subsidies of tunnage and poundage, not being granted by parliament, he shall likewise be reputed a betrayer of the liberties of England, and an enemy to the same.

Rushworth, *Historical Collections*, I, 660.

93. ACTS OF THE ROYAL GOVERNMENT (1630-35)

(A) PROCLAMATION FOR DISTRAINT OF KNIGHTHOOD (1630)[1]

Whereas we have heretofore granted our commission under the great seal of England to sundry of the lords and others of our privy council to treat and compound with such of our loving subjects as by law ought to make their fines with us for not making their appearance at the time and place by our writs appointed for receiving the order of knighthood—wherein our commissioners have so far proceeded that many have compounded with them and paid their fines agreed upon accordingly—and we are resolved constantly to hold the like course with all others who are liable by law to pay the like fines : nevertheless, because many parts of this our kingdom are so remote from our city of London as the travel from thence thither would be very chargeable and troublesome and at this time dangerous . . . , in favour of our good and loving subjects whom it concerneth, we have resolved to send our commissions to the several counties of this our realm, to whom they may with more ease and safety repair for their dispatch ; whereof we have thought fit by these presents to give notice to all whom it may concern, hereby letting them know that, if they shall neglect this our grace and not attend our commissioners in their several counties where they dwell and with them make agreement on our behalf . . . , we shall leave them to the just proceedings of our laws, and to that end to attend our commissioners at Whitehall or our court of exchequer. And if it shall so fall out to be more charge or trouble unto them, they shall have just cause to lay the blame upon themselves, and to acknowledge our grace and favour if in time it had been accepted. Given at our court at Westminster, the 13th day of July.

Rymer, *Foedera*, XIX, 175 f.

(B) WRIT FOR THE COLLECTION OF SHIP MONEY (1634)[2]

Carolus rex, etc., to the mayor, commonalty, and citizens of our city of London, and to the sheriffs of the same city and good men in the said city and in the liberties and members of the same, greet-

---

[1] Cf. no. 50A.

[2] In this year writs like the one given here were sent only to seaports; but in 1635 and 1636 the system was extended throughout all the counties of England and Wales. The modified writs dispatched for this purpose demanded quotas of ships from all communities, both urban and rural, and ordered the sheriffs to raise the necessary money by assessing lands within their bailiwicks. For the judicial problems involved, see no. 94B, C; and for historical precedent, cf. nos. 41D, 46F, I.

ing. Because we are given to understand that certain thieves, pirates, and robbers of the sea, as well Turks, enemies of the Christian name, as others . . . [are] wickedly taking by force and spoiling the ships and goods and merchandises, not only of our subjects, but also of the subjects of our friends in the sea, which hath been accustomed anciently to be defended by the English nation; . . . also, the dangers considered which on every side do hang over our heads, that it behooveth us and our subjects to hasten the defence of the sea and kingdom with all expedition or speed that we can; . . . and, although that charge of defence which concerneth all men ought to be supported by all . . . , you, constituted in the sea-coasts . . . , are chiefly bound to set your helping hand: we command firmly, enjoining you . . . that you cause to be prepared and brought to the port of Portsmouth before the first day of March now next ensuing one ship of war of the burden of 900 tons, with 350 men at the least, as well expert masters as very able and skilful mariners; one other ship of war of the burden of 800 tons, with 260 men at the least . . . ; four other ships of war, every of them of the burden of 500 tons and every of them with 200 men at the least . . . ; and one other ship of war of the burden of 300 tons, with 150 men. . . . And also every of the said ships [is to be equipped] with ordnance, as well greater as lesser, gunpowder and spears and weapons and other necessary arms sufficient for war, and with double tackling and with victuals until the said first of March competent for so many men; and from that time for twenty-six weeks at your charges as well in victuals as men's wages and other things necessary for war. . . . Also we have assigned you, the aforesaid mayor and aldermen of the city aforesaid . . . , to assess all men in the said city and in the liberties and members of the same . . . to contribute to the expenses about the necessary provision of the premises. . . .

Witness myself at Westminster, the 20th day of October in the tenth year of our reign.

Rushworth, Historical Collections, II, 257 f.

(C) COMMISSION FOR LEVYING FINES UNDER FOREST LAW (1635)[3]

Charles, by the grace of God king . . . , to our right trusty and right well-beloved cousin and councillor, Henry, earl of Holland; lord chief justice and justice in eyre of all our forests, chases, parks, and warrens on this side Trent, [and to the chancellor of the exchequer, the chief justices of king's bench and common pleas, the attorney general, the solicitor general, and a serjeant-at-law,] greeting. Whereas we are pleased for the ease and benefit of our subjects, upon reasonable fines and compositions to be paid into our exchequer to our use, to pardon and discharge them of all encroachments, purprestures, damages, detriments, trespasses, and offences whatsoever by them committed or done as well in our forest of Dean in

---

[3] Cf. nos. 35, 45.

our county of Gloucester as also in our forest of Essex in our county of Essex, and the perambulations, meets, bounds, and purlieus thereof . . . , and for the time to come to free them and exempt them, their lands, tenements, possessions, leases, and hereditaments of and from all common or depasturing of our deer, laws, liberties officers, and jurisdictions of forest, and to disafforest the same . . . : know ye therefore that we . . . by these presents do assign, make, and constitute you to be our commissioners, and we do hereby give full power and authority unto you, or any three or more of you . . . , in our name and behalf to compound, contract, and agree with all such persons as shall desire the same for pardons, releases and discharges . . . concerning all and all manner of encroachments, purprestures, damages, detriments, trespasses, and offences whatsoever by them in any wise committed or done in our said several forests . . . ; and also for grants and charters . . . for the fully, clearly, and absolutely disafforesting, discharging, releasing, freeing, and exempting of them, their heirs . . . , and their . . . hereditaments whatsoever of and from our deer and their commoning . . . or depasturing there, and of and from all laws, liberties, privileges, jurisdictions, assize, and ordinances of forest whatsoever, and of and from the view, cognizance, or jurisdiction of all swanimote courts. justice seats, courts or pleas to be holden before justices itinerant. and of and from the view or jurisdictions of justices itinerant, verderers, foresters, regardors, and other officers or ministers of forest. . . .

Rymer, Foedera, XIX, 688 f.

94. RECORDS OF JUDICIAL CASES (1627-38)

(A) The Case of the Five Knights (1627) [1]

. . . This is a case of very great weight and great expectation, and it had been fit we should have used more solemn arguments of it than now for the shortness of the time we can do. . . . I am sure you expect justice from hence, and God forbid we should sit here but to do justice to all men according to our best skill and knowledge, for it is our oaths and duties so to do. . . . We are sworn to maintain all prerogatives of the king; that is one branch of our oath. And we are likewise sworn to administer justice equally to all people. . . . That which is now to be judged by us is this: whether

---

[1] Following up his demand for a forced loan, Charles I in 1627 imprisoned various persons who had refused to contribute. Five of the prisoners—Sir Thomas Darnel, Sir John Corbet, Sir Walter Earl, Sir John Heveningham, and Sir Edmund Hampden—thereupon sued for writs of *habeas corpus* from the court of king's bench. The writs, thus being granted, were returned by the warden of the Fleet Prison with the statement that he had acted by virtue of a warrant from two members of the privy council ordering the prisoners committed "by the special command of his majesty." The points at issue, as well as the judgment of the court, are clearly stated by Chief Justice Hyde.

any one that is committed by the king's authority, and no cause declared of his commitment, according as here it is upon this return—whether we ought to deliver him by bail or to remand him back again. . . .

The exceptions which have been taken to this return were two: the one for the form, the other for the substance. . . . In our case the cause of the detention is sufficiently answered, which is the demand of the writ; and therefore we resolve that the form of this return is good. The next thing is the main point in law, whether the substance or matter of the return be good or no—wherein the substance is this: he doth certify that they are detained in prison by the special command of the king. And whether this be good in law or no, that is the question. . . .[2]

The precedents are all against you, every one of them. And what shall guide our judgments, since there is nothing alleged in this case but precedents? That, if no cause of the commitment be expressed, it is to be presumed to be a matter of state, which we cannot take notice of. You see we find none—no, not one that hath been delivered by bail in the like cases, but by the hand of the king or his direction. . . . Now here I shall trouble you with no more precedents; and you see your own, what conclusion they produce. And as to those strong precedents alleged on the other side, we are not wiser than they that went before us. And the common custom of the law is the common law of the land, and that hath been the continual common custom of the law, to which we are to submit; for we come not to change the law, but to submit to it. . . .

But the question now is whether we may deliver this gentleman or not. . . . Mr. Attorney hath told you that the king hath done it, and we trust him in great matters. And he is bound by law, and he bids us proceed by law as we are sworn to do, and so is the king. And we make no doubt but the king, if you seek to him . . . , will have mercy. But we leave that. If in justice we ought to deliver you, we would do it; but upon these grounds and these records, and the precedents and resolutions, we cannot deliver you, but you must be remanded. . . . I have endeavoured to give the resolutions of us all.

Howell, *State Trials*, III, 51-59.

(B) The Question of Ship Money (1637)[3]

. . . We, desirous to avoid such inconveniences, and out of our princely love and affection to all our subjects, being willing to prevent such errors as any of our loving subjects may happen to run into,

---

[2] The chief justice here takes up in detail the precedents cited by attorneys for the prisoners.

[3] In connection with the writs for the levy of ship money already issued (no. 93B), Charles I directed to his judges the letter which in part follows. And he received the answer which is quoted in full.

have thought fit in a case of this nature to advise with our judges, who, we doubt not, are all well studied and informed in the right of our sovereignty. And because the trial in our several courts, by the formality in pleading, will require a long protraction, we have thought it expedient, by this our letter directed to you all, to require your judgments in the case, as is set down in the enclosed paper, which will not only gain time but also be of more authority to over-rule any prejudicate opinions of others in the point. Given under our signet at our court at Whitehall, the 2nd day of February, in the twelfth year of our reign. . . .[4]

May it please your most excellent majesty: We have, according to your majesty's command—every man by himself and all of us together—taken into consideration the case and question signed by your majesty and enclosed in your royal letter. And we are of opin·ion that, when the good and safety of the kingdom in general is concerned and the whole kingdom is in danger, your majesty may, by writ under the great seal of England, command all the subjects of this your kingdom at their charge to provide and furnish such number of ships, with men, munition, and victuals, and for such time as your majesty shall think fit, for the defence and safeguard of the kingdom from such danger and peril; and that by law your majesty may compel the doing thereof in case of refusal or refractoriness. And we are also of opinion that in such case your majesty is the sole judge both of the danger and when and how the same is to be prevented and avoided. John Bramston. John Finch. Humphrey Davenport. John Denham. Richard Hutton. William Jones. George Crooke. Thomas Trevor. George Vernon. Francis Crawley. Robert Berkeley. Richard Weston.

Ibid., III, 843 f.

(C) The King v. John Hampden (1638)[5]

Robert Berkeley: . . . The grand question is shortly this: whether . . . in this special case . . . the charges imposed by the king upon his subjects for provision of shipping, without common consent in parliament, be good in law—yea or no. . . . I hope that

---

[4] The substance of the king's question is repeated in the judges' answer.

[5] John Hampden, a freeholder of Buckinghamshire, refused to pay 20s. assessed upon his land as ship money in accordance with the king's writ of 1636 (see above, p. 455, n. 2). On being summoned before the court of exchequer to show cause for non-payment, Hampden through his attorneys declared the levy illegal; and, as a test case, the matter was taken into exchequer chamber to be discussed before all the justices of the central courts. After twelve days of argument by counsel on the two sides, the court, by a vote of seven to five, gave judgment against Hampden. How these five—Crooke, Hutton, Denham, Davenport, and Bramston—thus came to differ from the view to which they had earlier subscribed is explained in the second of the following opinions, that of George Crooke. The first, in which the majority of the court concurred, is that of Robert Berkeley. Both men were justices of the king's bench.

none doth imagine that it either is or can be drawn by consequence to be any part of the question in this case whether the king may at all times and upon all occasions impose charges upon his subjects in general without common consent in parliament. If that were made the question, it is questionless that he may not. The people of the kingdom are subjects, not slaves—freemen, not villeins to be taxed *de alto et basso*. Though the king of England hath a *monarchical power and hath *jura summae majestatis* and hath an absolute trust settled in his crown and person for the government of his subjects, yet his government is to be *secundum leges regni*. . . . By those laws the subjects are not tenants at the king's will of what they have. . . . They have a birthright in the laws of the kingdom. No new laws can be put upon them; none of their laws can be altered or abrogated without common consent in parliament. Thus much I speak to avoid misapprehensions and misreports upon that which I shall say in this case, not as if there were cause of saying so much upon anything challenged on the king's side. . . .[6]

It is to be observed that the principal command in the shipping-writ is not to levy money; it is to provide a ship—which ship being to be provided at the charge of a multitude . . . , the thing cannot be done any manner of way but by . . . money. Therefore, the instructions in the shipping-writ are not only apt but necessary. . . . And thereupon it may be said that the sum assessed upon every one, and in our case upon Mr. Hampden, is . . . a duty to be performed as a means conducing to the principal end; the refusal of performance of which duty is a refusal to obey the principal thing commanded . . . , being of a kind concerning the commonwealth. The king, who is the head, the sovereign of the commonwealth, and who hath as incident to his regal office power of coercion, is by law to exercise such his power of coercion to enforce such as refuse to join with others in performance of that which is commanded for the commonwealth. . . .

I would be loath to irritate any differing in opinion from me with provoking or odious terms; but I cannot more fully express myself . . . than in saying that it is a dangerous tenet, a kind of Judaizing opinion to hold that the weal public must be exposed to the peril of utter ruin and subversion, rather than such a charge as this, which may secure the commonwealth, may be imposed by the king upon the subject without common consent in parliament. . . . All know that the Jews were so strict that they would not use means for defence of themselves and their country upon their Sabbath. Their enemies took the advantage and ruined their state. . . .

Mr. Holbourne[7] supposed a fundamental policy in the creation of the frame of this kingdom that, in case the monarch of England

---

[6] Berkeley here reviews the long series of precedents cited by Hampden's counsel.

[7] Counsel for Hampden.

should be inclined to exact from his subjects at his pleasure, he should be restrained, for that he could have nothing from them but upon a common consent in parliament. He is utterly mistaken herein. I agree the parliament to be a most ancient and supreme court, where the king and peers, as judges, are in person, and the whole body of the commons representatively. There peers and commons may . . . , amongst other things, make known their grievances, if there be any, to their sovereign and humbly petition him for redress. But the former fancied policy I utterly deny. The law knows no such king-yoking policy. The law is itself an old and trusty servant of the king's; it is his instrument or means which he useth to govern his people by. I never read nor heard that Lex was Rex; but it is common and most true that Rex is Lex, for he is . . . a living, a speaking, an acting law. . . .

There are two maxims of the law of England which plainly disprove Mr. Holbourne's supposed policy. The first is that the king is a person trusted with the state of the commonwealth. The second of these maxims is that the king cannot do wrong. Upon these two maxims the *jura summae majestatis* are grounded, with which none but the king himself—not his high court of parliament without leave —hath to meddle: as, namely, war and peace, value of coin, parliament at pleasure, power to dispense with penal laws, and divers others; amongst which I range . . . also . . . power to command provision—in case of necessity—of means from the subjects, to be adjoined to the king's own means for the defence of the commonwealth. . . . Otherwise I do not understand how the king's majesty may be said to have the majestical right and power of a free monarch. . . .

And so I have done at this time. And what I have said I have spoken to the best of my understanding and in discharge of my conscience. . . . And, it being high time now for me to give over, I conclude upon all my reasons and authorities cited that, as this case is upon the pleading of it, the charge of 20s. imposed on Mr. Hampden towards the provision of a ship commanded by the writ . . . is consonant to law, and consequently that judgment ought to be given against him. . . .

Sir George Crooke: . . . That which hath moved me most and maketh me distrust my own judgment in this case is that my brothers that have argued before me . . . have all argued one way; with whose opinions I should willingly have concurred if I could have satisfied my own judgment with their reasons. But, not being satisfied, I have learned that I must not come with a multitude against mine own conscience. . . . And therefore I shall show reasons and leave myself to the judgment of my lords and others my brethren. And whatsoever shall be adjudged I must submit unto, and so do with all others; and do now declare my opinion to be that, as this case is, judgment ought to be given for the defendant. My reasons and grounds that I shall insist upon are these: (1) that the command by this writ . . . for to have ships at the charge of the inhabitants of the county . . . is illegal and contrary to the common laws, not being by authority of parliament; (2) that, if at the common laws it had been lawful, yet now this writ is illegal, being expressly contrary to divers statutes prohibiting a general charge to be laid upon the commons in general without consent in parliament; (3) that it is not to be maintained by any prerogative or power royal, nor allegation of necessity or danger; (4) admitting it were legal to lay such a charge upon maritime ports, yet to charge any inland county, as the county of Bucks is, with making ships and furnishing them with masters, mariners, and soldiers at their charge . . . is illegal and not warranted by any former precedent. . . .[8]

To this opinion I confess I then, with the rest of the judges, subscribed my hand; but I then dissented to that opinion and then signified my opinion to be that such a charge could not be laid by any such writ but by parliament. And so absolutely in that point one other did agree with me, and dissented from that opinion; and four others in some other particulars from that which was subscribed. But the greater part seeming absolutely to be resolved upon that opinion—some of them affirming that they had seen divers records and precedents of such writs satisfying them to be of that judgment—I was pressed to subscribe with them. . . . And this by more ancient judges than myself was affirmed to be the continual practice; and that it was not fit—especially in a case of this nature, so much concerning the service of the king—for some to subscribe and some to forbear their subscriptions; and that, although we did subscribe, it did not bind us, but that in point of judgment, if the case came in question judicially before us, we should give our judgments as we should see cause. . . .

Ibid., III, 1089-1145.

(D) STAR CHAMBER REPORTS (1631)[9]

In the star chamber, Trinity term of the seventh year of King Charles: in the council of the lord king at that same place, before Thomas, lord of Coventry, lord keeper of the great seal; Henry, earl of Manchester, lord keeper of the privy seal; John, earl of Bridgewater; William, bishop of London; Richard, bishop of Winchester; Nicholas Hyde, knight, lord chief justice of the king's bench; Thomas Richardson, knight, lord chief justice of the [common] bench.

Between John Smith, plaintiff, and Benjamin Crokew and Thomas Wright, defendants. The plaintiff's bill showed that there had been

[8] Crooke here refers to the answer given by the judges in the previous February.

[9] The following cases are taken from various sessions of the court, each of which is preceded by a list of those present similar to the one that is given here. These lists are normally in Latin.

a long suit in the chancery between the plaintiff Smith and the defendant Crokew about lands belonging to the free school of [Wooton Underedge] in Gloucestershire, and this suit was directed to be there sued by the judges of the common law. And this was heard so far: the possession was decreed to the school, and all other estates to be cancelled, and the school's estate to be surrendered to the king with purpose to grant the same back again to the school. It was ordered further that, whereas Smith had been in possession of the manor or lordship of Wallens Court, being his own fee simple, and his lands lying intermixed with the school lands, he should have a lease . . . of the said lands in question. The king made a new grant by his letters patents and founded the school; and the lease is made to Mr. Smith accordingly. That divers good ordinances were made for the ordering of the school, 40*m*. per annum raised for the master and £4 a year for four poor scholars going to the university; that Mr. Smith hath improved it to the payment of £4 more to a poor scholar. That the defendant Crokew had—to the scandal of the court of chancery, of the late lord chancellor, of the lord keeper, and the king's counsel—printed and divulged a scandalous book to the number of 400 copies, divulged them in Somersetshire and Gloucestershire and London; and Wright the defendant, being a bookseller in Bristol, sold many of the books. And [the plaintiff] complained particularly that the said book contained a scandalous frontispiece and twelve principal slanders and scandalous passages in the book, naming the several pages; and that it was also to the scandal of the plaintiff Smith. The bill prayed the calling in of this scandalous libel to be burnt, and for repair of the plaintiff's reputation.

The defendants made no defence by counsel but, after an affidavit read for serving of the subpoena . . . , the defendants' answers were read. Crokew answered that there had been many unjust suits between the plaintiff and him, wherein the plaintiff had wronged him; that he caused a brief relation of all to be printed to inform the court of parliament, and kept his book, being printed, from publishing till the parliament was sitting, and then gave some of them to his friends. He intended not to lay scandal upon any, but to lay the fault upon the plaintiff only, and he hath not put to sale any of the books—and so not guilty.

Thomas Wright answered that Crokew told this defendant he had printed such books and would desire him to sell some of them for him; and after thirty books were sent by the carrier to him; that he sold them, not thinking they were scandalous, and he thought they were not when he read the book—and so not guilty.

The plaintiff's counsel showed the scandals of the book and the frontispiece: A True Relation of the Strange Passages in Causes between Smith and Crokew, especially in a Cause about the Statute of 43 of Elizabeth of Charitable Uses—wherein Smith hath abused his majesty that late was, my lord bishop of Canterbury, my lord chancellor, my lord keeper, in getting the possession of the said school lands, for which Crokew hath a bill now depending in the parliament. . . . The defendant Crokew confessed he caused it to be penned, and it was done by a servant of the now master of the court of wards, and agreed with one for £9 to print them, etc.

The court in their sentence condemned this book for a libellous and scandalous book, and declared that to print or write briefs of a cause before the hearing and to divulge and publish them is to be accounted scandalous and libellous, because it tendeth to make a private information of the cause. The court therefore ordered that this book, as many of them as could be gotten, should be brought to the public assizes at Gloucester and there burnt; Crokew to pay £500 fine to the king; and Wright £100 for selling some of the books (for if libels are printed, it is not warrant enough to any bookseller to put them to sale); and both to be imprisoned according to the course of the court; and the sentences to be drawn up to clear Smith in his reputation. . . .

Between Richard Waterhouse, plaintiff, and Sir Arthur Ingram, defendant. . . . The plaintiff's counsel opened the bill, consisting of three several charges: (1) for forging a deed of assignment of an old lease . . . of certain lands at Halifax in Yorkshire . . . ; (2) . . . for procuring a release of the said lands in question from Robert Waterhouse . . . while the said Robert was *non compos mentis*; (3) . . . for endorsing the plaintiff's name as a witness to a deed of indenture . . . whereas the plaintiff was no witness to the same deed. It was confessed by the plaintiff's counsel that two of these charges were mistaken . . . ; but for the third charge they showed that divers trials at the law there had been and verdicts and judgments for the plaintiff. . . .

The defendant justified his purchase and denied the forgery and the other crimes and justified an assignment by one Miller dated 1612 . . . , and produced the same to this court. . . .

The sentence of the court was that Sir Arthur Ingram was clear of the forgery and other crimes; that the bill should be taken off the file; that the plaintiff should pay a fine of £100 to the king *pro falso clamore*, and £500 damages to Sir Arthur Ingram; and the plaintiff to make confession of his fault at the assizes at York, standing upon a stool, and at the block at Halifax. . . .

Between Keld, plaintiff, and Fairside, defendant. . . . The plaintiff brought his bill charging the defendants of perjury, subornation of perjury, and confederacy to indict the plaintiff of high treason at York for saying these words . . . : "If it were the king's pleasure that these exactions be made, then we must needs think he is a very beggarly prince. . . ." That the grand jury found an *ignoramus*.[10]

The defendant was a constable and demanded benevolence[11] of

---

[10] A refusal to indict.
[11] One of the levies made by James I; cf. no. 69H.

the plaintiff for the king, and the defendant answered upon his oath that the plaintiff did speak these words unto him upon his second coming to him from Sir Thomas Hobby for a larger contribution; and confessed he did give evidence to the grand jury to this purpose, yet the jury would not find the bill.

The court was opinioned the words were spoken, though the jury in favour of life would not take notice of it by a single witness. And therefore, if this man should be punished for this, it would be a dangerous precedent; for that every single witness must run upon this rock, either to be perjured or punished. The plaintiff's bill was therefore dismissed and he was fined £20 *pro falso clamore*. . . .

One Archer of Southchurch in Essex was brought *ore tenus*,[12] being then charged by Mr. Attorney General for keeping in his corn and consequently for enhancing the price of corn the last year; which offence Mr. Attorney affirmed to be of high nature and evil consequence, to the undoing of the poor and *malum in se*, and then desired his examination taken before the lord keeper might be read. His examination purported that he had seen at the time of his examining a presentment that was made against him by the grand jury at the last assizes in Essex before Justice Vernon for the said offence of keeping in his corn and enhancing; and for that he had made a bargain to sell the poor of the town where he dwelt rye for 7s. a bushel, and afterwards refused to perform his bargain unless he might have 9s. a bushel. He denied this bargain, but for his excuse said he sold to the towns about him, for the poor, wheat at 7s. and 8s. a bushel, and at the latter end of the year for 5s.; and rye for 7s. and 6s., etc., and some for 3s. and 6d. the bushel. He confessed he kept in his corn till June, and that he had 8 quarters of wheat, 60 quarters of rye, and 100 quarters of oats; and that his family were himself and his wife and daughters, two maids, and a man. He confessed that he sold none or very little of his corn in Rochford Hundred where he dwelt, though he were commanded so to do by the earl of Warwick. Yet for his defence he further alleged that his barn was not visited by any justices or officers according to his majesty's late proclamation and orders for that purpose. . . .

Justice Harvey . . . was of opinion that this man's punishment and example will do a great deal more good than all their orders which they might have made at the sessions. And therefore he declared his offence to be very great and fit to be punished in this court; and adjudged him to pay 100m. fine to the king and £10 to the poor, and to stand upon the pillory in Newgate Market an hour with a paper, wherein the cause of his standing there was to be written, put upon his hat—"For enhancing the price of corn"—and then to be led through Cheapside to Leadenhall Market, and there likewise to stand upon the pillory one hour more with the same

---

[12] To answer in person.

paper upon his hat, and after this to be sent to Chelmsford, and there likewise in the market to stand upon the pillory.

Sir Thomas Richardson affirmed this offence to be an offence at the common law long before the king's proclamation and orders, and also against some statutes. . . . He therefore condemned the said Archer to be guilty . . . and agreed in his said fine to the king. . . . The bishop of London observed, with Mr. Attorney, that this was *malum in se*, and that this Archer was guilty of a most foul offence. . . . The earl of Danby consented to the sentence in all. . . . The earl of Dorset concurred in his sentence with the earl of Danby. . . . Lord privy seal gave his sentence in few words, that Archer was guilty by his own confession of a very great offence and well worthy the sentence aforesaid. . . . The lord keeper did affirm that it was indeed a good work to bring this man forth to be here sentenced. . . . His said lordship consented to the highest censure against the said Archer . . . and committed Archer to the Fleet. . . .

The king's attorney general, plaintiff; Charley Moody, Richard Strode . . . and others, defendants. The bill set forth that his majesty, being seised of divers lands and waste grounds called the Fens . . . surrounded with water and barren . . . , by advice of his council took order with Sir Cornelius Vermuyden for the draining of the Fens, if it might be. And articles of agreement were made between his majesty and the said Sir Cornelius Vermuyden . . . for the doing thereof; and a special provision [was made] that those that had any title of common should repair to the commissioners appointed for that purpose by commission and, upon their showing their title or interest, they should have full recompense. The king's letters were sent to warn them to come to the commission and demand their recompense. . . . The king provided workmen, the work was brought to good forwardness, and divers ditches and banks made, and Sir Cornelius Vermuyden was at great charge thereabouts. . . . The defendants with others came together in companies to throw down and demolish what was done: although divers proclamations were made, and no right they could pretend. . . . They made their assemblies by hundreds and five-hundreds; they demolish the work; they . . . burn the spades, shovels, wheelbarrows, planks, and beat the workmen; set up a pair of gallows for to terrify the workmen; threw some of them into the water and held them under a while. They had a signal to assemble themselves by, sometimes by a bell, sometimes by an horn. They threatened to kill the workmen if they came thither to work again. . . . They had fourteen several times in riotous and rebellious manner assembled themselves and done these riots, etc., to the slander of his majesty's government, to the hindrance of the work, and to the damage of Sir Cornelius Vermuyden £5000. . . . Some of them put those that served the king's process out of this court upon them into the stocks.

The defendants' answers some were read and the rest opened by counsel. They all claimed their common of pasture with all manner of cattle and common of turbary at all times of the year. . . . They never agreed with Sir Cornelius Vermuyden. . . . The country receiveth no profit by the work. The grounds are made rather worse. They confess, some of them, that they did with others enter into their grounds to go to their cattle there depasturing; that they cut down the banks and ditches and levelled them for stopping their way. This they did to claim their right, which they hope this court will maintain; seeing they have had possession and seisin . . . time out of mind. And as to the unlawful assemblies, riots, routs, plots, confederacies, woundings, beatings, etc., not guilty. . . .

It was unanimously declared by the whole court that his majesty proceeded herein legally and rightfully for the benefit of his crown and people. . . . And many of the defendants were found guilty of the several riots charged in the bill: namely, Toxie, James Moody, Henry Scott, and Hezekias Browne, who were fined £1000 apiece; the widow Smith, who married the minister after the riots, £500; and the several women who were proved to be at the said riots, 500m. apiece. And they were adjudged to pay for damages to Sir Cornelius Vermuyden, the relator, £2000. . . .

> Gardiner, *Cases in Star Chamber and High Commission*, pp. 37-65.

(E) HIGH COMMISSION REPORTS (1631)

In the court of high commission, Thursday, 20th October, 1631; before George, archbishop of Canterbury; William, bishop of London; Thomas, bishop of Coventry and Lichfield; Theophilus, bishop of St. David's; Francis, bishop of Norwich; John, bishop of Rochester; Sir Dudley Digges, knight; Sir Henry Martin, knight, doctor of law; Sir John Lambe, knight, doctor of law; Sir Nathaniel Brittaine, knight, doctor of law—commissioners.

The cause against Samuel Pretty, clerk. [Article 1:] That the said Samuel, being a minister, was commonly reported for the space of two years last past as a schismatical man. [Answer:] He confesseth himself to be a minister, but denieth that other part of the article. [Article 2:] That he had within twelve months last past preached in the church called St. Michael Pater Noster Royal, London, without licence of the bishop of that diocese. [Answer:] He confesseth that he hath preached in the said church and that he had licence from the late bishop of London. [Article 3:] That the said Samuel in his sermon there delivered these erroneous doctrines and assertions following, *viz.*, that Christians cannot, as touching their reconciliation with God, be too secure—nay, they ought to sing all care away. [Answer:] He saith that he hopeth these words may be spoken, because a favourable construction may be made of them. . . .[13]

The archbishop: "Pretty, tell me, if you had been in Jerusalem

---

[13] Three other articles charge Pretty with doctrinal errors and these charges are supported by three witnesses.

in the Temple among the buyers and sellers, would not Christ have whipped you out with them? What think you?" Samuel Pretty: "If there were not favourable construction of my words to be made, I think I should have been whipped out if I had been there." Then he fell down upon his knees and acknowledged he had given just offence, as by the articles was alleged; and humbly desired mercy of the court.

The archbishop then would only have imprisoned and suspended him from his ministerial office; but it was moved by the bishop of London[14] that he might undergo the censure of the court . . . , for that he and others were minded to degrade him. . . .[15] The archbishop concluded, briefly but sharply reproving him for his phrase of singing all care away. "Yea," saith the archbishop, "drink it away, too; but to what purpose then are all those rules of mortification and growing in sanctification, as 'The night is past, the day is at hand; let us therefore cast away the works of darkness,' etc." And [he] gave his sentence thus: "Let him be imprisoned, suspended, degraded, and kept in prison till he bring in his licence."

[24 November 1631.] A cause against Dr. Hooke, parson of Nettleham in Yorkshire, came to be heard this day. The articles against Dr. Hooke were six or seven: (1) for saying he resigned his archdeaconry because he would be rid of those caterpillars and cankerworms, the ecclesiastical officers; (2) for delivering his opinion at York before the justices of assize that he held it unlawful for priests to exercise any temporal jurisdiction; (3) for making licences for marriages without publishing any banns at his vicarage of Castor . . . and that he used a little seal, and that he married some himself and took money of them for the licences, etc.; (4) he was accused of six or seven several adulteries, he himself being a married man; (5) he was charged with the simoniacal resignation and bestowing of his vicarage of Castor upon a young man, a minister that was no party to this suit; (6) he was articled against for a contempt offered to this court by words, etc. . . .[16]

I give my sentence against this man, for his making of lawless churches, to be suspended three years. For his saying against the officers that they are caterpillars, I let that pass. For his simony I vehemently suspect him, and therefore [he is] to purge himself *septima manu*.[17] For the matters of adultery, it seemeth to me a wondrous thing that a man of his years should so carry himself to be subject to suspicion. These may be pardoned . . . ; I think him not guilty of these obliquities. . . . But for the other thing, that no clergyman may be so much as a justice of peace, this is fantastical and

---

[14] William Laud, subsequently archbishop of Canterbury.

[15] All but one member of the court spoke in favour of his degradation.

[16] After long argument, the members of the court gave their opinions and the archbishop of Canterbury delivered the following sentence.

[17] With six oath-helpers; see immediately below. Cf. no. 14F.

makes such a breach in the church that he cannot easily make satisfaction. . . . Well, sir, I must admonish you for your contempt
. . . ; you are to pay the charges of the suit and to be committed. . . .

[26 April, 1632.] Dr. Hooke maketh faith that the certificate of
the purgation to be made this day by him was read in the parish
church of Nettleton. . . . Then he produced his compurgators: by
name, John Shiboy, doctor of divinity; Francis Bradshaw, Thomas
Holt, Dennis Squire, Matthew Miller, Thomas Clare, bachelors of
divinity. Dr. Hooke and the rest came in their cloaks, and the said
Holt in a careless ruff and his hair somewhat long. For which their
coming they were chidden, and especially Mr. Holt. And they were
rejected till they should come as divines in their gowns. And they
went and got them gowns and scarfs; and Mr. Holt had another ruff
and a black satin night-cap on. And they appeared again, and then
the cause was opened by the doctors both on the one side and the
other. The promoter's counsel showed the accusations and the proofs
against the doctor, and his counsel showed his defence. Which done,
Dr. Hooke took his oath, swearing that he was not guilty of the
crimes laid against him, nor any of them. And the said compurgators
were first demanded severally whether they, notwithstanding all that
had been said, thought the doctor to be clear and innocent. And they
all did answer severally Yes. Then they took their oaths, swearing
that they thought in their consciences that Dr. Hooke had taken a
true oath. . . .

[3 May 1632.] This day were brought to the court out of prison
divers persons . . . which were taken on Sunday last at a conventicle met at the house of Barnett, a brewer's clerk, dwelling in the
precinct of Black Friars. . . .

Then came in Mr. Latropp, who is asked what authority he had
to preach and keep this conventicle. And saith the bishop of London:
"How many women sat cross-legged upon the bed whilst you sat
on one side and preached and prayed most devoutly?" Latropp: "I
keep no such evil company; they were not such women." London:
"Are you a minister?" . . . He answered that he was a minister.
London: "How and by whom qualified? Where are your orders?"
Latropp: "I am a minister of the gospel of Christ, and the Lord hath
qualified me." "Will you lay your hand on the Book and take your
oath?" said the court. He refuseth the oath. . . .

Samuel Eaton and two women and a maid appeared, who were
demanded why they were assembled in that conventicle when others
were at church. Eaton: "We were not assembled in contempt of
the magistrate." London: "No, it was in contempt of the Church
of England." Eaton: "It was in conscience to God. . . ." Canterbury:
"What did you?" "We read the Scriptures and catechized our families," said Eaton; "and may it please this honourable court to hear
us speak the truth, we will show you what was done . . . ; we did

nothing but what you will allow us to do." London: "Who can free you? These are dangerous men; they are a scattered company sown in all the city. . . . Hold them the Book." Eaton: "I dare not swear nor take this oath. . . . I know not what I shall swear to." King's advocate: "It is to give a true answer to articles put into the court against you, or that shall be put in touching this conventicle of yours and divers your heretical tenets, and what words and exercises you used, and things of this nature." Eaton: "I dare not." . . .[18] Archbishop of Canterbury: "Take them away." So they were all committed to the New Prison.

[14 June 1632.] . . . Sound, Hollingsworth, Gerard, John Osborne, and Thomas Pocock, having answered for setting up and continuing the seats above the communion table in St. Austin's Church by Paul's, they being churchwardens and parishioners there, Dr. Duck, the chancellor of London, moved that their answers and their cause might be considered, and they ordered to take down and remove their seats newly set up above the communion table. London: "You say you have not room for your parishioners, and therefore you must have seats above God Almighty and above Christ in His own house. Judge you, is it reason? The church of St. Leonard's, Foster Lane, is in the same case; but I made them pull down their seats. And so I will you. . . ." Parishioners: "If the court will order us to take them down, we will; or else we dare not, for the vestry hath ordered it that they shall be built upon the old foundation." . . . Rochester: "The power of vestries and churchwardens, this is to hatch a lay presbytery."

[21 June, 1632.] . . . Ralph Grafton, an upholsterer, dwelling in Cornhill, London, was required to take his oath to answer the articles. He was said to be a principal ringleader of those conventiclers that met at Black Friars. King's advocate: "This is a rich man, dwelling within the city. My motion is that your grace and the court would set a fine upon this man if he shall refuse to answer, that others may be warned for contemning of the court." London: "Mr. Advocate. I thank you for this motion." King's advocate: "I require you and the court requireth you to take your oath to answer to matters of your own fact, as far as you know and are bound by law." Grafton: "An oath is a matter of an high nature and must not be taken rashly. I dare not, therefore, take this oath. We have done nothing against the law. It was no conventicle. There was nothing spoken against the king, nor against the state. I dare not take the oath and I am no ringleader of any to evil." Canterbury: "You met without law; you had no authority. . . ." Wherefore the court for his contempt in refusing the oath set a fine of £200 upon him and committed him to prison. Grafton: "I have bail here ready; if you please to take

---

[18] The other prisoners also refused to take the oath.

it, I tender it to you." . . . Canterbury: "No, away with him to prison!" . . .

Ibid., pp. 181 f., 246 f., 276 f., 306 f., 315 f.

95. RECORDS OF THE SHORT PARLIAMENT (1640)

(A) Speech of the Lord Keeper (13 April)

My lords, and you, the knights, citizens, and burgesses of the house of commons: . . . I doubt not but you rejoice at this day's meeting . . . ; and good reason you have so to do, and with all humbleness of heart to acknowledge the great goodness of his majesty who, sequestering the memory of all former discouragements in preceding assemblies, is now, out of a fatherly affection to his people and a confidence that they will not be failing in their duty to him, pleased graciously to invite you and all his loving subjects to a sacred unity of hearts and affection in the service of him and of the commonwealth, and in execution of those counsels that tend only to the honour of his majesty and to the good preservation of you all. His majesty's kingly resolutions are seated in the ark of his sacred breast, and it were a presumption of too high a nature for any Uzzah, uncalled, to touch it. Yet his majesty is now pleased to lay by the shining beams of majesty . . . , that the distance between sovereignty and subjection should not bar you of that filial freedom of access to his person and counsel. Only let us . . . ever remember that, though the king sometimes lays by the beams and rays of majesty, he never lays by majesty itself.

In former parliaments you have been advised for the preventing and diverting of those dangers which by foreign and remote counsels might have tended to the ruin and to the dishonour of this nation. Therein his majesty's great wisdom and providence hath, for many years, eased you of that trouble; his majesty having with great judgment and prudence, not only foreseen and prevented our dangers, but kept up the honour and splendour of the English crown, of which we all this day find a happy and comfortable experience. . . . But what avails this the kingdom? . . . You are now summoned to counsels and resolutions that more nearly concern you—to prevent a danger and dishonour that knocks at our gates, and that moves from such from whom we had little reason to suspect it. . . .

When his majesty had most reason to expect a grateful return of loyalty and obedience from all the Scottish nation, some men of Belial, some Shebahs, have blown the trumpet there, and by their insolencies and rebellious actions drawn many after them, to the utter desertion of his majesty's government. . . . They have taken up arms against the Lord's anointed, their rightful prince and undoubted sovereign . . . ; they have seized on the trophies of honour and invested themselves with the regal power and authority—such and so many acts of disloyalty and disobedience as, let their pretences be what they will be, no true English Christian heart but must acknowledge them to be the effects of foul and horrid treasons. . . .

His majesty doth therefore desire you, upon these pressing and urgent reasons, that you will for a while lay aside all other debates, and that you would pass an act for such and so many subsidies as you, in your hearty affections to him and to the common good, shall think fit and convenient for so great an action; and withal that you would hasten the payment of it as soon as may be, with a proviso in the act that his majesty's royal assent shall not determine this session. . . . And his majesty is most graciously pleased to give you his royal word that . . . he will give you time for considering of such petitions as you shall conceive to be good for the commonwealth. . . .

Journals of the Lords, IV, 46 f.

(B) Speech of the Lord Keeper (22 April)

This day the lord keeper delivered to the house the effect of what was yesterday delivered, by the command of his majesty, at the meeting of the lords spiritual and temporal and the house of commons at Whitehall, *viz.*: ". . . That which I then delivered was, by his majesty's command, to this purpose—to put your lordships and the house of commons in mind of the cause of the calling of this parliament, which was for the supply of his majesty. . . . His majesty hath taken notice of some scruples that did remain in men's minds touching the shipping business. And for the clearing of those doubts and scruples . . . , it was declared to your lordships, first, that the king never had it in his thought or heart to make any revenue of the shipping business, nor to make the least penny of profit or advantage to himself; that *de facto* he had not done it. . . . He hath no ends or aims for himself, nor hath he any thought but to keep up the glory and honour of this nation. . . . His majesty is not wedded to this particular way. . . . If your lordships and the house of commons will think of any other way to maintain him in such a manner as is fit for his majesty . . . to live in, put it into what way you please; settle it with as much security and safety as you can invent, that you may be sure there can come nothing to the king but in that way, that you may be sure it shall be employed for your good and safety. . . . Nothing shall be propounded for the securing of the propriety of your estates and the liberties of your persons but his majesty will as graciously and readily grant the same as it is possible for you to ask it. His majesty doth bring with him wishes and royal desires that this may prove a happy and blessed parliament, and was pleased to put you into the way how to make it so; which was by putting obligations and trust and confidence upon his royal word, which it becomes us in duty and good manners fit for subjects to take from our king. . . . For there is a trust that must always be reposed in a king; and, when the king is pleased to declare himself so gracious and so free that he will perform this trust to the uttermost with royal heaped measure, it is the greatest security. No security of law, no other security that parliament can invent, can match it. . . ."

Ibid., IV, 62 f.

(C) PROCEEDINGS IN THE COMMONS (23-24 APRIL)

Mr. Lenthall reported from the committee of the whole house that the committee had resolved upon the question that we shall consult with the lords to prevent innovation in matter of religion and concerning the property of our goods and liberties and privileges of parliament, the better to give a present supply to his majesty. Upon this report it was ordered, upon the question, that we shall consult with the lords, to prevent innovation in matter of religion and concerning the property of our goods and liberties and privileges of parliament, the better to prepare us to give an answer to his majesty touching supply. . . .

These heads following were by the committee, according to yesterday's order, brought in as inducements and matter for the conference to be desired with the lords . . . :

I. Concerning innovation in matter of religion. (1) The commission that was lately granted to the convocation house. . . . (2) The complaints arising from petitions brought in from the several counties by the members of the house against innovations in religion. (3) The molesting and depriving of godly and conformable ministers for not yielding to matters enjoined without warrant of law. (4) The publishing of papist tenets in licensed books, sermons, and disputations. (5) Restraining of conformable ministers from preaching in their own charges.

II. Concerning propriety of goods. (1) Monopolies and restraint of trade. (2) Ship money. (3) Enlarging the bounds of forests. . . . (4) Military charges: namely, coat and conduct money, wages, arms taken from the owners, forcing the countries to buy or provide at their charges horses and carts by way of tax. (5) The denial of justice in the courts at Westminster to the subject's prejudice in point of the propriety of his goods. (6) Frequent imprisonments and vexations for non-payment of unwarrantable taxes and not submitting to unlawful monopolies.

III. Liberties and privileges of parliament. (1) Punishing men out of parliament for things done in parliament. (2) That which is already voted in the house concerning privilege of parliament. . . .

Journals of the Commons, II, 10 f.

(D) THE KING'S SPEECH AND ITS RESULTS (24-29 APRIL)

"My lords: The necessity of calling this parliament makes me to come this day hither contrary to expectation. You remember what the lord keeper said concerning the occasion of this meeting the first and second days. . . . The house of commons did seem to take into consideration my weighty affairs; but they have in a manner concluded the contrary and, instead of preferring my occasions in the first place, they have held consultation of innovation of religion, property of goods, and privileges of parliament, and so have put the cart before the horse. If it were a time to dispute, I should not much stand upon it; but my necessities are so urgent that there can be no delay. If the house of commons will trust me, I will make good what I have promised by my lord keeper. As for religion, my heart and conscience with the religion now established in the Church of England shall go together. For the ship money, God is my witness I never converted any of it to my own profit, but to the end of preserving the dominion of the seas. . . . As for property of goods, it is a thing I never but intended; and it is my desire to be king of a free and rich people; and if no property in goods, no rich people. I told the commons that, if they would speedily supply my occasions for the present, I would give them further time at winter to present and debate all their just grievances. If they will not trust me first, all my business this summer will be lost; and before the year goeth about I must be trusted at last, for in the winter I must call them to give me a greater supply. If the house of commons will not join to prefer my occasions before their grievances, I conjure your lordships to consider your own honours and mine, and the preposterous course of the house of commons; and desire that your lordships will not join with them, but leave them to themselves. . . . If the supply come not in time, I will not say what mischief may and must follow."

. . . Their lordships taking into consideration that which his majesty delivered to them this morning . . . , these two questions were agreed upon to be proposed to the house:—

First, as many of your lordships as are of opinion his majesty's supply should have precedency and be resolved of before any other matter whatsoever say Content.

[Second,] as many of your lordships as think fit there should be a conference desired with the house of commons to dispose them thereunto say Content. . . .

Then the first question was put and carried by the Contents; and likewise the second question carried in like manner.

The lord keeper reported the conference with the house of commons . . . to this effect. Mr. Pym did say he was commanded by the knights, citizens, and burgesses of the house of commons to represent to your lordships their desire and care to preserve a union and correspondence with your lordships. . . . The great privileges belonging to this high court of parliament are not airy and matters of pomp, but have in them reality and efficacy; whereby this great council of the kingdom is enabled to perform all those noble functions which belong to them in respect of the legislative power and conciliary power. . . . As there are general privileges belonging to the whole body, so there are others more peculiar belonging to either house. . . . Among these peculiar privileges there is one great privilege which was acknowledged by your lordships in the last conference—that the matter of subsidy and supply ought to begin in the house of commons. . . . Yet, after, you were pleased to declare that you have voted in your lordships' house that it was most necessary and fit that matter of supply should have the precedency of all other business and, this being done, your lordships would freely join with them in all things concerning matter of religion, propriety of goods, and liberty of parliament. Now, my lords, if you have voted this, you have not only meddled with matter of supply but, as far as in you lies, you have concluded both the matter and order of proceeding—which the house of commons takes to be a breach of their privilege; for which he was commanded to desire reparation from your lordships. . . .

Journals of the Lords, IV, 66-73.

(E) DISSOLUTION OF PARLIAMENT (5 May)

His majesty came this day in person to the house, apparelled in his regal robes, and, having ascended his royal throne, the lords spiritual and temporal sitting in their robes uncovered, the house of commons were called in with their speaker. And being all present, his majesty was pleased to express his pleasure to them in these words following . . . :—

"My lords: For my own part, I hope you remember what the first day of the parliament the lord keeper said to you in my name, what he said . . . at the banqueting house at Whitehall, and what I said the last day myself. I named it to you, not in any doubt that you do not remember, but to show you that I never said anything that way in favour to my people but, by the grace of God, I will punctually and really perform it. . . . My lords, you know at the first I expressed myself by my lord keeper that delay was worse danger than refusing. I would not put this fault on all the whole house; I will not judge so uncharitably. But it hath been some few cunning and some ill-affectioned men that have been the cause of this misunderstanding. I shall only end as I began, giving your lordships thanks for the care you have had of my honour and affairs, desiring you to go on and assist me for the maintaining of government and the liberties of the people that they so much start at. For, my lords, no king in the world shall be more careful to maintain the propriety of their goods, the liberties of their persons, and true religion than I shall be. And now, my lord keeper, do as I have commanded you."

Then the lord keeper said: "My lords, and ye knights, citizens, and burgesses of the house of commons, the king's majesty doth dissolve this parliament."

Ibid., IV, 81.

96. RECORDS OF THE LONG PARLIAMENT (1640-42)

(A) TRIENNIAL ACT (1641)

An act for the preventing of inconveniences happening by the long intermission of parliaments. Whereas by the laws and statutes of this realm the parliament ought to be holden at least once every year for the redress of grievances, but the appointment of the time and place for the holding thereof hath always belonged, as it ought, to his majesty and his royal progenitors; and whereas it is by experience found that the not holding of parliaments accordingly hath produced sundry and great mischiefs and inconveniences to the king's majesty, the church, and commonwealth: for the prevention of the like mischiefs and inconveniences in time to come, be it enacted by the king's most excellent majesty, with the consent of the lords spiritual and temporal and the commons in this present parliament assembled, that the said laws and statutes be from henceforth duly kept and observed. And your majesty's loyal and obedient subjects, in this present parliament now assembled, do humbly pray that it be enacted, and be it enacted accordingly by the authority of this present parliament, that, in case there be not a parliament summoned by writ under the great seal of England and assembled and held before the 10th day of September which shall be in the third year next after the last day of the last meeting and sitting in this present parliament . . .—and so from time to time and in all times hereafter, if there shall not be a parliament assembled and held before the 10th day of September which shall be in the third year next after the last day of the last meeting and sitting in parliament before that time assembled and held . . . —that then . . . the parliament shall assemble and be held in the usual place at Westminster in such manner and by such means only as is hereafter in this present act declared and enacted, and not otherwise, on the second Monday which shall be in the month of November then next ensuing. And in case this present parliament now assembled and held, or any other parliament which shall at any time hereafter be assembled and held . . . , shall be prorogued or adjourned . . . until the 10th day of September which shall be in the third year next after the last day of the last meeting and sitting in parliament . . . , that then . . . every such parliament so prorogued or adjourned . . . shall from the said 10th day of September be thenceforth clearly and absolutely dissolved, and the lord chancellor of England, the lord keeper of the great seal of England, and every commissioner and commissioners for the keeping of the great seal of England, for the time being, shall within six days after the said 10th day of September, in every such third year as aforesaid, in due form of law and without any further warrant or direction from his majesty, his heirs, or successors, seal, issue forth, and send abroad several and respective writs to the several and respective peers of this realm, commanding every such peer that he personally be at the parliament to be held at Westminster on the second Monday which shall be in November next following the said 10th day of September . . . ; and shall also seal and issue forth . . . several and respective writs to the several and respective sheriffs of the several and respective counties, cities, and boroughs of England and Wales . . . , and to all and every other officers and persons to whom writs have used to be directed, for the electing of the knights, citizens, barons, and burgesses of and for the said counties, cities, Cinque Ports, and boroughs of England and Wales respectively, in the accustomed form, to appear and serve in parliament to be held at Westminster on the said second Monday, which shall be in November aforesaid; which said peers, after the said writs received, and which said knights, citizens, barons, and burgesses chosen by virtue of the said writs, shall then and there appear and serve in parliament accordingly. And the said lord chancellor, lord keeper, commissioner and commissioners aforesaid, shall respectively take a solemn oath upon the Holy Evangelists for the due issuing of writs according to the tenor of this act. . . .[1]

And it is lastly provided and enacted, that his majesty's royal assent to this bill shall not thereby determine this present session of parliament, and that all statutes and acts of parliament which are to have continuance unto the end of this present session shall be of full force after his majesty's assent, until this present session be fully ended and determined. And if this present session shall determine by dissolution of this present parliament, then all the acts and statutes aforesaid shall be continued until the end of the first session of the next parliament.

Statutes of the Realm, V, 54 f.; 16 Charles I, c. 1.

(B) ACT FOR THE ATTAINDER OF STRAFFORD (1641)

An act for the attainder of Thomas, earl of Strafford, of high treason. Whereas the knights, citizens, and burgesses of the house of commons in this present parliament assembled, have, in the name of themselves and of all the commons of England, impeached Thomas, earl of Strafford, of high treason for endeavouring to subvert the ancient and fundamental laws and government of his majesty's realms of England and Ireland and to introduce an arbitrary and tyrannical government against law in the said kingdoms, and for exercising a tyrannous and exorbitant power above and against the laws of the said kingdoms over the liberties, estates, and lives of his majesty's subjects, and likewise for having by his own authority commanded the laying and sessing of soldiers upon his majesty's subjects in Ireland, against their consents, to compel them to obey his unlawful summons and orders, made upon paper petitions in causes between party and party, which accordingly was executed upon divers of his

---

[1] Elaborate provision is made for the assembling of parliament even should such royal officials fail to carry out their oath. Penalties are established for disobedience. And it is provided that this act shall be read annually in local courts and assizes.

majesty's subjects in a warlike manner within the said realm of Ireland; and [whereas] in so doing [he] did levy war against the king's majesty and his liege people in that kingdom; and also for that he, upon the unhappy dissolution of the last parliament, did slander the house of commons to his majesty and did counsel and advise his majesty that he was loose and absolved from rules of government, and that he had an army in Ireland which he might employ to reduce this kingdom—for which he deserveth to undergo the pains and forfeitures of high treason—and [whereas] the said earl hath also been an incendiary of the wars between the two kingdoms of England and Scotland; all which offences hath been sufficiently proved against the said earl upon his impeachment: be it therefore enacted by the king's most excellent majesty and by the lords and commons in this present parliament assembled, and by authority of same, that the said earl of Strafford, for the heinous crimes and offences aforesaid, stand and be adjudged attainted of high treason, and shall suffer such pains of death, and incur the forfeitures of his goods and chattels, lands, tenements, and hereditaments of any estate of freehold or inheritance in the said kingdoms of England and Ireland, which the said earl or any other to his use, or in trust for him, have or had the day of the first sitting of this . . . parliament, or at any time since. . . .

Ibid., V, 177 f.: 16 Charles I, c. 38.

(C) Act to Continue the Existing Parliament (1641)

An act to prevent inconveniences which may happen by the untimely adjourning, proroguing, or dissolving of this present parliament. . . . Be it declared and enacted by the king our sovereign lord with the assent of the lords and commons in this present parliament assembled, and by the authority of the same, that this present parliament now assembled shall not be dissolved unless it be by act of parliament to be passed for that purpose, nor shall be, at any time or times during the continuance thereof, prorogued or adjourned, unless it be by act of parliament to be likewise passed for that purpose; and that the house of peers shall not at any time or times during this present parliament be adjourned, unless it be by themselves or by their own order; and in like manner, that the house of commons shall not, at any time or times during this present parliament, be adjourned, unless it be by themselves or by their own order; and that all and every thing or things whatsoever done or to be done for the adjournment, proroguing, or dissolving of this present parliament contrary to this act shall be utterly void and of none effect.

Ibid., V, 103 f.: 16 Charles I, c. 7.

(D) Tunnage and Poundage Act (1641)

A subsidy granted to the king of tunnage, poundage, and other sums of money payable upon merchandise exported and imported. Whereas, upon examination in this present parliament of divers of the farmers, customers, and collectors of the customs upon merchandise, and likewise upon their own confession, it appeared that they have taken divers great sums of money of his majesty's subjects, and likewise of merchants aliens for goods imported and exported by the names of a subsidy of tunnage and poundage, and by colour of divers other impositions laid upon merchandise, which have been taken and received against the laws of the realm, in regard the said sums of money and impositions were not granted by common consent in parliament . . . : be it therefore declared and enacted by the king's most excellent majesty and the lords and commons in this present parliament assembled, and it is hereby declared and enacted, that it is and hath been the ancient right of the subjects of this realm that no subsidy, custom, impost, or other charge whatsoever ought or may be laid or imposed upon any merchandise exported or imported by subjects, denizens, or aliens without common consent in parliament.

Yet, nevertheless, the commons . . . , taking into their consideration the great peril that might ensue to this realm by the not guarding of the seas and the other inconveniences which might follow in case the said sums of money should upon the sudden be forborne to be paid, by and with the advice of the lords in this present parliament assembled and by the authority of the same, do give and grant to our supreme liege lord and sovereign one subsidy called tunnage—that is to say, of every tun of wine that is or shall come into this realm or any his majesty's dominions by way of merchandise the sum of 3s. . . .—and also one other subsidy called poundage—that is to say, of all manner of goods and merchandise of every merchant, denizen, and alien carried or to be carried out of this realm, or any his majesty's dominions, or to be brought into the same by way of merchandise, of the value of every 20s. of the same goods and merchandise 12d. . . .[2]—to have, take, enjoy, and perceive the subsidies aforesaid, and other the forementioned sums and every of them . . . from the five-and-twentieth of May, 1641, to the fifteenth of July next ensuing. . . .

Ibid., V, 104: 16 Charles I, c. 8.

(E) Act Abolishing Arbitrary Courts (1641)

An act for the regulating the privy council and for taking away the court commonly called the star chamber. . . . Forasmuch as all matters examinable or determinable . . . in the court commonly called the star chamber may have their proper remedy and redress and their due punishment and correction by the common law of the land and in the ordinary course of justice elsewhere; and forasmuch as the reasons and motives inducing the erection and con-

---

[2] The poundage on tin was double the normal rate. Wool, wool-fells, and woolen cloth were excepted from the force of this article, being taxed according to a separate schedule placed in the article following. Finally, it was provided that tobacco from the English plantations should pay only 2d. on the pound.

tinuance of that court do now cease, and the proceedings, censures, and decrees of that court have by experience been found to be an intolerable burden to the subjects and the means to introduce an arbitrary power and government; and forasmuch as the council table hath of late times assumed unto itself a power to intermeddle in civil causes and matters only of private interest between party and party, and have adventured to determine of the estates and liberties of the subject contrary to the law of the land and the rights and privileges of the subject, by which great and manifold mischiefs and inconveniences have arisen and happened, and much uncertainty by means of such proceedings hath been conceived concerning men's rights and estates: for settling whereof and preventing the like in time to come, be it ordained and enacted by the authority of this present parliament that the said court commonly called the star chamber, and all jurisdiction, power, and authority belonging unto or exercised in the same court, or by any the judges, officers, or ministers thereof, be from the first day of August, in the year of our Lord God 1641, clearly and absolutely dissolved, taken away, and determined. . . .

And be it likewise enacted that the like jurisdiction now used and exercised in the court before the president and council in the marches of Wales; and also in the court before the president and council established in the northern parts; and also in the court commonly called the court of the duchy of Lancaster, held before the chancellor and council of the court; and also in the court of exchequer of the county palatine of Chester, held before the chamberlain and council of that court . . . shall, from the said first day of August, 1641, be also repealed and absolutely revoked and made void. . . .

Be it likewise declared and enacted by authority of this present parliament, that neither his majesty nor his privy council have or ought to have any jurisdiction, power, or authority by English bill, petition, articles, libel, or any other arbitrary way whatsoever, to examine or draw into question, determine, or dispose of the lands, tenements, hereditaments, goods, or chattels of any the subjects of this kingdom, but that the same ought to be tried and determined in the ordinary courts of justice and by the ordinary course of the law.

Ibid., V, 110: 16 Charles I, c. 10.

(F) Act Abolishing the Court of High Commission (1641)

An act for the repeal of a branch of a statute . . . concerning commissioners for causes ecclesiastical. Whereas in the parliament holden in the first year of the reign of the late Queen Elizabeth . . . there was an act made . . . ;[3] and whereas, by colour of some words in the foresaid . . . act whereby commissioners are authorized to execute their commission according to the tenor and effect of the king's

---

[3] Here is recited the clause in the statute of 1559 (no. 81A) establishing the court of high commission.

letters patents and by letters patents grounded thereupon, the said commissioners have, to the great and insufferable wrong and oppression of the king's subjects, used to fine and imprison them, and to exercise other authority not belonging to ecclesiastical jurisdiction restored by that act, and divers other great mischiefs and inconveniences have also ensued to the king's subjects by occasion of the . . . commissions issued thereupon and the executions thereof : therefore, for the repressing and preventing of the foresaid abuses, mischiefs, and inconveniences in time to come, be it enacted by the king's most excellent majesty and the lords and commons in this present parliament assembled, and by the authority of the same, that the foresaid branch, clause, article, or sentence contained in the said act . . . shall from henceforth be repealed . . . and utterly made void forever. . . .

And be it also enacted by the authority aforesaid that no archbishop, bishop . . . , nor any other person or persons whatsoever exercising spiritual or ecclesiastical power, authority, or jurisdiction . . . shall from and after the first day of August, which shall be in the year of our Lord God 1641, award, impose or inflict any pain, penalty, fine, amercement, imprisonment, or other corporal punishment upon any of the king's subjects for any contempt, misdemeanour, crime, offence, matter, or thing whatsoever belonging to spiritual or ecclesiastical cognizance or jurisdiction, or shall *ex officio*, or at the instance or promotion of any other person whatsoever . . . , minister unto any . . . person whatsoever any corporal oath, whereby he or she shall or may be charged or obliged to make any presentment of any crime or offence, or to confess or to accuse him or herself of any crime, offence, delinquency, or misdemeanour, or any neglect . . . , or thing whereby, or by reason whereof, he or she shall or may be liable or exposed to any censure, pain, penalty, or punishment whatsoever. . . .[4]

And be it further enacted that, from and after the said first day of August, no new court shall be erected, ordained, or appointed within this realm of England or dominion of Wales which shall or may have the like power, jurisdiction, or authority as the said high commission court now hath or pretendeth to have; but that all and every such letters patents, commissions, and grants made or to be made by his majesty, his heirs, or successors, and all powers and authorities granted or pretended or mentioned to be granted thereby, and all acts, sentences, and decrees to be made by virtue or colour thereof shall be utterly void and of none effect.

Ibid., V, 112 f.: 16 Charles I, c. 11.

(G) Act Abolishing Ship Money (1641)

An act for the declaring unlawful and void the late proceedings touching ship money and for the vacating of all records and process

---

[4] See above, p. 470.

concerning the same. Whereas divers writs of late time issued under the great seal of England, commonly called ship writs, for the charging of the ports, towns, cities, boroughs, and counties of this realm respectively to provide and furnish certain ships for his majesty's service; and whereas, upon the execution of the same writs . . . , process hath been thence made against sundry persons pretended to be charged by way of contribution for the making up of certain sums assessed for the providing of the said ships, and in especial . . . against John Hampden, esquire . . . ;[5] and whereas some other actions and process depend . . . against other persons for the like kind of charge grounded upon the said writs commonly called ship writs, all which writs and proceedings as aforesaid were utterly against the law of the land: be it therefore declared and enacted by the king's most excellent majesty and the lords and the commons in this present parliament assembled, and by the authority of the same, that the said charge imposed upon the subject for the providing and furnishing of ships commonly called ship money . . . , and the said writs . . . and the said judgment given against the said John Hampden, were and are contrary to and against the laws and statutes of this realm, the right of property, the liberty of the subjects, former resolutions in parliament, and the Petition of Right made in the third year of the reign of his majesty that now is.

And it is further declared and enacted . . . that all . . . particulars prayed or desired in the said Petition of Right shall from henceforth be put in execution accordingly, and shall be firmly and strictly holden and observed as in the same petition they are prayed and expressed; and that all . . . the records . . . of all . . . the judgment, enrolments . . . , and proceedings as aforesaid, and all . . . the proceedings whatsoever, upon or by pretext . . . of any of the said writs commonly called ship writs . . . , shall be deemed . . . to be utterly void. . . .

Ibid., V, 116 f.: 16 Charles I, c. 14.

(H) Act Defining Forests and Forest Law (1641)

An act for the certainty of forests and of the meers, metes, limits, and bounds of the forests.[6] . . . Be it declared and enacted by the king's most excellent majesty and the lords and commons in this present parliament assembled, and by the authority of the same, that from henceforth the metes . . . and bounds of all and every the forests respectively shall be to all intents and purposes taken, adjudged, and deemed to extend no further respectively than the metes . . . and bounds . . . were commonly known, used, or taken to be the metes . . . and bounds of the said forests respectively in the twentieth year of the reign of our late sovereign lord, King James, and not beyond in any wise—any perambulation or perambu-

---

[5] The preamble here reviews the proceedings in Hampden's case (no. 94c).

[6] The preamble recites the recent abuses in this connection; cf. no. 93c.

lations, presentments, extents, surveys, judgments, records, decrees, or other matter or thing whatsoever to the contrary notwithstanding—and that all and every the presentments since the said twentieth year made . . . and all and every judgment and award upon or by reason or pretext of any such presentment or presentments . . . , and all and every fine and fines, and amercement and amercements, upon or by reason or colour of any such presentment or presentments shall from henceforth be adjudged, deemed, and taken to be utterly void and of no force or effect—any law, statute, record, or pretence whatsoever to the contrary notwithstanding.

And be it further enacted by the authority aforesaid that no place or places within this realm of England or dominion of Wales, where no such justice seat, swainmote, or court of attachment have been held or kept, or where no verderers have been chosen or regard made, within the space of sixty years next before the first year of his majesty's reign that now is, shall be at any time hereafter judged, deemed, or taken to be forest or within the bounds or metes of the forests; but the same shall be from henceforth forever disafforested and freed and exempted from the forest laws. . . .[7]

Ibid., V, 119: 16 Charles I, c. 16.

(I) Act Abolishing Fines for Distraint of Knighthood (1641)

An act for the prevention of vexatious proceedings touching the order of knighthood.[8] . . . Be it declared and enacted by the king's most excellent majesty and the lords and commons in this parliament assembled, and by the authority of the same, that from henceforth no person or persons of what condition, quality, estate, or degree soever, shall at any time be distrained or otherwise compelled by any writ or process of the court of chancery or court of exchequer, or otherwise by any means whatsoever, to receive or take upon him or them respectively the order or dignity of knighthood; nor shall suffer or undergo any fine, trouble, or molestation whatsoever by reason or colour of his or their having not received or not taken upon him or them the said order or dignity . . . ; and that all and every process, proceeding, and charge now depending by reason or colour of the said pretended custom or writs aforesaid, or of any the dependants thereof, shall from henceforth cease, and stand, be, and remain discharged and utterly void—any former law or custom, or any pretence of any former law or custom, or any other matter whatsoever to the contrary in any wise notwithstanding.

Ibid., V, 131: 16 Charles I, c. 20.

(J) Reply of Charles I to the Commons' Petition (1641)[9]

We having received from you soon after our return out of Scot-

---

[7] Other articles provide for inquests under parliamentary commission to enforce these enactments.

[8] The preamble recites the recent exactions made for this purpose; see no. 93A.

[9] This royal letter, dated December 23, was made in answer to a petition of

land a long petition consisting of many desires of great moment, together with a declaration of a very unusual nature annexed thereunto, we had taken some time to consider of it, as befitted us in a matter of that consequence, being confident that your own reason and regard to us, as well as our express intimation by our comptroller to that purpose, would have restrained you from the publishing of it till such time as you should have received our answer to it; but, much against our expectation finding the contrary, that the said declaration is already abroad in print by directions from your house, as appears by the printed copy, we must let you know that we are very sensible of the disrespect. Notwithstanding, it is our intention that no failing on your part shall make us fail in ours of giving all due satisfaction to the desires of our people in a parliamentary way; and therefore we send your this answer to your petition, reserving ourself in point of the declaration, which we think unparliamentary, and shall take a course to do that which we shall think fit in prudence and honour.

To the petition we say that . . . there are divers things in the preamble of it which we are so far from admitting that we profess we cannot at all understand them—as of "a wicked and malignant party prevalent in the government," of "some of that party admitted to our privy council and to other employments of trust and nearest to us and our children," of "endeavours to sow among the people false scandals and imputations to blemish and disgrace the proceedings of the parliament"—all or any of them, did we know of, we should be as ready to remedy and punish as you to complain of; so that the prayers of your petition are grounded upon such premises as we must in no wise admit. Yet, notwithstanding, we are pleased to give this answer to you.

To the first, concerning religion . . . , we say that, for preserving the peace and safety of this kingdom from the design of the popish party, we have and will still concur with all the just desires of our people in a parliamentary way; that for the depriving of the bishops of their votes in parliament, we would have you consider that their right is grounded upon the fundamental law of the kingdom and constitution of parliament. . . . As for the abridging of the inordinate power of the clergy, we conceive that the taking away of the high commission court hath well moderated that; but if there continue any usurpations or excesses in their jurisdictions, we therein neither have nor will protect them. Unto that clause which concerneth corruptions (as you style them) in religion, in church government,

the house of commons, dated December 1, that accompanied the Grand Remonstrance. The latter document was a long enumeration of parliamentary grievances alleging in particular a "malignant and pernicious design of subverting the fundamental laws and principles of government" on the part of papists, certain members of the clergy, and unscrupulous courtiers. The articles of the petition, which was designed to meet the evils thus enumerated, are clearly rehearsed in the king's reply.

and in discipline and the removing of such unnecessary ceremonies as weak consciences might check at . . . , for any illegal innovations which may have crept in, we shall willingly concur in the removal of them. . . . If our parliament shall advise us to call a national synod, which may duly examine such ceremonies as give just cause of offence to any, we shall take it into consideration and apply ourself to give due satisfaction therein. . . .

To the second prayer of the petition, concerning the removal and choice of councillors, we know not any of our council to whom the character set forth in the petition can belong. . . . By those whom we had exposed to trial, we have already given you sufficient testimony that there is no man so near unto us in place or affection, whom we will not leave to the justice of the law, if you shall bring a particular charge and sufficient proofs against him. And of this we do again assure you; but in the meantime we wish you to forbear such general aspersions as may reflect upon all our council, since you name none in particular. That for the choice of our councillors and ministers of state, it were to debar us that natural liberty all freemen have; and as it is the undoubted right of the crown of England to call such persons to our secret counsels, to public employment, and our particular service as we shall think fit, so we are and ever shall be very careful to make election of such persons in those places of trust as shall have given good testimonies of their abilities and integrity, and against whom there can be no just cause of exception whereon reasonably to ground a diffidence. And to choices of this nature we assure you that the mediation of the nearest unto us hath always concurred.

To the third prayer of your petition, concerning Ireland, we understand your desire of not alienating the forfeited lands thereof to proceed from much care and love, and likewise that it may be a resolution very fit for us to take. But whether it may be seasonable to declare resolutions of that nature before the events of a war be seen, that we much doubt of. Howsoever, we cannot but thank you for this care and your cheerful engagement for the suppression of that rebellion. . . .

Rushworth Historical Collections, IV, 452 f.

(K) Orders of the Commons with Regard to Printing

[13 February 1641.] Ordered that the sub-committee heretofore appointed by the grand committee for religion concerning abuses in licensing and printing of books be now made a committee from the house and enlarged to take into consideration and examine all abuses in printing, licensing, importing, and suppressing of books of all sorts, and in denying licence to some books and expunging several passages out of other books. . . .

[28 March 1642.] Resolved upon the question that what person soever shall print, [publish, or] sell any act or passages of this house under the name of a diurnal or otherwise, without particular licence of this house, shall be reputed a high contemner and breaker of the privilege of parliament, and so punished accordingly. . . .

Journals of the Commons, II, 84, 501.

(L) Act Abolishing Temporal Power of the Clergy (1641)

An act for disenabling all persons in holy orders to exercise any temporal jurisdiction or authority. Whereas bishops and other persons in holy orders ought not to be entangled with secular jurisdiction, the office of the ministry being of such great importance that it will take up the whole man; and for that it is found by long experience that their intermeddling with secular jurisdictions hath occasioned great mischiefs and scandal both to church and state: his majesty, out of his religious care of the church, and souls of his people, is graciously pleased that it be enacted, and by authority of this present parliament be it enacted, that no archbishop or bishop or other person that now is or hereafter shall be in holy orders, shall . . . have any seat or place, suffrage, or voice, or use, or execute any power or authority in the parliaments of this realm, nor shall be of the privy council of his majesty, his heirs, or successors, or justice of the peace . . . or execute any temporal authority by virtue of any commission; but shall be wholly disabled and be incapable to have, receive, use, or execute any of the said offices, places, powers, authorities, and things aforesaid. . . .

Statutes of the Realm, V, 138: 16 Charles I, c. 27.

(M) The Militia Ordinance (1642)[10]

An ordinance of parliament for the safety and defence of the kingdom of England and dominion of Wales. Whereas there hath been of late a most dangerous and desperate design upon the house of commons, which we have just cause to believe to be an effect of the bloody counsels of papists and other ill-affected persons, who have already raised a rebellion in the kingdom of Ireland; and [whereas] by reason of many discoveries we cannot but fear they will proceed not only to stir up the like rebellion and insurrections in this kingdom of England but also to back them with forces from abroad: for the safety, therefore, of his majesty's person, the parliament, and kingdom in this time of imminent danger, it is ordained by the lords and commons now in parliament assembled, that Henry, earl of Holland, shall be lieutenant of the county of Berks; Oliver, earl of Bolingbroke, shall be lieutenant of the county of Bedford. . . .[11] And [they] shall severally and respectively have power to assemble and call together all and singular his majesty's subjects within the said several and respective counties and places, as well within liberties as

[10] When the king refused to sign this enactment in the form of a bill, it was turned into an ordinance of parliament.

[11] Similar appointments are made for the other counties.

without, that are meet and fit for the wars, and them to train and exercise and put in readiness, and them after their abilities and faculties well and sufficiently from time to time to cause to be arrayed and weaponed, and to take the muster of them in places most fit for that purpose; and . . . shall severally and respectively have power . . . to nominate and appoint such persons of quality as to them shall seem meet to be their deputy lieutenants, to be approved of by both houses of parliament; and . . . shall have power to make colonels and captains and other officers . . . as they shall think fit for that purpose; and . . . shall have power to lead, conduct and employ the persons aforesaid arrayed and weaponed, for the suppression of all rebellions, insurrections, and invasions that may happen within the several and respective counties and places; and shall have power and authority to lead, conduct, and employ the persons aforesaid arrayed and weaponed, as well within their said several and respective counties and places as within any other part of this realm of England or dominion of Wales, for the suppression of all rebellions, insurrections, and invasions that may happen, according as they from time to time shall receive directions. . . .

Journals of the Lords, IV, 587.

(N) ROYAL PROCLAMATION (27 MAY 1642)

. . . Whereas we understand that, expressly contrary to the . . . laws of this our kingdom, under colour . . . of an ordinance of parliament, without our consent or any . . . warrant from us, the trained bands and militia of this kingdom have been lately, and are intended to be, put in arms and drawn into companies in a warlike manner, whereby the peace and quiet of our subjects is or may be disturbed: we, being desirous . . . to prevent that some malignant persons in this our kingdom do not by degrees seduce our good subjects from their due obedience to us and the laws of this our kingdom . . . , do therefore, by this our proclamation, expressly charge and command all our sheriffs, and all colonels, lieutenant-colonels, sergeant-majors, captains, officers, and soldiers belonging to the trained bands of this our kingdom, and likewise all high and petty constables and other our officers and subjects whatsoever, upon their allegiance and as they tender the peace of this our kingdom, not to muster, levy, raise, or march, or to summon or warn, upon any warrant, order or ordinance from one or both our houses of parliament, whereunto we have not, or shall not, give our express consent, any of our trained bands or other forces to rise, muster, march, or exercise without express warrant under our hand or warrant from our sheriff of the county, grounded upon a particular writ to that purpose under our great seal. And in case any of our trained bands shall rise or gather together contrary to this our command, we shall then call them in due time to a strict account and proceed legally against them as violators of the laws and disturbers of the peace of this kingdom.

Ibid., V, 111 f.

(O) Declaration of the Lords and Commons (27 May 1642)

The lords and commons, having perused his majesty's proclamation forbidding all his majesty's subjects belonging to the trained bands or militia of this kingdom, to rise, march, muster, or exercise, by virtue of any order or ordinance of one or both houses of parliament without consent or warrant from his majesty, upon pain of punishment according to the laws, do thereupon declare that . . . it is acknowledged that the king is the fountain of justice and protection; but the acts of justice and protection are not exercised in his own person, nor depend upon his pleasure, but by his courts and by his ministers, who must do their duty therein though the king in his own person should forbid them. And therefore, if judgments should be given by them against the king's will and personal command, yet are they the king's judgments. The high court of parliament is not only a court of judicature, enabled by the laws to adjudge and determine the rights and liberties of the kingdom against such patents and grants of his majesty as are prejudicial thereunto, although strengthened both by his personal command and by his proclamation under the great seal; but it is likewise a council to provide for the necessities, prevent the imminent dangers, and preserve the public peace and safety of the kingdom, and to declare the king's pleasure in those things as are requisite thereunto. And what they do herein hath the stamp of the royal authority although his majesty, seduced by evil counsel, do in his own person oppose or interrupt the same; for the king's supreme and royal pleasure is exercised and declared in this high court of law and council, after a more eminent and obligatory manner than it can be by personal act or resolution of his own.

Seeing therefore the lords and commons, which are his majesty's great and high council, have ordained that, for the present and necessary defence of the realm, the trained bands and militia of this kingdom should be ordered according to that ordinance . . . , the lords and commons do require and command all constables, petty constables, and all other his majesty's officers and subjects whatsoever to muster, levy, raise, march, and exercise, or to summon or warn any, upon warrants from the lieutenants, deputy lieutenants, captains, or other officers of the trained bands, and all others, according to the said ordinance of both houses; and [they] shall not presume to muster, levy, raise, march, or exercise by virtue of any commission or other authority whatsoever, as they will answer the contrary at their perils. And in their so doing they do further declare that they shall be protected by the power and authority of both houses of parliament; and that whosoever shall oppose, question, or hinder them in the execution of the said ordinance, shall be proceeded against as violators of the laws and disturbers of the peace of the kingdom.

Ibid., V, 112 f.

(P) THE NINETEEN PROPOSITIONS (1 JUNE 1642)

Your majesty's most humble and faithful subjects, the lords and commons in parliament, having nothing in their thoughts and desires more precious and of higher esteem—next to the honour and immediate service of God—than the just and faithful performance of their duty to your majesty and this kingdom . . . , do in all humility and sincerity present to your majesty their most dutiful petition and advice, that out of your princely wisdom . . . you will be pleased to grant and accept these their humble . . . propositions, as the most necessary effectual means, through God's blessing, of removing those jealousies and differences which have unhappily fallen betwixt you and your people . . . :—

1. That the lords and others of your majesty's privy council and . . . great officers and ministers of state, either at home or beyond the seas, may be put from your privy council and from those offices and employments, excepting such as shall be approved of by both houses of parliament; and that the persons put into the places and employments of those that are removed may be approved of by both houses of parliament; and that all privy councillors shall take an oath for the due execution of their places in such form as shall be agreed upon by both houses of parliament.

2. That the great affairs of the kingdom may not be concluded or transacted by the advice of private men, or by any unknown or unsworn councillors; but that such matters as concern the public and are proper for the high court of parliament, which is your majesty's great and supreme council, may be debated, resolved, and transacted only in parliament, and not elsewhere. And such as shall presume to do anything to the contrary shall be reserved to the censure and judgment of parliament. And such other matters of state as are proper for your majesty's privy council shall be debated and concluded by such of the nobility and others as shall from time to time be chosen for that place, by approbation of both houses of parliament. And that no public act concerning the affairs of the kingdom, which are proper for your privy council, may be esteemed of any validity, as proceeding from the royal authority, unless it be done by the advice and consent of the major part of your council, attested under their hands. And that your council may be limited to a certain number, not exceeding twenty-five, nor under fifteen. And if any councillor's place happen to be void in the intervals of parliament, it shall not be supplied without the assent of the major part of the council; which choice shall be confirmed at the next sitting of parliament, or else to be void.

3. That the lord high steward of England, lord high constable, lord chancellor, or lord keeper of the great seal, lord treasurer, lord privy seal, earl marshal, lord admiral, warden of the Cinque Ports, chief governor of Ireland, chancellor of the exchequer, master of the wards, secretaries of state, two chief justices, and chief baron,

may always be chosen with the approbation of both houses of parliament. . . .

4. That he or they unto whom the government and education of the king's children shall be committed shall be approved of by both houses of parliament. . . .

5. That no marriage shall be concluded or treated for any of the king's children with any foreign prince or other person whatsoever, abroad or at home, without the consent of parliament. . . .

6. That the laws in force against Jesuits, priests, and popish recusants be strictly put in execution, without any toleration or dispensation to the contrary. . . .

7. That the votes of popish lords in the house of peers may be taken away. . . .

8. That your majesty would be pleased to consent that such a reformation be made of the church government and liturgy as both houses of parliament shall advise. . . .

9. That your majesty will be pleased to rest satisfied with that course that the lords and commons have appointed for ordering the militia until the same shall be further settled by a bill; and that your majesty will recall your declarations and proclamations against the ordinance made by the lords and commons concerning it.

10. That such members of either house of parliament as have, during this present parliament, been put out of any place and office may either be restored to that place and office or otherwise have satisfaction for the same, upon the petition of that house whereof he or they are members.

11. That all privy councillors and judges may take an oath, the form whereof to be agreed on and settled by act of parliament, for the maintaining of the Petition of Right and of certain statutes made by this parliament, which shall be mentioned by both houses of parliament. . . .

12. That all the judges and all the officers placed by approbation of both houses of parliament may hold their places *quam diu bene se gesserint.*[12]

13. That the justice of parliament may pass upon all delinquents, whether they be within the kingdom or fled out of it. . . .

14. That the general pardon offered by your majesty may be granted, with such exceptions as shall be advised by both houses of parliament.

15. That the forts and castles of this kingdom may be put under the command and custody of such persons as your majesty shall appoint with the approbation of your parliament. . . .

16. That the extraordinary guards and military forces now attending your majesty may be removed and discharged; and that for the future you will raise no such guards or extraordinary forces, but according to the law, in case of actual rebellion or invasion.

---

[12] During good behaviour.

17. That your majesty will be pleased to enter into a more strict alliance with the states of the United Provinces, and other neighbouring princes and states of the Protestant religion. . . .

18. That your majesty will be pleased, by act of parliament, to clear the lord Kimbolton and the five members of the house of commons[13] in such manner that future parliaments may be secured from the consequence of that evil precedent.

19. That your majesty will be graciously pleased to pass a bill for restraining peers made hereafter from sitting or voting in parliament, unless they be admitted thereunto with the consent of both houses of parliament.

And these our humble desires being granted by your majesty, we shall forthwith apply ourselves to regulate your present revenue in such sort as may be for your best advantage; and likewise to settle such an ordinary and constant increase of it as shall be sufficient to support your royal dignity in honour and plenty, beyond the proportion of any former grants of the subjects of this kingdom to your majesty's royal predecessors. . . .

Ibid., V, 97 f.

---

[13] The five members whom Charles had tried to arrest in the famous scene on 4 January 1642.

97. DECREE OF THE CLERGY ON REGAL POWER (1640)

Whereas sundry laws, ordinances, and constitutions have been formerly made for the acknowledgment and profession of the most lawful and independent authority of our dread sovereign lord, the king's most excellent majesty, over the state ecclesiastical and civil: we, as our duty in the first place binds us and so far as to us appertaineth, enjoin them all to be carefully observed by all persons whom they concern, upon the penalties in the said laws and constitutions expressed. And for the fuller and clearer instruction and information of all Christian people within this realm in their duties in this particular, we do further ordain and decree that every parson, vicar, curate, or preacher, upon some one Sunday in every quarter of the year at morning prayer, shall in the place where he serves treatably and audibly read these explanations of the regal power here inserted :—

The most high and sacred order of kings is of divine right, being the ordinance of God Himself, founded in the prime laws of nature, and clearly established by express texts both of the Old and New Testaments. A supreme power is given to this most excellent order by God Himself in the Scriptures, which is that kings should rule and command in their several dominions all persons of what rank or estate soever, whether ecclesiastical or civil, and that they should restrain and punish with the temporal sword all stubborn and wicked doers. . . . For any person or persons to set up, maintain, or avow in any their said realms or territories respectively, under any pretence whatsoever, any independent coactive power either papal or popular, whether directly or indirectly, is to undermine their great royal office and cunningly to overthrow that most sacred ordinance which God Himself hath established; and so is treasonable against God as well as against the king. For subjects to bear arms against their kings, offensive or defensive upon any pretence whatsoever, is at the least to resist the powers which are ordained of God; and though they do not invade but only resist, St. Paul tells them plainly they shall receive to themselves damnation. And although tribute and custom, and aid and subsidy, and all manner of necessary support and supply be respectively due to kings from their subjects by the law of God, nature, and nations, for the public defence, care, and protection of them; yet, nevertheless, subjects have not only possession of, but a true and just right, title, and property to and in all their goods and estates and ought so to have. And these two are so far from crossing one another that they mutually go together for the honourable and comfortable support of both; for, as it is the duty of the subjects to supply their king, so is it part of the kingly office to support his subjects in the property and freedom of their estates.

And if any parson, vicar, curate, or preacher shall voluntarily or carelessly neglect his duty in publishing the said explications and conclusions, according to the order above prescribed, he shall be suspended by his ordinary till such time as, upon his penitence, he shall give sufficient assurance or evidence of his amendment. And in case he be of any exempt jurisdiction, he shall be censurable by his majesty's commissioners for causes ecclesiastical. And we do also hereby require all archbishops, bishops, and all other inferior priests and ministers, that they preach, teach, and exhort their people to obey, honour, and serve their king; and that they presume not to speak of his majesty's power in any other way than in this canon is expressed. And if any parson, vicar, curate, or preacher, or any other ecclesiastical person whatsoever, any dean, canon, or prebendary of any collegiate or cathedral church, any member or student of college or hall, or any reader of divinity or humanity in either of the universities, or elsewhere, shall in any sermon, lecture, commonplace, determination, or disputation, either by word or writing, publicly maintain or abet any position or conclusion in opposition or impeachment of the aforesaid explications, or any part or article of them, he shall forthwith by the power of his majesty's commissioners for causes ecclesiastical be excommunicated till he repent, and suspended two years from all the profits of his benefice, or other ecclesiastical, academical or scholastical preferments. And if he so offend a second time, he shall be deprived from all his spiritual promotions, of what nature or degree soever they be. Provided always, that if the offence aforesaid be given in either of the universities by men not having any benefice or ecclesiastical preferment, that then the delinquent shall be censured by the ordinary authority in such cases of that university respectively where the said fault shall be committed.

Laud, *Works,* V, pt. ii, 613 f.

98. RECORDS OF LOCAL GOVERNMENT (1616-37)

(A) SPEECH OF JAMES I TO THE JUDGES (1616)

. . . Let the judges be never so careful and industrious, if the justices of peace under them put not to their helping hands, in vain is all your labour; for they are the king's eyes and ears in the country. It was an ancient custom that all the judges, both immediately before their going to their circuits and immediately upon their return, repaired to the lord chancellor of England, both to receive what directions it should please the king by his mouth to give unto them, as also to give him an account of their labours, who was to acquaint the king therewith. And this good ancient custom hath likewise been too much slacked of late. And therefore, first of all, I am to exhort and command you that you be careful to give a good account to me and my chancellor of the duties performed by all justices of peace in your circuits. Which government by justices is so laudable and so highly esteemed by me that I have made Scotland to be governed by justices and constables as England is. And let not gentlemen be ashamed of this place, for it is a place of high honour and great reputation, to be made a minister of the king's justice in service of the commonwealth. Of these are two sorts, as there is of all companies, especially where there is a great number: that is, good and bad justices. For the good, you are to inform me of them, that I may know them, thank them, and reward them as occasion serves. For I hold a good justice of peace in his country to do me as good service as he that waits upon me in my privy chamber, and as ready will I be to reward him. . . . I esteem the service done me by a good justice of peace three hundred miles—yea, six hundred miles—out of my sight as well as the service done me in my presence. For, as God hath given me large limits, so must I be careful that my providence may reach to the farthest parts of them. . . . Therefore let none be ashamed of this office, or be discouraged in being a justice of peace, if he serve worthily in it. . . .

The good justices are careful to attend the service of the king and country for thanks only of the king and love to their country, and for no other respect. The bad are . . . idle slow-bellies, that abide always at home, given to a life of ease and delight, liker ladies than men, and think it is enough to contemplate justice; whenas . . . contemplative justice is no justice, and contemplative justices are fit to be put out. Another sort of justices are busybodies, and will have all men dance after their pipe and follow their greatness, or else will not be content. . . . These proud spirits must know that the country is ordained to obey and follow God and the king, and not them. Another sort are they that go seldom to the king's service, but when it is to help some of their kindred or alliance; so as when they come it is to help their friends or hurt their enemies, making justice to serve for a shadow to faction and tumultuating the country. Another sort are gentlemen of great worth in their own conceit, and cannot be content with the present form of government; but must have a kind of liberty in the people, and must be gracious lords and redeemers of their liberty; and in every cause that concerns prerogative give a snatch against a monarchy, through their Puritanical itching after popularity. Some of them have shown themselves too bold of late in the lower house of parliament; and when all is done, if there were not a king, they would be less cared for than other men.

McIlwain, *Political Works of James I*, pp. 339 f.

(B) The Lord Keeper's Instructions to the Justices (1632)

My lords the judges: The time draweth near that you are now to enter upon your several circuits, before which I am, according to my place and duty, to declare unto you his majesty's pleasure in four things especially. . . .

First, his majesty is informed that papists and recusants that have great estates in the country have the greater favour, contrary to that which is right; which his majesty would have you to look unto, and accordingly to instruct the people of your counties in your charges.

The second thing his majesty would have you to regard and to commend to noblemen and gentlemen in the counties is that you inform them of the grounds and reasons of his majesty's now present proclamation, ready to come forth, commanding their repair to their houses in the country, and not to lie about the cities of London and Westminster, and the places adjacent. And this is necessary in these days, wherein men dispute upon proclamations, whether they should be obeyed. You know that such a thing as the pleasure of the king made known in this court was sufficient; but I persuade myself, for the ground and reasons of this his majesty's command at this time, you know better than myself what they are. Yet for the present occasion I shall name some of them. . . .

There are a multitude of precedents whereby the kings of this realm have, upon due considerations, commanded their subjects to dwell at their own houses. . . . The sheriff of every shire takes his oath to be present in his county and there dwelling. And justices of peace take such an oath that, if they be non-resident, they cannot perform. It is no discharge from their oath to live at London; but they remove hither to London, where they must of necessity live idle. They cannot govern here—that the charter of London inhibiteth. And what do they, their wives, and servants? Themselves go from ordinaries to dicing houses, and from thence to playhouses. Their wives dress themselves in the morning, visit in the afternoon, and perhaps make a journey to Hyde Park, and so home again. Their servants [go] to playhouses, brothel-houses, drunkenness, to any vice. . . . This appeareth to be an offence against many laws, and very hurtful to the common good. It is therefore a great and a gracious providence to take care to prevent it, as his majesty doth. I pray give the countries warning of this; and his majesty will give no more warning in this kind, but expecteth all men to be left without excuse by this his proclamation, if they offend against it.

There is another [proclamation], and that is for the observation of Lent and fish-days, touching which likewise he will give this as his last warning. . . . Some pretend that one meat is not holier than another, and some that their stomachs will not endure fish and therefore they are to be excused. . . . Their stomachs will not bear it, but they can sit all day long at sack and tobacco. Nay, I have heard of some that must needs drink tobacco on the bench; but, if I understand of any such hereafter, they shall not sit upon the bench any more. Some pretend that there is not fish enough. It is truth that the scarcity of fish cometh by the discouragement of fishermen. The king therefore hath very providently set out this proclamation at this time; that men may not pretend shortness of warning, but have fit time to furnish themselves, and the fishermen to provide that there may be plenty. The unsufferable resort and residence of multitudes to the city of London hath heretofore been one means to make fish the scarcer. This is intended to be remedied, and commandment shall be given to the lord mayor and aldermen that they shall see the fishmongers sell at reasonable prices. Therefore your lordships are to give a strict charge and warning that the offenders against these good laws and proclamations shall be strictly dealt withal, both here and in other courts; and you in your assizes are to deal strictly with them.

Another thing there is to be remembered: that, whereas his majesty lately set forth . . . certain orders for the execution of the laws against idle vagrants and rogues . . . , unless execution be done in all, it will but drive them from one county to another. Therefore you are likewise to enforce this upon the justices of peace and other officers, and take care it be observed.

And one thing more you are to look unto in the middle shires of the kingdom: that you suffer no enclosures tending to depopulation.

For all other things, you are to do universal justice, that his majesty may have honour and his people comfort and quiet by your industry.

Gardiner, Cases in Star Chamber and High Commission, pp. 176 f.

(C) YORKSHIRE QUARTER SESSIONS RECORDS (1610-12)

The oath of a high constable. You shall well and truly exercise your office of high constable within the wapentake of A, and duly and truly shall keep your petty sessions and receive and take all informations and presentments to you made and presented, and return and certify the same accordingly. All manner of bloodsheds, assaults, affrays, and outcries done and committed within the same wapentake according to your best knowledge you shall present; all manner of writs, warrants, and precepts to you lawfully directed you shall duly and truly execute. You shall diligently endeavour to take felons and vagabonds and do your office upon them according to the laws and statutes made and provided in that behalf. You shall inquire of the faults in all under-constables within the said wapentake and the same with their names certify to the sessions of peace next following after the same inquiry had. The king's majesty's peace in your own person you shall, as much as in you lieth, conserve and keep. And in all other things that appertain to your office you shall well and truly behave yourself. So help you God and the contents of this Book.

Petty constable's oath. You shall duly exercise your office of constable of the township of A, and well and truly present all manner of bloodsheds, assaults, and affrays, and outcries there . . . committed against the king's majesty's peace. All manner of writs, warrants, and precepts to you lawfully directed you shall truly execute. The king's majesty's peace in your own person you shall conserve and keep, as much as in you lieth. And in all other things that appertain to your office you shall well and truly behave yourself. So help you God and the contents, etc.

High constables. All and every the high constables within the North Riding shall keep precisely the orders presented unto them in calling the churchwardens and petty constables at convenient times before them between every quarter sessions, and give them several copies of the said orders or articles for 8d. a copy. And [they are] to take their presentments to every the several articles upon their oaths . . . ; and if any difficulty happen in any of their presentments, to let it be censured by the justices at the next sessions. And if there be default of presentment in any of the offices abovesaid . . . , then the same defaulters [are] to be presented by the high constables at every general quarter sessions. And the head constables for every division [are] to enter in a fair book all such presentments as they shall so receive of the petty constables from time to time; and [they] shall attend some of the justices of the division with the said book of presentments and of defaults of petty constables and churchwardens and overseers of the poor one month before every sessions, to the end that such justices, upon consideration thereof, may give order to enjoin such of the offenders to appear at the then next sessions as they shall think fit to be ordered, as to justice shall appertain. And it is ordered that every of the said officers and ministers shall carefully behave themselves therein for the good example of the commonwealth . . . , freeing the good subjects from oppression and reforming common disorders, at their . . . perils.

Orders made, etc. [at Helmsley.] Ordered that all such freeholders as hereafter shall be summoned to appear at the quarter sessions and do make default shall be fined, the gentlemen to 40s. and yeomen to 30s. apiece. By the general consent of all the justices here assembled, the next general quarter sessions for the body of the whole North Riding shall be holden at Topcliffe upon Tuesday, the 2nd day of October next; and all surveyors [and] collectors for bridges [are] then to make their account there. The several proportions for the rates of these bridges underwritten, due within Richmondshire: *viz.*, for Whitby Bridge £46. 13/4; Yafforth Bridge, £3. 6/8; Isell Bridge, £3. 6/8; Yeddingham Bridge, £3. 6/8—amounting in all to £90, with the proportion of Richmondshire for Katherick Bridge being £33. 6/8. And further it is ordered that the other £10, to make up £100, shall be paid forth of Birdforth. . . .

Whereas the sessions have been holden these two days past and adjourned with a continuance to be held and concluded tomorrow, being the twelfth day at Allerton, these are to direct clerks of the peace to be there attendant for those services. And forasmuch as the sheriff's deputy here present hath refused to disburse his majesty's allowance to the justices now present for their wages, we do therefore, and in respect of his contempt in this behalf, with one consent set upon Mr. Sheriff's head, for a fine to be presently estreated, the sum of £10—and this to be entered amongst the orders of this sessions. . . .

Orders made at this said sessions holden at Thirske. . . . Forasmuch as it doth appear unto them, upon perusal of divers sundry former orders in the sessions . . . , that there was nothing effectually performed for the erecting of the house of correction formerly intended by the said orders . . . to be seated within the town of Richmond: therefore we, his majesty's said justices, do this day further order that all former orders touching the said house shall be resumed; and that all and every of us, and as many other of the justices of peace of the North Riding as will be pleased to be present at Helmsley upon Wednesday, the 27th day of May next, by eight of the clock in the forenoon of the same day, shall then give their meeting there further to consult and conclude in what place the said house of correction shall be erected and established, with all such further due consideration both for orders, governors, ministers, and taxing, assessing, and levying of sums of money and all other things whatsoever requisite and necessary for the full accomplishment and finishing of the aforesaid house of correction, according to his majesty's laws in that case formerly made and provided. . . .

Atkinson, *Quarter Sessions Records,* I, 118, 182 f., 193-95, 254-55.

(D) WORCESTERSHIRE QUARTER SESSIONS RECORDS (1637)

[Presentment of Henry Brian, constable of Bayton.] *Imprimis,* I present Humphrey Cooke for a recusant. Item, John Timberlett doth sell ale and doth keep good order in his house, as far as rightly known. Item, our poor are provided for according to the law. Item, our highways are in good repair. Item, we have punished rogues and vagrants and presented their names to the justices of the peace at our monthly meeting. To the rest of the articles I have not any matter worthy of presentment. . . .

[Presentment by John Hunt and Nicholas Rindon, constables of Chadgsley Corbett.] For recusants we do present Richard Leayght; Mary Bach, widow; and Mary Hunt, widow; Parnell, the wife of Gregory Munk; Elizabeth, the wife of William Leight; and Elizabeth Jordan. Our poor are well and sufficiently provided for. Our highways and bridges are in good repair. Rogues and vagabonds have been punished according to law. Riots or routs or unlawful assemblies we know none. Cards and dicing or other unlawful gaming we know none. Our alehouses are all licensed. For other matters worthy to present, we know none at the present time. . . .

[Presentment of Henry Hewes and John Finchar, constables, and Robert Bolton and Thomas Hewes, churchwardens, of Feckenham and Home.] We have punished one George Stevens of Derby as a rogue and sent him away with a pass according to the law. We have punished one Matthew Garrette of Birmingham as a rogue and sent him away with a pass according to the law. We present these persons hereunder written that absent themselves from church. . . .

[Presentment by Humphrey Wright, constable of Astley.] For recusants, we have none in our parish. John Highley, the younger, sells ale without licence. For our highways, they are in repair. Our poor are well provided for according to the statute. . . .

[Presentment by Thomas Harvey, constable of Inkbarrow.] We keep watch and warding duly. Our poor are provided for by a weekly contribution. Our alehouses do keep very good order. Common drunkards we have none. I present . . for recusants. Our bridges and highways are sufficiently repaired. No tobacco planted. . . .

[Presentment by Humphrey Brian, constable of Bayton.] I do present Humphrey Cooke as a recusant. That Edward Griffen, and Robert Brian, and John Timberlette sell ale. Robert Brian hath been fined in 20s. for selling ale and he yet doth continue selling of ale, but there could be no distress found worth 20s. Our poor are relieved according to the law. Our highways are in good repair. I have punished rogues and vagrants; presented their names to the justices of the peace at our monthly meetings. I do present Humphrey Winwood and Edward Winwood for making assault and affray and bloodshed upon me, being constable about the king's business, and swearing many grievous oaths they would beat me blind. Our watch and ward hath been duly kept, but William Whopper and Humphrey Winwood, being warned by me to watch, told me they would not and were as good as their words. I do present Edward Ashcrotte and John Hill for an affray and bloodshed. . . .

[Presentment by the constable of the township of St. John Bedwardine.] That there are no taverners, vintners, nor cooks; nor any baker that sell above the rate of thirteen to the dozen. That there are none that exceed the rate of 2s. a meal for the master, or above 8d. a meal for his servant attending him. That no unlawful games are used in the victualling houses, as far as our knowledge extends to know. That no inn-keeper exceeds the rate of 6*d.* a peck for oats, or 2*d.* for standing a horse at hay for the space of a day. That we know of none that doth harbour or lodge any vagabond rogues or suspected persons within our township. That no rogues or vagabonds do wander, to our knowledge, or do pass unpunished. That watch and ward hath been duly kept, as far as we know. That George Wigfall, Richard Frewin, Philip Callow, John Deakins, and Widow Hopkins are licensed ale-sellers, and John Webb unlicensed. That no victuallers do suffer any drinking in the time of divine service, or unreasonable times in the night. That we know of no inordinate haunts of tippling or drinking within our township. . . . That the highways and bridges are sufficiently mended and repaired within our township. That no loafers have passed unpunished through our default or neglect.

Worcestershire Quarter Sessions Papers, I, 638-45.

99. RECORDS CONCERNING VIRGINIA (1606-25)

(A) JAMES I: CHARTER TO THE VIRGINIA COMPANY (1606)

James, by the grace of God king of England, Scotland, France, and Ireland, defender of the faith, etc. Whereas our loving and well-disposed subjects, Sir Thomas Gates and Sir George Somers, knights; Richard Hackluit, clerk, prebendary of Westminster; and Edward Maria Wingfield, Thomas Hanham, and Ralegh Gilbert, esquires; William Parker and George Popham, gentlemen, and divers others of our loving subjects have been humble suitors unto us that we would vouchsafe unto them our licence to make habitation, plantation, and to deduce a colony of sundry of our people into that part of America commonly called Virginia . . . , situate, lying, and being all along the sea-coasts between four-and-thirty degrees of northerly latitude from the equinoctial line and five-and-forty degrees of the same latitude . . . ; and to that end, and for the more speedy accomplishment of their said intended plantation and habitation there, are desirous to divide themselves into two several colonies and companies— the one consisting of certain knights, gentlemen, merchants, and other adventurers of our city of London and elsewhere . . . , which do desire to begin their plantation and habitation in some fit and convenient place between four-and-thirty and one-and-forty degrees of the said latitude alongst the coasts of Virginia and the coasts of America aforesaid; and the other consisting of sundry knights, gentlemen, merchants, and other adventurers of our cities of Bristol and Exeter, and of our town of Plymouth, and of other places . . . , which do desire to begin their plantation and habitation in some fit and convenient place between eight-and-thirty degrees and five-and-forty degrees of the said latitude . . . .—we, greatly commending . . . so noble a work . . . , do by these our letters patent graciously accept of and agree to their humble and well-intended desires. . . .

And we do also ordain, establish, and agree, for us, our heirs, and successors, that each of the said colonies shall have a council, which shall govern and order all matters and causes which shall arise, grow, or happen to or within the same several colonies, according to such laws, ordinances, and instructions as shall be, in that behalf, given and signed with our hand or sign manual and pass under the privy seal of our realm of England; each of which councils shall consist of thirteen persons, to be ordained, made, and removed from time to time, according as shall be directed and comprised in the same instructions . . . ; and that also there shall be a council established here in England which shall . . . consist of thirteen persons to be for that purpose appointed by us, our heirs, and successors, which shall be called our Council of Virginia, and shall from time to time have the superior managing and direction . . . for all matters that shall or may concern the government as well of the said several colonies as of . . . any other . . . place within the aforesaid precincts. . . .

Also we do, for us, our heirs, and successors, declare by these presents that all and every the persons, being our subjects, which shall dwell and inhabit within every or any of the said several colonies and plantations, and every of their children which shall happen to be born within any of the limits and precincts of the said several colonies and plantations, shall have and enjoy all liberties, franchises and immunities within any of our other dominions to all intents and purposes as if they had been abiding and born within this our realm of England, or any other of our said dominions. . . .

Poore, Constitutions, II, 1888 f.

(B) Ordinance of the Virginia Council (1621)

An ordinance and constitution of the treasurer, council, and company in England, for a council of state and general assembly. To all people to whom these presents shall come . . . the treasurer, council, and company of adventurers and planters for the city of London for the first colony of Virginia send greeting. Know ye that we . . . , taking into our careful consideration the present state of the said colony of Virginia and intending by the divine assistance to settle such a form of government there as may be to the greatest benefit and comfort of the people . . . , have thought fit to make our entrance by ordering and establishing such supreme councils as may not only be assisting to the governor for the time being . . . , but also by their vigilant care and prudence may provide as well for a remedy of all inconveniences . . . as also for advancing of increase, strength, stability, and prosperity of the said colony.

We therefore . . . , by authority directed to us from his majesty under the great seal . . . , do hereby order and declare that from henceforward there shall be two supreme councils in Virginia. . . . The one of which councils, to be called the council of state—and whose office shall chiefly be assisting with their care, advice, and circumspection to the said governor—shall be chosen, nominated, placed, and displaced . . . by us, the said treasurer, council, and company . . . , and this council to be always or for the most part residing about or near the governor. The other council, more generally to be called by the governor once yearly, and no oftener but for very extraordinary and important occasions, shall consist for the present of the said council of state, and of two burgesses out of every town, hundred, or other particular plantation, to be respectively chosen by the inhabitants; which council shall be called the general assembly, wherein, as also in the said council of state, all matters shall be decided . . . by the greater part of the voices then present, reserving to the governor always a negative voice. And this general assembly shall have free power to treat, consult, and conclude as well of all emergent occasions concerning the public weal of the said colony . . . as also to make, ordain, and enact such general laws and orders for the behoof of the said colony . . . as shall . . . appear necessary or requisite. . . . We require the said general assembly, as also the said council of state, to imitate and follow the policy of the form of government, laws, customs, and manner of trial, and other administration of justice used in the realm of England as near as may be. . . .

Provided that no law or ordinance made in the said general assembly shall be or continue in force or validity unless the same shall be solemnly ratified and confirmed in a general quarter court of the said company here in England. . . .

Stith, *History of Virginia,* App. 4.

(C) Charles I: Proclamation concerning Virginia (1625)

Whereas the colony of Virginia, planted by the hands of our most dear father of blessed memory for the propagation of Christian religion, the increase of trade, and the enlarging of his royal empire, hath not hitherto prospered so happily as was hoped and desired . . . , and therefore his late majesty . . . did desire to resume that popular government and accordingly the letters patent . . . were . . . questioned and thereupon judicially repealed and adjudged to be void . . . ; and whereas we continue the like care of those colonies and plantations as our late dear father did, and . . . are of the same judgment that our said father was of for the government of that colony of Virginia . . . : we have thought fit to declare, and by our royal proclamation to publish, our own judgment and resolution in these things . . . , and therefore we . . . declare . . . that we hold those territories of Virginia and of the Summer Islands, as also that of New England, where our colonies are already planted . . . , to be a part of our royal empire descended upon us and undoubtedly belonging and appertaining unto us . . . ; and that our full resolution is that there may be one uniform course of government in and through all our whole monarchy; that the government of the colony of Virginia shall immediately depend upon ourself, and not be com-

mitted to any company or corporation—to whom it may be proper
to trust matters of trade and commerce, but cannot be fit or safe to
communicate the ordering of state affairs, be they of never so mean
consequence. . . .

We do hereby declare that we are resolved . . . to establish a
council consisting of a few persons of understanding and quality, to
whom we will give trust for the immediate care of the affairs of that
colony . . . ; also . . . another council to be resident in Virginia,
who shall be subordinate to our council here for that colony. . . .

Rymer, Foedera, XVIII, 72 f.

SAINTS' DAYS AND OTHER FESTIVALS
MENTIONED IN THE FOREGOING DOCUMENTS

All Saints: 1 November
All Souls: 2 November
Annunciation of the Virgin, The: 25 March
Ascension of the Lord, The: the fortieth day after Easter
Ash Wednesday: the first day of Lent
Assumption of the Virgin, The: 15 August
Bartholomew, St.: 24 August
Candlemas: 2 February
Chair of St. Peter, The: 18 January
Close of Easter, The: the Sunday after Easter
Conception of the Virgin, The: 8 December
Corpus Christi: the first Thursday after Trinity Sunday
Cuthbert, St.: 20 March
Dunstan, St.: 19 May
Easter: the first Sunday after the first full moon after the vernal
  equinox (21 March)
Edmund the King, St.: 20 November
Edward the Confessor, St.: 13 October
Epiphany: 6 January
Exaltation of the Holy Cross, The: 14 September
Faith, St.: 1 August
Giles, St.: 1 September
Gregory the Great, St.: 3 November
Helen, St.: 18 August
Hilary, St.: 13 January
Hokeday: the second Tuesday after Easter
James the Apostle, St.: 25 July
John, St.: 27 December
John the Baptist, St.: 24 June
Lent: the forty week-days preceding Easter
Martin, St.: 12 November
Matthew, St.: 21 September
Michael, St. (Michaelmas): 29 September
Mid-Lent: the fourth Sunday in Lent
Nativity of the Lord, The (Christmas): 25 December

Nativity of the Virgin, The: 8 September
Pentecost: the seventh Sunday after Easter
Peter and Paul, Sts.: 29 June
Purification of the Virgin, The: 2 February
Rogation Days: the three days before the feast of the Ascension
Simon and Jude, Sts.: 28 October
Stephen, St.: 26 December
Thomas the Martyr, St.: 6 September
Trinity, The Holy: the eighth Sunday after Easter
Vincent, the Martyr, St.: 22 January
Whitsuntide (Whit Sunday): the seventh Sunday after Easter

BIBLIOGRAPHY

Acts of the Privy Council. New Series. London, 1890———.

Adams, G. B. *Constitutional History of England.* Revised. edition, by R. L. Schuyler. New York, 1934.

Adams, G. B. *Council and Courts in Anglo-Norman England.* New Haven, Conn., 1926.

Adams, G. B. *The Origin of the English Constitution.* New edition. New Haven, Conn. 1920.

American Historical Review, The. New York, 1895———.

Amos, M. *The English Constitution.* London, 1930.

Anniversary Essays in Mediaeval History by Students of C. H. Haskins. Boston, 1929.

Anonimalle Chronicle, The. Edited by V. H. Galbraith. Manchester, 1927.

Anson, W. R. *The Law and Custom of the Constitution.* Fourth edition. 2 vols. Oxford, 1935.

Archaeologia Aeliana. Fourth Series Newcastle-upon-Tyne, 1925———.

Atkinson, J. C. (editor). *Quarter Sessions Records.* North Riding Record Society, vol. I-IX. London, 1884-92.

Attenborough, F. L. (editor). *The Laws of the Earliest English Kings.* Cambridge, 1922.

Aylmer, G. E. *The King's Servants: the Civil Service of Charles I.* London, 1961.

Baildon, W. P. (editor). *Select Cases in Chancery, 1364-1471.* Selden Society, vol. X. London, 1896.

Baker, R. L. *The English Customs Service, 1307-1343.* Philadelphia, 1961.

Baldwin, J. F. *The King's Council in England during the Middle Ages.* Oxford, 1913.

Ballard, A., and Tait, J. (editors). *British Borough Charters.* 2 vols. Cambridge, 1913-22.

Barlow, F. *The English Church, 1000-1066: A Constitutional History.* Hamden, Conn., 1963.

Bateson, M. (editor). *Borough Customs.* Selden Society, vols. XVIII, XXI. London, 1904-06.

Bateson, M. (editor). *Records of the Borough of Leicester, 1103-1603.* 3 vols. Cambridge, 1899-1905.

Baumer, F. L. V. *Early Tudor Theory of Kingship*. New Haven, Conn., 1940.

Bigelow, M. M. (editor). *Placita Anglo-Normannica*. Boston, 1879.

Bindoff, S. T. *et al.* (editors). *Elizabethan Government and Society: Essays presented to Sir John Neale*. London, 1961.

Birch, W. de Gray (editor). *Cartularium Saxonicum*. 3 vols. London, 1885-93.

Black, J. B. *The Reign of Elizabeth, 1558-1603*. Oxford, 1959.

Boussard, J. *Le gouvernment d'Henri II, Plantagenet*. Paris, 1956.

Brady, R. *An Historical Treatise of Cities and Burghs or Boroughs*. New edition. London, 1777.

Bristol Record Society Publications. Bristol, 1930——.

Brunton, D., and Pennington, D. H. *Members of the Long Parliament*. London, 1954.

Calendar of the Charter Rolls. Rolls Series. London, 1903——.

Calendar of the Patent Rolls. Rolls Series. London, 1891——.

Calendar of Treasury Books. Rolls Series. London, 1904——.

Cam, H. M. *The Hundred and the Hundred Rolls*. London, 1930.

Cam, H. M. *Law Finders and Law Makers in Medieval England: Collected Studies in Legal and Constitutional History*. New York, 1963.

Cam, H. M. *The Legislation of Medieval England*. London, 1945.

Cam, H. M. *Local Government in Francia and England*. London, 1912.

Cam, H. M. *Studies in the Hundred Rolls*. Oxford, 1921.

Cambridge Medieval History, The. 8 vols. Cambridge, 1911-36.

Cantor, N. F. *Church, Kingship, and Lay Investiture, 1089-1135*. Princeton, N.J., 1958.

Chadwick, H. M. *Studies on Anglo-Saxon Institutions*. Cambridge, 1905.

Charters Granted to the East India Company from 1601. London, 1773.

Cheney, C. R. *From Becket to Langton: English Church Government, 1170-1216*. Manchester, 1956.

Cheyney, E. P. *History of England from the Defeat of the Spanish Armada to the Death of Elizabeth*. 2 vols. New York, 1914-26.

Chrimes, S. B. *English Constitutional Ideas in the Fifteenth Century*. Cambridge, 1935.

Chrimes, S. B. *Introduction to the Administrative History of Medieval England*. London, 1959.

Chrimes, S. B., and Brown, A. L. *Select Documents of English Constitutional History, 1307-1485*. New York, 1961.

Clarke, M. V. *Medieval Representation and Consent*. London, 1936.

Close Rolls of the Reign of Henry III. Rolls Series. London, 1902——.

Coke, Sir Edward. *Institutes of the Laws of England*. 4 vols. London, 1628-44.

Coke, Sir Edward. *Reports*. (See *English Reports*.)

Collections for a History of Staffordshire. William Salt Archaeological Society. New Series. London, 1898——.

Cross, C. *The Royal Supremacy in the Elizabethan Church*. London, 1969.

Davies, E. T. *Episcopacy and the Royal Supremacy in the Church of England in the Twentieth Century*. Oxford, 1950.

Davies, G. *Bibliography of British History: Stuart Period*. Oxford, 1928.

Davies, G. *The Early Stuarts, 1603-1660*. Oxford, 1959.

Davies, J. C. *The Baronial Opposition to Edward II*. Cambridge, 1918.

Davis, H. W. C. (editor). *Regesta Regum Anglo-Normannorum, 1066-1154*. Vol. I. Oxford, 1913.

Denholme-Young, N. *Seignorial Administration in England*. Oxford, 1937.

D'Ewes, Simonds. *Journals of All the Parliaments during the Reign of Queen Elizabeth*. London, 1682.

Dialogus de Scaccario. Edited by C. G. Crump, A. Hughes, and C. Johnson. Oxford, 1902.

Dicey, A. V. *Introduction to the Study of the Law of the Constitution*. London, 1902.

Domesday Book seu Liber Censualis Wilhelmi Primi Regis Angliae. Record Commission. 2 vols. London, 1783.

Dunham, W. H., Jr. *Lord Hastings' Indentured Retainers, 1461-1483: The Lawlessness of Livery and Retaining under the Yorkists and Tudors*. New Haven, Conn., 1955.

Edwards, J. G. *The Commons in Medieval English Parliaments*. London, 1958.

Elton, G. R. *The Tudor Constitution: Documents and Commentary*. Cambridge, 1960.

Elton, G. R. *The Tudor Revolution in Government*. Cambridge, 1953.

Elyot, Thomas. *The Boke Named the Governour.* Edited by H. H. S. Croft. 2 vols. London, 1883.

English Historical Documents (general editor, D. C. Douglas). Vols. I, II, IV, V. London, 1955-69.

English Historical Review, The. London, 1886——.

English Reports, The. 176 vols. Edinburgh, 1900-30. (A full reprint with the paging of the original editions, to which paging reference is made in the foregoing citations.)

Evans, F. M. G. *The Principal Secretary of State.* Manchester, 1923.

Finberg, H. P. R. *The Early Charters of Wessex.* Leicester, 1964.

Finn. R. W. *Domesday Studies: The Liber Exoniensis.* Hamden, Conn., 1964.

Finn, R. W. *The Domesday Inquest and the Making of Domesday Book.* London, 1961.

Fortescue, Sir John. *De Laudibus Legum Angliae.* Edited and translated by S. B. Chrimes. Cambridge, 1942.

Fortescue, Sir John. *The Governance of England.* Edited by C. Plummer. Oxford, 1885.

Furnivall, F. J. (editor). *Life Records of Chaucer.* Chaucer Society. London, 1876.

Galbraith, V. H. *The Making of Domesday Book.* Oxford, 1961.

Ganshof, F. L. *Feudalism.* Translated by P. Greison. London, 1952.

Gardiner, S. R. (editor). *Constitutional Documents of the Puritan Revolution, 1625-1660.* Third edition. Oxford, 1906.

Gardiner, S. R. *History of England . . . , 1603-1642.* 10 vols. London, 1883-85.

Gardiner, S. R. (editor). *Parliamentary Debates in 1610.* Camden Society, vol. LXXXI. London, 1862.

Gardiner, S. R. (editor). *Reports of Cases in the Courts of Star Chamber and High Commission.* Camden Society, New Series, vol. XXXIX. London, 1886.

Gee, H., and Hardy, W. T. (editors). *Documents Illustrative of English Church History.* London, 1896.

Glanville, Ranulf de. *Tractatus de Legibus et Conseutudinibus Regni Angliae.* Edited by G. E. Woodbine. New Haven, Conn., 1932.

Gooch, G. P. *English Democratic Ideas in the Seventeenth Century.* Second edition, by H. J. Laski. Cambridge, 1927.

Gough, J. W. *Fundamental Law in English Constitutional History.* Oxford, 1955.

Gras, N. S. B. *The Early English Customs System*. Cambridge, Mass., 1918.

Gray, H. L. *The Influence of the Commons on Early Legislation*. Cambridge, Mass., 1932.

Green, V. H. *The Later Plantagenets*. London, 1955.

Grose, F. *Military Antiquities Respecting a History of the English Army*. New edition. 2 vols. London, 1801.

Gross, C. *The Gild Merchant*. 2 vols. Oxford, 1890.

Gross, C. (editor). *Select Cases from Coroners' Rolls, 1270-1638*. Selden Society, vol. IX. London, 1896.

Hakluyt, R. *Principal Navigations.* . . . Hakluyt Society. 12 vols. Glasgow, 1903-05.

Halmota Prioratus Dunelmensis. Surtees Society, vol. LXXXII. Durham, 1889.

Hamilton, N. E. S.A. (editor). *Inquisitio Comitatus Cantabrigiensis*. Royal Society of Literature. London, 1876.

Harding, N. D. (editor). *Bristol Charters, 1155-1373*. Bristol Record Society, vol. I. Bristol, 1930.

Harland, J. *The Lancashire Lieutenancy*. Chetham Society, vols. XLIX-L. Manchester, 1859.

Hart, C. R. *The Early Charters of Eastern England*. Leicester, 1966.

Hastings, Margaret. *The Court of Common Pleas in Fifteenth-Century England: A Study of Legal Administration and Procedure*. Ithaca, N.Y., 1947.

Hatsell, J. Precedents and Proceedings in the House of Commons. 4 vols. Dublin, 1786-96.

Historical Essays in Honour of James Tait. Manchester, 1933.

Hodgkin, R. H. *History of the Anglo-Saxons*. 2 vols. Oxford, 1952.

Holdsworth, W. S. A History of English Law. 16 vols. London, 1956——.

Hollister, C. W. *Anglo-Saxon Military Institutions on the Eve of the Norman Conquest*. Oxford, 1962.

Hollister, C. W. *The Military Organization of Norman England*. Oxford, 1965.

Holt, J. C. *Magna Carta*. Cambridge, 1965.

Howell, M. *Regalian Right in Medieval England*. London, 1962.

Howell, T. B. (editor). *A Complete Collection of State Trials to 1783; Continued to the Present Time*. Second edition. 33 vols. London, 1816-26.

Hughes, P. L., and Larkin, J. F. (editors). *Tudor Royal Proclamations*. 3 vols. London, 1964-69.

Hunnisett, R. F. *The Medieval Coroner*. Cambridge, 1961.

Jacob, E. F. *The Fifteenth Century, 1399-1485*. Oxford, 1961.

Jenkinson, H., and Formoy, B. E. R. (editors). *Select Cases in the Exchequer of Pleas*. Selden Society, vol. XLVIII. London, 1932.

Johnson, C. *The Course of the Exchequer by Richard, Son of Nigel. (Dialogue of the Exchequer)*. London, 1950.

Jolliffe, J. E. A. *Angevin Kingship*. London, 1955.

Jolliffe, J. E. A. *The Constitutional History of Medieval England*. London, 1954.

Journals of the House of Commons. 117 vols. London, 1803-63.

Journals of the House of Lords. 119 vols. London,   -1887.

Judson, M. A. *The Crisis of the Constitution: An Essay in Constitutional and Political Thought in England, 1603-1645*. Rutgers, N.J., 1949.

Kantorowicz, H. *Bractonian Problems*. Glasgow, 1941.

Kantorowicz, H. *The King's Two Bodies: A Study in Medieval Theology*. Princeton, N.J., 1957.

Keller, Mary F. *The Long Parliament*. Philadelphia, 1954.

Keeton, B. C. *Judgment by Peers*. Cambridge, Mass., 1949.

Keeton, G. W. *The Norman Conquest and the Common Law*. New York, 1966.

Keir, D. L. *Constitutional History of Modern Britain*. London, 1961.

Kemble, J. M. (editor). *Codex Diplomaticus Aevi Saxonici*. English Historical Society. 6 vols. London, 1839-48.

Kern, F. *Kingship and Law in the Middle Ages*. Edited and translated by S. B. Chrimes. Oxford, 1939.

Lambarde, W. *Archeion: or a Discourse upon the High Courts of Justice in England*. Edited by C. H. McIlwain and P. L. Ward. Cambridge, Mass., 1957.

Lambarde, W. *Eirenarcha, or the Office of the Justices of Peace*. London, 1581.

Lapsley, G. *Crown, Community and Parliament in the Later Middle Ages: Studies in English Constitutional History*. Edited by H. M. Cam and G. Barraclough. Oxford, 1951.

Laud, William. *Works*. Edited by W. Scott and J. Bliss. 7 vols. Oxford, 1847-60.

Leadam, I. S. (editor). *Select Cases before the King's Council in the Star Chamber, A.D. 1477-1544.* Selden Society, vols. XVI, XXV. London, 1903-11.

Leadam, I. S., and Baldwin, J. F. (editors). *Select Cases before the King's Council, 1243-1482.* Selden Society, vol. XXXV. London, 1918.

Lehmberg, S. E. *Sir Walter Mildmay and Tudor Government.* Austin, Tex., 1964.

Levine, M. *The Early Elizabethan Succession Question, 1558-1568.* Stanford Calif., 1966.

Liber Niger Scaccarii. Edited by T. Hearne. Oxford, 1728.

Liebermann, F. (editor). *Gesetze der Angelsachsen.* 3 vols. Halle, Ger., 1903-16.

Liebermann, F. *The National Assembly in the Anglo-Saxon Period.* Halle, Ger., 1913.

Lodge, E. C., and Thornton, G. A. (editors). *English Constitutional Documents, 1307-1485.* Cambridge, 1935.

Lunt, W. E. *The Financial Relations of the Papacy with England to 1327.* Cambridge, Mass., 1939.

Lyon, B. *A Constitutional and Legal History of Medieval England.* New York: 1960.

Lyon, B. *From Fief to Indenture: the Transition from Feudal to Non-Feudal Contract in Western Europe.* Cambridge, Mass., 1957.

Mackie, J. D. *The Earlier Tudors, 1485-1558.* Oxford, 1952.

Magna Carta Commemoration Essays. Royal Historical Society. London, 1917.

Maitland, F. W. *Constitutional History of England.* Edited by H. A. L. Fisher. Cambridge, 1961.

Maitland, F. W. *Domesday Book and Beyond.* Cambridge, 1897.

Maitland, F. W. (editor). *Memoranda de Parliamento.* Rolls Series. London, 1893.

Maitland, F. W. (editor). *Select Pleas of the Crown, 1200-1225.* Selden Society, vol. I. London, 1888.

Maitland, F. W. (editor). *Select Pleas in Manorial and Other Seignorial Courts.* Selden Society, vol. II. London, 1889.

Maitland, F. W. (editor). *Three Rolls of the King's Court, 1194-1195.* Pipe Roll Society, vol. XIV. London, 1891.

Marcham, F. G. *Constitutional History of Modern England, 1485 to the Present.* New York, 1960.

McIlwain, C. H. *The High Court of Parliament and Its Supremacy.* New Haven, Conn., 1910.

McIlwain, C. H. (editor). *Political Works of James I.* Cambridge, Mass., 1918.

McKechnie, W. S. *Magna Carta.* Second edition. Glasgow, 1914.

McKisack, M. *The Fourteenth Century: 1307-1399.* Oxford, 1959.

McKisack, M. *The Parliamentary Representation of the English Boroughs during the Middle Ages.* London, 1932.

Mitchell, S. K. *Studies in Taxation under John and Henry III.* New Haven, Conn., 1914.

Mitchell, S. K. *Taxation in Medieval England.* Edited by S. Painter. New Haven, Conn., 1951.

More, Thomas. *Utopia.* Edited and translated by J. H. Lupton. Oxford, 1895.

Morris, W. A. *The Early English County Court.* Berkeley, 1926.

Morris, W. A. *The Frankpledge System.* London, 1910.

Morris, W. A. *The Mediaeval English Sheriff to 1300.* Manchester, 1927.

Mosse, G. L. *The Struggle for Sovereignty in England: From the Reign of Queen Elizabeth to the Petition of Right.* East Lansing, Mich., 1950.

Munimenta Gildhallae Londoniensis. Edited by H. T. Riley. Rolls Series. 3 vols. London, 1859-62.

Murray, K. M. E. *Constitutional History of the Cinque Ports.* Manchester, 1935.

Myers, A. R. *The Household of Edward IV.* Manchester, 1959.

Neale, J. E. *Elizabeth I and Her Parliaments, 1559-1581.* London, 1953.

Neale, J. E. *Elizabeth and Her Parliaments, 1581-1602.* London, 1957.

Neale, J. E. *The Elizabethan House of Commons.* London, 1949.

Nicholas, E. *Proceedings and Debates in the House of Commons in 1620 and 1621.* 2 vols. Oxford, 1766.

Nicolas, H. *Proceedings and Ordinances of the Privy Council of England.* Record Commission. 7 vols. London, 1834-37.

Notestein, W. (editor). *The Journal of Sir Simonds D'Ewes.* New Haven, Conn., 1923.

Notestein, W., and Relf, F. H. (editors). *Commons Debates for 1629.* Minneapolis, Minn., 1921.

Notestein, W., Relf, F. H., and Simpson, H. (editors). *Commons Debates, 1621.* 7 vols. New Haven, Conn., 1935.

Ogilvie, C. *The King's Government and the Common Law, 1471-1641*. Oxford, 1958.

Oleson, T. *The Witenagemot in the Reign of Edward the Confessor*. Toronto, 1955.

Oliver, G. (editor). *Monasticon Dioecesis Exoniensis*. Exeter, 1846.

Otway, R. *The King's Secretary and Signet Office in the Fifteenth Century*. Cambridge, 1939.

Oxford Essays in Mediaeval History Presented to H. E. Salter. Oxford, 1934.

Page, W. *London: Its Origin and Early Development*. London, 1929.

Painter, S. *The Rise of the Feudal Monarchies*. Ithaca, N.Y., 1951.

Palgrave, F. (editor). *Parliamentary Writs*. Record Commission. 2 vols. London, 1827-34.

Pasquet, D. *Essays on the Origins of the English House of Commons*. Translated by R. G. D. Laffan, with a preface and notes by G. Lapsley. Cambridge, 1925.

Patent Rolls, 1216-1225. Rolls Series. London, 1901.

Petit-Dutaillis, C., and Lefebvre, G. *Studies and Notes Supplementary to Stubbs' Constitutional History*. 3 vols. Manchester, 1930.

Pickthorn, K. W. M. *Early Tudor Government: Henry VII*. Cambridge, 1934.

Pickthorn, K. W. M. *Early Tudor Government: Henry VIII*. Cambridge, 1934.

Pike, L. O. *Constitutional History of the House of Lords*. London, 1894.

Pipe Roll of 31 Henry I. Record Commission. London, 1833. Reprinted by the Pipe Roll Society. London, 1929.

Pipe Roll of 33 Henry II. Pipe Roll Society, vol. XXXVII. London, 1915.

Plucknett, T. F. T. *Concise History of the Common Law*. London, 1955.

Plucknett, T. F. T. *Legislation of Edward I*. Oxford, 1949.

Plucknett, T. F. T. *Statutes and Their Interpretation in the First Half of the Fourteenth Century*. Cambridge, 1922.

Pocock, J. G. A. *The Ancient Constitution and the Feudal Law: A Study in English Historical Thought in the Seventeenth Century*. Cambridge, 1957.

Pollard, A. F. *England under Protector Somerset.* London, 1900.

Pollard, A. F. *The Evolution of Parliament.* London, 1920.

Pollock, F., and Maitland, F. W. *History of English Law.* Second edition. 2 vols. Cambridge, 1899.

Poole, A. L. *From Domesday Book to Magna Carta,* Oxford, 1951.

Poole, A. L. *Obligations of Society in the Twelfth and Thirteenth Centuries.* Oxford, 1946.

Poole, R. L. *The Exchequer in the Twelfth Century.* Oxford, 1912.

Post, G. *Studies in Medieval Thought, Public Law, and the State, 1100-1322.* Princeton, N.J., 1964.

Powell, J. E., and Wallis, K. *The House of Lords in the Middle Ages.* London, 1968.

Powicke, Sir Maurice. *King Henry III and the Lord Edward: Community of the Realm in the Thirteenth Century.* 2 vols. Oxford, 1947.

Powicke, Sir Maurice. *The Thirteenth Century, 1216-1307.* Oxford, 1962.

Proceedings of the British Academy. London, 1903——.

Prothero, G. W. (editor). *Select Statutes and Other Constitutional Documents Illustrative of the Reigns of Elizabeth and James I.* Oxford, 1894.

Putnam, B. H. *The Place in Legal History of Sir William Shareshull, Chief Justice of the King's Bench, 1350-1361. A Study of Judicial and Administrative Method in the Reign of Edward III.* London, 1950.

Putnam, B. H. *Proceedings before the Justices of the Peace in the Fourteenth and Fifteenth Centuries.* London, 1938.

Read, C. *Bibliography of British History: Tudor Period, 1485-1603.* Oxford, 1959.

Red Book of the Exchequer, The. Edited by H. Hall. Rolls Series. 3 vols. London, 1896.

Redlich, J., and Hirst, F. W. *Local Government in England.* 2 vols. London, 1903.

Reid, R. R. *The King's Council in the North.* London, 1921.

Relf, F. H. *The Petition of Right.* Minneapolis, Minn., 1917.

Reports from the Lords' Committees . . . Touching the Dignity of a Peer. 5 vols. London, 1820-29.

Reports of State Trials. New Series. 8 vols. London, 1888-98.

Reppy, A. *The Ordinance of William the Conqueror, 1072: Its Implication in the Law of Succession.* New York, 1954.

Richardson, H. G., and Sayles, G. *The Governance of Medieval England from the Conquest to Magna Carta.* Edinburgh, 1963.

Richardson, H. G., and Sayles, G. *Rotuli Parliamentorum Anglie hactenus Inediti, MCCLXXIX-MCCCLXXIII.* Camden Society, Third Series, vol. LI. London, 1935.

Richardson, W. C. *The History of the Court of Augmentations, 1536-1554.* Baton Rouge, La., 1961

Richardson, W. C. *Tudor Chamber Administration.* Baton Rouge, La., 1952.

Robertson, A. J. (editor). *Anglo-Saxon Charters.* Cambridge, 1939.

Robertson, A. J. (editor). *The Laws of the Kings of England from Edmund to Henry I.* Cambridge, 1925.

Roskell, J. S. *The Commons and Their Speakers in English Parliaments, 1376-1523.* Manchester, 1965.

Roskell, J. S. *The Commons in the Parliament of 1422: English Society and Parliamentary Representation under the Lancastrians.* Manchester, 1954.

Roskell, J. S. *The Knights of the Shire for the County Palatine of Lancaster, 1377-1460.* Manchester, 1937.

Rotuli de Liberate ac de Misie et Praestitis Regnante Johanne. Record Commission. London, 1844.

Rotuli Litterarum Clausarum. Record Commission. 2 vols. London, 1833-44.

Rotuli Litterarum Patentium, 1201-1216. Record Commission. London, 1835.

Rotuli Parliamentorum. 6 vols. (London, 1776-1777.)

Round, J. H. (editor). *Ancient Charters, Royal and Private, Prior to 1200.* Pipe Roll Society, vol. X. London, 1888.

Round, J. H. *The Commune of London and Other Studies.* Westminster, 1899.

Round, J. H. *Feudal England.* London, 1895.

Round, J. H. *Geoffrey de Mandeville.* London, 1892.

Round, J. H. *The King's Serjeants and Officers of State.* London, 1911.

Round, J. H. *Studies on the Red Book of the Exchequer.* London, 1898.

Rushworth, J. (editor). *Historical Collections, 1618-1648.* 8 vols. London, 1721.

Rymer, T. (editor). *Foedera, Conventiones, Litterae, et . . . Acta Publica.* . . . 20 vols. London, 1704-35. (Vols. XVI-XX edited by A. Sanderson.)

Sanders, I. J. *English Baronies: A Study of Their Origin and Descent, 1086-1327.* Oxford, 1960.

Sanders, I. J. *Feudal Military Service in England: A Study of the Constitutional and Military Powers of the Barones in Medieval England.* Oxford, 1956.

Sayles, G. O. *The Medieval Foundations of England.* London, 1950.

Sayles, G. O. (editor). *Select Cases in the Court of King's Bench under Edward I.* Selden Society, vol. LV. London, 1936.

Sheehan, M. M. *The Will in Medieval England from the Conversion of the Anglo-Saxons to the End of the Thirteenth Century.* Toronto, 1963.

Simpson, A. W. B. *An Introduction to the History of Land Law.* Oxford, 1961.

Smith, H. M. *Henry VIII and the Reformation.* London, 1948.

Smith, Thomas. *De Republica Anglorum.* Edited by L. Alston. Cambridge, 1906.

Speculum: A Journal of Mediaeval Studies. Cambridge, Mass., 1926———.

Squibb, G. D. *The High Court of Chivalry: A Study of the Civil Law in England.* Oxford, 1959.

State Papers: Henry VIII. Rolls Series. 2 vols. London, 1830-52.

Statutes at Large. 105 vols. Cambridge, 1762-1865.

Statutes at Large: Ireland. 8 vols. Dublin, 1765.

Statutes of the Realm. Record Commission. 2 vols. London, 1810-28.

Steel, A. *The Receipt of the Exchequer, 1377-1485.* Cambridge, 1954.

Stenton, D. B. *English Justice between the Norman Conquest and the Great Charter, 1066-1215.* Philadelphia, Pa., 1964.

Stenton, Sir Frank. *Anglo-Saxon England, 550-1087.* Oxford, 1947.

Stenton, Sir Frank. *The First Century of English Feudalism, 1066-1166.* Oxford, 1932.

Stenton, Sir Frank. *The Latin Charters of the Anglo-Saxon Period.* Oxford, 1955.

Stenton, Sir Frank. *Norman London.* Historical Association Leaflet no. 93. London, 1934.

Stephen, J. F. *A History of the Criminal Law of England.* 3 vols. London, 1883.

Stephenson, C. *Borough and Town.* Cambridge, Mass., 1933.

Stephenson, C. *Medieval Feudalism.* Ithaca, N.Y., 1942.

Stevenson, W. H. (editor). *Records of the Borough of Nottingham.* 5 vols. London, 1882-1900.

Stewart-Brown, R. *The Serjeants of the Peace in Medieval England and Wales.* Manchester, 1936.

Stith, W. *History of the First Discovery and Settlement of Virginia.* Williamsburg, Va., 1747.

Stocks, J. E. (editor). *Records of the Borough of Leicester.* 4 vols. London, 1899-1923. (A continuation of Mary Bateson's work.)

Strype, J. *Life and Acts of Matthew Parker.* 3 vols. Oxford, 1821.

Strype, J. *Life and Acts of John Whitgift.* 3 vols. Oxford, 1822.

Stubbs, W. *Constitutional History of England.* Fifth edition. 3 vols. Oxford, 1891-96.

Stubbs, W. (editor). *Select Charters and Other Illustrations of English Constitutional History.* Ninth edition, by H. W. C. Davis. Oxford, 1913.

Tait, J. (editor). *The Domesday Survey of Cheshire.* Chetham Society, New Series, vol. LXXV. Manchester, 1916.

Tait, J. *The Medieval English Borough.* Manchester, 1936.

Tanner, J. R. (editor). *Constitutional Documents of the Reign of James I, A.D. 1603-1625.* Cambridge, 1930.

Tanner, J. R. (editor). *English Constitutional Conflicts of the Seventeenth Century, 1603-1689.* Cambridge, 1928.

Tanner, J. R. (editor). *Tudor Constitutional Documents, 1485-1603.* Cambridge, 1922.

Taswell-Langmead, I. P. *English Constitutional History.* Revised by T. F. T. Plucknett. London, 1949.

Thompson, F. *The First Century of Magna Carta.* Minneapolis, Minn., 1925.

Thompson, F. *Magna Carta: Its Role in the Making of the English Constitution, 1300-1629.* Minneapolis, Minn., 1948.

Thompson, F. *A Short History of Parliament, 1295-1642.* Minneapolis, Minn., 1953.

Thompson, G. S. *Lords Lieutenants in the Sixteenth Century.* London, 1923.

Thorpe, B. (editor). *Diplomatarium Anglicum Aevi Saxonici.* London, 1865.

Tout, T. F. *Chapters in the Administrative History of Mediaeval England*. 6 vols. Manchester, 1920-33.

Tout, T. F. *The Place of the Reign of Edward II in English History*. Manchester, 1914.

Tudor Studies Presented by the Board of Studies in History in the University of London to A. F. Pollard. London, 1924.

Turner, E. R. *The Privy Council of England in the Seventeenth and Eighteenth Centuries, 1603-1784*. 2 vols. Baltimore, Md., 1927-28.

Turner, G. J. (editor). *Select Pleas of the Forest*. Selden Society, vol. XIII. London, 1901.

Ullman, W. *Principles of Government and Politics in the Middle Ages*. New York, 1961.

Usher, R. G. *The Rise and Fall of the High Commission*. Oxford, 1913.

Victoria History of the Counties of England, The. Westminster, 1909——.

Vinogradoff, P. *Villainage in England*. Oxford, 1892.

Webb, S., and Webb, B. *English Local Government*. 6 vols. London, 1906-29.

Wedgwood, J. C., and Holt, A. D. *History of Parliament, 1439-1509: Biographies of Members of the Commons House*. London, 1936.

Weinbaum, M. *The Incorporation of Boroughs*. Manchester, 1937.

Weinbaum, M. *London unter Eduard I und II*. 2 vols. Stuttgart, 1923.

Weinbaum, M. *Verfassungsgeschichte Londons, 1066-1268*. Stuttgart, 1929.

West, F. *The Justiciarship in England, 1066-1232*. Cambridge, 1966.

White, A. B. *Self-Government at the King's Command*. Minneapolis, Minn., 1933.

Wilkins, D. (editor). *Concilia Magnae Britanniae et Hiberniae*. 4 vols. London, 1737.

Wilkinson, B. *Constitutional History of England in the Fifteenth Century, 1399-1485*. London, 1964.

Wilkinson, B. *Constitutional History of Medieval England*. 3 vols. London, 1948-1958.

Willard, J. F. *Parliamentary Taxes on Personal Property, 1290-1334*. Cambridge, Mass., 1934.

Willard, J. F., Morris, W. A., Strayer, J. R., and Dunham, W. H. (editors). *The English Government at Work, 1327-1336*. 3 vols. Cambridge, Mass., 1940-1950.

William Lambarde and Local Government: His "Ephemeris", and Twenty-Nine Charges to Juries and Commissions. Ithaca, N.Y., 1962.

Williams, P. *The Council in the Marches of Wales under Elizabeth I*. Cardiff, 1958.

Willson, D. H. (editor). *The Parliamentary Diary of Robert Bowyer, 1606-1607*. Minneapolis, Minn., 1931.

Worcestershire Quarter Sessions Papers. Worcestershire County Records, Division I, vol. I. Worcester, 1900.

Wright, H. G. *Life and Works of Arthur Hall*. Manchester, 1919.

Young, C. R. *The English Borough and Royal Administration*. Durham, N.C., 1961.

Zeeveld, W. G. *Foundations of Tudor Policy*. Cambridge, Mass., 1948.

84 85 86   10